PRIMITIVISM AND RELATED IDEAS IN ANTIQUITY

CONTRIBUTIONS TO THE HISTORY OF PRIMITIVISM

PRIMITIVISM AND RELATED IDEAS IN ANTIQUITY

BY

ARTHUR O. LOVEJOY

GEORGE BOAS

WITH SUPPLEMENTARY ESSAYS

BY

W. F. ALBRIGHT

AND

P.-E. DUMONT

1965

OCTAGON BOOKS, INC.

New York

Reprinted 1965
by special arrangement with The Johns Hopkins Press

OCTAGON BOOKS, INC.
175 FIFTH AVENUE
NEW YORK, N. Y. 10010

LIBRARY OF CONGRESS CATALOG CARD NUMBER: 65-25872

Printed in U.S.A. by
NOBLE OFFSET PRINTERS, INC.
NEW YORK 3, N. Y.

The Editors gratefully acknowledge the assistance of the American Council of Learned Societies through grants in aid of the preparation and publication of this volume.

PREFACE

The story which the present and subsequent volumes of this series are to tell in part is, broadly described, that of man's reflection upon the general course of his own history and upon the value of those achievements of his which have been most distinctive of that history. Perhaps by the early Pleistocene time protoplasm had taken form in a structure unique among its myriad combinations and metamorphoses — the brain of *homo sapiens*; and with the emergence of a creature endowed with this peculiar organ, a strange, long process, unknown to all the rest of nature, began. One of the feebler and more ungainly of the vertebrates set out, though with no prevision of the outcome, upon the singular business of transforming his environment and himself. Having been endowed, for better or worse, with an irrepressible propensity for taking thought, he found, through this, means which no instinct had taught him, means ever more various and more complex, of satisfying, first, impulses and aversions which he shared with other animals, and then, along with these, a multiplying host of other desires, as alien to himself at the outset as they were, and remain, to his animal kindred. The history of this process of man's cultural development is, in its outlines and in much of its variegated detail, now familiar. It is not with it, but with a somewhat less familiar accompaniment of it, that the present work is concerned. Probably among most races in which the process was not arrested at a very early stage, certainly among most of those the history of whose ideas is best known to us through their literatures, men long ago began an appraisal both of the historic process in general and of the predominant tendency which was manifested in it — the tendency which we call the progress of civilization. As the generations pass, does the condition of mankind grow better, or grow worse, or remain, except in external and relatively unimportant ways, the same; has the advance of civilization been a gain or a loss for the species responsible for it; is it a manifestation of man's superiority among the creatures, a legitimate ground for racial pride, or is it an evidence of his folly or depravity; are those peoples the most fortunate among whom it never began, or was speedily halted? It is the record of the opinions which men, chiefly in the Occident, have held upon such questions, at least down to a century and a half ago, that these volumes are — if the project can be carried out — designed to present: the record, especially, of civilized man's misgivings about his performances, about his prospects — and about himself. Some parts of the story, mainly in modern times, have been well told by others in various special studies; what is here attempted is a somewhat fuller, more connected and more integrated presentation of it — and therefore one which, so far as the literary material available permits, begins at the beginning.

ix

The history of any idea, or complex of ideas, is best presented through the citation of the *ipsissima verba* of the writers who have expressed it. No scholar is likely to be satisfied merely with a series of *précis* or interpretations of the opinions and reasonings of those writers, unless he is already intimately familiar with them; he will wish to have the texts under his own eye. It is, therefore, an essential feature of the plan of the present series that it shall be chiefly — so far as is practicable — a documentary history of the ideas with which it is concerned. There are, however, unfortunately or fortunately, limits to the practicability of this plan. When the modern period is reached, the increasing multiplicity and voluminosity of the material will make unavoidable a relatively more restricted selection from among the whole number of relevant writings, supplemented by references to, or bibliographies of, passages which are less important in their historic influence, or are mere repetitions of already trite themes. This limitation, in the case of later volumes of the series, can, however, perhaps in sufficient degree, be offset by the publication of critical editions of the longer texts of major importance in the history of modern primitivism and of the idea of progress (where such editions are still lacking), and of special monographs on particular episodes in that history.[1] In the present volume a nearer approximation to a comprehensive *corpus* of texts illustrative of the principal ideas dealt with is possible, though even here some resort to summarization or bare reference has been necessary, to keep the book within a moderate length; and examples of a number of other tendencies of thought having some connection with these ideas have been omitted. It is all too likely, also, that there are other omissions due to the limitations of the editors' knowledge.

It is hoped that this initial volume may be of some interest and use to students of classical literature, but it is not chiefly with them in view that it has been compiled. Most of the texts will be familiar to them, though these texts have not hitherto, so far as the editors are aware, been brought together and comprehensively studied in their interconnections and contrasts, as illustrations of ancient reflection upon a single group of related issues. But the principal purpose of this volume is to exhibit the classical background — and thereby, in many cases, the probable classical sources — of the manifold expressions of primitivism, and also of ways of thinking opposed to it, in modern literature, early modern historiography, and modern

---

[1] In the collateral series of *Contributions to the History of Primitivism* the following volumes have already appeared or are shortly to appear: Lahontan's *Dialogues curieux entre l'auteur et un sauvage de bon sens qui a voyagé, et Mémoires de l'Amérique septentrionale*, edited by Gilbert Chinard, 1931; *The Happy Beast in French Thought of the Seventeenth Century*, by George Boas, 1933; *Primitivism and the Idea of Progress in English Popular Literature of the Eighteenth Century*, by Lois Whitney, 1934, all published by The Johns Hopkins Press, Baltimore. An edition of Diderot's *Supplément au voyage de Bougainville*, by Gilbert Chinard, is in preparation.

social philosophy and ethics. There is some reason to think that this background is not universally familiar to those whose special fields of study lie within the period from the Renaissance to our own time; it is, in any case, certain that without a fairly full acquaintance with it a good many passages in modern writings, and the ideas contained in them, cannot be seen in their true historical perspective. Even in the works of learned authors it is sometimes still possible to find indications of the supposition that primitivism was essentially a novelty in the seventeenth or the eighteenth century; and in the minds of the less learned the belief appears still widely to prevail that it was a queer paradox introduced chiefly by Rousseau — the fact being that it was then beginning to go (temporarily) out of fashion, and that Rousseau contributed something to bring about its obsolescence. The texts given in the following pages will at least suffice to show that most of the various aspects of primitivistic thought conspicuous in those centuries had their counterparts in classical antiquity; and since most modern writers before the present century had more or less classical education, it may frequently be presumed — and is in numerous cases fairly evident from similarities in particular expressions or turns of thought — that these counterparts were also the originals. To our own age ancient primitivism has a different relation. Of direct, or even indirect, influence of the classical primitivistic tradition there is probably little. But since the beginning of the present century, Western man has become increasingly sceptical concerning the nineteenth-century " myth of progress ", increasingly troubled with misgivings about the value of the outcome of civilization thus far, about the future to which it tends, and about himself as the author of it all; and similar doubts and apprehensions found expression two millennia and more ago. In spite of the more complex and sophisticated general ideology of the contemporary exponents of these moods, there are striking parallels to be observed between certain of the texts that follow and some passages in, e. g., such writings as Freud's *Civilization and its Discontents* and Spengler's *Man and Technics*.

This volume, then, has been planned chiefly to be of convenient use to those whose primary interest is in the history of ideas in modern times. A large proportion of such users, it has been assumed, will wish to have before them the relevant texts in their original tongues; on the other hand, the addition of translations has seemed likely to make the compilation serviceable to a wider public. Some explanatory matter has been added which would, doubtless, be superfluous for specialists in the classics. Texts have been taken from approved editions of the works cited, in the main without alterations and without *variae lectiones*, though occasionally the editors have ventured emendations of punctuation, and, in a few cases, of readings. The translations, except a few indicated in footnotes, are new, but as a rule the best former translations have been " diligently compared," and where special felicities of rendering have been found in them, they have been adopted. Platonic passages have usually been given in Jowett's classic version, with some emendations; and the rule of printing the originals *in extenso* has been departed from in the chapter on Plato, in view of their general accessibility. Non-classical readers should perhaps be warned that a number of the historical matters touched upon are deeply involved in controversy among specialists; there is, indeed, not a great deal in classical literature and philosophy, from the dates and the authenticity of texts to the interpretation of them, which is not in some degree involved in controversy. It is, for example, not universally agreed among competent scholars that any of the ideas in the Platonic dialogues are the ideas of Plato. About the history of Cynicism, for another example, there has been, and still is, much division of learned opinion, and it has, partly because of the paucity of material from the first century of that school, been a fertile field for ingenious, and sometimes discordant, hypotheses. Into these disputes and conjectures the editors have for the most part avoided entering; to have done so would have been to convert a considerable part of the volume into a series of controversial chapters of minute analysis of texts, possibly of interest to specialists, but not serviceable to the principal objects in view. The general policy adopted has been to adhere to what appear to be the more commonly accepted views of contemporary classical scholars, while indicating the more important points about which dubiety has arisen. The main outlines of the history to be related are not, in most cases, greatly affected by these disputes; and whatever views be taken concerning them, the body of texts given remains as the background of modern primitivism and anti-primitivism.

The problem of arranging the material in the manner likely to be the most illuminating and convenient has been difficult; and, since the reasons for the solution adopted may not be evident, an explanation of it may be desirable. In the historiography of ideas, it is the fortunes of distinct ' unit-ideas ', and their interrelations of congruity or opposition, that are to be exhibited, not the ' systems ' of philosophers or schools, in which heterogeneous notions and reasonings on a variety of subjects are conjoined in a manner often determined chiefly by the peculiarities of the philosophers' temperaments. An analysis and anatomizing of texts, and a separating-out of the passages pertinent to the several ideas of which the history is under investigation, are therefore the first essentials in such a study. The passages illustrative of a given unit of this kind, and of its vicissitudes, need then to be brought together as a separate division of the story. These methodological preconceptions have chiefly determined the arrangement of the passages herein cited.[2] They precluded a merely chronological sequence of long passages, where these ranged over a number of ideas which it

---

[2] The general conception of the method of the history of ideas which will be followed in this series has been more fully set forth by one of the editors in the introductory chapter of a volume shortly to appear: *The Great Chain of Being*, by A. O. Lovejoy.

appeared important to discriminate and present separately. The reader will therefore sometimes find portions of a given text in one chapter of the volume, other portions in another; and he will likewise find different writings of the same period cited, or referred to, in widely separated parts of the book. As, however, probable dates of texts are indicated, the chronological relations of the passages in question may be readily observed by the reader. Such has been the general plan of arrangement. But the plan has — perhaps mistakenly — not been used as a bed of Procrustes. Four philosophical writers, Plato, Aristotle, Lucretius and Cicero, have been dealt with in separate chapters, chiefly because of their special importance as individual influences in the movement of ideas with which the book has to do; and for a similar reason, separate treatment has been given to the rôles in the history of primitivism of two philosophical 'schools', the Cynics and Stoics.

The editors have collaborated throughout the volume, but Mr. Lovejoy is chiefly responsible for Chapters I, II, § D, III-X, and the Appendix, and Mr. Boas for Chapters II, §§ A, B, C, E, and XI-XIII. They are deeply indebted to colleagues of the faculty of Johns Hopkins University for cooperation, especially to Professors Albright and Dumont for the valuable Supplementary Essays which extend the perspective of the history of primitivism into two important regions in which it has not hitherto received special study. The chapters dealing with primitivism in Greek and Roman literature would have been far more imperfect than they are if the editors had not been able to profit by the advice and assistance, at many points, of colleagues in the classical departments, especially the late Professors Roger M. Jones and Wilfred P. Mustard, and Professors Tenney Frank and David M. Robinson. Especially grateful acknowledgment is due Dr. Harold Cherniss for generous and indispensable cooperation through the progress of the work. The editors are notably indebted also to Mr. Panos P. Morphopoulos, who, as research assistant, has rendered able and invaluable services throughout; to Mr. Paul Clement for his careful proof-reading of Greek and Latin texts; and to Miss M. D. Boehm for assistance in the preparation of the manuscript for publication and of the first index.

ARTHUR O. LOVEJOY
GEORGE BOAS

TABLE OF CONTENTS

CHAPTER ONE

PROLEGOMENA TO THE HISTORY OF PRIMITIVISM

'Primitivism,' as the term has come to be used by historical and philosophical writers, is a name for two distinct tendencies in human thought which appear to have had separate historic origins, but early began to fuse and interpenetrate. It is necessary, for any clear understanding of the phenomena with which we are to deal, to begin by distinguishing these tendencies. One of them we shall call 'chronological,' the other 'cultural' primitivism. They are ways of thinking which, in spite of their usual association with one another, are primarily answers to different questions, which have in all periods presented themselves vaguely or definitely to men's minds.

CHRONOLOGICAL PRIMITIVISM

Chronological primitivism is one of the many answers which may be and have been given to the question: What is the temporal distribution of good, or value, in the history of mankind, or, more generally, in the entire history of the world? It is, in short, a kind of philosophy of history, a theory, or a customary assumption, as to the time — past or present or future — at which the most excellent condition of human life, or the best state of the world in general, must be supposed to occur.

There are, it is evident, a number of views with respect to this matter which are logically conceivable; and most of these have found historical exemplification either in popular belief or philosophical opinion. The meaning of chronological primitivism can best be understood if the conception is given its place in a classified enumeration of all the principal types of theory concerning the general question. These types fall into two classes according as the time-process as a whole, or the history of the human race in particular, is assumed to be finite or infinite.

A. *Finitist theories.* Finitist theories are those in which the history in question is assumed to be a succession of events having a beginning at some more or less determinable time in the past. Two varieties of this type are obviously possible: those in which the process is conceived as having both a beginning and an end; those in which it is conceived as having a beginning, but no end in the future — or in which, at least, no definite assumption of the future termination of it is made. The former may be called, for brevity of reference, bilateral, the latter unilateral, finitist theories.[1]

---

[1] A conceivable theory would, of course, be to the effect that the process had no beginning but will have an end. But, in this and other cases which the discriminating reader will recognize, it has not been thought necessary or useful to complicate the enumeration by the inclusion of types of view which have neither natural plausibility nor historical importance.

I. *Bilateral finitist theories.* These, which in philosophical doctrines or popular beliefs in the West since the introduction of Christianity have been the most usual general type, may appear in any one of three forms; i. e., if the assumption that history has both a beginning and an end is explicitly or implicitly made, the temporal distribution of good — or, indeed, of any particular kind of good — may be, as it has been, conceived in any of the following ways.

1. *The Theory of Undulation.* It may be supposed that, if any considerable periods of history are taken, there is no material difference between them in the amount of good that exists. The movement of history with respect to the realization of value is like the undulation of the sea. From time to time there may be brief improvement. A wave rises above the general level. But it always soon sinks again to or below that level, which on the whole is maintained unaltered from age to age. Mankind in the long run grows neither better nor worse, neither, on the average, happier nor unhappier, even though it may, in the external conditions and circumstances of its life, undergo great changes, and, conceivably, changes in a single general direction. History, on this view, has, so far as value is concerned, no course; if it is a drama, it is a drama without a plot. The thing which has been is the thing which shall be; between priority or posteriority in time and the degree or the extent of existing good there is no fixed or definite relation, either positive or negative. This theory sometimes takes the form, in later times, of the conception of a succession of empires or civilizations, each of which goes through a rise, decline, and fall, after the analogy of the life-history of an individual.

2. *The Theory of Decline.* It may be supposed that the highest degree of excellence or happiness in man's life existed at the beginning of history. This, of course, is the general assumption of chronological primitivism. It may, however, take four principal forms, according to the view held as to the course of history since the beginning — i. e., between the beginning and the present, in the present, and in the future. The following are therefore the variants of chronological primitivism, when it occurs as a mode of the bilateral finitist theory:

(a) The best time was at the beginning, but since man fell from the original happy condition, history has, with respect to value, been undulatory; man and the conditions of his existence have, on the whole, neither improved nor deteriorated; and this will continue to be the case in the future, until the process is terminated (at least so far as 'this world' is concerned) by a final catastrophe, supervening either through natural or supernatural forces. This may be called the Theory of a Fall without Subsequent Decline.

(b) The best time was at the beginning, and — in spite, perhaps, of minor transitory undulations — the subsequent course of human history has been downward, and this will continue to be the case in the future, until the process is ended either as a direct consequence of this deterioration, or by some catastrophe arising through external causes. This we shall call the Theory of Progressive Degeneration.

(c) It may be supposed that the best age of mankind hitherto was at the beginning; that there has been in the past, on the whole, a progressive decline; that this will, or may, continue for some longer or shorter time in the future, but that at some future time there will, or may, be a restoration of man's primeval goodness, or happiness, or both. This may be called the Theory of Decline and Future Restoration. The recovery may be held to be the result either, (i) of a sudden intervention of some external power, as in Christian chiliasm; or (ii) of a recognition by men of the superiority of their primeval mode or life, and, in consequence, a voluntary return to it or to some close approximation to it. This future renewal of the primitive excellence and felicity of the race may be supposed to be destined to be followed by some sudden catastrophe — such as, in certain phases of Christian belief, has been expected to bring the millennium, the future earthly paradise, to an end. Form ii of this conception, however, has not always, especially in modern times, been combined with any definite supposition of a termination of the renewed Golden Age; the question of the duration of that age has often been ignored, or left pleasantly vague, by those who have looked forward hopefully towards it, or have labored to bring men to it. The temper which is expressed in such a view is thus congenial to one of the other broad types of theory — either the 'unilateral finitist' or the 'infinitist' assumption.

(d) It may be supposed that the best age was the first; that subsequently, either in the past or present or future, some approximate renewal of this primeval excellence has been or will be attained; but that thereafter the process of history has been or will be, on the whole, one of gradual and continuous degeneration. This, though it rarely appears in a very well defined form in the history of ideas in the Occident, seems in some cases to have been adumbrated; and it is therefore worth including in our list. If it needs a name, it may be called the Three-Phase Theory of Decline.

3. *The Theory of Ascent.* It may be supposed that the least excellent and least desirable phase of the existence of the human race came at the beginning of the assumed finite historic process. This, of course, is the view antithetic to chronological primitivism. It appears in the history of thought in two main forms.

(a) *The Theory of Continuous Progress.* In this it is held that the course of things since the beginning — in spite of possible minor deviations and the occasional occurrence of backwaters in the stream of history — has been characterized by a gradual progressive increase, or a wider diffusion, of goodness, or happiness, or enlightenment, or of all of these; that the best time of all is yet to come; and that this progress will continue in the future up to the moment when history, or at all events the history of the human race, is brought to an end by a sudden catastrophe, either through some natural cosmic accident or through supernatural intervention.

(b) *The Theory of Successive Progress and Decline.* In this case, while the poorest and least desirable stage of human history is supposed to have been the earliest, and while this is conceived to have been followed by a more or less long upward movement, it is also assumed that this will inevitably be succeeded by a period of gradual deterioration, either through causes inherent in human nature or through alteration in the external physical conditions of human life. The eventual end of the whole affair may be regarded as destined to result from the culmination of this gradual change in external — e. g. in climatic — conditions; or from some suicidal folly of mankind itself; or through some catastrophe, natural or supernatural, supervening from without. Whatever assumption is made — if any definite one is made — upon the last question, there will evidently be an important difference in the effect of this type of view upon the imagination, and upon moral and religious feeling, according as the climax of the upward movement is placed, (*i*) in the past, (*ii*) in the present, or (*iii*) in the near or remote future. A good deal that has been called primitivism, both in ancient and modern thought, has, as the texts will show, been in fact the first variety of the theory of progress and decline. While a state of things far superior to the present has been assumed to have existed in a much earlier age, this condition has been conceived, not only as not primeval, but also as the result of a more or less definite series of prior stages of cultural or moral advance.

II. *Unilateral finitist theories.* These differ from the former only in omitting the assumption of a future term to the mundane process. All the sub-varieties mentioned under type A, I, may, *mutatis mutandis,* be held with this qualification; it is therefore unnecessary to repeat the enumeration.

B. *Infinitist Theories.* Where the infinity of the series of events *a parte ante* is asserted, as by Aristotle, chronological primitivism in the rigorous sense is obviously excluded; the thesis of an infinite process of deterioration — or, *per contra,* of an infinite progress — in the past remains abstractly possible, but lacks plausibility, not to say intelligible meaning.[2] In ancient reflective thought, however, the infinitist conception usually appears in the form of a species of compromise with its opposite, viz.:

1. *The Theory of World-Cycles.* Here the infinite succession of changes which constitute history is conceived as an endless reiteration of essentially

---

[2] The idea of a progress which has been going on for an infinite past time and will continue infinitely in the future has some obscure manifestations in the thought of the nineteenth and twentieth centuries, but its concrete signification is difficult to gather, and in any case these periods do not fall within the present history.

the same states of the world as a whole, in precisely the same order. This theory, like the theory of indefinite undulation, implies that, in the long run, the time-process as such has no moral or religious significance, that between better or worse, on the one hand, and earlier or later, on the other, there is no fixed correlation, that the cosmic drama is not the working out of any destiny, either good or ill. But with respect to the course of each cycle, all of the types of view which have been mentioned many conceivably find a place: every cycle, and therefore the one in which we now find ourselves, may be supposed to be itself also merely undulatory; or to be at its best either at its beginning or just before its close; and each of the two latter views may be taken in different ways, analogous to those already defined. If a given philosopher or religious teacher or reflective poet supposes himself and those whom he addresses to be at or near the beginning of an ascending process in the cycle, his outlook upon the immediate future will, of course, be a cheerful one, while if he supposes his generation to be involved in a process of decline the depressing implications for the imagination of most men of the theory of the *ewige Wiederkehr* itself will obviously be intensified by the expectation of an immediate future worse than the past experienced by their ancestors. The possible sub-varieties of the cyclic conception of universal history, being thus analogous to those indicated under A, I, need not be elaborated in detail. We shall find that in European thought, and especially in antiquity, the theory of cosmic cycles, where it has been accepted, has often been combined with a theory of decline with respect to the process going on within each cycle. The tendency has been to conceive of the beginning of a cycle as a period when all things are made new and therefore have not yet suffered from the attrition of time — an age when the energies of nature are at their fullest, when not only man but all things are in their vigorous and happy youth. The conception of world-cycles, therefore, has not infrequently been a special form of chronological primitivism.

It is evident that the theory of cycles combines certain advantages of both the finitist and infinitist ways of thinking. It makes the number of kinds of events and of phases of history finite, and therefore escapes, in part, the difficulties, both for the imagination and for the logical understanding, of the conception of the numerical infinite; and if it ascribes no single direction to the total temporal succession, it nevertheless makes it possible to conceive of this as composed of a series of repetitions of intelligibly ordered sequences, of genuine dramas — tragedies or comedies, as the case may be — of a vast temporal span. In its philosophical forms, ancient or modern, it has usually involved the assumption of the quantitative finitude of the stuff of which the world is composed, and upon the rearrangement of which in diverse patterns its history depends. On the other hand, the theory escapes the difficult conception of an absolute beginning *e nihilo,* or — in its religious forms — of the commencement at some arbitrarily chosen moment, by divine fiat, of a creation which might, it would appear, have equally reasonably received the boon of existence long before; and it similarly avoids the supposition of the sheer annihilation of matter, or of the absolute winding-up of all the processes which make up the natural order of the world. In these characteristics of it may perhaps be seen the ultimate reasons why it has so often attracted reflective minds in both the Orient and the Occident, especially in antiquity. When the assumption of recurrent cycles is not made, there remains, as the only plausible form of the infinitist conception:

2. *The Theory of Endless Undulation.* This is the supposition that the assumed infinite succession of events is neither repetitious in any fixed order, nor yet characterized by any definite tendency towards either the augmentation or decrease of value. It is the infinitist counterpart of A, I, 1, differing from that only in excluding — or in not including — the anticipation of a future termination of the process. As applied to the history of the human race upon the earth, it has been relatively unusual in the West, but has had the potent support of Aristotle.

It need hardly be said that in popular thought, in unsystematic reflection, and even in the reasonings of philosophers, the conceptions of the history of either man or the world he lives in have not always been so sharply discriminated as in the foregoing enumeration. Different ways of thinking about the matter have often been incongruously combined, or there has been neglect to distinguish consciously between different possible assumptions — for example, between the theory of finite and that of endless undulation, and, in general, between finitist and infinitist theories of the same mode. The historically current beliefs cannot, therefore, in all cases be classified with confidence and precision under the heads which have been set down. It is none the less desirable, not only to recognize the significant possible variations at the outset in a fairly definite way, but to keep them in mind throughout our survey of the highly various and complex phenomena which constitute the history of chronological primitivism and of the conflict between it and opposing conceptions.

It is evident from the foregoing that the idea of progress cannot without qualification be said to be the antithesis to chronological primitivism, as defined. The latter asserts only that there has been on the whole no progress in the past; but it is compatible with both hopeful and despondent views about the future. It is strictly antithetic only to the belief (A, I, 3, a) in a general and necessary *law* of progress, a tendency inherent in nature or in man to pass through a regular sequence of stages of development in past, present and future, the later stages being — with perhaps occasional retardations or minor retrogressions — superior to the earlier. This, however, appears to be what is usually meant by the 'idea of progress' in contemporary usage; and since it is an idea which has played so great a part in the thought of the last two hundred years, and especially of the nine-

teenth century, it is through contrast with it that the history of chronological primitivism has its greatest interest. If such a natural law of the augmentation of value in time is assumed, on the one hand all the past phases
of the historic process will appear to afford encouragement and instruction — and they can be regarded as showing the general direction of a
curve of progress which can be hypothetically projected into the future;
while, on the other hand, that assumption will chiefly make for a forward-
looking habit of mind. Since, for the race, the best is yet to come, it is
upon what is to come that the imagination will most fondly dwell. But
chronological primitivism can obviously find in the process of history in
general small encouragement, and only such instruction as may be obtained
from examples of evils and aberrations to be avoided, if possible; yet, even
if not without hope for the future, it is essentially a backward-looking habit
of mind. At most, nothing better is to be anticipated than a recovery of
what has been lost; and it is upon a single, brief and remote bygone episode
in history that it fixes the imagination. How largely man has, in this
sense, been a backward-looking animal, this and the following volumes will
show. It is a part of their purpose to exhibit the principal manifestations
of both of these contrasting habits, or temporal orientations, of the mind,
and to provide material for estimating their relative prevalence in different
periods.

Cultural Primitivism

Cultural primitivism is the discontent of the civilized with civilization,
or with some conspicuous and characteristic feature of it. It is the belief
of men living in a relatively highly evolved and complex cultural condition
that a life far simpler and less sophisticated in some or in all respects is
a more desirable life. Its temper, when combined, as it very commonly
has been, with chronological primitivism is summed up in the words of
the Preacher, which, indeed, in the history of Judaism and Christianity
seemed to give it a definite biblical sanction: " God hath made man
upright; but they have sought out many devices."

But ' civilization ' is, of course, a relative term. To men living in any
phase of cultural development it is always possible to conceive of some
simpler one, and usually possible to point to other men, past or present,
in whose life it is exemplified. Cultural primitivism has thus had enduring
roots in human nature ever since the civilizing process began. It is a not
improbable conjecture that the feeling that humanity was becoming over-
civilized, that life was getting too complicated and over-refined, dates from
the time when the cave-man first became such. It can hardly be supposed —
if the cave-men were at all like their descendants — that none among them
discoursed with contempt upon the cowardly effeminacy of living under
shelter or upon the exasperating inconvenience of constantly returning for
food and sleep to the same place instead of being free to roam at large in
the wide-open spaces.

The cultural primitivist has almost invariably believed that the simpler life of which he has dreamed has been somewhere, at some time, actually lived by human beings. He has not merely enunciated an ideal but has pointed to its exemplars. When these have been conceived as having existed at the beginning of history, or of a cycle of it, cultural primitivism fuses with one or another form of chronological primitivism. But the former may be, and fairly frequently has been, dissociated from the latter. It may be held by minds having no especial interest in a philosophy of history, no tendency to generalize about the distribution of value in time, no temperamental propensity to idealize the remote past. It has sometimes been one of the forms, above mentioned, of the theory of progress and decline. A remote, not primeval, but culturally extremely primitive, phase of human society has been set up as the ideal one. But above all the cultural primitivist's model of human excellence and happiness is sought in the present, in the mode of life of existing primitive, or so-called 'savage' peoples. These contemporary embodiments of this ideal have usually been found among races not intimately known to, and existing at some considerable distance from, the people to whom the preacher of primitivism commends them as examples to be followed, or exhibits them as more fortunate branches of our species whose state is to be envied. The fact is perhaps not without significance; for it suggests that one of the roots of primitivism may be common to it and certain other conspicuous phenomena in the history of thought and feeling — the charm of the remote and strange, the craving to imagine, and even to experience, some fashion of life which is at least *different* from the all too familiar visage of existence as it has hitherto presented itself to one whose imagination or whose action has been crampingly confined at home. In so far as the love of strangeness and the revolt against the familiar is an element in cultural primitivism — whether or not combined with the chronological variety — the phenomena of which we are to examine the history are forms of what has been called 'exoticism'; and their literary expression is a phase of the 'literature of escape.'

It will be seen that primitivism of the combined chronological and cultural type has thus had characteristic moods both of youth and age on its side. The love of strangeness, the desire to wander, in mind if not in body, in remote regions of space or among men unlike the tedious and unadventurous old fellows one has always been surrounded by, is an impulse likely to be strongest in adolescence and youth; while the *laudator temporis acti* is traditionally depicted as an old man resenting some departure from the fashions or standards to which he has been accustomed, and, in general, inclined, by virtue of his age, to idealize the past. But primitivism has been able to gratify, in some degree, both propensities — especially in the form in which the cultural and chronological types coexist without subordination of the former to the latter — in which, that is, the realization of the ideal simple life is seen not exclusively in the past but also in extant

savage peoples, living replicas of the character and life of the civilized
man's ancestors.

But it is evident that when you have found the springs of exoticism in
well-known, though by no means universal, traits of human nature, you
have not accounted for primitivism as such — for the fact that the type
of exotic life, remote in space or time or both, which has oftenest attracted
the curiosity or stirred the envy of civilized men, or aroused admiration
and set in play the imitative impulse in them, has been primitive life, or
some approximation to it. It is perhaps worth while to suggest briefly —
in advance of the presentation of the concrete and detailed historical pano-
rama of primitivism — some of its probable motives. They are not only
more numerous but more antithetic than most recent accounts of the matter would lead one to suppose. The unending revolt of the civilized against
something, or everything, characteristic of civilization, has been prompted
by diverse tempers or impulses, and it has been directed against diverse
objectives; and this diversity compels us to recognize a number of signifi-
cantly distinct primitivisms, and — if we are to avoid grossly confusing
essentially unlike phenomena — to keep these distinctions in view
throughout.

The civilized man, contrasting the mode of life of his age with that of a
less civilized people or epoch, will obviously find that the two differ in two
opposite respects. The existence of primitive men, as it has usually been
conceived, is both easier and harder than that of the civilized. It is easier
precisely *because* it is (or has, in part erroneously, been imagined to be)
simpler; it is less burdened with apparatus and (as has been supposed)
with a multitude of restrictive rules and regulations and conventionalities.
The individual in primitive society has often — by those who have known
little of the complexity and terrible force of primitive *tabus* — been pictured
as relatively exempt from constraint by the social group, more free to do
as he pleases; his native impulses and emotions and modes of self-expres-
sion had not yet been confined in a strait-jacket. Civilization, again, because
it has multiplied goods, has increased the necessity for labor to produce
them, has compelled man to satisfy his supposed needs in the sweat of his
brow, or, preferably, of his neighbor's brow; whereas the savage, primeval
or contemporary, has seemed, in comparison — at least the male savage,
who has usually been more prominent in the picture — a fellow of infinite
leisure. Thus cultural primitivism, whether as a mere escape for the
imagination or as a practical ideal, has often owed its appeal to men's
recalcitrance to some or most of the inhibitions imposed by current moral
codes, or to the alluring dream, or the hope, of a life with little or no toil
or strain of body or mind.

On the other hand, the life of many savage peoples, and those the best
known throughout the greater part of European history, is manifestly in
certain respects, or when regarded in a certain light, harder than that of

civilized mankind — at least of the more prosperous portion of it. It is, that is to say, characterized by a greater degree of physical hardship; if happier on the whole, it has fewer 'enjoyments,' and fewer 'goods' in the economic sense. It is, in short, a life of extreme poverty measured by the standards of civilization; and it has often been supposed to be so because fewer desires existed in the savage bosom. He wanted less, and therefore knew how to be content with little; he was inured to hardship, and therefore bore it courageously and cheerfully. Consequently primitivism has been throughout history a not less marked tendency among the preachers of an ethics of renunciation, of austerity, of self-discipline; among the lovers of Lady Poverty; and among those subtler hedonistic moralists who have taught that the only sure way to happiness for man lies in bringing down his desires to some exiguous, irreducible minimum. For the distinction between these two strains in primitivism by no means runs parallel with the conventional distinction between hedonistic and non-hedonistic schools of moral philosophy. In antiquity especially, as this volume will illustrate, even the hedonists usually tended to assume that the desire for 'goods' was inimical to the attainment of 'the good.' Unhappiness was identified with the state of unsatisfied desire; the Romantic notion that an insatiable and interminable outreach after a perpetually flying goal is itself a moral excellence was foreign to most ancient thought; therefore, to have desires not surely and easily capable of satisfaction, through all the vicissitudes of life, was the essence of irrationality; the equalization of desire and attainment, which is the good, is to be reached by "lessening one's denominator."

> *Multa petentibus*
> *Desunt multa: bene est, cui deus obtulit*
> *Parca quod satis est manu.*[3]

Thus one of the chief premises of cultural primitivism was laid down scarcely less insistently by most of the hedonistic moralists of antiquity than by their opponents, though the full primitivistic consequence was less often drawn by them.[4]

To express the distinction between these two types of cultural primitivism no terms as yet exist; we shall call them 'soft' and 'hard' primitivism. In antiquity the men of the Golden Age under the Saturnian dispensation were soft primitives, and the imaginary Hyperboreans were usually soft savages; on the other hand, the 'noble savages' *par excellence,* in the later primitivism of the classical period — the Scythians and the Getae, and later the Germans — were rude, hardy fellows to whom 'Nature' was no gentle or indulgent mother. Their food did not drop into their laps, they were obliged to defend themselves against predatory animals,

---

[3] Horace, *Odes*, III, 16.

[4] For the elements in Greek popular religion which tended to support cultural and chronological primitivism, see the introduction to Chapter VII.

they were not exempt from the infirmities of age; and they were extolled
for the fewness of their desires and their consequent indifference to the
luxuries and even the comforts of civilized life.　The Cynics and Stoics
were the principal promoters of primitivism in antiquity, and they were so
chiefly because they found, as they supposed, in primeval man and in certain savage peoples both the exemplification of the type of virtue which
they preached and the evidence that the practice of these virtues was in
truth the life *secundum naturam.*　(Cf. Chapters IV and X.)　Between
the spirit of such a hard primitivism and the idyll of the Golden Age there
is manifestly a profound opposition.　The same contrast persists throughout history; it is essentially misleading to label as " primitivism," without
qualifying adjectives, both the temper of Diderot's *Supplément au Voyage
de Bougainville,* or even of Joseph Warton's *Enthusiast,* and that of Col-
lins's eulogy of " Kilda's race,"

> On whose bleak rocks, which brave the wasting tides,
> Fair nature's daughter, virtue, yet abides;

who live " blest in primal innocence,"

> Suffic'd and happy with that frugal fare
> Which tasteful toil and hourly danger give.[5]

The latter mood is exemplified, again, in so highly conventional a primitivistic passage as Churchill's picture of

> the savage of those early times,
> 'Ere Europe's sons were known, or Europe's crimes:
> .　.　.　.　.　.　.　.　.　.
> In full Content he found the truest wealth;
> In Toil he found Diversion, Food and Health;
> Stranger to ease and luxury of Courts,
> His Sports were Labours and his Labours Sports.[6]

A good deal of recent writing about primitivism has been marked by a
failure to observe this elementary distinction and by an extraordinary confusion of the ' Romantic ' ideal of ' expansion ' with the primitivistic ethics
of, so to say, reduction.　The child of nature has probably, as our texts
will show, more frequently been held up as a model by the ethical rigorists
and the teachers of the wisdom of not-wanting than by the amoralists and
antinomians or by those who found their ideal in insatiability.

'NATURE' AS NORM

The history of primitivism is in great part a phase of a larger historic
tendency which is one of the strangest, most potent and most persistent

---

[5] *Ode on the Popular Superstitions of the Highlands of Scotland,* 1749.　Cf. Van
Tieghem, " L'homme primitif et ses vertus dans le pré-romantisme européen," in
Bull. de la Soc. d'histoire moderne, June, 1922.

[6] *Gotham,* Bk. I (1765).

factors in Western thought — the use of the term 'nature' to express the standard of human values, the identification of the good with that which is 'natural' or 'according to nature.' The primitive condition of mankind, or the life of 'savage' peoples, has usually been extolled because it has been supposed to constitute 'the state of nature.' The phenomena to be exhibited in these volumes can not, therefore, be adequately comprehended without an understanding of the way in which this fashion of appealing to something called 'nature' for norms came about, and of the extraordinary multiplicity of meanings latent in the term in its normative uses. Little, indeed, in the history of Western ideas about what is good or bad in conduct, in social and political institutions, and in art, is intelligible without a constant realization of the fact that the sacred word 'nature' is probably the most equivocal in the vocabulary of the European peoples; that the range of connotation of the single term covers conceptions not only distinct but often absolutely antithetic to one another in their implications; and that the writers who have used it have usually been little aware of its equivocality and have at all times tended to slip unconsciously from one of its senses to another. A knowledge of the range of its meanings, and of the processes of thought — logical, pseudo-logical, or merely associative — by which one sense of it gives rise to, or easily passes over into, others — is an indispensable prerequisite for any discriminating reading of a large part of classical, medieval and modern literature and philosophy.

The beginning of the custom of looking to 'nature' for standards falls — so far as historical evidence is available — within the period covered by the present volume, and will be dealt with in some detail in Chapter III, and, as an aid to the reader in discriminating the principal historic senses of the term, both in the early and later periods, a (doubtless incomplete) enumeration of these senses is given in the Appendix, with an attempt to indicate the probable derivation of one meaning from another; this last, however, must be regarded as in many cases merely conjectural. Not all of the normative meanings or implications which 'nature' took on even by the fourth century B. C. tended to promote primitivistic ways of thinking; some of them had precisely the opposite tendency. The most important, in relation to the history of primitivism, are the senses, or groups of kindred senses, defined by the following antitheses:

(a) That which anything is 'by nature' as its intrinsic or objective character, in contrast with subjective appearances or with human beliefs about it — an antithesis applied first to the objects of the external world (Nos. 9, 10, 11).[7]

(b) 'Nature' in contrast with 'law,' 'custom' or 'convention,' as the objectively valid in the realm of morals, existing positive law or custom being assumed to deviate from this objective standard partially or completely (Nos. 40, 41).

[7] These numbers refer to those of the Appendix.

(c) That which is true or valid 'by nature' as what is universally known to or accepted by mankind, in contrast with beliefs or standards peculiar to particular nations, periods or individuals — an interpretation of the criterion of objective validity implied by (b) (No. 60).

(d) 'Nature' as the general cosmic order, optimistically conceived as good, or as divinely ordained, in contrast with supposed deviations from this order arising from human error or depravity — 'Nature' in this sense tending from an early period to be more or less vaguely personified (Nos. 13, 14, 15).

(e) The 'natural' state of a living being as its healthy condition, in contrast with conditions of disease or impairment of functions — a sense already common in the Hippocratic writings (No. 7).

(f) The 'natural' state of any being as its congenital or original condition; hence, in the case of mankind, or of a given people, its primeval state, in contrast with subsequent historic alterations or accretions (Nos. 2, 21).

(g) 'Nature' as that which exists apart from man and without human effort or contrivance, in contrast with 'art,' i. e., with all that is artificial or man-made (Nos. 17, 22).

(h) 'Nature' as that *in* man which is not due to taking thought or to deliberate choice: hence, those modes of human desire, emotion, or behavior which are instinctive or spontaneous, in contrast with those which are due to the laboring intellect, to premeditation, to self-consciousness, or to instruction (Nos. 16, 18).

(i) The 'natural' state of human social life as that in which the only government is that of the family or the patriarchal clan, in contrast with that in which there exist formal and 'artificial' political institutions and laws (No. 23).

In senses (b), (c), (d) and (e) — which themselves have in all periods tended to be interchanged and confused with one another — 'nature' is merely a generic designation for the valid norm of human life, or for whatever is in accord with such a norm. But these, with the partial exception of (c), do not themselves indicate in what specific ways the individual must act, or society must be framed, in order to conform to this norm. A great part of the history of morals and of political thought in the West, since the fifth century B. C., has consisted in giving concrete meaning to this abstract and general sense of 'nature' as the normal, or the objectively valid standard, by reading into the signification of the word some one or more of the many other senses which it had assumed. This substitution of meanings was frequently unconscious, though even then the processes of association, or the latent desires, which psychologically explain the substitutions, are not beyond probable conjecture; in some cases the transition from one sense to another was reached through explicit (though usually highly dubious) philosophical reasonings. It does not fall within the scope of the present work to present exhaustively the evidence for these generalizations.[8] What concerns us is the fact that both chronological and

---

[8] Some indications of this evidence may be gathered from Chapter III and the Appendix.

cultural primitivism, in so far as they have been assertions of the superiority of the 'state of nature,' are, *inter alia,* examples of such substitutions of meanings, and could hardly have played the rôle in history which they have if, from an early period of classical antiquity, the word 'nature' had not had the specific diversity of senses above indicated, and had not thus permitted an easy and more or less unconscious transition in thought from one of these to another.

THE VARIETIES OF THE STATE OF NATURE

Partly in consequence of the differences between the four last mentioned senses of 'nature,' partly for other reasons, the term 'state of nature' has had at least seven distinguishable, though frequently combined, meanings.

1. *The temporal state of nature* — cf. (b) and (d) above: the original condition of things, and especially the state of man as nature first made him, whatever this condition may be supposed to have been. When this alone is conceived as the ideal state, chronological primitivism may be found apart from explicit cultural primitivism. The remaining six senses designate modes or aspects of the ideal of the latter.

2. *The technological state of nature* — cf. (g): the condition of human life in which it is most free from the intrusion of 'art,' i. e., in which none, or at most only the simplest and most rudimentary, of the practical arts are known. With this is often and naturally associated a more or less extreme sort of practical anti-intellectualism — the view that intellectual pursuits are in themselves a sort of abnormality and that the progress of knowledge has not made man happier or better, but rather the reverse.

3. *The economic state of nature*: human society without private property, and in particular, without property in land — in other words, economic communism. With this, in consequence partly, perhaps, of Plato's influence, was closely associated, especially in the minds of ancient primitivistic writers, another sort of communism, viz.:

4. *The marital state of nature*: community of wives and children; in its extreme form, sexual promiscuity, including incest.

5. *The dietetic state of nature*: vegetarianism, an early and rather frequent feature of ancient chronological primitivism, not usually on hygienic grounds but as an expression of the feeling that bloodshed in all its forms is sinful, that man in an ideal state should, or at all events once did, live at peace with the animals as well as with his own kind. It was therefore commonly associated with the denunciation of animal sacrifices. With the cultural primitivism which eulogized savage peoples it could, naturally, not easily be combined.

6. *The juristic state of nature* — cf. (i): society without organized political government, or without any except the 'natural' government of

the family or clan — in other words, anarchism, in the proper sense of the term.

7. *The ethical state of nature* — cf. (b) and (h) : the control of human life by so-called ' natural ' — which does not, in this connection, always imply egoistic or purely sensuous — impulses, without deliberate and self-conscious moral effort, the constraint of rules, or the sense of sin : man in unity with himself, with no " civil war in the cave."

The complete ' state of nature ' would, of course, combine all of these characteristics. The term and its synonyms occur sometimes in this generalized sense; but usually it implies only one or a few of them. It is always important to note in any expression of cultural primitivism which of the last six senses the writer has — or has chiefly, or primarily — in mind ; for the motivation of his primitivism, the reasons why he believes the state of nature to be the best, will be reflected in his conception of what the essential state of nature is. Writers chiefly interested in political theory are likely, of course, to consider only the juristic state of nature; and that conception has had a development more or less independent of the others, and largely, though by no means exclusively, at the hands of anti-primitivistic theorists. The state of nature is for these writers a condition for the intolerable evils of which the civil state is the necessary remedy. Many such political theorists, however, have nevertheless assumed that there is *something* essentially good in the juristic natural state — namely, the natural liberty of the individual, his freedom from coercion — which must somehow be conserved even in the political state.

In antiquity, it may be said at once, the most frequent and on the whole the most emphasized elements in the conception are the second and third — the technological and economic states of nature, which were commonly conceived to be interconnected. The absence of the arts and of the luxuries which they make possible, and the absence of private ownership and of the passions which at once generate it and are fed by it, usually were held to be the marks of man's truly natural state and the necessary condition for the peacefulness and happiness of men in that state. Technological primitivism has had, from an early period, a definite and increasingly persuasive ground in a very natural and reasonable consideration. It can hardly have long escaped man's notice, after he became in any degree reflective, that some of the arts, if not all of them, were by no means unmixed blessings; and that it was at least questionable whether many of them had not been instruments rather of mischief than of benefit to mankind. This was especially apparent in the case of the arts which had made war more deadly than it could have been in primitive times — even supposing that it occurred in those times. The introduction of mining and metallurgy and even of fire-making, in so far as it was instrumental to metallurgy, were the most conspicuous examples of this melancholy truth, to which subsequent, and especially recent, history has added so much confirmation. Man's propensities being what they are and apparently always have been, it could be — and early was — suspected that such an animal would have been less harmful to himself and his fellows if he had never gained the powers which technological progress has put into his hands. But, on one ground or another, nearly all of the crafts — as distinct from the play-arts of music, dancing, painting and sculpture — could more or less plausibly be, and, as the texts show, in antiquity already were, brought under a similar indictment.

The Primitivistic Reformer

Since the elements or aspects of the state of nature were thus various, primitivism throughout its history has been, among other things, a special form — and, until the last century and a half, one of the commonest forms — assumed by the polemic of a number of differing types of would-be reformers of society. Equalitarians, communists, philosophical anarchists, pacifists, insurgents against existing moral codes, including those of sexual relations, vegetarians, to whom may be added deists, the propagandists of ' natural religion,' who also had their ancient counterparts — all these have sought and, as they believed, found a sanction for their preachments and their programs in the supposed example of primeval men or of living savages. The Golden Age of Greek mythology was originally, indeed — so far as the texts indicate — irrelevant to man's life as it now is; it was enjoyed by a different breed of mortals, in a different condition of the world and (in one version) under different gods, and no practical moral could therefore consistently be drawn from it for the guidance of the present race. It was by implication irrecoverable, at least by men's own efforts. But the Golden Age was soon converted into an embodiment not only of one but of numerous ideals which could be held up to one's contemporaries or to posterity for realization. Merely, for example, to point out and to lament the horrors of war was less effective than to picture the felicity of a past and early, or absolutely primeval, condition in which war had been unknown; for this implied that it was not inseparable from human existence and not inherent in the original and universal, and therefore the true, or normal, nature of man; and more vaguely, it could be denounced, from this point of view, in the sacred name of ' nature.' Most primitivism, especially in poetry, has, no doubt, been rather the expression — often the pessimistic expression — of an emotional nostalgia or an idyllic day-dream, than an instrument of propaganda; and one may in principle distinguish ' sentimental ' from ' practical ' primitivism, whether the example of the state of nature be found in the earliest age or in surviving primitive peoples. But the one naturally shades off into the other; a mood of intense dissatisfaction with some or all the characteristics of the civilized life of one's own time will obviously produce in some minds a hope and an endeavor to put an end to them. Thus, as has already been remarked, primitivism need not be, and often has not been, hostile to a certain faith in progress.

tions of man's differentiating peculiarities which gave rise to it — had as their emotional concomitant a strange disgust of man with himself, of which the very possibility could be regarded as an evidence of something abnormal in the constitution of the species. It was the foreshadowing of the mood which was to manifest itself in the unflattering but penetrating analyses of human behavior and motives in Hobbes, La Rochefoucauld, La Bruyère, Mandeville, in the series of poetic "satires on man" in the late seventeenth and the eighteenth century, and most intensely of all in Swift — the feeling that it is no casual and remediable symptom, such as over-civilization, that afflicts man, but the more desperate malady of being human. From the beginning this self-disparagement of man arose, not merely from reflections upon the poverty of his physical equipment, the painful and disgusting manner of his birth, or the irrational self-destructiveness of his collective behavior, shown chiefly in his addiction to almost continuous war, but also from a consideration of his distinctive mental qualities, intellectual and affective (cf. XIII, 1, 4, 5, 6, 8 *ad fin.*; also IV, 6, II, 58, VIII, 8).

His boasted reason has seemed, to writers of this temper, a poor thing in comparison with the sureness and directness of instinct; while its achievements flatter his vanity and now and then perhaps serve some genuine utility, its most indubitable and characteristic effects are, it was observed, to lead him into doubts and perplexities, into error, into an endless diversity of contradictory beliefs and codes of conduct, into disagreement and wrangling, into a curiosity about things he cannot know and a concern about future events which he cannot control, and into a general habit of worrying and 'taking thought' about life which is inimical to the enjoyment of it. All this was, of course, merely an adaptation to a different use of the anti-intellectualist strain in primitivism. And though neither primitivists nor animalitarians, in antiquity at least, seem to have recognized in man's self-consciousness his most marked mental differentia — unique in degree and in its pervasion of his general affective life, if not absolutely peculiar to him — some of them, as the texts will show, did not fail to point to traits which are in fact conditioned by it as the major causes of the unnaturalness and unhappiness of his existence: the individual's preoccupation with the opinions of others about him and their feelings towards him, which results in an extreme emotional vulnerability and renders him incapable of that (for the Greeks) supreme good which is 'self-sufficiency' and self-containment; his insincerities and affectations; his concern about appearances and about proprieties, especially in connection with sex and other natural functions of the body; his susceptibility to shame and self-reproach, which is the shadow and nemesis of his irrational pride. In so far as these psychic peculiarities of man were increasingly reflected upon, in the course of his scrutiny and appraisal of himself, the sense of his unlikeness to all the rest of the animate creation became sharpened, and, to thinkers of a tough-minded or a melancholic type, it came to seem the more evident that he is a perverted creature profoundly alienated from ' nature.'

(b) On the other hand, the argument could be, and by some eventually was to be, reversed. From the thesis of the ' unnaturalness' of man it could equally consistently be argued that ' imitating ' or ' being in harmony with nature ' must, at best, be a perilous formula for the norm of human life, and, in its most usual senses, an essentially false one. Since few ancient moralists were wholly free from the habit of using ' nature ' with some normative connotation, this possible deduction, though in substance discernible enough in Plato, seldom emerges very clearly in antiquity. But it had an obvious affinity with the logic of Christian otherworldliness, just as the animalitarians' reflections upon the depravity and generic inner abnormality of man had with the doctrine of original sin. Finally, among the phases of the Romantic transformation of values was a tendency to find the supreme excellence of man in many of the traits which both primitivists and animalitarians had often reckoned among his abnormalities — his insatiability, restlessness, variability, his consciousness of his own inner states, the dissatisfaction and disharmony with himself which this engendered, his propensity to attempt intellectual and moral achievements beyond his powers; and the departure from ' nature,' which had so often been declared the source of all evil, came to be described as his chief glory and the beginning of wisdom and of virtue; as a Victorian poet wrote:

> Man must begin, know this, where Nature ends.
> Nature and man can never be fast friends.
> Fool, if thou canst not pass her, rest her slave!

It is a far cry from the starting-point of this history to such later episodes, which can here be only summarily called to mind; yet if they are not in some measure kept in view from the outset, the implicit antitheses which give significance to certain of the earlier phases of the history are likely to be overlooked and the perspective of the spectacle as a whole to be missed.

CHAPTER TWO

CHRONOLOGICAL PRIMITIVISM IN GREEK AND ROMAN MYTHOLOGY AND HISTORIOGRAPHY

A. THE THEORY AND LEGEND OF PROGRESSIVE DEGRADATION

THE AGE OF HEROES IN HOMER

While the earliest Greek version of the story of man's progressive degradation is found in Hesiod, there is already in Homer the recall of a past which is better than the present. It may be nothing more than *laus temporis acti,* yet it seems to refer to what in Hesiod becomes the Age of Heroes.

II, 1. *Iliad,* I, 260-268.

> ἤδη γάρ ποτ' ἐγὼ καὶ ἀρείοσιν ἠέ περ ὑμῖν
> ἀνδράσιν ὡμίλησα, καὶ οὔ ποτέ μ' οἵ γ' ἀθέριζον.
> οὐ γάρ πω τοίους ἴδον ἀνέρας οὐδὲ ἴδωμαι,
> οἷον Πειρίθοόν τε Δρύαντά τε ποιμένα λαῶν,
> Καινέα τ' Ἐξάδιόν τε καὶ ἀντίθεον Πολύφημον
> [Θησέα τ' Αἰγείδην, ἐπιείκελον ἀθανάτοισιν].
> κάρτιστοι δὴ κεῖνοι ἐπιχθονίων τράφεν ἀνδρῶν·
> κάρτιστοι μὲν ἔσαν καὶ καρτίστοις ἐμάχοντο,
> φηρσὶν ὀρεσκῴοισι, καὶ ἐκπάγλως ἀπόλεσσαν.[1]

For already I [Nestor] have consorted with men better even than you, and never did they belittle me. For I never have seen such men nor shall I ever again, as Pirithous and Dryas, shepherd of the people, and Caeneus and Exadius and godlike Polyphemus [and Theseus, son of Aegeus, like to the deathless gods]. Strongest were they of men upon earth; they were strongest and they fought with the strongest, with the wild men who dwell in the mountains,[2] and they entirely destroyed them.

The superiority of the heroes over Nestor's younger contemporaries, who were among the heroes and demigods of Hesiod, seems to have consisted largely in physical strength and courage.[3] No mention is made of their having lived in primitive times, and indeed their mountain enemies seem to have been more primitive than they. The tendency to refer to their times with longing did not die out with the Homeric poems. We find, for instance, Pindar in the opening lines of *Pyth.* III lamenting the disappear-

---

[1] Ed. Dindorf-Hentze, Leipzig, 1893, I.

[2] φηρσὶν ὀρεσκῴοισι is traditionally translated, "with the centaurs."

[3] The future of the idea that primitive men were stronger and, perhaps by implication, bigger than contemporary man is given below in Nos. 62-65.

ance of those days when " that rugged monster," Chiron, was alive, and
Catullus in his *Marriage of Peleus and Thetis* (LXIV, lines 16-23, 384-
408) plays upon the same theme.

The Legend of the Ages

The elements in Greek mythology which are most significant in relation
to the general history of primitivism are two — the legend of the Golden
Age and of the ages which came after it, and the story of Prometheus.
The one is the oldest known manifestation of chronological primitivism in
Western thought, dating, probably, from an antiquity more remote than
that of its earliest literary expression. It is a folk-belief of which the
genesis is hidden in the mists of pre-history, though some more or less
probable conjecture can be made as to how it originated. Thus, perhaps,
from long before the earliest Greek literature, the dream of a lost paradise
haunted the imagination of the Greeks — and with it the gloomy conception
of human history as a progressive deterioration, of which the end is not yet.
The Prometheus myth, on the other hand, which there is some reason for
supposing to be, in some simpler form, a still older piece of folk-belief,
implied a very different conception of the course of history, at least in the
past. It is, of course, a story of a type current among primitive peoples —
the story of the culture-hero of the tribe or race, the human or superhuman
benefactor who first taught the practical arts, especially those of fire-making
and agriculture. Such a story assumes, when it does not expressly say, that
a very early (usually the earliest) state of mankind, or of one's own people,
was an inferior one — a condition of comparative helplessness and physical
misery; that this was due to an ignorance of the arts of life, and that the
great event in past history, the innovation ever to be thankfully remembered, was the introduction of certain artificial contrivances — the firestick,
the plow, the spindle, and the loom.

While these two types of myth thus expressed essentially incongruous ways
of thinking about the past history of one's people, or of men in general, they
not only both found a place in that extraordinarily confused product of
religious syncretism which we call Greek mythology, but they both were connected with the same episode — with the story of the Titanomachia, the
struggle for supremacy between Zeus and the Olympian pantheon, on the
one hand, and his father Cronus and the rest of the Titans, on the other,
which ended in the defeat and dethronement of Cronus, the casting-down
of the Titans into Tartarus, and the establishment of the present dynasty
of gods in the control of celestial and earthly affairs. The one almost constant factor in the variations of the tale of the Golden Age is that it was
coincident with the reign of Cronus, and that it ceased with, or soon after,
the accession of Zeus to power. Men already existed in the age of Titans — at
least males did, for according to one version in Hesiod (Ch. VII, 1), there
were no women in the Golden Age, Pandora being the first of her sex and

the immediate source of human misery; and so long as the gods of the older generation reigned, all went well with mortals. By the eighth century B. C., then, and doubtless much earlier, both the story of man's rise from a state of wretchedness due to ignorance and the legend of a progressive deterioration had already been interwoven with the myth of the Titanomachia; and in the *Works and Days* the Tale of the Ages and that of the Firebringer make their initial appearance in literature together. The two contrasting streams of ideas with which this volume will be largely concerned thus flow from a single historic source, though both were later to be fed from many confluents. The purpose of the present study requires that their courses be traced separately. Though Hesiod tells first the story of Prometheus, priority must here be given to the Legend of the Ages; for early versions of the other myth, cf. Chapter VII.

THE AGES IN HESIOD

In the Hesiodic history of the Five Ages there is, no doubt, to be recognized, as Grote long since pointed out, a fusion of two distinct and incongruous myths. The first, manifestly pre-Hesiodic, is the myth of the Four Ages, all bearing the names of metals, and apparently arranged in a descending order of excellence; the second is the legend of the Age of the Heroes, which Hesiod, or some precursor, interpolated between the third and the last of the other ages.

II, 2. *Works and Days*, 109-201 (Translation on p. 27 ff.).

> Χρύσεον μὲν πρώτιστα γένος μερόπων ἀνθρώπων
> ἀθάνατοι ποίησαν Ὀλύμπια δώματ' ἔχοντες.
> οἳ μὲν ἐπὶ Κρόνου ἦσαν, ὅτ' οὐρανῷ ἐμβασίλευεν·
> ὥστε θεοὶ δ' ἔζωον ἀκηδέα θυμὸν ἔχοντες
> νόσφιν ἄτερ τε πόνων καὶ ὀιζύος· οὐδέ τι δειλὸν
> γῆρας ἐπῆν, αἰεὶ δὲ πόδας καὶ χεῖρας ὁμοῖοι
> τέρποντ' ἐν θαλίῃσι κακῶν ἔκτοσθεν ἁπάντων·
> θνῆσκον δ' ὥσθ' ὕπνῳ δεδμημένοι· ἐσθλὰ δὲ πάντα
> τοῖσιν ἔην· καρπὸν δ' ἔφερε ζείδωρος ἄρουρα
> αὐτομάτη πολλόν τε καὶ ἄφθονον· οἳ δ' ἐθελημοὶ
> ἥσυχοι ἔργ' ἐνέμοντο σὺν ἐσθλοῖσιν πολέεσσιν.
> ἀφνειοὶ μήλοισι, φίλοι μακάρεσσι θεοῖσιν.
> Αὐτὰρ ἐπεὶ δὴ τοῦτο γένος κατὰ γαῖ' ἐκάλυψε, —
> τοὶ μὲν δαίμονες ἁγνοὶ ἐπιχθόνιοι καλέονται
> ἐσθλοί, ἀλεξίκακοι, φύλακες θνητῶν ἀνθρώπων,
> [οἵ ῥα φυλάσσουσίν τε δίκας καὶ σχέτλια ἔργα
> ἠέρα ἑσσάμενοι πάντη φοιτῶντες ἐπ' αἶαν,]
> πλουτοδόται· καὶ τοῦτο γέρας βασιλήιον ἔσχον —,
> δεύτερον αὖτε γένος πολὺ χειρότερον μετόπισθεν
> ἀργύρεον ποίησαν Ὀλύμπια δώματ' ἔχοντες,
> χρυσέῳ οὔτε φυὴν ἐναλίγκιον οὔτε νόημα.
> ἀλλ' ἑκατὸν μὲν παῖς ἔτεα παρὰ μητέρι κεδνῇ
> ἐτρέφετ' ἀτάλλων, μέγα νήπιος, ᾧ ἐνὶ οἴκῳ.
> ἀλλ' ὅτ' ἄρ' ἡβήσαι τε καὶ ἥβης μέτρον ἵκοιτο,
> παυρίδιον ζώεσκον ἐπὶ χρόνον, ἄλγε' ἔχοντες

ἀφραδίῃς· ὕβριν γὰρ ἀτάσθαλον οὐκ ἐδύναντο
ἀλλήλων ἀπέχειν, οὐδ' ἀθανάτους θεραπεύειν
ἤθελον οὐδ' ἔρδειν μακάρων ἱεροῖς ἐπὶ βωμοῖς,
ἣ θέμις ἀνθρώποις κατὰ ἤθεα. τοὺς μὲν ἔπειτα
Ζεὺς Κρονίδης ἔκρυψε χολούμενος, οὕνεκα τιμὰς
οὐκ ἔδιδον μακάρεσσι θεοῖς, οἳ Ὄλυμπον ἔχουσιν.

Αὐτὰρ ἐπεὶ καὶ τοῦτο γένος κατὰ γαῖ' ἐκάλυψε, —
τοὶ μὲν ὑποχθόνιοι μάκαρες θνητοῖς καλέονται,
δεύτεροι, ἀλλ' ἔμπης τιμὴ καὶ τοῖσιν ὀπηδεῖ —,
Ζεὺς δὲ πατὴρ τρίτον ἄλλο γένος μερόπων ἀνθρώπων
χάλκειον ποίησ', οὐκ ἀργυρέῳ οὐδὲν ὁμοῖον,
ἐκ μελιᾶν, δεινόν τε καὶ ὄβριμον· οἷσιν Ἄρηος
ἔργ' ἔμελεν στονόεντα καὶ ὕβριες· οὐδέ τι σῖτον
ἤσθιον, ἀλλ' ἀδάμαντος ἔχον κρατερόφρονα θυμόν,
ἄπλαστοι· μεγάλη δὲ βίη καὶ χεῖρες ἄαπτοι
ἐξ ὤμων ἐπέφυκον ἐπὶ στιβαροῖσι μέλεσσιν.
τῶν δ' ἦν χάλκεα μὲν τεύχεα, χάλκεοι δέ τε οἶκοι
χαλκῷ δ' εἰργάζοντο· μέλας δ' οὐκ ἔσκε σίδηρος.
καὶ τοὶ μὲν χείρεσσιν ὕπο σφετέρῃσι δαμέντες
βῆσαν ἐς εὐρώεντα δόμον κρυεροῦ Ἀίδαο
νώνυμνοι· θάνατος δὲ καὶ ἐκπάγλους περ ἐόντας
εἷλε μέλας, λαμπρὸν δ' ἔλιπον φάος ἠελίοιο.

Αὐτὰρ ἐπεὶ καὶ τοῦτο γένος κατὰ γαῖ' ἐκάλυψεν,
αὖτις ἔτ' ἄλλο τέταρτον ἐπὶ χθονὶ πουλυβοτείρῃ
Ζεὺς Κρονίδης ποίησε, δικαιότερον καὶ ἄρειον,
ἀνδρῶν ἡρώων θεῖον γένος, οἳ καλέονται
ἡμίθεοι, προτέρη γενεὴ κατ' ἀπείρονα γαῖαν.
καὶ τοὺς μὲν πόλεμός τε κακὸς καὶ φύλοπις αἰνὴ
τοὺς μὲν ὑφ' ἑπταπύλῳ Θήβῃ, Καδμηίδι γαίῃ,
ὤλεσε μαρναμένους μήλων ἔνεκ' Οἰδιπόδαο,
τοὺς δὲ καὶ ἐν νήεσσιν ὑπὲρ μέγα λαῖτμα θαλάσσης
ἐς Τροίην ἀγαγὼν Ἑλένης ἔνεκ' ἠυκόμοιο.
ἔνθ' ἤτοι τοὺς μὲν θανάτου τέλος ἀμφεκάλυψε,
τοῖς δὲ δίχ' ἀνθρώπων βίοτον καὶ ἤθε' ὀπάσσας
Ζεὺς Κρονίδης κατένασσε πατὴρ ἐς πείρατα γαίης.
καὶ τοὶ μὲν ναίουσιν ἀκηδέα θυμὸν ἔχοντες
ἐν μακάρων νήσοισι παρ' Ὠκεανὸν βαθυδίνην,
ὄλβιοι ἥρωες, τοῖσιν μελιηδέα καρπὸν
τρὶς ἔτεος θάλλοντα φέρει ζείδωρος ἄρουρα.
τηλοῦ ἀπ' ἀθανάτων· τοῖσιν Κρόνος ἐμβασιλεύει.
τοῦ γὰρ δεσμὸ]ν ἔλυσε πα[τὴρ ἀνδρῶν τε θεῶν τε.
τοῖσι δ' ὁμῶς ν]εάτοις τιμὴ [καὶ κῦδος ὀπηδεῖ.

Πέμπτον δ' αὖτις ἔτ ἄ]λλο γένος θῆκ' [εὐρύοπα Ζεὺς
ἀνδρῶν, οἳ] γεγάασιν ἐπὶ [χθονὶ πουλυβοτείρῃ.]

Μηκέτ' ἔπειτ' ὤφελλον ἐγὼ πέμπτοισι μετεῖναι
ἀνδράσιν, ἀλλ' ἢ πρόσθε θανεῖν ἢ ἔπειτα γενέσθαι.
νῦν γὰρ δὴ γένος ἐστὶ σιδήρεον· οὐδέ ποτ' ἦμαρ
παύονται καμάτου καὶ ὀιζύος, οὐδέ τι νύκτωρ
φθειρόμενοι. χαλεπὰς δὲ θεοὶ δώσουσι μερίμνας·
ἀλλ' ἔμπης καὶ τοῖσι μεμείξεται ἐσθλὰ κακοῖσιν.
Ζεὺς δ' ὀλέσει καὶ τοῦτο γένος μερόπων ἀνθρώπων,
εὖτ' ἂν γεινόμενοι πολιοκρόταφοι τελέθωσιν.
οὐδὲ πατὴρ παίδεσσιν ὁμοίιος οὐδέ τι παῖδες,

οὐδὲ ξεῖνος ξεινοδόκῳ καὶ ἑταῖρος ἑταίρῳ,
οὐδὲ κασίγνητος φίλος. ἔσσεται, ὡς τὸ πάρος περ.
αἶψα δὲ γηράσκοντας ἀτιμήσουσι τοκῆας·
μέμψονται δ' ἄρα τοὺς χαλεποῖς βάζοντες ἔπεσσι
σχέτλιοι οὐδὲ θεῶν ὄπιν εἰδότες· οὐδέ κεν οἵ γε
γηράντεσσι τοκεῦσιν ἀπὸ θρεπτήρια δοῖεν
χειροδίκαι· ἕτερος δ' ἑτέρου πόλιν ἐξαλαπάξει.
οὐδέ τις εὐόρκου χάρις ἔσσεται οὔτε δικαίου
οὔτ' ἀγαθοῦ, μᾶλλον δὲ κακῶν ῥεκτῆρα καὶ ὕβριν
ἀνέρες αἰνήσουσι· δίκη δ' ἐν χερσί, καὶ αἰδὼς
οὐκ ἔσται· βλάψει δ' ὁ κακὸς τὸν ἀρείονα φῶτα
μύθοισιν σκολιοῖς ἐνέπων, ἐπὶ δ' ὅρκον ὀμεῖται.
ζῆλος δ' ἀνθρώποισιν ὀιζυροῖσιν ἅπασι
δυσκέλαδος κακόχαρτος ὁμαρτήσει, στυγερώπης.
καὶ τότε δὴ πρὸς Ὄλυμπον ἀπὸ χθονὸς εὐρυοδείης
λευκοῖσιν φάρεσσι καλυψαμένα χρόα καλὸν
ἀθανάτων μετὰ φῦλον ἴτον προλιπόντ' ἀνθρώπους
Αἰδὼς καὶ Νέμεσις· τὰ δὲ λείψεται ἄλγεα λυγρὰ
θνητοῖς ἀνθρώποισι· κακοῦ δ' οὐκ ἔσσεται ἀλκή.[4]

The Golden Age

First of all the deathless gods having homes on Olympus made a
golden race of mortal men. These lived in the time of Cronus when
he was king in heaven. Like gods they lived with hearts free from
sorrow and remote from toil and grief; nor was miserable age their
lot, but always unwearied in feet and hands they made merry in
feasting, beyond the reach of all evils. And when they died, it was
as though they were given over to sleep. And all good things were
theirs. For the fruitful earth spontaneously bore them abundant
fruit without stint. And they lived in ease and peace upon their
lands with many good things, rich in flocks and beloved of the
blessed gods.[5]

This passage established the following traditions: (1) the designation
of the primitive happy people as a " Golden Race," whence the subsequently
more famous term "The Golden Age." [6] (2) That this race lived when

---

[4] Ed. Evelyn-White, *Loeb Class. Library.*

[5] Cf. Hesiod, *Fragm.* 82 (216), Rzach, Leipzig, 1902:

Ξυναὶ γὰρ τότε δαῖτες ἔσαν, ξυνοὶ δὲ θόωκοι
ἀθανάτοισι θεοῖσι καταθνητοῖς τ' ἀνθρώποις

For they ate their meals in common, and sat together,
Both the immortal gods and mortal men.

This quotation is used by Origen (*Contra Cels.* IV, 79) to show that in the
beginning of human history men were placed under the protection of a supernatural
power so that a union of the divine and human natures might be found. It was
probably used by Hesiod to indicate no such thing, but merely the specially privileged lot of the Golden Race. Cf. *Schol. Arat.* 103, 4 (Maas).

[6] The use of the terms "golden," "silver," and "bronze" to indicate the comparative value of classes of beings is shown in Stobaeus in a quotation from Bion.
There are, according to this fragment, three classes of scholars, the golden, the
silver, and the bronze. The golden teach and learn, the silver teach and do not

Cronus was king, i. e., before the Olympian revolution which put Zeus upon the throne. Hence the name " the Age of Cronus " (Saturn) as a synonym for the Golden Age, which will later be contrasted with the Age of Zeus. (3) Soft primitivism: the life of this race was idle and merry and full of feasting. This will be satirized by the Comic Poets of the 5th century [7] (see below, II, Nos. 10-15, inc.). (4) That the earth produced spontaneously. When the primitive condition is identified with the " state of nature " this feature will develop into " technological primitivism." (5) The Golden Race lived without war or violence. To sum up, the earliest human family, according to Hesiod, lived almost in a state of luxury — its life was far from ascetic — and in perpetual peace.

Since the Prometheus myth does not figure in Hesiod's second tale, the issue of cultural primitivism is not even suggested. That the primeval life without toil and without sickness was the most desirable life Hesiod assumes; but that, for man under the present conditions of his existence, the simple life is the better, is not intimated, nor is any view implied as to whether the introduction of the arts and the labor of the intellect were a blessing or a curse to mortals under such conditions.

The Age of Silver

> But when this race had been covered by earth — they are called pure daimons who haunt the earth, noble, delivering from evil, guardians of mortal men (for they guard justice and ward off wicked deeds) clothed in mist as they roam everywhere over the earth, and are givers of wealth; and they received this kingly privilege too — then the dwellers on Olympus made another race much worse by far, a race of silver, and like the golden race neither in outward appearance nor in mind. But a hundred years a child was reared by his dear mother's side, a booby skipping about in his home. But when they were full grown and had arrived at the measure of manhood, they lived but a little while, and that in sorrow because of their foolishness; for they were unable to refrain from savage insolence towards one another, nor would they serve the immortals, nor sacrifice on the holy altars of the blessed ones, as is right for men according to custom. Then Zeus, son of Cronus, in anger hid them away, because they did not honor the blessed gods who dwell on Olympus.

With respect to the second or Silver Race, the following facts are to be noted: (1) The men of that race are not descendants of the Golden Race but a new creation. (2) They differ for the worse from their predecessors both physically [8] and mentally. (3) Their physical inferiority is shown in

---

learn, the bronze learn and do not teach. See Stobaeus (Meineke), Vol. IV, p. 202, *Excerpta e MS. Flor. Ioan. Damasc.* part II, 97.

[7] But see Campbell Bonner's article, " Dionysiac Magic and the Greek Land of Cockaigne." *Transactions and Proceedings of the American Philological Association*, 1910, Vol. XLI, 175 ff.

[8] Cf. below II, 4 (from Theognis).

their prolonged infancy and short maturity. (4) Their mental inferiority is shown in their impiety and belligerency. (5) The substitution of this new and inferior race is not explained as a consequence of any moral or other decline of their predecessors. But (6) the new race is destroyed by Zeus because of their impiety.

The Age of Bronze

But when this race too had been covered by earth — they are called the blessed ones of the underworld by mortals, a second rank, but nevertheless honor accompanies them too — Zeus, the father, made a third race of mortal men of bronze, in no way like the silver race, from the ash-tree,[9] terrible and strong. To them the lamentable deeds of Ares and violence were a delight. Nor did they eat bread, but they had dauntless hearts of adamant, fearful men. Great was their strength, and invincible their arms grew from their shoulders on their strong limbs. And of bronze was their armor and of bronze their houses and they worked in bronze; and there was no black iron. They were destroyed by their own hands and went to the mouldy house of chill Hades nameless. And black death seized them though they were terrible, and they left the bright light of the sun.

The third race, like the second, are not descended from their predecessors, but are either a fresh creation from ash-trees, or children of the Meliae. That they were inferior to the Silver Race is not clear from the description. It is hard to see why any eighth-century Greek should have considered them to be so.[10] For the men of the Silver Race, even at the age of one hundred, were childish simpletons; and soon after their belated maturity they were extirpated " because of their foolishness." But the Bronze Race, though violent and cruel, were mighty men of their hands, clearly superior physically and mentally to their precursors. It is therefore possible that the original tale of the Four Ages did not imply a continuous decline; but in the form in which it was used by Hesiod the sequence was probably represented as a progressive deterioration. This is suggested by the order of the

---

[9] Cf. Apoll. Rhod. *Argonautica*, IV, 1638 ff. where the bronze race is also said to be born of ash-trees. Evelyn-White in his translation of Hesiod (Loeb Library), p. 13, n. 1, adds that " Eustathius refers to Hesiod as stating that men ' spring from oaks and stones and ashtrees.' Proclus believed that the Nymphs called Meliae (*Theogony*, 187) are intended. Goettling would render: 'A race terrible because of their (ashen) spears.' "

Paley in his *The Epics of Hesiod*, London, 1883, cites Virgil, *Aen.* VIII, 315, " Gensque virum truncis et duro robore nata," in support of the version we have adopted. Ovid, as Paley says, leaves the matter ambiguous. See *Met.* I, 125. Mair in *Hesiod, the Poems and Fragments*, Oxford, 1908, translates, " begotten of the Meliai," following apparently Proclus. Mazon in his Commentary (*Hésiode, Les Travaux et les Jours*, 1914, p. 66), accepts the tradition that they are born of ash-trees and cites Pindar, *Fragm.* 74, 7. Cf. also Juvenal, *Sat.* VI, 12.

[10] Hesiod does not say, as Mr. Evelyn-White makes him do, that this race " was in no way equal to the Silver Age." He says that they were not at all like the weaklings of that age.

metals, for which the successive races are named, and by the paradoxical identification of the dull-witted and violent Silver Race after death with some divinities of the underworld, of honorable, if secondary, rank. The disappearance of the third race, it is to be noted, was a consequence of their own moral characteristics and conduct; they were not destroyed by Zeus as were the men of the preceding ages.

The Age of Heroes

But when this race too had been covered by earth, Zeus, son of Cronus, made another, the fourth, upon the fruitful earth, juster and more righteous, a divine race of hero-men who are called demi-gods — the race immediately preceding our own throughout the boundless earth. And these evil war and dread battle destroyed, some by seven-gated Thebes, the land of Cadmus, fighting because of the flocks of Oedipus, and some who had gone in ships over the great depths of the sea to Troy for fair-haired Helen. There the doom of death engulfed them. But to them Zeus, son of Cronus, the father, gave a life and a dwelling apart from men, at the ends of the earth. And they dwell with hearts free of sorrow [11] in the islands of the blessed by deep-eddying Ocean, happy heroes, for whom the grain-giving earth bears honeyed fruit, flourishing thrice a year. They are far from the immortals. Cronus rules over them. For the father of gods and men loosed his fetters. And these have equal honor and glory.

The Fourth Race is an interlude in human deterioration. It is not named after a metal but is called the Race of Heroes. The later writers, who adhere to the theory of continuous decline, smooth out this inconsistency by eliminating the incident and either reducing the number of ages to four or, as will be seen, to two.

The Heroes are (1) the superiors both of their immediate predecessors and their successors. (2) They were, however, destroyed by war. (3) But after death they live in the Islands of the Blessed.[12] There their life is a return to that of the Golden Age in that the earth produces food for them with wonderful abundance, and that they are ruled over by Cronus.

The Age of Iron

The Fifth Race continues the degradation interrupted by the Age of Heroes.

And then, fifth, Zeus, the far-seeing, made still another race of men upon the fruitful earth.

Would that I were not among the fifth race, but had either died before or were born afterwards. For now the race is iron. Neither by day does it have an end of toil and sorrow nor by night of wasting away. But the gods shall give them toilsome anxiety. Nevertheless for these too good shall be mixed with their evils. But Zeus will destroy this race of men too when they reach the point of being born

[11] Cf. Simonides, *Fragm.* 36 (51), in Bergk's *Poetae medici.*
[12] For the tradition of the Islands of the Blessed see Ch. XI, p. 290.

with greying temples.[13]   Nor will father agree with child nor child with father, nor guest with host nor comrade with comrade, nor will brother be dear to brother as before.   But soon men will dishonor their aging parents and will carp at them, scolding them with bitter words, merciless, knowing no fear of the gods.   Nor will they, whose right is in their fists, repay their aged parents for their nurture. And one man will sack another's city.   Nor will there be any favor for the man who keeps his word nor for the just and good, but rather will men praise the evil-doer and his crime ($\ddot{v}\beta\rho\iota\varsigma$).   And right will be in might, and modesty will no longer exist.   And the evil man will injure the better man, speaking with crooked tales and swearing an oath thereto.   And envy, foul-mouthed, of hateful visage, delight-ing in evil, will accompany all miserable men.   And then Shame (Aidos) and Indignation (Nemesis), with their fair forms wrapped in white robes, will go from the wide-pathed earth to Olympus and to the people of the gods, abandoning men.   And bitter sorrows will be left for mortal men, and there will be no help against evil.

The Fifth Race, our own, is: (1) apparently the worst of races, and is, moreover, in process of continuous deterioration, physical and moral.   Yet it may possibly be followed by a better race, since the poet wishes he had been born before *or after*.   (2) Its condition is the opposite of that of the Golden Race, consisting in suffering, toil, internal and external war, instead of pleasure, leisure, and peace.   (3) It will continue until its children are born senile.   (4) Force will take the place of justice and evil passions the place of good.   (5) The goddesses who sponsor right living will leave the earth.   These two goddesses, Aidos and Nemesis, will appear later as the one goddess, Astraea (see Aratus, II, 7 below), whose departure recalls not only the Hesiodic account of men being forsaken by the goddesses of right-living but also the substitution of Might for Right.   But this event, placed by the later writers in the past, is for Hesiod still future.

The Hesiodic story gives no explanation of the progressive degradation of mortals.   It is, apparently, arbitrarily woven into the texture of things, as in the Empedoclean if not in the Stoic theory of cycles.   Nor do the races disappear for any one reason.   The Golden Race disappears for no assigned cause; the Silver because of *hybris* and impiety; the Bronze by internecine war; the Heroes by external war; the Iron by exhaustion, or perhaps because of their evil-doing.   It remained for later poets to take up the elements of the confused Hesiodic "outline of history," to attempt to reduce them to some sort of coherency, and to give to them a rational meaning or a morally edifying significance.

The Hesiodic Ages in Greek Writers of the Sixth Century

The story of the Golden Age was doubtless as popular after Hesiod's time as before.   But the one record we have of a work of literature on the subject

---

[13] The development of the idea of man's physical degeneration will be suggested in Section E below.

is that of the Epicurean, Philodemus (early 1st century B. C.), who mentions the author of the *Alcmaeonid* as having, like Hesiod, written an account of " the most happy life in the time of Cronus." [14]

II, 3.

> Κα[ὶ τῆς ἐπ]ὶ Κρόνου ζω[ῆς εὐ]δαιμονεστά[της οὔσ]ης, ὡς ἔγραψ[αν
> Ἡσί]οδος καὶ ὁ τὴν ['Αλκμ]εωνίδα ποή[σας].

At the same time Theognis (*ca.* 544 B. C.) dwells upon the occurrence of a time, probably his own, when justice and piety died out and a man's word was no longer sacred. But the fragment in which this occurs does not contain any explicit description of primitive life nor give any account of the ages.

II, 4. Theognis, *Elegies*, A, 1135 ff.

> 'Ελπὶς ἐν ἀνθρώποισι μόνη θεὸς ἐσθλὴ ἔνεστιν,
> ἄλλοι δ' Οὐλυμπόνδ' ἐκπρολιπόντες ἔβαν.
> ᾤχετο μὲν Πίστις, μεγάλη θεός. ᾤχετο δ' ἀνδρῶν
> Σωφροσύνη· Χάριτές τ', ὦ φίλε, γῆν ἔλιπον.
> ὅρκοι δ' οὐκέτι πιστοὶ ἐν ἀνθρώποισι δίκαιοι,
> οὐδὲ θεοὺς οὐδεὶς ἅζεται ἀθανάτους.
> εὐσεβέων δ' ἀνδρῶν γένος ἔφθιται, οὐδὲ θέμιστας
> οὐκέτι γινώσκουσ' οὐδὲ μὲν εὐσεβίας.[15]

> The good goddess, Hope, alone dwells among men, but the others have gone off to Olympus. The great goddess, Good-faith, has departed, and there has departed from men Moderation (Sophrosyne). And the Graces, friend, have left the earth and just oaths no longer are held among men and no one dreads the deathless gods, and the race of pious men is past and justice and piety are no longer known.

In such a poem it is a moral rather than a material contrast which is made between our own time and that of primitive man.

EARLY PRIMITIVISTIC PACIFISM AND VEGETARIANISM

A similar exaltation of the virtues of primitive man is to be found in Empedocles (*fl. ca.* 444), with the difference that he is referring largely to the superiority of primitive religion. The details are perhaps of no great importance; the essential is that primitive man was better than contemporary man, chiefly by reason of his vegetarianism and the absence of animal sacrifices and of war. The supposition that men were once innocent of slaughter is connected with the Empedoclean cosmology. Love and Strife are two opposing forces which control the history of the cosmos: the four elements, Earth, Water, Air and Fire, are brought into composition and their compounds into dissolution by the action of these forces (*Fragm.* 17).[16]

[14] V. *Epicorum graecorum fragmenta*, ed. Kinkel, Leipzig, 1877, I, 313.

[15] Ed. Hudson-Williams, London, 1910.

[16] We follow the numbering of Diels (4th edition) in citing the Pre-Socratic philosophers.

The following texts refer to the period of the dominance of Love.

II, 5. Empedocles, *Fragm.* 128.

> οὐδέ τις ἦν κείνοισιν Ἄρης θεὸς οὐδὲ Κυδοιμός
> οὐδὲ Ζεὺς βασιλεὺς οὐδὲ Κρόνος οὐδὲ Ποσειδῶν,
> ἀλλὰ Κύπρις βασίλεια.
> τὴν οἵ γ᾽ εὐσεβέεσσιν ἀγάλμασιν ἱλάσκοντο
> γραπτοῖς τε ζώιοισι μύροισί τε δαιδαλεόδμοις
> σμύρνης τ᾽ ἀκρήτου θυσίαις λιβάνου τε θυώδους,
> ξουθῶν τε σπονδὰς μελιτῶν ῥίπτοντες ἐς οὖδας·
> ταύρων δ᾽ ἀκρήτοισι φόνοις οὐ δεύετο βωμός,
> ἀλλὰ μύσος τοῦτ᾽ ἔσκεν ἐν ἀνθρώποισι μέγιστον,
> θυμὸν ἀπορραίσαντας ἐνέδμεναι ἠέα γυῖα.[17]

[In a former age men] had neither Ares for a god nor Kudoimos [the Din of Battle], nor King Zeus nor Cronus nor Poseidon, but Queen Cypris[18] . . . Her they propitiated with holy statues and painted pictures and cleverly mixed perfumes, with offerings of pure myrrh and fragrant frankincense, pouring on the ground libations of tawny honey. And the altar did not reek of the unmixed blood of bulls, but this was the greatest abomination among men, to snatch out the life and eat the goodly limbs.[19]

II, 6. Empedocles, *Fragm.* 130.

> ἦσαν δὲ κτίλα πάντα καὶ ἀνθρώποισι προσηνῆ,
> θῆρές τ᾽ οἰωνοί τε, φιλοφροσύνη τε δεδήει.[20]

All were gentle and obedient to men, both animals and birds, and they glowed with kindly affection towards one another.

The full sense of the former passage comes out when it is referred to its context. It has survived through Porphyry's *De abstinentia* (II, 20-21), a work of the third century of our era. This work is a plea for vegetarianism. The basis of the plea in this particular passage is that if men were dominated by Love (Cypris) they would be vegetarian; and in proof of this Porphyry cites the lines of Empedocles as demonstrating that primitive man was thus dominated. The sentiment is of course in accord with Hesiod, for strife did not enter human affairs until after the disappearance of the Golden Race.[21]

---

[17] Ed. Diels, *Fragmente der Vorsokratiker*, 4th ed. 1922, I, 271-2.

[18] Cf. Theocritus, XII, 15-16, where the equal love of two individuals is the reason why they were called "golden" men. See also Diog. Laert. IV, 4, Life of Crates, and Porphyry on Dicaearchus in *De abstinentia*, IV, 2, cited below, II, 57.

[19] There is an amusing fragment of Antiphanes in Athenaeus, IV, 130, satirizing the *leaf-eating* Greeks whose ancestors ate whole oxen. Whether these ancestors were of the Golden Age or not we have no way of telling. The fragment does illustrate, however, the diversity of Greek opinion about the value of vegetarianism.

[20] Ed. Diels, I, 273.

[21] That there was an early tradition of primitive vegetarianism would appear from Plato, *Laws*, 782 E. But Plato there notes it as a fact, not as a program. Porphyry's argument is like that attributed to Pythagoras in Ovid, *Metamorphoses* (see below, II, 17).

Passed on to later Greek [22] and Roman and so to modern writers, the Empedoclean picture of man's former amicable relations with the animals became a part of the literary convention of chronological primitivism; e. g. almost the whole of Pope's description of the state of nature (*Essay on Man*, III, 147-160) is devoted to this theme, and some of the couplets might serve for free translations of some of Empedocles's lines.

THE MORALIZING OF THE HESIODIC STORY OF THE AGES

Aratus

How thoroughly ethical and religious motives become mingled with the myth of human degradation may be seen in the lines from Aratus which follow. The poem is a century and three-quarters later than that of Empedocles, and undoubtedly could not have been written had there not been already developed an elaborate philosophic tradition of human history.[23] Its author is said to have been a pupil of Timon of Phlius, the famous skeptic, but was more probably associated with Zeno, the founder of Stoicism.[24]

Aratus is describing the constellations and comes to Virgo.

II, 7. *Phaenomena*, 96-136.

> Ἀμφοτέροισι δὲ ποσσὶν ὕπο σκέπτοιο Βοώτεω
> Παρθένον, ἥ ῥ' ἐν χερσὶ φέρει Στάχυν αἰγλήεντα.
> εἴτ' οὖν Ἀστραίου κείνη γένος, ὅν ῥά τέ φασιν
> ἄστρων ἀρχαῖον πατέρ' ἔμμεναι, εἴτε τευ ἄλλου,
> εὔκηλος φορέοιτο. λόγος γε μὲν ἐντρέχει ἄλλος
> ἀνθρώποις, ὡς δῆθεν ἐπιχθονίη πάρος ἦεν,
> ἤρχετο δ' ἀνθρώπων κατεναντίη, οὐδέ ποτ' ἀνδρῶν
> οὐδέ ποτ' ἀρχαίων ἠνήνατο φῦλα γυναικῶν,
> ἀλλ' ἀναμὶξ ἐκάθητο καὶ ἀθανάτη περ ἐοῦσα.
> καί ἑ Δίκην καλέεσκον· ἀγειρομένη δὲ γέροντας
> ἠέ που εἰν ἀγορῆι ἢ εὐρυχόρωι ἐν ἀγυιῆι
> δημοτέρας ἤειδεν ἐπισπέρχουσα θέμιστας.
> οὔπω λευγαλέου τότε νείκεος ἠπίσταντο
> οὐδὲ διακρίσιος πολυμεμφέος οὐδὲ κυδοιμοῦ,
> αὔτως δ' ἔζωον· χαλεπὴ δ' ἀπέκειτο θάλασσα,
> καὶ βίον οὔπω νῆες ἀπόπροθεν ἠγίνεσκον,
> ἀλλὰ βόες καὶ ἄροτρα καὶ αὐτή, πότνια λαῶν,
> μυρία πάντα παρεῖχε Δίκη, δώτειρα δικαίων.
> τόφρ' ἦν, ὄφρ' ἔτι γαῖα γένος χρύσειον ἔφερβεν.
> ἀργυρέωι δ' ὀλίγη τε καὶ οὐκέτι πάμπαν ἑτοίμη
> ὡμίλει ποθέουσα παλαιῶν ἤθεα λαῶν,
> ἀλλ' ἔμπης ἔτι κεῖνο κατ' ἀργύρεον γένος ἦεν·
> ἤρχετο δ' ἐξ ὀρέων ὑποδείελος ἠχηέντων
> μουνάξ, οὐδέ τεωι ἐπεμίσγετο μειλιχίοισιν,
> ἀλλ', ὁπότ' ἀνθρώπων μεγάλας πλήσαιτο κολώνας,

---

[22] Cf. e. g. the passage from Babrius below (II, 18).
[23] See particularly the section on Plato, Ch. V below.
[24] See Zeller's *Stoics, Epicureans and Skeptics*, p. 43 f.

ἠπείλει δῆπειτα καθαπτομένη κακότητος,
οὐδ᾽ ἔτ᾽ ἔφη εἰσωπὸς ἐλεύσεσθαι καλέουσιν·
" οἵην χρύσειοι πατέρες γενεὴν ἐλίποντο
χειροτέρην. ὑμεῖς δὲ κακώτερα τεξείεσθε·
καὶ δή που πόλεμοι, καὶ δή που ἀνάρσιον αἷμα
ἔσσεται ἀνθρώποισι, κακὸν δ᾽ ἐπικείσεται ἄλγος."
ὣς εἰποῦσ᾽ ὀρέων ἐπεμαίετο, τοὺς δ᾽ ἄρα λαούς
εἰς αὐτὴν ἔτι πάντας ἐλίμπανε παπταίνοντας.
ἀλλ᾽ ὅτε δὴ κἀκεῖνοι ἐτέθνασαν, οἱ δ᾽ ἐγένοντο
χαλκείη γενεή, προτέρων ὀλοώτεροι ἄνδρες
(οἳ πρῶτοι κακοεργὸν ἐχαλκεύσαντο μάχαιραν,
εἰνοδίην, πρῶτοι δὲ βοῶν ἐπάσαντ᾽ ἀροτήρων),
δὴ τότε μισήσασα Δίκη κείνων γένος ἀνδρῶν
ἔπταθ᾽ ὑπουρανίη, ταύτην δ᾽ ἄρα νάσσατο χώρην,
ἧχί περ ἐννυχίη ἔτι φαίνεται ἀνθρώποισι
Παρθένος ἐγγὺς ἐοῦσα πολυσκέπτοιο Βοώτεω.[25]

And beneath both feet of Boötes behold the Maiden, who in her hands bears the Ear of Corn gleaming. Whether she be of the race of Astraeus, who they say was the ancient father of the stars, or of another, may she be borne on in safety. Now another tale is current among men, to wit, how formerly she was on earth, and met men face to face, and neither disdained the tribes of ancient men nor women, but sat amid them, immortal though she was. And they called her Justice; and assembling the elders, either in the market place or in the wide streets, she spoke aloud urging judgments more advantageous to the people. Not yet did men understand hateful war or vituperative disputes or din of battle, but they lived simply, and the cruel sea was concealed, nor did ships carry men's livelihood from afar; but oxen and the plough and Justice herself, mistress of the people, giver of just things, furnished all things a thousand fold. This continued as long as the earth nourished the Golden Race. But with the Silver [Race] she mingled seldom and no longer with great eagerness, longing for the manners of the ancient peoples. Nevertheless she was still there during the time of the Silver Race. But she came down from the echoing mountains only towards evening, nor did she deal with anyone with gentle words. But when she had filled the great hills with men, then assailing them she would threaten them because of their wickedness, and say that she would never come again before their eyes when they called to her. "What an inferior race the golden fathers have left! But you will breed worse. And wars and monstrous bloodshed will be among men and evil pain will be laid upon them." Thus speaking she sought the mountains and left the people all staring after her. But when this race was dead and the Bronze Race was born, men more deadly than their predecessors, the first to forge the evil-working sword of the roadside [26] and the first to eat of oxen who draw the plough, then Justice hated the race of those men and flew to Heaven. And she dwelt in that country where still at night she appears to men, the Maiden being near to far-seen Boötes.

[25] Ed. E. Maas, Berlin, 1893.
[26] Of the highwayman?—See G. R. Mair's translation in the Loeb Library.

The most notable changes which have here been worked into the story of man's deterioration are its consistent moral tone and the assumption of a blood-relationship between the races. The various races are no longer, as in Hesiod, fresh creations, but are of one descent. It is the increasing wickedness of man that brings on his present misery, and the gradual withdrawal of the goddess is a symbol for the gradual growth of injustice. In the Golden Age all men were just "by nature": — she sat amidst them.[27] In the Silver Age she spoke only occasionally and became, so to say, retributive justice. In the Bronze Age [28] she no longer dwelt among men.

The primitivism of Aratus is still a description, not a program; but it is a description in which the supernatural traits of Hesiod's Golden Age have been omitted. The Golden Race lived a life which could presumably be lived again, were men so minded. The features of primitive life which are emphasized by Aratus are its freedom from war, the absence of foreign trade, and vegetarianism — for oxen were still put to their proper use, drawing the plough. It is a "simple life" and thus approaches hard rather than soft primitivism, as was to be expected from a pupil of the Stoics. The hardness, however, is tempered by absence of pain. But that, too, is explicable if Aratus was a Stoic (or a skeptic, for that matter), for then primitive man would be simply living the life of the Sage — who was 'apathetic.'

The Fortunes of Aratus

The poem of Aratus appears to have had a considerable popularity in ancient times. An introduction is said to have been written for it by Achilles Tatius, who is also credited with a commentary on it, and another commentary was produced by Hipparchus. There were at least three poetical Latin translations, one by Cicero in De natura deorum, ii, 41, one ascribed to Caesar Germanicus, and one to Festus Avienus.

Not much later than the poem was written a commentary is said to have been composed by Eratosthenes, of which we have a version. From this we take the following extract:

II, 8. Ps.-Eratosthenes, Catasterismi, I, 244.

Παρθένου.

Ταύτην Ἡσίοδος ἐν Θεογονίᾳ εἴρηκε θυγατέρα Διὸς καὶ Θέμιδος, καλεῖσθαι δὲ αὐτὴν Δίκην· λέγει δὲ καὶ Ἄρατος παρὰ τούτου λαβὼν τὴν ἱστορίαν ὡς οὖσα πρότερον ἀθάνατος καὶ ἐπὶ τῆς γῆς σὺν τοῖς ἀνθρώποις ἦν καὶ ὅτι Δίκην αὐτὴν ἐκάλουν· μεταστάντων δὲ αὐτῶν καὶ μηκέτι τὸ δίκαιον συντηρούντων, οὐκέτι σὺν αὐτοῖς ἦν, ἀλλ᾽ εἰς τὰ ὄρη ὑπεχώρει· εἶτα στάσεων καὶ πολέμων αὐτοῖς ὄντων [διὰ] τὴν παντελῆ αὐτῶν ἀδικίαν ἀπομισήσασαν εἰς τὸν οὐρανὸν ἀνελθεῖν. λέγονται δὲ καὶ ἕτεροι λόγοι περὶ αὐτῆς πλεῖστοι· οἱ μὲν γὰρ αὐτὴν

---

[27] Is this a foreshadowing of a juristic state of nature — as in the passage from the Metamorphoses, II, 17, below?

[28] Aratus does not mention the Iron Age.

φασιν εἶναι Δήμητρα διὰ τὸ ἔχειν στάχυν, οἱ δὲ Ἶσιν, οἱ δὲ Ἀταργάτιν, οἱ δὲ Τύχην, διὸ καὶ ἀκέφαλον αὐτὴν σχηματίζουσιν.[29]

Hesiod in the *Theogony* says she (Astraea) was the daughter of Zeus and Themis, and calls her Justice. And Aratus in his turn, taking the story from him, says that she, though immortal, formerly lived on earth with men, and that they called her Justice. And when men changed and no longer observed justice, she stayed with them no longer but went off to the mountains. Then when there were factions and wars among them because of their absolute wickedness which she hated, she went off to heaven. And many other tales are told about her. For some say she is Demeter because she holds the Ear of Wheat, and some Isis, some Atargatis, and some Fortune (Τύχη). Hence she is represented [in the heavens] without a head.

This version is very poor in details and serves merely as a sample of how Aratus's story was kept alive. It will be noticed that war and discord are the causes of man's fall.

The Aratean tradition was passed on to Rome in the translations of the *Phenomena*, but the *Catasterismi* itself was imitated by Hyginus. If our text is by the Hyginus who Suetonius says was Ovid's friend, we may have here the source of Ovid's story of the Ages, if any special source need be assumed.

II, 9. Hyginus, *Poetica astronomica*, II, ch. 25.

Hanc Hesiodus Jovis et Themidis filiam dicit: Aratus autem Astraei et Aurorae filiam existimari, quod eodem tempore fuerit cum aurea secula hominum, et eorum principem fuisse, demonstrat: quam propter diligentiam et aequitatem Justitiam appellatam: neque illo tempore ab hominibus exteras nationes bello lacessitas esse, neque navigio quemquam usum esse, sed agris colendis vitam agere consuevisse. Sed post eorum obitum, qui sint nati, eos minus officiosos, magis avaros coepisse fieri: quare minus Justitiam inter homines fuisse conversatam. Denique causam pervenisse usque eo, dum diceretur: aeneum genus hominum natum. Itaque jam non potuisse pati amplius, et ad sidera evolasse. Sed hanc alii Fortunam, alii Cererem dixerunt: et hoc magis non convenit inter eos, quod caput ejus nimium obscurum videtur.[30]

Her Hesiod calls the daughter of Jupiter and Themis. Aratus, however, thinks her the daughter of Astraeus and Aurora, because she lived at the same time as the Golden Age of men and was their leader. Because of her faithfulness and equity she was called Justice. And at that time foreign nations were not harassed by men in war, nor was there any use of navigation, but people were accustomed to spend their life cultivating their fields. But after the death of these, those who were born were less dutiful. They began to be more avaricious. Wherefore Justice associated less with men. Finally

[29] Ed. Olivieri, Leipzig, 1897, pp. 11-12.

[30] *Mythographi Latini*, ed. van Staveren, Leyden and Amsterdam, 1742, p. 477 f. The edition of Hyginus by Chatelain and Legendre (1909) from a MS in Milan adds nothing to this passage.

things came to the point where, it was said, the Bronze Race of men was born. Then she was unable to endure more and flew off to the stars. But some call her Fortune and others Ceres. And for this reason the more there is no agreement among them, because her head appears too dimly.

Before passing on to the next great figure in the growth of this tradition, we must return to Athens of the fifth century B. C., during which the Golden Age seems to have been a fairly common literary theme.

PARODIES OF THE GOLDEN AGE IN GREEK COMIC POETS

The life free from toil and pain, when earth produced spontaneously the necessities and many of the luxuries of life, when all men were equal and all at peace, became an object of satire to the old comic writers. Athenaeus discussing them (*Deipnos.* VI, 267) is our authority for taking the following passages as referring to the Golden Age.

Cratinus in his *Plutoi* dwells on the abundance of foods:

II, 10. Cratinus, in Athenaeus, *Deipnos.* VI, 267.

Οἷς δὴ βασιλεὺς Κρόνος ἦν τὸ παλαιόν,
ὅτε τοῖς ἄρτοις ἠστραγάλιζον, μᾶζαι δ᾽ ἐν ταῖσι παλαίστραις
Αἰγιναῖαι κατεβέβληντο δρυπεπεῖς βώλοις τε κομῶσαι.[31]

Cronus was their king in ancient days, when men played dice with wheaten loaves, and Aeginetan barley cakes all cooked were thrown into the arena streaming with curds[?].

The same type of picture is drawn by Pherecrates (*fl. ca.* 438) in his *Metalles.* His land of Cockaigne seems to be situated in the Lower World.

II, 11. Pherecrates, in Athenaeus, *Deipnos.* VI, 268-269.

A. Πλούτῳ δ᾽ ἐκεῖν᾽ ἦν πάντα συμπεφυρμένα,
ἐν πᾶσιν ἀγαθοῖς πάντα τρόπον εἰργασμένα.
ποταμοὶ μὲν ἀθάρης καὶ μέλανος ζωμοῦ πλέῳ
διὰ τῶν στενωπῶν τονθολυγοῦντες ἔρρεον
αὐταῖσι μυστίλαισι, καὶ ναστῶν τρύφη,
ὥστ᾽ εὐμαρῆ γε καὐτομάτοις τὴν ἔνθεσιν
χωρεῖν λιπαρὰν κατὰ τοῦ λάρυγγος τοῖς νεκροῖς·
φύσκαι δὲ καὶ σίζοντες ἀλλάντων τόμοι
παρὰ τοῖς ποταμοῖσιν ἐξεκέχυντ᾽ ἀντ᾽ ὀστράκων.
καὶ μὴν παρῆν τεμάχη μὲν ἐξωπτημένα,
καταχυσματίοισι παντοδαποῖσιν εὐτρεπῆ·
τεύτλοισί τ᾽ ἐγχέλεια συγκεκαλυμμένα.
σχελίδες δ᾽ ὁλόκνημοι πλησίον τακερώταται
ἐπὶ πινακίσκοις, καὶ δίεφθ᾽ ἀκροκώλια
ἥδιστον ἀπατμίζοντα καὶ χόλικες βοὸς
καὶ πλευρὰ δελφάκει᾽ ἐπεξανθισμένα
χναυρότατα παρέκειτ᾽ ἐπ᾽ ἀμύλοις καθήμενα.
παρῆν δὲ χόνδρος γάλατι κατανενιμμένος
ἐν καταχύτλοις λεκάναισι καὶ πύου τόμοι.

---

[31] Ed. E. Kaibel, Leipzig, 1887, II, 94.

B. οἴμ' ὡς ἀπολεῖς μ' ἐνταῦθα διατρίβουσ' ἔτι,
παρὸν κολυμβᾶν ὡς ἔχω 's τὸν Τάρταρον.
A. τί δῆτα λέξεις, τἀπίλοιπ' ἤνπερ πύθῃ;
ὀπταὶ κίχλαι γὰρ εἰς ἀνάβραστ' ἠρτυμέναι
περὶ τὸ στόμ' ἐπέτοντ' ἀντιβολοῦσαι καταπιεῖν,
ὑπὸ μυρρίναισι κἀνεμώναις κεχυμέναι.
τὰ δὲ μῆλ' ἐκρέματο τὰ καλὰ τῶν καλῶν ἰδεῖν
ὑπὲρ κεφαλῆς, ἐξ οὐθενὸς πεφυκότα.
κόραι δ' ἐν ἀμπεχόναις τριχάπτοις ἀρτίως
ἠβυλλιῶσαι καὶ τὰ ῥόδα κεκαρμέναι
πλήρεις κύλικας οἴνου μέλανος ἀνθοσμίου
ἤντλουν διὰ χώνης τοῖσι βουλομένοις πιεῖν·
καὶ τῶνδ' ἑκάστοτ' εἰ φάγοι τις ἢ πίοι,
διπλάσι' ἐγίνετ' εὐθὺς ἐξ ἀρχῆς πάλιν.[32]

A. All things down there were mingled with wealth, and had good things mixed with them in every way. Rivers full of porridge and black soup flowed gurgling through the narrows with the very gravy sops and lumps of cheese cake, so that easily and of their own accord the mouthfuls would travel, as if they were grease, down the gullets of the dead. And blood puddings, sizzling slices of sausage, lay scattered along the rivers like oysters. And there were sliced [fish] all cooked, well prepared with all sorts of condiments. And there were eels covered with herbs. And whole hams, shins and all, were near-by, ready to melt in one's mouth, on platters, and well-boiled trotters steaming most sweetly and ox-guts and ribs of young pigs browned most daintily were laid on meal cakes. And there were grits covered over with milk in watering pots and slices of beestings.
B. Oh, you will kill me delaying here any longer, so that I shall dive into Tartarus just as I am.
A. What will you say when you have heard the rest? For roast thrushes prepared for a ragout[?] flew about our mouths begging us to swallow them as we lay among the myrtle and anemone. And the apples, the finest of the fine hung above our heads, growing on nothing. And girls in fine hair-cloth shawls,[33] quite young, their roses shorn, filled cups through a funnel brimful of dark wine, flower-fragrant, for those willing to drink. And if anyone ate or drank of these things, twice as much as there was first spurted up again.

Pherecrates seems to have repeated these ideas in the *Persians* (Athen. VI, 269 C). Similar satire is to be found in Aristophanes, Nicophon, and Metagenes (*ib.*).

Crates (*fl. ca.* 449) in his *Beluae* gives a comic explanation of the absence of slavery in the Golden Age. The fragment is cast in the form of a prophecy, but Athenaeus includes it as a description of primitive times.

II, 12. Crates, *Beluae* in Athenaeus, *Deipnos.* VI, 267.

A. ἔπειτα δοῦλον οὐδὲ εἷς κεκτήσετ' οὐδὲ δούλην,
ἀλλ' αὐτὸς αὑτῷ δῆτ' ἀνὴρ γέρων διακονήσει;
B. οὐ δῆθ'· ὁδοιποροῦντα γὰρ τὰ πάντ' ἐγὼ ποιήσω.

[32] Ed. E. Kaibel, II, 97-98.
[33] But see C. B. Gulick's translation of this passage in Loeb Library.

A. τί δῆτα τοῦτ' αὐτοῖς πλέον; B. πρόσεισιν αὖθ' ἕκαστον
τῶν σκευαρίων, ὅταν καλῇ τι· παρατίθου τράπεζα·
αὕτη παρασκεύαζε σαυτήν. μάττε θυλακίσκε.
ἔγχει κύαθε. ποῦσθ' ἡ κύλιξ; διάνιζ' ἰοῦσα σαυτήν.
ἀνάβαινε μᾶζα. τὴν χύτραν χρῆν ἐξερᾶν τὰ τεῦτλα.
ἰχθύ, βάδιζ'. ἀλλ' οὐδέπω 'πὶ θάτερ' ὀπτός εἰμι.
οὔκουν μεταστρέψας σεαυτὸν ἁλὶ πάσεις ἀλείφων; [34]

A. Then no one will have a man slave or a woman slave. But
will an old man wait upon himself [at meals]?
B. Certainly not. For I shall make things walk about.
A. What difference will that make?
B. Each object will automatically approach when ordered to.
"Table, set yourself. Get yourself ready. Mixing trough, start
kneading. Wine cup, fill yourself! Where is the cup? Wash yourself! Rise, barley cake! The pipkin must disgorge the beets. Fish,
advance!" "But I am not baked on the other side." "Then will
you turn yourself over and salt yourself, stupid?"

This is followed by a speech of the actor playing opposite, to the effect
that the hot bath will flow until ordered to stop, and the perfume, sponge,
and sandals will advance of their own accord.

Teleclides (*fl. ca.* 440 B. C.) in the *Amphictyons* indicates by his emphasis
on peace and the lack of fear and disease that he certainly parodies the
Golden Age. The antecedent of " I " is not known.

II, 13. Teleclides, *Amphictyons* in Athenaeus, *Deipnos.* VI, 268.

Λέξω τοίνυν βίον ἐξ ἀρχῆς ὃν ἐγὼ θνητοῖσι παρεῖχον·
εἰρήνη μὲν πρῶτον ἁπάντων ἦν ὥσπερ ὕδωρ κατὰ χειρός.
ἡ γῆ δ' ἔφερ' οὐ δέος οὐδὲ νόσους, ἀλλ' αὐτόματ' ἦν τὰ δέοντα·
οἴνῳ γὰρ ἅπασ' ἔρρει χαράδρα, μᾶζαι δ' ἄρτοις ἐμάχοντο
περὶ τοῖς στόμασιν τῶν ἀνθρώπων ἱκετεύουσαι καταπίνειν,
εἴ τι φιλοῖεν τὰς λευκοτάτας. οἱ δ' ἰχθύες οἴκαδ' ἰόντες
ἐξοπτῶντες σφᾶς αὐτοὺς ἂν παρέκειντ' ἐπὶ ταῖσι τραπέζαις.
ζωμοῦ δ' ἔρρει παρὰ τὰς κλίνας ποταμὸς κρέα θερμὰ κυλίνδων·
ὑποτριμματίων δ' ὀχετοὶ τούτων τοῖς βουλομένοισι παρῆσαν,
ὥστ' ἀφθονία τὴν ἔνθεσιν ἦν ἄρδονθ' ἁπαλὴν καταπίνειν.
λεκανίσκαισιν δ' ἂν ψαιστὰ παρῆν ἡδυσματίοις κατάπαστα,
ὀπταὶ δὲ κίχλαι μετ' ἀμητίσκων εἰς τὸν φάρυγ' εἰσεπέτοντο·
τῶν δὲ πλακούντων ὠστιζομένων περὶ τὴν γνάθον ἦν ἀλαλητός.
μήτρας δὲ τόμοις καὶ χναυματίοις οἱ παῖδες ἂν ἠστραγάλιζον.
οἱ δ' ἄνθρωποι πίονες ἦσαν τότε καὶ μέγα χρῆμα Γιγάντων. [35]

I shall then recount from the beginning the life which I provided
for mortals. First there was peace among all things like water
covering one's hands. And the earth bore neither fear nor disease,
but all needed things appeared of their own accord. For every
stream flowed with wine, and barley cakes fought with wheat cakes
to enter the mouths of men, pleading to be gulped down if they loved
the whitest. And fishes, coming to men's houses and baking them-

[34] Ed. Kaibel, II, 94.
[35] Ed. Kaibel, II, 95.

selves, would serve themselves upon the tables. And a river of soup flowed by the couches, swirling hot meats. And pipes conducting sharp sauces ran beside those wishing them, so that there was a plenty to moisten one's mouthfuls and permit one to swallow them tender. And on the dishes would appear honeyed barley cakes strewn over with spices, and roasted thrushes with milk cakes flew down one's gullet. And there were pancakes elbowing each other aside at one's jaw and shouting their war cries. And the [slave] boys shot dice with slices of sow-belly and dainties. Men were fat then, and like monstrous giants.

Sometimes, as in the *Chirones* of Cratinus, we find the spiritual blessings emphasized above the material.

II, 14. Cratinus, *Chirones, Fragm.* 1.

Μακάριος ἦν ὁ πρὸ τοῦ βίος βροτοῖσι
πρὸς τὰ νῦν, ὃν εἶχον ἄνδρες
ἀγανόφρονες ἡδυλόγῳ σοφίᾳ βροτῶν περισσοκαλλεῖς.[36]

Blessed was the life of mortals in those days as compared with that of today. Men lived in peace of mind and sweet-voiced wisdom, exceedingly fair beyond all mortals.[37]

The spirit of parody found in these comic fragments is paralleled by a feeling of impatience with the theme of the Golden Age found in the following fragment of Timotheus (early 4th c. B. C.).

II, 15. Timotheus, in Athenaeus, *Deipnos.* III, 122 d.

οὐκ ἀείδω τὰ παλαιά· τὰ γὰρ ἀμὰ κρείσσω.
νέος ὁ Ζεὺς βασιλεύει· τὸ πάλαι δ' ἦν
Κρόνος ἄρχων. ἀπίτω μοῦσα παλαιά.[38]

I do not sing of ancient things, for things of my own time are far better; young Zeus now rules whereas Cronus was lord in olden days. Ancient Muse, begone!

THE AGES IN LATER WRITERS

Tibullus

The following passage from Tibullus illustrates the use of the legend of the Ages for poetical purposes. Pillage is characteristic of the present age and is the source of war, navies, large estates, luxury. The Golden Age, on the contrary, was a reign of love. Freedom in love was apparently, for Tibullus, a sufficient commendation for any age in which it existed.

---

[36] Meineke, *Fragmenta comicorum graecorum*, Berlin, 1839, vol. II, 145.

[37] Or if one reads βρωτῶν περίσσ' ἔκηλοι, one would translate " abundantly provided with food."

[38] Ed. Kaibel, I, 279.

II, 16. *Elegies,* II, iii, 35-46, 63-74.

> ferrea non Venerem sed praedam saecula laudant:
>> praeda tamen multis est operata malis.
> praeda feras acies cinxit discordibus armis:
>> hinc cruor, hinc caedes mors propiorque venit.
> praeda vago iussit geminare pericula ponto,
>> bellica cum dubiis rostra dedit ratibus.
> praedator cupit immensos obsidere campos,
>> ut multa innumera iugera pascat ove:
> cui lapis externus curae est, urbisque tumultu
>> portatur validis mille columna iugis,
> claudit et indomitum moles mare, lentus ut intra
>> neglegat hibernas piscis adesse minas.
>
> . . . .
>
> et tu, Bacche tener, iucundae consitor uvae,
>> tu quoque devotos, Bacche, relinque lacus.
> haud impune licet formosas tristibus agris
>> abdere: non tanti sunt tua musta, pater.
> o valeant fruges, ne sint modo rure puellae:
>> glans alat, et prisco more bibantur aquae.
> glans aluit veteres, et passim semper amarunt:
>> quid nocuit sulcos non habuisse satos?
> tunc quibus aspirabat Amor praebebat aperte
>> mitis in umbrosa gaudia valle Venus.
> nullus erat custos, nulla exclusura dolentes
>> ianua: si fas est, mos precor ille redi.[39]

The iron age sings the praises not of love but of pillage. Yet pillage has brought about many evils. Pillage has girt the savage blade with the arms of strife. From it comes blood, from it slaughter and death draw nearer. Pillage ordered perils to be doubled upon the restless sea, when she gave the prows of war to unsteady ships. The pillager desires to hem in huge fields that he may pasture countless flocks upon his many acres. He yearns for foreign stone, and in the city's tumult a monolith is drawn by a hundred teams of strong oxen, a mole shuts out the unconquered sea, so that the sluggish fish may disdain the presence of threatening winter storms.

Tibullus continues to list the luxuries of contemporary life.

And thou, tender Bacchus, planter of the jocund grape, do thou also leave the accursed vats! Not without punishment may fair maidens be hidden in the gloomy fields; thy must is not worth so much, Father Bacchus. Oh that vines might disappear so that the girls would not linger in the country! The acorn would give food and water would be drunk in the primitive manner. The acorn nourished our elders, and they loved here and there without ceasing. What harm did it do not to have sown furrows? At that time to him upon whom Love was breathing gentle Venus gave open joys in a shady nook. There was no guardian, no gate to shut out grieving lovers. If it is permissible, I pray that custom may return. . . .

---

[39] Ed. Kirby Flower Smith, 1913, pp. 139-140.

Ovid

The version of the Ages as developed out of Hesiod by Aratus is continued by Ovid in the *Metamorphoses*. Before the composition of that work the legend had been greatly simplified [40] and two Ages alone were described — that of Cronus (Saturn) and that of Zeus, the former being that of fortunate primitive man, the latter that of unfortunate 'modern' man. Further passages of this type are given in Section B of this chapter.

The influence of Aratus on this account of the Ages is apparent in Ovid's emphasis upon the reign of justice in primitive life. It will be noticed that none of the races of Ovid is our own. We are children of the stones which Deucalion and Pyrrha cast behind them to repopulate the earth after the Deluge.

II, 17. *Metamorphoses*, I, 76-215 (Translation on p. 46 ff.).

> Sanctius his animal mentisque capacius altae
> deerat adhuc, et quod dominari in cetera posset.
> natus homo est: sive hunc divino semine fecit
> ille opifex rerum, mundi melioris origo,
> sive recens tellus seductaque nuper ab alto
> aethere cognati retinebat semina caeli;
> quam satus Iapeto, mixtam fluvialibus undis,
> finxit in effigiem moderantum cuncta deorum.
> pronaque cum spectent animalia cetera terram,
> os homini sublime dedit, caelumque videre

[40] The notion of degradation had, meanwhile, become a commonplace. The banality of the Golden Age is amusingly presented in the *Aetna* 9-16, a poem whose date is uncertain, but which legend ascribed to Virgil. Robinson Ellis in his edition of the poem, Oxford, 1901, finds (p. xlvii) two possible conclusions as to its date and authorship: (1) that it is by an unknown author writing not long after the death of Virgil; (2) that it is by an author of the late Claudian or early Neroian era, perhaps Lucilius Junior. Vessereau dates it between 55 B. C. and 79 A. D., possibly between 50 and 46 B. C. See his edition of the poem, Paris, 1923, pp. viii, xi. It would be particularly interesting to know the date, in order to know how early the theme became platitudinous. The author obviously takes much the same attitude towards the legend as was taken by the Greek comic writers and Timotheus.

> Aurea securi quis nescit saeculi regis?
> Quum domitis nemo cererem jactaret in arvis,
> Venturis que malas prohiberet fructibus herbas;
> Annua sed saturae complerent horrea messes,
> Ipse suo flueret Bacchus pede, mellaque lentis
> Penderent foliis, et pingui Pallas oliva
> Secretos amnis ageret: tum gratia ruris:
> Non cessit cuiquam melius sua tempora nosse.   [*Aetna*, 9-16.]

Who does not know of the Golden Age, of the king who was free from care, when no one sowed wheat in the plowed fields or kept weeds out of the future crops, but brimming harvests yearly filled the granaries? The wine pressed itself and honey dripped from sticky leaves and Pallas caused mysterious rivers of fat olive oil to flow. Then was the time of rural charm. No one could know his own age better than this.

iussit et erectos ad sidera tollere vultus.
sic, modo quae fuerat rudis et sine imagine, tellus
induit ignotas hominum conversa figuras.
  Aurea prima sata est aetas, quae vindice nullo,
sponte sua, sine lege, fidem rectumque colebat.
poena metusque aberant; nec verba minacia fixo
aere legebantur, nec supplex turba timebat
iudicis ora sui, sed erant sine vindice tuti.
nondum caesa suis, peregrinum ut viseret orbem,
montibus in liquidas pinus descenderat undas;
nullaque mortales praeter sua litora norant.
nondum praecipites cingebant oppida fossae;
non tuba directi, non aeris cornua flexi,
non galeae, non ensis erat; sine militis usu
mollia securae peragebant otia gentes.
ipsa quoque immunis rastroque intacta nec ullis
saucia vomeribus per se dabat omnia tellus:
contentique cibis nullo cogente creatis
arbuteos fetus montanaque fraga legebant
cornaque et in duris haerentia mora rubetis,
et quae deciderant patula Iovis arbore glandes.
ver erat aeternum, placidique tepentibus auris
mulcebant zephyri natos sine semine flores.
mox etiam fruges tellus inarata ferebat,
nec renovatus ager gravidis canebat aristis:
flumina iam lactis, iam flumina nectaris ibant,
flavaque de viridi stillabant ilice mella.
  Postquam, Saturno tenebrosa in Tartara misso,
sub Iove mundus erat, subiit argentea proles
auro deterior, fulvo pretiosior aere.
Iuppiter antiqui contraxit tempora veris,
perque hiemes aestusque et inaequales autumnos
et breve ver spatiis exegit quattuor annum.
tum primum siccis aër fervoribus ustus
canduit, et ventis glacies astricta pependit.
tum primum subiere domus: domus antra fuerunt
et densi frutices et vinctae cortice virgae.
semina tum primum longis Cerealia sulcis
obruta sunt, pressique iugo gemuere iuvenci.
  Tertia post illas successit aërea proles,
saevior ingeniis et ad horrida promptior arma,
non scelerata tamen. — de duro est ultima ferro.
protinus irrupit venae peioris in aevum
omne nefas. fugere pudor verumque fidesque:
in quorum subiere locum fraudesque dolique
insidiaeque et vis et amor sceleratus habendi.
vela dabant ventis (neque adhuc bene noverat illos
navita), quaeque diu steterant in montibus altis,
fluctibus ignotis insultavere carinae.
communemque prius, ceu lumina solis et auras,
cautus humum longo signavit limite mensor.
nec tantum segetes alimentaque debita dives
poscebatur humus, sed itum est in viscera terrae:
quasque recondiderat Stygiisque admoverat umbris,

effodiuntur opes, irritamenta malorum.
iamque nocens ferrum ferroque nocentius aurum
prodierat; prodit Bellum, quod pugnat utroque,
sanguineaque manu crepitantia concutit arma.
vivitur ex rapto; non hospes ab hospite tutus,
non socer a genero; fratrum quoque gratia rara est.
imminet exitio vir coniugis, illa mariti:
lurida terribiles miscent aconita novercae:
filius ante diem patrios inquirit in annos.
victa iacet pietas; et virgo caede madentes
ultima caelestum terras Astraea reliquit.
    Neve foret terris securior arduus aether,
affectasse ferunt regnum caeleste Gigantas
altaque congestos struxisse ad sidera montes.
tum pater omnipotens misso perfregit Olympum
fulmine et excussit subiectae Pelion Ossae.
obruta mole sua cum corpora dira iacerent,
perfusam multo natorum sanguine Terram
immaduisse ferunt calidumque animasse cruorem,
et, ne nulla suae stirpis monimenta manerent,
in faciem vertisse hominum. sed et illa propago
contemptrix superum saevaeque avidissima caedis
et violenta fuit: scires e sanguine natos.
    Quae pater ut summa vidit Saturnius arce,
ingemit et, facto nondum vulgata recenti
foeda Lycaoniae referens convivia mensae,
ingentes animo et dignas Iove concipit iras
conciliumque vocat. tenuit mora nulla vocatos.
est via sublimis, caelo manifesta sereno:
lactea nomen habet, candore notabilis ipso.
hac iter est superis ad magni tecta Tonantis
regalemque domum. dextra laevaque deorum
atria nobilium valvis celebrantur apertis;
plebs habitat diversa locis; a fronte potentes
caelicolae clarique suos posuere Penates.
hic locus est, quem, si verbis audacia detur,
haud timeam magni dixisse Palatia caeli.
ergo ubi marmoreo superi sedere recessu,
celsior ipse loco sceptroque innixus eburno
terrificam capitis concussit terque quaterque
caesariem, cum qua terram, mare, sidera movit.
talibus inde modis ora indignantia solvit:
'non ego pro mundi regno magis anxius illa
tempestate fui, qua centum quisque parabat
inicere Anguipedum captivo bracchia caelo.
nam quamquam ferus hostis erat, tamen illud ab uno
corpore et ex una pendebat origine bellum.
nunc mihi, qua totum Nereus circumsonat orbem,
perdendum est mortale genus. per flumina iuro
infera sub terra Stygio labentia luco:
cuncta prius temptata. sed immedicabile vulnus
ense recidendum est, ne pars sincera trahatur.
sunt mihi semidei, sunt rustica numina Nymphae
Faunique Satyrique et monticolae Silvani:

quos quoniam caeli nondum dignamur honore,
quas dedimus, certe terras habitare sinamus.
an satis, o superi, tutos fore creditis illos,
cum mihi, qui fulmen, qui vos habeoque regoque,
struxerit insidias notus feritate Lycaon? '
confremuere omnes studiisque ardentibus ausum
talia deposcunt. sic, cum manus impia saevit
sanguine Caesareo Romanum extinguere nomen,
attonitum tanto subitae terrore ruinae
humanum genus est totusque perhorruit orbis.
nec tibi grata minus pietas, Auguste, tuorum est,
quam fuit illa Iovi. qui postquam voce manuque
murmura compressit, tenuere silentia cuncti.
substitit ut clamor, pressus gravitate regentis,
Iuppiter hoc iterum sermone silentia rupit:
'ille quidem poenas — curam hanc dimittite — solvit.
quod tamen admissum, quae sit vindicta, docebo.
contigerat nostras infamia temporis aures:
quam cupiens falsam, summo delabor Olympo
et deus humana lustro sub imagine terras.
longa mora est, quantum noxae sit ubique repertum,
enumerare: minor fuit ipsa infamia vero.[41]

An animal more sacred than these and more capable of lofty thought was still lacking, one which could rule the others. Man was born; either the Maker of things, source of the better world, had made him from the divine seed, or the young earth recently separated from the lofty aether had retained the seed from her kinsman, the sky. The scion of Iapetus fashioned it, mixed with rainwater, in the image of the gods who regulate all things, and while the other animals look downwards towards the ground, he gave to man an upright posture, and bade him look upon the heavens and bear his countenance turned towards the stars. Thus she who had been recently unwrought and shapeless, earth, transformed, took on the hitherto unknown forms of men.

The first age was golden. In it faith and righteousness were cherished by men of their own free will without judges or laws. Penalties and fears there were none, nor were threatening words inscribed on unchanging bronze; nor did the suppliant crowd fear the words of its judge, but they were safe without protectors. Not yet did the pine cut from its mountain tops descend into the flowing waters to visit foreign lands, nor did deep trenches gird the town, nor were there straight trumpets, nor horns of twisted brass, nor helmets, nor swords. Without the use of soldiers the peoples in safety enjoyed their sweet repose. Earth herself, unburdened and untouched by the hoe and unwounded by the ploughshare, gave all things freely. And content with foods produced without constraint, they gathered the fruit of the arbute tree and mountain berries and cornel berries and blackberries clinging to the prickly bramblethickets, and acorns which had fallen from the broad tree of Jupi-

[41] Ed. Riese, Leipzig, 1872.

ter. Spring was eternal, and the placid Zephyrs with warm breezes lightly touched the flowers, born without seeds; untilled the earth bore its fruits and the unploughed field grew hoary with heavy ears of wheat. Rivers of milk and rivers of nectar flowed, and yellow honey dripped from the green oaks.

The characteristics of Ovid's version are (a) its juristic primitivism: in the first age all men were good by nature, and therefore had no need of lawyers, judges or courts. (b) Pacifism: they made no use of armies either for defensive or offensive warfare. (c) The absence of foreign trade or travel. (d) A technological primitivism. (e) Vegetarianism. (f) The soft primitivism of the Hesiodic Golden Age is still retained along with the definite moralization of the picture of that age: primeval innocence in a Land of Cockaigne.

After Saturn had been sent to shadowy Tartarus [42] and the world was under the reign of Jupiter, the Silver Race appeared, inferior to the Golden, more precious than the tawny Bronze. Jupiter shortened the length of the former spring, and with winter and summer and changeful autumn and a brief spring divided the year into four parts. Then for the first time the glowing air burned with dry heat, and slim icicles hung in the wind. Then first men lived in houses; their homes were caves and thick tree-trunks and faggots bound together with bark. Then grain was first cut down with long sickles and bullocks groaned under the weight of the yoke.

After this, a third race, of bronze, succeeded, more savage than its predecessors and prompter to [take up] bristling arms, yet not utterly wicked.[43]

Of hard iron is the last [race]. Immediately there broke out in the age of baser metal all manner of evil, and shame fled, and truth and faith. In place of these came deceits and trickery and treachery and force and the accursed love of possession. Sails were spread to the winds, for not yet had the sailor known them; trees still stayed in the high mountains, the wood of keels grew up ignorant of the waves. And the land, hitherto a common possession like the light of the sun and the breezes, the careful surveyor now marked out with long-drawn boundary line. Not only were corn and needful foods demanded of the rich soil, but men bored into the bowels of the earth, and the wealth she had hidden and covered with Stygian darkness was dug up, an incentive to evil.[44] And now noxious iron and gold more noxious still were produced: and these produced war — for wars are fought with both — and rattling weapons were hurled by blood-stained hands. Men lived by plunder, guest was not safe from host, father-in-law from son-in-law, and the love of brothers was rare. The husband's life was not safe from his wife, nor the wife's from her husband. Terrible stepmothers mixed the

[42] Note that he is not here sent to the Islands of the Blessed.

[43] It will be noted that Ovid follows Aratus rather than Hesiod in omitting the Age of Heroes.

[44] Cf. *Amores*, III, viii, 35-56; II, 28 below.

deadly wolf's-bane; sons sought to know how long their fathers would live.

Duty (*Pietas*) lay vanquished and the Virgin Astrea, last of the heavenly beings, left the lands which ran with blood. That the lofty aether might be no safer than earth, the giants strove to reach the heavenly kingdom and piled up mountains to the high stars. Then the omnipotent father, hurling a thunderbolt, split Olympus and shook off Pelion from Ossa. When their awful bodies lay buried under its mass, they made Earth drip with the blood of her children; and they gave life to the steaming gore, and lest no reminders of their race might remain, they converted it into the likeness of man. But that brood too was contemptuous of the gods and most eager for savage slaughter and violent: you would know they were born of blood.

In contrast with the Golden Race the Iron Race is characterized by trickery, avarice, bellicosity, navigation and trade; mining and metallurgy were introduced. The use of money was initiated and private ownership of property. Enmity among men arose in place of brotherly love.

It is noteworthy that Ovid does not suggest here the possibility of a return to the Golden Age. He is not touched, as far as one can see, by the Stoic theory of cycles, though the plan and purpose of his poem perhaps did not permit him to make use of that.[45]

As the Saturnian father saw these things from his high citadel, he groaned, and recalling a recent deed not yet noised abroad, the loathsome dish of the Lycaonian table, he conceived in his mind an anger mighty and worthy of Jove, and called a council. Nought delayed those who were summoned. There is on high a road, easily seen in a clear sky; it is called the Milky Way, known by its gleaming whiteness. This is the road the gods take to the abode of the mighty Thunderer and the royal home. On right and left with open doors are the dwellings occupied by the noble gods; the lesser deities (*plebs*) inhabit different places. In front and round about the glorious and powerful inhabitants of heaven have placed their penates. This is the place which, if my words may be so bold, I should not fear to call the Palatine of the great heavens.

Therefore when the gods were seated in the marble retreat, he himself on a higher level, leaning on his ivory sceptre, shook three or four times his terrible locks with which he moves the earth, sea, and stars. Then he gave utterance to his angry thoughts in this wise: "I was not more anxious over the rule of the world when each of the hundred serpent-footed monsters prepared to capture heaven with their arms [than I am now]. For although the enemy was savage, yet that war arose from one body and one source. Now I must destroy the mortal race, wherever Nereus resounds throughout the whole globe. By the rivers of the underworld I swear it, by those rivers which wash the Stygian grove beneath the earth. Everything else has been tried; but an incurable wound must be reopened with the sword, lest the healthy part be contaminated. I have demi-

[45] There is a hint, however, of the great conflagration in lines 253-255.

gods, rustic divinities, nymphs, fauns, satyrs, and the sylvani, mountain dwellers; these, since we do not yet deem them worthy of the honors of heaven, let us permit to inhabit unmolested the earth which we have given them. Do you believe, O gods, that they will be safe, when against me, who wield the thunderbolt, who own and rule you, Lycaon, famed for ferocity, wove his plots?"

They, trembling all and with burning zeal, begged him to punish him who had dared such deeds. So when an impious hand madly tried to blot out the Roman name with Caesar's blood, the human race was stunned by great terror of sudden ruin and the whole world was horrified. The loyalty (*pietas*) of thy subjects, Augustus, is no less welcome to thee than was that of Jupiter's subjects to him. After he had stilled their murmurs by voice and hand, all were silent. As the clamor, repressed by the sternness of their ruler, subsided, Jupiter again broke the silence with these words:

"That man has paid the penalty. Dismiss his case from your minds. Yet what did he commit, what was his punishment? I shall show you. The evil report of the times had reached our ears. Hoping it was false, I descended from lofty Olympus and, a god in human shape, I traversed the earth. It would take too long to enumerate how much villainy I found everywhere; the report was less than the truth. . . ."

A lengthy description of the Deluge follows, concluding with the production of the new race of men from the stones cast by Deucalion and Pyrrha.

The Ovidian story of the ages was probably more potent than any other in its historic influence; the echoes of it in later literature are innumerable. The Greek poets were largely forgotten in medieval Europe. It was chiefly through the *Metamorphoses* that the Hesiodic tradition was kept alive. We find in Ovid's account a quantity of detail missing in the earlier legends; and the passage is of especial importance in relation to primitivistic communism in medieval and modern times. In Ovid, too, the races between the Golden Age and our own are relegated to the background, and the tendency towards a single contrast, between the Age of Saturn and the Age of Zeus, is reënforced. As we have said above, this simplification had already been made by other writers, and as there were patriotic reasons why the Latins should particularly enhance the glory of Saturn, we shall find Roman literature more occupied than Greek with the version of two rather than four or more ages.[46]

Babrius

Meanwhile the same legend was kept alive in Greek popular literature. We find an interesting use of it in the version of Aesop's *Fables* given by Babrius. This version plays upon the theme of the friendly intercourse between man and nature, as was fitting for an introduction to such a work.

[46] Further passages from Ovid, in which only two ages appear will be given in Section B of this chapter. See pp. 53, 60, 63.

4

II, 18. *Fab. Aesop.* Preamb. 1-13.

Γενεὴ δικαίων ἦν τὸ πρῶτον ἀνθρώπων,
ὦ Βράγχε τέκνον, ἣν καλοῦσι χρυσείην.

.   .   .   .   .

τρίτη δ᾽ ἀπ᾽ αὐτῶν τις ἐγενήθη χαλκείη,
μεθ᾽ ἣν γενέσθαι φασὶ θείαν ἡρώων.
πέμπτη σιδηρᾶ ῥίζα καὶ γένος χεῖρον.
ἐπὶ τῆς δὲ χρυσῆς καὶ τὰ λοιπὰ τῶν ζῴων
φωνὴν ἔναρθρον εἶχε καὶ λόγους ᾔδει·
ἀγοραὶ δὲ τούτων ἦσαν ἐν μέσαις ὕλαις.
ἐλάλει δὲ πέτρα καὶ τὰ φύλλα τῆς πεύκης,
ἐλάλει δὲ πόντος, Βράγχε, νηὶ καὶ ναύτῃ,
στρουθοὶ δὲ συνετὰ πρὸς γεωργὸν ὡμίλουν.
ἐφύετ᾽ ἐκ γῆς πάντα μηδὲν αἰτούσης,
θνητῶν δ᾽ ὑπῆρχε καὶ θεῶν ἑταιρείη.[47]

In the first place, O my son Branchus, there was a race of just
men called golden . . . [*lacuna in the text*]. But the third race
born of these was of bronze, after which they say was born the
divine race of heroes. And the fifth race was a stock of iron and
the worst. During the time of the golden race the other animals
had articulate speech and knew the use of words. And they held
meetings in the middle of the forests; and the stones spoke, and
the needles of the pine tree, and the sea spoke, Branchus, to ship
and to sailor, and the sparrow spoke wise words to the farmer. And
all things grew from the earth spontaneously, and there was com-
radeship between gods and men.

Pseudo-Seneca

In the Neronian period we find the legend combined with the Stoic
theory of recurrent world-cycles,[48] in the pseudo-Senecan *Octavia*.

II, 19. *Octavia*, 388-448 (Translation on p. 52).

> Quid me potens fortuna fallaci *nimis*
> blandita vultu sorte contentum mea
> alte extulisti, gravius ut ruerem edita
> receptus arce totque prospicerem metus?
> melius latebam procul ab invidiae malis
> remotus inter corsici rupes maris,
> ubi liber animus et sui iuris mihi
> semper vacabat studia recolenti mea.
> o quam iuvabat, quo nihil maius parens

---

[47] Ed. F. G. Schneidewin, Leipzig, 1865. Since the publication of this Teubner
text, a new text of the first thirteen lines of Babrius has been discovered. This
new version gives three ages, the golden, the silver, and the iron. It is believed by
the scholars who have examined it to be the original, whereas our traditional version is a rearrangement to make the verses agree with the Hesiodic legend. For the
text itself, see P. Jouget and P. Perdrizet, " Le Papyrus Bouriant no. 1," in *Studien
zur Palaeographie und Papyruskunde, herausg. von C. Wessely*, VI (*Kolotes und
Menedemos*, by W. Crönert), Leipzig, 1906, p. 160.

[48] On this in general see II, 50-52 below.

natura genuit operis immensi artifex,
caelum intueri solis et currus sacros
[*mundique motus solis alternas vices*]
orbemque Phoebes astra quem cingunt vaga
lateque fulgens aetheris magni decus.
qui si senescit tantus in caecum chaos
casurus iterum: nunc adest mundo dies
supremus ille qui premat genus impium
caeli ruina, rursus ut stirpem novam
generet renascens melior, ut quondam tulit
iuvenis tenente regna Saturno poli.
tunc illa virgo numinis magni dea
iustitia caelo missa cum sancta fide
terrae regebat mitis humanum genus.
non bella norant non tubae fremitus truces
non arma gentes, cingere assuerant suas
muris nec urbes. pervium cunctis iter,
communis usus omnium rerum fuit.
et ipsa tellus laeta fecundos sinus
pandebat ultro tam piis felix parens
et tuta alumnis. alia sed soboles minus
conspecta mitis. tertium solers genus
novas ad artes extitit sanctum tamen.
mox inquietum quod sequi cursu feras
auderet acres, fluctibus tectos graves
extrahere pisces rete, vel calamo levi
decipere volucres, crate vel *texta pecus*
tenere la*etum,* premere subiectos iugo
tauros feroces, v*om*ere immunem prius
sulcare terram laesa quae fruges suas
interior alte condidit sacro sinu.
sed in parentis viscera intravit suae
deterior aetas: eruit ferrum grave
aurumque saevas mox et armavit manus.
partita fines regna constituit, novas
extruxit urbes, tecta defendit suis
aliena telis aut petit praedae imminens.
neglecta terras fugit et mores feros
hominum et cruenta caede pollutas manus
Astraea virgo siderum magnum decus.
cupido belli crevit atque auri fames.
totum per orbem maximum exortum est **malum**
luxuria pestis blanda, cui vires dedit
roburque longum tempus atque error gravis.
collecta vitia tot per aetates diu
in nos redundant. saeculo premimur gravi
quo scelera regnant, saevit impietas furens,
turpi libido venere dominatur potens,
luxuria victrix orbis immensas opes
iampridem avaris manibus ut perdat rapit.
sed ecce gressu fertur attonito Nero
trucique vultu. quid ferat mente horreo.[49]

[49] Ed. R. Piper and G. Richter, Leipzig, 1867.

[Seneca is speaking]

Why hast thou, powerful goddess Fortuna, with thy too deceptively flattering countenance, raised me, when I was satisfied with my lot, to lofty station, so that I might fall the more heavily and find before me so many terrors? Better did I lie hidden, remote from the evils of envy, among the rocks of the Corsican sea, where my mind, free and master of itself, always gave me leisure to pursue my studies. Ah, what a pleasure it used to be (a pleasure greater than any Mother Nature, creator of the huge universe, has produced) to look upon the heavens and the sacred pathway of the sun [and the motion of the world and the successive changes of the sun], and the orb of Phoebe girt by wandering stars, and the far gleaming beauty of the wide aether. If this great world grows old, there will be a return again to blind chaos, and the world's last day will be at hand, which will crush a wicked race in the downfall of the sky, so that a world born again in better form may bring forth a new stock, as once it bore in its youth, when Saturn reigned in heaven.

Then that virgin goddess of great power, Justice, sent to earth from heaven with holy Faith, gently ruled humankind. The nations knew neither wars nor the savage blast of bugles nor arms, nor were they wont to gird their cities with walls. The highways were open to all. The use of all things was common, and Earth herself gladly opened her fertile womb, a happy parent to such dutiful men, safe among her nurselings.

Here we have Justice accompanied by Faith, instead of ruling alone. Otherwise the account is faithful to tradition.

The intermediate races are briefly mentioned and dismissed, and the recital ends with the contemporary age.

But another breed less gentle then appeared. A third race arose, cunning in new arts, yet holy. Soon came a restless race which dared pursue the wild beasts in the chase, to draw out fishes in nets or by the light rod from their deep hiding places in the waters, to catch birds, or with wicker stockades to fence in the fat cattle, to master fierce bulls by subjecting them to the yoke, to dig the earth, until then immune, with the wounding plough, earth who hid her fruits deep in her sacred womb. But this degenerate age dug into its mother's bowels; it dragged forth heavy iron and gold, and soon armed its savage hands. Boundaries marked out divided kingdoms, and new cities were built. Men defended their roof-trees with their own weapons, or, threatening plunder, invaded the dwellings of other men. Astraea the Virgin, great glory of the stars, neglected fled from earth and the savage ways of men and hands polluted by gory slaughter. Desire for war grew and hunger for gold. Throughout the whole world the greatest evil arose, luxury, an alluring plague, to which the long lapse of time and grievous error gave strength and power. All these many vices, heaped up through long ages, now overflow on us. We are crushed beneath the heavy burden of an age in which crime rules, mad impiety rages, violent lust dominates in shameful love, and triumphant luxury has long since seized the huge wealth of the world with greedy hands, only to lose it. But lo! with thundering step and savage countenance Nero comes. I shudder in my mind at what he may bring.

Contrasted with the pacifism, communism, and technological ignorance of primitive man are modern man's belligerency, his subjection of the animal and vegetable kingdoms, his technological skill, his private ownership of property, his luxury, and his general immorality and impiety. It is worth pointing out that the age which is so berated here was in another writing, which will be cited in its proper place (II, 56), hailed in terms similar to those in which Vergil hailed the Age of Augustus in the Fourth Eclogue.

We can now turn to accounts of the Ages which omit epochs intermediate between the Age of Saturn and their own, contrasting simply the Ages of Saturn and of Zeus.[50]

B. THE AGE OF SATURN AND THE AGE OF JUPITER

THE AGE OF SATURN AS THE ANCIENT PAST

We have already seen that as the legend of the progressive degradation of mankind develops, the intermediate ages tend to become obscured, leaving the primitive and the contemporary ages in sharp contrast. In many ancient writers, especially in Roman literature, two ages alone are mentioned, the Age of Saturn (the Golden Age) and the Age of Jupiter (contemporary times). Sometimes the Age of Saturn is simply used as a synonym for "the remote past" with, indeed, a suggestion that the Age of Jupiter was the better. Thus Plato in the *Gorgias* (523) points out that in the Age of Cronus judgment was passed on men before their death, whereas now under Zeus men are judged after death. This is evidently held by Plato, at least for its literary effect, to be an improvement. Or in Ovid's *Heroides* (IV, 129-133) Phaedra says to Hippolytus, "nor, because I seem to be a step-mother who would mate with her step-son, let empty names terrify your mind. That old-fashioned virtue (*pietas*) which was to die in a later age prevailed in Saturn's rustic reign. Jupiter decreed that whatever any man desired to do was virtuous."

II, 20. Ovid, *Heroides,* IV, 129-133.

> Nec, quia privigno videar coitura noverca,
>   terruerint animos nomina vana tuos.
> ista vetus pietas, aevo moritura futuro,
>   rustica Saturno regna tenente fuit.
> Iuppiter esse pium statuit, quodcumque iuvaret . . . [51]

---

[50] For another form of the legend of Five Ages, see below, II, 45, p. 75.

[51] Ed. Riese, 1871, I, 13. There may be some difference of opinion as to whether Ovid thought Jupiter's decision an improvement on Saturnian morals or whether he

Even when the virtues of this age were admitted, it was sometimes introduced merely as a conventional literary ornament. Thus Silius Italicus (imitating Apollonius Rhodius, I, 503 ff.) has Teuthras say that Chiron sang of " the chaste age of father Saturn."

II, 21. Silius Italicus, *Punics,* XI, 458.

Castaque Saturni monstrabat secula patris.[52]

There is obviously no evidence here of anything more than the popularity of the legend. The same might be said of the poem on Maecenas, ascribed to Vergil, and in any case of the Augustan Age. Celebrating the virtues of the Etruscan, it remarks that his *animi simplicitas* redeemed his love of luxury:

II, 22. *Fragm.* 760a (olim 779), ll. 23-24.

Sic illi vixere, quibus fuit aurea virgo,
    Quae bene praecinctos postmodo pulsa fugit.[53]

Thus they lived who knew the golden maiden, who was driven out and fled from men girt for toil.[54]

So, too, in Statius, references to the Golden Age are mainly used for literary effect. Thus we find

II, 23. Statius, *Silvae,* I, iv, 1-3.

Estis, io, superi, nec inexorabile Clotho
volvit opus, videt alma pios Astraea Iovique
conciliata redit . . . [55]

You are present, ye gods, and Clotho no longer spins her inexorable web: benigant Astraea looks upon her pious followers and, reconciled with Jupiter, returns.

Or again,

II, 24. Statius, *Silvae,* III, iii, 1-7.

Summa deum, Pietas, cuius gratissima coelo

meant such an opinion to have merely dramatic relevancy. It is fairly likely, considering the erotic character of the *Heroides* and of the other early poems of Ovid, that not only the character Phaedra, but the poet, believed in following one's inclinations. In any event the poet apparently expected Phaedra's plea to win sympathy from Hippolytus and from his readers. For a similar speech of Phaedra's nurse in Seneca's play, with the reaction to it of Hippolytus, as the spokesman of Stoic primitivism, see Ch. X, 4, p. 281 ff.

[52] Ed. L. Bauer, Leipzig, 1892, II, 17.

[53] *Anth. lat.* 2d ed. 1906, Pt. I, fasc. 2, p. 235. The *aurea virgo* is of course Astraea.

[54] There seems to be here a play upon words. Maecenas in line 21 is mentioned as having been criticised for being too *discinctus*. Here the poet indicates that Justice fled from primitive men who were nevertheless *praecincti*. The metaphor of loose clothes as a sign of loose living is carried on in the lines which follow.

[55] Ed. Alf. Klotz, Leipzig, 1911.

rara profanatas inspectant numina terras,
huc vittata comam niveoque insignis amictu,
qualis adhuc praesens nullaque expulsa nocentum
fraude rudes populos atque aurea regna colebas,
mitibus exequiis ades.[56]

Greatest of the gods, Piety, whose godhead, most welcome in
heaven, rarely visits the corrupted earth, come to us again, with
hair bound in a fillet, shining in snowy robes, as thou wast amongst
us before, ere yet the treachery of wicked men had driven thee away,
and thou watchedst over the untutored peoples of the reign of gold —
come to these gentle rites.

THE IDENTIFICATION OF CRONUS AND SATURN

Although according to one tradition Cronus and Rhea dethroned earlier
rulers of the universe, Uranus and Gaia, and according to another, Ophion
and Eurynome,[57] Cronus was frequently believed to be the eldest of the
gods. In Hesiod, as we have seen, he was dethroned by Zeus, and sent to
the Islands of the Blest to be their king.

There were three features of the legend of Cronus which were especially
important in shaping its future history: (a) Cronus was generally believed
to have ruled the world before Zeus. (b) His reign was specially noteworthy for the various blessings which his subjects enjoyed: roughly,
leisure, peace, abundance of food, absence of private property, absence of
evil passions, and often absence of slaves. (c) At the same time he had
two bloodthirsty acts to his discredit: the swallowing of his children, and
the castrating of his father.

Relatively early in Greek thought an attempt was made to explain away
the supernatural elements in Pagan mythology. Although the initiation
of this attempt is usually attributed to Euhemerus, Geffcken in his article
on *Euhemerism* in Hastings' *Encyclopedia* points out that he was preceded
by Herodotus, the Cynics, and Hecataeus. Hecataeus particularly had a
Euhemeran touch in his theory that the gods were ancient monarchs.

Of Euhemerus we have no original fragments. Certain pagan authors
thought him an atheist. Thus the pseudo-Plutarchan *De placitis* (I, vii, 1)
definitely includes him in a list of those who deny the existence of the gods,[58]
quoting some insulting iambics of Callimachus. Aelian does the same in
his *Varia historia* (II, 31), though he increases the number of Euhemerus's
atheistic associates. The Christian Fathers often used him in their polemic
against paganism. He is quoted by Lactantius[59] and Minucius Felix[60]
and others to prove that the gods could not be divine. And we learn from

---

[56] Ed. Alf. Klotz.
[57] See Apoll. Rhod. *Argonaut.* I, 503 f. and *Schol. ad Lycophron*, 1191 f.
[58] Cf. Plutarch's *Isis and Osiris*, 23.
[59] *Div. inst.* I, i, 12, 14, among other places.
[60] *Octavius*, XXI, 1.

Eusebius [61] that he had treated the gods as glorified men, a thesis corroborated by Sextus Empiricus.[62]

It was, then, part of the Euhemeristic method to identify the gods with primitive men of power. Servius (*Aeneid,* VIII, 319), writing after Cronus was identified with Saturn, says that he was king of Crete, and later (*Aen.* VIII, 356) maintains that even Virgil thought Saturn was a man.

The first step in the history of this myth is the identification of Cronus and Saturn. This confusion can not be dated, but it was common knowledge, one gathers.[63]

How the confusion occurred is not easy to determine. We shall find that Cronus was identified with any god who was the oldest of gods or the chief god, in some cases with startling results. As Schmitz has pointed out,[64] the resemblance between Saturn and Demeter is much stronger than that between Saturn and Cronus. But, as Dionysius Halicarnassensis (I, 38) says, people thought " this daimon " to be the giver of all happiness and the "lord bountiful " (πληρωτής) to men. And as Italy was supposed to have enjoyed blessings under its early King, Saturn, analogous to those which human beings in general enjoyed under Cronus, the identification was probably based on the similarity of the two reigns.

The work of Euhemerus is said by Cicero (*De nat. deor.* I, xlii, 119) to have been translated by Ennius; [65] it was from this translation that the Christian writers usually quoted. In the fragment, in accordance with the theory that the gods were early kings and the myths about them historical incidents,[66] the god who was evidently Cronus in the original is called " Saturn " throughout. The author relates how Saturn, who had been king of Crete, was imprisoned by his uncle, Titan; how he was released by Jupiter and restored to his throne; how he then plotted to kill Jupiter lest he seize the power, and had to flee to Italy, where " he was with difficulty concealed." [67] Nothing is said or implied about the beneficence of Cronus's reign in Crete, and in fact at least one of the usual features of

[61] *Praep. evang.* II, ii, 52 ff.

[62] *Adv. math.* IX, 51.

[63] Cf. *Scholia ad Lycophron,* 1232; Cicero, *Nat. deor.* II, xxv, 64; Dion. Halic. *Ant. rom.* I, xxxvi, speaking of the place name *Saturnia* explains it by the legend of Cronus's having ruled in the place to which the name was given before the rule of Zeus; and Accius, as quoted by Macrobius (*Sat.* I, vii, 37), identifies the Saturnalia and the Cronia.

[64] See his art. " Saturnus " in Smith's *Dict. of Gk. and Rom. Biog. and Mythol.*

[65] He says, in fact, that he translated him *praeter ceteros.*

[66] For a good specimen of the Euhemeristic doctrine see the *De incredibilibus* of Palaephatus. On Saturn, see *Excerpta vaticana,* XIX, in Festa's *Mythog. graeci* (Leipzig, 1902), III, 2, p. 97.

[67] Ennius, *Euhem. Fragm.* III, IV, V (Vahlen); Lactantius, *Div. inst.* I, xiv, 1. 10. This story, says Lactantius, is repeated by the Erythraean Sibyl. See J. Geffcken's *Oracula sibyllina,* III, 110 ff. (Leipzig, 1902, p. 54 f.).

the Golden Age, its freedom from war, is strikingly absent. Moreover, he and his wife and "the other men of that time" were accustomed to eat human flesh, and it was Jupiter who first forbade it;[68] whereas we have seen that in many accounts of the Golden Age not only are its people not anthropophagous, but are vegetarians.

The fragments of the *Annals* are too shattered for us to know more than that Ennius did introduce into it a section on the reign of Saturn [*Ann.* I, xix, xx, xxi], and that in it he identified Saturn and Cronus.[69] But there is no indication that this ancient race was any happier or nobler than the author's own contemporaries.

It is not until we come to Virgil and his contemporary, Tibullus, that the Age of Saturn and the Golden Age are identified in extant literature. But in the Virgilian passage we are about to quote, it will be observed that Saturn has become a culture-hero and that his subjects are not primitive men — as are the people of Hesiod's Golden Race — but post-primitive. They would seem to be rather "the Melian Race" of the *Works and Days*; and they were found by Saturn, upon his arrival in Italy from Crete, living without government, morals, religion, husbandry, in complete ignorance, and apparently in a state of war. It is this primitive condition which Saturn improves by introducing laws and peace. It is obvious that though Virgil may have profited by Ennius's translation of Euhemerus in identifying Cronus with the legendary king, he could not have derived his account of Saturn's reign from the same work. This conception of Saturn as a culture-hero lingered on in Roman literature alongside of the older tradition, and we find it surviving in such a work as the Pseudo-Victor's *Origo gentis romanae* (1-3) whose date is uncertain.[70] The part which concerns us is, moreover, largely a commentary on the following passage of the *Aeneid*.

II, 25. Virgil, *Aeneid,* VIII, 314-327.

> 'haec nemora indigenae Fauni Nymphaeque tenebant
> gensque virum truncis et duro robore nata,
> quis neque mos neque cultus erat, nec iungere tauros
> aut componere opes norant aut parcere parto,
> sed rami atque asper victu venatus alebat.
> primus ab aetherio venit Saturnus Olympo,
> arma Iovis fugiens et regnis exul ademptis.
> is genus indocile ac dispersum montibus altis
> composuit legesque dedit Latiumque vocari
> maluit, his quoniam latuisset tutus in oris.

---

[68] Ennius, *Euhem. Fragm.* IX; Lactantius, *Div. inst.* I, xiii, 2, quotes this in reference to the legend of Cronus's eating his children.

[69] *Saturno quem Caelus genuit, Ann.* I, xxi.

[70] See Teuffel's *History of Roman Literature* (rev. by Schwabe), English translation, London, 1892, § 414, 5, which inclines to ascribe it to the 5th or 6th century of our era.

> aurea quae perhibent illo sub rege fuere
> saecula: sic placida populos in pace regebat,
> deterior donec paulatim ac decolor aetas
> et belli rabies et amor successit habendi.[71]

In these groves the native Fauns and Nymphs once dwelt and a race of men born of tree trunks and hard oak, who had neither a rule of life nor civilization, nor did they know how to yoke bulls or store up their wealth or husband their gains, but fed themselves from trees and the rough fare of the huntsman. Saturn first came from aethereal Olympus,[72] fleeing the weapons of Jupiter, an exile from his stolen kingdom. He brought together that ignorant race scattered on the mountain tops and gave them laws. And he wished the country to be called Latium, since he had safely lived in hiding (*latuisset*) in these parts.[73] Golden is called the age in which that king reigned. He ruled the people in calm peace, until little by little the age grew worse, its brilliance dimmed, and the madness of war and love of possession took its place.[74]

The Complementary Legend: Saturn, the Dethroned God

Virgil's contemporary, Tibullus (*ca.* 65-19 B. C.), differs from Virgil in not trying to reconcile the legend of Saturn, the dethroned god, with that of Saturn, the culture-hero. His Saturnian race were presumably primitive men. He, too, extols a technological, economic, and pacificistic state of nature combined with a generally " soft " condition. This type of satire of contemporary life will be repeated in Juvenal, XIII, 28-59 (No. 38 below), and VI, 1-23 (No. 39 below), except that Juvenal's primitivism is hard.[75]

[71] Ed. Ribbeck-Ianell, Leipzig, 1930.

[72] It will be recalled that he went to the Islands of the Blessed in Hesiod, and came from Crete in Euhemerus.

[73] This fills Arnobius with scorn. *Vide* his *Adv. gentes*, IV, 24.

[74] This passage should be compared with the close of *Georgics*, II (lines 536 to end), where navigation takes the place of avarice, the point being—as in Ovid, *Metamorph.* I, 130 ff.—that navigation's purpose was to increase wealth. Cf. quotation from Tibullus, no. 26 below.

[75] K. F. Smith has pointed out an Alexandrian example of this tradition in his edition of Tibullus, p. 245, from *Oxyrhynchus papyri*, XIV, text of H. Weil, *Rev. des Études Grecques*, XI, 241:

> [Τοῖος ἔην θνητοῖσι νόος, ῥῆστον βίον εὖτε
>   ἠλλάξαντ' αἰν]ῆς ἀντὶ γεωτομίης,
> [οἶος ἔην Γλαύ]κῳ Λυκίῳ, ὅτε σιφλὸς ἔπειγε
>   [ἀνθ ἑκατομβοί]ων ἐννεάβοια λαβεῖν.
> [πρὶν δ' οὔτις σ]μινύην, πέλεκυν π[αχὺν οὔτε δίκελλαν
>   χάλκευεν θη]κτὴν ἀμφοτέρῳ στόμα[τι,
> ὄφρα δίκην σκαπα]νῆος ὀρειτύπου ἐργάζηται
>   [ἀμπολέων γα]ίης ὀκρυόειν ἔδαφος,
> [αὔλακι δ' οὐ βάλλε]σκεν ἔνι σπόρον οὔτε ν[έαινεν,
>   ἀλλ' ἤνει Κρο]νίδου δῶρα κυθηγενέος·
> [πᾶσιν ἀτερθε πόνοι]ο σαρωνίδας οὖδας ἔνε[γκε
>   καὶ βαλάνους μερόπω]ν δαῖτα παλαιοτάτην.

[Such was the mind of mortals when they changed from the easiest life] to grim plowing; [such that of Glau]cus, the Lycian, when he hastily took

II, 26. Tibullus, *Elegies*, I, iii, 35-52.

> quam bene Saturno vivebant rege, prius quam
>   tellus in longas est patefacta vias!
> nondum caeruleas pinus contempserat undas,
>   effusum ventis praebueratque sinum,
> nec vagus ignotis repetens compendia terris
>   presserat externa navita merce ratem.
> illo non validus subiit iuga tempore taurus,
>   non domito frenos ore momordit equus,
> non domus ulla fores habuit, non fixus in agris,
>   qui regeret certis finibus arva lapis.
> ipsae mella dabant quercus, ultroque ferebant
>   obvia securis ubera lactis oves.
> non acies, non ira fuit, non bella, nec ensem
>   immiti saevus duxerat arte faber.
> nunc Iove sub domino caedes et vulnera semper,
>   nunc mare, nunc leti mille repente viae.
> parce, pater. timidum non me periuria terrent,
>   non dicta in sanctos impia verba deos.[76]

How well they lived under King Saturn, before long roads made the land accessible to all! Not yet had the ship of pine affronted the blue waters, nor offered its open bosom to the winds. Not yet had the wandering sailor, seeking riches on unknown shores, loaded his ships with foreign merchandise. In those days the stalwart bull did not submit to the yoke, nor did the horse clench the bit with servile mouth. Houses had no doors; nor were stones planted in the fields, fixing the boundaries with definite limits. The oaks themselves gave honey and ewes offered their udders full of milk to untroubled men. There was neither army, nor wrath, nor war, nor had the cruel smith beaten out the sword with pitiless art.

Now under Lord Jupiter, there are always murders, always wounds;[77] now there are shipwrecks; now there are a thousand roads to sudden death. Spare me, Father; false oaths do not terrify me nor impious words spoken against the sacred gods.

In addition to the story of Five Ages (II, 17) Ovid also presents the form of chronological primitivism in which only two ages appear. In the following passage from the *Metamorphoses,* Pythagoras is exhorting his

the value of nine oxen [for a hecatomb's]. [Up to then no one wrought in bronze] the mattock, the [sturdy] ax or [two-edged hoe to] labor like a miner in the mountains turning up [the cold soil. Nor did he sow] grain in [the furrow nor did he plow, but he was contented with] the gifts of the Son of [Cronus], born in secret. [To all without labor] earth brought forth oaks [and gave acorns] the oldest food [of men].

Κρονίδου is curious, since the Son of Cronus was not then reigning. Weil, who emended the text, seemed, however, to have no other choice. There is, of course, the possibility that the original poem did not refer to the Age of Cronus at all but to another early period in which Zeus was reigning.

[76] Ed. Kirby Flower Smith, New York, 1913.

[77] Note how this contradicts the Euhemeristic account as given in Ennius, *Euhem. Fragm.* IX (Vahlen).

fellows to give up a carnivorous diet.[78]   It will be noted that his second
argument suggests a kind of animalitarianism, appealing to the beasts as
moral exemplars, an argument which Seneca was later to find so
objectionable.

II, 27. Ovid, *Metamorph.* XV, 75-142 (Translation on p. 61 f.).

'parcite, mortales, dapibus temerare nefandis
corpora! sunt fruges, sunt deducentia ramos
pondere poma suo, tumidaeque in vitibus uvae;
sunt herbae dulces, sunt quae mitescere flamma
mollirique queant. nec vobis lacteus umor
eripitur nec mella thymi redolentia florem.
prodiga divitias alimentaque mitia tellus
suggerit atque epulas sine caede et sanguine praebet.
carne ferae sedant ieiunia: nec tamen omnes.
quippe equus et pecudes armentaque gramine vivunt:
at quibus ingenium est inmansuetumque ferumque,
Armeniae tigres iracundique leones
cumque lupis ursi, dapibus cum sanguine gaudent.
heu quantum scelus est, in viscera viscera condi,
congestoque avidum pinguescere corpore corpus,
alteriusque animantem animantis vivere leto!
scilicet in tantis opibus, quas optima matrum
terra creat, nil te nisi tristia mandere saevo
vulnera dente iuvat ritusque referre Cyclopum?
nec, nisi perdideris alium, placare voracis
et male morati poteris ieiunia ventris?
at vetus illa aetas, cui fecimus aurea nomen,
fetibus arboreis et, quas humus educat, herbis
fortunata fuit, nec polluit ora cruore.
tunc et aves tutae movere per aëra pennas,
et lepus impavidus mediis erravit in arvis,
nec sua credulitas piscem suspenderat hamo:
cuncta sine insidiis nullamque timentia fraudem
plenaque pacis erant. postquam non utilis auctor
victibus invidit, quisquis fuit ille, ferinis,
corporeasque dapes avidam demersit in alvum,
fecit iter sceleri. primoque e caede ferarum
incaluisse putes maculatum sanguine ferrum:
idque satis fuerat, nostrumque petentia letum
corpora missa neci salva pietate fatemur.
sed quam danda neci, tam non epulanda fuerunt.
longius inde nefas abiit, et prima putatur
hostia sus meruisse mori, quia semina pando
eruerat rostro spemque interceperat anni;
vite caper morsa Bacchi mactatus ad aras
dicitur ultoris: nocuit sua culpa duobus.
quid meruistis, oves, placidum pecus inque tuendos
natum homines, pleno quae fertis in ubere nectar,

---

[78] The vegetarianism of the Pythagoreans is of course an old legend. Cf. Epi-
phanius, in Diels, *Dox. graec.* I (587), III, 8 (590), and Diog. Laert. VIII, 33.

mollia quae nobis vestras velamina lanas
praebetis vitaque magis quam morte iuvatis?
quid meruere boves, animal sine fraude dolisque,
innocuum, simplex, natum tolerare labores?
immemor est aequi nec frugum munere dignus,
qui potuit curvi dempto modo pondere aratri
ruricolam mactare suum, qui trita labore
illa, quibus totiens durum renovaverat arvum,
tot dederat messes, percussit colla securi.
nec satis est, quod tale nefas committitur: ipsos
inscripsere deos sceleri, numenque supernum
caede laboriferi credunt gaudere iuvenci.
victima labe carens et praestantissima forma
(nam placuisse nocet) vittis insignis et auro
sistitur ante aras auditque ignara precantem
imponique suae videt inter cornua fronti,
quas coluit, fruges, percussaque sanguine cultros
inficit in liquida praevisos forsitan unda.
protinus ereptas viventi pectore fibras
inspiciunt mentesque deum scrutantur — et illis
(unde fames homini vetitorum tanta ciborum est?)
audetis vesci, genus o mortale? quod, oro,
ne facite, et monitis animos advertite nostris:
cumque boum dabitis caesorum membra palato,
mandere vos vestros scite et sentite colonos.' [79]

Refrain, mortals, from profaning your bodies with wicked viands. There are grains, there are fruits bending down the branches with their weight, and swollen clusters on the vine. There are sweet herbs, there are things which can be mellowed, softened by the flame, nor is milk denied you, nor honey smelling of the thyme flower. The prodigal earth offers riches and gentle nourishment and furnishes banquets without bloody slaughter. The wild beasts still their hunger with meat, but yet not all, for horses and cattle and sheep live on grass. But those whose character (*ingenium*) is cruel and savage, the Armenian tiger and the raging lion, the wolf and bear, rejoice in meals of blood. Ah what a crime it is for flesh to be filled with flesh, for a greedy body to stuff itself with another body and grow fat, for a living being to live on the death of another living being! Thus amid so great wealth which earth, the best of mothers, has produced, you please to inflict pitiful wounds with savage teeth and to repeat the customs of the Cyclôpes. Nor, unless you should cause another to perish, could you placate the hunger of your voracious and nasty bellies.

The argument (supposedly of Pythagoras) now turns to the Golden Age, showing that it was vegetarian and pacific. So universal was the reign of peace that, as in Empedocles, it even included the beasts.

But that ancient age, to which we have given the name of Golden, was blessed with the fruit of trees and the herbs which the soil

---

[79] Ed. A. Riese, Leipzig, 1871.

brings forth, and it did not pollute its mouth with gore. Then the birds in safety winged their way through the air and the hare fearlessly wandered through the fields, nor was the fish caught through its witlessness. There were no snares, and none feared treachery, but all was full of peace. But after some innovator — whoever he was — introducing no useful change, began to envy the provender of the wild beasts, and stuffed bodies into his greedy belly for food, a way was made for crime. Beginning with the first slaughter of the wild beasts, you would think that iron had been tempered and dyed in blood. This was enough; now we grant that bodies which tend to cause our own death may be slaughtered without offense to piety. But though the wild animals deserved death, yet they should not have been feasted upon.

From this resulted far greater wickedness. The sow is thought first to have merited death as a victim because she uprooted seeds with her curved snout and cut off the hope of the year. The goat having nibbled the vine of Bacchus is said to have been slain at the altars of the avenger. Their own guilt harmed them both. But what have you sheep done to merit death, a peaceful flock born to help men, who produce nectar in your full udders and furnish us soft clothing from your wool? You favor us by your life rather than by your death. What have the oxen merited, animals without treachery, harmless, innocent, simple, born to labor? Forgetful of justice is he, and unworthy of the gift of grain, who, when the weight of the curved plough had been just removed, could slaughter the tiller of his land, who struck with his ax that neck, worn with toil, by which he had so often renewed the hard soil and produced so many crops. Nor was it enough to commit such sin: they ascribed the crime to the gods themselves and believed that the celestial deities rejoiced in the slaughter of the laboring bullock. A victim free from blemish and of outstanding beauty (for it is his ruin to have been pleasing), marked with golden fillets, is led before the altars and hears unwittingly the prayers and sees placed between the horns on his own forehead the grain he has produced, and struck down he stains with his blood the knife which he has perhaps already seen in the limpid water. At once they inspect his entrails, snatched from his living breast, and scrutinize in them the mind of the gods. Upon this — wherefore is man's hunger for forbidden food so great? — do you dare to feed. O mortal race! Refrain from this, I pray, and attend to our warnings! And when you give the limbs of slain cattle to your palates, know and feel that you are eating your fellow farmers.

A passage in the *Amores* emphasizes the lack of money in the Age of Saturn, contrasting, as it were, the Age of Agriculture with the Age of Commerce. One notes economic primitivism and another hint that avarice has been the cause of our degradation.[80] Ovid has just been lamenting his

[80] There is a suggestion of technological primitivism in a later line, in speaking of an ancient altar—*per antiquas facta sine arte manus*, as if the *sine arte* were important. *Amores*, III, xiii, 10.

mistress's preference for a soldier and says that Jupiter won a maid by turning into gold.

II, 28. Ovid, *Amores,* III, viii, 35-56.

> at cum regna senex caeli Saturnus haberet,
>   omne lucrum tenebris alta premebat humus:
> aeraque et argentum cumque auro pondera ferri
>   manibus admorat, nullaque massa fuit.
> at meliora dabat; curvo sine vomere fruges
>   pomaque, et in quercu mella reperta cava.
> nec valido quisquam terram findebat aratro,
>   signabat nullo limite mensor humum,
> non freta demisso verrebant eruta remo,
>   ultima mortali tum via litus erat.
> contra te sollers, hominum natura, fuisti
>   et nimium damnis ingeniosa tuis.
> quo tibi, turritis incingere moenibus urbes?
>   quo tibi, discordes addere in arma manus?
> quid tibi cum pelago? terra contenta fuisses!
>   cur non et caelum tertia regna facis?
> [qua licet, adfectas caelum quoque: templa Quirinus,
>   Liber et Alcides et modo Caesar habent.]
> eruimus terra solidum pro frugibus aurum:
>   possidet inventas sanguine miles opes.
> curia pauperibus clausast: dat census honores:
>   inde gravis iudex, inde severus eques.[81]

But when old Saturn had the rule of heaven,[82] the deep earth kept all lucre in darkness, and bronze and silver with gold and heavy iron she hid from all hands, and there was no massy metal. But she gave better things — grains without the curved plough-share, and apples, and honey found within the hollow oak. And no one broke the earth with strong plough; no surveyor marked off the soil with boundaries. No one swept the seas stirred by low-ered oar. The shore in those days was man's last road.

You have been too clever for your own good, O human nature (*hominum natura*)! and gifted beyond measure to your ruin. Of what avail to you to gird cities with turreted walls? Of what avail to arm hands in strife? What had you to do with the sea — you might have been satisfied with the land! Why do you not seek the sky as well — a third kingdom? In so far as you may, you do annex the sky also — Quirinus has his temple, and Liber and Alcides, and now Caesar. We draw from the earth solid gold instead of grains. The soldier possesses riches made from his blood. The curia is closed to the poor — a man's rating in the tax assessors' books pro-cures him public office; from that come the grave judge and the stern knight![83]

---

[81] Ed. R. Ehwald, Leipzig, 1916, with slight changes in punctuation.

[82] Here he is not confused with King Saturn of Italy.

[83] This passage emphasizing the lack of money in the Golden Age should be com-pared with *Ars Amat.* II, 277 f. where Ovid bitterly says that his own time might be called golden, since gold was given the highest honors and won even a woman's love.

Both ethical and what may be called epistemological primitivism is illustrated by the following query of Plutarch about an epithet of Cronus (1st c. A. D.).

II, 29.   Plutarch, *Aetia romana*, 12.

' Διὰ τί δὲ τὸν Κρόνον πατέρα τῆς ἀληθείας νομίζουσι; ' πότερον, ὥσπερ ἔνιοι τῶν φιλοσόφων, χρόνον οἴονται τὸν Κρόνον εἶναι, τὸ δ' ἀληθὲς εὑρίσκει χρόνος· ἢ τὸν μυθολογούμενον ἐπὶ Κρόνου βίον, εἰ δικαιότατος ἦν, εἰκός ἐστι μάλιστα μετέχειν ἀληθείας; [84]

Why do the Romans consider Cronus the Father of Truth? Is it, as some philosophers think, because Cronus is Time (*Chronos*), and time brings truth to light; or because the life of the mythical age of Saturn, if it was the most righteous, is likely to have possessed a greater measure of truth?

A return to the traditional view of the Age of Cronus as an age of plenty freely given is found in Lucian's *Saturnian Letters* (2d c. A. D.), where the legend is used to heighten the picture of the misery of the author's time.

II, 30.   Lucian, *Saturnian Letters*, I, 20, 402 f.

καίτοι ἀκούω τῶν ποιητῶν λεγόντων ὡς τὸ παλαιὸν οὐ τοιαῦτα ἦν τοῖς ἀνθρώποις τὰ πράγματα σοῦ ἔτι μοναρχοῦντος, ἀλλ' ἡ μὲν γῆ ἄσπορος καὶ ἀνήροτος ἔφυεν αὐτοῖς τὰ ἀγαθά, δεῖπνον ἕτοιμον ἑκάστῳ ἐς κόρον, ποταμοὶ δὲ οἱ μὲν οἴνον, οἱ δὲ γάλα, εἰσὶ δὲ οἳ καὶ μέλι ἔρρεον· τὸ δὲ μέγιστον, αὐτοὺς ἐκείνους φασὶ τοὺς ἀνθρώπους χρυσοῦς εἶναι, πενίαν δὲ μηδὲ τὸ παράπαν αὐτοῖς πλησιάζειν. ἡμεῖς δὲ αὐτοὶ μὲν οὐδὲ μόλυβδος ἂν εἰκότως δοκοίημεν, ἀλλ' εἴ τι καὶ τούτου ἀτιμότερον, ἡ τροφὴ δὲ μετὰ πόνων τοῖς πλείστοις, ἡ πενία δὲ καὶ ἀπορία καὶ ἀμηχανία καὶ τὸ οἴμοι καὶ τὸ πόθεν ἄν μοι γένοιτο καὶ ὦ τῆς τύχης πολλὰ τοιαῦτα παρὰ γοῦν ἡμῖν τοῖς πένησι. καὶ ἧττον ἄν, εὖ ἴσθι, ἠνιώμεθα ἂν ἐπ' αὐτοῖς, εἰ μὴ τοὺς πλουσίους ἑωρῶμεν τοσαύτῃ εὐδαιμονίᾳ συνόντας, οἳ τοσοῦτον μὲν χρυσόν, τοσοῦτον δὲ ἄργυρον ἐγκλεισάμενοι, ἐσθῆτας δὲ ὅσας ἔχοντες, ἀνδράποδα δὲ καὶ ζεύγη καὶ συνοικίας καὶ ἀγρούς, πάμπολλα δὲ ταῦτα ἕκαστα κεκτημένοι οὐχ ὅπως μετέδοσαν ἡμῖν ποτε αὐτῶν, ἀλλ' οὐδὲ προσβλέπειν τοὺς πολλοὺς ἀξιοῦσι. [85]

Now I hear poets saying that in the old days when you [Cronus] were still king things were not so with men, but earth brought forth her goods for them unsown and unploughed; there were meals more than sufficient made ready for each man; rivers ran wine and milk and honey. Most important of all, they say that the men of that time themselves were of gold, and poverty never approached them. But we would hardly seem to be of lead, but rather of something cheaper than this. Most of us earn our food by toil, live in poverty, want and helplessness, with cries of " Ah me! " " Whence comes this? " and " Oh that such a fate should be! " — such is the lot of us poor men. And we should suffer less, mark you, in these things if we did not find the rich enjoying such a happy lot. They have

[84] In *Moralia*, II, ed. G. N. Bernardakis, Leipzig, 1889.
[85] Ed. C. Jacobitz, Leipzig, 1867, III, 312-313.

such stores of gold and silver, such wardrobes, slaves and carriages and houses and fields, and, though they own such abundance, they share none of it with us, but deem the many unworthy of even a glance.

THE SATURNALIA AS A RETURN TO THE AGE OF SATURN

We have seen that there were at least two theories of the Age of Saturn in Latin literature; one that it was an age common to the world as a whole, and primitive; the other that it was an age peculiar to Italy, and post-primitive. But both theories, or rather legends, emphasized the blessings of the period. Meanwhile the celebration of the Feast of Saturn, or Saturnalia, had become customary. The origin of this festival is assigned to various dates by Roman historians, but by all it is recognized as ancient.[86] It corresponded to the Greek Cronia, and in later authors who wrote of matters Roman in Greek, the word *Cronia* was used to denote the Saturnalia as the name *Cronus* was used for Saturn.

The Greek Cronia

Very little is known from early authors of the Greek Cronia. It is mentioned by Aristophanes (*Nubes*, 398), but much in the spirit of his fellow comic writers when they spoke of the Age of Cronus. Demosthenes dates it for us in the month Hecatombaeon (*Adv. Timoc.* 708, 26) which would place it in the summer rather than in December, which was the month of the Saturnalia, and lets us infer that during the festival the Senate did not sit. Whether this was a reminiscence of the happy anarchism of the Golden Age or not, we have no way of telling.[87] Alciphron (*Epist.* III, 57, (21 Schepers)), who lived at a time when Roman and Greek customs may have become confused, informs us that gifts were exchanged; it is impossible to be sure whether he is speaking of the Greek Cronia or the Saturnalia. We are in the same predicament regarding Lucian, whose *Saturnalia, Saturnian Letters,* and *Cronosolon* give us such a lively picture of the feast. In the *Saturnalia* (§ 7) Cronus, when asked why he resigned his kingdom to Zeus, replies that it was because of old age and the degeneracy of the times. He returns for seven days a year simply to remind men how different life was in his time, when bread and meat were provided

---

[86] Macrob. *Sat.* I, vii; Dion. Halic. *Ant. rom.* II, 50, III, 32, VI, 1; Livy, XXII, i, 19, 20; Plut. *Quaest. rom.* xi.

[87] Suidas (Κρόνια) tells us that it was a festival both of Cronus and the mother of the gods, which might have made it quite different from the Saturnalia, and certainly would have tended to obscure its meaning as a recalling of the Golden Age. For the mother of the gods never figures in that particular legend. Yet see Macrobius's reference to Philochorus in *Sat.* I, x, 22; *Philochorus Saturno et Opi primum in Attica statuisse aram Cecropem dicit eosque deos pro Jove Terraque coluisse instituisseque ut patresfamiliarum et frugibus et fructibus iam coactis passim cum servis vescerentur, cum quibus patientiam laboris in colendo rure toleraverant. delectari enim deum honore servorum contemplatu laboris.*

all cooked, wine flowed in rivers, milk and honey spurted up in fountains, all men were good and free and there were no slaves.

II, 31. Lucian, *Saturnalia*, VII.

πλὴν ὀλίγας ταύτας ἡμέρας ἐφ' οἷς εἶπον ὑπεξελέσθαι μοι ἔδοξε καὶ ἀναλαμβάνω τὴν ἀρχήν, ὡς ὑπομνήσαιμι τοὺς ἀνθρώπους οἷος ἦν ὁ ἐπ' ἐμοῦ βίος, ὁπότε ἄσπορα καὶ ἀνήροτα πάντα ἐφύετο αὐτοῖς, οὐ στάχυες, ἀλλ' ἕτοιμος ἄρτος καὶ κρέα ἐσκευασμένα, καὶ ὁ οἶνος ἔρρει ποταμηδὸν καὶ πηγαὶ μέλιτος καὶ γάλακτος· ἀγαθοὶ γὰρ ἦσαν καὶ χρυσοῖ ἅπαντες. αὕτη μοι ἡ αἰτία τῆς ὀλιγοχρονίου ταύτης δυναστείας, καὶ διὰ τοῦτο ἀπανταχοῦ κρότος καὶ ᾠδὴ καὶ παιδιὰ καὶ ἰσοτιμία πᾶσι καὶ δούλοις καὶ ἐλευθέροις· οὐδεὶς γὰρ ἐπ' ἐμοῦ δοῦλος ἦν.[88]

This passage is obviously written in the spirit of the Old Comedy (see II, 10-15 above) and must not be taken seriously. It is obvious that Lucian had no great faith in the historicity of the Golden Age; the passage is largely of interest to us as indicating the survival of the legend and suggesting that the Cronia were a fictitious return to the Age of Cronus. In what spirit the festival was taken is seen in the laws which Cronosolon is asked by Cronus to compose, of which we quote the first table as most germane to our subject.

II, 32. Lucian, *Cronosolon*, 13.

ΝΟΜΟΙ ΠΡΩΤΟΙ.

Μηδένα μηδὲν μήτε ἀγοραῖον μήτε ἴδιον πράττειν ἐντὸς τῆς ἑορτῆς ἢ ὅσα ἐς παιδιὰν καὶ τρυφὴν καὶ θυμηδίαν, ὀψοποιοὶ μόνοι καὶ πεμματουργοὶ ἐνεργοὶ ἔστωσαν. ἰσοτιμία πᾶσιν ἔστω καὶ δούλοις καὶ ἐλευθέροις καὶ πένησι καὶ πλουσίοις. ὀργίζεσθαι ἢ ἀγανακτεῖν ἢ ἀπειλεῖν μηδενὶ ἐξέστω. λογισμοὺς παρὰ τῶν ἐπιμελουμένων Κρονίοις λαμβάνειν μηδὲ τοῦτο ἐξέστω. μηδεὶς τὸν ἄργυρον ἢ τὴν ἐσθῆτα ἐξεταζέτω μηδὲ ἀναγραφέτω ἐν τῇ ἑορτῇ μηδὲ γυμναζέσθω Κρονίοις μηδὲ λόγους ἀσκεῖν ἢ ἐπιδείκνυσθαι, πλὴν εἴ τινες ἀστεῖοι καὶ φαιδροὶ σκῶμμα καὶ παιδιὰν ἐμφαίνοντες.[89]

First laws: No one may do anything of a public or private nature during the feast except such as pertains to games and wantonness and good cheer. Only cooks and bakers may engage in business.

There shall be equal honor to all, both slaves and free, both poor and rich.

Let there be no anger nor irritation nor threatening on the part of anyone. Nor shall there be given a reckoning during the Cronia from stewards. Let no one count his money nor his raiment nor make records during the feast, and let there be no physical drill nor composing and delivery of speeches, unless they be witty and jolly, displaying jokes and playfulness.

The Roman Saturnalia

Although many writers believed the Saturnalia to be a distinctly Roman

[88] Ed. C. Jacobitz, Leipzig, 1867, III, 305. This passage has been introduced by so complete a paraphrase that no translation has been thought necessary.
[89] Ed. C. Jacobitz, Leipzig, 1867, III, 308.

custom, one writer at least is quoted as suggesting that this festival was an imitation of the Cronia. Accius (b. 170 B. C.) is cited by Macrobius as follows:

II, 33. Macrobius, *Saturnalia*, I, vii, 37.

> Maxima pars Graium Saturno et maxime Athenae
> conficiunt sacra, quae Cronia esse iterantur ab illis,
> eumque diem celebrant: per agros urbesque fere omnes
> exercent epulis laeti, famulosque procurant
> quisque suos nostrique itidem, et mos traditus illinc
> iste, ut cum dominis famuli epulentur ibidem.[90]

> Most of the Greeks, especially the Athenians, perform rites to Saturn, which are called by them the Cronia, and this day they celebrate. Throughout the fields and cities nearly everyone joyfully prepares banquets and each one serves his slaves, and we do likewise, and our custom comes down from this, so that our slaves dine in the same place with their masters.

That the Saturnalia were recognized as a brief return to the Age of Saturn is shown in the following passage from Pompeius Trogus (early 1st c. A. D.), in which the economic state of nature and the absence of slavery in the Golden Age are emphasized.

II, 34. Pompeius Trogus, in Justin, *Hist. phil. epit.* XLIII, i, 3-4.

> Italiae cultores primi Aborigines fuere, quorum rex Saturnus tantae iustitiae fuisse dicitur, ut neque servierit quisquam sub illo neque quicquam privatae rei habuerit, sed omnia communia et indivisa omnibus fuerint, veluti unum cunctis patrimonium esset. Ob cuius exempli memoriam cautum est, ut Saturnalibus exaequato omnium iure passim in conviviis servi cum dominis recumbant.[91]

> The first inhabitants of Italy were the Aborigines, whose king, Saturn, is said to have been so just that there were no slaves under him nor any private property, but all things belonged to all in common and undivided, as if all men had one patrimony. In memory of this precedent it was decreed that during the Saturnalia, by a leveling of all men's rights, slaves should sit down at banquets with their masters indiscriminately.[92]

The theory of Pompeius Trogus is in accord with the actual characteristics of the Saturnalia. Not only were slaves treated as if free, but no wars could be begun nor criminals punished — thus again recalling men's freedom from war and exemption from government in the Golden Age.[93] It was essentially a time of relaxation of restraints — the *libertas Decem-*

---

[90] Ed. F. Eyssenhardt, Leipzig, 1893.

[91] Ed. Fr. Ruehl, Leipzig, 1915, p. 238.

[92] This reversal of rôles between master and slave became a source of many literary decorations. *Vide* e. g. Horace, *Sat.* II, vii, 4 f.; Pliny's Letter to Tacitus, *Letters*, VIII, 7.

[93] See Macrobius, *Sat.* I, ix. Cf. Suetonius, *Oct. Aug.* XXXII, end.

bri [94] becoming a sort of literary cliché. Perhaps no better impression of the Saturnalian spirit could be found than in a section of the *Silvae* (I, vi, 1-45) of Statius, which, however, describes a festival of the Kalends of December and not the annual festival of Saturn. It emphasizes, as was only natural, considering the circumstances, the soft primitivism of the traditional account (as in the passages from the Greek comic poets), rather than the simplicity of primitive life. The passage ends on the following lines:

II, 35. Statius, *Silvae,* I, vi, 39-45.

> I nunc saecula compara, Vetustas,
> antiqui Iovis aureumque tempus:
> non sic libera vina tunc fluebant
> nec tardum seges occupabat annum.
> una vescitur omnis ordo mensa,
> parvi, femina, plebs, eques, senatus:
> libertas reverentiam remisit.[95]

Go now, Antiquity, compare the times of ancient Jupiter and the Golden Age. Not thus freely did wine then flow nor did the harvest continue until so late in the year. Every social rank eats at one table, the lowly, women, the plebeians, the knights, the senate. Freedom has relaxed reverence.

It is, moreover, this Saturnalian spirit which undoubtedly inspired the following passage from Fronto's *Eulogy of Negligence* (? 139 A. D.), so curiously in the spirit of the " Paradoxes " of the 15th and 16th centuries.

II, 36. Fronto, *Laudes negligentiae.*

> Iam illud a poetis saeculum aureum memoratum, si cum animo reputes, intellegas neglegentiae saeculum fuisse, cum ager neglectus fructus uberes ferret, omniaque utensilia neglegentibus nullo negotio suppeditaret. Hisce argumentis neglegentia bono genere nata, dis accepta, sapientibus probata, virtutum particeps, indulgentiae magistra, tuta ab insidiis, grataque bene factis, excusata ingratis et ad postremum aurea declaratur.[96]

Now that Golden Age commemorated by the poets, if you reflect upon it, you will understand to have been an age of negligence, when the fields neglected bore rich crops, and supplied without any labor all necessaries to those who neglected them. By these arguments negligence is shown to have been born of a good family, accepted by the gods, approved by the wise, a comrade of the virtues, a teacher of indulgence, safe from trickeries, welcome for her

---

[94] Cf. not only the passages referred to in Horace and Pliny, but also Martial, XI, vi and XIV, i.

[95] Ed. Fr. Vollmer, Leipzig, 1898.

[96] Ed. S. A. Naber, Leipzig, 1867, p. 215. Fronto's letters were discovered in 1815, and hence were not accessible to early modern writers.

benefactions, excused for her misdeeds,[97] and finally proclaimed to be golden.

Our last document in this section shows the survival of the old literary tradition of soft primitivism. Both its author and date are uncertain.

II, 37. Anon. *Elegy,* in *Anthologia Latina,* No. 914, 63-80.

> Quam bene, cum ferrum nondum prodiret in auras,
>   Omnia pacis erant, et sua cuique satis!
> Dives erat, si quis parvi possessor agelli.
>   Severat ille prius, deinde coquebat holus.
> Non locus invidiae, quamvis vicinus habunde
>   Et pecus et messes mustaque haberet ager.
> Liber amor, nulli mulier suspecta marito,
>   Casta satis, norat si qua negare palam.
> Tunc Venus . . . . spirabat dulciter ignes
>   Spiculaque in silvis tuta vibrabat Amor.
> Cur mihi non illis nasci, mea vita, diebus
>   Contigit? invidit quis bona tanta deus?
> O niveas luces! o tempora dulcia! vere
>   Aurea Saturni saecla fuere senis.
> Nunc ferrum erupit (rabiesque asperrima ferri),
>   Nunc furor et caedes . . . .
> Forsan et hic noster tinget cruor hospitis arma
>   Aut cadet unanimis frater ab ense meo.[98]

How happily, before iron was brought to light, were all things at peace, while each man found his own possessions sufficient! He was rich who was the owner of a little plot of ground. First he sowed, then cooked his vegetables. There was no place for envy, although one's neighbor's property had abundant flocks and harvests and wine. Love was free and no woman an object of suspicion to her husband.[99] She was chaste enough if she knew what to deny in public. Then Venus kindled her fires gently and Love sped his quivering darts safely in the woods. Why did I not begin my life in those days? What god envied me such good things? O snow-white days! O happy times! Truly that age of old Saturn was of gold. Now iron has broken loose, and the bitter madness of iron. Now rage and slaughter. . . . Perhaps my blood will stain the weapon of a guest, or my brother, now of one mind with me, will fall by my sword.

---

[97] We have retained the reading " ingratis " in preference to Buttman's suggestion " erratis," in spite of its difficulties. There seems to be a rhetorical effect in the contrast between the word " grata " and " ingratis," and by a stretch of the imagination one may roll up into " ingratis " " the things negligence does which are unwelcome." We preserve the contrast in the words " benefactions " and " misdeeds." But the dubiousness of the rendering must be granted.

[98] Ed. A. Riese, Leipzig, 2d ed. 1906. This was first published in Florence in 1590 by Aldus Manutius. Its present editor suggests that it is by Maximianus, the ambassador from Theodoric to the Emperor Anastasius, the friend of Boethius.

[99] Contrast Juvenal in the passage quoted below, II, 38.

Here there is a re-echo of the more idyllic note, in which the free love of primitive days is emphasized. But the old strains of the simple life, peace, and the absence of envy and avarice, also resound. It will be observed, however, that primitive man is not represented as communistic outside of his marital relations, but enjoys private property. The passage has little historical significance. It is obviously for the most part 'mere literature,' whereas such passages as Juvenal's are definite criticisms of the author's time.

Hard Primitivism in Juvenal

It is noticeable that the Saturnalia revived mainly that aspect of the nostalgia for the Age of Saturn which we have called soft primitivism. With the exception of the pretended equality between man and master and the prohibition of war and law-suits, there seems to have been little if any reminder of the moral virtues often ascribed to the men of that epoch. The Saturnalia were a festival of revelry and merry-making, not a return to simple pastoral innocence. In Juvenal a very different note is struck. A new age is said to have arrived, an age for which there is no metal base enough to give it a name. By contrast with this period, the Age of Saturn was one of simplicity in living, of righteousness, of respect. The "Age of Negligence" finds no echo here.

II, 38. *Sat.* XIII, 28-59.

> nunc aetas agitur peioraque saecula ferri
> temporibus, quorum sceleri non invenit ipsa
> nomen et a nullo posuit natura metallo.
> nos hominum divumque fidem clamore ciemus,
> quanto Faesidium laudat vocalis agentem
> sportula? dic, senior bulla dignissime, nescis
> quas habeat veneres aliena pecunia? nescis
> quem tua simplicitas risum vulgo moveat, cum
> exigis a quoquam ne peieret et putet ullis
> esse aliquod numen templis araeque rubenti?
> quondam hoc indigenae vivebant more, priusquam
> sumeret agrestem posito diademate falcem
> Saturnus fugiens, tunc cum virguncula Iuno
> et privatus adhuc Idaeis Iuppiter antris,
> nulla super nubes convivia caelicolarum
> nec puer Iliacus formonsa nec Herculis uxor
> ad cyathos, et iam siccato nectare tergens
> bracchia Vulcanus Liparaea nigra taberna,
> prandebat sibi quisque deus, nec turba deorum
> talis ut est hodie, contentaque sidera paucis
> numinibus miserum urguebant Atlanta minori
> pondere, nondum aliquis sortitus triste profundi
> imperium aut Sicula torvus cum coniuge Pluton,
> nec rota nec Furiae nec saxum aut vulturis atri
> poena, sed infernis hilares sine regibus umbrae.
> inprobitas illo fuit admirabilis aevo,

credebant quo grande nefas et morte piandum
si iuvenis vetulo non adsurrexerat et si
barbato cuicumque puer, licet ipse videret
plura domi fraga et maiores glandis acervos;
tam venerabile erat praecedere quattuor annis,
primaque par adeo sacrae lanugo senectae.[100]

Now an age is here, an age worse than that of iron, for whose crimes no name has been found, nor does nature provide one from any metal. We invoke the faith of men and gods with cries as loud as those with which the noisy populace at the games applauds Faesidius in action. Tell me, childish old man, do you not know what loves a stranger's money may obtain? Do you not know how your simplicity moves the crowd to laughter, when you exact from someone that he swear not falsely and that he think some divinity owns the temples and the glowing altar? Once the aborigines did live according to this rule of life, before Saturn fleeing laid aside the crown to take up the rustic sickle, when Juno was a little girl and Jupiter still a private citizen in the caves of Ida. The dwellers in heaven had no banquets above the clouds: neither the Ilian boy nor the shapely wife of Hercules were at the wine-ladle. Nor did Vulcan, having drained his nectar, wipe his arms, black from his Liparean workshop. Each god dined alone, nor was the crowd of gods such as it is to-day. The heavens, satisfied with a few divinities, weighed less heavily on poor Atlas. Not yet had any of them received by sorry lot the empire of the deep, nor did gloomy Pluto reign with his Sicilian wife. There were neither wheel nor furies nor rock nor punishment by the black vulture, but the shades made merry without the kings of hell. Dishonesty[101] was a thing for wonder in that age, in which it was deemed a great crime and punishable by death for a youth not to rise before an old man and for a boy not to do likewise before a person with a beard, although he might have at home more fruits and greater heaps of acorns. So venerable was a few years' seniority, and so equal first down to sacred age.[102]

This picture of an Age of Saturn whose moral virtues were pre-eminent is completed in Juvenal by a more rounded-out account of primitive life. Satirizing an age of luxury, he lays special emphasis upon the roughness of primitive life and is one of the earliest of our authors to see the merit not only in simplicity but in crudity. There is no attempt here to depict primitive men as resembling shepherds of Theocritus. These sylvan folk are very close to the savages. Yet in spite of their ugliness and coarseness they are our moral superiors.

II, 39. *Sat.* VI, 1-24.

Credo Pudicitiam Saturno rege moratam
in terris visamque diu, cum frigida parvas

---

[100] Ed. H. L. Wilson, New York, 1903.

[101] *Impietas* would be a reading fitting the context much better than *improbitas*.

[102] The last line is intelligible only if taken as ironical.

praeberet spelunca domos ignemque Laremque
et pecus et dominos communi clauderet umbra,
silvestrem montana torum cum sterneret uxor
frondibus et culmo vicinarumque ferarum
pellibus, haut similis tibi, Cynthia, nec tibi, cuius
turbavit nitidos extinctus passer ocellos,
sed potanda ferens infantibus ubera magnis
et saepe horridior glandem ructante marito.
quippe aliter tunc orbe novo caeloque recenti
vivebant homines, qui rupto robore nati
compositive luto nullos habuere parentes.
multa Pudicitiae veteris vestigia forsan
aut aliqua exstiterint et sub Iove, sed Iove nondum
barbato, nondum Graecis iurare paratis
per caput alterius, cum furem nemo timeret
caulibus et pomis, et aperto viveret horto.
paulatim deinde ad superos Astraea recessit
hac comite, atque duae pariter fugere sorores.
anticum et vetus est alienum, Postume, lectum
concutere atque sacri genium contemnere fulcri.
omne aliud crimen mox ferrea protulit aetas:
viderunt primos argentea saecula moechos.[103]

I believe that what Saturn was king Shame still lingered on earth,
and was to be seen continually in the days when an icy cavern provided a man's little home and enclosed the hearth and the lares, the
flocks and their masters in common darkness; when the mountain
wife laid a sylvan bed of leaves and stalks and skins of the neighboring beasts. Not like you, Cynthia, was she, nor like you whose
shining eyes a dead sparrow clouded. But she bore breasts to feed
great children and was often more savage than her acorn-belching
mate. Then when the earth was new and heaven young, men lived
otherwise than now, those who, born of a riven oak and compounded
of mud, had no parents. Perhaps there were many traces of ancient
Shame, or some at least, still existing even under Jupiter, but under
a Jupiter not yet bearded, when the Greeks were not yet ready to
swear by the head of the other, when no one feared the theft of his
cabbages and apples, and men lived in an open garden. Then little
by little Astraea withdrew to the heavenly regions with this companion [viz. Shame] and the two sisters fled together. It is now
an old and ancient custom, Postumus, to defile the bed of another,
and to defy the genius of the chamber. The iron age soon produced every other crime. The silver age saw the first adulterer.

The hard primitivism of this version still retains certain features of the
more idyllic passages. In the Age of Saturn there was, for instance, no
theft; there was presumably no private ownership of land; there was no
adultery. But the spontaneous gifts of mother earth are replaced by the
acorns, which anti-primitivists scorned, or by apples and cabbages. No
effort is made to prettify the dark caves in which men and flocks lived

[103] Ed. H. A. Wilson, 1903.

together. The theme of two divine sponsors of right living, Astraea and Shame, is a definite echo of Hesiod's *Aidos* and *Nemesis* (See above, II, 2).

SATURN THE MALIGNANT PLANET

The third element in the life of Cronus-Saturn which interests us is the story of his pedophagy, if the neologism is permissible. We have already seen that in Ennius's translation of Euhemerus this was explained as a symbol of the cannibalism prevalent in primitive times. The fact remained that Cronus had swallowed his children. That he was the father of the gods gave him, moreover, a position of pre-eminence, so that, in spite of Dionysius Halicarnassensis (*Ant. rom.* I, 38), he was identified with other chief gods, and with one in particular, who was famous for his love of human flesh.

Sextus Empiricus, (*Hyp.* III, 208), discussing cannibalism says that some people sacrifice a man to Cronus just as the Scythians sacrifice strangers to Artemis. There is, of course, no telling whether by Cronus Sextus means the Greek Cronus or one of the barbarian gods identified with him. So Dionysius Halicarnassensis says:

II, 40. Dionysius Halicarnassensis, *Ant. rom.* I, 38, 2.

> λέγουσι δὲ καὶ τὰς θυσίας ἐπιτελεῖν τῷ Κρόνῳ τοὺς παλαιούς, ὥσπερ ἐν Καρχηδόνι τέως ἡ πόλις διέμεινε καὶ παρὰ Κελτοῖς εἰς τόδε χρόνου γίνεται καὶ ἐν ἄλλοις τισὶ τῶν ἑσπερίων ἐθνῶν ἀνδροφόνους.[104]

> And it is said that the ancients made human sacrifices to Cronus, just as was done in Carthage so long as the city existed, and as is done to this very day among the Celts, as well as among certain other peoples of the west.

Here Dionysius is obviously identifying Cronus with the other chief gods.

Among the gods with whom he was eventually identified, not, of course, because of his pedophagy but because of his hierarchical position and the fact that his day was Saturday, was Jehovah. Tacitus made Saturn a hero of the Jews, as Plutarch seems to.[105] In speaking of the origin of the Jews, he says that they have been said to come from Crete, whence they fled to the confines of Libya when Saturn was expelled by Jupiter (*Hist.* V, ii). They celebrate the Sabbath, some say, in honor of Saturn, *seu principia religionis tradentibus Idaeis, quos cum Saturno pulsos et conditores gentis accepimus* (" or because they got the principles of their religion from the Idaeans, whom we believe to have been expelled with Saturn and to have been the founders of this people ").[106] But in general Cronus-Saturn was identified with Ba'al or Moloch. The following texts will illustrate this.

[104] Ed. C. Jacoby, Leipzig, 1885.
[105] *Cessation of Oracles*, 21, in reference to the Solymi.
[106] *Hist.*, V, v.

II, 41. Eusebius (*ca.* 264-*ca.* 340 A. D.), *Praep. evang.* I, x, 16.

παραλαβὼν δὲ ὁ Οὐρανὸς τὴν τοῦ πατρὸς ἀρχὴν ἄγεται πρὸς γάμον τὴν ἀδελφὴν Γῆν, καὶ ποιεῖται ἐξ αὐτῆς παῖδας τέσσαρας, Ἤλον, τὸν καὶ Κρόνον, κτλ.[107]

When Uranus took over his father's power, he married his sister Earth and had from her four children, El, who is also called Cronus. . . .

Here Cronus is identified with the Phoenician *El* or Chaldean *Bel*.[108] Who the father of Uranus was, Eusebius does not tell us. That he had a father is, of course, contrary to the Hesiodic genealogy of the gods.

II, 42. Servius on *Aen.* I, 729, *Apud Assyrios Bel dicitur quadam sacrorum ratione et Saturnus et Sol.*

The *Life of Isidorus*[109] by Damascius (§ 115) corroborates this.[110]

II, 43.

Φοίνικες καὶ Σύροι τὸν Κρόνον Ἤλ καὶ Βὴλ καὶ Θολάθην ἐπονομάζουσιν.

II, 44. Q. Curtius Rufus (1st c. A. D.), *Hist. Alex.* IV, iii, 23.

Sacrum quoque, quod equidem dis minime cordi esse crediderim, multis seculis intermissum repetendi auctores quidam erant, ut ingenuus puer Saturno immolaretur — quod sacrilegium verius quam sacrum Carthagenienses a conditoribus traditum usque ad excidium urbis suae fecisse dicuntur —, ac nisi seniores obstitissent, quorum consilio cuncta agebantur, humanitatem dira superstitio vicisset.[111]

The restoration of a certain sacrifice, which the gods, I should have imagined, would have but little heart for, was, after having been abandoned for many centuries, proposed by some persons — that a free-born boy be offered up to Saturn: which sacrilege (rather than sacrifice), handed down by the founders of the city, the Carthaginians are said to have made, up to its downfall; and if their elders, at whose advice all things used to be carried on, had not been opposed to it, dire superstition would have conquered humanity.[112]

---

[107] Ed. Dindorf, Leipzig, 1867, I.

[108] See Bouché-Leclercq, *L'Astrologie Grecque*, 93, n. 2. He was also identified with Ninib, *Id.* 69.

[109] This may be found in the Didot edition of Diogenes Laertius, Append. 131, Paris, 1861, taken from the *Bibliotheca* of Photius.

[110] More extensive information may be found in Roscher, art. *Kronos.* If the dialogue *Minos* is Platonic, it is the earliest document which identifies Cronus and Baal.

[111] Ed. Ed. Hedicke, Leipzig, 1908. Cf. the Pseudo-Platonic *Minos*, 315 C; Ennius, *Annals*, VII; Pliny, *Nat. hist.* xxxvi, 5, 37; Porphyry, *De abstin.* II, 56; Justin, *Hist. phil.* XVIII, 6, 2; XIX, 1, 1.

[112] Cf. Minucius Felix, XXX, 3. The way this idea lingered on may be seen by the following quotation from the seventeenth century French author:

Les hommes commencerent à s'adonner à l'idolatrie et la plus commune

This side of Cronus-Saturn no doubt facilitated the identification of a god-king whose reign was sung as the epoch of man's greatest happiness with a *sidus triste* [113] whose influence on man is peculiarly gloomy and indeed maleficent. So extreme is this paradox that in a list of the planets and their powers, which is given by Apuleius (*Florida,* X), the power of Jupiter is *benefica* and that of Saturn *perniciosa.*[114] And not only that, but Saturn, under whose reign there was usually supposed to be neither money nor navigation, is said by Ptolemy to have the peculiar property of increasing wealth by agriculture — which is understandable — or maritime traffic.[115]

But it is next to hopeless to find any logical coherence between the characters of the planet Saturn and the god Saturn, and one astronomer, Firmicus (4th c. A. D.), became so convinced of the astrological account that he refused to believe that the first age, when Saturn ruled, was one of gold at all, but insisted that the first men were like the planet, rustic, savage, and inhuman.

II, 45. Firmicus, *Mathesis,* III, i, 11-15.

> Voluerunt Lunam ⟨ita⟩ constituere, ut primum se Saturno coniungeret eique temporum traderet principatum, nec inmerito; quia enim prima origo mundi inculta fuit et horrida et agresti conversatione effera, et quia rudes homines prima et incognita sibi vestigia lucis ingressos politae humanitatis ratio deserebat, Saturni hoc agreste et horridum tempus esse voluerunt, ut ad imitationem huius sideris ⟨in⟩ initiis vitae constituta mortalitas agresti se conversatione et inhumana feritatis exasperatione duraret. Post Saturnum Iuppiter accepit temporum potestatem (nam huic secundo loco Luna coniungitur), ut deserto pristini squaloris horrore et agrestis conversationis feritate seposita cultior vita hominum purgatis moribus redderetur. Tertio vero loco Marti se Luna coniungens ei temporum tradidit potestatem, ut rectum vitae iter ingressa mortalitas et iam humanitatis quadam moderatione composita omnia artium ac fabricationum ornamenta conciperet. Post Martem dominandi Venus tempus accepit; et quia per gradus crescens hominum disciplina etiam prudentiae ornamenta concepit, hoc tempus, quo mores hominum sermo doctus excoluit et quo homines singularum disciplinarum naturali scientia formati sunt, Veneris esse voluerunt, ut laeti ac salutaris numinis maiestate provecti errantes actus providentiae magisterio gubernarent. Ultimum vero tempus Mercurio dandum esse putaverunt, cui se novissimo Luna coniungit. Quid hac potest inveniri dispositione subtilius? Purgatis agrestibus

opinion est que Nynus Roy des Assyriens fut le premier idolatre, et Bel le premier des faux dieux auquel le culte divin fut rendu, le nom duquel est diversifié entre diverses nations, comme Baal, Baalim, Belfegor, Belsebut, *et les Grecs l'ont nommé* Kronos, *les Latins* Saturne.

Scipion Dupleix, *Mem. des Gaules,* Paris, 1627, Bk. II, p. 57.

[113] Juvenal, *Sat.* VI, 569. Cf. Propertius III, i, 83-84.

[114] Cf. Lucan, *Phars.* I, 645 f.

[115] Bouché-Leclercq, *op. cit.* 436 f.

studiis, repertis artibus disciplinisque compositis per diversos actus humani se generis exacuit intentio, et quia mobile ingenium in homine unum vitae cursum servare non potest, ex variis institutis moribusque confusis malitiae crevit inprobitas, et vitae scelerum flagitia gens hominum hoc tempore facinorosis machinationibus et invenit et tradidit. Hac ex causa ultimum tempus Mercurio esse tradendum putaverunt, ut ad imitationem istius sideris intenta gens hominum plenam malitiae conciperet potestatem. Ex his itaque, quae per ordinem gesta sunt, et his, quicumque hominum succedentium temporum mutationem fecerunt, genitura mundi divina coniecturae interpretatione composita est; et nobis hactenus et origo et cursus humani generis traditur, [et] ut hoc esset, quod in genituris hominum sequeremur exemplum. Ne quid autem a nobis praetermissum esse videatur, omnia explicanda sunt, quae probant hominem ad imitationem mundi similitudinemque formatum.[116]

They so wished to locate the Moon that she would at the first be in conjunction with Saturn and bestow upon him the primacy of the ages, and that not undeservedly. Because mankind in its origin was without civilization and barbarous and savage in its rustic way of living, and because the procedure of civilized society was unknown to the rough men then for the first time following the hitherto unknown path of light, they wished this rustic and coarse age to be Saturn's, that in imitation of this star primitive human beings might live in a rude kind of association and inhuman and extreme savagery. After Saturn Jupiter took over the control of temporal things (for in the second period the Moon was in conjunction with him), that when the loathsomeness of their original squalor had been abandoned and the savagery of their rustic way of living laid aside, a more cultured life might be produced by purifying human manners.

In the third period the Moon was in conjunction with Mars and gave him the control over temporal things, so that mortals already embarked upon the right road of life and, already settled in a certain order of humanity, might receive all the adornments of the arts and crafts.

After Mars Venus took control, and because human discipline increased step by step and assumed the adornments of foresight, this age, in which learned discourse improved human manners and in which men were formed by natural knowledge of the several disciplines, they wished to be Venus's, that, guided by the power of a happy and benevolent deity, they might govern their wandering acts by the authority of foresight. The last age they thought should be given to Mercury, with whom the Moon was last in conjunction. What cleverer arrangement could be found than this? When their rude efforts were set aside, when arts were found and sciences organized, the mind of mankind was stimulated by various activities; and because the fickle spirit in one man can not preserve a single course of living, from various institutions and confused customs the wickedness of evil burst forth, and mankind at this time discovered and passed on the shame of a sinful life [117] with maleficent

[116] Ed. W. Kroll and F. Skutsch, Leipzig, 1897.
[117] Note that the text of this passage is corrupt.

wiles. For this reason they thought the last age was Mercury's as mankind striving to imitate this planet assumed a power full of evil. And so from these things which occur by natural order and from those [gods] who have produced the change of the successive generations of men, the divine horoscope of the world was described by inference. And thus far the origin and history of mankind have been related to us so that we might follow it generation by generation in the case of individuals. That we may not appear to overlook anything, we must explain all as proving man to be formed in the image of the world.

Firmicus, who takes no credit for this theory himself, adheres, however, to the legend of five ages, each of which is determined by the supremacy of a planet with which the Moon is in conjunction. As a consequence, the Age of Jupiter is an improvement upon that of Saturn, in that man's morals are purified, a direct reversal, as we have said, of the traditional legend. In the third age, that of Mars, the arts and crafts develop; in the fourth, that of Venus, the sciences; in the fifth, that of Mercury (our own age), crimes break out because man's restless mind can not preserve a single direction. Firmicus then points out how an individual's life recapitulates the life of humanity as a whole and his composition the composition of the cosmos. This curious theory of the Ages is perhaps allied with the Stoic theory of cycles. Its interest here is in its exemplification of the influence of astrology upon the interpretation not only of Saturn but of his Age.

CRONUS AS A SYMBOL OF DOTAGE

Surprising as it is to find this beneficent god become a maleficent planet, it is not less surprising to find him a symbol of dotage and imbecility. As early as Aristophanes adjectives derived from his name become terms of ridicule. This, however, occurs only in Greece. The Latin authorities cite no derivatives from the name *Saturnus* which correspond to κρονικός. Our " saturnine " comes, of course, from astrology, and has no classical Latin analogue.[118] This interesting difference in linguistic development is no doubt attributable to the fact that Saturn occupied a privileged position in Roman history as a culture-hero which Cronus did not occupy in Greece. For although Pausanias tells us (I, xviii, 7), that there was an altar to Cronus in Athens, which, according to Macrobius, was built by Cecrops himself [*Sat.* I, x, 22], there was no legend to connect him with the beginnings of Athenian culture, as for instance Athene was connected, and the Athenian sense of humor saw him as a ridiculous old man who passed his time in feasting and was driven off the throne by his son.

---

[118] The first example of " Saturnine " as " gloomy " in the *NED* is dated 1433, and comes from Lydgate's *St. Edmund*, ll. 275. "This cursid Bern, enuyous and riht fals, And of complexioun verray saturnyne." But neither the god nor the king Saturn was saturnine. It was the planet alone which had that property.

We need no better evidence of the popularity of this side of the Cronus story than that furnished by Suidas. We find the following examples furnished by him.

II, 46. Suidas, *Lexicon*.[119]

a. κρονικαὶ λῆμαι. παροιμία, ὥσπερ τὸ "χύτραις λημῶν καὶ κολοκύνταις," ἐπὶ τῶν ἀμβλυωπούντων.

Here "Cronic rheums" is used proverbially for the "dim-sighted."

b. κρονικαῖς γνώμαις λημῶν τὴν φρένα [Aristoph. *Pluto* 581] ἤγουν ἀρχαίαις μωρίαις ἐσκοτισμένε τὸ φρονεῖν, τουτέστιν ἀμβλυωπῶν. λήμη δέ ἐστι τὸ πεπηγὸς δάκρυον, ὅπερ ἐπικαθεζόμενον βλάπτει τοὺς ὀφθαλμούς. σημαίνει οὖν τὸ τετυφλωμένε τὰς φρένας, ὥσπερ οἱ τὰς λήμας ἔχοντες.

In this passage "Cronic judgments" are said to refer to senile foolishness which has, so to speak, the watery eyes of Cronus.

c. κρονικώτερα: ἀρχαιότερα, μωρότερα. καὶ Ἀριστοφάνης [Vesp.] "Καὶ τοὺς τραγῳδοὺς φησιν ἀποδείξειν Κρόνους τὸν νοῦν,[120] διορχησάμενος ὀλίγον ὕστερον."

"More Cronic" as more old-fashioned, more foolish, in Aristophanes [Vesp.]: "And he says he will show the tragedians to have the mind of Cronuses, dancing in competition with them a little later."

d. κρόνιππος ὁ μέγας λῆρος, κατ' ἐπίτασιν λαμβανομένου τοῦ ἵππου. "σὺ δ' εἰ κρόνιππος" [Arist. *Nub.* 1070], ἢ ὑβριστής, τρυφητής, πόρνης.

"Cronippos" is defined as "great nonsense," with reference to the horse (ἵππος). A quotation is made from the *Clouds* of Aristophanes, in which the term is used, and "wanton," "voluptuary," and "prostitute" are given as synonyms. As a matter of fact, the term in Aristophanes is used of one no longer capable of being a voluptuary and means rather "an old Cronus of a nag."

e. κρονίων ὄζων: Ἀριστοφάνης Νεφέλαις [398] "καὶ πῶς, ὦ μῶρε σὺ καὶ κρονίων ὄζων;" τουτέστιν ἀρχαϊσμοῦ γέμων καὶ μωρίας. ἤτοι ὅτι ἑορτή τις παλαιὰ ἤγετο τῷ Κρόνῳ, ἢ ὅτι τὰ παλαιὰ πάντα καὶ εὐήθη κρόνια ἐκάλουν, καὶ Κρόνους τοὺς λήρους.

"Smelling of Cronia" [Suidas again gives an Aristophanic reference]. "How so, you fool, smelling of dark ages." [Liddell and Scott.] He equates it with being full of antiquated phrases and foolishness, either because of the ancient festival of Cronus or because all ancient and simple things are called *Cronia* and nonsense was called *Cronus*.

f. Κρόνου πυγή: τό ἀρχαῖον καὶ ἀναίσθητον κρέας.

Cronus's rump — old and insensible flesh.

---

[119] Ed. Ada Adler, Leipzig, 1933.

[120] Modern editors of Aristophanes read τοὺς νῦν. We read διορχησάμενος to conform to the best Aristophanes MSS.

This list, which dates from the twelfth century, may be supplemented by Liddell and Scott, where reference is made to Plato's *Lysis* (205 c) in which old platitudes are called *Cronic* and the *Euthydemus* (287 c) where Cronus is clearly a synonym for " an old fool," to the lexicographer Pollux (2. 16), and the *Anecdota graeca* (p. 46) of Bekker.

This lexicographical exercise brings to a close our section on the Age of Saturn. Its purpose is to show how one attribute of Cronus, his age, was selected for emphasis in order to convert the god under whose realm mankind had been at its best into a comic figure.

As a matter of fact, the story of Cronus and the Golden Age is still incomplete. At times his name was confused with Χρόνος (as for example in II, 29) and a Neoplatonistic interpretation of the myth was evolved.[121] But to treat this would lead us beyond the limits we have set for ourselves.

C. CYCLES AND THE RETURN OF THE GOLDEN AGE

The philosophic theory of recurrent world-cycles is pertinent to the history of primitivism only in so far as, on the one hand, it tended to take the form of the belief that the world is at its best at the beginning of each cycle and grows progressively worse until the cycle reaches its term; and in so far as, on the other hand, it implied that the Golden Age (like all the others) will return. While the general doctrine clearly was widely current, its forms were various, and the two features mentioned are not invariably present.

HERACLITUS

It was generally believed by the Stoics that Heraclitus was the father of the theory of cycles and of the conflagration (*ecpyrosis*) which brings each of them to an end. The most trustworthy account of this part of the Heraclitean philosophy, according to Burnet,[122] is that given by Diogenes Laertius (IX, 7); it includes both the theory of cycles and the ecpyrosis, which could not in fact be easily separated.[123]

II, 47. Diog. Laert. IX, 7-9.

> Ἐκ πυρὸς τὰ πάντα συνεστάναι καὶ εἰς τοῦτο ἀναλύεσθαι· πάντα δὲ γίνεσθαι
> καθ᾽ εἱμαρμένην καὶ διὰ τῆς ἐναντιοδρομίας ἡρμόσθαι τὰ ὄντα· . . . πῦρ
> εἶναι στοιχεῖον καὶ πυρὸς ἀμοιβὴν τὰ πάντα, ἀραιώσει καὶ πυκνώσει γινόμενα.
> σαφῶς δ᾽ οὐδὲν ἐκτίθεται. γίνεσθαί τε πάντα κατ᾽ ἐναντιότητα καὶ ῥεῖν τὰ
> ὅλα ποταμοῦ δίκην, πεπεράνθαι τε τὸ πᾶν καὶ ἕνα εἶναι κόσμον· γεννᾶσθαί τε
> αὐτὸν ἐκ πυρὸς καὶ πάλιν ἐκπυροῦσθαι κατά τινας περιόδους ἐναλλὰξ τὸν σύμ-
> παντα αἰῶνα· τοῦτο δὲ γίνεσθαι καθ᾽ εἱμαρμένην. τῶν δὲ ἐναντίων τὸ μὲν ἐπὶ τὴν
> γένεσιν ἄγον καλεῖσθαι πόλεμον καὶ ἔριν, τὸ δ᾽ ἐπὶ τὴν ἐκπύρωσιν ὁμολογίαν

---

[121] The identification of Κρόνος and Χρόνος was also made by some Stoics. See Arnim, *Stoicorum veterum fragmenta*, II, fragm. 1087-1091.

[122] See *Early Greek Philosophy*, 3rd ed. London, 1920, p. 147.

[123] This passage is partly given in Ritter and Preller 36, but unfortunately without the sentences which interest us.

καὶ εἰρήνην, καὶ τὴν μεταβολὴν ὁδὸν ἄνω κάτω, τόν τε κόσμον γίνεσθαι
κατ᾽ αὐτήν. πυκνούμενον γὰρ τὸ πῦρ ἐξυγραίνεσθαι συνιστάμενόν τε γίνεσθαι
ὕδωρ, πηγνύμενον δὲ τὸ ὕδωρ εἰς γῆν τρέπεσθαι· καὶ ταύτην ὁδὸν ἐπὶ τὸ
κάτω εἶναι. πάλιν τε αὖ τὴν γῆν χεῖσθαι, ἐξ ἧς τὸ ὕδωρ γίνεσθαι, ἐκ δὲ
τούτου τὰ λοιπά, σχεδὸν πάντα ἐπὶ τὴν ἀναθυμίασιν ἀνάγων τὴν ἀπὸ τῆς
θαλάττης· αὕτη δέ ἐστιν ἡ ἐπὶ τὸ ἄνω ὁδός.[124]

All things [Heraclitus says] are organized out of fire and resolved
into it. And all things come into being according to fate, and are
harmonized by conversion into their opposites. . . . Fire is the element and all things are an exchange for fire and are brought into
being by rarefaction and condensation. But nothing is clearly
expounded. And all things are born through opposition and all are
in flux like a river. And the whole is limited and the cosmos is one.
It arises from fire and again is consumed by fire in certain periods
throughout all eternity. And this takes place in accordance with
fate. And of the opposites, that which leads to the genesis is called
war and strife, and that which leads to the *ecpyrosis* concord and
peace. And change he calls the way up and down, and the cosmos
is produced through this. For fire when condensed grows moist and
forms water, and water when congealed is turned into earth. And
this road is said to be the way down. And again earth is liquefied
and from it water arises, and from this the rest, virtually all things
being referred to evaporation from the sea. And this is the road up.

Though Diogenes Laertius is a figure of the third century of our own era,
the account he gives is derived from the Theophrastan tradition,[125] which
would put its essential features perhaps in the fourth century B. C. Hence,
whether Heraclitus himself really believed in an *ecpyrosis* or not,[126] we
have a fairly early tradition that gave the weight of his authority to the
theory. This tradition also ascribed to Heraclitus a definite measure of the
length of a cycle. According to Aetius (II, 32, 3) he believed its length
to be 18,000 years.[127]

EMPEDOCLES

Empedocles's "Age of Love," of which the description has already been
cited,[128] appears to have been only one phase of a cycle. Love and Strife
gradually become dominant in turn, so that after a period of maximal
disintegration (Strife) there follows a period of maximal integration
(Love).

II, 48. In Simplicius, *Phys.* 158, 1.

δίπλ᾽ ἐρέω· τοτὲ μὲν γὰρ ἓν ηὐξήθη μόνον εἶναι
ἐκ πλεόνων, τοτὲ δ᾽ αὖ διέφυ πλέον᾽ ἐξ ἑνὸς εἶναι.

[124] Ed. R. D. Hicks, *Loeb Class. Library*, 1925, II.
[125] See Burnet, *op. cit.* p. 148.
[126] See Burnet, *op. cit.* p. 158 f.
[127] In Censorinus, Heraclitus and Linus both make it 10,800 years long. See Diels,
Heracl. A, 13.
[128] See II, 5 above.

δοιὴ δὲ θνητῶν γένεσις, δοιὴ δ' ἀπόλειψις·
τὴν μὲν γὰρ πάντων σύνοδος τίκτει τ' ὀλέκει τε,
ἡ δὲ πάλιν διαφυομένων θρεφθεῖσα διέπτη.
καὶ ταῦτ' ἀλλάσσοντα διαμπερὲς οὐδαμὰ λήγει,
ἄλλοτε μὲν Φιλότητι συνερχόμεν' εἰς ἓν ἅπαντα,
ἄλλοτε δ' αὖ δίχ' ἕκαστα φορεύμενα Νείκεος ἔχθει.
οὕτως ᾗ μὲν ἓν ἐκ πλεόνων μεμάθηκε φύεσθαι
ἠδὲ πάλιν διαφύντος ἑνὸς πλέον' ἐκτελέθουσι,
τῇ μὲν γίγνονταί τε καὶ οὔ σφισιν ἔμπεδος αἰών·
ᾗ δὲ διαλλάσσοντα διαμπερὲς οὐδαμὰ λήγει,
ταύτῃ δ' αἰὲν ἔασιν ἀκίνητοι κατὰ κύκλον.
ἀλλ' ἄγε μύθων κλῦθι· μάθη γάρ τοι φρένας αὔξει·
ὡς γὰρ καὶ πρὶν ἔειπα πιφαύσκων πείρατα μύθων,
δίπλ' ἐρέω· τοτὲ μὲν γὰρ ἓν ηὐξήθη μόνον εἶναι
ἐκ πλεόνων, τοτὲ δ' αὖ διέφυ πλέον' ἐξ ἑνὸς εἶναι,
πῦρ καὶ ὕδωρ καὶ γαῖα καὶ ἠέρος ἄπλετον ὕψος,
Νεῖκός τ' οὐλόμενον δίχα τῶν, ἀτάλαντον ἁπάντῃ,
καὶ Φιλότης ἐν τοῖσιν, ἴση μῆκός τε πλάτος τε·
τὴν σὺ νόῳ δέρκευ, μηδ' ὄμμασιν ἧσο τεθηπώς·
ἥτις καὶ θνητοῖσι νομίζεται ἔμφυτος ἄρθροις,
τῇ τε φίλα φρονέουσι καὶ ἄρθμια ἔργα τελοῦσι,
Γηθοσύνην καλέοντες ἐπώνυμον ἠδ' Ἀφροδίτην·
τὴν οὔ τις μετὰ τοῖσιν ἑλισσομένην δεδάηκε
θνητὸς ἀνήρ· σὺ δ' ἄκουε λόγου στόλον οὐκ ἀπατηλόν.
ταῦτα γὰρ ἶσά τε πάντα καὶ ἥλικα γένναν ἔασι,
τιμῆς δ' ἄλλης ἄλλο μέδει, πάρα δ' ἦθος ἑκάστῳ,
ἐν δὲ μέρει κρατέουσι περιπλομένοιο χρόνοιο.[129]

I shall tell a double tale. At one time there grew to be one only out of many, and at another it is separated into many from one. And there is a double becoming of mortal things and a double passing away. For the latter (i. e., passing away) the union of all things both begets and destroys; and the former (becoming) when it is complete is scattered again by the separation of things. And these [elements] never cease this continuous change, now all coming together into one because of Love, now each pulled apart by the hatred engendered by Strife. Thus, inasmuch as they have learned to grow into one out of many, and again when the one separates to become many, so far they are in a state of becoming and their life is not stable. But inasmuch as their change is eternal, they are immutable, in a cycle.

But come, listen to my story. For learning increases wisdom. As I was just saying, declaring the ends of my story, I shall recite a double tale. For at one time it grew to be one out of many, and at another it split into many out of one, fire and water and earth and air's boundless height, and dreadful Strife apart from these, equal in weight to all of them, and Love among them equal also in length and width. Contemplate her with your mind: do not sit with dazzled eyes. She is acknowledged to be implanted in mortal limbs, and because of her men have thoughts of love and achieve the works of peace. And they call her by the names of Joy and Aphrodite. Not yet has mortal man seen her moving about among

[129] Diels, *Fragm.* 17.

them, but listen to the undeceitful course of my speech. For all these things are equal and of equal age; but one has one province, another another, according to the character of each of them; and in turn they hold sway as time moves round. . . .

This passage contains no reference either to an identification of the Age of Love with the Age of Cronus nor to an *ecpyrosis*. Indeed, as Burnet has shown,[130] Fire plays a predominant part in building up, not in tearing down the world in the Empedoclean system. The ideal age, in its last previous recurrence, seems to have been preceded by one in which, Love not yet being more potent than Strife, the proper mixtures of the four elements necessary for the existence of normal organisms had not yet been produced. At this period "there grew many creatures with double faces and double breasts; offspring of cattle with human faces and conversely human bodies with the heads of oxen sprang up, and mixed kinds partly male and partly female, having ambiguous members" (*Fragm.* 61); and these, or still earlier and still more rudimentary creatures, lacking "the lovely form of the limbs, and voices, and organs [or sexual organs] such as are usual in men" (*Fragm.* 62), Empedocles describes as "the sprouts of lamentable men and women" which "first sprang up as earth's rudimentary sketches, in their wholly natural state" (*ibid.* line 4).[131] As such forms are no longer generated, the present age should, it would appear, be regarded by Empedocles as one in which Love has decidedly the upper hand; yet in the passage earlier cited (II, 5) it is implied that Love is no longer dominant because men now destroy one another and the animals. The notion that the earlier, autochthonous organisms were ill-adapted and abortive types reappears in Lucretius (*De rer. nat.* V, 837-848), but the supposition that there can ever have existed creatures *duplici natura et corpore bino ex alienigenis membris compacta* is attacked by him (*ibid.* 877-881).

THE PYTHAGOREANS

A similar theory was evidently held by the Pythagoreans, if we may believe Simplicius (*Phys.* 732, 26). Aristotle's pupil, Eudemus, is quoted as saying:

II, 49. Eudemus, *Phys.* B. III, *Fragm.* 51.

. . . εἰ δέ τις πιστεύσειε τοῖς Πυθαγορείοις, ὥστε πάλιν τὰ αὐτὰ ἀριθμῷ, κἀγὼ μυθολογήσω τὸ ῥαβδίον ἔχων ὑμῖν καθημένοις οὕτω, καὶ τὰ ἄλλα πάντα ὁμοίως ἕξει, καὶ τὸν χρόνον εὔλογόν ἐστι τὸν αὐτὸν εἶναι.[132]

---

[130] *Op. cit.* p. 236 f.

[131] The meaning of *Fragm.* 62, line 4, is uncertain; Diels renders the line "zuerst tauchten rohgeballte Erdklumpen auf." The interpretation of the details of Empedocles's account of the genesis of animals and men, and its correlation with his general cosmology, are involved in controversies into which, for the purposes of this volume, it is not necessary to enter. Cf. Aristotle *Met.* 1000a 25, 32; Dümmler, *Akademika*, 1889, pp. 217-222; Millerd, *On the Interpretation of Empedokles*, 1908.

[132] Diels, *Vors.* 4th ed. (1922), *Pythag.* B 34. Plato and Aristotle, whose views on cycles would normally follow, are treated in Chapters V and VI.

And if one were to believe the Pythagoreans, things exactly the same numerically will again occur, and I with my wand shall converse with you seated as you are, and everything else will recur in like manner, and the time will reasonably appear to be the same.

THE STOICS

Our knowledge of the date and origin of the Stoic theory of cycles is not wholly certain, coming as it does largely from authors of much later times. Simplicius (Arist. phys. 480) [133] definitely relates the doctrine to that of Heraclitus. It was accepted by Zeno, Cleanthes, Chrysippus and Posidonius, but rejected by Panaetius, according to Diogenes Laertius (VII, 142). Eusebius also testifies to the place of this theory in the original doctrine of the school.

II, 50. Eusebius, Praep. evang. XV, 18, 1-3.

'Αρέσκει δὲ τοῖς πρεσβυτάτοις τῶν ἀπὸ τῆς αἱρέσεως ταύτης ἐξαιθεροῦσθαι πάντα κατὰ περιόδους τινὰς τὰς μεγίστας εἰς πῦρ αἰθερῶδες ἀναλυομένων πάντων. Καὶ ἑξῆς ἐπάγει·

'Εκ τούτων δὲ δῆλον, ὅτι Χρύσιππος ἐπὶ τῆς οὐσίας οὐ ταύτην παρείληφε τὴν σύγχυσιν (ἀδύνατον γάρ), ἀλλὰ τὴν ἀντὶ τῆς μεταβολῆς λεγομένην· οὐ γὰρ ἐπὶ τῆς τοῦ κόσμου κατὰ περιόδους τὰς μεγίστας γινομένης φθορᾶς κυρίως παραλαμβάνουσι τὴν φθορὰν οἱ τὴν εἰς πῦρ ἀνάλυσιν τῶν ὅλων δογματίζοντες, ἣν δὴ καλοῦσιν ἐκπύρωσιν· ἀλλ' ἀντὶ τῆς κατὰ φύσιν μεταβολῆς χρῶνται τῇ προσηγορίᾳ τῆς φθορᾶς. ἀρέσκει γὰρ τοῖς Στωϊκοῖς φιλοσόφοις τὴν ὅλην οὐσίαν εἰς πῦρ μεταβάλλειν οἷον εἰς σπέρμα, καὶ πάλιν ἐκ τούτου αὐτὴν ἀποτελεῖσθαι τὴν διακόσμησιν, οἷα τὸ πρότερον ἦν. καὶ τοῦτο τὸ δόγμα τῶν ἀπὸ τῆς αἱρέσεως οἱ πρῶτοι καὶ πρεσβύτατοι προσήκαντο, Ζήνων τε καὶ Κλεάνθης καὶ Χρύσιππος. τὸν μὲν γὰρ τούτου μαθητὴν καὶ διάδοχον τῆς σχολῆς Ζήνωνά φασιν ἐπισχεῖν περὶ τῆς ἐκπυρώσεως τῶν ὅλων.[134]

The oldest members of this [Stoic] school believed that all things would become aether at certain very long periods, being dissolved again into an aether-like fire. And this occurs again and again. From this it is clear that with respect to substance Chrysippus did not accept the theory of actual destruction (for that is impossible), but used the term 'destruction' as equivalent to 'change.' For those who assert the resolution of all things into fire (which they call ecpyrosis) do not regard this as a literal destruction of the cosmos taking place at immense intervals of time. But to designate this natural change they use the term 'destruction.' For the Stoic philosophers liked to believe that all substance changes into fire as its elemental stuff, and that again from this arises the ordered universe as it was before. And this doctrine was accepted by the first and eldest teachers of their school, Zeno and Cleanthes and Chrysippus. For they say that his (Chrysippus's) disciple and suc-

---

[133] Arnim, Stoic Vet. Fragm. II, p. 185, Fragm. 603. The most complete collection of passages bearing on the Stoic theory of cycles is to be found in Arnim, II, Fragm. 596-632. For illustrations of the currency of the idea of a terrarum omnium deflagratio, cf. Cicero, De fin. III, ix, 64; De div. 11.

[134] Arnim, II, 184, Fragm. 596.

cessor in the school, Zeno,[135] suspended judgment concerning the
ecpyrosis of all things.

The attribution of this doctrine to the founders of Stoicism is made in
the same words by Stobaeus (*Eclog.* I, p. 171, 2W; Arnim II, 183 f.).[136]
Again Tatianus (second century A. D.) writes:

II, 51.   Tatianus *Adv. graec.* c. 5.

τὸν Ζήνωνα διὰ τῆς ἐκπυρώσεως ἀποφαινόμενον ἀνίστασθαι πάλιν τοὺς
αὐτοὺς ἐπὶ τοῖς αὐτοῖς, λέγω δὲ καὶ Ἄνυτον καὶ Μέλητον ἐπὶ τῷ κατηγορεῖν,
Βούσιριν δὲ ἐπὶ τῷ ξενοκτονεῖν καὶ Ἡρακλέα πάλιν ἐπὶ τῷ ἀθλεῖν, παραιτητέον.[137]

Zeno has shown that after the *ecpyrosis* these men will be resur-
rected as they were.   And I say that this must imply that Anytus
and Meletus will again bring their accusation, and Busiris slay the
strangers, and Hercules perform his labors.

Nemesius (fifth century A. D.), attributing the same doctrine to the
Stoics, represents them as basing it upon astrological grounds.

II, 52.   Nemesius, *De nat. hom.* c. 38.

Στωϊκοί φασιν ἀποκαθισταμένους τοὺς πλάνητας εἰς τὸ αὐτὸ σημεῖον κατά
τε μῆκος καὶ πλάτος, ἔνθα τὴν ἀρχὴν ἕκαστος ἦν, ὅτε τὸ πρῶτον ὁ κόσμος
συνέστη, ἐν ῥηταῖς χρόνων περιόδοις ἐκπύρωσιν καὶ φθορὰν τῶν ὄντων ἀπερ-
γάζεσθαι καὶ πάλιν ἐξ ὑπαρχῆς εἰς τὸ αὐτὸ τὸν κόσμον ἀποκαθίστασθαι,
καὶ τῶν ἀστέρων ὁμοίως πάλιν φερομένων ἕκαστον ἐν τῇ προτέρᾳ περιόδῳ
γενόμενον ἀπαραλλάκτως ἀποτελεῖσθαι. ἔσεσθαι γὰρ πάλιν Σωκράτην καὶ
Πλάτωνα καὶ ἕκαστον τῶν ἀνθρώπων σὺν τοῖς αὐτοῖς καὶ φίλοις καὶ πολίταις
καὶ τὰ αὐτὰ πείσεσθαι καὶ τοῖς αὐτοῖς συντεύξεσθαι καὶ τὰ αὐτὰ μεταχειριεῖσ-
θαι, καὶ πᾶσαν πόλιν καὶ κώμην καὶ ἀγρὸν ὁμοίως ἀποκαθίστασθαι· γίνεσθαι
δὲ τὴν ἀποκατάστασιν τοῦ παντὸς οὐχ ἅπαξ, ἀλλὰ πολλάκις, μᾶλλον δὲ εἰς
ἄπειρον, καὶ ἀτελευτήτως τὰ αὐτὰ ἀποκαθίστασθαι.[138]

And the Stoics say that the planets will be restored to the same
zodiacal sign, both in longitude and latitude, as they had in the
beginning when the cosmos was first put together; that in stated
periods of time a conflagration (*ecpyrosis*) and destruction of things
will be accomplished, and once more there will be a restitution of the
cosmos as it was in the very beginning.   And when the stars move
in the same way as before, each thing which occurred in the previous
period will without variation be brought to pass again.   For again
there will exist Socrates and Plato and every man, with the same
friends and fellow citizens, and he will suffer the same fate and will
meet with the same experiences and undertake the same deeds.   And
every city and village and field will be restored.   And there will be
a complete restoration of the whole, not once only but many times,
or rather interminably, and the same things will be restored without
end.

---

[135] Zeno of Tarsus.
[136] See also Aetius and Hippolytus in Arnim, II, 184, *Fragm.* 597, 598.
[137] Arnim, I, 32, *Fragm.* 109. The same idea is in Arnim, II, 190, *Fragm.* 626.
[138] Ritter and Preller, *Hist phil. graec.* 10th ed. Gotha, 1934, p. 417.

The Return of the Golden Age in Virgil's Fourth Eclogue

The literature which has grown up about the so-called "Messianic Eclogue" of Virgil is enormous, and the problem of its precise meaning is perhaps insoluble. At all events, it does not fall within the scope of this volume to examine the rival theories concerning the circumstances which gave rise to the poem and concerning the identity of the child. The Eclogue is pertinent here only as the most famous expression of the conception of an idyllic period in the future which will repeat the Golden Age.

Virgil is faithful to the literary traditions: he has intertwined them in associating the Golden Age both with King Saturn and the Virgin Astraea — for there can be no doubt of the identity of the maiden referred to — and in describing this period as one of peace, without arts or commerce or navigation. This appears to be the first (extant) suggestion of the 'return of Astraea' and of the paradisiacal condition of human life which she symbolized. That Virgil intended anything more than a gracefully hyperbolic compliment to the father of the child is uncertain. In any case, there is no evidence that Virgil's contemporaries took the passage seriously; and it became in later writers, doubtless because of the Virgilian example, a literary convention to greet the birth of a royal heir or the accession of a new monarch as the promise of a new Age of Gold.

What prophecies of the Cumaean Sibyl had the poet in mind? As has been pointed out by Mayor,[139] they could not have been those preserved in the *Sibylline Books,* for these writings were destroyed by fire in 83 B. C. Though some of the prophecies may have leaked out, we have no factual evidence that they predicted a return of a Golden Age.

We still have, however, passages in the *Sibylline Oracles* which recall the ideas of the Messianic Eclogue. The age and origin of these verses are unfortunately too much a matter of dispute for us to do more than quote them here, reserving judgment as to their historical relationship to Virgil. According to Lanchester [140] the date of this portion of the Sibyllina is about the middle of the second century B. C. and its point of view that of an Egyptian Jew. But the second book, in which there is a passage prophesying the coming of the Tenth Race and a great conflagration, the downfall of Roman power and the coming of Christ with the distribution of rewards to the righteous is dated by the same authority in the second century A. D.[141] This shows at most that certain metaphors common to the Pythagorean and Stoic tradition [142] had crept into apocalyptic literature; it is of interest to us mainly in that it describes — as Virgil does — the future happy state of

---

[139] "Sources of the Fourth Eclogue," in *Virgil's Messianic Eclogue,* London, 1907.

[140] Hasting's *Encyclopaedia,* art. "Sibylline Books."

[141] It is worth noting that line II, 155, on the horrors of the future, mentions children who are born "gray at the temples," an obvious reminiscence of Hesiod.

[142] The story of the ages is given in Books, I, II, IV, and XI. The number of ages varies between ten and twelve.

mankind in soft-primitivistic terms. Otherwise, particularly since it locates man's happy condition in the future, the tradition is more closely allied to anti-primitivism than to primitivism.

II, 53. *Oracula sibyllina*, III, 743-759; 787-795.

γῆ γὰρ παγγενέτειρα βροτοῖς δώσει τὸν ἄριστον
καρπὸν ἀπειρέσιον σίτου οἴνου καὶ ἐλαίου
[αὐτὰρ ἀπ' οὐρανόθεν μέλιτος γλυκεροῦ ποτὸν ἡδύ
δένδρεά τ' ἀκροδρύων καρπὸν καὶ πίονα μῆλα
καὶ βόας ἔκ τ' ὀίων ἄρνας αἰγῶν τε χιμάρους·]
πηγάς τε ῥήξει γλυκερὰς λευκοῖο γάλακτος·
πλήρεις δ' αὖτε πόλεις ἀγαθῶν καὶ πίονες ἀγροί
ἔσσοντ'· οὐδὲ μάχαιρα κατὰ χθονὸς οὐδὲ κυδοιμός·
οὐδὲ βαρὺ στενάχουσα σαλεύσεται οὐκέτι γαῖα·
οὐ πόλεμος οὐδ' αὖτε κατὰ χθονὸς αὐχμὸς ἔτ' ἔσται,
οὐ λιμὸς καρπῶν τε κακορρέκτειρα χάλαζα·
ἀλλὰ μὲν εἰρήνη μεγάλη κατὰ γαῖαν ἅπασαν,
καὶ βασιλεὺς βασιλῆι φίλος μέχρι τέρματος ἔσται
αἰῶνος, κοινόν τε νόμον κατὰ γαῖαν ἅπασαν
ἀνθρώποις τελέσειεν ἐν οὐρανῷ ἀστερόεντι
ἀθάνατος, ὅσα πέπρακται δειλοῖσι βροτοῖσιν.

. . . .

ἐν σοὶ δ' οἰκήσει· σοὶ δ' ἔσσεται ἀθάνατον φῶς·
ἠδὲ λύκοι τε καὶ ἄρνες ἐν οὔρεσιν ἄμμιγ' ἔδονται
χόρτον, παρδάλιές τ' ἐρίφοις ἅμα βοσκήσονται·
ἄρκτοι σὺν μόσχοις νομάδες αὐλισθήσονται·
σαρκοβόρος τε λέων φάγεται ἄχυρον παρὰ φάτνῃ
ὡς βοῦς· καὶ παῖδες μάλα νήπιοι ἐν δεσμοῖσιν
ἄξουσιν· πηρὸν γὰρ ἐπὶ χθονὶ θῆρα ποιήσει.
σὺν βρέφεσίν τε δράκοντες ἅμ' ἀσπίσι κοιμήσονται
κοὐκ ἀδικήσουσιν· χεὶρ γὰρ θεοῦ ἔσσετ' ἐπ' αὐτούς.[143]

For the all-bearing earth will give her best fruit without end to mortals, bread, wine, and wild olive [and from heaven sweet streams of sugared honey and fruits of fruit trees and fat sheep and beeves and lambs from ewes and kids from she-goats]. And streams will flow with sweet white milk, and cities will be full of goods and the fields will be fat; nor will there be swords nor the din of battle on the face of the earth; nor will earth be shaken with heavy lamentations; nor will war nor drought be upon earth, nor famine nor hail working evil on the fruits of the earth. But a great peace will fall upon all the lands and king shall be friend to king until the end of time and the immortal in the starry heaven shall proclaim a common law for men over all the earth, as far as can be done for wretched mortals. . . .

And in thee [exultation] will dwell. In thee will be immortal light. And the wolves and sheep will graze together on the mountains, and the panther shall feed with the kid, and the wandering bear shall lie down to sleep with the calf and the flesh-eating lion shall eat hay in the manger like the ox. And tender children shall

[143] Ed. J. Geffcken, Leipzig, 1902.

drive them in chains, for he shall render the wild beast helpless on earth. And dragons and wicked asps shall be lulled by infants, and will do not harm, for the hand of god will be among them.

II, 54. Virgil, *Eclogue*, IV (Translation on p. 88).

Sicelides Musae, paulo maiora canamus!
Non omnes arbusta iuvant humilesque myricae;
si canimus silvas, silvae sint consule dignae.
    Ultima Cumaei venit iam carminis aetas;
magnus ab integro saeclorum nascitur ordo.
Iam redit et virgo, redeunt Saturnia regna;
iam nova progenies caelo demittitur alto.
Tu modo nascenti puero, quo ferrea primum
desinet ac toto surget gens aurea mundo,
casta fave Lucina: tuus iam regnat Apollo.
Teque adeo decus hoc aevi, te consule inibit,
Pollio, et incipient magni procedere menses;
te duce, siqua manent sceleris vestigia nostri,
inrita perpetua solvent formidine terras.
Ille deum vitam accipiet divisque videbit
permixtos heroas, et ipse videbitur illis,
pacatumque reget patriis virtutibus orbem.
At tibi prima, puer, nullo munuscula cultu
errantis hederas passim cum baccare tellus
mixtaque ridenti colocasia fundet acantho.
Ipsae lacte domum referent distenta capellae
ubera, nec magnos metuent armenta leones.
Ipsa tibi blandos fundent cunabula flores.
Occidet et serpens, et fallax herba veneni
occidet; Assyrium vulgo nascetur amomum.
At simul heroum laudes et facta parentis
iam legere et quae sit poteris cognoscere virtus,
molli paulatim flavescet campus arista,
incultisque rubens pendebit sentibus uva,
et durae quercus sudabunt roscida mella.
Pauca tamen suberunt priscae vestigia fraudis,
quae temptare Thetim ratibus, quae cingere muris
oppida, quae iubeant telluri infindere sulcos.
Alter erit tum Tiphys, et altera quae vehat Argo
delectos heroas; erunt etiam altera bella,
atque iterum ad Troiam magnus mittetur Achilles.
Hinc, ubi iam firmata virum te fecerit aetas,
cedet et ipse mari vector, nec nautica pinus
mutabit merces: omnis feret omnia tellus.
Non rastros patietur humus, non vinea falcem;
robustus quoque iam tauris iuga solvet arator;
nec varios discet mentiri lana colores,
ipse sed in pratis aries iam suave rubenti
murice, iam croceo mutabit vellera luto;
sponte sua sandyx pascentes vestiet agnos.
'Talia saecla' suis dixerunt 'currite' fusis
concordes stabili fatorum numine Parcae.
Aggredere o magnos (aderit iam tempus) honores,

cara deum suboles, magnum Iovis incrementum.
Aspice convexo nutantem pondere mundum,
terrasque tractusque maris caelumque profundum,
aspice, venturo laetantur ut omnia saeclo!
O mihi tum longae maneat pars ultima vitae,
spiritus et, quantum sat erit tua dicere facta;
non me carminibus vincat nec Thracius Orpheus,
nec Linus, huic mater quamvis atque huic pater adsit,
Orphei Calliopea, Lino formosus Apollo.
Pan etiam, Arcadia mecum si iudice certet,
Pan etiam Arcadia dicat se iudice victum.
Incipe, parve puer, risu cognoscere matrem;
matri longa decem tulerunt fastidia menses.
Incipe, parve puer: cui non risere parentes,
nec deus hunc mensa, dea nec dignata cubili est.[144]

Sicilian Muses, let us sing of greater themes! The groves and lowly tamarisk do not please all; if we sing of the woods, let them be worthy of our consul.

The last age of the Cumaean song has come; the great succession of the ages begins anew. Now the Maiden returns and the reign of Saturn; now a new race is sent down from high heaven. Favor, O chaste Lucina, this new born babe, at whose coming the iron race will disappear and the golden race arise throughout the whole world. Now let thine Apollo reign. It is in thy consulship, Pollio, that this glorious age shall commence and the great months shall begin their course. While thou art leader, if any traces of our guilt remain they shall be purged away, and earth shall thus be free from its age-long fear. The child shall be born to a godlike life, and shall see heroes mingling with the gods, and shall himself be seen amongst them, and shall rule a world restored to peace by his father's virtues. On thee, oh child, shall Earth, untilled, bestow thy earliest playthings — trailing ivy with foxgloves and lilies with laughing acanthus. The she-goats shall bring their udders swollen with milk to thy abode and the herds shall not fear the mighty lions. Thy cradle shall be hung with smiling flowers. The serpent shall disappear and the deceitful poisonous herbs. Assyrian balsam shall spring up on every roadside. And when thou art of age to read the praises of the heroes and the deeds of thy sire and to know what virtue is, then one by one the fields now bare shall bloom with mellow grain, and the purple grape shall hang from the wild thornbush, and honey shall form like dew upon the sturdy oaks. Yet still some vestiges of the old wickedness shall survive to bid men tempt the sea with ships, gird towns with walls, and dig the plough in earth. Then there will be another Tiphys and another Argo to bear the chosen heroes; there will be other wars, and once again great Achilles shall be sent to Troy. At last, when riper age shall have made thee man, even the voyager will desert the sea, and ships of pinewood shall no longer carry merchandise from land to land; for each land will produce all things. The soil will not suffer the harrow nor the vine the sickle; the rude ploughman will free his oxen from the yoke; wool will not be taught deception by the dyers' art, but in the fields

[144] Ed. O. Ribbeck-Ianell, Leipzig, 1930.

the ram's own fleece will shine with ruddy purple or with crocus gold; spontaneously will vermilion clothe the grazing lambs. "Through such ages run"—so to their spindles speak the Parcae, who pronounce in concert the unchanging will of fate.

Begin thy great career, dear child of the gods, Jove's mighty progeny;[145] the time is now at hand. See how the world trembles beneath its massive vault, the lands and ocean wastes and lofty sky: see how all rejoices at the age that comes to birth. Oh, were these latter days of my life long enough and were breath given me to recite thy deeds, not Thracian Orpheus would conquer me in song nor Linus, although his mother aid the one, his father the other, Calliope aiding Orpheus, fair Apollo Linus. Even Pan, if he should strive with me, calling Arcadia to be his judge, even Pan, by Arcadia's own judgment, should acknowledge himself vanquished. Begin, child, to recognise thy mother with a smile: thy mother who has borne the long weariness of ten months. Begin, child: him upon whom his parents have not smiled, him God has not seated at his table nor has a goddess been appointed for his bed.

IMITATIONS OF THE FOURTH ECLOGUE

The Fourth Eclogue, which had a peculiar charm for Christians, furnished a model also for certain Pagan writers. The first of these is Calpurnius Siculus, an author of Nero's time, of whom we have eleven eclogues. In the first of these Ornitus and Corydon withdraw into a grotto sacred to Faunus to escape the heat of the day, and Ornitus reads the verses which follow, engraved by the god himself on the bark of a tree.

II, 55. Calpurnius, *Eclogue*, I, 33-88 (Translation on p. 90).

> Qui iuga, qui silvas tueor, satus aethere, Faunus
> Haec populis ventura cano: iuvat arbore sacra
> Laeta patefactis incidere carmina fatis.
> Vos o praecipue nemorum gaudete coloni,
> Vos populi gaudete mei: licet omne vagetur
> Securo custode pecus, nocturnaque pastor
> Claudere fraxinea nolit praesepia crate.
> Non tamen insidias praedator ovilibus ullas
> Afferet, aut laxis abiget iumenta capistris.
> Aurea secura cum pace renascitur aetas,
> Et redit ad terras tandem squalore situque
> Alma Themis posito, iuvenemque beata sequuntur
> Saecula, maternis causam qui vicit in ulnis.
> Dum populos deus ipse reget, dabit impia victas
> Post tergum Bellona manus, spoliataque telis
> In sua vesanos torquebit viscera morsus,
> Et modo quae toto civilia distulit orbe,
> Secum bella geret. Nullos iam Roma Philippos
> Deflebit, nullos ducet captiva triumphos.
> Omnia Tartareo subigentur carcere bella,
> Immergentque caput tenebris, lucemque timebunt.

---

[145] Warde Fowler and some others would render: "promise of a Jove to be."

Candida pax aderit, nec solum candida vultu,
Qualis saepe fuit, quae, libera Marte professo,
Quae, domito procul hoste, tamen grassantibus armis,
Publica diffudit tacito discordia ferro.
Omne procul vitium simulatae cedere pacis
Iussit, et insanos Clementia contudit enses.
Nulla catenati feralis pompa senatus
Carnificum lassabit opus, nec carcere pleno
Infelix raros numerabit curia patres.
Plena quies aderit, quae, stricti nescia ferri,
Altera Saturni referet Latialia regna,
Altera regna Numae, qui primus ovantia caede
Agmina, Romuleis et adhuc ardentia castris,
Pacis opus docuit, iussitque silentibus armis
Inter sacra tubas, non inter bella sonare.
Iam nec adumbrati faciem mercatus honoris,
Nec vacuos tacitus fasces et inane tribunal
Accipiet consul, sed legibus omne reductis
Ius aderit, moremque fori vultumque priorem
Reddet, et afflictum melior deus auferet aevum.
Exsultet, quaecumque Notum gens ima iacentem
Erectumque colit Boream, quaecumque vel ortu
Vel patet occasu, mediove sub aethere fervit.
Cernitis, ut puro nox iam vicesima coelo
Fulgeat, et placida radiantem luce cometem
Proferat? ut liquidum nutet sine vulnere plenus?
Numquid utrumque polum, sicut solet, igne cruento
Spargit, et ardenti scintillat sanguine lampas?
At quondam non talis erat, cum, Caesare rapto,
Indixit miseris fatalia civibus arma.
Scilicet ipse deus Romanae pondera molis
Fortibus excipiet sic inconcussa lacertis,
Ut neque translati sonitu fragor intonet orbis,
Nec prius ex meritis defunctos Roma penates
Censeat, occasus nisi quum respexerit ortus.[146]

I who protect the hills and woodlands, child of heaven, Faunus, sing unto the peoples these events to come. I am happy to carve upon this sacred tree the joyful tidings which the fates have revealed.

Rejoice, first of all, dwellers in the forests, rejoice, O my people. Though all your flocks wander without a guardian, and the shepherd neglect to close them in at night with beechen bolt, yet no thief shall lay his traps near the sheep-fold nor loosen the tethers of the beasts of burden to drive them off. The golden age of untroubled peace is born again, and kindly Themis returns to earth freed from stain and rust. The happy times are ruled by a youth [147] who won the victory while still in his mother's arms. When he shall himself reign as a god, wicked Bellona, her hands bound behind her back, stripped of her weapons, will savagely gnaw her own vitals and, as she once tore asunder the whole world with civil

---

[146] Ed. C. H. Keene, London, 1887.
[147] Presumably Nero.

wars, so shall she now wage war upon herself. Now Rome will cease to bewail Philippi, and, captive herself, will lead no future triumphs. All wars will be buried in the prison-house of Tartarus, and will hide their heads in the shadows and fear the light. Shining Peace will appear — shining not in countenance only, as she often was when, free from open war, and with the enemies once conquered, she nevertheless, stealthily preparing her armaments, spread public discord with silenced sword. She has bidden all this crime of pretended peace be gone, and Clemency has broken in pieces the weapons of madness. No processions of senators going to their death in chains shall again cause exhausting labor for the executioners, nor shall the unhappy Curia number but few Fathers in its seats while the prisons are full. Full peace will come upon us, a peace which, drawing of swords unknown, shall bring back a second reign of Saturn, like that in Latium of old, another reign of Numa, who first taught the ways of peace to the soldiers of Romulus rejoicing in slaughter and thirsting for camp-life, and who bade the trumpets blow, not for war, but for sacrifices when the clash of arms was stilled. No longer will a consul buy the appearance of a shadowy honor, and receive the empty fasces and a meaningless office. But, with law restored, Right shall return and restore the ancient customs and give to the forum its ancient aspect. A better god will then raise up our prostrate age. Let the peoples who worship the placid South Wind or the resolute North exult, and those who live beside the rising or the setting sun or burn with heat beneath the middle sky! Do you not see how now for twenty nights the clear sky has been radiant and shows a comet shining with a gentle light, and how, full and unbroken, it twinkles with limpid beam? It does not, as comets are wont to do, spread blood-red fire over both poles, nor does its torch shine with flaming gore. Once it was otherwise, when at Caesar's death it foretold disastrous wars to our unhappy citizens. But the god himself will take up the unshaken mass of Roman power in his strong arms, and the world transformed will make no sound, nor shall Rome know its penates to have died as they deserved until she looks upon the newly risen star.

Here the Virgilian theme is simply the praise of a new ruler, as if he were a Messiah restoring the Golden Age. The same effect is sought in an eclogue published contemporaneously with that of Calpurnius and preserved for us in the Codex Einsidlensis.[148] It too makes no use of the Great Year beyond the attenuated metaphor of the return of the Golden Age, but does retain in its last lines the eschatological note of the *Sibyllina*.

II, 56. Anonymous (*ca.* 50 A. D.) in *Anthologia Latina,* 726, 17-end.

> Spirant templa mero, resonant cava tympana palmis,
> Maenalides teneras ducunt per sacra choreas,
> Tibia laeta canit, pendet sacer hircus ab ulmo
> Et iam nudatis cervicibus exuit exta.
> Ergo non dubio pugnant discrimine nati:

[148] *Anthol. Lat.* no. 726.

Et negat huic aevo stolidum pecus aurea regna?
Saturni rediere dies Astraeaque virgo,
Totaque in antiquos redierunt saecula mores.
Condit securus tuta spe messor aristas,
Languescit senio Bacchus, pecus errat in herba.
Nec gladio metimus nec clausis oppida muris
Bella tacenda parant, nullo iam noxia partu
Femina quaecumque est hostem parit. arva iuventus
Nuda fodit tardoque puer domifactus aratro
Miratur patriis pendentem sedibus ensem.
Sed procul a nobis infelix gloria Sullae
Trinaque tempestas, moriens cum Roma supremas
Desperavit [opes] et Martia vendidit arma.
Nunc tellus inculta novos parit ubere fetus,
Nunc ratibus tutis fera non irascitur unda,
Morden frena tigres, subeunt iuga saeva leones.
Casta fave Lucina, tuus iam regnat Apollo! [149]

The temples are redolent of pure wine; the hollow drums resound under the palms of the drummers; the Maenalids lead graceful choruses in sacred dances; the glad flutes sing; the sacred goat hangs upon the elm, his entrails exposed on his naked back. No longer, therefore, do the youth fight, with doubtful outcome. Can the stupid mob deny that this is a golden age? The days of Saturn have returned and the virgin Astraea, and our whole age has returned to the ancient customs. The reaper in safety stores up his grain with hope secure; Bacchus grows languid with age; the flocks wander through the grass. Nor do we reap with the sword; nor do towns, their walls shut tight, prepare for unspeakable war. No longer do women with baneful womb bring forth enemies. Youth ploughs up the fields unarmed and the boy trained to the plough wonders at the sword hanging in his father's house. Far from us the unhappy glory of Sulla and the triple storm, when Rome dying abandoned her last hope and sold her martial weapons. Now earth untilled bears new fruits in her bosom; the wild waves no longer threaten with their rage the safety of ships; tigers clench the bit, lions bear the stubborn yoke.[150] Chaste Lucina, be gracious unto us, now thine Apollo reigns.[151]

D. PRIMEVAL MAN IN THE HISTORIANS

The opinions of the ancients about the life of primeval man are mostly contained in writings which involve the legend of the Golden Age or that of the Age of Cronus. There is, however, still extant a small group of fragments which show that the Greek and Latin historians, as well as the

---

[149] Ed. A. Riese.

[150] Cf. *Sibyllina*, III, 790 ff.

[151] For modern imitations of the Fourth Eclogue see among others Clement Marot's *Eglogue sur la Naissance*; J. Leochaeus Scotus's [John Leech?] *Ecl. Bucol.* 4 (*Carolus*); René Rapin's *Ecl. Sacr.* VI (*Sibylla*); Shelley's final chorus in *Hellas*; perhaps Pope's *Messiah*.

mythographers and poets, considered the question. Though the legend of the Ages may have had some influence in orienting the thoughts of these writers, it does not appear explicitly in these fragments.

DICAEARCHUS

As the author of " the earliest *Kulturgeschichte* "[152] Dicaearchus naturally began his Βίος Ἑλλάδος (late fourth century B. C.) with an account of primeval man. Though a pupil of Aristotle and commonly classified by ancient writers as a Peripatetic, he was clearly a heterodox one, on this and other matters. A materialistic philosopher, who denied not only the immortality but the existence of the soul,[153] and a historian who rejected the traditional mythology, he nevertheless regarded the legend of the age of Cronus as probably a 'non-natural' version of a historic fact. As he was read and utilized by Eratosthenes, Panaetius, Posidonius, Josephus and Plutarch[154] and especially extolled by Cicero and Varro,[155] the fragment cited must be regarded as one of the more important, as well as one of the most extreme, expressions of chronological primitivism — even though the most ardent admirers of Dicaearchus did not all follow him on this point. Whether his description of the state of nature is fully reproduced by Porphyry, through whom it has come down to us, is dubious; but it is in any case evident that it dwelt upon both the physical and moral superiority of primitive men and suggested two psychological roots of the evils of civilization, which were to be made much of by later, and especially by modern, writers: (a) a multiplication of desires which led, even in the second or pastoral stage, to the pursuit of economic goods not needful for happiness, and to mutual conflict; and (b) the craving for distinction (φιλοτιμία). In connecting the origin of war with the termination of the supposed primeval peace between man and the other animals, Dicaearchus (following Empedocles) contributed to the literary tradition of primitivism an idea (surprising in a naturalistic historian) which persisted down to the time of Pope:

> Ah! how unlike the man of times to come!
> Of half that live the butcher and the tomb. . . .
> The fury-passions from that blood began,
> And turned on Man, a fiercer savage, Man.[156]

[152] Christ, *Gesch. d. gr. Litt.* 1905, p. 610; Bury, *Anc. Greek Historians*, 1909, p. 187; Martini in Pauly-Wissowa, *Realencyclopädie*, V, col. 546.

[153] Cicero, *Tusc. disp.* I, 10, 21.

[154] Cf. Martini in Pauly-Wissowa, *loc. cit.* In view of the scantiness of the text of the first three authors mentioned, the extent of their use of Dicaearchus can hardly be determined.

[155] He is called by Cicero *deliciae meae* (*Tusc. disp.* I, 31, 77), *mirabilis vir* (*Ad. Att.* II, 2), *peripateticus magnus et copiosus* (*De off.* II, 5, 16), and by Varro *doctissimus homo* (*De re rustica*, I, 2). For Varro's Latin paraphrase of the same passage cf. below, Ch. XII, 1, 2.

[156] *Essay on Man*, III, 161-2, 167-8.

II, 57. *Vita Graeciae, Fragm*. I, in Porphyry, *De abstinentia,* IV, i, 2.

τῶν τοίνυν συντόμως τε ὁμοῦ καὶ ἀκριβῶς τὰ Ἑλληνικὰ συναγαγόντων ἐστὶν
καὶ ὁ περιπατητικὸς Δικαίαρχος, ὃς τὸν ἀρχαῖον βίον τῆς Ἑλλάδος ἀφη-
γούμενος, τοὺς παλαιοὺς καὶ ἐγγὺς θεῶν φησὶ γεγονότας, βελτίστους τε
ὄντας φύσει καὶ τὸν ἄριστον ἐζηκότας βίον, ὡς χρυσοῦν γένος νομίζεσθαι
παραβαλλομένους πρὸς τοὺς νῦν, κιβδήλου καὶ φαυλοτάτης ὑπάρχοντας ὕλης,
μηδὲν φονεύειν ἔμψυχον. ὃ δὴ καὶ τοὺς ποιητὰς παριστάντας χρυσοῦν μὲν
ἐπονομάζειν γένος, ἐσθλὰ δὲ πάντα, λέγειν,

τοῖσιν ἔην· καρπὸν δ' ἔφερεν ζείδωρος ἄρουρα
αὐτομάτη πολλόν τε καὶ ἄφθονον· οἳ δ' ἐθελημοὶ
ἥσυχοι ἔργ' ἐνέμοντο σὺν ἐσθλοῖσιν πολέεσσιν.

ἃ δὴ καὶ ἐξηγούμενος ὁ Δικαίαρχος τὸν ἐπὶ Κρόνου βίον τοιοῦτον εἶναι φησίν·
εἰ δεῖ λαμβάνειν μὲν αὐτὸν ὡς γεγονότα καὶ μὴ μάτην ἐπιπεφημισμένον, τὸ δὲ
λίαν μυθικὸν ἀφέντας, εἰς τὸ διὰ τοῦ λόγου φυσικὸν ἀνάγειν. αὐτόματα μὲν
γὰρ πάντα ἐφύετο, εἰκότως· οὐ γὰρ αὐτοί γε κατεσκεύαζον οὐθὲν διὰ τὸ μήτε
τὴν γεωργικὴν ἔχειν πω τέχνην μήθ' ἑτέραν μηδεμίαν ἁπλῶς. τὸ δ' αὐτὸ καὶ
τοῦ σχολὴν ἄγειν αἴτιον ἐγίγνετο αὐτοῖς καὶ τοῦ διάγειν ἄνευ πόνων καὶ
μερίμνης, εἰ δὲ τῇ τῶν γλαφυρωτάτων ἰατρῶν ἐπακολουθῆσαι δεῖ διανοίᾳ, καὶ
τοῦ μὴ νοσεῖν. οὐθὲν γὰρ εἰς ὑγίειαν αὐτῶν μεῖζον παράγγελμα εὕροι τις
ἂν ἢ τὸ μὴ ποιεῖν περιττώματα, ὧν διὰ παντὸς ἐκεῖνοι καθαρὰ τὰ σώματα
ἐφύλαττον. οὔτε γὰρ τῆς φύσεως ἰσχυροτέραν τροφὴν [ἀλλ' ἧς ἡ φύσις
ἰσχυροτέρα] προσεφέροντο, οὔτε τὴν πλείω τῆς μετρίας διὰ τὴν ἑτοιμότητα,
ἀλλ' ὡς τὰ πολλὰ τὴν ἐλάττω [τῆς ἱκανῆς] διὰ τὴν σπάνιν. ἀλλὰ μὴν οὐδὲ
πόλεμοι αὐτοῖς ἦσαν οὐδὲ στάσεις πρὸς ἀλλήλους· ἆθλον γὰρ οὐθὲν ἀξιόλογον
ἐν τῷ μέσῳ προκείμενον ὑπῆρχεν, ὑπὲρ ὅτου τις ἂν διαφορὰν τοσαύτην ἐνε-
στήσατο. ὥστε τὸ κεφάλαιον εἶναι τοῦ βίου συνέβαινεν σχολήν, ῥᾳθυμίαν
ἀπὸ τῶν ἀναγκαίων, ὑγίειαν, εἰρήνην, φιλίαν. τοῖς δὲ ὑστέροις ἐφιεμένοις
μεγάλων καὶ πολλοῖς περιπίπτουσι κακοῖς ποθεινὸς εἰκότως ἐκεῖνος ὁ βίος
ἐφαίνετο. δηλοῖ δὲ τὸ λιτὸν τῶν πρώτων καὶ αὐτοσχέδιον τῆς τροφῆς τὸ
μεθύστερον ῥηθὲν ἅλις δρυός, τοῦ μεταβάλλοντος πρώτου, οἷα εἰκός, τοῦτο
φθεγξαμένου. ὕστερον ὁ νομαδικὸς εἰσῆλθεν βίος, καθ' ὃν περιττοτέραν ἤδη
κτῆσιν προσπεριεβάλοντο καὶ ζώων ἥψαντο, κατανοήσαντες ὅτι τὰ μὲν ἀσινῆ
ἐτύγχανεν ὄντα, τὰ δὲ κακοῦργα καὶ χαλεπά· καὶ οὕτω δὴ τὰ μὲν ἐτιθάσευαν,
τοῖς δὲ ἐπέθεντο, καὶ ἅμα τῷ αὐτῷ βίῳ συνεισῆλθεν πόλεμος. καὶ ταῦτα,
φησίν, οὐχ ἡμεῖς, ἀλλ' οἱ τὰ παλαιὰ ἱστορίᾳ διεξελθόντες εἰρήκασιν. ἤδη γὰρ
ἀξιόλογα κτήματα ἦν ὑπάρχοντα, οἱ μὲν ἐπὶ τὸ παρελέσθαι φιλοτιμίαν
ἐποιοῦντο, ἀθροιζόμενοί τε καὶ παρακαλοῦντες ἀλλήλους, οἱ δ' ἐπὶ τὸ δια-
φυλάξαι. προϊόντος δὲ κατὰ μικρὸν οὕτω τοῦ χρόνου, κατανοοῦντες ἀεὶ τῶν
χρησίμων εἶναι δοκούντων, εἰς τὸ τρίτον τε καὶ γεωργικὸν ἐνέπεσον εἶδος.

ταυτὶ μὲν Δικαιάρχου τὰ παλαιὰ τῶν Ἑλληνικῶν διεξιόντος μακάριόν τε
τὸν βίον ἀφηγουμένου τῶν παλαιοτάτων, ὃν οὐχ ἧττον τῶν ἄλλων καὶ ἡ ἀποχὴ
τῶν ἐμψύχων συνεπλήρου. διὸ πόλεμος οὐκ ἦν, ὡς ἂν ἀδικίας ἐξεληλαμένης·
συνεισῆλθεν δὲ ὕστερον καὶ πόλεμος καὶ εἰς ἀλλήλους πλεονεξία ἅμα τῇ τῶν
ζῴων ἀδικίᾳ.[157]

Among those who have at once concisely and accurately collected the facts of Greek history is Dicaearchus the Peripatetic. In
his account of the primeval life of Greece, he says of the men of
the earliest age, who were akin to the gods and were by nature the
best men and lived the best life, so that they are regarded as a

[157] Ed. A. Nauck, Leipzig, 1886.

Golden Race in comparison with the men of the present time, made of a base and inferior matter — of these primeval men he says that they took the life of no animal. To this, he remarks, the poet bears witness [quotes Hesiod, *Works and Days*, 116].[158] In explanation of which lines Dicaearchus tells us of what sort the life of the Age of Cronus was: if it is to be taken as having really existed and not as an idle tale, when the too mythical parts of the story are eliminated it may by the use of reason be reduced to a natural sense. For all things then presumably grew spontaneously, since the men of that time themselves produced nothing, having invented neither agriculture nor any other art. It was for this reason that they lived a life of leisure, without care or toil, and also — if the doctrine of the most eminent medical men is to be accepted — without disease. For no counsel of theirs will be found more conducive to health than that of avoiding the production of excremental matter [or impure humors], of which these physicians seek to keep the body wholly free. For they [primitive men] did not eat food too strong for their constitutions, but such food as their constitutions could absorb, nor did they exceed the limits of moderation, in consequence of having so much food available; on the contrary, by reason of scarcity they often ate less than they needed. And there were no wars or feuds between them; for there existed among them no objects of competition of such value as to give anyone a motive to seek to obtain them by those means. Thus it was that their whole life was one of leisure, of freedom from care about the satisfaction of their needs, of health and peace and friendship. Consequently this manner of life of theirs naturally came to be longed for by men of later times who, because of the greatness of their desires, had become subject to many evils. How simple and ready-to-hand the food of primeval men was is shown by the later proverb, *Enough of the oak-tree!*[159] which was probably uttered by the man who first departed from this way of living. Later came the wandering pastoral life, in which they already sought to obtain superfluous possessions and laid hands on animals, having observed that certain of these are harmless, though others are fierce and dangerous. The former therefore they domesticated, the latter they attacked. And simultaneously with the beginning of this way of life war also was introduced. All this, says Dicaearchus, is not asserted merely by us, but by those who have thoroughly investigated the history of early times. For possessions which they thought worth obtaining for themselves already existed. Some men summoned others and gathered them together in groups in order to gain distinction, others

---

[158] Cf. above, II, 2.

[159] This commonplace had become tedious later on, just as the whole legend of the Golden Age bored the writer of the *Aetna*. The proverb, ἅλις δρυός, became popular, as is shown by Cicero's letter to Atticus (*Ep.* II, xix, 1). This phrase, according to the paroemiographers, was used by primitive man when he grew tired of eating acorns and turned to the cultivated fruits of Demeter. See Zenobius, *Centuria*, II, 40 in Leutsch-Schneidewin, *Paroemiographi Graeci*, Göttingen, 1839, I, 42 f.; Diogenianus, I, 62, *ibid.* I, 190; Apostolius, II, 42, *ibid.* II, 275; Macarius, I, 88; *ibid.* II, 142. That the proverb was used as late as the fourth century A. D. is shown by Libanius, *Ep.* MLXXXII.

did the same for the sake of greater security. And so by degrees, in the process of time, as they always fixed their minds upon seeming goods, they passed on to a third kind of life, the agricultural. In this way Dicaearchus in his account of the ancient history of the Greeks explains the happiness of the life of the men of the earliest time — to the completeness of which their abstinence from animal food contributed not less than any of its other features. For this reason there was no war, since every kind of wrong-doing had been excluded. But simultaneously with wrong-doing against animals, war and the desire to possess more than others came in.

That the primitivism of Dicaearchus was associated with what would now be called pacifist propaganda is further indicated by the fact that in his *De interitu hominum* he attempted to show that (civilized) man is man's worst enemy, and that war has caused more destruction than all natural catastrophes taken together.

II, 58. *Fragm.* 67, in Cicero, *De off.* II, 5.

Est Dicaearchi liber de interitu hominum, Peripatetici magni et copiosi, qui, collectis ceteris causis eluvionis, pestilentiae, vastitatis, belluarum etiam repentinae multitudinis quarum impetu docet quaedam hominum genera esse consumpta, deinde comparat, quanto plures deleti sunt homines hominum impetu, id est bellis aut seditionibus, quam omni reliqua calamitate.[160]

There is a book on *The Destruction of Men* by the great and eloquent Peripatetic Dicaearchus. In it, after bringing together all other causes — floods, pestilence, drought, and even sudden attacks of great multitudes of wild animals, by which he maintains that some tribes of men have been wiped out — he then calculates how many more men have been destroyed by the aggression of other men, that is, by wars and seditions, than by every other kind of calamity.

POMPEIUS TROGUS

The writings of Trogus were based upon those of his Greek predecessors and it is likely that if the whole of his universal history were preserved, there would be a chapter on the life of primitive man. In what survives of this work there is a passage in which the goodness of our earliest ancestors is emphasized, a goodness which was reflected in the juristic state of nature. This in itself might not be a sign of their superiority, but we can see from the beginning of his history that in his opinion the rise of kings and the judicial system was a degeneration rather than an improvement. The juristic state of nature was, of course, a commonplace in descriptions of the Golden Age.

II, 59. In Justin, *Hist. phil.* I, i, 1-3.

Principio rerum gentium nationumque imperium penes reges erat, quos ad fastigium huius maiestatis non ambitio popularis, sed

---

[160] Ed. Mueller, Leipzig, 1879, Part IV, Vol. III.

spectata inter bonos moderatio provehebat. Populi nullis legibus tenebantur [arbitria principum pro legibus erant]. Fines imperii tueri magis quam proferre mos erat; intra suam cuique patriam regna finiebantur.[161]

In the beginning of things the power over peoples and nations was in the hands of kings, who had been raised to the height of this majesty not by popular ambition but by the sight of their moderation among good men. The peoples were not checked by laws [the will of the princes took the place of laws]. It was the custom to defend the boundaries of one's empire rather than to extend them; the power of each was limited to his own country.

TACITUS

The *Annals* of Tacitus contains a typical expression of the three-phase theory of the general course of political history. It is fundamentally a piece of chronological primitivism. The first men were the best, and they lived in a juristic state of nature, as in Trogus. But there was, of course, a 'fall'; the primeval virtue was lost, and with it the primeval equality. The originally latent defect in human nature which chiefly caused the fall was apparently 'ambition,' the desire to have more power or distinction or possessions than one's neighbor. An evil state of arbitrary monarchical rule followed, to be eventually replaced, among some peoples, by a 'government of laws and not of men.'

II, 60. *Annals,* Book III, 26.

Vetustissimi mortalium, nulla adhuc mala libidine, sine probro, scelere eoque sine poena aut coercitionibus agebant. neque praemiis opus erat, cum honesta suopte ingenio peterentur; et ubi nihil contra morem cuperent, nihil per metum vetabantur. at postquam exsui aequalitas et pro modestia ac pudore ambitio et vis incedebat, provenere dominationes multosque apud populos aeternum mansere. quidam statim, aut postquam regum pertaesum, leges maluerunt. eae primo rudibus hominum animis simplices erant; maximeque fama celebravit Cretensium, quas Minos, Spartanorum, quas Lycurgus, ac mox Atheniensibus quaesitiores iam et plures Solo perscripsit. nobis Romulus, ut libitum, imperitaverat: dein Numa religionibus et divino iure populum devinxit, repertaque quaedam a Tullo et Anco. sed praecipuus Servius Tullius sanctor legem fuit, quis etiam reges obtemperarent.[162]

The most ancient human beings lived with no evil desires, without guilt or crime, and therefore without penalties or compulsions. Nor was there any need of rewards, since by the prompting of their own nature they followed righteous ways. Since nothing contrary to morals was desired, nothing was forbidden through fear. But after equality began to be abandoned and in place of modesty and shame ambition and force appeared, despotisms arose, and among

[161] Ed. F. Ruehl, Leipzig, 1915.
[162] Ed. Percival Frost, London, 1872.

many peoples still persist. But some peoples at once, or else after they had become disgusted with kings, preferred laws. These at first were simple, for the uncultivated souls of men; and tradition especially has celebrated those of the Cretans which Minos, and those of the Spartans which Lycurgus, drew up; and not long after Solon prescribed more carefully considered and more numerous laws for the Athenians. Over us [Romans] Romulus ruled as he pleased; then Numa made the people subject to binding duties and divine law, and some also were devised by Tullus and Ancus. But Servius Tullius was foremost establisher of laws which even the kings must obey.

PAUSANIAS

One final passage, from Pausanias, concerns not the earliest state of human civilization but what in Hesiod was called the Age of Heroes. Here again the greater goodness of men is emphasized and their supernatural relations. The passage in itself contributes nothing to the history of primitivism, but is important as an ancient specimen of what in the Middle Ages and Renaissance became what might be called nationalistic primitivism, which asserts that the earliest period in the history of a given nation is the best, in some of the many senses of the word " best."

II, 61. Pausanias, *Graeciae descr.* VIII, 2, 4-5.

οἱ γὰρ δὴ τότε ἄνθρωποι ξένοι καὶ ὁμοτράπεζοι θεοῖς ἦσαν ὑπὸ δικαιοσύνης καὶ εὐσεβείας, καί σφισιν ἐναργῶς ἀπῆντα παρὰ τῶν θεῶν τιμή τε οὖσιν ἀγαθοῖς καὶ ἀδικήσασιν ὡσαύτως ἡ ὀργή, ἐπεί τοι καὶ θεοὶ τότε ἐγίνοντο ἐξ ἀνθρώπων, οἳ γέρα καὶ ἐς τόδε ἔτι ἔχουσιν . . . ἐπ' ἐμοῦ δὲ—κακία γὰρ δὴ ἐπὶ πλεῖστον ηὔξετο καὶ γῆν τε ἐπενέμετο πᾶσαν καὶ πόλεις πάσας—οὔτε θεὸς ἐγίνετο οὐδεὶς ἔτι ἐξ ἀνθρώπου, πλὴν ὅσον λόγῳ καὶ κολακείᾳ πρὸς τὸ ὑπερέχον, καὶ ἀδίκοις τὸ μήνιμα τὸ ἐκ τῶν θεῶν ὀψέ τε καὶ ἀπελθοῦσιν ἐνθένδε ἀπόκειται.[163]

For men of that time [the time of Cecrops] were guests and table companions of the gods because of their justice and piety, and honor was openly done to them by the gods if they were good and wrath visited upon them if they were unrighteous. And at that time gods arose from the ranks of men and they are worshipped to this day. . . . But in our day — for wickedness has grown to great proportions and covers the whole earth and every city — no man any longer is deified, except in name and in exaggerated flattery, and the punishment which comes from the gods to the wicked is reserved until such a time as they shall have departed from this life.

E. HUMAN AND COSMIC SENESCENCE [164]

The legends of the Ages were largely concerned with the degeneration of society in a moral sense. But at some point in their history a new ele-

---

[163] Ed. Fr. Spiro, Leipzig, 1903, p. 260.

[164] Lucretius's treatment of this subject will be found in Ch. VIII. There is a hint of cosmic perfection in time in an opinion attributed to Empedocles by the author of the Aristotelian *De plantis* (817 b, 35) which is repeated by Plutarch in *De plac. phil.* V, 26.

ment was introduced which was to have important consequences. This is that form of the theory of progressive decline which is based upon the analogy of human senescence. The world is like a human being who grows old and weak only to die. This conception fitted in best with the doctrine of world-cycles; we cite here a few expressions of it unconnected with that doctrine.

The infancy of a human life is obviously not (*pace* some of the poets) its best period, and one of the passages cited below seems to indicate a certain uneasiness on the author's part caused by the failure of the analogy at this point. Nevertheless, the infant, though physically weak, is like the Spring, full of promise.

PHILO JUDAEUS

As early as Philo there is established the notion of the "world's vernal prime," a notion which, as we shall see in the second volume of this *History,* was paralleled in Philo's mind with that of continuous degeneration. In this passage, however, the process of degeneration is not described.

II, 62. *Quaestiones solutae earum quae sunt in Exodo, in Exod.* 12, 2.

Tempus autem mundi conditi, siquis opportuno examinis consilio utens inquirere velit veritatem, vernum tempus est; hoc enim tempore omnia universim florescunt ac germinantur et suos terra perfectos generat fructus. Nihil autem imperfectum erat, ut dixi, in prima procreatione universorum. Nam opera data constitutum erat, ut gens ista optime conversaretur in mundo, sortita propriam partem meliorem pro honore pietatis, magnam hanc urbem, mundum inquam, et urbanitatem, qua dispensatione bene conversatur.[165]

The time when the world was created — if any one will with proper consideration inquire into the truth of the matter — was the spring-time; for at this time all things germinate and come to flower, and the earth brings forth its perfect fruits; but, as I have said, nothing was imperfect at the first creation of all things. For the completed work was so constituted that the people of that time might live together in the world in the best manner, having allotted to them, as their own, because of their piety, the best part, this great city — I mean the universe — and the civility by virtue of which men are able to live well together.

DIO CHRYSOSTOM

The conception that the world will grow old and worn out is commented on by Lucretius (see Ch. VIII) and Pliny the Younger (Ch. XII, 15) and appears in Seneca (Ch. X, pp. 285 f.). The following passage from Dio Chrysostom (2nd c. A. D.) gives a Neoplatonic version of the Ages of

---

[165] *Philonis opera omnia*, Leipzig, 1830, VII, p. 263. The text is the Latin translation by J. B. Aucher, Venice, 1826, of the fifth century Armenian version of Philo's "explanations" of passages in *Genesis* and *Exodus*. Other passages from Philo bearing upon this subject will appear in Volume II.

the World. In this passage the earlier ages are referred to obscurely under the terms familiarly used in Neoplatonic and Orphic allegory which need not concern us here. But as soon as the cosmos is finally created, it is in its best state. It is a child, to be sure, yet not weak like a human child, " but young and in its prime from the beginning."

II, 63. *Oratio,* xxxvi (*Borysthenitica*), 58-61.

ἐργασάμενος δὲ καὶ τελεώσας ἀπέδειξεν ἐξ ἀρχῆς τὸν ὄντα κόσμον εὐειδῆ καὶ καλὸν ἀμηχάνως, πολὺ δὴ λαμπρότερον ἢ οἷος ὁρᾶται νῦν. πάντα γάρ που καὶ τἄλλα ἔργα τῶν δημιουργῶν καινὰ ἀπὸ τῆς τέχνης καὶ τῶν χειρῶν παραχρῆμα τοῦ ποιήσαντος κρείττω καὶ στιλπνότερα. καὶ τῶν φυτῶν τὰ νεώτερα εὐθαλέστερα τῶν παλαιῶν ὅλα τε βλαστοῖς ἐοικότα. καὶ μὴν τά γε ζῷα εὐχάριτα καὶ προσηνῆ ἰδεῖν μετὰ τὴν γένεσιν, οὐ μόνον τὰ κάλλιστα αὐτῶν, πῶλοί τε καὶ μόσχοι καὶ σκύλακες, ἀλλὰ καὶ θηρίων σκύμνοι τῶν ἀγριωτάτων. ἡ μὲν γὰρ ἀνθρώπου φύσις νηπία τότε καὶ ὑδαρὴς ὁμοία Δήμητρος ἀτελεῖ χλόῃ, προελθοῦσα δὲ εἰς τὸ μέτρον ὥρας καὶ νεότητος παντὸς ἀτεχνῶς φυτοῦ κρεῖττον καὶ ἐπιφανέστερον βλάστημα. ὁ δὲ ξύμπας οὐρανός τε καὶ κόσμος, ὅτε πρῶτον συνετελέσθη, κοσμηθεὶς ὑπὸ τῆς σοφωτάτης τε καὶ ἀρίστης τέχνης, ἄρτι τῶν τοῦ δημιουργοῦ χειρῶν ἀπηλλαγμένος, λαμπρὸς καὶ διαυγὴς καὶ πᾶσι τοῖς μέρεσι παμφαίνων, νήπιος μὲν οὐδένα χρόνον ἐγένετο οὐδὲ ἀσθενὴς κατὰ τὴν ἀνθρωπίνην τε καὶ θνητὴν τῆς φύσεως ἀσθένειαν, νέος δὲ καὶ ἀκμάζων εὐθὺς ἀπὸ τῆς ἀρχῆς. ὅτε δὴ καὶ ὁ δημιουργὸς αὐτοῦ καὶ πατὴρ ἰδὼν ἥσθη μὲν οὐδαμῶς· ταπεινὸν γὰρ ἐν ταπεινοῖς τοῦτο πάθος· ἐχάρη δὲ καὶ ἐτέρφθη διαφερόντως

ἥμενος Οὐλύμπῳ, ἐγέλασσε δέ οἱ φίλον ἦτορ
γηθοσύνη, ὅθ' ὁρᾶτο θεοὺς

τοὺς ἅπαντας ἤδη γεγονότας καὶ παρόντας. τὴν δὲ τότε μορφὴν τοῦ κόσμου, λέγω δὲ τήν τε ὥραν καὶ τὸ κάλλος ἀεὶ καλοῦ ὄντος ἀμηχάνως, οὐδεὶς δύναιτ' ἂν ἀνθρώπων διανοηθῆναι καὶ εἰπεῖν ἀξίως οὔτε τῶν νῦν οὔτε τῶν πρότερον, εἰ μὴ Μοῦσαί τε καὶ Ἀπόλλων ἐν θείῳ ῥυθμῷ τῆς εἰλικρινοῦς τε καὶ ἄκρας ἁρμονίας.[166]

And when [the Creator] had brought forth his work to completion, the primordial reality stood forth a cosmos, good to look upon and inconceivably beautiful, much more splendid then than as it now appears. For all things everywhere, including the other works of creators, when they are newly made and fresh from the hands of the maker, are better and more radiant. And of plants the younger are more flourishing than the older, and so are all things which grow. And even the animals are more charming and pleasanter to see immediately after birth, not only the most beautiful of them, such as colts and calves and puppies, but also the young of the wildest beasts. The nature of man in that time of life is childish and fluid like an unripe ear of wheat, but when it has come to the fullness of its youth and beauty, it is a better and more beautiful growth than anything which is simply a plant. And the universe, both heaven and cosmos, when it was first completed, adorned by the wisest and best art, freshly released from its creator's hands, was shining and radiant and gleaming in all its parts, a child which had

[166] Ed. J. von Arnim, Berlin, Weidmann, 1896, Vol. II.

lived no time, not weak by nature, in the human and mortal fashion, but young and in its prime from the beginning. Yet when its creator and father saw it, he did not feel pleasure. For this emotion is the lowest of all low things. But he did rejoice, and was satisfied in a different way: " going to Olympus, his kind heart laughed in glee when he saw the gods," all those then existing and present. And as for the form of the cosmos at that time, I say that of both the youthfulness and the beauty of the inconceivably ever-beautiful no man could ever be able to conceive and speak worthily, either of men now living or of the ancients; but only the Muses and Apollo, in the divine rhythm of pure and lofty harmony.

PLINY

Hesiod had predicted that the day would come when man would be born senile. That idea, which is an obvious parallel to the idea of cosmic degeneration, apparently developed concomitantly with the legend of the Ages, for we find in Pliny, who invented nothing, a passage — which was to have repeated echoes in later literature — on the decrease of human stature.

II, 64. *Nat. hist.* VII, 15(16).

In trimatu suo cuique dimidiam esse mensuram futurae certum est. in plenum autem cuncto mortalium generi minorem in dies fieri propemodum observatur, rarosque patribus proceriores, consumente ubertatem seminum exustione, in cuius vices nunc vergat aevom. in Creta terrae motu rupto monte inventum est corpus stans XLVI cubitorum, quod alii Orionis, alii Oti esse arbitrabantur. Orestis corpus oraculi iussu refossum septem cubitorum fuisse monimentis creditur. iam vero ante annos prope mille vates ille Homerus non cessavit minora corpora mortalium quam prisca conqueri. Naevii Pollionis amplitudinem annales non tradunt, sed quia populi concursu paene sit interemptus, vice prodigii habitum. procerissimum hominem aetas nostra Divo Claudio principe Gabbaram nomine ex Arabia advectum novem pedum et totidem unciarum vidit. . . . [167]

At the age of three it is certain that each has attained half the measure of his future height. On the whole, however, it is observed throughout the entire human race that it grows shorter almost as the days go by, and that men are rarely taller than their fathers. This happens through the consuming exhaustion of the fertility of the seed, to which turn the age may well have come by now. In Crete on a hill broken open by an earthquake a body was found forty-six cubits tall, which some said was the body of Orion, others of Otus. The body of Orestes which was exhumed by an order of the oracle is believed, according to the records, to have been seven cubits tall.[168]

[167] Ed. D. Detlefsen, Berlin, 1866.

[168] See Herodotus, I, 68. There was also a legend that Hercules was unusually tall. Herodorus Heracleensis is reported to have said that he measured four cubits and one foot. See Herodorus, *Fragm.* 6, in Müller's *Fragm. hist. graec.* II, 29.

It is now nearly a thousand years since, when the poet Homer did not cease to complain that the bodies of men were shorter than in earlier times.[169]   The annals do not relate the height of Naevius Pollio, but since he was killed only by a great mob, it is held to have been prodigious.   The tallest man whom our age has seen, during the reign of Claudius, Gabbara by name, was brought from Arabia; his height was nine feet and as many inches.

AULUS GELLIUS

The matter is disputed by Aulus Gellius, but his very questioning is proof that the belief in the decrease of human stature was still held in his time.   It is to be noted he correlates the idea with that of a senescent world.

II, 65.   Aulus Gellius: *Noctes Atticae*, III, 10.

> . . . Esse dicit [Varro] summum adolescenti humani corporis septem pedes.   Quod esse magis verum arbitramur, quam quod Herodotus, homo fabulator, *in primo historiarum* inventum esse sub terra scripsit Oresti corpus cubita longitudinis habens septem, quae faciunt pedes duodecim et quadrantem, nisi si, ut Homerus opinatus est, vastiora prolixioraque fuerunt corpora hominum antiquiorum et nunc quasi iam mundo senescente rerum atque hominum decrementa sunt.[170]

> [Varro] says that the greatest height of the human body in youth is seven feet.   This we may believe to be truer than what Herodotus, a man given to fictitious tales, wrote in the first book of his *History*,[171] that the body of Orestes, discovered underground, was seven cubits tall, which makes twelve and a quarter feet — unless it be true that, as Homer thought, the bodies of the ancients were broader and taller than ours and that now, as if in a world already senescent, things and men have shrunk.

---

[169] This is presumably a reference to such passages as *Iliad*, V, 304 and XII, 383, which imply nothing as to continuous degeneration.   Velleius Paterculus comments on this in his *Roman History*, I, 5.

[170] Ed. C. Hosius, Teubner, Leipzig, 1903, I, 161-162.

[171] I, 68.

CHAPTER THREE

GENESIS OF THE CONCEPTION OF 'NATURE' AS NORM

Primitivism, as has been remarked in the Prolegomena, is closely related throughout most of its history to the assumption that correctness in opinion and excellence in individual conduct or in the constitution of society consists in conformity to some standard or norm expressed by the term 'nature' or its derivatives. The word had already acquired a peculiar sanctity in Greek usage by the fifth century B. C., and carried a definitely eulogistic connotation. It is therefore necessary to indicate at this point — so far as the historical evidence permits — how this usage came about and how such diverse significations as have already been noted originated.

The etymology of the word φύσις does not obviously explain its acquisition of a normative signification. The word is in form a verbal substantive derived from φύειν, "to beget, produce, give birth to," or more probably from the passive φύεσθαι, "to be born or produced, or to come into being"; and its original meaning, which it had already largely lost in classical Greek, was doubtless simply 'birth' or 'origin.' Primarily, in short, the word was synonymous with γένεσις, and this possible equivalence of meanings was still recognized by Aristotle.[1] From this meaning most, if not all, of the manifold senses of 'nature' must be supposed to have developed, since *natura* is the Latin equivalent of φύσις and inherited its literary and philosophical connotations from the Greek term. Yet 'genesis' has shown no such amazing proliferation of meanings as 'nature.' How, then, from this signification of the latter word did its other senses arise? The question is perhaps the largest, as it is the most curious, of its kind in the science of semantics. It cannot be fully considered here; but some early stages of the process, pertinent to our subject, can be made out with some degree of historical probability, though the subject is much involved in learned controversies.[2]

---

[1] *Metaphysics*, 1014 b 17: "In one sense φύσις signifies the genesis of things that come into being, as if one should pronounce the υ long."

[2] On this cf. especially the important monograph of J. W. Beardslee, Jr.: *The Use of Φύσις in Fifth Century Greek Literature*, 1918; also Hardy, *Der Begriff der Physis in der griechischen Philosophie*, 1884; Burnet, *Early Greek Philosophy*, 2d ed. 1908, pp. 12 ff., 3d ed. pp. 10 ff.; "Law and Nature in Greek Ethics" (1927) in *Essays and Addresses*, 1930, pp. 23 ff.; Lovejoy, "The Meaning of φύσις in the Greek Physiologers," *Philosophical Rev.* 1909, pp. 369 ff.; Heidel, "περὶ φύσεως," *Proc. of the Amer. Acad. of Arts and Sciences*, 1910; B. Bauch, *Das Substanzproblem in der griechischen Philosophie*, 1910; E. Barker, *Greek Political Theory*, 1918, pp. 64-77; J. L. Myres, *The Political Ideas of the Greeks*, 1927, pp. 241-318. We are unable to accept the view of Myres and some other writers that φύσις meant "the way things grow," or "the process of becoming," and that the normative senses of the

1. In its earliest literary uses, the word already has the meaning of 'quality,' 'character,' the 'what' of anything. So in its sole occurrence in Homer (*Od.* X, 303): Hermes gives Odysseus the herb moly, and "shows him its nature, that it was black at the root and its flower was white like milk." In Pindar and Aeschylus it usually signifies "the visible characteristics of the person or object under consideration," though it is also used of the moral and intellectual qualities of men.[3] Behind this lies presumably a semasiological transition from 'birth' to '*innate* characteristic or quality' and from this to 'characteristic' in general, the derivation from 'birth' being then largely forgotten.

2. Nevertheless, there are indications, especially in the usage of Sophocles, that, from 'innate quality' the sense of 'inherent' or 'real' or 'permanent nature,' in contrast with superficial, transitory, or merely apparent characteristics, had also developed. Thus in *Philoctetes*, 902: "When a man forsakes his own nature and doth unseemly deeds." Here there is, as the context shows, an antithesis between the essential character of a man and his acts in aberrant moments. Neoptolemus had been persuaded by the wily tongue of Odysseus to play a despicable trick upon the helpless Philoctetes; remorse comes over him, but in self-justification he says, in substance: "I am not really that kind of man." Similarly in *Ajax*, 472: Ajax, rendered mad by Athene, rests under an imputation of blustering cowardice; he resolves to vindicate his character by some last bold stroke, crying: "Some enterprise must yet be sought to show my aged sire that his son is not, in his real nature ($\phi\acute{\nu}\sigma\epsilon\iota$), a coward." In these and other passages it is evident that the word was one which a Greek writer of the fifth century tended to employ when he had occasion to make the distinction between reality and appearance.[4]

3. This is especially apparent in the use of the term by the Greek pre-Socratic philosophers who speculated about the constitution of matter. Most, at least, of these philosophers were commonly said by the later doxographers to have written or discoursed "Concerning Nature"; and this is confirmed, and the meaning of the word in the terminology of these 'physiologers' is indicated, by a decisive and somewhat neglected passage

term are chiefly derivative from this. So far as the historical period is concerned, the literary evidence seems to us to fail to show such a meaning, which can be read into the relevant passages only by violent and improbable interpretations. The remark of Burnet (*Early Greek Philosophy*, 3d ed. p. 163) that even the sense "birth" is derivative, since the root $\phi\nu$ is equivalent to the English "be," is, no doubt, philologically correct, but it also is of dubious pertinence to the meanings of $\phi\acute{\nu}\sigma\iota\varsigma$ in the extant texts. Our reasons for not adopting these renderings in the explanation of the genesis of the normative use of the term may be gathered from what follows.

[3] Beardslee, *op. cit.* Ch. II, where the relevant passages are examined.

[4] Cf. *Electra*, 1023; *Oedipus Coloneus*, 1194; and for fuller comment on all these passages, Lovejoy, *op. cit.* 1909, pp. 377-8.

in Plato's *Laws* (891c): "One who talks in this fashion conceives fire
and water and earth and air to be the first elements of things, and these
he calls the 'nature.'" Such, Plato adds, are "the unreasonable opinions
of all those who have devoted themselves to inquiries concerning 'nature.'"
Aristotle also, in a passage manifestly referring to the early physiologers,
writes (*Physics*, II, 193a 9f): "By some the nature and true being
(οὐσία) of natural things is said to consist in the primary element inhering
in each thing, . . . just as wood is the 'nature' of a couch and bronze of
a statue," . . . this "true being of the thing being that which continuously
abides while undergoing alterations. And if things are thus subject, each
in its own way, to reduction to something else — as bronze or gold to water,
bones and wood to earth, etc., these latter are said to be the φύσις — the real
nature — and the οὐσία — the true being. Wherefore some say that fire,
some that earth, some that air, some that water, some that more than one
of these, and some that all of them, constitute the nature of things (φύσις
τῶν ὄντων). For what any one of these men conceives to have the character
mentioned, that, he says, is the entire essence of the thing, but the other
[qualities] are merely affections and states and conditions of things. And
the former are all eternal, for there occurs in them no change from what
they themselves are; but the latter are perpetually coming into existence
and passing out of it again." [5]

As a technical term in pre-Socratic philosophy, then, and especially in
the writings of the cosmologists, φύσις meant 'the intrinsic and permanent
qualitative constitution of things,' or, more colloquially, 'what things
really are, or are made of.' [6] Now things do not, in general, appear to be
what, according to one or another of the pre-Socratics, they are 'by
nature'; bronze does not seem to be, or to be composed of, water, or wood
of earth — any more than they appear to be composed of electrons and
protons. The distinction between the intrinsic qualities of matter and
those which are perceived by us thus presents itself — doubtless at first
somewhat dimly and confusedly — almost at the beginning of extant
Greek philosophy, and 'nature' was the term chiefly used to designate
either the former qualities or the substance or substances which possess
them. This antithesis, expressed on its positive side by the same term,
becomes explicitly and fully defined in the atomism of Democritus. [7] The

[5] For further discussion of these Platonic and Aristotelian passages, cf. Lovejoy,
op. cit. 1909, pp. 377-383 and 372.

[6] Cf. the same. Beardslee, *op. cit.* 1918, p. 11, finds this interpretation "quite
correct."

[7] For the doxographic evidence, cf. Aristotle, *Phys.* VIII, 265 b 24; Simplicius,
Phys. 1318, 34, in Diels, *Fragmente der Vorsokratiker*, 4th ed. *Fragm.* 168; and
especially Theophrastus, *De sensibus*, 63 (text and translation in G. M. Stratton,
Greek Physiological Psychology): "As for the other sensory qualities, he (Democritus) holds that none has an objective reality (φύσιν), but that one and all are
effects in our sensuous faculty, and that from this faculty arises the inner presenta-

atoms which, with the empty space in which they move, are the sole physical realities, have only the attributes of size, shape and weight; these properties alone, then, exist 'objectively' (φύσει), while all the other sensible qualities are merely subjective appearances (φαντασίαι).[8]   The school which in some respects stood at the opposite pole from the Democritic, the Pythagorean, seems to have made much of an analogous contrast between the inherent and unchanging nature of reality and the forms in which this manifests itself to human minds.[9]

While φύσις had thus by the fifth century, and probably earlier, come to signify, in the vocabulary of cosmology and metaphysics, the objective qualities or independent realities of the external world, and hence to express also the abstract concept of objectivity, νόμος had come, as the result of another long process of semasiological development,[10] to signify not only ancient rules, established custom, accepted moral standards, and positive law, but also 'prevalent but erroneous opinion' and 'merely subjective appearance.'   This disparaging sense is already apparent in Empedocles, who, in summarizing a current view which he does not accept, adds: "but in this I am myself using words νόμῳ," i. e., in a usual but incorrect way.[11]   In a sentence of Democritus preserved by Galen we read: "Νόμῳ things possess color, νόμῳ they are sweet, νόμῳ they are bitter; but in reality (ἐτεῇι) there exist only atoms and the void." [12]   It is evident, then, that when a fifth-century philosopher wished to express the doctrine of the subjectivity of the secondary qualities of matter, νόμος was the word most suitable to convey his meaning.   It was, obviously, an ethically significant phenomenon in linguistic history when the expression which usually meant either 'by law' or 'in accordance with accepted mores' also took on the sense, not only of 'subjectively,' but of the latter adverb with an unfavorable connotation, i. e. erroneously.

A curious illustration of the degree to which the antithesis of φύσις and

tion; for not even of heat and cold is there for him an objective reality (φύσιν). . . . Proof that these (qualities) are not objectively real is found in the fact that they do not appear the same to all living creatures."   Cf. also *id.* 70.

[8] Cf. Simplicius, *Phys.* 512, 28, and Sextus Empir. *Adv. mathematicos*, VII, 135, in Diels, *op. cit. Fragm.* 9; Galen, *De elem. sec.—Hipp.* I, 2, *ibid.* 25.

[9] Cf. the fragment of Philolaus in Stobaeus, *Ecl.* I, 21, 7d: "As regards Nature and Harmony the case stands thus: the substance of things, which is eternal and their very nature, is the object of divine and not of human knowledge, except indeed that none of the things that exist could have become known by us did there not exist the underlying substance of the things of which the cosmos consists, both of the indeterminates and determinants."   *Vide* on this the article of W. R. Newbold, *Archiv f. Gesch. der Philosophie*, XIX, 1905, pp. 176 ff.

[10] For the etymology and early meanings of the word, cf. Myres, *op. cit.* pp. 243-255.

[11] *Fragm.* 9, Diels.

[12] Democr., *Fragm.* 125, Diels.   Cf. also the sentence of Antisthenes reported by Philodemus (*Dox. graec.* p. 538) that "κατὰ νόμον, according to the usual but false belief, there are many gods, but κατὰ φύσιν, in reality, only one."

νόμος, and the search for that which is " according to nature," had penetrated to the most diverse provinces of thought, is to be seen in an early
controversy about language of which we find an echo in Plato's *Cratylus*.
Two of the interlocutors, Cratylus and Hermogenes, appeal to Socrates to
settle an argument which they have been having on the question whether
words, the names of things, have any objective or intrinsic meaning.
Cratylus has maintained that names " are natural and not conventional —
not sounds which men merely agree to utter, but that there is a truth or
correctness about them which is the same for Hellenes and barbarians."
Hermogenes is of the opposite opinion. " I cannot convince myself," he
says, " that there is any principle of correctness in names other than convention and agreement; any name which you give [a thing], in my judgment, is the right one, and if you change that and give another, the new
name is as correct as the old: we frequently change the names of our
slaves, and the newly imposed name is as good as the old, for there is
no name given to anything by nature: all is convention and the habit of
the users " (384 d). Odd as we may think the notion of Cratylus, which
was probably that of the Sophistic teacher Prodicus, there was something of
it at the bottom of the so-called dialectic method of Socrates. For he
went about asking people to tell what they meant by certain important
words, such as justice, temperance, etc.; his function as man-midwife was
to deliver them of the real meaning which these words had for them, though
without his help they had not realized it themselves. And to assume that
you can find out something more than a linguistic fact — a fact about
usage — by getting people to discover what they really mean by a certain
word, suggests a tacit assumption that that word has a real as distinct
from a conventional meaning ·which can be discovered by the dialectic
process. A similar assumption runs tacitly through not a little modern
philosophical discussion.

4. It is a commonplace of the history of Greek civilization that in
Athens by the second half of the fifth century, and probably earlier in some
of the Ionian colonies, faith in the νόμοι, the traditional moral rules and
existing laws, had become greatly weakened. The causes of this have often
been set forth by other writers; it suffices here to recall only the most
evident and potent. The νόμοι were found to be local affairs, varying from
people to people, as Herodotus showed; even those of the Greeks were sometimes in conflict with one another — one of the themes of Greek tragedy;
in so far as they took form in positive law, they seemed to be man-made
things, and, in a time of frequent political revolutions, and especially in
democracies, they were subject to frequent and sudden change. They had,
in short, when critical reflection was brought to bear upon them, the look
of local historical accidents, or of group-prejudices, and thus seemed to have
no binding force. " Things fair and things just," as Aristotle said, in
summing up the whole story, " are characterized by so much diversity and

variability that they are believed to exist *only* by custom (νόμῳ) and not by nature." [13]   The result was two-fold: in some cases mere ethical scepticism,[14] in others the quest for new moral criteria which could somehow be regarded as having objective and universal validity.   Some other basis than tradition or convention for the conduct of individual life and for positive law and institutions must be found.   This quest was the most characteristic and historically momentous development in the Greek Enlightenment of the sixth to the fourth centuries.

But if the νόμοι, purely as such, were open to the suspicion of mere subjectivity, where and how was an objective norm to be discovered?   Here the linguistic facts outlined above came to have crucial importance.   The recognized antithesis to νόμος was φύσις; the adverbial derivatives of the one already, as we have seen, *meant*, in the language of the natural philosophers, ' subjectively,' or ' according to customary but erroneous opinion,' of the other ' objectively.'   The desiderated norm was therefore described as that which is good or right or just ' by nature ' or ' according to nature.' This carrying over of the word into the vocabulary of ethics was promoted also by other senses which the term had acquired or was acquiring.   In the *Hippocratica* it often signifies (among many other things) the condition of an organ, or of the body as a whole, when unaffected by disease or injury, i. e. its normal condition;[15] in short, the ' natural state ' tended in medical usage to be synonymous with health.   ' Nature ' is also used by some Hippocratic writers to designate the (physiological) characteristics of all humanity, anything that is common to the race, or even, by a simple metonymy, ' all men ' distributively.[16]   Thus the notion of universality among mankind could be conveyed by ' nature '; and the word was consequently appropriate to express that universal recognition and acceptance which was assumed to be an indication, or even the decisive criterion, of objective validity; when transferred to the terminology of morals, in short,

[13] *Eth. Nic.* I, 1094b 14.

[14] Best illustrated by Thrasymachus in Bk. I of Plato's *Republic* and by the speech of the Athenian envoys in Thucydides, I, 76, 2-4.

[15] Cf. Beardslee, *op. cit.* pp. 34, 37.   Our ignorance of the dates of many of the treatises included in the Hippocratic corpus makes the priority of this usage to the ethical senses uncertain, but in any case these medical significations of the word gave support to the tendency to find in ' nature ' the moral norm.   For the antithesis νόμος-φύσις in the *Hippocratica*, cf. *On Diet*, 476: ὁ νόμος γὰρ τῇ φύσει περὶ τούτων ἐνάντιος: " The usual opinion on these matters is contrary to nature," i. e. to the real facts of the case.

[16] Beardslee, *op. cit.* pp. 36-7.   Cf. the treatise *On Ancient Medicine*, I, 578 (cited below, Ch. VII, no. 6), where it is said that the beginning of civilization came when men began to mix and cook foods, " adapting all to the nature and digestive powers of man," πρὸς τὴν τοῦ ἀνθρώπου φύσιν τε καὶ δύναμιν.   The word in the sense of " generic human nature " is oftenest, Beardslee remarks, employed in the *Hippocratica* " with the addition of some noun or adjective such as ἀνθρώπου or ἀνθρωπίνη, but also without such addition "; cf. his citations.

it readily served as a synonym for ' that which is attested by the *consensus gentium.*' [17] Finally, at a time which cannot with certainty be determined, but pretty certainly before the end of the fifth century, ' nature ' had come to have, *inter alia*, the sense of ' the cosmic system as a whole,' or the properties or laws of that system, as distinguished from that which is done or created by man. Thus in Euripides's *Troades* (884-888), which was produced in 415, Hecuba, in what Menelaus in surprise calls " a strange, new-fangled way of praying to the gods," uses ἀνάγκη φύσεως in antithesis to " the minds of mortals ":

> O Earth's upholder, who on earth dost dwell,
> Whoe'er thou art, past finding out, whate'er
> Thy name be, Zeus, or Necessary Law
> Of Nature, or the Mind of Mortal Man,
> I worship thee, for still with noiseless tread,
> Thou guid'st all human things the righteous way.[18]

Here Euripides seems to be echoing — as one of three views which he contrasts — a contemporary conception in which the cosmic law is on the one hand set over against man, but is at the same time credited with a moral purpose or tendency. Those who held such a conception (and probably Euripides himself) [19] had substituted " the laws of Nature " for the commands of Zeus, but still conceived them as normative and invested with a quasi-religious sanctity. ' Nature,' in short, was taking on the attributes of divinity and becoming an object of piety. It was a result to which the several uses of the term already mentioned naturally tended.

5. To identify the objective ethical norm with those rules of conduct which are valid ' by ' or ' according to ' nature gave no logical answer to any concrete moral question; it was merely another way of saying that whatever is objectively right is objectively right, or that what is normal is normal. Yet it was to these questions that answers were required. And here the already manifold ambiguities of the word came in to supply — in great part by pure confusions of thought — the answers that were demanded; one or another of its numerous other meanings could be taken — without any consciousness of a shift from one sense to another — as

---

[17] This equation of ' by nature ' with ' universal ' was turned to their own uses by the Pyrrhonian sceptics in the third century: *Diog. Laert.* IX, 101: the Pyrrhonists argued that " there is nothing good or bad by nature, for if there is anything good or bad by nature, it must be good or bad for all persons alike, just as snow is cold to all. But there is no common good or bad; therefore there is no such thing as good or bad by nature." So also Sextus Empir. *Hyp.* III, 182, 190.

[18] The translation is Lewis Campbell's, *Guide to Greek Tragedy*, 1891, p. 248; while it is admirably close to the original for a metrical version, " past finding out " is somewhat too strong (Euripides says merely " hard to find out "), and the question implied in 886 concerns not the name but the nature of the Power to which the prayer should be addressed.

[19] Cf. Campbell, *op. cit.* p. 258.

clues to those specific modes of life or types of character which *are* 'by nature' right. It was, it will be seen, in a sense a historical accident that, when Greek thinkers had occasion to formulate the demand for objectively true principles, in contrast with mere conventions or subjective prejudices, in the realm of moral judgments, the term which they found made ready for them by the cosmologists and by the theorists about sense-perception was 'nature.' It is a historical accident in the sense that is quite conceivable that the expression chiefly used for 'the objective' might have been some other word — some much more inert and colorless and less ambiguous word — than 'nature.' If it had happened so, the history of European thought in many fields would doubtless have had a very different course. The cosmologists and the theorists about sense-perception might, for example, have used, to express the idea of the manner in which things exist in themselves, or of the way in which they should be thought of after correction is made for the subjective sources of error, some term more nearly approximating our adverb 'objectively.' They might have spoken (as they sometimes did) of what things are 'in reality,' ἐτεῇ, or ὄντως, 'in their very being'; or of what they are 'in truth,' κατ' ἀλήθειαν; and from such terms for the epistemological contrast no such consequences for ethics would have flowed as flowed from the use of φύσει. Or again, the notion of the objectively valid, as against mere seeming, might have been expressed by a reference to the type of mental process employed in reaching it. Such a physical philosopher as Anaxagoras with his ὁμοιομερῆ, or as Democritus with his almost qualityless atoms, obviously arrived at these conceptions by a process of logical thought, of conceptual reasoning, which transcended and even conflicted with the testimony of the senses. The objective, then, as such a philosopher conceived it, might have been expressed by a word derived from the peculiarities of the function or faculty by which you discovered the world of real things as they unchangeably and intrinsically are; or again, it might have been indicated by a word formed by negating the name of the mental process by which you do *not*, as these thinkers declared or implied, apprehend 'reality.' Then the term for the objectively valid would have been the 'rational,' or that which belongs to the 'intellectual system,' or the 'non-sensual,' or even the 'supersensible.' This would *not* have been an inert expression, without consequences in the general tone and tendency of ideas among philosophers or the general cultivated public; but the consequences would have been quite different from those produced by the word 'nature.' This last is what in fact happened in certain schools of Greek thought, beginning about this time, notably in Platonism. But with these we are not here concerned. Despite the fact that alternative expressions for the distinction of 'subjective' and 'objective' (in both existential and moral judgments) were available and were sometimes used, none of the alternatives was destined to have the extraordinary historic fortunes of the antithesis of φύσις and νόμος; and the reason for this lies apparently in the great number of other conceptions which were expressed by or associated with 'nature' and could therefore be tacitly put in the place of its purely formal or epistemological sense — and thus, on the one hand, fill that out with more or less definite practical ideals, and on the other hand, invest these with a seemingly self-evident authority and cogency. It is not, in all this, implied that pure verbal confusions were the only or even the major causes of the development of the multitude of distinct and largely conflicting doctrines concerning what is, in moral, social or aesthetic matters, the valid norm. Those doctrines, no doubt, have usually had also their own sources in human feeling and imagination, and were not all of them the parthenogenetic offspring of the equivocality of a word. But any desire, any imagined ideal of individual or social life, any moral preference, to which the adjectives or adverbial phrases derived from 'nature' were already commonly applied, or could easily be made to apply, seemed to gain thereby an immediate certificate of legitimacy; its credentials need not be further scrutinized. Thus in any argument about ethical or political questions the word 'nature,' and consequently its ambiguity, often played a decisive part. In their reasonings men use words as counters; and when the words employed in the premises are ambiguous — and their ambiguities are not recognized — the conclusions drawn will be diverse, or will be diversely interpreted by different readers. One of the best illustrations of the way in which the ambiguity of 'nature' could be used to justify theses which could not easily have been made plausible by the use of any other designation for 'that which, objectively considered, is morally legitimate,' may be seen in the argumentation of Callicles in Plato's *Gorgias*; and numerous apparently unconscious transitions from one sense to another can be discerned even in Aristotle (cf. Ch. VI). Other examples are to be found in profusion throughout the entire history of Western philosophy and literature from the fifth century onward. Only a part of this further story is pertinent to the theme of this volume: the reading into the general and, in itself, indeterminate normative sense of 'nature,' 'natural,' etc., of such other more specific senses as made for chronological or cultural primitivism or both. Those senses have been enumerated in the Prolegomena; we need here note only the manner in which they became associated and the species of logic whereby they converged to give apparent justification to a single conclusion. By virtue of its (probably) original signification, 'nature' suggested the condition in which human society existed at its genesis; if, then, that which is 'by nature' is *eo ipso* the best or the normal condition, the primeval state of man must have been his normal and best state. But this implication was greatly re-enforced by the sense of 'nature' as that which is not made by man, not due to his contrivance, and the associated assumption that 'nature' — as a quasi-divine power — does all things better than man. Cultural as well as chronological primitivism thus seemed to be in accord with the norm of 'nature'; all man's

alterations of or additions to the 'natural' order of things are changes
for the worse. The same conclusion was further facilitated by the fact that
'nature' — in the senses of 'original endowment' or 'spontaneous tendency' — was in familiar usage antithetic, not only to νόμος, but also to
art (τέχνη) and to culture or instruction (διδαχή). If 'nature' is accepted
as the name for what is 'objectively right,' or for what is 'healthy,' anything which is opposed to it becomes suspect; and therefore 'art' and
'the artificial' become disparaging terms, and whatever is acquired by
deliberate teaching or cultivation seems, by definition, to be, at the least,
inferior to the native intuitions or unsophisticated feelings of the mind.
Finally, in so far as 'nature,' without a qualifying adjective, could serve
as a name for what is fundamental and universal in man's own constitution, the beliefs and customs of primitive men could, on this ground also,
be regarded as solely 'in accordance with nature,' and therefore as alone
in keeping with an objective standard of truth or of morals. For it was,
as texts to be later cited will show, sometimes assumed in antiquity, and
still more frequently in modern times, that the really universal elements
in human nature are to be seen in their simplicity and purity only in
savages or in primeval mankind; these were conceived as the least common
denominator of humanity, while the 'progress' of civilization has been
characterized by the multiplication of differences: the religions, the moral
ideas and customs, the entire cultures, of the peoples who have departed
from the state of nature appeared to have become increasingly dissimilar
and conflicting. If, in short, it was taken for granted that there is a
common *fond* of insights and impulses 'natural' to man as such, and
alone valid and needful, this manifestly could not be discovered, undisguised
by the accretions due to divergent cultural developments, except among
primitive folk. The fundamental antithesis νόμος — φύσις itself thus had
latent in it this primitivistic implication; 'customs' had come to be the
name for those moral rules, practices and beliefs which were observably
local and diverse, and their diversity could be explained only as the consequence of a process of gradual historic change, taking place in different
ways among different peoples, by which the one objective and therefore
invariant norm had become corrupted or overlain with 'unnatural' re-
dundancies.

But even when the period of self-conscious Enlightenment and of revolt
against mere tradition set in, the Greek mind was doubtless predisposed to
an emphasis upon the primitivistic senses of the norm of 'nature' by the
influence of tradition — by those preconceptions about the historic process
which were embodied in the Legend of the Ages and other elements of the
racial mythology which have been illustrated in Chapter II. It has been
pertinently remarked by Chiappelli that "in the moral teaching of the
earliest Sophists" — or, at all events, in that of certain of the most influential of them — the subjects of their discourses "were drawn from the

Heroic Age; and this mental habit of taking the themes of the new teaching from the mythical and heroic past joined with that ancient tendency of the Greek mind which may be called genealogical — the tendency always to turn backward to the origins of nature or of human life. Such a tendency was wholly natural in a people which did not have as the centre of gravity in its life a future ideal state, like that to which the Messianic hopes, the prophetic and apocalyptic vision, of Jewish thought turned, but found the highest point of its history in the past which the national legend had represented as heroic and divine, the picture of which had received artistic form in the Homeric Epos." [20]

6. Just when and through whom the appeal to ' nature ' for standards first took a definitely primitivistic turn it is not easy to determine. In the scanty evidence which we have concerning the doctrines of the early Sophists who sought to base a constructive ethics upon φύσις in contradistinction to νόμος, a full-blown primitivism can hardly be discerned. That there was already a controversy over e. g. the virtues of ' savages ' among the intellectuals at the time in which Plato dates the conversation in his *Protagoras* (*ca.* 435) is strongly suggested by that dialogue; [21] but who the Sophistic protagonists of primitivism were is not made clear. Some historians of Greek philosophy [22] have attributed that rôle to Prodicus of Ceos and Hippias of Elis, of whose enormous reputation for wisdom among the Athenian youth the *Protagoras* gives sufficient evidence. That both made much of the distinction between the ' natural ' and the ' conventional,' [23] and that there were in the moral teaching of both ideas tending towards primitivism, and destined to be taken up into the primitivistic tradition, is plain; but neither can be shown to have been an enthusiast for the state of nature in both the chronological and cultural senses.

The fullest indication of the character of the teaching of Prodicus which we have is his celebrated apologue of " The Choice of Hercules," given by Xenophon in *Memorabilia* (II, 1, 21 ff.). In the Xenophontic version it is possibly somewhat diluted by having passed through Xenophon's rather commonplace mind; [24] but as it stands, it is in the main an edifying

[20] " Per la storia della sofistica greca " in *Archiv für Gesch. der Philosophie*, III, 1890, p. 19.

[21] See Ch. V, p. 167.

[22] Notably Benn, *The Greek Philosophers*, 1882, and Chiappelli, *op. cit.* pp. 1-21, 240-274.

[23] Dümmler (*Akademika*, p. 256) has sought to show that Hippias was the originator of this antithesis as applied to moral and social questions. The evidence for this conclusion appears to us insufficient. Barker credits its origination to Archelaus, which is somewhat more probable (*op. cit.* p. 53); but Beardslee scarcely overstates the fact in saying that " there is absolutely no evidence showing to whom it first occurred to oppose natural and conventional morals " (*op. cit.* p. 76).

[24] That Prodicus wrote such a dialogue is attested by other writers, e. g. Plato, in *Symposium*, 177b: some of " the good Sophists have written in praise of Hercules

but conventional piece of moralizing, in which the allegorized figures of
Virtue and Vice compete in self-laudation to win over the youthful
Hercules. In the speeches of Virtue, however, there are notes which were
to be taken up by the Cynics and to be recurrent in later primitivism of
the hard type. (a) The denunciation of luxury and the demand for the
limitation of desires: "Thou (Vice) dost not even await the desire of
pleasant things, but fillest thyself with all things before thou desirest them,
eating before thou art hungry, drinking before thou art thirsty; devising
cooks to make eating more pleasurable, procuring costly wines and running
about in search of snow in summer to make drinking more pleasurable.
To soothe thy slumbers thou must not only have soft coverlets but rockers
for thy beds. Not from being tired with labor but from the boredom of
having nothing to do thou desirest sleep. Thou forcest lust before there is
need, resorting to many devices, and using men as women." (b) The
eulogy of strenuous labor: "Of the things that are good and fair the gods
give none to men without toil and diligence." (c) The selection, for the
model of human virtue, of Hercules, who was soon to become the hard
primitivists' hero *par excellence*.[25]

But in all this none of the paradoxical extreme of cultural primitivism
appears, and of chronological primitivism the only hint is the fact that the
hero of the tale was a relatively primeval figure of Greek legend. And that
Prodicus was no zealot for the simple life — and also no primitivistic
pacifist — is shown by the same dialogue. Labor is extolled because it
leads to wealth;[26] and the learning of the arts of war is commended, because it increases power and enables a man "to liberate his friends and
subdue his enemies."

For the chronological primitivism of Hippias we have more definite
evidence. We are told in a probably pseudo-Platonic dialogue that he was
much occupied with "ἀρχαιολογία in general," which does not, of course,
mean 'archaeology' in the modern sense, but the study of primitive
times;[27] and that this interest was connected with a conviction of the
superiority of those times is shown by the declaration also attributed to him
in the same dialogue: "For my part, I am accustomed to praise the men of

. . . , as, for example, the excellent Prodicus"; *Schol. Aristoph.* in Diels, 4th ed. II,
p. 270. But that it is faithfully reproduced by Xenophon is dubious; as Diels
remarks, "the style is certainly Xenophontic," and Xenophon admits that he gives
the story "as well as he can from memory."

[25] In Xenophon's version of the allegory we are not explicitly told which of the
rival ladies Hercules chose to follow; but the sequel was, of course, too familiar to
need telling.

[26] That Prodicus was no disparager of wealth is indicated also by the bromidic
remark attributed to him in the pseudo-Platonic *Eryxias*, 379 d: "Riches are a
good to good men and to those who know how to make use of them, to bad and
ignorant men an evil."

[27] *Hippias Minor*, 285d.

early ages (τοὺς παλαιούς) and those that were before us more than those of the present."[28] In accord with this conviction, Hippias discoursed with predilection on the typical sage of the Age of Heroes, Nestor, who gave the wisest counsels to the young Neoptolemus and in his own life exemplified all manner of moral excellences in the highest degree.[29] As an evidence of the departure from 'nature' in the later course of history Hippias seems to have pointed especially to the growth of national states and of nationalistic prejudices and antipathies: "All of you who are here present I consider to be kinsmen and friends and fellow-citizens by nature, though not by law; for by nature like is akin to like, but law is a tyrant over mankind, and in many things does violence to nature."[30] The cosmopolitan temper which passed on through Cynicism to Stoicism, and was in them connected with primitivistic ideas, thus probably had its historic origin in Hippias's teaching. In so far, then, as the advance of civilization has involved the development of a diversity of moral ideas and codes it was for Hippias a progressive degeneration. He is said to have once appeared at the Olympic games boasting that everything that he wore had been made by himself;[31] it has been suggested that this was not a mere display of vanity but an object-lesson in primitivism: before the development of specialized trades, every man provided for all his needs by his own exertions.[32] But the story hardly suggests any acceptance of technological primitivism by Hippias, for the home-made outfit in which he exhibited himself was of an elaborate and showy sort; it included an engraved finger-ring, an oil-flask, a tiara, and a girdle "similar to the most expensive Persian kinds." As little did Hippias, according to Plato, hesitate to display his proficiency in poetic composition and the polymathy for which, indeed, he was celebrated. That he was a spokesman of cultural primi-

---

[28] *Ibid.* 282a.

[29] *Hippias Major*, 286a. On the authenticity of the two Hippias dialogues the weight of critical opinion is almost equally divided; for a review of the controversy, see D. Tarrant, *The Hippias Major*, 1928, Introd. pp. ix-xvii, xxx-xxxii, who accepts as "the most probable hypothesis" with respect to that dialogue the view that we have in it "the work of a young student of the Academy in Plato's own time."

[30] *Protagoras*, 337b. There is no reason to suppose that Plato here puts into the mouth of Hippias an idea foreign to his teaching.

[31] *Hippias Minor*, 368b.

[32] So Benn, *The Greek Philosophers*, 1882, I, p. 83: "Here we have precisely the sort of versatility which characterises uncivilised society, and which believers in a state of nature love to encourage at all times. . . . If we must return to Nature, our first step should be to learn a number of trades, and so be better able to shift for ourselves." The remark is repeated—with reference to the same story about Hippias—by Chiappelli (*op. cit.* p. 248), who adds that the "enthusiasts for the state of nature in all periods" have held that "in that state every man should seek for himself the highest possible culture"(!). These writers have curiously forgotten the place of cultural, and especially of technological, primitivism in most conceptions of the state of nature, ancient and modern.

tivism is therefore not inferrible from the available evidence. On the other hand, he was apparently an early, and perhaps the first, representative of the identification of 'the natural,' in ethical use, with that which is supported by the universal agreement of mankind, and of at least one inference from this which we shall see playing a part in later primitivism, that incest is not contrary to nature; in a dialogue which Xenophon represents him as having with Socrates, he will not admit that " it is a law of the gods that parents should not intermarry with their children," on the ground that " some (peoples) reject (or transgress) it." [33]

We cannot, then, identify either Prodicus or Hippias as the originator of the phase of thorough-going primitivism which was associated with the ideal of " the life that is in accord with nature." But, as the next chapter will show, in the generation following Prodicus and Hippias, and in the teaching of one of their pupils, it appears as a fully developed doctrine and as a program of life put into actual practice.

[33] *Memorabilia*, IV, 4, 5.

CHAPTER FOUR

A. CYNIC PRIMITIVISM

From the later period of the life of Socrates to the beginnings of Stoicism (*ca.* 308 B. C.), the principal representatives of both cultural and chronological primitivism were the Cynics. Our knowledge of the early Cynic doctrine, however, is fragmentary and largely indirect, resting chiefly upon the speech ascribed to the founder of the school, Antisthenes, in the *Banquet* of Xenophon (No. 3 below); the account of Diogenes in Dio Chrysostom's fourth, sixth, eighth, ninth, and tenth *Discourses*, probably written in the ninth or tenth decade of the first century A. D. (Nos. 6, 16, 20); some passages of Epictetus; the sixth book of Diogenes Laertius, before the middle of the third century, which incorporates many extracts from earlier but not, as a rule, authoritative expositors and compilers of anecdotes;[1] two of the *Orations* (VI and VII) of the Emperor Julian; and fragments, numerous but seldom of indubitable authenticity, in some of the Fathers, and in the *Florilegium* of Stobaeus, of the fifth century.[2] That the primitivistic strain in Stoicism, with much else in that doctrine, was directly derivative from the Cynic teachers, may be safely assumed; Zeno of Citium was a pupil of Crates who was a pupil of Diogenes, and himself adhered to the Cynic dress and regimen;[3] Cicero spoke of the Stoics before his time, or of many of them, as virtually Cynics, *paene*

---

[1] The historical value of many of the anecdotes both of Antisthenes and of Diogenes the Cynic which Diogenes Laertius borrowed is more than dubious; on this cf. Kurt von Fritz, *Quellenuntersuchungen zu Leben und Philosophie des Diogenes von Sinope* (*Philologus*, Supplementband XVIII, Heft I, 1926, especially pp. 33-60), who nevertheless thinks it possible to distinguish, by means of a careful source-analysis, between the stories and sayings which are "pure inventions" and those which can be held with some probability to be authentic. The traditional picture of the early Cynic sage, as conceived by the ancients after the fourth century, and handed down to modern writers, remains clear, in spite of the questionable character of many of the sources.

[2] For these, *vide* Mullach, *Fragmenta philos. graec.* II, pp. 261-395. Mullach's numberings of the fragments is here followed. It has been maintained by Dümmler with some force that Dio Chrysostom's *Disc.* XIII contains "a dialogue which can only have been written shortly after 393," and that "all the indications point to Antisthenes as its author" (*Akademika*, 1889, p. 1 ff.). If this opinion, which is rejected by some other scholars, is correct, the greater part, at least, of an original work of Antisthenes is extant. Plato's *Cratylus* is doubtless, as Schleiermacher has argued (*Platons Werke*, 1857, II, 2, p. 12), in part a presentation—with a good deal of parody—of the theory of "natural language" which Antisthenes probably learned from Prodicus. The so-called *Letters of Diogenes* are obviously spurious, and of almost no value as historical sources except for the development of the Diogenes legend.

[3] Diog. Laert. VII, 26-7.

Cynici,[4] and Epictetus, traditionally described as the principal Roman expositor of the Stoic ethics, called his own ideal " Cynic," and cited the example and the words of Diogenes more frequently than those of any of the philosophers of the Porch. But aside from the continuance (with a good deal of toning-down and with the addition of a logical and metaphysical theory) of fundamental elements of its moral teaching in Stoicism, the Cynic school itself had an unbroken existence and considerable influence for more than eight centuries;[5] and although there were minor variations in and accretions to its doctrine, and periods of laxity among its adherents in the practice of its principles, its distinctive temper and ideas remained much the same throughout. This was largely due to the fact that the Cynic ethics had been early embodied, dramatized and standardized in the figures of Antisthenes and (especially) Diogenes, and of the legendary Hercules; more than any of the other post-Socratic schools, Cynicism had the advantage of having not only a doctrinal tradition, but persons—salient, racy and venerated characters—in whom its spirit and ideals were concretely exemplified.[6] There is, indeed, reason to think that these historic models of the Cynic life were early given a somewhat heightened coloring; but since it is probable that in the main the later presentations of that life here given, and of the philosophy inspiring it, followed closely the Cynicism of the fourth century, we have brought together in a single chapter relevant texts from all periods of the history of the school.

The Cynic ethics may be said to reduce, in its practical outcome, almost wholly to primitivism. Cynicism was the first and most vigorous philosophic revolt of the civilized against civilization in nearly all its essentials — except ' philosophy ' itself. And in the fragments of Cynic writings which have survived and the expositions of their doctrine by other ancient writers we find for the first time a fairly clear indication of certain of the most significant ethical ideas underlying thorough-going primitivism as a philo-

---

[4] *De off.* I, xxxv, 128. Cf. Juvenal: "The Stoics differ from the Cynics only by a tunic." *Sat.* XIII, 122.

[5] It has been supposed by some historians that Cynicism virtually disappeared in the second and first centuries B. C. and had a renascence about the beginning of the Christian era in consequence of the vogue of Stoicism. That this is an error has been shown by Helm, art. "Kynismus," in Pauly-Wissowa, XII, 1 (1925), col. 5. For the degeneracy of some of those who professed and called themselves Cynics in the fourth century A. D., cf. Julian, *Orat.* VI. But Cynics of the original type were still extant at late as the sixth century; then (as Helm remarks) "Cynicism disappeared with the disappearance of paganism, after monachism had taken over into itself in part the characteristic features of the Cynic life" (*op. cit.*). The relation of Cynicism to early Christianity will be dealt with in the second volume of this history.

[6] The accounts of Diogenes's teachings to be found in the pertinent dialogues of Dio Chrysostom are possibly, as some modern scholars have held, to be regarded rather as applicable to Antisthenes and as echoes of his writings. Cf. K. von Fritz, *op. cit.* pp. 82-4.

sophical doctrine — ideas which, implicitly or explicitly, run through much of the subsequent history of the tendency. It therefore seems necessary here to attempt a connected account of these ideas. Two major conceptions were combined in the premises of the Cynic doctrine. Antisthenes was a devoted pupil at once of Socrates[7] and of the 'Sophists' Hippias and Prodicus; in Xenophon's *Banquet* Socrates jokingly calls him a pander, because he brought Callias to these wise men and thereby made him a lover of philosophy.[8] Probably from the one source Antisthenes derived the conception of 'self-sufficiency' (αὐτάρκεια), independence of 'things' and of other persons, as the essence of the good, and from the other the assumption that the norm of life lies in 'conformity to nature.' The former became the common and characteristic conception of the *summum bonum* in all the schools through which the Socratic influence persisted, with the qualified exception of some of those heterodox 'Socratics,' the Cyrenaics,[9] but it manifested itself at different points in their systems: in the ethical ideals of ataraxy and apathy in the Epicureans and Stoics; in the definition of the absolute good in Plato's *Philebus*;[10] and in the Aristotelian, and one aspect of the Platonic, conception of God. In all these applications of the equation of the *finis bonorum* with self-sufficiency, even the theological and metaphysical ones, the emphasis was upon its negative sense of not-wanting, of indifference to all that is external to the individual, human or divine, rather than upon the positive idea of the attainment of specific objects of possible desire; it suggested, in short, that the good is to be reached, not by getting anything, but by being able to dispense with everything extraneous to 'oneself,' while maintaining an inner state of untroubled satisfaction. And this, it would appear, was the practical moral which Antisthenes drew from the Socratic teaching and example. But the ideal of self-sufficiency manifestly implied that man will be unhappy and irrational in proportion to the multiplicity of his desires; and it thus led directly to cultural primitivism. For the principal psychological source of technological progress

---

[7] H. von Arnim, *Leben und Werke des Dio von Prusa*, 1898, p. 32: "Antisthenes was undoubtedly influenced more profoundly than any other pupil of Socrates except Plato by the personality and teaching of his master." Cf. also *Memor.* III, 12.

[8] Cf. Mullach, *Fragm.* II, 280-281.

[9] The distinctively Socratic element in the hedonism of Aristippus was his insistence that the seeker of sensual pleasures, even while he enjoys them, should be independent of them (ἔχω ἀλλ' οὐκ ἔχομαι, Diog. Laert. II, 75; cf. Stobaeus, *Flor.* XVII, 18). In later Cyrenaics, notably Hegesias and his followers, this emphasis was so extreme that their position closely approximated that of the Cynics (Diog. Laert. II, 94-95). On the *rapprochement* of "the later Cynics" to Aristippus, cf. Dümmler, *Akademika*, 1889, pp. 166 ff., especially p. 186. But the Cynic and Cyrenaic doctrines were throughout, as Dümmler's analysis of the latter shows, less completely antithetic than has usually been supposed.

[10] *Philebus* 60 b: "The good differs from all other things in that the being who possesses it always, everywhere, and in all things, has the most perfect sufficiency and is never in need of anything else."

has obviously been the expansiveness of human desires, the craving, which to the Cynics seemed purely pathological, to obtain possessions and to enjoy new pleasures which were not indispensable to man's existence or content- ment — as was shown by the fact that before new inventions were devised he had existed contentedly without them; and the advance of the practical arts has made most men increasingly dependent upon external things and less capable of finding an assured satisfaction within themselves alone. The Cynic program, therefore, was to destroy this evil at its source, to persuade men that nearly all economic goods have no real value, because their supposed value arises from subjective desires which, once the reins have been given to them, are insatiable, and make in the end neither for happiness nor rational self-possession. It was thus a program which would have arrested all cultural progress in the future and have abandoned most of the results of it in the past. Though the radical application given by the Cynics to the notion of self-sufficiency went beyond that of Socrates, whose philosophy — whatever view be taken of its content as a whole — was certainly more many-sided, that notion may be set down as the Socratic element in the ideology of primitivism; and Socrates's personal temper and habit of life was regarded by the Cynics as a foreshadowing of their own [11] (cf. No. 1).

This strain in Cynicism, however, was at once reënforced, in some points intensified, and in others modified, by the notion of 'nature' as norm. This seems to have been used by the Cynic teachers in at least four of its senses. 'In accordance with nature' is: (a) Anything which is uncon- taminated with 'art.' Things are best as 'Nature' made them; hence, for a second reason, the thesis that the progress of the arts and sciences has been harmful to mankind, the strain of anti-intellectualism, and the degrading of Prometheus, or the function of which he was the legendary embodiment, from the rôle of hero to that of villain in the early history of humanity (No. 16). Hence, also, the dietetic moral which, according to Julian, Diogenes drew — that it is more 'natural' to eat food uncooked (No. 18). (b) Anything which is characteristic of the primeval age. This naturally followed from the preceding, on the assumption that the primeval age was not a civilized one, but was prior to the development of most (at least) of the arts and sciences. (c) With respect to human desires: those are 'natural' which are primary, universal, instinctive and irrepressible, spontaneous rather than factitious, not prompted by emula- tion or vanity or the lust of possession for possession's sake, and are shown to be 'natural' by the fact that they can be easily and equally gratified by all men. This element in the Cynic doctrine prevented the ideal of self- sufficiency from taking an extreme ascetic form. Not all desires are to be repressed; and while a rigorous discipline of the desires was an essential

[11] Cf. Joël, *Der echte und der xenophontische Sokrates*, Berlin, II, 1901, p. 352.

part of the original Cynic rule of life, the mortification of the flesh was not. On the contrary there is a conspicuous, and not altogether incongruous, mixture of hedonistic and rigoristic tendencies in the Cynic ethics. According to one reported saying of his (No. 4), Antisthenes denounced the desire for pleasure as intrinsically evil; but it appears upon rather better authority that both he and Diogenes paradoxically professed to be the only intelligent voluptuaries (Nos. 5, 6, 7). The pleasure which attends the gratification of the primary and natural desires — provided even they are not permitted to become excessive — is harmless and legitimate. The Cynic life was especially commended, by those who practised it, for general adoption because it made for health and physical vigor and for keenness of sensible enjoyment. To lack food occasionally is a good thing because it is real hunger that makes eating most pleasurable. Antisthenes was not averse to drinking good wine now and then — if someone else provided it for him; and Diogenes, a pioneer of summer tourists, is said to have changed his climate with the seasons — nature affording him in this the example of the birds [12] (Nos. 3, 6). The sexual impulse, since it is natural and universal, is not to be repressed, but on the contrary to be gratified as promptly and easily as possible; and with respect to this the Cynics, according to the the tradition, preached, and even exemplified in practise, an ἀναίδεια, a freedom from psychological 'repressions,' in the modern sense, which went far beyond that of any modern counterparts. All conventional refinements and rules of decorum, in this or other matters, had for them no warrant in 'nature'; and the most famous of the Cynics, if the stories told of him are true (which is questionable), delighted in shocking his contemporaries by ostentatious indecencies.[13] The 'plain-speaking' which was one of the boasts of the Cynics was similarly a rejection of the refinements and courtesies which had become conventional in civilized social intercourse; though it was conceived by Epictetus as merely the expression of the right and duty of the truly virtuous man to rebuke evil in others (*Disc.* III, 22, 13). (d) With respect to laws, customs and moral codes: those are not 'natural' which are not attested by the *consensus gentium*, not accepted *semper ubique et ab omnibus*. Anything is conformable to nature if it is regarded as approvable or permissible by any people. Hence neither incest nor anthropophagy can be said to be against nature, since they are practised by some races (Nos. 20, 21).

[12] For the Cynic use of the idea of learning the ways of nature from the animals, *vide* Ch. XIII, Nos. 2, 3, 4.

[13] Diog. Laert. VI, 69. "It was his (Diogenes's) habit to do everything in public, both the works of Demeter and those of Aphrodite." The reverence of, e. g. Epictetus for Diogenes makes it improbable that the more extreme obscenities ascribed to the latter were regarded by the Cynics themselves as in keeping with his character; and they are at least as probably libels invented by rival schools or by the ancient composers of *scabreux* anecdotes. But their ascription to him is nevertheless indicative of a Cynic characteristic.

Since the 'natural' desires are few, and since one of their distinguishing marks is that they are appeasable with very little effort, the Cynic moral theory tended, on one side, to a glorification of laziness — a glorious leisure like that of the gods or of the men of the Golden Age. Those who are self-sufficient have nothing to work for; and the fact that a thing requires much trouble to procure is good evidence that Nature did not mean us to have it (Nos. 6, 23). But there is here a conflict of tendencies in the Cynic preaching. From the outset — probably under the influence of Prodicus — they took Hercules as their model among the heroes of Greek antiquity.[14] The aspects of the character traditionally ascribed to Hercules which primarily made him the object of their hero-worship were doubtless his rudeness of life, strength of will, indifference to luxury, superiority to all external circumstance. But to hold up as the supreme exemplar for all mankind the man of many and arduous labors was to be committed to a 'gospel of work,' a glorification of the strenuous life which the founders of Cynicism nevertheless at times deprecated and were apparently far from practising.

What especially distinguishes the fourth-century Cynics, and those who later imitated them, in the history of primitivism — if the accounts of them given by other writers are in any degree historical — is that they not only praised but in the main lived the life of primitive men, or what they conceived to be such, and did so in the midst of a civilized society. They apparently had no yearning to retire to a desert or to live with shepherds or peasants; they were essentially urban, and loved to be amongst the crowds they despised. It is suggested by some of the most current anecdotes of them that, in spite of their special denunciation of the desire for distinction and the regard of other men, a species of inverted vanity and ostentation was one of their conspicuous characteristics — as Socrates is said to have frankly told Antisthenes, and Plato, Diogenes [15] — and that their austerity of life would have had less charm for them without its foil. But a more charitable and perhaps a fairer explanation of their preference for living in the midst of a society differing as widely as possible from the state of nature has been offered by a modern writer: that they conceived themselves as essentially missionaries of a saving gospel and therefore naturally passed their lives *in partibus infidelium*. "The Cynics were not so concerned with saving their own souls that they neglected the salvation of mankind; on the contrary, they undertook the duty of delivering those enslaved by vices or false opinions from their chains. Therefore they did not, like other philosophers, seek out sequestered gardens to philosophize in, but wandered about in the streets, temples, gymnasiums, preaching their new

---

[14] For a comprehensive and important but sometimes over-ingenious discussion and interpretation of the texts pertinent to the Hercules-cult of the Cynics, *vide* Joël, *Der echte und der xenophontische Sokrates*, II, 1901, pp. 253-332.

[15] Diog. Laert. VI, 8; VI, 26.

doctrine. How, then, could a Cynic so fail in his duty as to retire to the solitude of the country or of deserts?"[16] Certainly there is much to indicate that both the early Cynics and those who in later centuries followed "with the stricter observance the rule of St. Diogenes"[17] were characterized by a more ardent missionary fervor than other ancient schools. The mendicant friars of antiquity, the Cynic preachers seem to have found their most sympathetic public amongst the poor and lowly — who needed their gospel least but naturally took most satisfaction in their pungent and unsparing satire of plutocrats and aristocrats.[18] But — unlike some ancient and medieval and much modern primitivism — Cynicism can hardly have given much encouragement to any proletarian insurgency. The rich were not to be envied or pillaged but pitied and despised. The communistic program was, so far as the extant evidence shows, not emphasized by the Cynics. They were less concerned that men should have economic goods in common than that they should have as few of them as possible; and their effort was not to establish a new social order but to persuade individuals to return to the life of nature, as individuals. The poor man was bidden to rejoice in his poverty — and, if it was not so extreme as that of the Cynic sages themselves, to seek to emulate them in the meagreness of his possessions; and what Epictetus the slave learned from Antisthenes and Diogenes (himself supposed to have been at one time a slave)[19] was not that slavery is contrary to nature but that it is as compatible with freedom of the soul as any other condition (No. 2). To ancient conservatives Cynicism may well have seemed an excellent philosophy for the lower classes.

Socrates as exemplar

IV, 1. Diog. Laert. II, 24-28.

24. Αὐτάρκης τε ἦν καὶ σεμνός. καί ποτε Ἀλκιβιάδου, καθά φησι Παμφίλη ἐν τῷ ἑβδόμῳ τῶν Ὑπομνημάτων, διδόντος αὐτῷ χώραν μεγάλην, ἵνα ἐνοικοδομήσηται οἰκίαν, φάναι, "καὶ εἰ ὑποδημάτων ἔδει, καὶ βύρσαν μοι ἐδίδους, ἵν' ἐμαυτῷ ὑποδήματα ποιησαίμην, καταγέλαστος ἂν ἦν λαβών." 25. πολλάκις δ' ἀφορῶν εἰς τὰ πλήθη τῶν πιπρασκομένων ἔλεγε πρὸς αὑτόν, "πόσων ἐγὼ χρείαν οὐκ ἔχω." . . . 27. Ἦν δ' ἱκανὸς καὶ τῶν σκωπτόντων [αὐτὸν] ὑπερορᾶν. καὶ ἐσεμνύνετο ἐπὶ τῇ εὐτελείᾳ, μισθόν τε οὐδένα εἰσεπράξατο. καὶ ἔλεγεν ἥδιστα ἐσθίων ἥκιστα ὄψου προσδεῖσθαι· καὶ ἥδιστα πίνων ἥκιστα τὸ μὴ παρὸν ποτὸν ἀναμένειν· καὶ ἐλαχίστων δεόμενος ἔγγιστα

---

[16] E. Weber: "De Dione Chrysostomo Cynicorum sectatore" (*Leipziger Studien*, X, 1887, p. 126). A mendicant Cynic, however, could hardly have subsisted in a desert.

[17] Wilamowitz-Moellendorf in *Philol. Untersuchungen*, IV, 1881, p. 299. On Teles as an itinerant Cynic preacher, cf. *id.* pp. 292-318.

[18] Cf. Weber, *op. cit.* p. 165 ff.; Joël, *op. cit.* II, 258 ff. The Cynic hero, Hercules, was *inter alia* a god of peasants and herdsmen.

[19] Kurt von Fritz has argued with considerable probability that "the entire story that Diogenes was a slave is an invention of Menippus" (*op. cit.* p. 26).

εἶναι θεῶν. . . . 28. τοῦτο δ' αὐτοῦ τὸ ὑπεροπτικὸν καὶ μεγαλόφρον ἐμφαίνει
καὶ Ἀριστοφάνης λέγων οὕτως,

ὅτι βρενθύει τ' ἐν ταῖσιν ὁδοῖς, καὶ τὠφθαλμὼ παραβάλλεις,
κἀνυπόδητος κακὰ πόλλ' ἀνέχει, κἂν ἡμῖν σεμνοπροσωπεῖς.[20]

24. He was self-sufficient and self-respecting. When — as Pam-
phila relates in the seventh book of her Commentaries — Alcibiades
once offered him a large piece of land on which to build a house,
he replied: "If I wanted shoes and you gave me a whole hide to
make them with, how ridiculous I should be if I accepted it." 25.
Often when he looked at the multitude of wares offered for sale,
he would say to himself, "How many things there are which I can
do without!"... 27. He was able to disdain those who scoffed
at him. He prided himself on his simplicity of life, and never took
a fee from anyone. He used to say that he most enjoyed the food
which had least need of seasoning and the drink which least made
him want to drink more, and that he was nearest to the gods because
he had fewest wants. . . . 28. This disdainful and proud spirit
of his is pointed out by Aristophanes when he says: "Because you
stride through the streets holding your head high and rolling your
eyes, and go barefoot and endure many hardships, and gaze proudly
up at us (the clouds)."

Self-sufficiency

IV, 2. Epictetus, *Disc.* III, xxiv, 67 f.

' ἐξ οὗ μ' Ἀντισθένης ἠλευθέρωσεν, οὐκέτι ἐδούλευσα.' πῶς ἠλευθέρωσεν;
ἄκουε τί λέγει· 'ἐδίδαξέν με τὰ ἐμὰ καὶ τὰ οὐκ ἐμά. κτῆσις οὐκ ἐμή· συγγενεῖς,
οἰκεῖοι, φίλοι, φήμη, συνήθεις τόποι, διατριβή, πάντα ταῦτα ὅτι ἀλλότρια. σὸν
οὖν τί; χρῆσις φαντασιῶν. ταύτην ἔδειξέν μοι ὅτι ἀκώλυτον ἔχω, ἀνανάγκαστον,
οὐδεὶς ἐμποδίσαι δύναται, οὐδεὶς βιάσασθαι ἄλλως χρήσασθαι ἢ ὡς θέλω. τίς
οὖν ἔτι ἔχει μου ἐξουσίαν; Φίλιππος ἢ Ἀλέξανδρος ἢ Περδίκκας ἢ ὁ μέγας
βασιλεύς; πόθεν αὐτοῖς; τὸν γὰρ ὑπ' ἀνθρώπου μέλλοντα ἡττᾶσθαι πολὺ
πρότερον ὑπὸ τῶν πραγμάτων δεῖ ἡττᾶσθαι.[21]

' Since Antisthenes set me (Diogenes) free I have no longer been
a slave.' 'How did he set you free?' 'Listen to what he says:
He taught me what things are my own concern [lit. 'mine'] and
what things are not my own concern: possessions are not my concern, nor kindred, nor family, nor friends, nor fame, nor familiar
places, nor the nature of my occupation; these, he pointed out, are
all alien to myself.' 'What, then, *is* your own concern?' 'The
use of appearances; in this, he showed me, I am free and subject
to no necessity; no one can hinder me, or compel me to use them
otherwise than as I will. Who then has any power over me? Philip,
or Alexander, or Perdiccas, or the Great King? Whence can they
obtain it? For one who is to be overpowered by men must long
before that have been overpowered by things?'

The luxury of poverty

The diners at Callias's banquet have agreed that each shall tell what it is that he is proudest of. " Of my wealth," says Antisthenes, when his turn comes.[22]

IV, 3. Xenophon, *Banquet,* IV, 34-44.

Ἀλλ' ἄγε δή, ἔφη ὁ Σωκράτης, σὺ αὖ λέγε ἡμῖν, ὦ Ἀντίσθενες, πῶς οὕτω βραχέα ἔχων μέγα φρονεῖς ἐπὶ πλούτῳ. Ὅτι νομίζω, ὦ ἄνδρες, τοὺς ἀνθρώπους οὐκ ἐν τῷ οἴκῳ τὸν πλοῦτον καὶ τὴν πενίαν ἔχειν ἀλλ' ἐν ταῖς ψυχαῖς. ὁρῶ γὰρ πολλοὺς μὲν ἰδιώτας, οἳ πάνυ πολλὰ ἔχοντες χρήματα οὕτω πένεσθαι ἡγοῦνται ὥστε πάντα μὲν πόνον, πάντα δὲ κίνδυνον ὑποδύονται, ἐφ' ᾧ πλείω κτήσονται, οἶδα δὲ καὶ ἀδελφούς, οἳ τὰ ἴσα λαχόντες ὁ μὲν αὐτῶν τἀρκοῦντα ἔχει καὶ περιτ-τεύοντα τῆς δαπάνης, ὁ δὲ τοῦ παντὸς ἐνδεῖται· αἰσθάνομαι δὲ καὶ τυράννους τινάς, οἳ οὕτω πεινῶσι χρημάτων ὥστε ποιοῦσι πολὺ δεινότερα τῶν ἀπορω-τάτων· δι' ἔνδειαν μὲν γὰρ δήπου οἱ μὲν κλέπτουσιν, οἱ δὲ τοιχωρυχοῦσιν, οἱ δὲ ἀνδραποδίζονται· τύραννοι δ' εἰσί τινες οἳ ὅλους μὲν οἴκους ἀναιροῦσιν, ἀθρόους δ' ἀποκτείνουσι, πολλάκις δὲ καὶ ὅλας πόλεις χρημάτων ἕνεκα ἐξανδραποδίζονται. τούτους μὲν οὖν ἔγωγε καὶ πάνυ οἰκτίρω τῆς ἄγαν χαλεπῆς νόσου. ὅμοια γάρ μοι δοκοῦσι πάσχειν ὥσπερ εἴ τις πολλὰ ἔχοι καὶ πολλὰ ἐσθίων μηδέποτε ἐμπίμπλαιτο. ἐγὼ δὲ οὕτω μὲν πολλὰ ἔχω ὡς μόλις αὐτὰ καὶ [ἐγὼ ἂν] αὐτὸς εὑρίσκω· ὅμως δὲ περίεστί μοι καὶ ἐσθίοντι ἄχρι τοῦ μὴ πεινῆν ἀφικέσθαι καὶ πίνοντι μέχρι τοῦ μὴ διψῆν καὶ ἀμφιέννυσθαι ὥστε ἔξω μὲν μηδὲν μᾶλλον Καλλίου τούτου τοῦ πλουσιωτάτου ῥιγοῦν· ἐπειδάν γε μὴν ἐν τῇ οἰκίᾳ γένωμαι, πάνυ μὲν ἀλεεινοὶ χιτῶνες οἱ τοῖχοί μοι δοκοῦσιν εἶναι, πάνυ δὲ παχεῖαι ἐφεστρίδες οἱ ὄροφοι, στρωμνήν γε μὴν οὕτως ἀρκοῦσαν ἔχω ὥστ' ἔργον μέγ' ἐστὶ καὶ ἀνεγεῖραι. ἂν δέ ποτε καὶ ἀφροδισιάσαι τὸ σῶμά μου δεηθῇ, οὕτω μοι τὸ παρὸν ἀρκεῖ ὥστε αἷς ἂν προσέλθω ὑπερασπάζονταί με διὰ τὸ μηδένα ἄλλον αὐταῖς ἐθέλειν προσιέναι. καὶ πάντα τοίνυν ταῦτα οὕτως ἡδέα μοι δοκεῖ εἶναι ὡς μᾶλλον μὲν ἥδεσθαι ποιῶν ἕκαστα αὐτῶν οὐκ ἂν εὐξαίμην, ἧττον δέ· οὕτω μοι δοκεῖ ἔνια αὐτῶν ἡδίω εἶναι τοῦ συμφέροντος. πλείστου δ' ἄξιον κτῆμα ἐν τῷ ἐμῷ πλούτῳ λογίζομαι εἶναι ἐκεῖνο, ὅτι εἴ μού τις καὶ τὰ νῦν ὄντα παρέλοιτο, οὐδὲν οὕτως ὁρῶ φαῦλον ἔργον ὁποῖον οὐκ ἀρκοῦσαν ἂν τροφὴν ἐμοὶ παρέχοι. καὶ γὰρ ὅταν ἡδυπαθῆσαι βουληθῶ, οὐκ ἐκ τῆς ἀγορᾶς τὰ τίμια ὠνοῦμαι (πολυτελῆ γὰρ γίγνεται), ἀλλ' ἐκ τῆς ψυχῆς ταμιεύομαι. καὶ πολὺ πλέον διαφέρει πρὸς ἡδονήν, ὅταν ἀναμείνας τὸ δεηθῆναι προσφέρωμαι ἢ ὅταν τινὶ τῶν τιμίων χρῶμαι, ὥσπερ καὶ νῦν τῷδε τῷ Θασίῳ οἴνῳ ἐντυχὼν οὐ διψῶν πίνω αὐτόν. ἀλλὰ μὴν καὶ πολὺ δικαιοτέρους γε εἰκὸς εἶναι τοὺς εὐτέλειαν μᾶλλον ἢ πολυχρηματίαν σκοποῦντας. οἷς γὰρ μάλιστα τὰ παρόντα ἀρκεῖ ἥκιστα τῶν ἀλλοτρίων ὀρέγονται. ἄξιον δ' ἐννοῆσαι ὡς καὶ ἐλευθερίους ὁ τοι-οῦτος πλοῦτος παρέχεται. Σωκράτης τε γὰρ οὗτος παρ' οὗ ἐγὼ τοῦτον ἐκτησάμην οὔτ' ἀριθμῷ οὔτε σταθμῷ ἐπήρκει μοι, ἀλλ' ὁπόσον ἐδυνάμην φέρεσθαι, τοσοῦτόν μοι παρεδίδου· ἐγώ τε νῦν οὐδενὶ φθονῶ, ἀλλὰ πᾶσι τοῖς φίλοις καὶ ἐπιδεικνύω τὴν ἀφθονίαν καὶ μεταδίδωμι τῷ βουλομένῳ τοῦ ἐν τῇ ἐμῇ ψυχῇ πλούτου. καὶ μὴν καὶ τὸ ἁβρότατόν γε κτῆμα, τὴν σχολὴν ἀεὶ ὁρᾶτέ μοι παροῦσαν, ὥστε καὶ θεᾶσθαι τὰ ἀξιοθέατα καὶ ἀκούειν τὰ ἀξιάκουστα καὶ ὃ πλείστου ἐγὼ τιμῶμαι, Σωκράτει σχολάζων συνδιημερεύειν.[23]

' Come, tell us, then, Antisthenes,' Socrates said, ' why it is that *you* boast of your riches, when you have so little.' ' Because, gentle-

---

[22] There is no reason to assume the literal authenticity of this or other speeches in Xenophon's dialogue. The passage is nevertheless contemporary evidence as to the sort of thing it would have been in character for Antisthenes to say on such an occasion.

[23] *Opera.* Ed. E. C. Marchant, Oxford, 2nd ed.

men,' he replied, ' I think that the wealth or poverty of men lies not in their houses but in their souls. For, in the first place, I see many men in private life who, though they have great possessions, yet think themselves so poor that they are willing to undergo any labor and risk any danger in order to get more. I know of brothers who have inherited equal fortunes, of whom one has enough and more than enough, and the other is in abject poverty. I observe certain tyrants, also, who so eagerly crave riches that they do far more shameful things than the neediest of men. It is true that poverty leads some men to thievery or housebreaking or slave dealing; but there are tyrants who, in order to enrich themselves, ruin whole families, slaughter multitudes, and even reduce whole cities to slavery. But for my part, I have great pity for those who suffer from so grievous a disease. For their condition seems to me like that of a man who, however much he possesses and eats, is never free from hunger. I, on the other hand, possess so many things that I myself hardly know where to find them. Nevertheless, when I am hungry, I have enough to eat until my hunger is satisfied, or when I am thirsty, enough to drink until my thirst is satisfied; and as for clothes, I don't suffer more from the cold when I am out of doors than this plutocrat Callias here. But when I am indoors, the walls seem to me a warm enough shirt and the roof a sufficient cloak; and I have such an abundance of bedclothes that it is hard to wake me up. And if my body ever has sexual needs, I am satisfied with whatever is at hand, so that the women to whom I go receive me kindly, since no other man desires them.[24]   And I find all these things so pleasant, that when I am experiencing any one of them I could wish the pleasure not increased but lessened — so much more enjoyable do some of them seem to me than it is good for them to be. But the thing that I think of most value in my sort of wealth is that, if anyone should deprive me of the goods I now possess, I should consider no labor so mean that it could not provide me with enough to live on. For when I wish to enjoy myself, I do not go and buy something at a high price — for the prices are extravagant — in the market-place; but I draw on the store-house of my soul. For there is much more pleasure in not eating until you are hungry than in enjoying costly luxuries like this Thasian wine, which I am drinking though I have no thirst. And it is pretty certain that they are honester men who prefer frugality to luxury; those who are content with what they have are least likely to crave what belongs to others. And it is worth considering, also, how generous this kind of wealth makes men — Socrates here, for example, from whom I acquired mine: he never counted or weighed any of it, but gave me as much as I could carry away. And so I too am now niggardly with no man, but show my bounty to all my friends and give to whoever wishes of the riches that are in my soul. Moreover, you see for yourselves how I am always in possession of that greatest luxury of all — leisure; so that I can see the things that are best worth seeing and hear the

---

[24] Diogenes Laertius, nevertheless (VI, 11), represents Antisthenes as an early eugenist: " The wise man will marry in order to have children by a woman of the best natural endowments, and such a one he will love; for only the wise man knows who are worthy to be loved." Cf. Joël, *op. cit.* II, 349 ff.

things best worth hearing — and, what I value most of all, can spend the whole day doing nothing but listen to Socrates talk.'

The life according to Nature

The following passages illustrate, among other things, the combination of an anti-hedonistic with a hedonistic strain in the Cynic conception of the life according to nature.[25] But the extreme anti-hedonism of the first citation is of dubious authenticity.

IV, 4. Eusebius, *Praeparatio evangelica,* XV, 13.

’Αντισθένης Ἡρακλεωτικός τις ἀνὴρ τὸ φρόνημα, ὃς ἔφη τοῦ ἥδεσθαι τὸ μαίνεσθαι κρεῖττον εἶναι· διὸ καὶ παρῄνει τοῖς γνωρίμοις μηδέποτε χάριν ἡδονῆς δάκτυλον ἐκτείνειν.[26]

Antisthenes was a man of Hercules' kind in the strength of his character. He said that it is better to be mad than to be pleased, and advised his disciples never even to stretch out a finger for the sake of pleasure.[27]

IV, 5. Diog. Laert. VI, 71.

δέον οὖν ἀντὶ τῶν ἀχρήστων πόνων τοὺς κατὰ φύσιν ἑλομένους ζῆν εὐδαιμόνως, παρὰ τὴν ἄνοιαν κακοδαιμονοῦσι. καὶ γὰρ αὐτὴ τῆς ἡδονῆς ἡ καταφρόνησις ἡδυτάτη προμελετηθεῖσα, καὶ ὥσπερ οἱ συνεθισθέντες ἡδέως ζῆν, ἀηδῶς ἐπὶ τοὐναντίον μετίασιν, οὕτως οἱ τοὐναντίον ἀσκηθέντες ἥδιον αὐτῶν τῶν ἡδονῶν καταφρονοῦσι. τοιαῦτα διελέγετο καὶ ποιῶν ἐφαίνετο, ὄντως νόμισμα παραχαράττων, μηδὲν οὕτω τοῖς κατὰ νόμον ὡς τοῖς κατὰ φύσιν διδούς· τὸν αὐτὸν χαρακτῆρα τοῦ βίου λέγων διεξάγειν ὅνπερ καὶ Ἡρακλῆς, μηδὲν ἐλευθερίας προκρίνων.[28]

[Diogenes said] that men ought to attain a happy life by choosing the labors that are according to nature, instead of stupid ones; but from their lack of intelligence they are unhappy. For the very contempt of pleasure, once we have grown used to it, is most pleasurable; and just as those who are accustomed to a voluptuous way of living do not willingly change to its opposite, so those who have by discipline become habituated to the opposite find a greater pleasure in their scorn of pleasures than in the pleasures themselves. Such were the things he used to say; and what he said he practised, really ' adulterating the current coin ' of custom,[29] giving to that

[25] The contention of K. von Fritz (*op. cit.* p. 44) that " the hedonistic element was first introduced into the picture of Diogenes's character at a later period " seems to us unconvincing. The same conjunction of two tendencies is also apparent in the speech of Antisthenes (No. 3) and in the characterization of Crates (No. 10); and there is in it no real inconsistency.

[26] Ed. Dindorf, 1867, II. Cf. Diog. Laert. VI, 3.

[27] This obviously is hardly in accord with the tone of the preceding and several of the following passages.

[28] Ed. R. D. Hicks.

[29] There is an often-repeated philosophic pun here. Legend had it that the father of Diogenes, a banker, had adulterated the coinage (νόμισμα); or, according to another version (among many), that the philosopher himself did so on the

which is in accord with law (or custom) no such regard as he gave to that which is in accord with nature, and declaring that his own manner of life was like that of Hercules, since he chose liberty in preference to everything else.

IV, 6.   Dio Chrysostom, *Orat.* VI, 30-34.

ὁπόσα μὲν οὖν πολυδάπανα καὶ δεόμενα πραγματείας καὶ ταλαιπωρίας, ταῦτα μὲν ἀφῄρει καὶ βλαβερὰ τοῖς χρωμένοις ἀπέφαινεν· ὅσα δὲ ῥᾳδίως καὶ ἀπραγμόνως ἔστιν ἐπικουρεῖν τῷ σώματι καὶ πρὸς χειμῶνα καὶ πρὸς λιμὸν καὶ πρὸς τὸ παῦσαί τινα ὄρεξιν τοῦ σώματος, οὐ παρέπεμπεν οὐδὲν αὐτῶν, ἀλλὰ καὶ τόπους ᾑρεῖτο τοὺς ὑγιεινοὺς μᾶλλον ἢ τοὺς νοσώδεις καὶ τοὺς εὐφόρους ἑκάστῃ ὥρᾳ, καὶ τροφῆς ὅπως εὐπορήσει τῆς ἱκανῆς ἐπεμελεῖτο καὶ ἐσθῆτος τῆς μετρίας, πραγμάτων δὲ καὶ δικῶν καὶ φιλονικιῶν καὶ πολέμων καὶ στάσεων ἐκτὸς ἦν. καὶ μάλιστα ἐμιμεῖτο τῶν θεῶν τὸν βίον· ἐκείνους γὰρ μόνους φησὶν Ὅμηρος ῥᾳδίως ζῆν, ὡς τῶν ἀνθρώπων ἐπιπόνως καὶ χαλεπῶς βιούντων. τὰ δὲ τοιαῦτα ἔφη καὶ τὰ θηρία διορᾶν. τοὺς μὲν γὰρ πελαργοὺς τὰ θερμὰ τοῦ θέρους ἀπολείποντας εἰς τὸν εὔκρατον ἀέρα ἀφικνεῖσθαι, καὶ διαγαγόντας ἐνταῦθα ὁπόσον ἥδιστον τοῦ χρόνου, μετὰ ταῦτα ἀθρόους ἀπιέναι, τὸν χειμῶνα ὑποχωροῦντας, τὰς δὲ γεράνους ἐπιφοιτᾶν τῷ σπόρῳ, χειμῶνα μετρίως φερούσας, καὶ τῆς τροφῆς ἕνεκα. τὰς δὲ ἐλάφους καὶ τοὺς λαγὼς τοῦ μὲν ψύχους εἰς τὰ πεδία καὶ τὰ κοῖλα καταβαίνειν ἐκ τῶν ὀρῶν, κἀνταῦθα ὑποστέλλειν τοῖς ἀπηνέμοις καὶ προσηνέσι, τοῦ δὲ καύματος εἰς τὴν ὕλην ἀποχωρεῖν καὶ τὰ βορειότατα τῶν χωρίων. ὁρῶν δὲ τοὺς ἄλλους ἀνθρώπους ἅπαντα μὲν τὸν βίον ταραττομένους, ἅπαντα δὲ ἀλλήλοις ἐπιβουλεύοντας, ἀεὶ δὲ ἐν κακοῖς ὄντας μυρίοις, μηδέποτε δὲ ἡσυχίαν δυναμένους ἄγειν, ἀλλὰ μηδὲ ἐν ταῖς ἱερομηνίαις μηδὲ ἂν ἐκεχειρίαν ἐπαγγέλλωσι, καὶ ταῦτα ξύμπαντα δι᾽ οὐδὲν ἕτερον τὰ μὲν δρῶντας, τὰ δὲ πάσχοντας, ἢ ὅπως ζῆν δυνήσονται, καὶ μάλιστα δὴ δεδιότας μήποτε αὐτοὺς ἐπιλίπῃ τἀναγκαῖα δὴ λεγόμενα, ἔτι δὲ φροντίζοντας καὶ ζητοῦντας ὅπως παισὶ τοῖς αὐτῶν καταλίπωσι πολλὰ χρήματα, ἐθαύμαζεν ὅτι μηδὲν αὐτὸς πράττοι τοιοῦτον, ἀλλὰ μόνος δὴ τῶν ἁπάντων ἐλεύθερός ἐστι καὶ οὐδεὶς ἄλλος συνίησι τῆς αὐτοῦ μάλιστα εὐδαιμονίας.[30]

[Diogenes] used to avoid everything that was costly or that involved trouble or much labor; such things, he showed, are harmful to those who use them. But if anything easily and without trouble helped the body to escape cold or hunger, or to satisfy any bodily appetite, he would by no means forgo it. On the contrary, he chose out places to live in that were healthful and adapted to the different seasons; and he took care to have sufficient food and a moderate amount of clothing. But from public business and lawsuits and contentions and wars and factions he kept clear. He imitated chiefly the life of the gods; for they alone, Homer says, live at ease — implying that the life of man is toilsome and hard. Even the beasts, he used to say, thoroughly understand these matters. The storks, for example, leaving the summer's heat, migrate to a

advice of the Delphian oracle. But νόμισμα means 'established usage' as well as 'coinage'; and in this sense, Diogenes, says the text, did as the oracle had bidden: he 'changed the currency.' It seems likely that the stories grew out of a pun used by Diogenes himself in one of his writings, not the pun out of the stories (cf. Diog. Laert. VI, 20-21; Julian, *Oration* VI, 188a, and K. von Fritz, *op. cit.* pp. 19-20).

[30] Ed. J. von Arnim, Berlin, 1893, I, pp. 89-90.

temperate clime; but after remaining there as long as it is comfortable, they depart in flocks before the advance of winter. Cranes, on the other hand, which bear winter-weather fairly well, revisit us at the seeding-time for food. Deer and rabbits come down from the mountains to the plains and valleys during the cold season, and take shelter in places where it is mild and there is no wind, but in summer withdraw into the woods and the most northern regions. When, then, he saw how other men spent their whole lives in disquiet, forever plotting against one another, always in the midst of a thousand ills, never able to attain peace, not even when a truce is declared during the great festivals; when he saw, too, that they did and suffered all these things merely for the sake of keeping alive and were, above all, in fear lest their so-called necessaries should fail them, and that, in addition to all this, they constantly schemed and struggled in order to leave riches to their sons — then he used to marvel at himself, that he did not behave as other men did, but was the one free man in the world, and that no one else understood how to attain his own greatest happiness.[31]

IV, 7. Diogenes: *Disputations,* in Stobaeus, *Florileg.* IX, 49.

οὐ γὰρ πειράσεται αὐτὸν ἀδικεῖν οὐδὲ καθ' ἕν μέρος. οὐδὲ γὰρ λύπης αὐτῷ
αἴτιός ἐστιν οὐδὲ νόσου· ἀλλὰ τὰ αἰσθητήρια τὰ τῆς φύσεως θεοὺς ὑπολαμ-
βάνων εἶναι, δικαίως χρήσεται αὐτοῖς, οὐδὲν μὲν ὑπὲρ τὴν δύναμιν πράττων,
φυλάττων δὲ τὰ μάλιστα καὶ ἡδονὰς καὶ ὠφελείας λαμβάνων διὰ τούτων. καὶ
γὰρ ἀπὸ ἀκοῆς καὶ ἀπὸ ὁράσεως καὶ ἀπὸ τῆς τροφῆς καὶ ἀπὸ τῶν ἀφροδισίων
ἡδοναὶ ἔσονται τῷ δικαίως ἑαυτῷ χρωμένῳ, τῷ δὲ μὴ δικαίως χρωμένῳ καὶ
κίνδυνοι γίνονται περὶ τὰ πλείστου ἄξια καὶ ἀναγκαιότατα.[32]

[A good man] endeavors not to harm himself in any way. For he does not cause himself either pain or disease; but, regarding the sense-organs which nature has given him as gods, he uses them rightly; and taking care not to exceed his powers, he derives from them pleasure and benefit. And so he who uses them rightly gets pleasure from seeing and from hearing, from food and from sex; while for him who uses them wrongly dangers arise from those things which are most valuable and necessary.

IV, 8. Diogenes, in Stobaeus, *Florileg.* CIII, 20.

Εὐδαιμονία γὰρ μία ἐστὶ τὸ εὐφραίνεσθαι ἀληθινῶς καὶ μηδέποτε λυπεῖσθαι,
ἐν ὁποίῳ δὴ ἂν τόπῳ ἢ καιρῷ ὑπάρχῃ τις.[33]

Happiness consists solely in this: that a man truly enjoy himself, and never be grieved, in whatever place or circumstances he may be.

[31] There is a similar passage at the opening of the same *Discourse* (1-17). Diogenes declares that his life is like that of the king of the Persians, except that it is more luxurious. He too changes his residence according to the seasons of the year, but has less far to travel, since he alternates only between Athens and Corinth. He is not neglectful of his body, as some stupid people suppose, but enjoys the pleasures of the senses more keenly than other men because he avoids surfeit and does not anticipate or stimulate his natural desires.

[32] Ed. A. Meineke, Leipzig, 1855, I.

[33] Ed. A. Meineke, 1856, IV.

IV, 9. Diog. Laert. VI, 104.

'Αρέσκει δ' αὐτοῖς καὶ λιτῶς βιοῦν, αὐτάρκεσι χρωμένοις σιτίοις καὶ τρίβωσι
μόνοις, πλούτου καὶ δόξης καὶ εὐγενείας καταφρονοῦσιν. ἔνιοι γοῦν καὶ
βοτάναις καὶ παντάπασιν ὕδατι χρῶνται ψυχρῷ σκέπαις τε ταῖς τυχούσαις καὶ
πίθοις, καθάπερ Διογένης, ὃς ἔφασκε θεῶν μὲν ἴδιον εἶναι μηδενὸς δεῖσθαι,
τῶν δὲ θεοῖς ὁμοίων τὸ ὀλίγων χρῄζειν.[34]

[The Cynics] hold that we should live simply, eating only such
food as any of us can readily obtain for himself,[35] and wearing only
a single garment. Wealth and reputation and high birth they
despise. Some, at least, are vegetarians, and drink only cold water,
and make use of any shelters that happen to be at hand — even tubs,
as Diogenes did, who used to say that the distinguishing characteristic of gods is that they need nothing, and of men who are like
gods, that they want but little.

IV, 10. Crates, *Fragm.* 40. In Plutarch, *De animi tranquillitate,* iv,
466.

Κράτης δὲ πήραν ἔχων καὶ τριβώνιον παίζων καὶ γελῶν ὥσπερ ἐν ἑορτῇ
τῷ βίῳ διετέλεσε.[36]

Crates, though he carried a beggar's wallet and wore a threadbare coat, went through life joking and laughing like one who is at
a festival.

' Sell all that thou hast '

When converted to the Cynic philosophy by Diogenes, Crates — according to the *Successions* of Antisthenes [37]—divested himself of all his worldly
goods.

IV, 11. Diog. Laert. VI, 87.

ἐξαργυρισάμενόν τε τὴν οὐσίαν—καὶ γὰρ ἦν τῶν ἐπιφανῶν—ἀθροίσαντα
πρὸς τὰ [ἑκατὸν] διακόσια τάλαντα, τοῖς πολίταις διανεῖμαι ταῦτα. αὐτὸν
δὲ καρτερῶς οὕτω φιλοσοφεῖν ὡς καὶ Φιλήμονα τὸν κωμικὸν αὐτοῦ μεμνῆσθαι.
φησὶ γοῦν·
      καὶ τοῦ θέρους μὲν εἶχεν ἱμάτιον δασύ,
      ἵν' ὡς Κράτης ᾖ, τοῦ δὲ χειμῶνος ῥάκος.
φησὶ δὲ Διοκλῆς πεῖσαι αὐτὸν Διογένη τὴν οὐσίαν μηλόβοτον ἀνεῖναι καὶ
εἴ τι ἀργύριον εἴη, εἰς θάλατταν βαλεῖν.[38]

He converted his landed property — for he came of a family of
high position — into money, and having thus got together about
two hundred talents, he distributed it to his fellow citizens. Moreover he lived the philosophic life so strenuously that he is mentioned
as an example of it by the comic poet Philemon, who says:

---

[34] Ed. R. D. Hicks, II.

[35] Lit. " self-sufficient foods; " the meaning may be " unbought," or " uncultivated,"
or even " consistent with the maintenance of αὐτάρκεια."

[36] Mullach, *Fragm.* II, p. 338.

[37] Not, of course, the Cynic philosopher but the historian of philosophy, Antisthenes of Rhodes.   [38] Ed. R. D. Hicks, II.

In summer he would wear a shaggy coat,
To be like Crates, but in winter rags.

Diocles, however, says that Diogenes persuaded him to turn his land
into sheep-pastures and throw whatever money he had into the sea.

A *Hymn to Frugality* by Crates opens:

IV, 12. *Fragm.* 4, in *Anthologia Graeca*.

> Χαῖρε θεὰ δέσποιν᾽, ἀνδρῶν ἀγαθῶν ἀγάπημα,
> Εὐτελίη, κλεινῆς ἔκγονε Σωφροσύνης.
> Σὴν ἀρετὴν τιμῶσιν, ὅσοι τὰ δίκαι᾽ ἀσκοῦσι.[39]

Hail, Lady Goddess, all good men's delight,
Frugality, fair Moderation's child!
All rev'rence thee who strive to do the right.

The happy city

IV, 13. Crates, in Diog. Laert. VI, 85.

> Πήρη τις πόλις ἐστὶ μέσῳ ἐνὶ οἴνοπι τύφῳ,
> καλὴ καὶ πίειρα, περίρρυπος, οὐδὲν ἔχουσα,
> εἰς ἣν οὔτε τις εἰσπλεῖ ἀνὴρ μωρὸς παράσιτος,
> οὔτε λίχνος πόρνης ἐπαγαλλόμενος πυγῇσιν·
> ἀλλὰ θύμον καὶ σκόρδα φέρει καὶ σῦκα καὶ ἄρτους,
> ἐξ ὧν οὐ πολεμοῦσι πρὸς ἀλλήλους περὶ τούτων,
> οὐχ ὅπλα κέκτηνται περὶ κέρματος, οὐ περὶ δόξης.[40]

There is a city, Pera, which wine-dark mists envelop; fair is it,
and fertile of soil, squalid in every way, and nought it possesses.
But into it never sails a fool, nor parasite, nor those who lust for
harlots' bodies. But thyme it yields and garlic, figs and wheaten
loaves; for such things men do not wage wars, nor take up arms
for money or for fame.

The Gospel of Work

IV, 14. Diog. Laert. VI, 2.

> Καὶ ὅτι ὁ πόνος ἀγαθὸν συνέστησε διὰ τοῦ μεγάλου Ἡρακλέους καὶ τοῦ
> Κύρου, τὸ μὲν ἀπὸ τῶν Ἑλλήνων, τὸ δὲ ἀπὸ τῶν βαρβάρων ἑλκύσας.[41]

[Antisthenes] showed that labor is a good by pointing to the
great Hercules and to Cyrus — taking one of his examples from
the Greeks and the other from the barbarians.[42]

IV, 15. Stobaeus, *Florileg.* XXIX, 65.

> Ἡδονὰς τὰς μετὰ τοὺς πόνους διωκτέον, ἀλλ᾽ οὐχὶ τὰς πρὸ τῶν πόνων.[43]

---

[39] Mullach, *Fragm.* II, p. 333.

[40] Ed. R. D. Hicks, II. There is a play upon words in the name Pera, which was
also the term for the characteristic emblem of the rigorous Cynic, the beggar's wallet.

[41] Ed. R. D. Hicks, II.

[42] In the list of the reputed works by Antisthenes given by Diogenes Laertius,
three have to do with Hercules and four with Cyrus, but these probably include
duplications, and the list is in general questionable.

[43] Ed. A. Meineke, Leipzig, 1855.

[Antisthenes].   The pleasures that come after labor are to be sought, but not those that come before it.

The vanity of the arts and sciences

IV, 16. Diogenes, in Dio Chrysostom, *Orat*. VI, 25-26, 28-30.

25. εἰς δὲ τὰς πόλεις συνελθόντας, ὅπως ὑπὸ τῶν ἔξωθεν μὴ ἀδικῶνται, τοὐναντίον αὐτοὺς ἀδικεῖν καὶ τὰ δεινότατα πάντα ἐργάζεσθαι, ὥσπερ ἐπὶ τούτῳ ξυνεληλυθότας. διὰ ταῦτα δὲ δοκεῖν αὐτῷ καὶ τὸν μῦθον λέγειν ὡς τὸν Προμηθέα κολάζοι ὁ Ζεὺς διὰ τὴν εὕρεσιν καὶ μετάδοσιν τοῦ πυρός, ὡς ἀρχὴν τοῦτο καὶ ἀφορμὴν τοῖς ἀνθρώποις μαλακίας καὶ τρυφῆς. οὐ γὰρ δὴ τοῦ Δία μισεῖν τοὺς ἀνθρώπους οὐδὲ φθονεῖν αὐτοῖς ἀγαθοῦ τινος. . . . 28. ἀλλὰ τὴν πανουργίαν τοῖς ὕστερον καὶ τὸ πολλὰ εὑρίσκειν καὶ μηχανᾶσθαι πρὸς τὸν βίον οὐ πάνυ τι συνενεγκεῖν. οὐ γὰρ πρὸς ἀνδρείαν οὐδὲ δικαιοσύνην χρῆσθαι τῇ σοφίᾳ τοὺς ἀνθρώπους, ἀλλὰ πρὸς ἡδονήν· διώκοντας οὖν τὸ ἡδὺ ἐξ ἅπαντος ἀεὶ ζῆν ἀηδέστερον καὶ ἐπιπονώτερον, καὶ δοκοῦντας προμηθεῖσθαι σφῶν αὐτῶν κάκιστα ἀπόλλυσθαι διὰ τὴν πολλὴν ἐπιμέλειάν τε καὶ προμήθειαν. καὶ οὕτως δὴ τὸν Προμηθέα δικαίως λέγεσθαι δεδεμένον ἐν πέτρᾳ κεῖρεσθαι τὸ ἧπαρ ὑπὸ τοῦ ἀετοῦ.[44]

[25] [Diogenes] said that men first came together in cities that they might not suffer wrong from those outside; but then they turned about and did all manner of wrong to one another and committed the most atrocious deeds, as though this had been the purpose of their coming together.   And the reason, as it seemed to him, why the myth says that Zeus punished Prometheus for the discovery and bestowal of fire was that that was the origin and starting-point of softness and luxury amongst men.   For Zeus surely did not hate men nor begrudge them any good. . . .   [28] But man's cleverness in having discovered and devised so many inventions has been of small benefit to the life of those of after times.   For men do not use their intelligence to promote manly virtue and justice, but in the pursuit of pleasure.   And so, from the very fact that they pursue it before everything else, their life becomes constantly less pleasurable and more wearisome; and while they imagine that they are exercising forethought about their own interests, they perish miserably through just this excess of care and forethought.   Thus Forethought [Prometheus] is altogether justly said to have been bound to the rock and to have had his liver torn out by the eagle.[45]

IV, 17. Diog. Laert. VI, 103.

ἀρέσκει οὖν αὐτοῖς τὸν λογικὸν καὶ τὸν φυσικὸν τόπον περιαιρεῖν . . . μόνῳ δὲ προσέχειν τῷ ἠθικῷ . . . παραιτοῦνται δὲ καὶ τὰ ἐγκύκλια μαθήματα. γράμματα γοῦν μὴ μανθάνειν ἔφασκεν ὁ Ἀντισθένης τοὺς σώφρονας γενομένους, ἵνα μὴ διαστρέφοιντο τοῖς ἀλλοτρίοις. περιαιροῦσι δὲ καὶ γεωμετρίαν καὶ μουσικὴν καὶ πάντα τὰ τοιαῦτα. ὁ γοῦν Διογένης πρὸς τὸν ἐπιδεικνύντα αὐτῷ ὡροσκοπεῖον, " χρήσιμον," ἔφη, " τὸ ἔργον πρὸς τὸ μὴ ὑστερῆσαι δείπνου."[46]

[44] Ed. J. von Arnim, Berlin, 1893, I, 88-89.
[45] For another example of the Cynics' disparagement of the typical culture-hero, Prometheus, cf. Dio Chrysostom's *Eighth Discourse*, 33.
[46] Ed. R. D. Hicks, II.

[The Cynics] hold that the subjects of logic and physical science may be dispensed with . . . It is to ethics alone that they give any attention. . . . They also omit even the studies of the ordinary school curriculum; Antisthenes used to say that those who have attained discretion ought not to learn to read, lest they be corrupted by the ideas of others.[47] They eliminate, likewise, geometry and music and all such studies. And so when somebody showed Diogenes a clock; ' a useful thing,' he said, ' to save you from being late for dinner.'

Natural diet

One of the acts by which Diogenes was reported to have shocked the Athenian sense of propriety was eating raw meat (according to one version, a squid) in the market-place (Diogenes Laertius, VI, 34) — though it did not agree with him.[48] Julian gives his interpretation of the philosophic purpose of the act.

IV, 18. Julian, *Orat.* VI, 191-193.

Τὴν σαρκοφαγίαν οἱ μὲν ἀνθρώποις ὑπολαμβάνουσι κατὰ φύσιν, οἱ δὲ ἥκιστα τοῦτο ἐργάζεσθαι προσήκειν ἀνθρώπῳ διανοοῦνται, καὶ πολὺς ὁ περὶ τούτου δείκνυται λόγος. ἐθέλοντι οὖν σοι μὴ ῥαθυμεῖν ἐσμοὶ περὶ τοῦ τοιούτου βίβλων φανήσονται. τούτους Διογένης ἐξελέγχειν ᾤετο δεῖν. διενοήθη γοῦν οὕτως· εἰ μὲν ἀπραγματεύτως ἐσθίων τις σάρκας, ὥσπερ οἶμαι τῶν ἄλλων ἕκαστον θηρίων, οἷς τοῦτο ἔνειμεν ἡ φύσις, ἀβλαβῶς αὐτὸ καὶ ἀνεπαχθῶς, μᾶλλον δὲ καὶ μετὰ τῆς τοῦ σώματος ὠφελείας ἐργάζοιτο, κατὰ φύσιν εἶναι πάντως τὴν σαρκοφαγίαν ὑπέλαβεν· εἰ δέ τις ἐντεῦθεν γένοιτο βλάβη, οὐχὶ τοῦτο ἀνθρώπου τὸ ἔργον ἴσως ἐνόμισεν, ἀλλ' ἀφεκτέον εἶναι κατὰ κράτος αὐτοῦ . . . αἰσθανόμενος οὖν ἴσως αὐτοῦ Διογένης ἐν μὲν τοῖς ἄλλοις ἅπασιν ἀπαθοῦς, ὑπὸ δὲ τῆς τοιαύτης ἐδωδῆς μόνον θραττομένου καὶ ναυτιῶντος καὶ δόξῃ κενῇ μόνον ἢ λόγῳ δεδουλωμένου· σάρκες γάρ εἰσιν οὐδὲν ἧττον, κἂν μυριάκις αὐτὰς ἑψήσῃ, κἂν ὑποτρίμμασι μυρίοις τις αὐτὰς καρυκεύσῃ· καὶ ταύτης αὐτὸν ἀφελέσθαι καὶ καταστῆσαι παντάπασιν ἐξάντη τῆς δειλίας ᾠήθη χρῆναι. δειλία γάρ ἐστιν, εὖ ἴσθι, τὸ γοῦν τοιοῦτον. ἐπεὶ πρὸς τῆς θεσμοφόρου [Δήμητρος] εἰ σαρκῶν ἡψημένων ἁπτόμεθα, τοῦ χάριν οὐχὶ καὶ ἁπλῶς αὐτὰς προσφερόμεθα, φράσον ἡμῖν. οὐ γὰρ ἔχεις ἕτερον εἰπεῖν ἢ ὅτι οὕτω νενόμισται καὶ οὕτω συνειθίσμεθα. οὐ γὰρ δὴ πρὶν μὲν ἑψηθῆναι βδελυρὰ πέφυκεν, ἑψηθέντα δὲ γέγονεν αὐτῶν ἁγνότερα . . . ἀλλ' ὅτι μὲν οὐ χαλεπὸν οὐδὲ

---

[47] So the MSS.; but it is possible that a negative has been omitted before σώφρονας: " Those who have not attained discretion." Alternative renderings of the concluding phrase might be " foreign literature " or " alien notions." In any case this anti-intellectualism of Antisthenes did not prevent him, if the list in Diogenes Laertius is even approximately correct, from writing some sixty essays and treatises, some of them apparently dealing with logical and physical questions. The passage also conflicts with what is recorded of the pedagogic methods of Diogenes (*ibid.* 29 ff. and 75); these, however, are regarded by K. von Fritz as derived from later educational writings, in fictional form, of which Diogenes was made the hero (*op. cit.* p. 22).

[48] One story ran that this dietetic indiscretion was the cause of Diogenes's death (Diog. Laert. VI, 76). It is probable, as Von Fritz has shown, that this is " a later version by a writer hostile to Diogenes " (*op. cit.* p. 30).

παράνομον οὐδὲ ἀσύνηθες ὑμῖν ὁ γενναῖος εἰργάσατο Διογένης, εἰ μὴ τῷ
σκληροτέρῳ καὶ μαλακωτέρῳ, ἡδονῇ τε λαιμοῦ καὶ ἀηδίᾳ τὰ τοιαῦτά τις ἐξετάζοι, πρόδηλον οἶμαι τοῖς ὁπωσοῦν ἕπεσθαι λόγῳ δυναμένοις. οὐκ ἄρα τὴν
ὠμοφαγίαν βδελύττεσθε οἱ τὰ παραπλήσια δρῶντες, οὐκ ἐπὶ τῶν ἀναίμων
μόνον ζῴων, ἀλλὰ καὶ ἐπὶ τῶν αἷμα ἐχόντων. καὶ τούτῳ δὲ ἴσως διαφέρεσθε
πρὸς ἐκεῖνον, ὅτι ὁ μὲν ἁπλῶς ταῦτα καὶ κατὰ φύσιν ᾠήθη χρῆναι προσ-
φέρεσθαι, ἁλσὶ δὲ ὑμεῖς καὶ πολλοῖς ἄλλοις ἀρτύσαντες ἡδονῆς ἕνεκα, τὴν
φύσιν ὅπως βιάσησθε. . . . Τῆς Κυνικῆς δὲ φιλοσοφίας σκοπὸς μέν ἐστι
καὶ τέλος, ὥσπερ δὴ καὶ πάσης φιλοσοφίας, τὸ εὐδαιμονεῖν, τὸ δὲ εὐδαιμονεῖν
ἐν τῷ ζῆν κατὰ φύσιν. . . .[49]

For men to eat meat is held by some to be in accordance with
nature, while others think that such food is not at all proper for
men. And about this question there has been much debate; if you
are not too lazy to look for them, you will find swarms of books on
the subject. These Diogenes thought it his duty to refute; at any
rate, his thought ran as follows: If one can eat meat without taking
trouble to prepare it, as can all other animals to which nature has
granted this diet, and if, also, one can do so without harm or discomfort — or rather, with actual benefit to the body — then he
thought that eating meat is entirely in accord with nature. But if
it should prove harmful he probably thought that it is not a practice
suitable for man, but is rather one which he must by all means
avoid. . . . Diogenes, then, saw, perhaps, that, since all other foods
caused him no discomfort and only raw meat gave him indigestion
and nausea, he was enslaved to vain opinion rather than reason;
for flesh is still flesh, though you cook it countless times and season
it with countless sauces. And this was the reason why he thought
that he should rid and free himself altogether of this cowardice —
for you may be sure that this sort of thing is cowardice. And in the
name of the law-giving Goddess [Demeter], tell us why, if we make
use of cooked meats, we do not use them in their raw state also. You
can give no answer, except that this has become a custom and a habit
with us. For manifestly it cannot be said that meat is by nature
disgusting before it is cooked and becomes more pure through cooking. . . . . . . It is now, I think, evident to those who are at all
able to follow an argument, that the excellent Diogenes was not
unreasonable nor regardless of custom and usage — unless one should
test such matters by hardness and softness and by the pleasure and
displeasure of his gullet. So, then, it is not really the eating of raw
food that disgusts you [the degenerate Cynics of Julian's age], either
in the case of bloodless animals or of those that have blood. But
perhaps there is this difference between you and Diogenes, that he
thought that he ought to eat such food raw and in its natural state,
whereas you think you must first prepare it with salt and many other
things for the sake of pleasure, whereby you do violence to nature. . . .
The object and end of the Cynic, as of all, philosophy is happiness;
but happiness consists in living according to nature.

Community of wives and children

IV, 19. Diog. Laert. VI, 72.

ἔλεγε δὲ καὶ κοινὰς εἶναι δεῖν τὰς γυναῖκας, γάμον μηδένα νομίζων, ἀλλὰ
τὸν πείσαντα τῇ πεισθείσῃ συνεῖναι· κοινοὺς δὲ διὰ τοῦτο καὶ τοὺς υἱέας.[50]

[49] Ed. Fr. C. Hertlein, Leipzig, 1875.   [50] Ed. R. D. Hicks, II.

He [Diogenes] said that there ought to be community of wives, considering marriage to consist in nothing but the union of the man persuading with the woman consenting. And for this reason he also thought that children should be held in common.

Incest not against nature

The passage, put into the mouth of Diogenes, may be based upon the play *Oedipus* attributed to him by Diogenes Laertius.[51]

IV, 20. Dio Chrysostom, *Disc.* X, 29-30.

ἔγνω γὰρ [Οἰδίπους] ὅτι τῇ μητρὶ συνεγένετο καὶ παῖδές εἰσιν αὐτῷ ἐξ ἐκείνης· καὶ μετὰ ταῦτα, δέον ἴσως κρύπτειν τοῦτο ἢ ποιῆσαι νόμιμον τοῖς Θηβαίοις, πρῶτον μὲν πᾶσιν ἐποίησε φανερόν, ἔπειτα ἠγανάκτει καὶ ἐβόα μεγάλα, ὅτι τῶν αὐτῶν πατήρ ἐστι καὶ ἀδελφὸς καὶ τῆς αὐτῆς γυναικὸς ἀνὴρ καὶ υἱός. οἱ δὲ ἀλεκτρύονες οὐκ ἀγανακτοῦσιν ἐπὶ τούτοις οὐδὲ οἱ κύνες οὐδὲ τῶν ὄνων οὐδείς, οὐδὲ οἱ Πέρσαι· καίτοι δοκοῦσι τῶν κατὰ τὴν Ἀσίαν ἄριστοι. πρὸς δὲ τούτοις ἐτύφλωσεν αὐτόν· ἔπειτα ἠλᾶτο τετυφλωμένος, ὥσπερ οὐ δυνάμενος βλέπων πλανᾶσθαι. καὶ ὃς ἀκούσας ἔφη, Σὺ μέν, ὦ Διόγενες, ἀναισθητότατον ἁπάντων ἀνθρώπων ἀποφαίνεις τὸν Οἰδίπουν· οἱ δὲ Ἕλληνες οἴονται οὐκ εὐτυχῆ μὲν γενέσθαι ἄνθρωπον, συνετὸν δὲ πάντων μάλιστα.[52]

'Oedipus discovered that he had had intercourse with his mother and had had children by her; whereupon — when he should, perhaps, have concealed this, or else have made it lawful for the Thebans — he first of all announced it to everybody, and then reproached himself and moaned loudly that he was father and brother to the same children, and husband and son of the same woman. But cocks do not see anything wrong in such unions, nor do dogs or asses, nor yet the Persians, who are considered the best people of Asia. And after this he put out his eyes and wandered about blind — as if he could not have wandered just as well with the use of his eyes.' At this one of the listeners said: 'Diogenes, you make Oedipus out to be the silliest of all men; but the Greeks think that, though he was not, indeed, a fortunate man, he was of all men the most intelligent.'

Anthropophagy not against nature

IV, 21. Diog. Laert. VI, 73.

Μηδ' ἀνόσιον εἶναι τὸ καὶ τῶν ἀνθρωπείων κρεῶν ἅψασθαι, ὡς δῆλον ἐκ τῶν ἀλλοτρίων ἐθῶν.[53]

[51] Sotion of Alexandria (2nd c. B. C.) whose *Successions* was one of the principal sources used by Diogenes Laertius, denied the authenticity of all the plays attributed to Diogenes; Satyrus, also of the second century, ascribed them to a pupil of Diogenes, Philiscus; and the same ancient historian of philosophy, and Sosicrates of Rhodes, declared that Diogenes left nothing in writing. This last view has been adopted by some modern scholars, but has not gained general acceptance. By whomever written, the seven plays in question appear to have been of early Cynic origin, and to have been satiric tragedies, or parodies of tragedies, not written for stage-representation. Cf. Diog. Laert. VI, 80 and Natorp in Pauly-Wissowa, s. v. "Diogenes," col. 769.

[52] Ed. J. von Arnim, 1893. Cf. Sext. Empir. *Hypotyp.* III, 205.

[53] Ed. R. D. Hicks, II. For other examples of the use of the *consensus gentium* as

[Diogenes said] that there is nothing wicked even in eating human flesh, as is evident from the customs of other nations.

A debate on the simple life

The authorship and date of this dialogue are uncertain. Long attributed to Lucian, it is regarded by most recent students of that author as spurious;[54] according to J. Bernays, it is probably the work of " a Cynic of the Byzantine period."[55] In any case it illustrates the persistent vitality of the ' hard ' or Cynic type of primitivism in later antiquity, as well as certain stock arguments against it which were still to be repeated in the eighteenth century by Voltaire and others; and because of its inclusion in the editions of Lucian it was one of the possible vehicles of the transmission of several elements of the primitivistic tradition to modern times.

IV, 22. Lucian, *Cynicus* (Translation on p. 140).

1. ΛΥΚΙΝΟΣ. Τί ποτε σύ, οὗτος, πώγωνα μὲν ἔχεις καὶ κόμην, χιτῶνα δὲ οὐκ ἔχεις καὶ γυμνοδερκῇ καὶ ἀνυποδητεῖς τὸν ἀλήτην καὶ ἀπάνθρωπον βίον καὶ θηριώδη ἐπιλεξάμενος καὶ ἀεὶ τοῖς ἐναντίοις τὸ ἴδιον δέμας οὐχ ὡς οἱ πολλοὶ διαχρησάμενος περινοστεῖς ἄλλοτε ἀλλαχοῦ εὐναζόμενος ἐπὶ ξηροῦ δαπέδου, ὡς ἄσην πάμπολλον τουτὶ τὸ τριβώνιον φέρειν, οὐ μέντοι καὶ τοῦτο λεπτὸν οὐδὲ μαλακὸν οὐδὲ ἀνθηρόν;

ΚΥΝΙΚΟΣ. Οὐδὲ γὰρ δέομαι· τοιοῦτον δὲ ὁποῖον ἂν πορισθείη ῥᾷστα καὶ τῷ κτησαμένῳ πράγματα ὡς ἐλάχιστα παρέχον· τοιοῦτον γὰρ ἀρκεῖ μοι.

2. σὺ δὲ πρὸς θεῶν εἰπέ μοι, τῇ πολυτελείᾳ οὐ νομίζεις κακίαν προσεῖναι;

ΛΥΚ. Καὶ μάλα.

ΚΥΝ. Τῇ δὲ εὐτελείᾳ ἀρετήν;

ΛΥΚ. Καὶ μάλα.

ΚΥΝ. Τί ποτε οὖν ὁρῶν ἐμὲ τῶν πολλῶν εὐτελέστερον διαιτώμενον, τοὺς δὲ πολυτελέστερον, ἐμὲ αἰτιᾷ καὶ οὐκ ἐκείνους;

ΛΥΚ. Ὅτι οὐκ εὐτελέστερόν μοι, μὰ Δία, τῶν πολλῶν διαιτᾶσθαι δοκεῖς, ἀλλ' ἐνδεέστερον, μᾶλλον δὲ τελέως ἐνδεῶς καὶ ἀπόρως· διαφέρεις γὰρ οὐδὲν σὺ τῶν πτωχῶν, οἳ τὴν ἐφήμερον τροφὴν μεταιτοῦσιν.

3. ΚΥΝ. Βούλει οὖν ἴδωμεν, ἐπεὶ προελήλυθεν ἐνταῦθα ὁ λόγος, τί τὸ ἐνδεὲς καὶ τί τὸ ἱκανόν ἐστιν;

ΛΥΚ. Εἴ σοι δοκεῖ.

ΚΥΝ. Ἆρ' οὖν ἱκανὸν μὲν ἑκάστῳ ὅπερ ἂν ἐξικνῆται πρὸς τὴν ἐκείνου χρείαν, ἢ ἄλλο τι λέγεις;

ΛΥΚ. Ἔστω τοῦτο.

ΚΥΝ. Ἐνδεὲς δὲ ὅπερ ἂν ἐνδεέστερον ᾖ τῆς χρείας καὶ μὴ ἐξικνῆται πρὸς τὸ δέον;

ΛΥΚ. Ναί.

ΚΥΝ. Οὐδὲν ἄρα τῶν ἐμῶν ἐνδεές ἐστιν· οὐδὲν γὰρ αὐτῶν ὅ τι οὐ τὴν χρείαν ἐκτελεῖ τὴν ἐμήν.

criterion of what is ' according to nature,' *vide* E. Weber, *De Dione Chrysostome*, etc. pp. 130-133.

[54] So Bernays, Croiset, Harmon. D. W. and F. G. Fowler, however, regard the arguments against authenticity of this dialogue as " unconvincing " (*The Works of Lucian of Samosata*, I, p. xiv). The attitude towards Cynicism is, however, quite opposite to that usual in Lucian's dialogues.

[55] Bernays, *Lucian und die Kyniker*, 1879, p. 105, n. 24.

4. ΛΥΚ. Πῶς τοῦτο λέγεις;

ΚΥΝ. Ἐὰν σκοπῇς πρὸς ὅ τι γέγονεν ἕκαστον ὧν δεόμεθα, οἷον οἰκία ἄρ᾽ οὐχὶ σκέπης;

ΛΥΚ. Ναί.

ΚΥΝ. Τί δὲ ἐσθὴς τοῦ χάριν; ἆρα οὐχὶ καὶ αὐτὴ τῆς σκέπης;

ΛΥΚ. Ναί.

ΚΥΝ. Τῆς δὲ σκέπης αὐτῆς πρὸς θεῶν τίνος ἐδεήθημεν ἕνεκα; οὐχ ὥστε ἄμεινον ἔχειν τὸν σκεπόμενον;

ΛΥΚ. Δοκεῖ μοι.

ΚΥΝ. Πότερ᾽ οὖν τὼ πόδε κάκιον ἔχειν δοκῶ σοι;

ΛΥΚ. Οὐκ οἶδα.

ΚΥΝ. Ἀλλ᾽ οὕτως ἂν μάθοις· τί ποδῶν ἔστ᾽ ἔργον;

ΛΥΚ. Πορεύεσθαι.

ΚΥΝ. Κάκιον οὖν πορεύεσθαί σοι δοκοῦσιν οἱ ἐμοὶ πόδες ἢ οἱ τῶν πολλῶν;

ΛΥΚ. Τοῦτο μὲν οὐκ ἴσως.

ΚΥΝ. Οὐ τοίνυν οὐδὲ χεῖρον ἔχουσιν, εἰ μὴ χεῖρον τὸ ἑαυτῶν ἔργον ἀποδιδόασιν.

ΛΥΚ. Ἴσως.

ΚΥΝ. Τοὺς μὲν δὴ πόδας οὐδὲν φαίνομαι χεῖρον διακείμενος τῶν πολλῶν ἔχειν.

ΛΥΚ. Οὐκ ἔοικας.

ΚΥΝ. Τί δέ; τοὐμὸν σῶμα τὸ λοιπὸν ἆρα κάκιον; εἰ γὰρ κάκιον, καὶ ἀσθενέστερον, ἀρετὴ γὰρ σώματος ἰσχύς. ἆρ᾽ οὖν τὸ ἐμὸν ἀσθενέστερον;

ΛΥΚ. Οὐ φαίνεται.

ΚΥΝ. Οὐ τοίνυν οὔθ᾽ οἱ πόδες φαίνονταί μοι σκέπης ἐνδεῶς ἔχειν οὔτε τὸ λοιπὸν σῶμα· εἰ γὰρ ἐνδεῶς εἶχον, κακῶς ἂν εἶχον. ἡ γὰρ ἔνδεια πανταχοῦ κακὸν καὶ χεῖρον ἔχειν ποιεῖ ταῦτα οἷς ἂν προσῇ. ἀλλὰ μὴν οὐδὲ τρέφεσθαί γε φαίνεται χεῖρον τὸ σῶμα τοὐμόν, ὅτι ἀπὸ τῶν τυχόντων τρέφεται.

ΛΥΚ. Δῆλον γάρ.

ΚΥΝ. Οὐδὲ εὔρωστον, εἰ κακῶς ἐτρέφετο· λυμαίνονται γὰρ αἱ πονηραὶ τροφαὶ τὰ σώματα.

ΛΥΚ. Ἔστι ταῦτα.

5. ΚΥΝ. Πῶς οὖν, εἰπέ μοι, τούτων οὕτως ἐχόντων αἰτιᾷ μου καὶ φαυλίζεις τὸν βίον καὶ φὴς ἄθλιον;

ΛΥΚ. Ὅτι, νὴ Δία, τῆς φύσεως, ἣν σὺ τιμᾷς, καὶ τῶν θεῶν γῆν ἐν μέσῳ κατατεθεικότων, ἐκ δὲ αὐτῆς ἀναδεδωκότων πολλὰ κἀγαθά, ὥστε ἔχειν ἡμᾶς πάντα ἄφθονα μὴ πρὸς τὴν χρείαν μόνον, ἀλλὰ καὶ πρὸς ἡδονήν, σὺ πάντων τούτων ἢ τῶν γε πλείστων ἄμοιρος εἰ καὶ οὐδενὸς μετέχεις αὐτῶν οὐδὲν μᾶλλον ἢ τὰ θηρία· πίνεις μὲν γὰρ ὕδωρ ὅπερ καὶ τὰ θηρία, σιτῇ δὲ ὅπερ ἂν εὑρίσκῃς, ὥσπερ οἱ κύνες, εὐνὴν δὲ οὐδὲν κρείττω τῶν κυνῶν ἔχεις· χόρτος γὰρ ἀρκεῖ σοι καθάπερ ἐκείνοις. ἔτι δὲ ἱμάτιον φορεῖς οὐδὲν ἐπιεικέστερον ἀκλήρου. καίτοι εἰ σὺ τούτοις ἀρκούμενος ὀρθῶς φρονήσεις, ὁ θεὸς οὐκ ὀρθῶς ἐποίησε τοῦτο μὲν πρόβατα ποιήσας ἔμμαλλα, τοῦτο δ᾽ ἀμπέλους ἡδυοίνους, τοῦτο δὲ τὴν ἄλλην παρασκευὴν θαυμαστῶς ποικίλην καὶ ἔλαιον καὶ μέλι καὶ τὰ ἄλλα, ὡς ἔχειν μὲν ἡμᾶς σιτία παντοδαπά, ἔχειν δὲ ποτὸν ἡδύ, ἔχειν δὲ χρήματα, ἔχειν δὲ εὐνὴν μαλακήν, ἔχειν δὲ οἰκίας καλὰς καὶ τὰ ἄλλα πάντα θαυμαστῶς κατεσκευασμένα· καὶ γὰρ αὖ τὰ τῶν τεχνῶν ἔργα δῶρα τῶν θεῶν ἐστι. τὸ δὲ πάντων τούτων ζῆν ἀπεστερημένον ἄθλιον μέν, εἰ καὶ ὑπὸ ἄλλου τινὸς ἀπεστέρητο καθάπερ οἱ ἐν τοῖς δεσμωτηρίοις· πολὺ δὲ ἀθλιώτερον, εἴ τις αὐτὸς ἑαυτὸν ἀποστεροίη πάντων τῶν καλῶν, μανία ἤδη τοῦτό γε σαφής.

6. ΚΥΝ. Ἀλλ᾽ ἴσως ὀρθῶς λέγεις. ἐκεῖνο δέ μοι εἰπέ, εἴ τις ἀνδρὸς πλουσίου προθύμως καὶ φιλανθρώπως ἔτι τε φιλοφρόνως ἑστιῶντος καὶ

ξενίζοντος πολλοὺς ἅμα καὶ παντοδαπούς, τοὺς μὲν ἀσθενεῖς, τοὺς δὲ ἐρρωμένους,
κἄπειτα παραθέντος πολλὰ καὶ παντοδαπά, πάντα ἁρπάζοι καὶ πάντα ἐσθίοι,
μὴ τὰ πλησίον μόνον, ἀλλὰ καὶ τὰ πόρρω τὰ τοῖς ἀσθενοῦσι παρεσκευασμένα
ὑγιαίνων αὐτός, καὶ ταῦτα μίαν μὲν κοιλίαν ἔχων, ὀλίγων δὲ ὥστε τραφῆναι
δεόμενος, ὑπὸ τῶν πολλῶν ἐπιτριβήσεσθαι μέλλων, οὗτος ὁ ἀνὴρ ποῖός τις
δοκεῖ σοι εἶναι; ἆρά γε φρόνιμος;

ΛΥΚ. Οὐκ ἔμοιγε.

ΚΥΝ. Τί δέ; σώφρων;

ΛΥΚ. Οὐδὲ τοῦτο.

7. ΚΥΝ. Τί δέ, εἴ τις μετέχων τῆς αὐτῆς ταύτης τραπέζης τῶν μὲν
πολλῶν καὶ ποικίλων ἀμελεῖ, ἓν δὲ τῶν ἔγγιστα κειμένων ἐπιλεξάμενος, ἱκανῶς
ἔχον πρὸς τὴν ἑαυτοῦ χρείαν, τοῦτο ἐσθίοι κοσμίως καὶ τούτῳ μόνῳ χρῷτο,
τοῖς δὲ ἄλλοις οὐδὲ προσβλέποι, τοῦτον οὐχ ἡγῇ σωφρονέστερον καὶ ἀμείνω
ἄνδρα ἐκείνου;

ΛΥΚ. Ἔγωγε.

ΚΥΝ. Πότερον οὖν συνίης, ἢ ἐμὲ δεῖ λέγειν;

ΛΥΚ. Τὸ ποῖον;

ΚΥΝ. Ὅτι ὁ μὲν θεὸς τῷ ξενίζοντι καλῶς ἐκείνῳ ἔοικε παρατιθεὶς πολλὰ
καὶ ποικίλα καὶ παντοδαπά, ὅπως ἔχωσιν ἁρμόζοντα, τὰ μὲν ὑγιαίνουσι, τὰ δὲ
νοσοῦσι, καὶ τὰ μὲν ἰσχυροῖς, τὰ δὲ ἀσθενοῦσιν, οὐχ ἵνα χρώμεθα ἅπασι πάντες,
ἀλλ' ἵνα τοῖς καθ' ἑαυτὸν ἕκαστος καὶ τῶν καθ' ἑαυτὸν ὅτουπερ ἂν τύχῃ
μάλιστα δεόμενος. 8. ὑμεῖς δὲ τῷ δι' ἀπληστίαν τε καὶ ἀκρασίαν ἁρπάζοντι
πάντα τούτῳ μάλιστα ἐοίκατε πᾶσι χρῆσθαι ἀξιοῦντες καὶ τοῖς ἁπανταχοῦ,
μὴ τοῖς παρ' ὑμῖν μόνον, οὐ γῆν οὐ θάλατταν τὴν καθ' αὑτοὺς αὐταρκεῖν
νομίζοντες, ἀλλὰ ἀπὸ περάτων γῆς ἐμπορευόμενοι τὰς ἡδονὰς καὶ τὰ ξενικὰ
τῶν ἐπιχωρίων ἀεὶ προτιμῶντες καὶ τὰ πολυτελῆ τῶν εὐτελῶν καὶ τὰ δυσ-
πόριστα τῶν εὐπορίστων, καθόλου δὲ πράγματα καὶ κακὰ ἔχειν μᾶλλον
ἐθέλοντες ἢ ἄνευ πραγμάτων ζῆν· τὰ γὰρ δὴ πολλὰ καὶ τίμια καὶ εὐδαιμονικὰ
παρασκευάσματα, ἐφ' οἷς ἀγάλλεσθε, διὰ πολλῆς ὑμῖν ταῦτα κακοδαιμονίας
καὶ ταλαιπωρίας παραγίνεται. σκόπει γάρ, εἰ βούλει, τὸν πολύευκτον χρυσόν,
σκόπει τὸν ἄργυρον, σκόπει τὰς οἰκίας τὰς πολυτελεῖς, σκόπει τὰς ἐσθῆτας
τὰς ἐσπουδασμένας, σκόπει τὰ τούτοις ἀκόλουθα πάντα, πόσων πραγμάτων
ἐστὶν ὤνια, πόσων πόνων, πόσων κινδύνων, μᾶλλον δὲ αἵματος καὶ θανάτου
καὶ διαφθορᾶς ἀνθρώπων πόσης, οὐ μόνον ὅτι πλέοντες ἀπόλλυνται διὰ ταῦτα
πολλοὶ καὶ ζητοῦντες καὶ δημιουργοῦντες δεινὰ πάσχουσιν, ἀλλ' ὅτι καὶ πολυ-
μάχητά ἐστι καὶ ἐπιβουλεύετε ἀλλήλοις διὰ ταῦτα καὶ φίλοις φίλοι καὶ πατράσι
παῖδες καὶ γυναῖκες ἀνδράσιν. [οὕτως οἶμαι καὶ τὴν Ἐριφύλην διὰ τὸν χρυσὸν
προδοῦναι τὸν ἄνδρα.] 9. καὶ ταῦτα μέντοι πάντα γίνεται, τῶν τε ποικίλων
ἱματίων οὐδέν τι μᾶλλον θάλπειν δυναμένων, τῶν δὲ χρυσορόφων οἰκιῶν οὐδέν
τι μᾶλλον σκεπουσῶν, τῶν δὲ ἐκπωμάτων τῶν ἀργυρῶν οὐκ ὠφελούντων τὸν
πότον οὐδὲ τῶν χρυσῶν, οὐδ' αὖ τῶν ἐλεφαντίνων κλινῶν τὸν ὕπνον ἡδίω
παρεχομένων, ἀλλ' ὄψει πολλάκις ἐπὶ τῆς ἐλεφαντίνης κλίνης καὶ τῶν πολυ-
τελῶν στρωμάτων τοὺς εὐδαίμονας ὕπνου λαχεῖν οὐ δυναμένους. ὅτι μὲν γὰρ
αἱ παντοδαπαὶ περὶ τὰ βρώματα πραγματεῖαι τρέφουσι μὲν οὐδὲν μᾶλλον,
λυμαίνονται δὲ τὰ σώματα καὶ τοῖς σώμασι νόσους ἐμποιοῦσι, τί δεῖ λέγειν;
10. τί δὲ καὶ λέγειν, ὅσα τῶν ἀφροδισίων ἕνεκα [πράγματα] ποιοῦσί τε καὶ
πάσχουσιν οἱ ἄνθρωποι; καίτοι ῥᾴδιον θεραπεύειν ταύτην τὴν ἐπιθυμίαν, εἰ μή
τις ἐθέλοι τρυφᾶν. καὶ οὐδ' εἰς ταύτην ἡ μανία καὶ διαφθορὰ φαίνεται τοῖς
ἀνθρώποις ἀρκεῖν, ἀλλ' ἤδη καὶ τῶν ὄντων τὴν χρῆσιν ἀναστρέφουσιν ἑκάστῳ
χρώμενοι πρὸς ὃ μὴ πέφυκεν, ὥσπερ εἴ τις ἀνθ' ἁμάξης ἐθέλοι τῇ κλίνῃ
καθάπερ ἁμάξῃ χρήσασθαι.

ΛΥΚ. Καὶ τίς οὗτος;

ΚΥΝ. Ὑμεῖς, οἳ τοῖς ἀνθρώποις ἅτε ὑποζυγίοις χρῆσθε, κελεύετε δὲ αὐτοὺς ὥσπερ ἁμάξας τὰς κλίνας τοῖς τραχήλοις ἄγειν, αὐτοὶ δ' ἄνω κατάκεισθε τρυφῶντες καὶ ἐκεῖθεν ὥσπερ ὄνους ἡνιοχεῖτε τοὺς ἀνθρώπους ταύτην, ἀλλὰ μὴ ταύτην τρέπεσθαι κελεύοντες· καὶ οἱ ταῦτα μάλιστα ποιοῦντες μάλιστα μακαρίζεσθε. 11. οἱ δὲ τοῖς κρέασι μὴ τροφῇ χρώμενοι μόνον, ἀλλὰ καὶ βαφὰς μηχανώμενοι δι' αὐτῶν, οἷοί γέ εἰσιν οἱ τὴν πορφύραν βάπτοντες, οὐχὶ καὶ αὐτοὶ παρὰ φύσιν χρῶνται τοῖς τοῦ θεοῦ κατασκευάσμασι;

ΛΥΚ. Μὰ Δία· δύναται γὰρ βάπτειν, οὐκ ἐσθίεσθαι μόνον τὸ τῆς πορφύρας κρέας.

ΚΥΝ. Ἀλλ' οὐ πρὸς τοῦτο γέγονεν· ἐπεὶ καὶ τῷ κρατῆρι δύναιτ' ἄν τις βιαζόμενος ὥσπερ χύτρᾳ χρήσασθαι, πλὴν οὐ πρὸς τοῦτο γέγονεν. ἀλλὰ γὰρ πῶς ἅπασαν τὴν τούτων τις κακοδαιμονίαν διελθεῖν δύναιτ' ἄν; τοσαύτη τίς ἐστι. σὺ δέ μοι, διότι μὴ βούλομαι ταύτης μετέχειν, ἐγκαλεῖς· ζῶ δὲ καθάπερ ὁ κόσμιος ἐκεῖνος, εὐωχούμενος τοῖς κατ' ἐμαυτὸν καὶ τοῖς εὐτελεστάτοις χρώμενος, τῶν δὲ ποικίλων καὶ παντοδαπῶν οὐκ ἐφιέμενος. 12. κἄπειτα εἰ θηρίου βίον βραχέων δεόμενος καὶ ὀλίγοις χρώμενος δοκῶ σοι ζῆν, κινδυνεύουσιν οἱ θεοὶ καὶ τῶν θηρίων εἶναι χείρονες κατά γε τὸν σὸν λόγον· οὐδενὸς γὰρ δέονται. ἵνα δὲ καταμάθῃς ἀκριβέστερον τό τε ὀλίγων καὶ τὸ πολλῶν δεῖσθαι ποῖόν τι ἑκάτερόν ἐστιν, ἐννόησον ὅτι δέονται πλειόνων οἱ μὲν παῖδες τῶν τελείων, αἱ δὲ γυναῖκες τῶν ἀνδρῶν, οἱ δὲ νοσοῦντες τῶν ὑγιαινόντων, καθόλου δὲ πανταχοῦ τὸ χεῖρον τοῦ κρείττονος πλειόνων δεῖται. διὰ τοῦτο θεοὶ μὲν οὐδενός, οἱ δὲ ἔγγιστα θεοῖς ἐλαχίστων δέονται. 13. ἢ νομίζεις τὸν Ἡρακλέα τὸν πάντων ἀνθρώπων ἄριστον, θεῖον δὲ ἄνδρα καὶ θεὸν ὀρθῶς νομισθέντα, διὰ κακοδαιμονίαν περινοστεῖν γυμνὸν δέρμα μόνον ἔχοντα καὶ μηδενὸς τῶν αὐτῶν ὑμῖν δεόμενον; ἀλλ' οὐ κακοδαίμων ἦν ἐκεῖνος, ὃς καὶ τῶν ἄλλων ἀπήμυνε τὰ κακά, οὐδ' αὖ πένης, ὃς γῆς καὶ θαλάττης ἦρχεν· ἐφ' ὅ τι γὰρ ἂν ὁρμήσειεν, ἁπανταχοῦ πάντων ἐκράτει καὶ οὐδενὶ τῶν τότε ἐνέτυχεν ὁμοίῳ οὐδὲ κρείττονι ἑαυτοῦ, μέχριπερ ἐξ ἀνθρώπων ἀπῆλθεν. ἢ σὺ δοκεῖς στρωμάτων καὶ ὑποδημάτων ἀπόρως ἔχειν καὶ διὰ τοῦτο περιιέναι τοιοῦτον; οὐκ ἔστιν εἰπεῖν, ἀλλ' ἐγκρατὴς καὶ καρτερικὸς ἦν καὶ κρατεῖν ἤθελε καὶ τρυφᾶν οὐκ ἐβούλετο. ὁ δὲ Θησεὺς ὁ τούτου μαθητὴς οὐ βασιλεὺς μὲν ἦν πάντων Ἀθηναίων, υἱὸς δὲ Ποσειδῶνος, ὥς φασιν, ἄριστος δὲ τῶν καθ' αὑτόν; 14. ἀλλ' ὅμως κἀκεῖνος ἤθελεν ἀνυπόδητος εἶναι καὶ γυμνὸς βαδίζειν καὶ πώγωνα καὶ κόμην ἔχειν ἤρεσκεν αὐτῷ, καὶ οὐκ ἐκείνῳ μόνῳ, ἀλλὰ καὶ πᾶσι τοῖς παλαιοῖς ἤρεσκεν· ἀμείνους γὰρ ἦσαν ὑμῶν, καὶ οὐκ ἂν ὑπέμειναν οὐδὲ εἷς αὐτῶν οὐδὲν μᾶλλον ἢ τῶν λεόντων τις ξυρώμενος· ὑγρότητα γὰρ καὶ λειότητα σαρκὸς γυναιξὶ πρέπειν ἡγοῦντο, αὐτοὶ δ' ὥσπερ ἦσαν, καὶ φαίνεσθαι ἄνδρες ἤθελον καὶ τὸν πώγωνα κόσμον ἀνδρὸς ἐνόμιζον ὥσπερ καὶ ἵππων χαίτην καὶ λεόντων γένεια, οἷς ὁ θεὸς ἀγλαΐας καὶ κόσμου χάριν προσέθηκέ τινα· οὕτωσὶ δὲ καὶ τοῖς ἀνδράσι τὸν πώγωνα προσέθηκεν. ἐκείνους οὖν ἐγὼ ζηλῶ τοὺς παλαιοὺς καὶ ἐκείνους μιμεῖσθαι βούλομαι, τοὺς δὲ νῦν οὐ ζηλῶ τῆς θαυμαστῆς ταύτης εὐδαιμονίας ἧς ἔχουσι περὶ τραπέζας καὶ ἐσθῆτας καὶ λεαίνοντες καὶ ψιλούμενοι πᾶν τοῦ σώματος μέρος καὶ μηδὲ τῶν ἀπορρήτων μηδέν, ᾗ πέφυκεν, ἔχειν ἐῶντες. 15. εὔχομαι δέ μοι τοὺς μὲν πόδας ὁπλῶν ἱππείων οὐδὲν διαφέρειν, ὥσπερ φασὶ τοὺς Χείρωνος, αὐτὸς δὲ μὴ δεῖσθαι στρωμάτων ὥσπερ οἱ λέοντες, οὐδὲ τροφῆς δεῖσθαι πολυτελοῦς μᾶλλον ἢ οἱ κύνες· εἴη δέ μοι γῆν μὲν ἅπασαν εὐνὴν αὐτάρκη ἔχειν, οἶκον δὲ τὸν κόσμον νομίζειν, τροφὴν δὲ αἱρεῖσθαι τὴν ῥάστην πορισθῆναι. χρυσοῦ δὲ καὶ ἀργύρου μὴ δεηθείην μήτ' οὖν ἐγὼ μήτε τῶν ἐμῶν φίλων μηδείς· πάντα γὰρ τὰ κακὰ τοῖς ἀνθρώποις ἐκ τῆς τούτων ἐπιθυμίας φύονται, καὶ στάσεις καὶ πόλεμοι καὶ ἐπιβουλαὶ καὶ σφαγαί. ταυτὶ πάντα πηγὴν ἔχει τὴν ἐπιθυμίαν τοῦ πλείονος· ἀλλ' ἡμῶν αὕτη ἀπείη, καὶ πλεονεξίας μήποτε ὀρεχθείην, μειονεκτῶν δ' ἀνέχεσθαι δυναίμην. 16. τοιαῦτά σοι τά γε ἡμέτερα, πολὺ δήπου διάφωνα τοῖς τῶν

πολλῶν βουλήμασι· καὶ θαυμαστὸν οὐδέν, εἰ τῷ σχήματι διαφέρομεν αὐτῶν,
ὁπότε καὶ τῇ προαιρέσει τοσοῦτον διαφέρομεν. θαυμάζω δέ σου πῶς ποτε
κιθαρῳδοῦ μέν τινα νομίζεις στολὴν καὶ σχῆμα καὶ αὐλητοῦ νὴ Δία γε σχῆμα
καὶ στολὴν τραγῳδοῦ, ἀνδρὸς δὲ ἀγαθοῦ σχῆμα καὶ στολὴν οὐκέτι νομίζεις,
ἀλλὰ τὴν αὐτὴν αὐτὸν οἴει δεῖν ἔχειν τοῖς πολλοῖς, καὶ ταῦτα τῶν πολλῶν
κακῶν ὄντων. εἰ μὲν δεῖ ἑνὸς ἰδίου σχήματος τοῖς ἀγαθοῖς, τί πρέποι ἂν
μᾶλλον ἢ τοῦθ’ ὅπερ ἀναιδέστατον τοῖς ἀκολάστοις ἐστὶ καὶ ὅπερ ἀπεύξαιντ’
ἂν οὗτοι μάλιστα ἔχειν; 17. οὐκοῦν τό γε ἐμὸν σχῆμα τοιοῦτόν ἐστιν,
αὐχμηρὸν εἶναι, λάσιον εἶναι, τρίβωνα ἔχειν, κομᾶν, ἀνυποδητεῖν, τὸ δ’ ὑμέτερον
ὅμοιον τῷ τῶν κιναίδων, καὶ διακρίνειν οὐδὲ εἷς ἂν ἔχοι, οὐ τῇ χρόᾳ τῶν ἱματίων,
οὐ τῇ μαλακότητι, οὐ τῷ πλήθει τῶν χιτωνίσκων, οὐ τοῖς ἀμφιάσμασιν, οὐχ
ὑποδήμασιν, οὐ κατασκευῇ τριχῶν, οὐκ ὀδμῇ· καὶ γὰρ ἀπόζετε ἤδη παραπλήσιον ἐκείνοις οἱ εὐδαιμονέστατοι οὗτοι μάλιστα. καίτοι τί ἂν δῴη τις
ἀνδρὸς τὴν αὐτὴν τοῖς κιναίδοις ὀδμὴν ἔχοντος; τοιγαροῦν τοὺς μὲν πόνους
οὐδὲν ἐκείνων μᾶλλον ἀνέχεσθε, τὰς δὲ ἡδονὰς οὐδὲν ἐκείνων ἧττον· καὶ
τρέφεσθε τοῖς αὐτοῖς καὶ κοιμᾶσθε ὁμοίως καὶ βαδίζετε, μᾶλλον δὲ βαδίζειν
οὐκ ἐθέλετε, φέρεσθαι δὲ ὥσπερ τὰ φορτία οἱ μὲν ὑπ’ ἀνθρώπων, οἱ δὲ ὑπὸ
κτηνῶν· ἐμὲ δὲ οἱ πόδες φέρουσιν ὅποιπερ ἂν δέωμαι. κἀγὼ μὲν ἱκανὸς καὶ
ῥίγους ἀνέχεσθαι καὶ θάλπος φέρειν καὶ τοῖς τῶν θεῶν ἔργοις μὴ δυσχεραίνειν,
διότι ἄθλιός εἰμι, ὑμεῖς δὲ διὰ τὴν εὐδαιμονίαν οὐδενὶ τῶν γινομένων ἀρέσκεσθε
καὶ πάντα μέμφεσθε καὶ τὰ μὲν παρόντα φέρειν οὐκ ἐθέλετε, τῶν δὲ ἀπόντων
ἐφίεσθε, χειμῶνος μὲν εὐχόμενοι θέρος, θέρους δὲ χειμῶνα, καὶ καύματος μὲν
ῥῖγος, ῥίγους δὲ καῦμα καθάπερ οἱ νοσοῦντες δυσάρεστοι καὶ μεμψίμοιροι
ὄντες· αἰτία δὲ ἐκείνοις μὲν ἡ νόσος, ὑμῖν δὲ ὁ τρόπος. . . . 19. ὁ δὲ τρίβων
οὗτος, οὗ καταγελᾶτε, καὶ ἡ κόμη καὶ τὸ σχῆμα τοὐμὸν τηλικαύτην ἔχει
δύναμιν, ὥστε παρέχειν μοι ζῆν ἐφ’ ἡσυχίας καὶ πράττοντι ὅ τι βούλομαι καὶ
συνόντι οἷς βούλομαι· τῶν γὰρ ἀμαθῶν ἀνθρώπων καὶ ἀπαιδεύτων οὐδεὶς ἂν
ἐθέλοι μοι προσιέναι διὰ τὸ σχῆμα, οἱ δὲ μαλακοὶ καὶ πάνυ πόρρωθεν ἐκ-
τρέπονται· προσίασι δὲ οἱ κομψότατοι καὶ ἐπιεικέστατοι καὶ ἀρετῆς ἐπιθυμοῦντες. οὗτοι μάλιστά μοι προσίασι· τοῖς γὰρ τοιούτοις ἐγὼ χαίρω ξυνών.
θύρας δὲ τῶν καλουμένων εὐδαιμόνων οὐ θεραπεύω, τοὺς δὲ χρυσοῦς στεφάνους
καὶ τὴν πορφύραν τῦφον νομίζω καὶ τῶν ἀνθρώπων καταγελῶ. . . .[56]

Lycinus.	You, there! what in the world are you, with your beard and long hair, shirtless, half-naked, barefoot — you who prefer a wandering and solitary life, more like a beast's than a man's; who, unlike most men, wear away your own body with hardships; who roam from place to place, sleeping alone on the hard ground, so that your threadbare cloak becomes covered with filth — though it was no delicate or soft or handsome garment to begin with?
Cynic.	For garments of that sort I have no use. The kind of cloak I have is easy to come by and gives its owner no trouble; so it is good enough for me. But tell me, don't you consider extravagance a vice?
Lyc.	Oh, yes.
Cyn.	And economy a virtue?
Lyc.	Yes, again.
Cyn.	Then, when you see me living more economically than other men, why do you blame me instead of them?

[56] Ed. C. Jacobitz, Leipzig, 1877, pp. 392 ff.

Lyc. Because I don't call your way of living more economical than other men's. I call it more destitute; in fact it is complete destitution and want. You are no better off than the beggars who cadge their daily bread.

Cyn. The question then comes to this: what is destitution and what is sufficiency? Shall we consider what the answer is?

Lyc. Yes, if you like.

Cyn. Shall we say that there is a sufficiency when a man's needs are satisfied? Have you any objection to that?

Lyc. Let it pass.

Cyn. And that there is want when what a man has falls short of his needs, when it does not satisfy his requirements?

Lyc. Yes.

Cyn. Very well, then, I am not at all in want; for there is not a thing that I have which does not satisfy my requirements.

Lyc. How so?

Cyn. Well, consider the purpose of anything we require. The purpose of a house, for example, is protection, isn't it?

Lyc. Yes.

Cyn. And clothes — what is their purpose? Protection too?

Lyc. Yes.

Cyn. But now, in God's name, what in turn is the purpose of the protection? Is it not that the protected shall be better off?

Lyc. I suppose so.

Cyn. Do you think, then, that my feet are worse off than yours?

Lyc. I don't know.

Cyn. Well, but consider, what are feet for?

Lyc. Walking.

Cyn. And do you think my feet walk worse than yours or most people's?

Lyc. No, perhaps not.

Cyn. They are not worse off, then, unless they do their work worse?

Lyc. Very likely not.

Cyn. So far as feet go, then, I appear to be no worse off than other people.

Lyc. No, I don't see that you are.

Cyn. Well, the rest of my body, then? If it is in a worse condition it must be weaker, since strength is the virtue of the body. Is mine weaker?

Lyc. Apparently not.

Cyn. It seems, then, that neither my feet nor the rest of my body need protection. If they did, they would be in a bad condition; for a need is always an evil and harmful to anything in which it is present. Again, my body does not appear to be any the worse nourished for being nourished on common food?

Lyc. Not at all the worse.

Cyn. It would not be healthy if it were badly nourished; for bad food injures the body.

Lyc. True.

Cyn. Well, since all these things are so, tell me on what grounds you blame me and disparage my manner of life and call it miserable.

Lyc. Why, on these grounds: Nature, which you honor, and the gods, have set the earth before us and given us out of it all manner of good things, which provide abundantly not merely for our needs but for our pleasures. But of none of these good things, or of hardly any of them, do you partake; you make no more use of them than the beasts. Your drink is water, like theirs; your food is what you pick up, as a dog's is; your bed is no better than a dog's, since a little straw is enough for either of you; and your clothes are no more presentable than a pauper's. Now if it is wisdom to be content with these things, God must have made a mistake when he made sheep woolly, and created grapes that yield sweet wine, and provided such a wonderful variety of oil and honey and the rest, so that we might have food of every sort, pleasant drinks, money, soft beds, fine houses, and all the other things that we have so wonderfully fashioned for ourselves — for the products of art are God's gifts too. To live without all these even under compulsion, as prisoners must, is miserable enough. It is far more so if a man deliberately deprives himself of all fine things: that is sheer madness.

Cyn. What you say may possibly be true. But tell me this: Suppose a rich man, out of a benevolent, humane and kindly disposition, gives a dinner for men of all sorts and conditions, some sick, others sound, the dishes being equally various; and suppose one of the guests helps himself to everything — not only to the eatables placed in front of him but also — though he is in good health — to those that are placed some way off and were intended for the invalids. Well, since he has after all only one stomach and needs but little to nourish him, it is quite certain that he will come to grief from partaking so liberally. Now what do you think of this gentleman? Is he a man of sense?

Lyc. Certainly not.

Cyn. Or of self-control?

Lyc. No.

Cyn. Suppose, now, there is another guest at the same table who, disregarding the number and variety of the dishes, chooses one close by him that is sufficient for his need, and eats moderately of it and of it alone, without so much as glancing at the rest: don't you consider him a better and more temperate man than the other?

Lyc. Certainly.

Cyn. Do you see the point, then, or must I explain it?

Lyc. What point?

Cyn. That God is like that generous host; he spreads before us many dishes of all kinds, so that each may have what is suitable for him: this for the healthy, that for the sick; this for the strong, that for the weak. They are not all meant to be eaten by everyone; each is to take what is in front of him, and of that only as much as he needs. But you and your kind are like that greedy and insatiable guest. You help yourselves to everything. Not content with what is near at hand, you reach out everywhere. Your own soil and seas are quite insufficient; you purchase your pleasures from the ends of the earth, always preferring the imported to the domestic article, the dear to the cheap, things that are hard to come by to those that can be had without trouble; in fact, you prefer to have troubles and annoyances, rather than to live without them. For all that costly array of means of enjoyment which you so gloat over is obtained only at the price of labor of the body and vexation of the mind. Consider, if you please, the gold that is so sought after, the silver, the luxurious houses, the elaborate clothing — and then remember through how much toil and trouble and danger these have been acquired — yes, and through how many men's blood and death and ruin. To bring these things to you, many seamen must perish; to find and fashion them, many laborers must endure misery. Nor is that all: conflicts often arise because of them, and the desire for them sets friend against friend, children against parents, wives against husbands. [In this way I believe Eriphyle also betrayed her husband for the sake of gold]. And all this goes on in spite of the fact that embroidered clothes are no warmer than others, houses with gilded roofs keep out the rain no better; a drink out of a silver cup — or a gold one, for that matter — is no more refreshing, and sleep is no sweeter on an ivory bed—the reverse, in fact, is true; your 'happy' man, between the delicate sheets on his ivory bed, is often unable to sleep. As for all the trouble that is devoted to the preparation of fancy dishes, it is needless to say that it contributes nothing to our nourishment; on the contrary, such dishes injure the body and breed diseases in it. No need, either, to mention all the things that men do and suffer for the sake of sexual gratification — though that desire is easy enough to satisfy, if one is not too fastidious about it. But it is not in this only that men show their madness and corruption; nowadays they pervert everything from its natural use — like a man who insists on treating a couch not as a couch but a carriage.

Lyc.   Does anybody do that?

Cyn.   Why, you do — you, who use men as beasts of burden, who make them bear your couch on their shoulders as a carriage, while you loll up there luxuriously, driving your men with reins like so many asses, and shouting gee! and haw! at them: and anyone who does so you consider a peculiarly happy fellow. Again, when people use edible things not for food but for making dyes — the murex, for example — are they not using the gifts of God in a way that is contrary to nature?

Lyc.   Not at all; the flesh of the murex can be just as well used for a dye as for food.

Cyn.   But it was not for that that it was made. You can force a mixing bowl to do the work of a stew-pot; but that is not what it was made for. — However, it is impossible to mention all the ways that such people have of being mad; the number is too great. And you reproach me because I will not join in this madness! *My* life is like that of the well-behaved guest I described; I fare excellently on whatever is placed before me, I enjoy the things that it costs least trouble to prepare, and I have no craving for all those numerous and variegated dishes.

Moreover, if you think that because I need and use but few things I live the life of a beast, you could by the same argument prove that the gods live worse than beasts; for they have no needs at all. But to understand more clearly what are the comparative advantages of having many and of having few needs, you have only to consider that children have more needs than grown people, women than men, the sick than the well, and in general, the inferior than the superior. Thus it is that the gods have no needs, and those men have the fewest who are nearest gods.

Take Hercules, the best man that ever lived, a divine man, and rightly reckoned a god. Was there something wrong with him, that he wandered about wearing nothing but a lion's skin, and felt no need of any of the things that you think needful? No, there was nothing wrong with him, who set right what was wrong with other men; nor was he poor who was master on land and sea. For in whatever he undertook he surpassed everyone else, and through all his life he never met a man who was his superior or equal. Do you suppose *he* went without sheets and shoes because he could not get them? No; but he had strength and endurance; mastery was what he wanted, not luxury.

And Theseus his pupil — king of the Athenians, son of Poseidon, as the legend says, the best man of his generation — he too chose to go naked and barefoot and to let his hair and beard grow; and not he only, but all the men of his time. They were better men than you; and they would no more have let any one shave their beards than a lion would. Soft smooth flesh was well enough, they thought, for women; but as for them, they were men, and preferred to look it. The beard they considered man's ornament, like a lion's or a horse's mane; just as God gave these appendages to those animals for beauty and adornment, so he gave beards to men. Now I admire the men of those early times and seek to imitate them; but I have not the least admiration for the present age and all that wonderful ' happiness ' that it enjoys — tables, clothes, bodies artificially polished and shaven all over, so that none even of their secret parts remain as nature made them.

My prayer is that my feet may be just like hoofs, like Chiron's in the story; that I may need bedclothes no more than the lion, and costly food no more than a dog. Let the whole earth be my sufficient bedchamber, the universe my house; and the food I would choose is that which is easiest to get. May neither I nor any friend of mine have need of silver or gold; for from the desire for these all human evils spring — factions and wars and conspiracies and murders. The source of all of these lies in the desire to have more. May that desire be far from me; may I never crave great possessions, but rather be able to endure poverty.

You see, then, what our aims are — very different from those of most men. Since our practical principles differ so widely from theirs, it is not surprising that we dress differently too. It seems curious to me that you allow a harpist his special costume — and even a flute-player his, and a tragic actor his — but will not recognize any costume for a good man; you think the good man ought to dress like the majority of men, in spite of the fact that the majority consists of bad men. Well, if the good are to have a costume of their own, can there be any more suitable than that which strikes the sensualist as most shocking, so that it is quite certain that *he* will not choose to wear it? Now *my* costume consists of a rough hairy skin, long hair, a threadbare cloak, and bare feet; but yours is like a male prostitute's. No one by looking at the two of you could tell you apart — either by the color of your cloaks or their texture or the number of your other garments or your shoes or the way your hair is dressed or your perfume. Yes, you even smell like those most 'happy' creatures. What value can be placed on a man of whom that can be said? So, too, you are no more given to work than they are, and no less given to pleasure. You eat like them, you sleep like them, you walk like them — except when you avoid walking, by having yourselves carried about like parcels by porters or animals. But as for me, my own feet carry me wherever I need to go. I am able to endure cold and heat alike, and so 'miserable' am I that I feel no discontent with any of the works of God; while you are so 'happy' that you are discontented with everything and grumble without ceasing. What is present you can't abide, what is not present you pine for — in winter for summer, in summer for winter; for cold when it is hot, for heat when it is cold. You are as querulous and hard to please as so many invalids; but the reason in their case is their illness, in yours is your character. . . .

This old cloak of mine that you laugh at, my long hair, my whole style, have this effect: they enable me to live a quiet life, to do what I want to do, to keep the company I want to keep. No ignorant and uneducated person will approach any one who dresses as I do, and nice people turn away as soon as they see me in the distance; but men of real refinement and reasonableness and character seek me out. They come to me because it is with such as they that I delight to associate. At the doors of your so-called 'happy' men I do not hang about. Their golden crowns and purple garments I regard as absurdities, and the men who wear them as ridiculous. . . .[57]

The Cynic life is that of the Golden Age

A philosophical essayist of the time of the Antonines, Maximus Tyrius was a not very critical eclectic who drew the elements of his doctrine more largely from Platonic than from other sources. Yet in one of his *Dissertations* he discusses and answers in the affirmative the question: " Whether the Cynic life is to be preferred? " and treats this as equivalent to the question whether the life of the Saturnian Age (interpreted chiefly in the spirit of hard primitivism) was superior to that of any subsequent period. Diogenes was a man who, living among the degenerate 'iron race,' exemplified the virtues and the happiness of mankind as it was when fresh from the hands of its creator, before its progressive corruption had begun. Prometheus, incidentally, appears in a rôle the reverse of his usual one: instead

---

[57] Two brief passages which are mainly repetitions have been omitted.

of culture-hero he is a deputy-creator whose handiwork, the human species, is spoiled by the introduction of the arts and of private property. Maximus's attempt to fuse the traditional materials which he brings together— especially the soft primitivism of the legend of the Golden Age and the Cynic rigorism — is weak and ineffective; on the other hand, the passage contains one of the more vigorous of ancient satires upon, nominally, civilized man, but perhaps by implication upon human nature as such. Maximus was not a consistent primitivist; *Diss. VI, What is knowledge?* contains a eulogy of the practical arts as an expression of the intelligence, though not of its highest form.[58]

IV, 23. Maximus Tyrius, *Diss.* XXXVI (Translation on p. 148).

. . . Ζεὺς ἦν καὶ οὐρανὸς καὶ γῆ· οὐρανῷ μὲν πολῖται θεοί· τὰ δὲ γῆς θρέμματα, οἱ ἄνθρωποι, οὔπω ποτὲ ἐν φωτὶ ἦσαν. Καλεῖ δὴ Ζεὺς Προμηθέα, καὶ αὐτῷ προστάττει κατανεῖμαι τῇ γῇ ἀποικίαν, ζῷον ἁπλοῦν, ʽκατὰ μὲν τὴν γνώμην ἐγγύτατα ἡμῖν τοῖς θεοῖς, τὸ δὲ σῶμα αὐτῶν ἔστω λεπτόν, καὶ ὄρθιον, καὶ σύμμετρον, καὶ ἰδεῖν ἥμερον, καὶ χειρουργεῖν εὔκολον, καὶ βαδίζειν ἀσφαλές.ʼ Πείθεται ὁ Προμηθεὺς Διί, καὶ ποιεῖ ἀνθρώπους, καὶ οἰκίζει τὴν γῆν. Οἱ δὲ ἐπεὶ γενέσεως ἐπελάβοντο, οὐ χαλεπῶς διέζων· καὶ γὰρ τροφὴν αὐτοῖς ἀποχρῶσαν γῆ παρείχετο, λειμῶνας δασεῖς, καὶ ὄρη κομῶντα, καὶ καρπῶν χορηγίαν, ὅσα γῆ φέρειν φιλεῖ μηδὲν ὑπὸ γεωργῶν ἐνοχλουμένη· . . . περιμάχητον δ' ἦν τούτων οὐδὲν ἐν ἀφθόνῳ τῇ τῶν αὐτομάτων χορηγίᾳ διαιτωμένοις. Δοκοῦσιν δέ μοι καὶ οἱ ποιηταὶ ἐγγύτατα εἶναι τῷ ἡμετέρῳ τούτῳ μύθῳ, ὑπὸ Κρόνῳ θεῶν βασιλεῖ τοιοῦτόν τινα αἰνιττόμενοι βίον, ἀπόλεμον, ἀσίδηρον, ἀφύλακτον, εἰρηνικόν, ἀπερίμαχητον, ὑγιεινόν, ἀνενδεᾶ· καὶ τὸ χρυσοῦν γένος τοῦτο, ὡς ἔοικεν, ὁ Ἡσίοδος καλεῖ, νεανιευόμενος πρὸς ἡμᾶς. Ἐμοὶ δὲ ὁ μῦθος ἀπελθὼν ἐκποδῶν, καὶ γενόμενος ἐκ μύθου αὐτὸ τοῦτο λόγος, προϊὼν παραβαλλέτω βίον βίῳ, τῷ προτέρῳ τὸν δεύτερον, εἴτε σιδηροῦν τις αὐτόν, εἴτε καὶ ἄλλῃ πη ὀνομάζων χαίρει, ἡνίκα ἤδη κληρουχήσαντες οἱ ἄνθρωποι τὴν γῆν, ἐπετέμοντο αὐτῆς ἄλλος ἄλλην μοῖραν, περιβάλλοντες αὐτοῖς ἕρκη καὶ τειχία, καὶ τὰ σώματα σπαργάνοις μαλθακοῖς καθειλίξαντες, καὶ τὼ πόδε σκύτεσιν χαρακώσαντες, καὶ χρυσὸν οἱ μὲν τοῖς αὐχέσιν, οἱ δὲ ταῖς κεφαλαῖς, οἱ δὲ τοῖς δακτύλοις περιαρτήσαντες, εὔφημόν τινα καὶ εὐπρόσωπον δεσμόν, καὶ στέγας οἰκοδομησάμενοι, καὶ κλεῖδας καὶ αὐλίους καὶ προπύλαια ἄττα ἐπιστήσαντες· καὶ παρέχοντες τῇ γῇ πράγματα, μεταλλεύοντες αὐτὴν καὶ σκάπτοντες καὶ ὀρύττοντες· καὶ μηδὲ τὴν θάλατταν κατὰ χώραν ἐῶντες, ἀλλὰ ἐπιτειχίσαντες καὶ ταύτῃ σκάφη πολεμιστήρια καὶ πορευτικὰ καὶ ἐμπορευτικά· καὶ μηδὲ τοῦ ἀέρος ἀπεχόμενοι, ἀλλὰ καὶ τοῦτον ληϊζόμενοι, τὰς ὀρνίθων ἀγέλας ἰξῷ καὶ ἕρκεσιν καὶ παντοδαπαῖς μηχαναῖς σαγηνεύοντες· ἀποσχόμενοι δὲ μήτε τῶν ἡμέρων ζῴων δι' ἀσθένειαν, μήτε τῶν ἀγρίων διὰ δέος, ἀλλὰ αἵματι καὶ φόνῳ καὶ λύθρῳ παντοδαπῷ γαστριζόμενοι· καὶ ἀεί τι ταῖς ἡδοναῖς εὑρίσκοντες νέον, καὶ τῶν ἑώλων ὑπερορῶντες· καὶ διώκοντες μὲν τὰ τερπνά, περιπίπτοντες δὲ τοῖς λυπηροῖς· πλούτου μὲν ὀρεγόμενοι, ἀεὶ δὲ τὸ παρὸν ἐνδεέστερον ἡγούμενοι τοῦ ἀπόντος, καὶ τό τε κτηθὲν ἔλαττον τοῦ προσδοκωμένου· δεδιότες μὲν ἔνδειαν, πληρωθῆναι δὲ μὴ δυνάμενοι· φοβούμενοι

---

[58] The Dissertations have been edited by H. Hobein (*Maximi Tyrii philosophumena*, Teubner, 1910), whose text (pp. 412-425) is here followed, with one alteration indicated below. There is an English translation by Thomas Taylor, the Platonist, 2 v. London, 1804 (*Diss.* XXXVI in vol. I, pp. 197-207).

μὲν θάνατον, μὴ φροντίζοντες δὲ τοῦ ζῆν· εὐλαβούμενοι νόσους, τῶν δὲ νοσερῶν οὐκ ἀπεχόμενοι· ὑποπτεύοντες μὲν ἄλλους, ἐπιβουλεύοντες δὲ τοῖς πλείστοις· δεινοὶ μὲν πρὸς τοὺς ἀνόπλους, δειλοὶ δὲ πρὸς τοὺς ὡπλισμένους· μισοῦντες μὲν τυραννίδα, τυραννεῖν δὲ αὐτοὶ ἐπιθυμοῦντες· ψέγοντες μὲν τὰ αἰσχρά, τῶν δὲ αἰσχρῶν οὐκ ἀπεχόμενοι· τὰς εὐτυχίας θαυμάζοντες, τὰς ἀρετὰς μὴ θαυμάζοντες· τὰς δυστυχίας ἐλεοῦντες, οὐκ ἀπεχόμενοι τῶν μοχθηρῶν· ἐν μὲν ταῖς εὐπραγίαις τολμηταί, ἐν δὲ ταῖς δυσπραγίαις ἀνάκλητοι· μακαρίζοντες μὲν τοὺς τεθνηκότας, γλιχόμενοι δὲ τοῦ ζῆν, μισοῦντες μὲν τὸ ζῆν, φοβούμενοι δὲ ἀποθανεῖν· προβεβλημένοι μὲν τοὺς πολέμους, εἰρήνην δὲ ἄγειν μὴ δυνάμενοι· ἐν μὲν δουλείᾳ ταπεινοί, ἐν δὲ ἐλευθερίᾳ θρασεῖς· ἐν μὲν δημοκρατίᾳ ἀκατάσχετοι, ἐν δὲ τυραννίδι ἐπτηχότες· παίδων μὲν ἐπιθυμοῦντες, γενομένων δὲ ὀλιγωροῦντες· εὐχόμενοι μὲν τοῖς θεοῖς, ὡς δυναμένοις ἐπαρκεῖν, καταφρονοῦντες δὲ ὡς οὐ δυναμένων τιμωρεῖν· καὶ δεδιότες μὲν ὡς κολάζοντας, ἐπιορκοῦντες δὲ ὡς οὐδὲν ὄντας.

Τοιαύτης τοίνυν στάσεως καὶ διαφωνίας τὸν δεύτερον τοῦτον κατεχούσης βίον, τίνι δῶμεν τὰ νικητήρια φέροντες; τίνα, ποῖον αὐτῶν φῶμεν ἁπλοῦν εἶναι βίον, καὶ ἀπερίστατον, καὶ ἐλευθερίας ἐπήβολον; καὶ ποῖον οὐχ ἁπλοῦν, ἀλλὰ ἀναγκαῖον, καὶ ἐλεεινόν, καὶ περιστάσεων γέμοντα; Φέρε ἐξ ἑκατέρων ἡκέτω τις ἡμῖν ἀνὴρ ἐπὶ διαιτητὴν τὸν λόγον· ὁ δὲ αὐτῶν ἐρέσθω ἑκάτερον, καὶ πρῶτον γε τὸν πρῶτον, τὸν γυμνὸν ἐκεῖνον καὶ ἄοικον καὶ ἄτεχνον, τὸν πάσης τῆς γῆς πολίτην καὶ ἐφέστιον· ἐρέσθω δὲ ἀντιτιθεὶς αὐτῷ τὸν τοῦ δευτέρου βίου καὶ τρόπου, πότερα αἱρεῖται μένειν ἐν τῇ πρόσθεν τροφῇ καὶ ἐλευθερίᾳ, ἢ τὰς τοῦ δευτέρου ἡδονὰς λαβὼν σὺν ταύταις καὶ τὰ λυπηρὰ ἔχειν; Ἴτω δὴ μετὰ τοῦτον ὁ ἕτερος· ἀντιτιθέτω δὲ αὐτῷ ὁ δικαστὴς τὴν τοῦ προτέρου δίαιταν καὶ ἐλευθερίαν· καὶ ἐρέσθω, πότερα αἱρεῖται τὰ αὑτοῦ ἔχειν, ἢ μετατίθεται καὶ μετοικίζεται ἐπὶ τὸν εἰρηναῖον ἐκεῖνον βίον καὶ ἄφετον καὶ ἀδεῆ καὶ ἄλυπον; Τίς τῶν ἀνδρῶν αὐτομολεῖ; τίς μετοικεῖ; τίς ἑκὼν ἀλλάττεται βίον βίου;

Τίς οὕτως ἀνόητος καὶ δύσερως καὶ κακοδαίμων ἀνήρ, ὥστε διὰ φιλίαν μικρῶν καὶ ἐφημέρων ἡδονῶν, καὶ ἀγαθῶν ἀμφισβητησίμων, καὶ ἀδήλων ἐλπίδων, καὶ ἀμφιβόλων εὐτυχημάτων, μὴ ἀνασκευάσασθαι, μηδὲ ἀνοικίσαι αὐτὸν εἰς ὡμολογημένην εὐδαιμονίαν; καὶ ταῦτα, εἰδὼς ὅτι ἀπαλλάξεται πολλαπλασίων κακῶν, ἃ τῷ δευτέρῳ τρόπῳ καὶ βίῳ ἀναπεφυρμένα, πῶς οὐ περιστατικὴν ποιεῖ κακοδαίμονά τε τὴν διαγωγὴν τοῦ βίου καὶ σφόδρα ἀτυχῆ; Ὥστε εἰκάσαιμ' ἂν ἔγωγε ἑκάτερον τῶν βίων, τὸν μὲν γενναῖον τοῦτον καὶ παντοδαπὸν δεσμωτηρίῳ χαλεπῷ κακοδαιμόνων ἀνδρῶν καθειργμένων ἐν ἀφεγγεῖ μυχῷ, πολὺν μὲν τοῖς ποσὶν σίδηρον περιβεβλημένων, βαρὺν δὲ κλοιὸν περὶ τῷ αὐχένι, κἀκ ταῖν χεροῖν ἐξηρτημένων δεσμὰ δυσχερῆ, ῥυπώντων, καὶ ἀγχομένων, καὶ ὀδυρομένων,[59] καὶ στενόντων· ὑπὸ δὲ χρόνου καὶ ἔθους εὐημερίας τινὰς ἑαυτοῖς ἔνδον καὶ εὐθυμίας μηχανωμένων, μεθυσκομένων ἐνίοτε ἐν τῷ δεσμωτηρίῳ, καὶ ᾀδόντων ἀναμίξ, καὶ γαστριζομένων, καὶ ἀφροδισιαζόντων, καὶ μηδὲ ἠρέμα ἑκάστου ἐμπιμπλαμένων διὰ δέος καὶ ἀπιστίαν καὶ μνήμην τῶν παρόντων κακῶν· ὥστε ἀκοῦσαι ἄν τις παρ' ἑκάστῳ δεσμωτηρίῳ οἰμωγῆς ὁμοῦ καὶ ᾠδῆς καὶ στόνου καὶ παιᾶνος. Τὸν δὲ ἕτερον αὖ βίον εἰκάζω ἀνδρὶ ἐν καθαρῷ φωτὶ διαιτωμένῳ, λελυμένῳ τὼ πόδε καὶ τὼ χεῖρε, καὶ τὸν αὐχένα πανταχοῦ περιστρέφοντι, καὶ τὰς ὄψεις πρὸς τὸν ἥλιον ἀνατείλαντ⟨α ἀνατείνοντ⟩ι, καὶ τοὺς ἀστέρας ὁρῶντι, καὶ διακρίνοντι νύκτα καὶ ἡμέραν, καὶ τὰς ὥρας τοῦ ἔτους ἀναμένοντι, καὶ τῶν ἀνέμων αἰσθανομένῳ, καὶ ἀέρα σπῶντι καθαρὸν καὶ ἐλεύθερον· ἀπεστερημένῳ δὲ τῶν ἔνδον ἐκείνων ἡδονῶν ὁμοῦ τοῖς δεσμοῖς, μὴ μεθυσκομένῳ, μηδὲ ἀφροδισιάζοντι, μὴ γαστριζομένῳ, μὴ στένοντι, μὴ

---

[59] Instead of ῥυττομένων, following Orelli, Meiser.

παιωνίζοντι, μὴ ᾄδοντι, μὴ οἰμώζοντι, μὴ ἐμπιμπλαμένῳ, ἀλλ' ὅσον ἀποζῆν
λεπτῷ καὶ διερρινημένῳ τὴν γαστέρα. Τίνα τῶν εἰκόνων μακαρίσωμεν; τίνα
οἰκτείρωμεν τῶν βίων; τίνα ἑλώμεθα; Τὸν ἐν τῷ δεσμωτηρίῳ, τὸν μικτὸν
ἐκεῖνον, τὸν ἀσαφῆ, πικραῖς καὶ ἐλεειναῖς ἡδοναῖς δελεασθέντες,

(Δ 450) ἔνθα δ' ἄρ' οἰμωγή τε καὶ εὐχωλὴ πέλεν ἀνδρῶν,
ἡδομένων ὁμοῦ καὶ στενόντων; Μὴ σύ γε, ὦ δειλαία ψυχή·

Ἀπολείπουσά μοι ταυτασὶ τὰς εἰκόνας αὐτοῖς μύθοις, ἴθι ἐπ' ἄνδρα, οὐ
κατὰ τὴν Κρόνου καὶ ἀρχὴν βιοτεύσαντα, ἀλλ' ἐν μέσῳ τῷ σιδηρῷ τούτῳ γένει,
ἐλευθερωθέντα ὑπὸ τοῦ Διὸς καὶ τοῦ Ἀπόλλωνος· Ἦν δὲ οὗτος οὐκ Ἀττικός,
οὐδὲ Δωριεύς, οὐδ' ἐκ τῆς Σόλωνος τροφῆς, οὐδ' ἐκ τῆς Λυκούργου παιδαγωγίας
(οὐ γὰρ χειροτονοῦσιν τὰς ἀρετὰς οἱ τόποι οὐδὲ οἱ νόμοι), ἀλλὰ ἦν μὲν
Σινωπεὺς ἐκ τοῦ Πόντου· συμβουλευσάμενος δὲ τῷ Ἀπόλλωνι τὰς περιστάσεις
πάσας ἀπεδύσατο, καὶ τῶν δεσμῶν ἐξέλυσεν αὐτόν, καὶ περιῄει τὴν γῆν ἄφετος,
ὄρνιθος δίκην νοῦν ἔχοντος, οὐ τύραννον δεδιώς, οὐχ ὑπὸ νόμου κατηναγκασ-
μένος, οὐχ ὑπὸ πολιτείας ἀσχολούμενος, οὐχ ὑπὸ παιδοτροφίας ἀγχόμενος,
οὐχ ὑπὸ γάμου καθειργμένος, οὐχ ὑπὸ γεωργίας κατεχόμενος, οὐχ ὑπὸ
στρατείας ἐνοχλούμενος, οὐχ ὑπὸ ἐμπορίας περιφερόμενος· ἀλλὰ τούτων
ἁπάντων τῶν ἀνδρῶν καὶ τῶν ἐπιτηδευμάτων κατεγέλα, ὥσπερ ἡμεῖς τῶν
σμικρῶν παίδων, ἐπειδὰν ὁρῶμεν αὐτοὺς περὶ ἀστραγάλους σπουδάζοντας,
τύπτοντας καὶ τυπτομένους, ἀφαιροῦντας καὶ ἀφαιρουμένους· . . . ἀλλ' οὕτως
ἄρα ἐθὰς ἦν τῇ τοῦ παντὸς φύσει, ὥστε ἐκ τοιαύτης διαίτης ὑγιεινός τε ἦν
καὶ ἰσχυρός, καὶ κατεγήρα εἰς τὸ ἀκρότατον· μηδὲν φαρμάκων δεηθείς, μὴ
σιδήρου, μὴ πυρός, μὴ Χείρωνος, μὴ Ἀσκληπιοῦ, μὴ Ἀσκληπιαδῶν, μὴ μάντεων
μαντευομένων, μὴ ἱερέων καθαιρόντων, μὴ γοήτων ἐπᾳδόντων. πολεμουμένης
δὲ τῆς Ἑλλάδος, καὶ πάντων πᾶσιν ἐπιτιθεμένων, (Γ 132) "οἳ πρὶν ἐπ'
ἀλλήλοισι φέρον πολύδακρυν Ἄρηα," ἐκεχειρίαν ἦγεν μόνος, ἐν ὡπλισμένοις
ἄοπλος, ἐν μαχομένοις ἔνσπονδος πᾶσιν.[60]

Zeus existed, and heaven and earth, and in heaven its citizens,
the gods; but the nurselings of earth, men, had not yet seen the
light of day. Zeus therefore called Prometheus and bade him settle
upon the earth an animal which should be simple, 'in mind
approaching very near to the gods, in body slender, erect and sym-
metrical, mild of aspect, apt for handicraft, firm of step.' Prometheus obeyed the command of Zeus, and made men and settled the
earth with them. And when the creation of them was completed,
they lived without difficulty. For the earth provided them with
food in abundance, grassy meadows and leafy mountains and plenti-
ful fruits, such as she is wont to bear when undisturbed by husbandmen. . . . Among men thus enjoying an unlimited wealth of goods
freely furnished them, strife was unknown. The poets seem to me
to have come very close to this myth of ours when, speaking in
parables, they describe a life of this kind under Saturn, king of
the gods; a life without war, without weapons, without guards,
quiet, peaceful, healthful, free from poverty. And it was this, it
seems, that Hesiod, speaking of it in a boastful way in comparison
with us, called the Golden Race.

But here I leave the myth. Let us turn to the argument which
arises from it, and proceed to compare one manner of life with
another, the earlier with the later, whether this be called 'iron' or
by some other name. When, then, men, having the earth allotted

[60] Ed. H. Hobein, Leipzig, 1910.

to them, divided it up in portions amongst themselves, they surrounded themselves with walls and fortifications, and wrapped soft cloths about their bodies, and protected their feet with skins; and some hung gold about their necks, others about their heads, others about their fingers, as a kind of charm, both for luck and for ornament; and they built themselves houses, and invented locks and halls and gateways. They began, also, to molest the earth by digging and burrowing in it for metals; nor did they leave the sea unvexed, but constructed on it ships for war and travel and trade. Even the air they could not let alone, but plundered it by catching birds with bird-lime and nets and all manner of devices. They abstained neither from tame animals on account of their weakness, nor from wild ones because they were dangerous, but filled their bellies through slaughter and bloodshed and ravin of every sort. And always they sought for new kinds of enjoyment, disdaining those to which they were accustomed. By thus pursuing pleasure, they fell into misery. When they sought after wealth, they always considered what they already possessed as mere poverty in comparison with what they lacked, and their acquisitions always fell short of their ambitions. Dreading poverty, they were incapable of being content with sufficiency; fearing death, they took no care of life; seeking to avoid disease, they never abstained from the things that cause it. Full of mutual suspicions, they plotted against most of their fellows. They were cruel to the unarmed and craven towards the armed. They hated tyranny and themselves desired to tyrannize; they blamed base actions but did not refrain from them. Good fortune they admired but not virtue; misfortune they pitied but knavery they did not avoid. When luck was with them they were bold, when it turned against them they were in despair. They declared that the dead are happy, yet themselves clung to life; and on the other hand they hated life, yet were afraid to die. They denounced wars and were incapable of living in peace. In slavery they were abject, in freedom insolent. Under democracy they were turbulent, under tyranny, timid. They desired children, but neglected them when they had them. They prayed to the gods, as to beings able to assist them, they scorned them, as unable to punish; or again, they feared them as avenging powers, and swore falsely, as if the gods had no existence.

Such, then, being the discord and dissension characteristic of this second kind of life, to which of the two shall we give the prize of victory? Which of them shall we say is the simple life, exempt from difficulties, and of ample liberty, and which the life that is not simple, but constrained, pitiable, full of difficulties? Let a representative of each of them come forward, so that the question may be put to the judgment. Let both be interrogated — first the man who lived the first kind of life, naked, without a house, without arts, who has the whole earth for his city and household. Let us put before him the contrast between his own and the other manner of existence, and ask him whether he prefers to continue in his former way of living and in liberty, or to gain the pleasures of the second sort of life at the cost of the evils which accompany them. After him, let the other present himself, and let the judge put before him, in contrast, the mode of life and the liberty of the former, and then ask him whether he prefers to remain as he is, or to change over to that peaceful and unrestrained life, exempt from fear and from suffering. Which of these men is the one who will prove the deserter? which will leave his dwelling-place? which will voluntarily exchange one mode of life for the other? Who is so stupid and insensible and wretched that, through love of small and ephemeral pleasures, dubious goods, uncertain hopes, and equivocal successes, he will not remove and migrate to what is admittedly a state of happiness; especially since he knows that he will by this means be freed from a multitude of evils which are involved in the second kind of life, and knows, too, how troublous and wretched and hapless existence is made by them?

To describe each of these lives by a simile: that 'noble' [61] and variegated kind is like a dreadful prison in which unhappy men, confined in a dark cell, with great irons on their feet, heavy weights about their necks, and grievous fetters on their hands, pass their days in filth, in torment, in weeping [62] and groaning. Nevertheless, through time and custom they devise for themselves, even in their prison, certain means of relief and enjoyment — sometimes by getting drunk, sometimes by all singing at once, sometimes by gourmandizing, sometimes by sexual indulgence. Yet fear and distrust and the recollection of the evils that are present to them prevent them from ever being quietly satisfied with these things; so that you may hear in the prison at one and the same time groans and songs of triumph, lamentation and rejoicing. But the other sort of life I will liken to that of a man living in the clear light of day, whose hands and feet are free, who can turn his neck in any direction, can lift his eyes to the rising sun, look at the stars, distinguish night from day, look forward to the changes of the seasons, feel the winds, and breathe the pure, free air. On the other hand, he is deprived of the pleasures which accompanied his confinement in the prison; so that he neither becomes intoxicated, nor is given to sexual indulgence, nor over-eats, nor groans, nor sings songs of triumph, nor laments, nor is satiated, but finds sufficient sustenance in a spare and meagre diet. Which of these shall we consider the image of happiness? Which sort of life shall we pity? Which shall we choose? Shall it be life in the prison, mixed and obscure as it is, ensnared in bitter and pitiful pleasures:

Where joyful shouts and groans promiscuous rise,[63]

from men who rejoice and weep at the same time? Let not such be *thy* choice, O fearful soul!

Let us, however, leave both similes and myths, and turn to a man who, though he lived, not in the reign of Saturn, but in the midst of this iron race, was nevertheless set free by Zeus and Apollo. This man was not Attic nor Dorian, he was not reared by Solon nor taught by Lycurgus (for the virtues do not depend upon the suffrages of places or of laws), but was a native of Sinope in Pontus.

---

[61] The text seems dubious; if the reading γενναῖον is accepted, it must be construed as ironical.

[62] Reading, with Meiser, in 125 a 20, ὀδυρομένων instead of ῥυττομένων.

[63] *Iliad*, IV, 450.

After he had taken counsel of Apollo, he divested himself of all unfavorable circumstances, freed himself from bonds and moved about the earth without ties, like a bird endowed with reason — fearing no tyrant, constrained by no law, occupied with no state's business, unencumbered by the care of children, unhampered by marriage, not fastened to a farm nor burdened with military affairs nor driven from one place to another by trade. Rather, he laughed at all such men and at their pursuits, as we laugh at little children when we see them quarreling over their playthings, beating one another and being beaten, plundering and being plundered.

[The eulogy of Diogenes continues in the usual vein; it consists largely of echoes of passages of Dio Chrysostom [64] and other earlier writers; two sentences will suffice for illustration.]

He was so adjusted to the nature of the universe that from this mode of life he became healthy and strong, and lived to a ripe old age, having no need of medicine, nor of the knife, nor of fire, nor of Chiron, nor of Aesculapius or his descendants, nor of the oracles of soothsayers, the lustrations of priests or the incantations of sorcerers. And when Greece was at war, and everyone was attacking someone else—

' Each against each then strove in dreadful fight ' [65] —

he alone maintained an armistice, moving unarmed among the armed and at peace with all the combattants.

Cynicism the primitive and universal philosophy

In the late fourth century A. D. we find Cynicism identified with the original and universal ' philosophy of nature ' — the truths known to all men from the beginning — in precisely the sense in which in the eighteenth century deism was presented by its adherents as the ' religion of nature.' Much as the Emperor Julian revered Antisthenes and Diogenes, he could not admit that they, or even Hercules, originated so ' natural ' a doctrine.

IV, 24. Julian, *Orat.* VI, 187.

λέγουσι μὲν γὰρ οἱ γενναιότεροι τῶν κυνῶν, ὅτι καὶ ὁ μέγας Ἡρακλῆς, ὥσπερ οὖν τῶν ἄλλων ἀγαθῶν ἡμῖν τις αἴτιος κατέστη, οὕτω δὲ καὶ τούτου τοῦ βίου παράδειγμα τὸ μέγιστον οὗτος κατέλιπεν ἀνθρώποις. ἐγὼ δὲ ὑπὲρ τῶν θεῶν καὶ τῶν εἰς θείαν λῆξιν πορευθέντων εὐφημεῖν ἐθέλων πείθομαι μὲν καὶ πρὸ τούτου τινὰς οὐκ ἐν Ἕλλησι μόνον, ἀλλὰ καὶ βαρβάροις οὕτω φιλοφῆσαι. αὕτη γὰρ ἡ φιλοσοφία κοινή πως ἔοικεν εἶναι καὶ φυσικωτάτη καὶ δεῖσθαι οὐδ' ἡστινοσοῦν πραγματείας.[66]

The nobler Cynics say that, as there has been someone who has been the cause of our other goods, so it was the great Hercules who left to men the greatest example of this way of life. But for my part, while I desire to speak with reverence of the gods and of those

---

[64] On the relation of Maximus to Dio, cf. A. E. Weber, *op. cit.* p. 121 f.

[65] *Iliad*, III, 132.

[66] Ed. Fr. C. Hertlein, Leipzig, 1875.

who have passed over to the condition of gods, I nevertheless believe that even before Hercules there were men, not only among the Greeks but among the barbarians also, who adhered to this philosophy. For it seems to be in some sense a universal philosophy, and the most natural of any, and to demand no special study whatsoever.

B. EPICUREANISM AND THE SIMPLE LIFE

No ancient ethical system was to be so commonly interpreted in modern times in the light of the libels of its adversaries as Epicureanism. The fact concerning the moral teaching of Epicurus — evident in both of the two principal sources of our knowledge of it, Cicero and Diogenes Laertius (Bk. X) — which is pertinent here is that it was second only to Cynicism in its demand for the cultivation of indifference to all the objects commonly sought after by men except those for which the desire is both 'natural' and 'necessary.' Thus there was in it a strain of hard moral primitivism based on hedonistic premises. Man's real needs are few, and nature has made the attainment of them easy and simple; and those who set their hearts upon more than these will never attain happiness. Without the exhibitionism of Diogenes, and without the Cynic's delight in shocking other men's sense of propriety, Epicurus inculcated in a more moderate tone much the same discipline of the desires, and in part on the same grounds. Like the Cynic, the Epicurean did not necessarily refuse good viands and the like if they occasionally came to him without desire or effort on his part, but the aim of his life was the 'self-sufficiency' which enabled him to live in complete contentment without these or any luxuries; and he cultivated the same scorn for reputation and distinction.[67]

IV, 25. Epicurus, *Epist.* III in Diog. Laert. X, 130-131.

τῇ μέντοι συμμετρήσει καὶ συμφερόντων καὶ ἀσυμφόρων βλέψει ταῦτα πάντα κρίνειν καθήκει· χρώμεθα γὰρ τῷ μὲν ἀγαθῷ κατά τινας χρόνους ὡς κακῷ, τῷ δὲ κακῷ τἄμπαλιν ὡς ἀγαθῷ. καὶ τὴν αὐτάρκειαν δὲ ἀγαθὸν μέγα νομίζομεν, οὐχ ἵνα πάντως τοῖς ὀλίγοις χρώμεθα, ἀλλ᾽ ὅπως ἐὰν μὴ ἔχωμεν τὰ πολλά, τοῖς ὀλίγοις ἀρκώμεθα, πεπεισμένοι γνησίως ὅτι ἥδιστα πολυτελείας ἀπολαύουσιν οἱ ἥκιστα ταύτης δεόμενοι, καὶ ὅτι τὸ μὲν φυσικὸν πᾶν εὐπόριστόν ἐστι, τὸ δὲ κενὸν δυσπόριστον. οἱ γὰρ λιτοὶ χυλοὶ ἴσην πολυτελεῖ διαίτῃ τὴν ἡδονὴν ἐπιφέρουσιν, ὅταν ἅπαξ τὸ ἀλγοῦν κατ᾽ ἔνδειαν ἐξαιρεθῇ· καὶ μᾶζα καὶ ὕδωρ τὴν ἀκροτάτην ἀποδίδωσιν ἡδονήν, ἐπειδὰν ἐνδέως τις αὐτὰ προσενέγκηται. τὸ συνεθίζειν οὖν ἐν ταῖς ἁπλαῖς καὶ οὐ πολυτελέσι διαίταις καὶ ὑγιείας ἐστὶ συμπληρωτικὸν καὶ πρὸς τὰς ἀναγκαίας τοῦ βίου χρήσεις ἄοκνον ποιεῖ τὸν ἄνθρωπον καὶ τοῖς πολυτελέσιν ἐκ διαλειμμάτων προσερχομένους κρεῖττον ἡμᾶς διατίθησι καὶ πρὸς τὴν τύχην ἀφόβους παρασκευάζει.[68]

---

[67] Cf. L. Robin, "Sur la notion épicurienne du progrès," *Rev. de Mét. et le Morale*, 1916, pp. 697 ff.; and for further illustrations of these aspects of Epicureanism, *vide* Ch. VIII, Nos. 4, 6.

[68] Ed. R. D. Hicks, *Loeb Class. Library*, 1925, Vol. II. The passage is from a letter, preserved by Diogenes Laertius, in which Epicurus gives a summary account of his ethical doctrine.

It is by measuring [pleasures and pains] against one another and by observing which are beneficial to us and which the contrary, that one ought to judge of all these matters. For sometimes we use the good as an evil, and conversely, the evil as a good. And we [Epicureans] regard self-sufficiency as a great good — not so that we may in all cases actually possess little, but so that, if we do not possess much, we may find a little sufficient. It is our sincere conviction that those who get the most enjoyment from luxury are those who want it least, that whatever is natural is easy to obtain, and only what is worthless is hard to acquire. Simple fare gives as much pleasure as sumptuous, when once the pain of need has been removed; and bread and water yield the very acme of pleasure to a man who is really hungry and thirsty. To habituate oneself, therefore, to a simple and frugal diet is fully sufficient for health; it makes a man resolute when confronted with any of the requirements of life; it enables us to get the more satisfaction from luxuries when they now and then come our way; and it renders us fearless of the vicissitudes of fortune.

IV, 26. Cicero: *Tusc. disp.* V, 89; 93; 97.

89. Hic vero ipse quam parvo est contentus! Nemo de tenui victu plura dixit. Etenim quae res pecuniae cupiditatem adferunt, ut amori, ut ambitioni, ut cotidianis sumptibus copiae suppetant, cum procul ab his omnibus rebus absit, cur pecuniam magnopere desideret vel potius cur curet omnino? . . . 93. Vides, credo, ut Epicurus cupiditatum genera diviserit, non nimis fortasse subtiliter, utiliter tamen: partim esse naturales et necessarias, partim naturales et non necessarias, partim neutrum; necessarias satiari posse paene nihilo; divitias enim naturae esse parabiles; secundum autem genus cupiditatum nec ad potiendum difficile esse censet, nec vero ad carendum; tertias, quod essent plane inanes neque necessitatem modo, sed ne naturam quidem attingerent, funditus eiciendas putavit. . . . 97. Atque his similia ad victum etiam transferuntur, extenuaturque magnificentia et sumptus epularum, quod parvo cultu natura contenta sit. Etenim quis hoc non videt, desideriis omnia ista condiri? [69]

With how little was Epicurus himself contented! No one has had more to say than he about plain living. For as to the things which cause men to desire money to provide for their daily luxuries or for love or for ambition — since he is far removed from all these things, why should he feel any great need of money, or rather, why should he care for it at all? . . . You know, I think, that Epicurus has divided the desires into classes, not very subtly, perhaps, but nevertheless usefully: in part, he says, they are both natural and necessary, in part natural but not necessary, in part neither.[70] Those

[69] Ed. M. Pohlenz, Leipzig, 1918, Teubner.

[70] This distinction is explained as follows by Diogenes Laertius, X, 149: "Those objects of desire are natural and necessary which put an end to pains, such as drink when we are thirsty; natural but not necessary are those which merely make pleasures more various but do not remove pain; neither natural nor necessary are such as crowns or the erection of statues [in one's honor]."

that are necessary, he says, can be satisfied with almost nothing, for the riches of nature are easy to come by; the second class of objects of desire, he thinks, are not difficult to attain, but neither are they difficult to go without; the third class he thought should be utterly rejected, because they are manifestly empty, having in them nothing either necessary or natural. . . . And he applied similar conclusions also to food, and depreciated magnificent and sumptuous banquets, since nature is content with little elaboration. For who does not see that it is need that gives savor to everything?

CHAPTER FIVE

PLATO AND PRIMITIVISM

The " Healthy City " in the Republic

In the *Republic* Plato's attitude towards the more moderate form of cultural primitivism is by no means unequivocal. Though the state in which the lineaments of " justice " are traced, and for which the ideal constitution is provided, is a complex one, and fairly far removed from the primitive, Plato dwells fondly upon the idyllic picture of an earlier and simpler society; and if (which is not wholly clear) he regards man's departure from this as necessary, he also plainly declares it to be an unhappy necessity. The "genuine and healthy city" (372 e) is that in which, while men have clothes and shoes and houses, practise the simpler crafts, exchange goods both directly and through middle-men, and use currency, they will limit their desires to the real " necessaries " of life (373 a). Their food will be cakes of barley and wheat, olives and cheese, and the " country fare of boiled onions and cabbage," with, for dessert, figs and peas and beans, myrtle berries and beech-nuts, " and wine in moderation." Spreading their modest viands " upon mats of reeds and clean leaves, and themselves reclining upon beds of yew and myrtle boughs, they and their children will fare excellently, drinking their wine, wearing garlands, singing the praises of the gods, having happy companionship with one another. They will not beget children beyond their means, so avoiding penury and war. . . . And thus passing their days in peace and health, they will, it is probable, live to a ripe old age, and dying, bequeath to their children a life similar to their own." The picture evokes from the young aristocrat Glaucon the usual outburst of the anti-primitivist of all ages: " If you were planning a city for pigs, Socrates, how else would you feed the beasts? " All the comforts and refinements that have become customary among men would be lacking. Socrates, however, does not take up the challenge. Since it is a " luxurious city," rather than a healthy one, that Glaucon wants, Socrates is willing to proceed to examine how such a city can best be constituted; " and perhaps it will not be amiss to do so; for by considering that sort of city we may the more easily see how both justice and injustice grow up in cities " (372 c-373).[1] The ideal commonwealth of the *Republic* is thus, at the outset of Plato's description of it, explicitly characterized as an abnormality — or rather, the remedy for an abnormality; its constitution will be that suitable to a city " suffering from an

---

[1] It is a not improbable conjecture that Plato has here in mind a primitivistic ideal state described by Antisthenes; *vide* Dümmler, *Antisthenica* (1882), pp. 3-4. But Plato cannot here be said to " make game " of this ideal, as Dümmler supposes.

inflammation." The form of organization which is "justice" will become necessary in it because injustice will otherwise prevail in it. With the progress of the dialogue this consideration seems to be forgotten; certainly it is not again emphasized, and the highly organized state rigorously ruled by philosophers appears as Plato's true ideal of human society.[2] Yet even in it much of the primitivistic strain is, of course, discernible; the rulers and the guardians live an even more austere if hardly a more simple life than the happy and innocent rustics of the earlier picture; and meanwhile, that picture remained unobliterated for the encouragement of subsequent primitivistic writers. That man's real "needs" are few and simple, that all desires and ambitions which go beyond these are a kind of disease, that the beginning of luxury is therefore the beginning of degeneration — these themes, at least, which were to be so endlessly repeated, found in the *Republic* Platonic sanction.

THE AGES

The passages in which Plato deals with the legend of the ages, or describes and evaluates the several stages of human culture, are: *States-man,* 269-274; *Timaeus,* 20 e-25 e; *Critias,* 108 ff.; *Laws,* IV, 713 and III. It would be superfluous to reproduce *in extenso* passages so familiar; but as Plato's treatment of the subject is involved and at some points seemingly equivocal, it is essential to analyze each of these loci (in their most probable chronological order) in order to determine, as nearly as may be, his position, and his relation to earlier, contemporary and later ideas on the subject.

In the Statesman

The passage in the *Statesman* concerning the Golden Age fits that myth into a peculiar form of the theory of world-cycles, which may have been suggested to Plato by Empedocles. The earlier part of this "famous tale" is so fanciful that, as Taylor[3] has remarked, it is wrong in principle to take it "as scientific cosmology meant seriously by Plato"; its conclud-ing portion, on the other hand, appears to be presented as an outline of the actual stages of development of human society and culture in the world as we now know it. The story runs as follows. The history of the world falls into two classes of cycles. There are times when the movement of the sun and other heavenly bodies, and all the changes which occur thereon, are under the direct guidance of the deity — when " God himself goes round

---

[2] Plato's plan in the *Republic* for discovering "justice" in the individual by first observing it writ large in the structure of the state required, of course, that the state in question should be one characterized by class differences and corresponding diversities of function and political authority. The "healthy state" with its simplicity and equality would not have served the purpose of this argument from analogy.

[3] A. E. Taylor: *Plato; the Man and his Work,* 1927, p. 396.

with the world and helps to roll it." But after the completion of a certain period, " God lets go, . . . and the world turns about and revolves in the opposite direction . . . during an immense cycle of years." This sudden reversal naturally produces a jolt, and is therefore accompanied by vast cosmic catastrophes. But when things settle down again, all natural phenomena, biological as well as astronomical, go on as before in the opposite order. Old men become young, young men become babies, and babies grow littler and littler and finally vanish away. Not only are all physical processes thus reversed, but the world and its inhabitants in all respects grow worse and worse, the longer they are left to their own devices. At the outset of this phase they retain much of the impress and memory of their divine origin; but it was inevitable that this should be gradually but continuously lost. For there are, and have always been, two contrary elements in the world's make-up. From " God, its Creator," indeed, " it received every good "; but " an admixture of matter was inherent in its original nature," and therefore in the constitution of all living beings; and this manifests itself in a tendency of all created things to fall into disorder and discord. The evil principle of " matter " is, in fact, the dominant one in the ordinary course of nature in the universe, when it operates in accordance with its own propensities, rather than under the external and supernatural control of higher powers.

V, 1. *Statesman,* 273 c-d.

> While the world was engendering creatures under the governance of God, the evil in it was small and the good was great. After the separation from him, when the world was let go, at first all went very well; then, as time went on, there was more and more forgetting, and the old discord began to prevail and at last came to full flower; small, then, was the good and great was the admixture of the elements of evil, so that there was danger of universal ruin of the world and of the things therein. Wherefore God, who made the world, seeing it was in great straits, took charge of it again, in order that it might not be overwhelmed by this confusion and dissolved into an infinite diversity, which is a state of misery. So he seated himself once more at the helm and reversed all that had been disordered and relaxed in the previous period when it had been left to itself, and set all things in order and restored them, and made the world ageless and immortal.[4]

Now the legend of the Golden Age under Cronus, says Plato, is a picture of the first of these cycles, " when God superintended the revolution of the universe as a whole, and the parts of the universe were distributed under the rule of certain inferior deities." And the supersession of Cronus by Zeus represents the moment when the creator left the world to itself. In the first age men had no responsibility for their own well-being; they were

---

[4] That the cause of evil is not God is strongly emphasized in *Rep.* 379 c.

controlled and shepherded by God and his subordinate local agents, the demigods, as the domestic animals are now controlled and shepherded by man. Mankind had then no arts, no governments, no property, no clothes and no houses; they lived in the open air and slept on soft couches of grass, and the earth gave them food in abundance, without labor. They also had no wars and no quarrels; and they and all other animals were vegetarians; "none then devoured another." Sexual reproduction did not exist; all arose out of, as they repeatedly returned to, the earth, and therefore, naturally, "separate possession of wives and children" was unknown.

The principal interlocutor in the dialogue (the Eleatic Stranger) here asks whether the life of man in the days of Cronus was happier than in the present age of Zeus; and answers that under certain circumstances — namely, if the men of that time "had used all these advantages with a view to philosophy," learning from the other creatures (whose speech they could understand) whatever special powers or wisdom the others possessed, they doubtless *would* have been happier. Or if they lived a merely animal existence, eating and drinking until they were satiated, and telling stories to one another and the animals — "the answer to that question also is easy." But, Plato adds, with a caution which primitivists have not usually imitated, "as there is no satisfactory reporter of the desires and thoughts of those times," the question must be left unanswered. It is, nevertheless, in the mythic age when God ruled the world directly that human life resembled the most extreme "state of nature" of later writers; and this passage of the *Statesman*, therefore, taken apart from its context, could plausibly be construed as giving support to cultural primitivism. In fact, however, Plato makes it clear that this part of the tale has no relevance whatever to the present race of men. This race is somewhat confusedly and inconsistently placed in a third period differing both from the age of Cronus and from the cycle in which all things went from greater to less and from better to worse. Our age is clearly subsequent to the stoppage of the process of reversal and the restoration of the world's movement to its normal direction (273 e). Men and animals are no longer generated, as in both the previous periods, directly from the earth, but by sexual reproduction, though their development is like that in the first cycle. They begin as infants, reach maturity, grow old and die. On the other hand, they are like the men of the second cycle, and unlike those of the first, in that they are not under the direct care and control of a paternalistic divinity. They must therefore look out for themselves, and be saved, if at all, through their own exertions. They must begin, moreover, where the preceding phase ended, i. e., in the condition of maximal evil. The beginning of the cycle to which we belong was not the best part of it; and man owes his escape from destruction, and all the goods that he has attained, not to nature but art. "Deprived of the care of the divinity who had possessed and tended them," men were left defenceless against the beasts — which, with the change of régime, had become wild and untractable — and continued to be so in the third stage.

V, 2. *Statesman,* 274 c-d.

> In the first ages men were without arts or inventions; the food which once had grown spontaneously had failed, and they knew not how to procure any more, because no necessity had hitherto compelled them. For all these reasons they were in great straits. Therefore the gifts spoken of in the old tradition were imparted to us by the gods, together with the necessary knowledge and instruction as to their uses; fire was given us by Prometheus, the arts by Hephaestus and his fellow-worker [i. e. Athene], seeds and plants by others. Out of these all the things that make up human life arose, since the care of the gods, as I was saying, had now failed men, and they had to order their course of life for themselves, and were their own masters.

Such, then, is the myth in the *Statesman.* Its preponderantly antiprimitivistic tone is unmistakable. In what he says of the third cycle Plato is no longer giving us a wholly fanciful cosmogony; he is dealing with the conditions of life as they actually exist. And here he accepts neither chronological nor cultural primitivism. The state of man at the beginning of the present chapter of world-history was an altogether miserable one, and there has subsequently taken place — at least up to a point — an improvement and enrichment of human life. And this progress has not been towards a restoration of the irresponsible animal happiness of the imaginary reign of Cronus; it has been a progress in civilization through man's own effort in making use of the knowledge of the arts bestowed by Prometheus, Hephaestus and Athene.

In the Timaeus and Critias

The passages in the *Timaeus* and the *Critias* form a unit, the *Critias* being an unfinished fragment of a sequel to the *Timaeus.* Of the story which concerns us the beginning is chiefly to be found in the *Timaeus,* the sequel in the *Critias,* the conclusion again in the *Timaeus.* It is " a tale which, though passing strange, is yet wholly true," as Solon, the wisest of the Seven Sages, declared; it was communicated to him by certain of the Egyptian priests of Neith, the goddess of Sais, " whose name in Greek, they say, is Athene " (*Timaeus,* 21 e). Shiftings of the positions of the heavenly bodies produce recurrent catastrophes upon the earth, sometimes by floods, at longer intervals through excessive heat; in consequence of these, or at times through other and lesser causes, the greater part of the populations of many regions have been, and always will be, from time to time destroyed. There usually remains, however, a small remnant; the character of the remnant varies with the nature of the catastrophe. When it is by flood, the cultivated city-dwellers of the plains and valleys are swept away, the rude herdsmen and shepherds of the mountain-heights remain;

when the destruction is by fire, the reverse is the case (*Timaeus,* 21 e-23 c). The particular story which Solon told relates to a previous period in the history of Attica between two deluges, and of the now vanished island of Atlantis. At the beginning the only survivors in Attica were the uncultured and unlettered mountain-folk; but of them little is said. The history is concerned with a much later phase of cultural development. Yet this phase was a sort of Golden Age; in it — as in the primitive era in the *Statesman* — the gods still effectually controlled the life of men.

V, 3. *Critias,* 109 b.

> [For] in the former ages, the gods had the whole earth divided amongst them by lot. . . . Each of them peopled their own districts; and when they had peopled them, they tended us human beings as shepherds tend their flocks, as their possessions and nurselings; except that it was not our bodies that they controlled, by blows and physical violence, as shepherds control their flocks, but they governed us as pilots steer a ship from its stern, by the rudder of persuasion, taking hold of our souls through pleasure, which is the easiest way to direct the movements of animals: thus did they direct and steer all mortal creatures.

Attica was the domain allotted to the divinities of wisdom and craftsmanship, Athene and Hephaestus, and in it dwelt " the noblest and best race amongst men "; Atlantis was ruled by Poseidon and peopled by his progeny. The constitution of Athens in these days was similar to that of Plato's ideal commonwealth in the *Republic,* Bks. I-IV. Its laws were established by the goddess herself; in them attention was first of all paid to the cosmic order and to the relation of divine things to human life (*Timaeus,* 24 c). There were distinct social classes, artisans, shepherds, farmers, priests, and a caste of warriors or " guardians," " originally set apart by divine men." This class " took a middle course between meanness and extravagance " . . . residing " in moderate houses on the summit of the Acropolis "; community of goods and of wives and children prevailed among them (*Critias,* 110 c; cf. *Timaeus,* 26 d) ; they lived a disciplined and austere life, " having virtue always as their great concern, and keeping free from other pursuits." In this age, then, the Athenian State " possessed the fairest works of art and the noblest polity of any nation now under heaven of which we have heard tell " (*Timaeus,* 23 c).

The people of Atlantis developed a far more elaborate social organization, and made extraordinary advances in engineering — all of which Plato describes in some detail, apparently not without gusto, in the *Critias.* Their harbors were " full of merchants, and vessels coming from all parts "; these traders and seamen, " from their numbers, kept up a multitudinous sound of human voices and din of all sorts by night and day." The picture of Atlantis, in short, is as near as Plato could well come to the representation of a great modern seaport. Yet, in spite of their wealth and luxury, the Atlantides also long remained uncorrupted:

V, 4. *Critias,* 120 e, 121 a.

> For many generations, as long as the divine nature lasted in them, they were obedient to the laws, and well-affected towards the gods, who were their kinsmen; for they possessed honorable and in every way great spirits, uniting gentleness with wisdom in the various chances of life. . . . They despised everything but virtue, little esteeming their present state of life, and bearing lightly the burden of the gold and other property they possessed; neither were they intoxicated by luxury, nor did wealth deprive them of their self-control and thereby cause their downfall. On the contrary, in their soberness of mind, they saw clearly that all these good things are increased by mutual good will combined with virtue, whereas to honor and strive after these goods destroys not only the goods themselves, but also virtue with them.

In time, however, the divine strain in their ancestry became more and more diluted, and their human nature got the upper hand. Thus they gradually became filled with unrighteous avarice and lust of power; whereupon Zeus determined to visit chastisement upon them for their improvement.

At this point, the story in the *Critias* abruptly breaks off; with some solution of continuity, the rest is told in the *Timaeus.* In the working out, presumably, of the design of Zeus, the people of Atlantis became, as we should now say, imperialists of the most ambitious sort. Their great maritime empire embarked upon a career of conquest in Europe, Asia and Africa, which was at first successful; their power extended in Africa from the pillars of Hercules as far as Egypt, and in Europe as far as Tyrrhenia. But at last the Athenians took the lead among the Hellenes in resisting this aggression, and, even when deserted by their allies, and at the very point of destruction, finally defeated and triumphed over the invaders and liberated, not only all Greece, but " all the others who dwell within the limits of Hercules," i. e. east of Gibraltar. But afterwards both races were destroyed in a great flood; the island of Atlantis disappeared under the sea, and of the population of Greece, only a few ignorant folk dwelling upon the tops of the mountains escaped, as before. These ancestors of the present Athenians, being assumed to have lost, or never known, the arts which had flourished among the vanished races, passed gradually through the same cultural phases until the existing — and inferior — social and political order was reached.

Here again, then, cultural primitivism is absent. Something of the legend of the Golden Age survives in the myth of a past more virtuous and more glorious than the present; but it is a past in which men lived in a relatively — and in the case of the Atlantides a highly — advanced cultural condition. There is nevertheless the suggestion that the excess of power and wealth and luxury of Atlantis was in the end its undoing; and that the people which, though far removed from savagery, lived the more simple, disciplined and austere life proved the better in the final conflict. As for the ultimate catastrophe, there is no suggestion that, like the Noachian deluge in the Hebrew myth, it was a punitive or purifying visitation; it overwhelms the just and the unjust, and is simply Plato's way of accounting for the partial extinction of the one and the complete disappearance of the other of the two imaginary peoples whom he has described.

In the Laws

The short passage in *Laws*, IV, 713, is a moralized version of the Golden Age story already suggested in the *Statesman*. There is in reality neither chronological nor cultural primitivism in it; the story is expressly introduced as a " fable " to illustrate a point in the argument, and the " reign of Cronus " is simply a figure of speech for the supremacy in the life of a community or an individual of the divine element in human nature, the Reason. The old " tradition of the happy life of mankind in the days when all things were spontaneous and abundant," says Plato, in substance, is a parable, and this is its meaning:

V, 5. *Laws,* IV, 713 c-714 a.

> Cronus knew that no human being invested with autocratic power is able to order human affairs and not overflow with insolence and wrong. Being, then, mindful of this, he appointed not men but demigods, who are of a higher and more divine race, to be the kings and rulers of our cities, . . . and they, with great ease and pleasure to themselves, and no less to us, taking care of us and giving us peace and reverence and order and justice without stint, made the tribes of men happy and peaceful. And even today this tale speaks with truth, declaring that cities of which some mortal man and not God is the ruler have no escape from evils and toils. Nevertheless, we must do all we can to imitate the life which is said to have existed in the days of Cronus; and in so far as the immortal element dwells in us, to that we must hearken, both in private and public life, and regulate our cities and houses by law, meaning by the very term " law " the diffusion of reason.

Plato, in short, here simply converts the myth of the Cronian Age into an allegory which serves him partly to express his favorite ethical doctrine, partly to suggest the dependence of the well-being of the State upon the moral education of its rulers, be they few or many.

Book III, 676-682 a, on the other hand, is not a parable, but an attempt at a theoretical reconstruction of the typical history of any society from its earliest phase. It is perhaps the Platonic passage which had most influence on the subsequent history of primitivism. Plato here is inquiring into the origin of government. This does not, he observes, mean going back to its chronological beginnings; no one " can reckon the time which has elapsed since cities first existed and men were citizens of them " (676). But to know the actual first state is unimportant, for the whole history has been

repeated in the same general outline many times over, and it is sufficient to
start with the initial phase of one of these typical cycles. For we may
reasonably accept, Plato's principal interlocutor suggests (as in the
Timaeus), the ancient tradition that mankind has been all but completely
destroyed many times, by flood and pestilence and other causes, leaving
each time but a remnant. Let us imagine the case in which the destruction
has been by flood and the only men who escaped were shepherds on the high
hills. Such survivors, Plato again assumes, would be unacquainted with
the arts, except weaving and the making of pottery, and would have no
written language. They would possibly know how to make fire, but would
have no use of metals. They would be a pastoral folk, living by the produce
of their flocks and herds, but also by the chase — i. e., they would not be
vegetarians. In this condition they would remain " for thousands and
thousands of years," for in our cycle of human history invention is relatively
but a thing of yesterday. Their life was comparatively easy, though not
without labor. This was no Golden Age of irresponsibility and indolence,
and these primitive folk did not live like the naked, houseless and homeless
creatures of the so-called divinely-ruled cycle in the *Statesman*. Government they had none, " except the patriarchal rule and sovereignty of . . .
parents, which of all sovereignties is the most just." Plato's picture of the
primitives is, in short, a description of the life of savage peoples in the later
Stone Age of technological development.

Upon the moral superiority of man in this stage of culture Plato seems
at first to insist strongly; and the passage is doubtless one of the sources
of the expression in later literature of the morally serious and 'hard'
type of primitivism. Conflict and war, Plato observes, must have been
unknown in those days, for several reasons; partly because " the desola-
tion of these primitive men," the very hardships and dangers of their
existence, " would create in them a feeling of friendship and affection
towards one another "; and also because everyone had enough of the necessaries of existence and none had any of the superfluities. " There was no
great poverty in those days; . . . and rich they could not be, since they
had no gold and silver. And a community which has neither poverty nor
riches will almost always produce the noblest characters; there is no insolence or injustice, nor do any envyings or contentions arise among them."
For these reasons, then, says Plato, the men of this age were " good "; and
for another reason too — " what is called their simple-mindedness; for
what they were told of the nature of good and evil, in their simplicity they
believed to be true, and practised. No one had the cleverness to suspect
another of a falsehood, as men now do." Would not, then (asks Plato),
many generations living in this way, " although ruder and more ignorant
of the arts generally, and in particular of the arts of war by land and sea,
and of those other sorts of war known in cities under the names of law-
suits and party conflicts, and including all conceivable ways of hurting one

another in word and deed — would they not, I say, be simpler and more manly and more temperate and in all ways better men?" (679 b-d).

Taken by itself, this obviously seems an expression of a fairly thorough-going cultural primitivism. But even here Plato himself is not really a primitivist. Though these simple and ignorant shepherds were better men than their civilized descendants, they were not, in his eyes, the best that men could become; it was not possible for man to attain his complete moral stature under such conditions. " How," exclaims his spokesman in the dialogue, the Athenian Stranger, — " how can we possibly suppose that those who knew nothing of all the good and evil of cities could have attained their full development, whether of virtue or of vice?" (678 b). The gradual process of civilization which followed these beginnings and has produced " cities and governments and arts and laws," while it has in many ways depraved man, has also produced virtues, or the possibility of them, which could find no place in the simple life and unsophisticated minds of a primitive people. Nor would the continuance of this state have been possible, even if it had been desirable. The growth of population and the desire for protection against wild beasts necessarily led to the group-ing of several clans in walled towns; and the patriarchal régime being no longer sufficient for communities unrelated by blood, they elected repre-sentatives of the clans living together, who must be supposed to have con-vened to adopt as their common laws " those usages which pleased them best," and to have chosen magistrates. Thus emerged by agreement out of the patriarchate " the first political constitution, aristocratic or perhaps monarchical in form." In another context Plato makes this social contract underlying the state specifically a compact between rulers and subjects. The former bind themselves by oath to govern only in accordance with the fundamental laws, and " not to make their rule more arbitrary"; and the consent of the subjects to obey is conditioned upon the observance of this pledge by the rulers (684 a). The principle, which was to play so great a part in political theories and movements in the sixteenth, seventeenth and eighteenth centuries, that the state should be " a government of laws and not of men," is especially insisted upon by Plato; " that state in which the law is subject, and has no authority, I perceive to be on the highway to ruin; but I see that the state in which the law is above the rulers, and rulers are the inferiors of the laws, has salvation, and every blessing which the gods can confer" (715 d).

Since it is not in the primitive age that Plato finds the best condition, it might have been expected that when he describes his new model com-monwealth, the " city of the second degree of excellence " — presented as less ideal but more practicable than that in the *Republic* — there would be no preaching of the gospel of going back. Yet in fact his final program may be said to be that of going half-way back. The ideal constitution, though not workable by a society composed of average human beings

(739 e), is still to be imitated as closely as possible; and this "super-excellent" polity is that "in which there is community of wives and children and all possessions, and all that is called 'private' is everywhere and by every means rooted out of life" (739 c). In the new state, therefore, land will still be regarded as the property of the state, but it will be permanently allotted for occupancy and cultivation by individual families (740 a); and though private and unequal wealth in land and other goods will be permitted (744 c), this inequality will be restricted by laws fixing a lower "limit of poverty" and forbidding any citizen to possess more than four times this minimum. If by some chance anyone acquires more, the surplus must be made over to the state (744 e-745 b). Foreign trade will apparently be forbidden (742 a, b, 705 a, b) and all trade will be discouraged (741 e) as the least honorable of permissible pursuits (743 d, e), and no claims to interest on loans will be either morally valid or legally enforcible (742 c). Slavery, however, will not be abolished (914 e). No private citizen will be allowed to possess gold and silver, but only a modicum of token-currency for daily use within the community (742 a). The legislator under his system, says Plato, will have "for the most part nothing to do with laws about shipowners and merchants and retailers and innkeepers and tax-collectors and mines and loans and interest and innumerable other things — bidding good-bye to these, he will give laws to husbandmen and shepherds and bee-keepers, and the guardians and superintendents of their implements" (842 d). The legislator will not seek to make the state as great and as rich as possible, and to this end to obtain for it "silver and gold and the greatest empire by land and sea." He will seek, rather, "to make the citizen happy and good; but very rich and good at the same time he cannot be" (742 e). Of all the offices of state, that of director of education will be "by far the most important," since upon the right training of citizens in youth the well-being of the state chiefly depends. "Man, as we say, is a tame animal; nevertheless, though he is wont to become a most godlike and tame one when he happens to have both a right education and a good nature, if his training is insufficient or bad, he is the wildest of all earth's offspring" (766 a). Plato is thus no believer in the "natural goodness" of man; "there is no great plenty or abundance of men eager to become as good as possible as speedily as possible," and Hesiod showed his wisdom when he wrote: "Before virtue the immortal gods have placed the sweat of labor; and long and steep is the road thereto, and rough the first ascent. But when you have reached the summit, what once was hard becomes easy" (718 d-719 a). It is to be borne in mind, however, that in another sense Plato does believe in the inherent rightness of the human will, since he accepts the Socratic doctrine that all voluntary choice is directed towards that end which the agent at the time believes to be the greatest good attainable by him: "the evil-doer is not an evil-doer voluntarily" (731 c) and "no man is voluntarily intemperate" (734 b), since

"no one would ever of his own free-will choose to possess the greatest of evils." Moral evil consists only in ignorance or lack of self-control (734 b).

In the scheme of education great place is given to certain of the arts, especially choral music and ritual dancing. But poets, and even prose writers, are not to be encouraged, and they may publish or exhibit their works, if at all, only under a rigorous censorship (801 c-d, 817 a-d). The reading of the youth will be the book of the *Laws* itself, or other "poems or prose writings" which say the same things (811 d-e). There is a definite, though not extreme, anti-intellectualism: "*much* learning (polymathy) brings danger to youth" (811 b); and there is complete rejection of freedom of thought and of the cultivation of diversity of characters and points of view. For the state must be *one*, not only outwardly but inwardly; it must implant and maintain in all its citizens identical beliefs and sentiments, so that "all men, so far as possible, are unanimous in the praise and blame they bestow, rejoicing and grieving at the same things, and conforming to the utmost of their ability to those laws which render the state in the highest degree unified" (739 d, cf. 659 d-660 a). In this part of the program the Platonic model state was an imaginary prototype of Soviet Russia, Fascist Italy, and Germany under National Socialism.

NATURE AND ART

Plato's account of the meaning of the antithesis of 'nature' and 'art,' and of the assertion of the superiority of the former by certain unnamed contemporaries, has already been cited (Ch. III, p. 113). His polemic against these teachers is chiefly to be found in the *Laws*.

(a) The antithesis itself he finds to be a spurious one: "law and also art exist by nature, or by that which is not inferior to nature" (890 d). The sense in which Plato is here using "nature" is not altogether clear; a probable interpretation, suggested by the context, is that he intends to say that "art" — i. e. the control of life by the conscious exercise of reason — is no less a product of universal nature than the non-rational elements in man's constitution; since man has been made capable of it, it is an essential part of the cosmic scheme, and therefore cannot be "contrary to nature." To say that positive and moral laws restrictive of the uncontrolled play of the other forces in individual and social life are "artificial" (889 a) is true; but this does not mean that they are unnatural in any sense which implies that they ought not to exist, or that "art," of which they are among the manifestations, produces "lesser works" than does the rest of nature. Plato here, in short, is apparently repeating what had probably already been said by Democritus (Ch. VII, p. 207) and is anticipating Shakespeare's

The art itself is nature.[5]

---

[5] *Winter's Tale*, IV, iii, 96.

(b) In the sense of "nature" in which it *is* antithetic to "art" — though Plato does not like this use of the term — the sense, namely, of that which operates without control by "mind" and "reason" — it is not nature but art which is primary and superior, both in the universe and in man:

V, 6. *Laws*, X, 892 b.

> Thought and foresight and mind and art and law will be prior to things hard and soft, and heavy and light [i. e. to the material elements]; and the great and primitive works and actions will be works of art; they will be first, and after them will come nature and the works of nature — which, however, is a wrong word to apply to them; these will follow and be under the government of art and mind.

Plato is here talking, primarily, cosmology rather than ethics; the cosmos is the product and manifestation of reason, as in the *Timaeus*. But the ethical application is evident, since, in the passage as a whole, it is constantly implied that what is true of the universe is true of "the soul." In man's constitution also, in so far as its condition is (in what is for Plato the proper sense) "natural," i. e. normal, the "government of art" is essential and supreme. Against the assumption — destined to play so great a part among the ideas underlying cultural primitivism for more than a millennium — that art, or the artificial, is a vitiation of nature, Plato thus made his protest almost as soon as that tendency manifested itself.

Nor was it only this general and abstract antithesis that Plato attacked. The anti-primitivistic speech ascribed to Protagoras (Ch. VII, No. 12) in the dialogue of that name was in accord, it can hardly be doubted, in this point, at least, with Plato's own attitude. Prometheus, when he gave men the mechanical arts, and therewith "the wisdom necessary to support life" in spite of man's physical inferiority to the other animals, was the benefactor of our race; and as for the "art of government," though it was beyond Prometheus's power to bestow that, it was conferred upon men by the beneficence of Zeus himself, since the race must have perished without it. And Plato was probably uttering his own conviction, even though he was doubtless also reporting that of Protagoras, in the passage comparing the life of savages and of civilized men even at their worst (*Protag.* 327 e).

Plato's position in the history of primitivism may be briefly summed up thus: (1) He, too, was in revolt against the civilization in which he lived. And his moral and social ideal was in great part compounded of the same ingredients as that of the many hard primitivists of all periods [6] — sim-

---

[6] Natorp has emphasized the affinity between Plato's political and social doctrines and the Cynics' revolt against the existing culture: "Hier wie dort dieselbe tiefe Ueberzeugung von der Unrettbarkeit der gegenwärtigen hellenischen Kultur; daher

plicity and austerity of life, limitation of desires, freedom from luxury, economic and even marital communism; though in the Utopias in the *Republic* and the *Timaeus* and the *Critias* this ideal was fully exemplified in the mode of life of only one select class in the community, and was not assumed to be possible for all men. (2) In some passages he gives a summary endorsement to the general thesis of chronological primitivism, in a phrase which was to be repeated by Cicero: " the men of early times were better than we and nearer to the gods ";[7] and Theophrastus attributes to him the proposition that " all that is by nature tends to good rather than evil."[8] (3) On the other hand, three anti-primitivistic motives were potent in Plato's thought. (a) With the belief in the superiority of the instinctive, unreflective elements in man's constitution he was wholly without sympathy. " The unexamined life is not to be lived by man "; reason is the " part of the soul " which is " by nature " fitted to rule the others; and it is only through philosophic insight made possible by rigorous intellectual discipline that the true nature of the good can become the object of knowledge and of love. (b) Akin to this was Plato's usual rejection of the eulogistic use of ' nature ' in senses 14, 16, 17, 18, 22, 23,[9] and of the dyslogistic use of ' art.' (c) His appraisal of human nature was such that his influence told heavily against equalitarianism and against any glorification of the juristic state of nature. Men are by nature unequal; the inferior should be ruled by the superior; and all must be subject to the restraints of an elaborate and unalterable constitution.[10]

---

zahlreiche Berührungen auch im einzelnen, mag man nun von Kynismen Platons oder von Platonismen des Kynikers sprechen " (Pauly-Wissowa, V, 1905, art. " Diogenes von Sinope," col. 772).

[7] *Philebus*, 16 c; cf. *Tim.* 40 d, and the quotation from the *Niobe* of Aeschylus, *Repub.* 391 e.

[8] Theophrastus, *De sensibus*, 32.

[9] *Vide* Appendix I.

[10] In an article on " Plato's Theory of Social Progress " (*Int. Jour. of Ethics*, XXXVIII, 1927-8, pp. 467 ff.) E. O. Bassett seeks to show that Plato held the view that " society executes an infinite progression. . . . The end of progress is progress; the aim is but a directing principle. . . . Since the social as well as the universal aim is maximum orderliness, progress must be perpetual" (p. 476). This interpretation seems to go beyond anything warranted by Plato's text, and in particular to overlook (a) Plato's large degree of sympathy with technological primitivism; (b) his assumption of periodic catastrophes; (c) the essentially static character of his political and social ideal. The rational state or the closest humanly possible approximation to it (as in the *Laws*) is the fixed goal; once attained it ought in principle never to be changed. The Romantic ideal of endless progress for progress' sake is alien to Plato's thought.

CHAPTER SIX

ARISTOTLE AND PRIMITIVISTIC IDEAS

Aristotle is in the main to be placed in the succession of philosophers hostile both to chronological and cultural primitivism. His conception of the general course of the historic process, however, was determined by the interplay of partially conflicting preconceptions peculiar to his own philosophy, and can only be understood in connection with these. And along with his opposition to various favorite theses of the primitivists, there are in his thought — and in his influential terminology — elements which had some affinity with primitivistic ideas or could be converted into supports for such ideas.

THE COURSE OF COSMICAL HISTORY

The Aristotelian cosmology was in principle antagonistic both to the theory of general progress and to that of general decline, for two reasons. (a) Since both views implied that cosmical and terrestrial history had a beginning, they were incongruous with the Aristotelian doctrine of the eternity of the world.[1] (b) Both also implied that some significant and continuous change — involving either improvement or deterioration — in the general constitution of the world has taken place. But Aristotle was averse to admitting any such change on a cosmical scale. Of physical conditions there are only local vicissitudes. One of the four qualities of matter (hot, cold, moist, dry), or of the four elements which are respectively characterized by certain pairs of them, may observably increase or decrease in a given region; but it is an error to suppose this to extend to the universe, or even to the earth as a whole, or to continue even locally for any long period.[2] The astronomical structure of the world and the motion of the *primum mobile,* and of the sun, by which terrestrial physical conditions are for the most part determined, are permanent and unalterable, and, while a rigid uniformity of the laws of nature in the sublunary region is not asserted by Aristotle,[3] there is a quantitative constancy of the 'primary matter,' if not of the elements;[4] and in general he conceives of the world and of the earth as having substantially the same constitution and manifesting essentially the same processes throughout infinite duration.

---

[1] *Metaph.* XI, 1072 a 23, 1075 b 33; *De caelo,* I, 279 b 18 ff.; II, 280 b 26; cf. also the pseudo-Aristotelian *De mundo,* 396 a 33 ff.

[2] *Meteorologica,* I, 352 a 15 ff.

[3] *Physics,* II, 195 b 31-196 b 27, 199 b 23 f.

[4] *De caelo,* I, 270 a 14. In *Meteor.* II, 357 b Aristotle seems to imply the quantitative constancy of each of the elements, though other passages are difficult to reconcile with this.

The notion of a general law of rectilinear and cumulative change in time, in any particular direction, was foreign to Aristotle's mind.

COSMICAL CYCLES

He might, therefore, have been expected to take refuge, as other believers in the infinity of the time-process have done, in the theory of recurrent world-cycles. The conception of cyclical change is, in fact, conspicuous in his thought; and in one passage he presents an argument for the necessary circularity of the sequence of causes and effects which would seem to entail the conclusion that everything is endlessly repeated.

VI, 1. *De generatione et corruptione,* 337 a–338 b.

τούτου δ' αἴτιον, [τοῦ γίνεσθαι ἀεὶ καὶ τῆς γενέσεως] ὥσπερ εἴρηται πολλάκις, ἡ κύκλῳ φορά· μόνη γὰρ συνεχής. διὸ καὶ τἆλλα ὅσα μεταβάλλει εἰς ἄλληλα κατὰ τὰ πάθη καὶ τὰς δυνάμεις, οἷον τὰ ἁπλᾶ σώματα, μιμεῖται τὴν κύκλῳ φοράν· ὅταν γὰρ ἐξ ὕδατος ἀὴρ γένηται καὶ ἐξ ἀέρος πῦρ καὶ πάλιν ἐκ τοῦ πυρὸς ὕδωρ, κύκλῳ φαμὲν περιεληλυθέναι τὴν γένεσιν διὰ τὸ πάλιν ἀνακάμπτειν· ὥστε καὶ ἡ εὐθεῖα φορὰ μιμουμένη τὴν κύκλῳ συνεχής ἐστιν. . . . 338 a. εἰ ἄρα τινὸς ἐξ ἀνάγκης ἁπλῶς ἡ γένεσις, ἀνάγκη ἀνακυκλεῖν καὶ ἀνακάμπτειν. ἀνάγκη γὰρ ἤτοι πέρας ἔχειν τὴν γένεσιν ἢ μή, καὶ εἰ μή, ἢ εἰς εὐθὺ ἢ κύκλῳ. τούτων δ', εἴπερ ἔσται ἀίδιος, οὐκ εἰς εὐθὺ οἷόν τε διὰ τὸ μηδαμῶς εἶναι ἀρχήν (μήτ' ἂν κάτω ὡς ἐπὶ τῶν ἐσομένων λαμβανομένων, μήτ' ἄνω ὡς ἐπὶ τῶν γενομένων)· ἀνάγκη δ' εἶναι ἀρχήν . . . μήτε πεπερασμένης οὔσης ἀίδιον εἶναι· διὸ ἀνάγκη κύκλῳ εἶναι. ἀντιστρέφειν ἄρα ἀνάγκη ἔσται, οἷον εἰ τοδὶ ἐξ ἀνάγκης, καὶ τὸ πρότερον ἄρα· ἀλλὰ μὴν εἰ τοῦτο, καὶ τὸ ὕστερον ἀνάγκη γενέσθαι. καὶ τοῦτο ἀεὶ δὴ συνεχῶς—οὐδὲν γὰρ τοῦτο δια-φέρει λέγειν διὰ δύο ἢ πολλῶν. ἐν τῇ κύκλῳ ἄρα κινήσει καὶ γενέσει ἐστὶ τὸ ἐξ ἀνάγκης ἁπλῶς· καὶ εἴτε κύκλῳ, ἀνάγκη ἕκαστον γίνεσθαι καὶ γεγονέναι, καὶ εἰ ἀνάγκη, ἡ τούτων γένεσις κύκλῳ. ταῦτα μὲν δὴ εὐλόγως, ἐπεὶ ἀίδιος καὶ ἄλλως ἐφάνη ἡ κύκλῳ κίνησις καὶ ἡ τοῦ οὐρανοῦ, ὅτι ταῦτα ἐξ ἀνάγκης γίνεται καὶ ἔσται, ὅσαι ταύτης κινήσεις καὶ ὅσαι διὰ ταύτην· 338 b. εἰ γὰρ τὸ κύκλῳ κινούμενον ἀεί τι κινεῖ, ἀνάγκη καὶ τούτων κύκλῳ εἶναι τὴν κίνησιν—οἷον τῆς ἄνω φορᾶς οὔσης ὁ ἥλιος κύκλῳ ὡδί, ἐπεὶ δ' οὕτως, αἱ ὧραι διὰ τοῦτο κύκλῳ γίνονται καὶ ἀνακάμπτουσιν, τούτων δ' οὕτω γινομένων πάλιν τὰ ὑπὸ τούτων. τί οὖν δή ποτε τὰ μὲν οὕτω φαίνεται, οἷον ὕδατα καὶ ἀὴρ κύκλῳ γινόμενα, καὶ εἰ μὲν νέφος ἔσται, δεῖ ὗσαι, καὶ εἰ ὕσει γε, δεῖ καὶ νέφος εἶναι, ἄνθρωποι δὲ καὶ ζῷα οὐκ ἀνακάμπτουσιν εἰς αὑτοὺς ὥστε πάλιν γίνεσθαι τὸν αὐτόν (οὐ γὰρ ἀνάγκη, εἰ ὁ πατὴρ ἐγένετο, σὲ γενέσθαι· ἀλλ' εἰ σύ, ἐκεῖνον), εἰς εὐθὺ δὲ ἔοικεν εἶναι αὕτη ἡ γένεσις; ἀρχὴ δὲ τῆς σκέψεως πάλιν αὕτη, πότερον ὁμοίως ἅπαντα ἀνακάμπτει ἢ οὔ, ἀλλὰ τὰ μὲν ἀριθμῷ τὰ δὲ εἴδει μόνον. ὅσων μὲν οὖν ἄφθαρτος ἡ οὐσία ἡ κινουμένη, φανερὸν ὅτι καὶ ἀριθμῷ ταὐτὰ ἔσται (ἡ γὰρ κίνησις ἀκολουθεῖ τῷ κινουμένῳ), ὅσων δὲ μὴ ἀλλὰ φθαρτή, ἀνάγκη τῷ εἴδει, ἀριθμῷ δὲ μὴ ἀνακάμπτειν. διὸ ὕδωρ ἐξ ἀέρος καὶ ἀὴρ ἐξ ὕδατος εἴδει ὁ αὐτός, οὐκ ἀριθμῷ· εἰ δὲ καὶ ταῦτα ἀριθμῷ, ἀλλ' οὐχ ὧν ἡ οὐσία γίνεται, οὖσα τοιαύτη οἷα ἐνδέχεσθαι μὴ εἶναι.[5]

The cause of this perpetual coming-to-be, as we have often said, is circular motion: for that is the only motion which is continuous. And it is for the same reason that all other things — the things, I

---

[5] Ed. Joachim, Oxford, 1922, pp. 57–61, with omissions.

mean, which are transformed into one another by virtue of their powers of acting and being acted upon, e. g. the simple bodies — imitate circular motion. For whenever water is transformed into air, air into fire, and the fire back into water, we say the coming-to-be 'has completed the circle,' because it reverts again to the beginning. Hence it is by imitating circular motion that rectilinear motion too is continuous. . . .

338 a. If, then, the coming-to-be of anything is absolutely necessary, it must be cyclical — i. e. it must return upon itself. For coming-to-be must either be limited or not limited: and if not limited, it must be either rectilinear or cyclical. But the first of these last two alternatives is impossible if coming-to-be is eternal, because there could not be any first cause whatever in an infinite rectilinear sequence, whether its members be taken forwards (as future events) or backwards (as past events). Yet coming-to-be must have a first cause. . . . But it cannot be eternal if it is limited. Consequently it must be cyclical. There will, then, necessarily be a reciprocal relation between what is prior and what is subsequent, so that the necessary occurrence of the subsequent involves the necessary occurrence of the prior, and conversely the necessary occurrence of the prior involves that of the subsequent. And this will hold continuously in all cases: for it makes no difference whether the sequence of which we are speaking is composed of two or of many members.

It is in circular movement, therefore, and in cyclical coming-to-be, that the absolutely necessary is to be found. And if the coming-to-be of things is cyclical, it is necessary that each of them is coming-to-be and has come-to-be: and if their coming-to-be is necessary, it is cyclical. It is, then, reasonable that this should be so (since the circular motion, i. e. the motion of the heavens, was shown to be eternal on other grounds also) because it is from necessity that things exist and will continue to exist, as many of them as are moments of this motion or are due to it. For since that which moves in a circle is always setting something else in motion, the movements of the things it moves are also necessarily circular. Thus because there is such a motion of the upper heaven, the sun also revolves in a circle; and because it does so, the seasons consequently come-to-be in a cycle, i. e. return upon themselves; and because they come-to-be cyclically, so in their turn do the things whose coming-to-be is caused by the seasons.

Why then do some things manifestly come-to-be in this cyclical fashion, as, e. g., showers and air, so that it must rain if there is to be a cloud and, conversely, there must be a cloud if it is to rain, while men and animals do not return upon themselves so that the same individual comes-to-be a second time (for though your coming-to-be necessarily presupposes your father's, his coming-to-be does not presuppose yours)? Why, on the contrary, does *this* coming-to-be seem to occur in a straight line? To answer this question we must begin by inquiring whether all things return upon themselves in the same manner or whether they do not, — so that in some cases what recurs is numerically the same, in others it is the same only in species [or form]. Now it is evident that those things whose substance throughout their motion is imperishable will be numerically, as well as specifically, the same in their recurrence: for the character of the motion is determined by the character of that which undergoes it. Those things, on the other hand, whose substance is perishable must return upon themselves in the sense that what recurs, though the same in species, is not the same numerically. That is why, when water comes-to-be from air and air from water, the air is the same in species but not numerically: and even if these too recur numerically the same, yet this does not happen with things whose substance is such that it is essentially capable of not-being.[6]

Here are two arguments, both of which would seem to lead logically to a theory of world-cycles. (a) The 'movement' (a term which for Aristotle covers also qualitative change and growth) of things in the lower world is (except for the occasional slight admixture of 'luck and chance' in natural processes) determined directly by the spatial motion of the sun and indirectly by that of the celestial bodies 'above' it. But this motion is circular; each body in the heavens returns repeatedly to the same point in every orbit which it traverses. Hence the circular motion of the heavens should have as its consequence a temporally cyclical repetition of the same kinds of qualitative change in the same order in the sublunary world. (b) The number of events or states of things which arise in time is infinite, but the sequence of causes and effects must be finite: it must have a first member. This combination of temporal infinity with finitude of the causal regress is conceivable only if the latter be regarded as cyclical. This should mean that the number of *kinds* of causes (and effects, which are in turn causes) is limited; i. e. that nature has a certain répertoire of states which it must go through in a fixed sequence (allowing, once more, for minor variations due to 'contingency'), and must then repeat this *ad infinitum*. There should then, it would appear, have been in the past infinitely many Aristotles uttering the same thoughts in the same phases of the cycle; and there should be infinitely many more to come. Doubtless each of these would be 'numerically' distinct from all the others; but the combination of attributes which distinguishes Aristotle or any present individual from any other should be reproduced again and again.

But the natural inference from his argument is not drawn by Aristotle. As his illustrations show, the cyclical character which he here ascribes to the natural processes in the lower world amounts to no more than a continuous repetition of the same generic types of entities or states. The annual circular motion of the sun results in the recurrent round of the seasons — which, however, are not precisely the same every year. Every individual organism goes through a cycle in a similar sense, i. e., it comes into existence, develops to maturity, declines and dies; but the cycle which Aristotle deduces by his dialectic here consists only in the fact that, while individuals are transitory, the same species is continued in other individuals; fathers are succeeded by sons who in turn become fathers, but

---

[6] Based upon Joachim's translation in Oxford edition.

the sons are obviously not exact, nor usually close, replicas of their parents. The cycles actually admitted, in short, are such only in a loose sense, and they too are apparently local, not cosmical or even terrestrial in magnitude. As for world-cycles such as were conceived by Empedocles, (probably) by Heraclitus, and by the Stoics — involving the periodic ' destruction' of the world as a whole, or its resolution into a single primary element with a consequent disappearance of the qualitative diversities or ' mixtures' which are now manifested by it — this is excluded by Aristotle's general assumption of the substantial constancy of the structure and constitution of the world.[7]

Thus, while Aristotle suggests arguments which could be used in support of the theory of the *ewige Wiederkunft,* he does not himself employ them to that end. And there is in his cosmology, even within the limits of any one of his larger so-called cyclical processes, no movement towards an end, and neither an augmentation nor a loss of value. Through the succession of generations, each species remains true to type and is not transformed into a ' higher' one; the world in general grows neither better nor worse, and the past as a whole was not, except in minor ways, different from what the present is and the future will be. His conception of cosmical history, in other words, is on the whole a form of what we have called the Theory of Endless Undulation.

CULTURAL CYCLES

On the other hand, the cyclical conception is applied in a somewhat more definite way by Aristotle to the history of the arts and sciences. These all go through a process of development (analogous to the life-cycle of the individual) which is limited. Its final outcome, once attained, is destroyed; and the sequence is subsequently repeated, without limit. *Within* each of these cycles, then, there is a more or less regular advance from a rudimentary beginning to a climax; but the supposition of an endless intellectual or cultural progress is excluded. The passage from the *Politics* suggests that there is not only such a process of development and decline in the case of each art, but also a more or less regular sequence in which the several arts are discovered. Aristotle does not, however, attempt (as some other ancient writers did) to trace this history in any detail, except in the case of the political art.

VI, 2. *Met.* XI, 1074 b 10.

> κατὰ τὸ εἰκὸς πολλάκις εὑρημένης εἰς τὸ δυνατὸν ἑκάστης καὶ τέχνης καὶ φιλοσοφίας καὶ πάλιν φθειρομένων. . . .[8]

---

[7] Aristotle, it is true, also asserts that the transformation of the elements into one another takes place in a regular cyclical order; but this also appears to be a local affair. It does not imply that at any given time the whole cosmical system is composed of one element, at another of another, and so on. Cf. *De gener. et corrupt.* II, 331 b 2 f.   [8] Ed. W. Christ, Leipzig, 1931.

It is probable that each of the arts and sciences has been many
times investigated as far as it is possible for it to be and has again
perished.[9]

VI, 3. *Politica,* VII, 1329 b 25.

σχεδὸν μὲν οὖν καὶ τὰ ἄλλα δεῖ νομίζειν εὑρῆσθαι πολλάκις ἐν τῷ πολλῷ
χρόνῳ, μᾶλλον δ' ἀπειράκις. τὰ μὲν γὰρ ἀναγκαῖα τὴν χρείαν διδάσκειν εἰκὸς
αὐτήν, τὰ δ' εἰς εὐσχημοσύνην καὶ περιουσίαν· ὑπαρχόντων ἤδη τούτων εὔλογον
λαμβάνειν τὴν αὔξησιν.[10]

It is perhaps necessary to believe that other things also have been
discovered repeatedly, or rather infinitely often, in the long course
of time. For necessity itself probably first taught them what is
needful and then by degrees led them to refinements and superfluities; and when these have once taken a start, it may reasonably be
supposed that they will increase.

THE NORMAL SEQUENCE OF THE FORMS OF SOCIAL ORGANIZATION

In the past political history of (at least) the Greeks Aristotle found a
certain law of progress exemplified. It has not, however, been fully realized even by all the Hellenic peoples, still less by the barbarians; nor is it
suggested that it is necessarily destined to be. Nevertheless, the phenomenon of " association " (κοινωνία) has, like an organism, its normal sequence
of stages, from its germinal to its fully developed form; and it can best
be understood in the light of its genesis and development.[11]

VI, 4. *Pol.* I, 1252 a 24 f.

Εἰ δή τις ἐξ ἀρχῆς τὰ πράγματα φυόμενα βλέψειεν, ὥσπερ ἐν τοῖς ἄλλοις,
καὶ ἐν τούτοις κάλλιστ' ἂν οὕτω θεωρήσειεν.[12]

As in other matters, so also in politics, it is by considering the
growth of things from their beginning that one will obtain the
clearest understanding of them.

Aristotle's enumeration of these typical successive phases of social
development is at the same time an account of their motivation, the desires
and needs from which they spring, and an appraisal of their relative value,
in terms of the degree to which they serve the " natural " ends of human
existence. The first cause of association is the sexual and parental instinct
(1252 a 27-30), common to man and other animals (and even plants!);
the second is " the union of those who are by nature rulers and those who
are by nature destined to be ruled," i. e. slaves, " for the sake of security.
For he who is able by his intelligence to exercise foresight is by nature

[9] Substantially the same remark is made in *De caelo,* I, 270 b 19-20.

[10] Ed. Otto Immisch, Leipzig, 1929.

[11] As the passage is probably the most familiar in all of Aristotle's writings, it
has seemed more useful to analyze it briefly than to reproduce the text in full.

[12] Ed. Immisch, Leipzig, 1929.

ruler and master, and he who can only carry out by using his body what the foreseeing man plans is by nature a slave " (1252 a 31 f.). It is apparently with the household (οἰκία) as already constituted by this dual relationship that Aristotle begins the sequence. Such a household " is the association which has arisen in accordance with nature to supply man's every-day wants " (1252 b 14).

A second stage arises when out of a number of households scattered villages are formed, of which the " most natural " kind is a consanguineous group, or clan, " ruled by the eldest." Thus the earliest form of Greek kingship arose, which among many barbarian peoples still persists (1252 b 19 f.). This type of society is already capable of satisfying something more than the most rudimentary, or " every-day," needs.

The third stage results when a " complete city-state which already possesses entire self-sufficiency " is formed through the union of several such villages. Thus the state, though (as arising out of the earlier forms of society) it originates in " the bare needs of life," continues in existence " for the sake of the good life " (1252 b 27-30), of which " self-sufficiency is the most excellent characteristic and the consummation " (1253 a 1).[13] The self-sufficiency of a state depends partly upon the number of its citizens and partly upon its territory. " A state when composed of too few is not self-sufficient (but self-sufficiency is what constitutes a state); when composed of too many, though self-sufficing in mere necessaries, it is not a state but only a people; for constitutional government (πολιτεία) can scarcely exist [when the number of citizens is very great]. For who can be the general of such an excessive multitude, or who the herald, unless he has the voice of a Stentor. Necessarily, then, a state begins to exist only when it has attained a population sufficient for the good life in the political community; it may, indeed, if it somewhat exceed this [minimal] number be a greater state, but this . . . will not be unlimited " (Pol. VII, 1326 b 2-11). Much the same holds good with respect to the territory of the state: " As to the question what kind of territory it ought to have, it is evident that everyone would agree that it should be such as to make the state completely self-sufficing; and such is necessarily that which bears every sort of products, for self-sufficiency means having a supply of everything and lacking nothing. In extent and magnitude the territory should, moreover, be sufficient to enable the inhabitants to live a life of leisure in a manner at once liberal and self-controlled " (ibid. 1326 b 27-34).

Yet it is not, apparently, these attributes alone which distinguish a " state " from the prior and inferior forms of social organization. Two other differentiae are elsewhere insisted upon by Aristotle. (a) A genuine state has a fixed constitution defining civil rights and the allocation of political powers, privileges and duties; it is a government of laws and not

---

[13] On the peculiar importance of the notion of self-sufficiency in nearly all Greek ethical doctrines, vide p. 119.

of men (*Pol.* III, 1278 b 10 ff.). " The rule of law is better than that of any one of the citizens; and for the same reason, even if it be better for certain individuals to govern, they should be appointed only as guardians of the laws and as subject to them " and as interpreters of their application to special cases not clearly covered by general statutes — with, however, the right " to introduce any amendments which experience leads them to consider an improvement on the laws already established." " He therefore who proposes that the laws shall govern, seems to propose that God and reason shall govern, but he who would have man govern, hands over the power to a wild beast; for desire is like a wild beast, and passion warps the rule even of the best men " (*Pol.* III, 1287 a 19-28). (b) But laws, in this sense — i. e. as definitions of rights — are not enough: " the law is a covenant, or, in the words of the Sophist Lycophron, a guarantee of men's just claims upon one another, but it does not as such make the citizens good and just " (III, 1280 b 10-12). Laws defining mutual rights are necessary even in " alliances ": " thus it is clear that any state that is properly so called, and is not a ' state ' in name only, must be concerned about virtue; for otherwise the association becomes merely an alliance " (*ibid.* 1280 b 6-9).

A society, then, when its normal development is not arrested, goes through a typical evolution which corresponds to, and results from, an increasing realization by men of the originally merely latent potentialities and needs of human nature — a gradual discovery of what " a good way of living " (εὖ ζῆν) for man is. The simplest and earliest form of social organization is the least excellent because it serves only the most rudimentary and least distinctively human of these needs.[14] Man is " by nature a political animal " in the sense that his specific nature can manifest itself fully only in the third stage, i. e. when he is a member of a πόλις. But since this final and best phase is for Aristotle one which assures to individuals " leisure " and abundant opportunity for " liberal " pursuits, its advantages must necessarily be confined to a limited class. The " virtue " to which the state is instrumental cannot be a universal possession. There must be tillers of the soil and artisans and tradesmen, and the functions which these perform should preclude them from citizenship in the best constituted state; " for such a life is ignoble and unfavorable to virtue, since leisure is needful for the production of virtue and for participation in politics " (*Pol.* VII, 1328 b 39-1329 a 2; III, 1278 a 9). Most of the property, also, should be in the hands of this ruling class, " for the citizens must necessarily possess abundant means. . . . The artisan class has no share in the

---

[14] Of democracy, however — which is not the ideal form of the state — the best type is the earliest, in which the population is composed of farmers and herdsmen, all of them too poor to covet one another's goods and too busy at making a living to find much time for politics or to be ambitious for political distinction (*Pol.* VI, 1318 b 6-17).

state, nor has any other that is not an 'artificer of virtue'"; and the tillers of the soil must obviously be without the right to hold property, "since these will necessarily be either slaves or immigrant aliens (*perioeci*)" (*Pol.* VII, 1329 a 18-26). Social progress thus consists chiefly for Aristotle in the gradual development of forms of government and other conditions favorable to the existence of a property-holding leisure class who, being free from manual labor and the petty concerns of retail trade, will be able to give themselves to intellectual pursuits and enjoyments, and to the disinterested management of the affairs of the state.[15] Aristotle does not assume that this consummation, once reached or approximated, will endure unchanged; all forms of government, even the best, are, because of the weaknesses of human nature, liable to "perversions" and "those which are faulty and perverted are necessarily subsequent to those which are perfect" (*Pol.* III, 1275 b 1-3); moreover, all actual governments fall short of perfection in some degree and are in that sense all "perversions" (*Pol.* IV, 1293 b 25-26) or "deviations" from the norm.[16] Of the mutability of all things under the moon, and of the tendency of all human achievements to degenerate, Aristotle has an abiding sense.

PRIMITIVE MEN

Of primitive peoples, whether in past or present, and of their customs and beliefs, Aristotle has the lowest opinion. Discussing the question "whether it is expedient to make any changes in the laws of a country"

[15] On the other hand in an earlier passage (*Pol.* III, 1281 a 39-1282 a 43), Aristotle admits that the argument for democracy may "have an element of truth," mainly on three grounds. (a) "The many, though not individually good men, yet when they come together, may be so collectively," since "it may be argued that each individual of the many has some portion of virtue and wisdom, and when these are combined, just as a multitude assembled together becomes one individual having many feet and many hands and many senses, so it also becomes one individual with respect to moral character and intelligence." This cannot, indeed, be assumed to be true of all multitudes, but it may well be true of some. (b) A state which excludes a great part of the population from participation in government is in a dangerous condition, "for when there is a large number of persons without political honors and in poverty, the state will necessarily be full of enemies." (c) The best judges of the merits of a product are often not the experts who make it but those for whose use it is made; thus the best judges of laws may similarly be those who are affected by them, i. e. the entire body of persons subject to them. "Hence the multitude is justly sovereign with respect to greater matters . . . and the rateable property of all members collectively greater than that of the individual or the few who hold the great offices of government." Though Aristotle thus presents (apparently at second-hand) some of the principal arguments for democracy which subsequent writers were to employ, the passage cannot be said to express his own final view.

[16] To enter further into the details of Aristotle's political theory, such as his comparison of the merits and demerits of the six typical forms of polity, does not fall within the subject-matter of this volume.

there are, he observes, two schools of opinion. One of these argues chiefly from the premises (a) that politics is an art and that any art is progressive; and (b) that the people of primeval times were unenlightened and their laws and customs obviously absurd.

VI, 5. *Pol.* II, 1268 b 36-1269 a 8.

ὥστ᾽ ἐπεὶ μίαν τούτων [τεχνῶν καὶ δυνάμεων] θετέον καὶ τὴν πολιτικήν, δῆλον ὅτι καὶ περὶ ταύτην ἀναγκαῖον ὁμοίως ἔχειν ["τὸ κινεῖν"]. σημεῖον δ᾽ ἂν γεγονέναι φαίη τις ἐπ᾽ αὐτῶν τῶν ἔργων· τοὺς γὰρ ἀρχαίους νόμους λίαν ἁπλοῦς εἶναι καὶ βαρβαρικούς. ἐσιδηροφοροῦντό τε γὰρ οἱ Ἕλληνες, καὶ τὰς γυναῖκας ἐωνοῦντο παρ᾽ ἀλλήλων, ὅσα τε λοιπὰ τῶν ἀρχαίων ἐστί που νομίμων, εὐήθη πάμπαν ἐστίν, οἷον ἐν Κύμῃ περὶ τὰ φονικὰ νόμος ἐστίν, ἂν πλῆθός τι παράσχηται μαρτύρων ὁ διώκων τὸν φόνον τῶν αὐτοῦ συγγενῶν, ἔνοχον εἶναι τῷ φόνῳ τὸν φεύγοντα. ζητοῦσι δ᾽ὅλως οὐ τὸ πάτριον ἀλλὰ τἀγαθὸν πάντες· εἰκός τε τοὺς πρώτους, εἴτε γηγενεῖς ἦσαν εἴτ᾽ ἐκ φθορᾶς τινος ἐσώθησαν, ὁμοίους εἶναι καὶ τοὺς τυχόντας καὶ τοὺς ἀνοήτους, ὥσπερ καὶ λέγεται κατὰ τῶν γηγενῶν, ὥστε ἄτοπον τὸ μένειν ἐν τοῖς τούτων δόγμασιν.[17]

If politics likewise is to be classed as one of these (arts and faculties), it is evident that in it also change is necessary; and the facts themselves show that it has been subject to change. For the old customs are exceedingly simple and barbarous. For the Greeks at one time went about armed and bought their women from one another; and all the other ancient customs which still persist anywhere are altogether foolish. For example, there is a law at Cyme concerning murders, that if the accuser bring forward a certain number of witnesses from among his own kinsmen, the accused is guilty of the murder. And in general, men desire the good and not merely what their fathers had. And it would seem that the primitive men, whether they were born from the earth or survived from some previous catastrophe, were like average and unintelligent men. This, indeed, is expressly said to have been the case with the earthborn race, so that it would be absurd to adhere to their notions.[18]

The moral of the passage might be taken to be that since changes (specifically in laws and institutions) have been made with advantage in the past, they should and will continue to be made in the future. But Aristotle admits this consequence only with hesitancy and much qualification. A

[17] Ed. O. Immisch, 1929, p. 53.

[18] In view of Aristotle's general conception of cosmical history, these "first" men cannot, of course, have been such in any absolute sense; and it would be unwarranted, also, to infer from the passage that Aristotle seriously entertained the notion of "earth-born men," or supposed each cultural cycle to begin with the spontaneous generation of human beings from the soil. "The men who are saved from some catastrophe," however, would correctly represent the first generation in the new cycle which, on Aristotle's theory, had been brought about by a natural (but local) cataclysm. Since they would be "average men" reduced to primitive necessities by the cataclysm, they would lose all but a memory of the arts and sciences their people had had before the flood or earthquake. This memory Aristotle elsewhere relies upon to find in language and myth indications of a pre-existent development of art and philosophy.

few changes may occasionally be desirable, but " the habit of changing laws lightly is an evil " (*Pol.* II, 1269 a 14 f.) ; the analogy from progress in the arts to progress in laws does not hold, because the law gets its efficacy from the habit of obedience, " which can only be given by time, so that a readiness to change from old to new laws weakens the power of law " (*ibid.*). And elsewhere Aristotle — referring primarily but apparently not exclusively to political and social matters — assumes that pretty much all the progress needful or possible in the present cultural cycle has already been accomplished. Everything good must by this time have been discovered and tried, and new, or new-old, schemes of society, such as Plato's, may be dismissed on this ground alone — though Aristotle does not fail to give other grounds. If Aristotle had no faith in — or illusions about — the excellence of primitive society, he had scarcely more faith in the possibility of any material improvement upon the social order existing in the Greece of his own day; that of the barbarians was another matter. The *ignava ratio* of the hopeless conservative finds in the following passage its most striking expression in classical literature.

VI, 6. *Pol.* II, 1264 a 1-5.

δεῖ δὲ μηδὲ τοῦτο αὐτὸ ἀγνοεῖν, ὅτι χρὴ προσέχειν τῷ πολλῷ χρόνῳ καὶ τοῖς πολλοῖς ἔτεσιν, ἐν οἷς οὐκ ἂν ἔλαθεν, εἰ ταῦτα καλῶς εἶχεν· πάντα γὰρ σχεδὸν εὕρηται μέν, ἀλλὰ τὰ μὲν οὐ συνῆκται, τοῖς δ' οὐ χρῶνται γινώσκοντες.[19]

We must not fail to keep in mind the length of time and multitude of years in which these things, if they had been good, would certainly not have remained unknown; for almost everything has been found out, though in some cases what is known has not been systematized, and in other cases men do not make use of the knowledge which they have.

Of contemporary savages Aristotle's opinion is no more favorable than of primeval men.

VI, 7. *Eth. Nic.* VII, 1149 a 9 f.

καὶ τῶν ἀφρόνων οἱ μὲν ἐκ φύσεως ἀλόγιστοι καὶ μόνον τῇ αἰσθήσει ζῶντες θηριώδεις, ὥσπερ ἔνια γένη τῶν πόρρω βαρβάρων.

And of the foolish, those who are irrational by nature and live only by their senses are like the beasts, as are some of the races of the distant barbarians.[20]

[19] Ed. Immisch, 1929.

[20] Cf. *Eth. Nic.* VII, 1145 a 30 ff. These distant barbarians are presumably the Scythians and their like. In one place (*Eth. Nic.* X, 1176 b 33), Aristotle quotes with approval Anacharsis, who was, however, not a typical Scythian and can hardly be regarded as relevant. In *Pol.* VII, 1324 b 12 ff. he includes the Scythians among his examples of the peoples excessively addicted to war, and refers to their custom of carrying around " at a certain festival a cup from which no one who had not killed any enemy was allowed to drink."

Aristotle's remoteness from the primitivistic temper is once more to be seen in his appraisal of the different levels of technological development. The cultural primitivist was wont to praise either the stage before the domestication of animals, or the pastoral stage — or, in the case of semi-primitivists, the incipient agricultural stage. But Aristotle has no belief in the superior virtues of hunters or shepherds or even farmers. Their modes of subsistence are sufficient for bare living, but not for " the good life."

VI, 8. *Pol.* 1256 a 30 ff.

πολὺ γὰρ διαφέρουσιν οἱ τούτων βίοι. οἱ μὲν οὖν ἀργότατοι νομάδες εἰσίν (ἡ γὰρ ἀπὸ τῶν ἡμέρων τροφὴ ζῴων ἄνευ πόνου γίνεται σχολάζουσιν· ἀναγκαίου δ' ὄντος μεταβάλλειν τοῖς κτήνεσι διὰ τὰς νομὰς καὶ αὐτοὶ ἀναγκάζονται συνακολουθεῖν, ὥσπερ γεωργίαν ζῶσαν γεωργοῦντες)· οἱ δ' ἀπὸ θήρας ζῶσι, καὶ θήρας ἕτεροι ἑτέρας, οἷον οἱ μὲν ἀπὸ λῃστείας, οἱ δ' ἀφ' ἁλιείας, ὅσοι λίμνας καὶ ἕλη καὶ ποταμοὺς ἢ θάλατταν τοιαύτην προσοικοῦσιν, οἱ δ' ἀπ' ὀρνίθων ἢ θηρίων ἀγρίων· τὸ δὲ πλεῖστον γένος τῶν ἀνθρώπων ἀπὸ τῆς γῆς ζῇ καὶ τῶν ἡμέρων καρπῶν. . . . ἡ μὲν οὖν τοιαύτη κτῆσις ὑπ' αὐτῆς φαίνεται τῆς φύσεως διδομένη πᾶσιν, ὥσπερ κατὰ τὴν πρώτην γένεσιν εὐθύς, οὕτω καὶ τελειωθεῖσιν. καὶ γὰρ κατὰ τὴν ἐξ ἀρχῆς γένεσιν τὰ μὲν συνεκτίκτει τῶν ζῴων τοσαύτην τροφὴν ὡς ἱκανὴν εἶναι μέχρις οὗ ἂν δύνηται αὐτὸ αὑτῷ πορίζειν τὸ γεννηθέν.[21]

Men's modes of life differ widely. The laziest are the nomadic shepherds, for they live an idle life getting their subsistence without labor from tame animals; as their flocks have to wander from one pasturage to another, they are obliged to follow them, cultivating, as it were, a living farm. Others live by various kinds of hunting, such as brigands, some — those who dwell beside lakes or marshes or rivers or a sea, — by fishing, still others live on birds and wild beasts. But the greater number of men obtain a living from the cultivated fruits of the soil. . . . Property in this sense seems to be given to all by nature, both at birth and when they are grown up. For at the beginning, after the birth of their offspring, some animals produce food in quantity sufficient for them until they are able to provide for themselves.

COMMUNISM

That primitive society was communistic Aristotle assumed (*Pol.* I, 1257 a 19 f.) ; but this was in his eyes one of the evidences of its inferiority and its non-accordance with ' nature' (in one sense). In view of the frequent prominence of the communistic ideal in ancient and later primitivism, the following passages, as the most important criticism of communism in classical literature, are relevant to our subject, though they are primarily directed against Plato.

VI, 9. *Pol.* II, 1261 a 2 ff. (Translation on p. 182).

ἀλλὰ πότερον ὅσων ἐνδέχεται κοινωνῆσαι, πάντων βέλτιον κοινωνεῖν τὴν μέλλουσαν οἰκήσεσθαι πόλιν καλῶς, ἢ τινῶν μὲν τινῶν δ' οὐ βέλτιον;

[21] Ed. Otto Immisch.

ἐνδέχεται γὰρ καὶ τέκνων καὶ γυναικῶν καὶ κτημάτων κοινωνεῖν τοὺς πολίτας
ἀλλήλοις, ὥσπερ ἐν τῇ πολιτείᾳ τῇ Πλάτωνος· ἐκεῖ γὰρ ὁ Σωκράτης φησὶ
δεῖν κοινὰ τὰ τέκνα καὶ τὰς γυναῖκας εἶναι καὶ τὰς κτήσεις. τοῦτο δὴ πότερον
ὡς νῦν οὕτω βέλτιον ἔχειν, ἢ κατὰ τὸν ἐν τῇ πολιτείᾳ γεγραμμένον νόμον;
Ἔχει δὴ δυσχερείας ἄλλας τε πολλὰς τὸ πάντων εἶναι τὰς γυναῖκας κοινάς,
καὶ δι' ἣν αἰτίαν φησὶ δεῖν νενομοθετῆσθαι τὸν τρόπον τοῦτον ὁ Σωκράτης,
οὐ φαίνεται συμβαῖνον ἐκ τῶν λόγων. ἔτι δὲ πρὸς τὸ τέλος ὅ φησι τῇ πόλει
δεῖν ὑπάρχειν, ὡς μὲν εἴρηται νῦν, ἀδύνατον, πῶς δὲ δεῖ διελεῖν, οὐδὲν διώρισται.
λέγω δὲ τὸ μίαν εἶναι τὴν πόλιν ὡς ἄριστον ὂν ὅτι μάλιστα πᾶσαν· λαμβάνει
γὰρ ταύτην ὑπόθεσιν ὁ Σωκράτης. Καίτοι φανερόν ἐστιν ὡς προϊοῦσα καὶ
γινομένη μία μᾶλλον οὐδὲ πόλις ἔσται· πλῆθος γάρ τι τὴν φύσιν ἐστὶν
ἡ πόλις, γινομένη τε μία μᾶλλον οἰκία μὲν ἐκ πόλεως ἄνθρωπος δ' ἐξ οἰκίας
ἔσται· μᾶλλον γὰρ μίαν τὴν οἰκίαν τῆς πόλεως φαίημεν ἄν, καὶ τὸν ἕνα τῆς
οἰκίας· ὥστ' εἰ καὶ δυνατός τις εἴη τοῦτο δρᾶν, οὐ ποιητέον· ἀναιρήσει γὰρ
τὴν πόλιν. . . .

1261 b 15. Ἀλλὰ μὴν οὐδ' εἰ τοῦτο ἄριστόν ἐστι, τὸ μίαν ὅτι μάλιστ'
εἶναι τὴν κοινωνίαν, οὐδὲ τοῦτο ἀποδείκνυσθαι φαίνεται κατὰ τὸν λόγον, ἐὰν
πάντες ἅμα λέγωσι τὸ ἐμὸν καὶ τὸ μὴ ἐμόν· τοῦτο γὰρ οἴεται ὁ Σωκράτης
σημεῖον εἶναι τοῦ τὴν πόλιν τελέως εἶναι μίαν. τὸ γὰρ πάντες διττόν. εἰ μὲν
οὖν ὡς ἕκαστος, τάχ' ἂν εἴη μᾶλλον ὃ βούλεται ποιεῖν ὁ Σωκράτης (ἕκαστος
γὰρ υἱὸν ἑαυτοῦ φήσει τὸν αὐτὸν καὶ γυναῖκα δὴ τὴν αὐτήν, καὶ περὶ τῆς
οὐσίας καὶ περὶ ἑκάστου δὴ τῶν συμβαινόντων ὡσαύτως)· νῦν δ' οὐχ οὕτως
φήσουσιν οἱ κοιναῖς χρώμενοι ταῖς γυναιξὶ καὶ τοῖς τέκνοις, ἀλλὰ πάντες μέν,
οὐχ ὡς ἕκαστος δ' αὐτῶν, ὁμοίως δὲ καὶ τὴν οὐσίαν πάντες μέν, οὐχ ὡς ἕκαστος
δ' αὐτῶν. . . . ὡδὶ δ' οὐδὲν ὁμονοητικόν· πρὸς δὲ τούτοις ἑτέραν ἔχει βλάβην
τὸ λεγόμενον. ἥκιστα γὰρ ἐπιμελείας τυγχάνει τὸ πλείστων κοινόν· τῶν γὰρ
ἰδίων μάλιστα φροντίζουσιν, τῶν δὲ κοινῶν ἧττον, ἢ ὅσον ἑκάστῳ ἐπιβάλλει·
πρὸς γὰρ τοῖς ἄλλοις ὡς ἑτέρου φροντίζοντος ὀλιγωροῦσι μᾶλλον, ὥσπερ ἐν
ταῖς οἰκετικαῖς διακονίαις οἱ πολλοὶ θεράποντες ἐνίοτε χεῖρον ὑπηρετοῦσι τῶν
ἐλαττόνων. γίνονται δ' ἑκάστῳ χίλιοι τῶν πολιτῶν υἱοί, καὶ οὗτοι οὐχ ὡς
ἑκάστου, ἀλλὰ τοῦ τυχόντος ὁ τυχὼν ὁμοίως ἐστὶν υἱός· ὥστε πάντες ὁμοίως
ὀλιγωρήσουσιν. ἔτι οὕτως ἕκαστος ἐμὸς λέγει τὸν εὖ πράττοντα τῶν πολιτῶν
ἢ κακῶς, ὁπόστος τυγχάνει τὸν ἀριθμὸν ὤν, οἷον ἐμὸς ἢ τοῦ δεῖνος, τοῦτον
τὸν τρόπον λέγων καθ' ἕκαστον τῶν χιλίων, ἢ ὅσων ἡ πόλις ἐστί, καὶ τοῦτο
διστάζων· ἄδηλον γὰρ ᾧ συνέβη γενέσθαι τέκνον καὶ σωθῆναι γενόμενον.
καίτοι πότερον οὕτω κρεῖττον τὸ ἐμὸν λέγειν ἕκαστον, τὸ αὐτὸ μὲν προσ-
αγορεύοντας δισχιλίων καὶ μυρίων, ἢ μᾶλλον ὡς νῦν ἐν ταῖς πόλεσι τὸ ἐμὸν
λέγουσιν; ὁ μὲν γὰρ υἱὸν αὑτοῦ ὁ δὲ ἀδελφὸν αὑτοῦ προσαγορεύει τὸν αὐτόν,
ὁ δ' ἀνεψιόν, ἢ κατ' ἄλλην τινὰ συγγένειαν, ἢ πρὸς αἵματος ἢ κατ' οἰκειότητα
καὶ κηδείαν αὑτοῦ πρῶτον ἢ τῶν αὑτοῦ, πρὸς δὲ τούτοις ἕτερος φράτορα
φυλέτην. κρεῖττον γὰρ ἴδιον ἀνεψιὸν εἶναι ἢ τὸν τρόπον τοῦτον υἱόν. . . .

1262 a 25. Ἔτι δὲ καὶ τὰς τοιαύτας δυσχερείας οὐ ῥᾴδιον εὐλαβηθῆναι
τοῖς ταύτην κατασκευάζουσι τὴν κοινωνίαν, οἷον αἰκίας καὶ φόνους (ἀκουσίους
τοὺς δὲ ἑκουσίους) καὶ μάχας καὶ λοιδορίας· ὧν οὐδὲν ὅσιόν ἐστι γίνεσθαι
πρὸς πατέρας καὶ μητέρας καὶ τοὺς μὴ πόρρω τῆς συγγενείας ὄντας, ὥσπερ
πρὸς τοὺς ἄποθεν· ἀλλὰ καὶ πλεῖον συμβαίνειν ἀναγκαῖον ἀγνοούντων ἢ
γνωριζόντων, καὶ γενομένων τῶν μὲν γνωριζόντων ἐνδέχεται τὰς νομιζομένας
γίνεσθαι λύσεις, τῶν δὲ μηδεμίαν. . . .

1262 b 15. ἐν δὲ τῇ πόλει τὴν φιλίαν ἀναγκαῖον ὑδαρῆ γίνεσθαι διὰ τὴν
κοινωνίαν τὴν τοιαύτην, καὶ ἥκιστα λέγειν τὸν ἐμὸν ἢ υἱὸν πατέρα ἢ πατέρα
υἱόν. ὥσπερ γὰρ μικρὸν γλυκὺ εἰς πολὺ ὕδωρ μειχθὲν ἀναίσθητον ποιεῖ τὴν
κρᾶσιν, οὕτω συμβαίνει καὶ τὴν οἰκειότητα τὴν πρὸς ἀλλήλους τὴν ἀπὸ τῶν

ὀνομάτων τούτων, δι' ἃ φροντίζειν ἥκιστα ἀναγκαῖον ἐν τῇ πολιτείᾳ τῇ τοιαύτῃ
ἢ πατέρα ὡς υἱῶν ἢ υἱὸν ὡς πατρός, ἢ ὡς ἀδελφοὺς ἀλλήλων. δύο γάρ ἐστιν
ἃ μάλιστα ποιεῖ κήδεσθαι τοὺς ἀνθρώπους καὶ φιλεῖν, τό τε ἴδιον καὶ τὸ
ἀγαπητόν· ὧν οὐδέτερον οἷόν τε ὑπάρχειν τοῖς οὕτω πολιτευομένοις.[22]

Should a well ordered state have all things, so far as possible, in
common, or some things in common and some not? For it is possible that citizens should have wives and children and property in
common, as Socrates proposes in the *Republic* of Plato. Which,
then, is better: our present custom or that which is described in
the *Republic*?

There are many difficulties in the community of women; and the
reason which Socrates gives for such a law does not appear to follow
from his argument. As a means to the end which he says the state
ought to realize, the plan, as thus far set forth, is impossible; and
how we are to interpret the argument is by no means precisely stated.
I refer to the argument that the more any state is a unity, the better
it is; for this Socrates takes as his premise. Yet it is evident that
a state may reach such a degree of unity that it will be no longer a
state. For the state is in its very nature a kind of plurality, and if
it comes to be more of a unity it becomes rather a family, and the
family in the same way becomes an individual; for the family may
be said to be more one than the state, and the individual than the
family. So that this degree of unity ought not to be realized, even
if it could be, for it would be the destruction of the state. . . .

1261 b 15 ff. But even if it were best for the community to have
this greatest degree of unity, such unity is by no means evidenced
by " all men's saying ' mine ' and ' not mine ' together " — which,
according to Socrates, is the sign of perfect unity in the state. For
the word " all " is ambiguous. If it refers to *each* man, perhaps
that would rather be what Socrates desires to attain; for each will
call the same person his wife and the same person his son, and so of
his property and of whatever else belongs to him. But this is not
the way in which people would speak who had their wives and children in common; they would say " all " and not " each "; similarly,
they would say that the property " belongs to all of us," not " to each
of us." . . . If the words are taken in [the former] sense, such a
way of speaking is by no means conducive to harmony. And there
is a further objection to the proposal. For that which is common
to the greatest number has the least care bestowed upon it. For
everyone thinks chiefly of his own and very little of the common
interest, or only so far as it affects him as an individual. For aside
from other considerations, men neglect what they regard as the concern of some one else, just as in households, many servants are often
less useful than a few. Every citizen will have thousands of sons,
who will not be his sons individually, but anyone of them will be
equally the son of everybody, and all will equally be neglected.
Further, upon this plan, everyone will call another " mine " according as he is a flourishing citizen or the reverse — whatever fraction
of the whole number of citizens may chance to be flourishing. Just
as one speaks of a thing as " mine or some other's." so he will speak
in this way of each of thousands — or whatever the number in the

[22] Ed. Immisch.

state may be — as "my" son, and that without any certainty
[whether any of them is actually his son]. For it will evidently be
impossible to know who chanced to have a son, or whether, if he was
born, he survived. But which is better — for each to say "mine"
in this way, attributing the same son to two thousand or ten thousand fathers, or to use the word "mine" as we do in the states that
now exist? For the same person is now called by one man his son,
by another his brother, by another his cousin, or some other relation,
whether by blood or marriage or kinship, or again, by another he is
called his fellow clansman or tribesman. For it is better to be a real
cousin of somebody than to be a son after such a fashion as this. . . .

1262 a 25. There will be other difficulties against which it will
not be easy for those who set up this sort of communism to guard,
such as assaults and homicides (voluntary or involuntary), quarrels
and slanders, all of which are most unholy acts when committed
against fathers and mothers and other near relations, but are not so
in the same degree when there is no relationship. Moreover, they
are much more likely to occur when the relationship is unknown
than when it is recognized; and when they have occurred, the customary expiations can be made when it is recognized, but not when
it is unknown. . . .

1262 b 15. And in the state having this sort of community, affection will be watery; the son will not say "my father," nor the
father "my son." As a little sweet wine mingled with a great deal
of water will be imperceptible in the mixture, so the sense of relationship which is based upon these names will be lost; consequently,
in such a polity, the son will not care about the father, or the father
about the son, or brother about brother. For there are two things
which chiefly arouse in man concern about anything and affection
for it — that a thing is his own and that it is his only one, and
neither can exist in such a state as this. . . .

VI, 10. *Pol.* 1262 b 37-1263 b 26.

Ἐχόμενον δὲ τούτων ἐστὶν ἐπισκέψασθαι περὶ τῆς κτήσεως, τίνα τρόπον
δεῖ κατασκευάζεσθαι τοῖς μέλλουσι πολιτεύεσθαι τὴν ἀρίστην πολιτείαν,
πότερον κοινὴν ἢ μὴ κοινὴν εἶναι τὴν κτῆσιν. τοῦτο δ' ἄν τις καὶ χωρὶς
σκέψαιτο ἀπὸ τῶν περὶ τὰ τέκνα καὶ τὰς γυναῖκας νενομοθετημένων, λέγω
δὲ τὰ περὶ τὴν κτῆσιν πότερον κἂν ᾖ ἐκεῖνα χωρίς, καθ' ὃν νῦν τρόπον ἔχει
πᾶσι, τάς τε κτήσεις κοινὰς εἶναι βέλτιον καὶ τὰς χρήσεις . . . ὅλως δὲ τὸ
συζῆν καὶ κοινωνεῖν τῶν ἀνθρωπικῶν πάντων χαλεπόν, καὶ μάλιστα τῶν τοιούτων. δηλοῦσι δ' αἱ τῶν συναποδήμων κοινωνίαι· σχεδὸν γὰρ οἱ πλεῖστοι
διαφερόμενοι ἐκ τῶν ἐν ποσὶ καὶ ἐκ μικρῶν προσκρούοντες ἀλλήλοις. ἔτι δὲ
τῶν θεραπόντων τούτοις μάλιστα προσκρούομεν οἷς πλεῖστα προσχρώμεθα
πρὸς τὰς διακονίας τὰς ἐγκυκλίους. τὸ μὲν οὖν κοινὰς εἶναι τὰς κτήσεις ταύτας
τε καὶ ἄλλας τοιαύτας ἔχει δυσχερείας· ὃν δὲ νῦν τρόπον ἔχει καὶ ἐπικοσμηθὲν
ἤθεσι καὶ τάξει νόμων ὀρθῶν, οὐ μικρὸν ἂν διενέγκαι. . . . αἱ μὲν γὰρ ἐπι-
μέλειαι διῃρημέναι τὰ ἐγκλήματα πρὸς ἀλλήλους οὐ ποιήσουσιν, μᾶλλον
δ' ἐπιδώσουσιν ὡς πρὸς ἴδιον ἑκάστου προσεδρεύοντος· δι' ἀρετὴν δ' ἔσται
πρὸς τὸ χρῆσθαι κατὰ τὴν παροιμίαν κοινὰ τὰ φίλων. . . . ἔτι δὲ καὶ πρὸς
ἡδονὴν ἀμύθητον ὅσον διαφέρει τὸ νομίζειν ἴδιόν τι. μὴ γὰρ οὐ μάτην τὴν
πρὸς αὑτὸν αὐτὸς ἔχει φιλίαν ἕκαστος, ἀλλ' ἔστι τοῦτο φυσικόν. τὸ δὲ
φίλαυτον εἶναι ψέγεται δικαίως· οὐκ ἔστι δὲ τοῦτο τὸ φιλεῖν ἑαυτόν, ἀλλὰ τὸ
μᾶλλον ἢ δεῖ φιλεῖν, καθάπερ καὶ τὸν φιλοχρήματον, ἐπεὶ φιλοῦσί γε πάντες

ὡς εἰπεῖν ἕκαστον τῶν τοιούτων. ἀλλὰ μὴν καὶ τὸ χαρίσασθαι καὶ βοηθῆσαι φίλοις ἢ ξένοις ἢ ἑταίροις ἥδιστον· ὃ γίνεται τῆς κτήσεως ἰδίας οὔσης. ταῦτά τε δὴ οὐ συμβαίνει τοῖς λίαν ἓν ποιοῦσι τὴν πόλιν, . . . Εὐπρόσωπος μὲν οὖν ἡ τοιαύτη νομοθεσία καὶ φιλάνθρωπος ἂν εἶναι δόξειεν· ὁ γὰρ ἀκροώμενος ἄσμενος ἀποδέχεται (νομίζων ἔσεσθαι φιλίαν τινὰ θαυμαστὴν πᾶσι πρὸς ἅπαντας), ἄλλως τε καὶ ὅταν κατηγορῇ τις τῶν νῦν ὑπαρχόντων ἐν ταῖς πολιτείαις κακῶν ὡς γινομένων διὰ τὸ μὴ κοινὴν εἶναι τὴν οὐσίαν, λέγω δὲ δίκας τε πρὸς ἀλλήλους περὶ συμβολαίων καὶ ψευδομαρτυριῶν κρίσεις καὶ πλουσίων κολακείας. ὧν οὐδὲν γίνεται διὰ τὴν ἀκοινωνησίαν ἀλλὰ διὰ τὴν μοχθηρίαν, ἐπεὶ καὶ τοὺς κοινὰ κεκτημένους καὶ κοινωνοῦντας πολλῷ διαφερο- μένους μᾶλλον ὁρῶμεν ἢ τοὺς χωρὶς τὰς οὐσίας ἔχοντας· ἀλλὰ θεωροῦμεν ὀλίγους τοὺς ἐκ τῶν κοινωνιῶν διαφερομένους πρὸς πολλοὺς συμβάλλοντες τοὺς κεκτημένους ἰδίᾳ τὰς κτήσεις. ἔτι δὲ δίκαιον μὴ μόνον λέγειν ὅσων στερήσονται κακῶν κοινωνήσαντες, ἀλλὰ καὶ ὅσων ἀγαθῶν· φαίνεται δ' εἶναι πάμπαν ἀδύνατος ὁ βίος.[23]

We must next consider how those who wish to live under the best form of government ought to arrange about property — whether it should be owned in common or not in common. And this question might be considered separately from the legislation concerning wives and children: I mean whether, even if the latter are held indi- vidually, as is now the universal practice, it is better that property and its use should be common. . . . But in general to live together and to share any human affairs is difficult; and this is especially the case in such affairs as these. This is shown in the companion- ships of travellers, for perhaps the majority of them fall into dis- agreements and quarrels over chance matters from small causes; and again, in the case of servants, we most frequently take offence at those whom we employ most for everyday services. Community of property, then, gives rise to these and other difficulties; and our present practice, improved by good morals and regulated by laws, would be not a little superior. . . . For when the care of things is divided among many, they will not complain of one another, but will rather prosper the more as each attends to his own property; yet, as a result of virtue, 'friends' goods will be common goods' (as the proverb goes) for purposes of use. . . . Moreover, one gets an inex- pressibly greater pleasure from thinking of a thing as one's private property. For the love which every man has for himself is not unreasonable, but is natural. Selfishness, indeed, is justly blamed; but this consists, not in self-love, but in loving oneself too much, just as covetousness [consists in loving money too much], for some love of both is, one may perhaps say, characteristic of all men. Furthermore, to do a kindness or a service to friends or guests or comrades is a great pleasure; but this can be enjoyed [only] when property is privately owned. These advantages, therefore, do not fall to the lot of those who carry the unification of the state too far. . . . Such a scheme of legislation has, indeed, an attractive and humani- tarian air; for men readily listen to it and are easily induced to believe that some wonderful love of everybody for everybody will result — especially when someone denounces the evils which now exist in states on the ground that they are consequences of the fact that property is not owned in common, e. g. lawsuits or breaches of

[23] Ed. Immisch.

contract, trials for perjury, and flattery of the rich.   But none of
these evils are due to the absence of communism, but to wickedness,
since we see those who jointly own or possess things quarreling a
great deal more than those whose property is separate; but we find
that those who quarrel because of joint-ownerships are few in comparison with the many who hold property individually.   And again,
justice requires that we state not only any evils from which those
who live under communism will be free but also any good things of
which they will be deprived; and [when this is done] life [under
such a system] is seen to be utterly impossible.

The Naturalness of War

The Empedoclean Golden Age, in which there was neither war nor
slaughter of animals, is for Aristotle not truly in accord with " nature."

VI, 11. *Pol.* I, 1256 b 23-26.

διὸ καὶ ἡ πολεμικὴ φύσει κτητική πως ἔσται (ἡ γὰρ θηρευτικὴ μέρος αὐτῆς),
ᾗ δεῖ χρῆσθαι πρός τε τὰ θηρία καὶ τῶν ἀνθρώπων ὅσοι πεφυκότες ἄρχεσθαι
μὴ θέλουσιν, ὡς φύσει δίκαιον τοῦτον ὄντα τὸν πόλεμον.[24]

Thus the art of war is a natural art of acquisition, for it includes
hunting, an art which we ought to practise against wild beasts, and
against men who were designed by nature to be ruled, but are unwilling to be.   This kind of war, then is just by nature.[25]

' Nature ' as Norm

No Greek writer whose works have come down to us was more prone than
Aristotle to use the word ' nature ' in a eulogistic or normative sense, and
none more richly illustrates its equivocality.   That it had, in its use in

---

[24] Ed. Immisch.

[25] Other kinds of war are, however, strongly condemned by Aristotle, and the
general failure of peoples and statesmen to recognize that moral principles apply to
international relations he finds " exceedingly strange."   " Most men are not ashamed
to do to other peoples things which they would declare to be unjust and injurious
if done to themselves as individuals; for in their own internal affairs they demand
just government, yet in their relations to other peoples they take no account of
justice."   It is therefore obligatory upon statesmen to keep in mind the distinction
between " those who by nature are intended to be despotically ruled and those who
are not; it is not proper to attempt to exercise despotic government over all peoples
but only over those who are designed for it."   Aristotle, in short, justifies not only
defensive but also imperialist wars against the ' inferior races '; but against these
only.   He censures extremely militaristic states such as Sparta and Crete, in which
" both the system of education and most of the laws are framed in the main with
a view to war "; and he observes that an " isolated state " might live happily without any military class or other provision for war.   (Cf. also VII, 1333 a 31-1334 a
10.)   Manifestly, however, he was not one of the more zealous pacifists of antiquity:
" While all military employments are to be considered honorable, they are not so
as being the supreme end of all things, but only as means to the end previously
mentioned " (*Pol.* VII, 1324 b 255-1325 a 7, *passim*).

cosmology and metaphysics, already become highly equivocal, he was himself aware; and he was perhaps the first to attempt to discriminate the descriptive senses in which it was employed by other philosophers or by himself. In the *Physics* (II, Ch. I, 192 b 8-193 b 20) he enumerates four and in the *Metaphysics* (IV, Ch. IV, 1014 b 16-1015 a 19) seven (nominally) distinct meanings of the term.[26] These do not concern us except in so far as normative uses are derivative from them. In Books I and II of the *Politics,* of which some passages have already been summarized, and elsewhere in that writing, it is his almost constant practice to justify any institution, law or custom which he regards as normal and desirable by declaring that — in one sense or another — it is " natural " or " exists by nature," and to condemn those which he disapproves on the ground that they are not " in accord with nature " (though seldom on that ground alone): οὐδὲν τῶν παρὰ φύσιν καλόν (*Pol.* VII, 1325 b 9). Unfortunately, while thus habitually using conformity to nature as a moral criterion, Aristotle had not taken pains to define and discriminate the ethical meanings of the term as he had, after a fashion, the metaphysical and cosmological senses. Sometimes ' natural ' seems to have no signification beyond that of vague moral eulogy. In a number of passages, however, the context makes fairly clear certain specific ideas associated with the word in Aristotle's mind, through which the logic or pseudo-logic of his applications of the norm of ' nature ' to special problems can be discerned. Only those which have some bearing upon the attitude of Aristotle or his successors towards primitivism on the one hand or the idea of progress on the other, need be enumerated here.

(a) Anything in human life exists " by nature " if it arises out of instincts or impulses common to all men — and, indeed, shared by them with the animals; it is in this sense that the family is a natural institution. The contrast here is with προαίρεσις, deliberate and reflective purpose (*Pol.* I, 1252 a 26-30) or with that which " arises through experience and art " (*ibid.* 1257 a 4-6). The word in this use has for Aristotle a limited normative import: these instinctive propensities, and the institutions to which they give rise, being inherent in the generic nature of man, are not to be suppressed or over-ridden, but are insufficient, because this is not an adequate meaning of "nature."

(b) Anything which is an indispensable means to the satisfaction of such instinctive desires and needs also arises " by nature "; it is first of all on this ground that slave-holding is justified. Master and slave need one another because of a natural desire for " security " which is realized by their association in that relationship (*Pol.* I, 1252 a 31-1252 b 1). Here a

---

[26] The distinctions in the *Metaph.* are not in all cases clear-cut; some of the senses which are enumerated seem to overlap; nor are all the definitions innocent of circularity. J. D. Logan (*Philos. Rev.* VI, 1897, pp. 34 ff.) reduces the Aristotelian metaphysical significations of the term to five. The important non-normative senses in Aristotle will be found briefly indicated in Appendix I.

rudimentary form of προαίρεσις appears, but is purely instrumental to " nature " in the first sense.

(c) The idea of adaptation to an end, implicit in the preceding, when applied to persons or classes of persons, gives rise to the conception (already made much of by Plato) of congenital fitness for specific functions or activities — in the *Politics* especially, the function of ruling. This is for Aristotle the chief ground of his justification of slavery (under certain conditions), of some aggressive wars, and of the existence of subject-classes in the state. Some men are " by nature " intellectually qualified to rule, others are fitted only for mechanical crafts, yet others are capable merely of unskilled physical labor. Here the factual " nature " of the individual determines what ought to be his economic and political status (*Pol.* I, 1252 a 31 ff., 1253 b 15 ff., 1259 b 21 ff.; VII, 1332 b 32).

(d) Aside from their instrumental value, some congenital powers and activities are " by nature " superior to others; here the normative use of nature becomes simply the vehicle for expressing Plato's hierarchical division of the parts of the soul, of which the highest is the " theoretical reason ": " the activities of the part that is by nature superior must be preferable," for those who are capable of them (*Pol.* VII, 1333 a 27).

(e) Underlying the foregoing uses is the general psychological sense of the nature or constitution of an individual, with which has become associated the assumption that this internal nature predestines different men for certain modes of life, which are therefore the modes they are morally obligated to adopt. But the teleological conception here introduced is transferred by Aristotle to ' Nature ' in a sense already popular — that of an external, sometimes half-personified, agency which gives men their qualities, a sort of ' power not ourselves.' This Nature is assumed to have " purposes " [27] and, indeed, to have made nothing, to have conferred no gift upon men, which was not " intended " to be used: " Nature, as we are accustomed to say, makes nothing in vain, and man is the only animal that has the gift of speech "; but " speech is designed to indicate the beneficial and the harmful, and therefore the just and the unjust " (*Pol.* I, 1253 a 7 ff.). It is partly from this curious teleological premise that Aristotle concludes that man " by nature is a political animal " and ought to behave as such; i. e. since Nature gave him the means of doing so, he is ethically bound to utilize this means, for the purpose of Nature ought not to be frustrated (*ibid.*). The premise contained the large and obviously perilous assumption that any power which Nature made it possible for man to exercise, or any natural product which she made it possible for him to utilize, *should* be employed. It is, again, from the same premise that " Nature makes nothing without an end in view, or in vain " (*Pol.* I, 1256 b 15 ff.) that Aristotle infers that animals and plants were made to serve

[27] On teleology in nature, cf. *Phys.* 198 b 10-199 b 34.

man or be eaten by him — possibly a remark directed against theriophiles and primitivistic vegetarians of the lineage of Empedocles. This quasi-religious sense of 'Nature,' with the vague but far-reaching assumption implicit in it, tends to interpenetrate or to reënforce most of the other Aristotelian normative uses.

(f) The most characteristically Aristotelian normative use of the term is determined by certain fundamental conceptions of his metaphysics, and especially by what may be called his metaphysical biology. Of the four senses of "the nature of a thing" distinguished in the *Physics*, the one which Aristotle prefers is: "the nature is the form ($\mu o \rho \phi \acute{\eta}$) and character-istic property ($\epsilon \ddot{\iota} \delta o s$) of things which have the source of their motion or change within themselves, this property not being separable from the thing itself except verbally." Here (i) "nature" is first of all identified with the logical 'what' of an entity, the defining attributes of its class ($\tau \grave{o}$ $\tau \acute{\iota}$ $\mathring{\eta} \nu$ $\epsilon \mathring{\iota} \nu a \iota$); but (ii) this use is limited to things which undergo change or development through causes inherent in their own constitution, not through external agents—in other words, to organisms. But (iii) the $\epsilon \ddot{\iota} \delta o s$, or formal cause, of anything, that which makes it what it is, in organisms (and sometimes, in a certain sense, in inanimate things as potential objects of transformation by art) exists at first only potentially ($\delta v \nu \acute{a} \mu \epsilon \iota$), not as actually realized ($\mathring{\epsilon} \nu \epsilon \rho \gamma \epsilon \acute{\iota} a$). The logical essence of the kind is conceived as a sort of inner force seeking to realize itself in the individual, but under the necessity of passing through a sequence of transitional phases before it can do so completely; a living being is thus not itself, it has not its own "nature," until the final stage of its development has been reached. These logico-metaphysical ideas, then, combined with those indicated under (e), lead to the conclusion that the "end," in the temporal sense, of the thing's possible evolution is also its "end" in the normative sense; and this phase of completed realization of its originally latent "nature" is "by nature" its best state.

VI, 12. *Pol.* I, 1252 b 32 ff.

> . . . ἡ δὲ φύσις τέλος ἐστίν· οἷον γὰρ ἕκαστόν ἐστι τῆς γενέσεως τελεσ-θείσης, ταύτην φαμὲν τὴν φύσιν εἶναι ἑκάστου, ὥσπερ ἀνθρώπου ἵππου οἰκίας. ἔτι τὸ οὗ ἕνεκα καὶ τὸ τέλος βέλτιστον.[28]

> The nature of a thing is its end, since that which each thing is when its development is completed we call its nature, e. g. of a man, a horse, a house. And, furthermore, that for the sake of which a thing is, and its end, is its chief good.

Thus most of all it is, for Aristotle, that the state "exists by nature" in a sense in which the family or primitive household does not; and the "apolitical" individual, if he is such "by nature" and not by some acci-dent, can scarcely be considered human at all (*ibid.* 1253 a 2-4). The

---

[28] Ed. O. Immisch.

shift from purely logical or descriptive to normative connotations of the term here is patent and curious.

It is evident from the foregoing that Aristotle at times used "nature" in certain senses beloved by the primitivists, i. e. as signifying both the primeval state of society, and the simple primary desires and universal needs inherent in man's constitution; and that in the latter sense it was not for him wholly devoid of eulogistic implication. But it is also evident that all the other normative uses of the term thus far distinguished contained explicit or implicit assumptions about what is good or bad, 'just' or 'unjust,' which were profoundly incongruous with either cultural or chronological primitivism. Aristotle's anti-primitivistic attitude, in short, was more definitely and deeply rooted in his general scheme of ideas than that of any other ancient representative of that attitude; and yet the blessed word of the primitivists of his own and of all ages was also *his* blessed word. What most distinguishes him in the history of the ideas with which we are concerned is that — merely, however, developing a theme of Plato's — he converted 'nature' into the expression of a standard of value opposite to that which it most commonly had been, and for centuries was to continue to be, used to convey: not the initial but the terminal, not the simple but the complex and highly evolved, is the most excellent condition of anything which is subject to change. "Art" is also, though not equally, equivocal in Aristotle. In so far as it consists in the transformation of a thing by an external agency, rather than by the spontaneous self-realization of the essence, it is antithetic to "nature"; and if Aristotle had developed this antithesis — as he did not — he would have been led at least into a kind of pedagogical primitivism, of the sort that was to be characteristic of some influential educational theories in the seventeenth and eighteenth centuries. Education is one of the arts,[29] and in the degree that it restricts or alters the free self-development by the individual of his innate potentialities and tendencies, it could have been regarded as a mischievous interference with "nature," in its most distinctively Aristotelian sense. But such a view was essentially antipathetic to Aristotle's mind. While Nature must provide the groundwork, instruction (διδαχή) and rigorous discipline are necessary to supplement it. The individual not subjected to these from infancy will *not* spontaneously become rational and virtuous: "he who is to become good must be properly brought up and habituated."[30] And art in general, though sometimes contrasted unfavorably with nature,[31] in the end ceases for Aristotle to be antithetic to it. Since men, or at least some men, are capable of the arts, "Nature" intended that this capacity should be fully exercised; until it is, the specific nature of man remains unrealized; and art as the manifestation of reason, is therefore itself "nature" in what

[29] *Pol.* 1337 a 1.
[30] *Eth. Nic.* X, 1179 b 20 ff.; cf. *Pol.* 1334 b 24 ff.
[31] *Eth. Nic.* 1106 b 14.

Aristotle considers the most appropriate meaning of the word: ὁ δὲ λόγος ἡμῖν καὶ ὁ νοῦς τῆς φύσεως τέλος (*Pol.* VII, 1334 b 15 ff.). When the antithetic use of the terms persists, the disadvantage, from this point of view, lies with nature: πᾶσα τέχνη καὶ παιδεία τὸ προσλεῖπον βούλεται τῆς φύσεως ἀναπληροῦν, "all art and education aim at filling up Nature's deficiencies"; [32] ὅλως ἡ τέχνη τὰ μὲν ἐπιτελεῖ ἃ ἡ φύσις ἀδυνατεῖ ἀπεργάσασθαι, τὰ δὲ μιμεῖται, "in general art partly completes what Nature cannot bring to completion, and partly imitates her" (*Phys.* 199 a 15 ff.). But even when art is said to complement nature, it is in reality nature completing itself, as "may be best illustrated by the case of a physician curing himself; for nature is like that" (*Phys.* 199 b 30).

If Aristotle had applied his favorite categories of δύναμις and ἐνέργεια to the universe, or to the organic world as a whole, and not solely to individuals and societies, his philosophy would have ended in a theory of cosmical or organic evolution. Though other elements in his doctrine prevented him from reaching this conclusion, it was so natural an extension of his principles that we find an eighteenth-century writer using Aristotelian premises to justify the thesis that *everything* passes through a necessary process of gradual development from rudimentary beginnings. Lord Monboddo, after insisting upon the fundamental importance of "the distinction between the *power* of becoming anything and the actually *being* that thing; or, as I chuse to express it in two words, *capacity* and *energy*," declared that "this distinction runs through all nature, in which there is a perpetual progress from one state to another, and that nothing *is* at first what it afterwards *becomes*." [33] From this (along with more empirical reasons) Monboddo concluded among other things that man was originally identical with one of the anthropoid apes, so that even his "rational soul" then existed only "in the possibility or capacity of acquiring it." The germ, at least, of what may be called the modern genetic habit of mind, and of a generalized evolutionistic conception of nature, was thus present in the Aristotelian system.

One further meaning given by Aristotle to "nature" must be noted, since it was destined to have great influence in later thought and become associated with primitivism. In the *Nicomachean Ethics* (V, 10, 1137 b) Aristotle writes: "The socially just is of two kinds, natural and conventional: the former being that which everywhere has the same force, and does not depend upon being received or not." Here he is speaking of a purely objective universal validity which, he assumes, a moral judgment possesses even (apparently) if no one should recognize its validity; but since such universality could not be observed and verified, the final clause of the definition tended to drop out, and the rest helped to give to "nature" the sense of "that which is *de facto* universal," i. e. is known to, or approved

[32] *Pol.* 1337 a 2.
[33] *Origin and Progress of Knowledge*, I, 2d ed. 1774, p. 438.

by, all mankind in all times. So in the *Rhetoric*: "Law is either particular (ἴδιος) or universal (κοινός). The 'particular' law is that which is determined by each people for itself; it includes both unwritten and written law. The universal law is that which is according to nature. For there exists, as all men in some degree divine, that which is universally just or unjust by nature, independently of men's membership with one another in the same society, and of any compact." [34] This sense, embodied in the classic definition of the *lex* or *jus naturae* in Cicero [35] and the Roman jurists, was later to provide one of the weapons in the armory of primitivists.

[34] *Rhet.* I, 1373 b 2. On the relation of such passages of Aristotle and other Greek writers to the development of the conception of the *jus gentium*, cf. C. Phillipson, *The International Law and Custom of Ancient Greece and Rome*, Chs. II and III.

[35] Cf. below, p. 256.

CHAPTER SEVEN

ANTI-PRIMITIVISM IN GREEK LITERATURE: EIGHTH TO FIRST CENTURIES B. C.

Almost, if not quite, from the earliest period about which we have literary evidence, both chronological and cultural primitivism were confronted with opposing modes of thought — as they have continued to be in all subsequent ages. The belief in man's primeval felicity subsisted side by side with the belief — which was perhaps an actual racial memory transmitted by tradition from generation to generation — that men's life had once been far less secure, peaceful and comfortable than it was in the present. And the latter conception was usually associated with the tradition or the assumption that the discovery of 'the arts,' or the invention of the tools which made the practice of them possible, was the means of this vast amelioration of the conditions of human life. The original culture-bringer, whether god or man, was the savior of mankind. Latent, though at the outset perhaps only latent, in this conviction was a species of apotheosis of the intellect, of the practice of 'taking thought beforehand' (προμήθεια, μέριμνα) through which man's deliverance had come, and consequently a sense of the potentially benign rôle of innovation.

But the anti-primitivistic tendency came into sharp conflict with a religious idea deeply rooted in the Greek mind, that of the gods' jealousy of men, their unwillingness that an upstart race of mortals should encroach upon the divine powers and prerogatives — a conception of which a Semitic form appears in *Genesis* in the *tabu* placed upon the fruit of the tree of knowledge and the story of the punishment visited upon men for the construction of the Tower of Babel. Thus we find (cf. the following section of this chapter) perhaps the earliest attack upon anti-primitivism in European literature taking the form of a myth telling of the gods' resentment of even the first step in man's technological progress. This widely diffused element in early folk-belief was not improbably the first (so to say) theoretical ground of the primitivistic distrust of the arts, and, in general, of man's tendency to pry into hidden things, his quest of new knowledge and of power through knowledge. Later illustrations of this conception of φθόνος as the characteristic attitude of the gods towards men are numerous and familiar; the most direct evidence of its wide acceptance in the early fifth century is dealt with below (Aeschylus, *Agamemnon*, 750-771).

But even when reflection brought a more elevated and moralized theology (such as is exemplified in Aeschylus) and when, for the most part a little later, the deification of 'nature' took place, a new difficulty, at first

192

implicit rather than explicit, arose for those who would reject at least chronological primitivism. It has already been suggested in the Prolegomena. If God is not envious but benignant, and if he created man — or if 'Nature,' the universal mother, does all things well — it followed by a natural if not, perhaps, a coercive logic that man must have been made perfect after his kind and placed at the outset in the condition in which he was intended to remain. The complications resulting from these assumptions, and the attempted solutions, belong in the main to the history of Judaeo-Christian rather than of Greek thought; but for any reflective pagan mind which accepted either assumption the difficulty was already present. Chronological primitivism could not easily be escaped, except at the cost of impiety towards God or 'Nature.' Thus, paradoxically, the purification of the idea of deity of its earlier and more sinister elements, its interpenetration by loftier ethical conceptions, tended to give support to much the same view as the earlier and less edifying form of religious belief. If the gods were envious, the departure of man (with the aid of the arts) from his original state must have been contrary to their will, and therefore disastrous; and if the gods were beneficent, his departure from his original state must not less evidently have been contrary to their will, and therefore disastrous.

There was, however, another strain in Greek religious thought, perhaps not less ancient than the conception of the gods as hostile to man's acquisition of the arts, which had precisely the opposite implication. Certain even of the great gods of the Olympic pantheon were technic divinities — inventors, sometimes practisers, of particular arts or crafts, bestowers of the knowledge of them upon man, and patrons of the mortals who followed these trades.[1] Thus Demeter was not only a goddess of agriculture, but according to an Attic and Sicilian legend, was the inventor of the mill; though the art of grinding grain was in other traditions ascribed to other deities, e. g. to certain special " Mill Gods," μυλάντειοι θεοί, and even Zeus had as one of his epithets " guardian of the mills," μυλεύς.[2] Hephaestus was the patron of all metal-workers and of potters and the protector of mints; Athena was probably in one of her early forms a goddess of handicrafts in general (*Athene Ergane*) and " peaceful protectress of her worshippers and their leader in all manner of skilled occupations," was the introducer of olive-culture in Attica, and the inventor of the taming of horses and the use of chariots.[3] The list of technic deities, and of the rôles of deities having many other attributes and functions in the communication of the arts and the protection of those who practised them, might be

---

[1] V. Blümner, *Technologie und Terminologie der Gewerbe und Künste bei Griechen und Römern*, 1875, I, p. 23; A. Kleingünther, ΠΡΩΤΟΣ ΕΥΡΕΤΗΣ, *Philologus*, Supplementband XXVI, 1933, pp. 26-39. Cf. Pliny, VII (191), 56 (57) cited below, Ch. XII.

[2] Cf. Blümner, p. 24, for the relevant texts.

[3] H. J. Rose, *Handbook of Greek Mythology*, 1922, pp. 108-111.

extended to considerable length; it would include minor divinities (perhaps 'etymological gods') named simply for the arts with which they were identified and which they had imparted to men. Thus there was an old Attic hero, Bouzyges (Ox-Yoker), the first ploughman, who became the object of a cult, and may still be seen in a fifth-century vase-painting giving instruction to Cecrops and Athene in the use of the plough; the picture has been described as " the most perfect epitome extant of the earliest stratum of religion in primitive Athens." [4] The idea that, though the gods were not averse to the acquisition of the arts by mankind, they left men to discover most of them gradually for themselves, is possibly reflected in a remark of Xenophanes: " Not from the beginning did the gods show men all things, but in time by searching they discover better things." [5] What concerns us here is merely the general conflict between these two elements in Greek popular religion. The second was obviously a traditional idea opposed to primitivism; the arts were favored and prompted by the higher powers, and their introduction was a blessing to man.

The anti-primitivistic strain was not only early apparent but increasingly conspicuous. It became fully and aggressively manifest in Athens in the Enlightenment of the late fifth and early fourth centuries. It is another of the paradoxes in the history of ideas that this age — or at least many of those who introduced or were most strongly affected by the new intellectual ferment that marked it — had two antithetic sacred words, φύσις and τέχνη, or their cognate terms. The vogue of the former, as is sufficiently shown elsewhere in this volume, was, as it for centuries continued to be, one of the most potent promoters of primitivism, both chronological and cultural. The influence of the ideas associated with the other cannot be adequately illustrated by a limited collection of texts; it is to be seen rather, on the one hand, in the general aim and presuppositions of the activity of many Sophists, and, on the other, in the copious production of technological writings on all manner of subjects, of most of which only the titles remain to us.[6] The claim of many of the Sophistic teachers was the ability to impart a new, non-traditional *technique* — a technique ostensibly based upon special knowledge or original reflection — in one or another practical activity, a novel and more intelligent way of doing things; and it was this claim which brought them eager bands of pupils from among the more ardent or ambitious of the Athenian youth. There were 'professors' of politics, oratory, the art of writing, medicine, mental healing, education,

    [4] *Vide* D. M. Robinson, " Bouzyges and the First Plough on a Krater," *Amer. Jour. of Archaeology*, XXXV, 1931, pp. 152-160. The vase is in the Baltimore Museum of Art. Cf. p. 387, below.

    [5] Diels, Xenophanes, *Fragm.* 18. But on these lines cf. Kleingünther, *op. cit.* p. 41.

    [6] Cf. A. Espinas, *Les origines de la technologie*, 1897, for numerous examples; Kleingünther, *op. cit.* 1933, Ch. V; P.-M. Schuhl, *Essai sur la formation de la pensée grecque*, 1934, pp. 342-7.

the improvement of the memory, painting, agriculture, pharmacology, household economics, boat-designing, as well as of the general art of life, i. e. ethics, and of the more theoretical subjects; even Socrates (if we may at all trust Xenophon) was not only much preoccupied with ascertaining the technical procedure of the successful practitioners of any art, however humble, but was also the author of what may be called a general theory of technique which could be usefully applied to any field of practice, the persistent preacher of the necessity of clearly defining the end aimed at in any art and then ascertaining the means to its attainment — a preaching which, however truistic it may now seem, was as inimical as that of any of the Sophists to all merely conventional or traditional procedures. The glorification of $\tau\acute{\epsilon}\chi\nu\eta$, in the sense of deliberate and reflective art, had, indeed, this in common with the fashion of appealing for norms to whatever could be called $\phi\acute{\nu}\sigma\iota\varsigma$ — that it also was hostile to the tyranny of custom, to all merely habitual and "unexamined" methods in any of the activities of life; and it is perhaps for that reason chiefly that both ideas, when they themselves were new, were so fascinating, not to say intoxicating, to the new generation. But the two enthusiasms — partly, indeed, because of the confusions of meaning attaching to 'nature' — tended to opposite consequences. The faith in conscious and premeditated 'art' necessarily made against most of the forms of primitivism. Not in the naïveté of a primeval age, not in the simple life of the savage or the rustic, lay man's good, but in the improvement of techniques, the invention of new devices, and the consequent increase in the complexity of civilization. There was, it may be conjectured, more unuttered anti-primitivism of this temper than appears in the extant literary record.

In the political conflicts of the fifth and fourth centuries anti-primitivists appear on the side alike of democracy and of aristocracy or dictatorship; thus we find Protagoras and Critias at one on this issue. In so far as the aristocratic or the oligarchical parties took an unfavorable view of the intelligence and character of the mass of mankind and emphasized the needfulness of strong and stable government controlling and disciplining the multitude from above, their natural tendency was anti-primitivistic; for both primeval men and savages, upon the primitivistic theory, exemplified a peaceful and admirable social order without such government. On the other hand, the doctrine of the superiority of $\phi\acute{\nu}\sigma\iota\varsigma$, in one of its senses, was, as Theognis and Pindar especially clearly illustrate, congenial to the aristocratic class. The assumption that "virtue could be taught," and therefore that the qualities required for participation in government were discoverable by the investigations of 'professors,'[7] and, once discovered, could be imparted by instruction to every man, was a detestable one to the old ruling families, since it implied that such virtue was not the peculiar

[7] This word, as colloquially used, is on the whole the nearest English equivalent of $\Sigma o\phi\iota\sigma\tau\acute{\eta}s$.

possession of the ' best people ' and of the inheritors of a special tradition.[8]
There was, manifestly, a latent incongruity between these two aspects of the
aristocratic position, and also a fundamental cleavage between two types of
anti-primitivists — those whose motives were of the sort mentioned, who
had no faith in the pretensions of the innovating Sophistic teachers of
τέχναι, and those who were enthusiasts about the advantages to be gained
through the escape from custom and tradition to a new art of life based
upon reasoned theory.

HESIOD

The earliest, i. e., the Hesiodic, version of the story of Prometheus is
favorable to chronological but adverse to cultural primitivism. According
to this part of Hesiod's jumble of incongruous myths, mankind " lived on
earth free from evils " not only during the reign of Cronus but also for a
time after the defeat of the Titans and the attainment of supreme power
by Zeus. Man's woes did not begin until after Prometheus stole the fire.
It is true that he is said to have done this for men's benefit. But as they
are described as extremely well off without it, the original philanthropist —
like some of his successors — would seem to have conferred upon them a
dubious boon. Enraged at the trick played upon him, the President of
the Immortals punishes, not (so far as this version relates) Prometheus,
but innocent mankind: he " gives men as the price of fire an evil thing,"
namely Pandora and her jar, from which countless plagues are let loose.
The myth is manifestly an expression of the idea of the envious and
monopolistic temper of the gods. Men, it is implied, were not meant to
possess and practise the arts; they once lived, and might have continued
to live, innocently and happily without them. The Hesiodic story also
appears to reflect — being in this, too, not unlike that in *Genesis* iii — a
tendency to misogyny on the part of early, presumably male, myth-makers.
Though the original offender was, indeed, a demigod of the male sex, the
creation of the first woman was the immediate cause of man's undoing.
The detail, otherwise incongruous, that one good gift, hope, was contained
in Pandora's jar, but that this remained unescapably shut up in it, is

[8] Cf. Theognis, 429-438: " by teaching you will never make the bad man good "
(438) ; and Pindar, *Nem.* III, 40 ff.: " by inborn honor (συγγενεῖ εὐδοξίᾳ) one man
surpasses others; but he who has only learning is a man obscure, uttering now
one thing, now another, nor does he walk with firm step, but with ineffectual mind
tries countless feats of excellence." *Pyth.* VIII, 44 ff.: " The spirit which is born
in one by nature and passed on from father to sons stands out before the eyes."
Cf. also *Ol.* XIII, 13. Some of the fifth and fourth century teachers, in Athens
doubtless in deference to this type of opinion, disclaimed any pretension to teach
ethics; so Gorgias in Plato's *Meno*, 95 c. Isocrates (*On the Sophists*, 21), while
arguing for the value of (his own) instruction for those who have the right sort
of nature to begin with, adds: " Yet let no one suppose me to say that justice can be
taught. For I believe absolutely that there is no sort of art which can implant
justice and virtue in one who is evil by nature (or birth)."

apparently a mythological way of emphasizing the irremediable nature of the disaster; no future redemption of man is forecast.

VII, 1. *Works and Days,* 42-105.

Κρύψαντες γὰρ ἔχουσι θεοὶ βίον ἀνθρώποισιν·
ῥηιδίως γάρ κεν καὶ ἐπ' ἤματι ἐργάσσαιο,
ὥστε σε κεἰς ἐνιαυτὸν ἔχειν καὶ ἀεργὸν ἐόντα·
αἶψά κε πηδάλιον μὲν ὑπὲρ καπνοῦ καταθεῖο,
ἔργα βοῶν δ' ἀπόλοιτο καὶ ἡμιόνων ταλαεργῶν.
ἀλλὰ Ζεὺς ἔκρυψε χολωσάμενος φρεσὶ ᾗσιν,
ὅττι μιν ἐξαπάτησε Προμηθεὺς ἀγκυλομήτης·
τοὔνεκ' ἄρ' ἀνθρώποισιν ἐμήσατο κήδεα λυγρά.
κρύψε δὲ πῦρ· τὸ μὲν αὖτις ἐὺς πάις Ἰαπετοῖο
ἔκλεψ' ἀνθρώποισι Διὸς πάρα μητιόεντος
ἐν κοΐλῳ νάρθηκι λαθὼν Δία τερπικέραυνον.
τὸν δὲ χολωσάμενος προσέφη νεφεληγερέτα Ζεύς·

Ἰαπετιονίδη, πάντων πέρι μήδεα εἰδώς,
χαίρεις πῦρ κλέψας καὶ ἐμὰς φρένας ἠπεροπεύσας
σοί τ' αὐτῷ μέγα πῆμα καὶ ἀνδράσιν ἐσσομένοισιν·
τοῖς δ' ἐγὼ ἀντὶ πυρὸς δώσω κακόν, ᾧ κεν ἅπαντες
τέρπωνται κατὰ θυμὸν ἑὸν κακὸν ἀμφαγαπῶντες.

Ὣς ἔφατ'· ἐκ δ' ἐγέλασσε πατὴρ ἀνδρῶν τε θεῶν τε·
Ἥφαιστον δ' ἐκέλευσε περικλυτὸν ὅττι τάχιστα
γαῖαν ὕδει φύρειν, ἐν δ' ἀνθρώπου θέμεν αὐδὴν
καὶ σθένος, ἀθανάτῃς δὲ θεῇς εἰς ὦπα ἐΐσκειν
παρθενικῆς καλὸν εἶδος ἐπήρατον· αὐτὰρ Ἀθήνην
ἔργα διδασκῆσαι, πολυδαίδαλον ἱστὸν ὑφαίνειν·
καὶ χάριν ἀμφιχέαι κεφαλῇ χρυσέην Ἀφροδίτην
καὶ πόθον ἀργαλέον καὶ γυιοκόρους μελεδῶνας·
ἐν δὲ θέμεν κύνεόν τε νόον καὶ ἐπίκλοπον ἦθος
Ἑρμείην ἤνωγε, διάκτορον Ἀργεϊφόντην.
Ὣς ἔφαθ'· οἱ δ' ἐπίθοντο Διὶ Κρονίωνι ἄνακτι.
αὐτίκα δ' ἐκ γαίης πλάσσεν κλυτὸς Ἀμφιγυήεις
παρθένῳ αἰδοίῃ ἴκελον Κρονίδεω διὰ βουλάς·
ζῶσε δὲ καὶ κόσμησε θεὰ γλαυκῶπις Ἀθήνη·
ἀμφὶ δέ οἱ Χάριτές τε θεαὶ καὶ πότνια Πειθὼ
ὅρμους χρυσείους ἔθεσαν χροΐ· ἀμφὶ δὲ τήν γε
Ὧραι καλλίκομοι στέφον ἄνθεσι εἰαρινοῖσι·
[πάντα δέ οἱ χροῒ κόσμον ἐφήρμοσε Παλλὰς Ἀθήνη.]
ἐν δ' ἄρα οἱ στήθεσσι διάκτορος Ἀργεϊφόντης
ψεύδεά θ' αἱμυλίους τε λόγους καὶ ἐπίκλοπον ἦθος
[τεῦξε Διὸς βουλῇσι βαρυκτύπου· ἐν δ' ἄρα φωνὴν]
θῆκε θεῶν κῆρυξ, ὀνόμηνε δὲ τήνδε γυναῖκα
Πανδώρην, ὅτι πάντες Ὀλύμπια δώματ' ἔχοντες
δῶρον ἐδώρησαν, πῆμ' ἀνδράσιν ἀλφηστῇσιν.

Αὐτὰρ ἐπεὶ δόλον αἰπὺν ἀμήχανον ἐξετέλεσσεν,
εἰς Ἐπιμηθέα πέμπε πατὴρ κλυτὸν Ἀργεϊφόντην
δῶρον ἄγοντα, θεῶν ταχὺν ἄγγελον· οὐδ' Ἐπιμηθεὺς
ἐφράσαθ', ὥς οἱ ἔειπε Προμηθεὺς μή ποτε δῶρον
δέξασθαι πὰρ Ζηνὸς Ὀλυμπίου, ἀλλ' ἀποπέμπειν
ἐξοπίσω, μή πού τι κακὸν θνητοῖσι γένηται.
αὐτὰρ ὁ δεξάμενος, ὅτε δὴ κακὸν εἶχ', ἐνόησεν.

Τὸ πρὶν μὲν ζώεσκον ἐπὶ χθονὶ φῦλ᾽ ἀνθρώπων
νόσφιν ἄτερ τε κακῶν καὶ ἄτερ χαλεποῖο πόνοιο
νούσων τ᾽ ἀργαλέων, αἵ τ᾽ ἀνδράσι κῆρας ἔδωκαν.
[αἶψα γὰρ ἐν κακότητι βροτοὶ καταγηράσκουσιν.]
ἀλλὰ γυνὴ χείρεσσι πίθου μέγα πῶμ᾽ ἀφελοῦσα
ἐσκέδασ᾽· ἀνθρώποισι δ᾽ ἐμήσατο κήδεα λυγρά.
μούνη δ᾽ αὐτόθι Ἐλπὶς ἐν ἀρρήκτοισι δόμοισιν
ἔνδον ἔμιμνε πίθου ὑπὸ χείλεσιν, οὐδὲ θύραζε
ἐξέπτη· πρόσθεν γὰρ ἐπέμβαλε πῶμα πίθοιο
[αἰγιόχου βουλῇσι Διὸς νεφεληγερέταο.]
ἄλλα δὲ μυρία λυγρὰ κατ᾽ ἀνθρώπους ἀλάληται.
πλείη μὲν γὰρ γαῖα κακῶν, πλείη δὲ θάλασσα·
νοῦσοι δ᾽ ἀνθρώποισιν ἐφ᾽ ἡμέρῃ ἠδ᾽ ἐπὶ νυκτὶ
αὐτόματοι φοιτῶσι κακὰ θνητοῖσι φέρουσαι
σιγῇ, ἐπεὶ φωνὴν ἐξείλετο μητίετα Ζεύς.
οὕτως οὔ τί πη ἔστι Διὸς νόον ἐξαλέασθαι.[9]

For the gods keep the means of life hidden from men. For otherwise you would easily accomplish enough in a day to have what you
need for a year, and that without working; and soon would you put
away your rudder over the smoke, and the labor of the oxen and the
drudging mules would be abandoned. But Zeus, angry in his heart,
hid it, for Prometheus the crafty had deceived him; and therefore
he planned sorrow and mischief against men. And he hid fire; but
the noble son of Iapetus stole it for men from Zeus wise in counsel,
in a hollow fennel-stalk, so that Zeus who delights in the thunder
did not see it. But Zeus the cloud-gatherer said to him angrily,

" Son of Iapetus, greater than all in cunning, you rejoice to have
stolen fire and to have outwitted my mind; and this is a great plague
to you yourself and to men yet to be. To them, as the price of fire,
I shall give an evil thing in which all will rejoice in their hearts,
embracing their own evil."

Thus he spoke. And the father of men and gods laughed. And
he ordered the renowned Hephaestus speedily to mix earth with
water and in it to put the voice and strength of man and to model
the fair form of a maiden in countenance like a deathless goddess;
and [he ordered] Athene to teach her crafts and how to weave the
highly wrought web; and golden Aphrodite to shower grace upon her
head, cruel longing and sorrows that weary the limbs. And Hermes,
the guide, the slayer of Argus, he ordered to implant in her a doglike
mind and a tricky disposition.

Thus he spoke. And they obeyed Zeus son of Cronus the king.
And straightway the famous lame one molded from earth an image
of a modest maiden, according to the will of Zeus. And the goddess,
bright-eyed Athene, girded her and clothed her, and the divine
Graces and lady Persuasion put golden necklaces upon her and the
fair-haired Hours crowned her with spring flowers and Pallas
Athene adorned her body with all things. And the Guide, the
Slayer of Argus, instilled in her lies and crafty words and a thievish
disposition, according to the will of Zeus the loud-thunderer. And
the herald of the gods gave her speech, and he called this woman

[9] Ed. A. Rzach, 1884, Leipzig, G. Freytag.

Pandora, because all who had homes on Olympus gave her a gift, a plague to bread-eating men.

But when he had finished the snare deep and inescapable, the Father sent renowned Argus-slayer, the messenger of the gods, to Epimetheus, bringing it as a gift. And Epimetheus did not think how Prometheus had told him not to accept a gift from Zeus the Olympian, but to send it back again lest it should be somehow an evil to mortals. But after he had received it, when he finally had discovered the evil thing it was, he understood.

For before this time the tribes of men lived on earth remote from evils and hard labor and heavy sicknesses which bring the Fates to men. For in an evil condition mortals age quickly. But the woman removed with her hands the great lid of the jar, and it vomited forth gloomy cares upon men. And Hope alone remained there in an unbreakable home under the rim of the jar and did not fly forth; for by the will of aegis-bearing Zeus, the cloud-gatherer, she (Pandora) closed the lid of the jar. But myriad ills wander about among men; for earth is full of evils and full is the sea. And diseases spontaneously come to man by day and by night bearing mischief to mortals silently; since wise Zeus deprived them of speech. Thus there is no way whatever to escape the mind of Zeus.[10]

Hesiod does not attempt to correlate this story intelligibly with the legend of the Ages; and no satisfactory synthesis of the two appears possible. In the *Theogony* (563) Zeus refuses to give fire to the Melian race, which, if the poet is thinking of the races as given in *Works and Days* (110-201), would be not primitive men at all but men of the third or Bronze Age.

HOMERIC HYMNS

In the Homeric Hymns, to which dates have been assigned ranging from the eighth to as late as the third century, the anti-primitivistic strain definitely appears. If an early date be accepted for the Hymn to Hephaestus, it gives evidence of the currency of a folk-legend opposed to, and perhaps as old as, the primitivistic one related by Hesiod. Prometheus does not figure in the story. The arts were freely imparted to man by the artisan-god and the goddess of wisdom.

VII, 2. *Hymn to Hephaestus.*

Ἥφαιστον κλυτόμητιν ἀείσεο, Μοῦσα λίγεια,
ὃς μετ' Ἀθηναίης γλαυκώπιδος ἀγλαὰ ἔργα
ἀνθρώπους ἐδίδαξεν ἐπὶ χθονός, οἳ τὸ πάρος περ
ἄντροις ναιετάασκον ἐν οὔρεσιν, ἠΰτε θῆρες.
νῦν δὲ δι' Ἥφαιστον κλυτοτέχνην ἔργα δαέντες
ῥηϊδίως αἰῶνα τελεσφόρον εἰς ἐνιαυτὸν
εὔκηλοι διάγουσιν ἐνὶ σφετέροισι δόμοισιν.[11]

Sing of Hephaestus famed for his skill, clear-voiced Muse — of him who with bright-eyed Athene taught glorious crafts to men on

[10] Based on Evelyn-White's translation (Loeb Lib.).
[11] Ed. Allen in *Opera*. V, 84. Oxford, Clarendon Press, 1912.

earth, who aforetime lived in caves in the mountains like wild beasts. But now having learned crafts from Hephaestus, the famous craftsman, they easily live out their life to its full span, abiding free from care in their own houses.[12]

AESCHYLUS

In the *Prometheus Bound* Aeschylus (if he is the author of the tragedy)[13] combines two different accounts of the early condition of mankind. As in the Hesiodic story, Prometheus confers the arts upon men and the jealous gods resent this and take vengeance for it, though it is Prometheus, not, as in Hesiod, the beneficiaries of his gifts, who suffers the punishment. On the other hand, the life of men under the reign of Zeus, a peculiarly jealous and unfriendly god, was, before the intervention of Prometheus, a miserable one. (What it may have been under an earlier régime Aeschylus does not say.) It is through pity for men's distress, not through an officious zeal to confer upon them a gift of which they had no need, that the Prometheus of Aeschylus is led to incur the wrath of Zeus against himself, by bestowing upon mortals not only the use of fire but many other arts besides, not all of them derivative from the first — metallurgy, architecture, the domestication of animals, navigation, astronomy, arithmetic, writing, medicine, divination. It was the introduction of the arts that was man's salvation — not only from his original condition of animal helplessness and wretchedness, but also from the actual destruction which Zeus was preparing for him; and his deliverer was the personification of practical intelligence, Foresight by name, the God of Taking Thought. (For whatever view be taken of Kuhn's etymology of the name, according to which it is derived from the word for ʻ fire-stick,' Skr. *pramanthas,* it is probable that no Greek of the historic period had any such notion of its meaning.) In short, the version followed (probably not created) by Aeschylus, though it could be reconciled with, and was perhaps not intended to exclude, a species of chronological primitivism, a belief in an original Golden Age, was nevertheless essentially opposed to cultural primitivism. He depicted the original condition of mankind, under the sort of climatic and other physical conditions which actually exist on the earth as we know it, as the worst possible condition; and he saw in the first of the arts the beginning of man's ascent, and in the addition of further arts the steps in his progress.

VII, 3.   *Prometheus Bound* (*ca.* 467 B. C.), 447–468; 478–506.

> Οἳ πρῶτα μὲν βλέποντες ἔβλεπον μάτην,
> κλύοντες οὐκ ἤκουον, ἀλλ' ὀνειράτων
> ἀλίγκιοι μορφαῖσι τὸν μακρὸν βίον

---

[12] In the Homeric *Hymn to Hermes* (III) that God is credited with the discovery of fire and the invention of the fire-stick. The line is perhaps spurious.

[13] See Schmid and Stählin's *Geschichte der Griechischen Literatur,* Munich, 1934, I, ii, p. 193, for a discussion of the authorship of *Prometheus Bound.*

ἔφυρον εἰκῇ πάντα, κοὔτε πλινθυφεῖς
δόμους προσείλους ᾖσαν, οὐ ξυλουργίαν,
κατώρυχες δ' ἔναιον ὥστ' ἀήσυροι
μύρμηκες ἄντρων ἐν μυχοῖς ἀνηλίοις.
Ἦν δ' οὐδὲν αὐτοῖς οὔτε χείματος τέκμαρ
οὔτ' ἀνθεμώδους ἦρος οὔτε καρπίμου
θέρους βέβαιον, ἀλλ' ἄτερ γνώμης τὸ πᾶν
ἔπρασσον, ἔστε δή σφιν ἀντολὰς ἐγώ
ἄστρων ἔδειξα τάς τε δυσκρίτους δύσεις.
Καὶ μὴν ἀριθμόν, ἔξοχον σοφισμάτων,
ἐξηῦρον αὐτοῖς, γραμμάτων τε συνθέσεις,
μνήμην ἁπάντων, μουσομήτορ' ἐργάνην.
Κἄζευξα πρῶτος ἐν ζυγοῖσι κνώδαλα
ζεύγλαισι δουλεύοντα σώμασίν θ', ὅπως
θνητοῖς μεγίστων διάδοχοι μοχθημάτων
γένοινθ', ὑφ' ἅρμα τ' ἤγαγον φιληνίους
ἵππους, ἄγαλμα τῆς ὑπερπλούτου χλιδῆς.
Θαλασσόπλαγκτα δ' οὔτις ἄλλος ἀντ' ἐμοῦ
λινόπτερ' ηὗρε ναυτίλων ὀχήματα.

.   .   .   .

Τὸ μὲν μέγιστον, εἴ τις ἐς νόσον πέσοι,
οὐκ ἦν ἀλέξημ' οὐδέν, οὔτε βρώσιμον,
οὐ χριστόν, οὐδὲ πιστόν, ἀλλὰ φαρμάκων
χρείᾳ κατεσκέλλοντο, πρίν γ' ἐγώ σφισιν
ἔδειξα κράσεις ἠπίων ἀκεσμάτων
αἷς τὰς ἁπάσας ἐξαμύνονται νόσους.
Τρόπους τε πολλοὺς μαντικῆς ἐστοίχισα
κἄκρινα πρῶτος ἐξ ὀνειράτων ἃ χρή
ὕπαρ γενέσθαι, κληδόνας τε δυσκρίτους
ἐγνώρισ' αὐτοῖς ἐνοδίους τε συμβόλους,
γαμψωνύχων τε πτῆσιν οἰωνῶν σκεθρῶς
διώρισ', οἵτινές τε δεξιοὶ φύσιν
εὐωνύμους τε, καὶ δίαιταν ἥντινα
ἔχουσ' ἕκαστοι, καὶ πρὸς ἀλλήλους τίνες
ἔχθραι τε καὶ στέργηθρα καὶ συνεδρίαι,
σπλάγχνων τε λειότητα, καὶ χροιὰν τίνα
ἔχοντ' ἂν εἴη δαίμοσιν πρὸς ἡδονήν,
χολῆς λοβοῦ τε ποικίλην εὐμορφίαν,
κνίσῃ τε κῶλα συγκαλυπτὰ καὶ μακράν
ὀσφῦν πυρώσας δυστέκμαρτον ἐς τέχνην
ὥδωσα θνητούς καὶ φλογωπὰ σήματα
ἐξωμμάτωσα πρόσθεν ὄντ' ἐπάργεμα.
Τοιαῦτα μὲν δὴ ταῦτ'· ἔνερθε δὲ χθονός
κεκρυμμέν' ἀνθρώποισιν ὠφελήματα,
χαλκόν, σίδηρον, ἄργυρον χρυσόν τε, τίς
φήσειεν ἂν πάροιθεν ἐξευρεῖν ἐμοῦ;
οὐδείς, σάφ' οἶδα, μὴ μάτην φλῦσαι θέλων.
Βραχεῖ δὲ μύθῳ πάντα συλλήβδην μάθε·
πᾶσαι τέχναι βροτοῖσιν ἐκ Προμηθέως.[14]

---

[14] Ed. Paul Mazon, Paris, 1920.

In the beginning their eyes looked vainly; listening, they did not hear, but like shapes seen in a dream they lived their long life to no purpose; nor had they sunny houses made of bricks, nor wood-work, but buried in the ground they lived like little ants in the recesses of sunless caves. And there was for them no fixed sign either of winter or of flowering spring or of fruitful summer, but without understanding they did all things, until I taught them the risings of the stars and their settings, hard to interpret. And then number, the noblest of inventions, I devised for them,[15] and the composition of letters, memory of all things — productive mother of the arts. I first harnessed together wild animals, that they might bear either the yoke or the human body, that they might take the place of mortals in the greatest labors, and to the chariot I led horses which obey the rein, glory of the rich man's luxury, and no one except me invented those sea-tossed vehicles of the sailors winged with sails. . . . If anyone fell ill, there was no help for it, neither solid food nor ointment, nor draughts, but they would have withered away for want of drugs before I showed them how to mix soothing remedies by which they might drive away all diseases. And the many ways of divination I first devised, and interpreted from dreams what must occur in waking life; omens hard to interpret I made known to them, and symbolic meetings, and I explained exactly the flight of crooked-taloned birds of prey, both those which are of good omen and those of bad, and the way of living which each has, and their hatred for one another and their love, and their manner of sitting together, and the smoothness of their viscera, and the color they must have, if they would be pleasing to the gods, the various propitious shapes of the bile and lobe of the liver; and I burned the members enveloped in fat and the great loins to guide mortals in the dark craft, and I made clear the fiery tokens which before that time were dark. Such were my deeds. And useful things buried beneath the earth from sight of mortals, bronze, iron, silver, gold — who can claim to have found them before me? No one, I know, unless he wishes to babble vainly. Take all together in a word: — all arts [come] to mortals from Prometheus.

In the *Agamemnon*, however, Aeschylus briefly presents another version, inspired by a less primitive theology. Three successive dynasties of gods are still recognized. That of Uranus was an evil one. The character of the reign of Cronus is not indicated, but there is at least no suggestion that it was a Golden Age. Zeus, however, is no longer a malignant deity; the

---

[15] In a fragment which is perhaps from Aeschylus, Nauck's *Fragm. Adespota* 470 (*olim* 393), we find Palamedes given as the inventor of number.

> ἔπειτα πάσης Ἑλλάδος καὶ ξυμμάχων
> βίον διῴκησ' ὄντα πρὶν πεφυρμένον
> θηρσίν θ' ὅμοιον. πρῶτα μὲν τὸν πάνσοφον
> ἀριθμὸν ηὕρηκ' ἔξοχον σοφισμάτων

"Then he put order into the life of all Hellas and of the allies, which was formerly confused and similar to the life of beasts. First he discovered all-wise number, greatest of the ways of pursuing wisdom." But see Plato, *Rep.* 522 e for satirical comment on Palamedes, and the idea that "number was invented."

ancient belief that the gods are envious of man's prosperity is definitely attacked by Aeschylus, through the Chorus (750-771), even though he " stands alone in this opinion " (δίχα δ' ἄλλων μονόφρων εἰμί). Though Zeus brings woes upon men, it is only in punishment of impious deeds. He is the bestower of wisdom upon mortals. The reference, however, is not to knowledge of the arts but to moral insight — the costly wisdom that comes through suffering. The words are spoken by the Chorus of Argive elders.

VII, 4. *Agamemnon*, 167-176.

> οὐδ' ὅστις πάροιθεν ἦν μέγας
> παμμάχῳ θράσει βρύων,
> οὐδὲ λέξεται πρὶν ὤν·
> ὃς δ' ἔπειτ' ἔφυ, τρια-
> κτῆρος οἴχεται τυχών.
> Ζῆνα δέ τις προφρόνως ἐπινίκια κλάζων
> τεύξεται φρενῶν τὸ πᾶν·
> τὸν φρονεῖν βροτοὺς ὁδώ-
> σαντα, τῶι πάθει μάθος
> θέντα κυρίως ἔχειν.
> στάζει δ' ἐνθ' ὕπνῳ πρὸ καρδίας
> μνησιπήμων πόνος· καὶ παρ' ἄ-
> κοντας ἦλθε σωφρονεῖν.
> δαιμόνων δέ που χάρις βίαιος
> σέλμα σεμνὸν ἡμένων.[16]

He who before was supreme [Uranus], bristling with martial might, is no longer to be reckoned with; he was of a former time; and he who followed also met his match and passed away; but if you raise the shout of triumph heartily to Zeus, you will be wholly wise — Zeus who guides mortals in the path of understanding, who has ordained that from suffering should arise wisdom. The painful memory of woe trickles before the heart sometimes in sleep; and wisdom comes to men even though they will it not, a grace forced on them by the gods who sit upon their august thrones.

EURIPIDES

Anti-primitivism is again expressed in Greek drama in a speech of Theseus in the *Suppliants* of Euripides (421 B. C.).

VII, 5. *Suppliants*, 201-213.

> αἰνῶ δ' ὃς ἡμῖν βίοτον ἐκ πεφυρμένου
> καὶ θηριώδους θεῶν διεσταθμήσατο,
> πρῶτον μὲν ἐνθεὶς σύνεσιν, εἶτα δ' ἄγγελον
> γλῶσσαν λόγων δούς, ὥστε γιγνώσκειν ὄπα,
> τροφήν τε καρποῦ τῇ τροφῇ τ' ἀπ' οὐρανοῦ
> σταγόνας ὑδρηλάς, ὡς τά γ' ἐκ γαίας τρέφῃ
> ἄρδῃ τε νηδύν· πρὸς δὲ τοῖσι χείματος
> προβλήματ', αἴθρον ἐξαμύνασθαι θεοῦ,
> πόντου τε ναυστολήμαθ', ὡς διαλλαγὰς

[16] Ed. Paul Mazon, Paris, 1925.

ἔχοιμεν ἀλλήλοισιν ὧν πένοιτο γῆ.
ἃ δ' ἔστ' ἄσημα κοὐ σαφῶς γιγνώσκομεν,
ἐς πῦρ βλέποντες καὶ κατὰ σπλάγχνων πτυχὰς
μάντεις προσημαίνουσιν οἰωνῶν τ' ἄπο.[17]

Let me praise him among the gods who brought order into our
way of life, out of disorder and brutishness, first by instilling reason,
then by giving the tongue, the messenger of thoughts, that we may
understand the meaning of words; and the nourishment of grain,
and for that nourishment raindrops from heaven, that the things
that arise from the earth might be fed and her belly given water;
and besides these things, shelter from winter's cold and shade from
the heat; and [the wit] to sail the sea in ships that we might have
commerce with one another in those things [our own] land might
lack; and, for such things as are unintelligible or confusedly known
to us, soothsayers who prophesy from the flight of birds and by
gazing into the fire and inspecting the folds of viscera.

HIPPOCRATIC WRITINGS

We now pass from the mythological expressions of anti-primitivism to
its manifestations in the Greek Enlightenment of the 5th-4th centuries.
Though the assumption of the beneficent working of 'nature' is frequent
in the writers of the Hippocratic Corpus, the members of a guild of trained
practitioners of an art newly based upon scientific inquiry were naturally
unsympathetic to the chronological and cultural primitivism of their time,
as is shown in the treatise on *Ancient Medicine*, probably of the fifth century. The deliverer of primitive mankind from its misery was he who first
introduced a diet which, though artificial, was nevertheless better suited to
man's physiological nature than that which unaided nature provided. These
first dietetic innovators are described as the founders of the medical art.

VII, 6.   *On Ancient Medicine*, III, 26 (576-578).

ἔτι δὲ ἄνωθεν ἔγωγε ἀξιῶ οὐδ' ἂν τὴν τῶν ὑγιαινόντων δίαιτάν τε καὶ τροφήν,
ᾗ νῦν χρέονται, εὑρεθῆναι, εἰ ἐξήρκει τῷ ἀνθρώπῳ ταὐτὰ ἐσθίοντι καὶ πίνοντι
βοΐ τε καὶ ἵππῳ καὶ πᾶσιν ἐκτὸς ἀνθρώπου, οἷον τὰ ἐκ [τῆς] γῆς φυόμενα,
καρπούς τε καὶ ὕλην καὶ χόρτον· ἀπὸ τούτων γὰρ καὶ τρέφονται καὶ αὔξονται
καὶ ἄπονοι διάγουσιν οὐδὲν προσδεόμενοι ἄλλης διαίτης. καί τοι τὴν ἀρχὴν
ἔγωγε δοκέω καὶ τὸν ἄνθρωπον τοιαύτῃ τροφῇ κεχρῆσθαι· τὰ δὲ νῦν διαιτήματα
εὑρημένα καὶ τετεχνημένα ἐν πολλῷ χρόνῳ γεγενῆσθαί μοι δοκέει· ὡς [γὰρ]
ἔπασχον πολλά τε καὶ δεινὰ ὑπὸ ἰσχυρῆς τε καὶ θηριώδεος διαίτης ὠμά τε καὶ
ἄκρητα καὶ μεγάλας δυνάμιας ἔχοντα ἐσφερόμενοι, οἷά περ ἂν καὶ νῦν ὑπ'
αὐτῶν πάσχοιεν πόνοισί τε ἰσχυροῖσι καὶ νούσοισι περιπίπτοντες καὶ διὰ
τάχεος θανάτοισιν. ἧσσον μὲν οὖν ταῦτα τότε εἰκὸς ἦν πάσχειν διὰ τὴν
συνήθειαν, ἰσχυρῶς δὲ καὶ τότε, καὶ τοὺς μὲν πλείστους τε καὶ ἀσθενεστέρην
φύσιν ἔχοντας ἀπόλλυσθαι εἰκός, τοὺς δὲ τούτων ὑπερέχοντας πλείω χρόνον
ἀντέχειν, ὥσπερ καὶ νῦν ἀπὸ τῶν ἰσχυρῶν βρωμάτων οἱ μὲν ῥηϊδίως ἀπαλ-
λάσσονται. οἱ δὲ μετὰ πολλῶν πόνων τε καὶ κακῶν. διὰ δὴ ταύτην τὴν αἰτίην
καὶ οὗτοί μοι δοκέουσι ζητῆσαι τροφὴν ἁρμόζουσαν τῇ φύσει καὶ εὑρεῖν

[17] Ed. G. Murray, Oxford, 1902-1909, II.

ταύτην, ᾗ νῦν χρώμεθα. ἐκ μὲν οὖν τῶν πυρῶν βρέξαντές σφας καὶ πτίσαντες
καὶ καταλέσαντές τε καὶ διασήσαντες· καὶ φορύξαντες καὶ ὀπτήσαντες ἀπε-
τέλεσαν ἄρτον, ἐκ δὲ τῶν κριθέων μᾶζαν, ἄλλα τε πολλὰ περὶ ταύτην πραγ-
ματευσάμενοι ἥψησάν τε καὶ ὤπτησαν καὶ ἔμιξαν καὶ ἐκέρασαν τὰ ἰσχυρά τε
καὶ ἄκρητα τοῖσιν ἀσθενεστέροις πλάσσοντες πάντα πρὸς τὴν τοῦ ἀνθρώπου
φύσιν τε καὶ δύναμιν, ἡγεύμενοι, ὡς, ἢν μὲν ἰσχυρὰ ᾖ, οὐ δυνήσεται κρατέειν
ἡ φύσις, ἢν ἐμφέρηται, ἀπὸ τούτων τε αὐτῶν πόνους τε καὶ νούσους καὶ
θανάτους ἔσεσθαι, ὁπόσων δ' ἂν δύνηται ἐπικρατέειν, ἀπὸ τούτων τροφήν τε
καὶ αὔξησιν καὶ ὑγιείην. τῷ δὲ εὑρήματι τούτῳ καὶ ζητήματι τί ἄν τις ὄνομα
δικαιότερον ἢ προσῆκον μᾶλλον θείη ἢ ἰητρικήν, ὅτι γε εὕρηται ἐπὶ τῇ τοῦ
ἀνθρώπου ὑγιείῃ τε καὶ σωτηρίῃ καὶ τροφῇ, ἄλλαγμα ἐκείνης τῆς διαίτης,
ἐξ ἧς οἱ πόνοι καὶ ναῦσοι καὶ θάνατοι ἐγίνοντο; [18]

I hold that not even the kind of diet and nourishment used at the
present time by men in health would have been discovered, had man
been satisfied with the same food and drink as satisfy an ox, a horse,
and every animal except man, for example the products of the
earth — fruits, wood, and grass. For on these the animals are
nourished, grow, and live without pain, having no need of any other
kind of sustenance. Yet I am of opinion that in the beginning man
also used this sort of nourishment. Our present diet has, I think,
been discovered and elaborated through a long period of time. For
many and terrible were the sufferings of men from crude and brutish
diet, when they partook of raw foods, unmixed and potent — the
same, in fact, as men would suffer at the present day, falling into
violent pains and diseases quickly followed by death. Formerly,
indeed, they probably suffered less, because they were used to it, but
they suffered severely even then. The majority naturally perished,
having too weak a constitution, while the stronger resisted longer,
just as at the present time some men easily deal with strong foods,
while others do so only with many and severe pains. For this reason
the ancients too seem to me to have sought for nourishment that
harmonized with their constitution, and to have discovered that
which we use now. So from wheat, after steeping it, winnowing,
grinding and sifting, kneading, baking, they produced bread, and
from barley they produced cake. Experimenting with food they
boiled or baked, after mixing, many other things, combining the
strong and violent with the weaker components so as to adapt all to
the constitution (nature) and power of man, thinking that from too
strong foods which the human constitution (nature) cannot assimi-
late when eaten, will come pain, disease, and death, while from such
as can be assimilated will come nourishment, growth and health.
To this discovery and research what juster or more appropriate name
could be given than divine medicine, seeing that it was discovered
with a view to the health, saving and nourishment of man, in place
of that diet from which came pain, disease and death.[19]

---

[18] Ed. I. L. Heiberg, Leipzig, 1927; but ἁρμόζουσιν has been corrected to ἁρμόζουσαν.
[19] Use has been made, with several emendations, of the translation of W. H. S.
Jones, *Loeb Classical Lib.* London, 1923, I, p. 17 ff.

ANAXAGORAS

Man's intellectual endowments are the source of the arts and enable him to dominate the animals, though physically inferior to them. Human practical intelligence is presumably for Anaxagoras a special manifestation of the pervasive cosmic Mind.

VII, 7. *Fragm.* 21 b (in Plut. *De fort.* 3, p. 98 F).

> . . . ἐν πᾶσι τούτοις ἀτυχέστεροι τῶν θηρίων ἐσμέν, ἐμπειρίᾳ δὲ καὶ μνήμῃ καὶ σοφίᾳ καὶ τέχνῃ κατὰ ᾿Αναξαγόραν σφῶν τε αὐτῶν χρώμεθα καὶ βλίττομεν καὶ ἀμέλγομεν καὶ φέρομεν καὶ ἄγομεν συλλαμβάνοντες.[20]

In all these (physical qualities) we are less fortunate than the animals, but we have the use of experience and memory and wisdom and art, according to Anaxagoras, and we take from the animals their honey and their milk, and in general appropriate them and their goods.

ARCHELAUS

Pupil of Anaxagoras and a teacher of Socrates, Archelaus held the theory, common to a number of the physiologers, of the original generation of animals from a primordial slime. Though man's origin and primitive condition were the same, he alone developed the arts and political institutions, which Archelaus apparently conceived as a higher expression of the mind, or reason, common to all creatures.

VII, 8. In Hippolytus, *Ref. omn. haer.* I, 9.

> περὶ δὲ ζῴων φησίν, ὅτι θερμαινομένης τῆς γῆς τὸ πρῶτον ἐν τῷ κάτω μέρει, ὅπου τὸ θερμὸν καὶ τὸ ψυχρὸν ἐμίσγετο, ἀνεφαίνετο τά τε ἄλλα ζῷα πολλὰ καὶ οἱ ἄνθρωποι, ἅπαντα τὴν αὐτὴν δίαιταν ἔχοντα ἐκ τῆς ἰλύος τρεφόμενα (ἦν δὲ ὀλιγοχρόνια) · ὕστερον δὲ αὐτοῖς ἡ ἐξ ἀλλήλων γένεσις συνέστη. καὶ διεκρίθησαν ἄνθρωποι ἀπὸ τῶν ἄλλων καὶ ἡγεμόνας καὶ νόμους καὶ τέχνας καὶ πόλεις καὶ τὰ ἄλλα συνέστησαν. νοῦν δὲ λέγει πᾶσιν ἐμφύεσθαι ζῴοις ὁμοίως. χρῆσθαι γὰρ ἕκαστον καὶ τῶν ζῴων τῷ νῷ τὸ μὲν βραδυτέρως, τό δὲ ταχυτέρως.[21]

Concerning the animals [Archelaus] says that, when the earth was at first in a heated state in the lower part, where the hot and the cold were mixed together, many other animals, and also men, came into existence, all living the same manner of life and being produced from the slime. But this continued only for a short time; afterwards arose the mode of birth in which one animal is produced from another. And men were differentiated from the other animals, and so rulers and laws and arts and cities and the like arose. But mind, he says, is implanted in all animals alike. For even of the animals each makes some use of mind, some in a duller, others a quicker fashion.

[20] Diels, 4th ed. I, 409.
[21] Diels, I, 412.

DEMOCRITUS

The fragments of Democritus contain some passages which were to have notable literary echoes in the Renaissance and after. The first contained an idea, probably not original with Democritus, which reappears in Cynic writers (cf. Ch. IV) and was to be a favorite theme for poetic elaboration as late as the eighteenth century: the notion that at least the simpler arts were acquired by man through imitation of the animals. The culture-hero was thus dispensed with; and the theory, since it traced these arts back to an undeniably instinctive and 'natural' origin, had a persistent appeal to moderate primitivists.

VII, 9. *Fragm.* 154. In Plutarch, *De Sollert. anim.* 20 (974 a).

Γελοῖοι δ' ἴσως ἐσμὲν ἐπὶ τῷ μανθάνειν τὰ ζῷα σεμνύνοντες, ὧν ὁ Δημόκριτος ἀποφαίνει μαθητὰς ἐν τοῖς μεγίστοις γεγονότας ἡμᾶς· ἀράχνης ἐν ὑφαντικῇ καὶ ἀκεστικῇ, χελιδόνος ἐν οἰκοδομίᾳ· καὶ τῶν λιγυρῶν, κύκνου καὶ ἀηδόνος, ἐν ᾠδῇ κατὰ μίμησιν.[22]

But perhaps we are absurd to put on airs, because we are teachers of the beasts; for Democritus declares that we have been their pupils in matters of the greatest importance: imitators of the spider in weaving and mending, of the swallow in architecture, and of the clear-voiced swan and nightingale in singing.

Whether acquired through imitation or otherwise, the arts are due to man's own efforts. The earliest were evolved under the pressure of necessity (i. e., presumably, were indispensable to the survival of the race); the fine arts were of later development.

VII, 10. *Fragm.* 144. In Philodemus, *De musica.*

. . . μουσικήν φησι [Δημόκριτος] νεωτέραν εἶναι καὶ τὴν αἰτίαν ἀποδίδωσι λέγων μὴ ἀποκρῖναι τἀναγκαῖον, ἀλλὰ ἐκ τοῦ περιεῦντος ἤδη γενέσθαι.[23]

Music, says Democritus, is one of the younger arts; the reason he gives [for this opinion] being that necessity did not decree it, but it arose only when there already existed a superabundance.

Another passage in Democritus manifests an aversion to the sharp antithesis of 'nature' and 'culture' which played so great a part in the ethical and political controversies of the period. The thought adumbrates, but can not be said to anticipate unequivocally, the passage in which Shakespeare (*Winter's Tale*, Act IV, Sc. iv, 89-90) made his devastating comment upon the primitivism of Montaigne: "Nature is made better by no mean, but Nature makes that mean." Democritus, however, at least appears to imply that the blessed word 'nature' ought not to be invoked for the disparagement of the processes which change man from his original condition.

[22] In Diels, II, 90. [23] Diels, II, 87.

VII, 11. *Fragm.* 33. In Clement, *Strom.* IV, 151.

'Η φύσις καὶ ἡ διδαχὴ παραπλήσιόν ἐστι. καὶ γὰρ ἡ διδαχὴ μεταρυσμοῖ τὸν ἄνθρωπον, μεταρυσμοῦσα δὲ φυσιοποιεῖ.[24]

Nature and culture are similar to one another. For culture, indeed, transforms man, but in transforming him it makes nature [or ' a nature '].

PROTAGORAS

The cultural and chronological primitivism of the late fifth century found its most notable opponent in the greatest of the Sophists who came to teach in Athens. In the dialogue of Plato which bears the name of Protagoras there is put into the mouth of that philosopher a speech which we have no reason to suppose not to have been in accord with his actual teaching.[25] In the course of this speech Protagoras takes occasion to satirize the ideas that men in a purely natural state, without education or the discipline of coercive political institutions, would be more just, or enjoy a happier existence, than civilized men: " He who appears to you the worst of those who have been brought up in laws and in the society of other men would appear a just man, aye, a master of justice, if he were compared with men who had no education or courts or laws, nor anything whatever to constrain them to practise virtue — with the savages, for example, whom the poet Pherecrates exhibited at last year's Lenaean festival. If you were living among men such as the man-haters in his chorus, . . . you would soon sorrowfully desire the wickedness of this part of the world " (*Protag.* 327 c). The remainder of the relevant part of the long speech of Protagoras follows.[26]

VII, 12. *Protagoras,* 320 c-323 a.

Once upon a time there were gods only, and no mortal creatures. But when the time came that these also should be created, the gods fashioned them out of earth and fire and various mixtures of both elements in the interior of the earth; and when they were about to bring them into the light of day, they ordered Prometheus and Epimetheus to equip them, and to distribute to them severally their proper qualities. Epimetheus said to Prometheus: ' Let me distribute, and do you inspect.' This was agreed, and Epimetheus made

[24] Diels, II, 71-72. Diels renders the last clause: " aber durch diese Umformung schafft sie eine *zweite* Natur." The compound verb φυσιοποιεῖν was apparently coined by Democritus, and the precise shade of meaning is difficult to determine; it possibly comes close to: " it carries on the creative work of nature."

[25] W. Uxkull-Gyllenband: *Griechische Kultur-Entstehungslehren,* 1924, maintains that " Plato in this myth probably gives us, in a much abridged form, an extract from one of the writings of the Sophist," and attempts a conjectural reconstruction of the contents of this writing.

[26] The Greek text of this, as of other Platonic passages, is omitted, because of its accessibility.

the distribution. There were some to whom he gave strength without swiftness, while he equipped the weaker with swiftness; some he armed, and others he left unarmed; and he devised for the latter some other means of preservation, making some large, and having their size as a protection, and others small, whose nature was to fly in the air or burrow in the ground; this was to be their way of escape. Thus did he compensate them with the view of preventing any species from becoming extinct. And when he had provided against their destruction by one another, he contrived also a means of protecting them against the seasons of heaven; clothing them with close hair and thick skins sufficient to defend them against the winter cold and able to resist the summer heat, and furnishing them with lairs, so that, when they wanted to rest, each might have a bed of its own suited to its nature; also he provided them with hoofs or claws or hard and callous skins under their feet. Then he gave them varieties of food — herbs of the soil to some, to others fruits of trees, and to others roots, and to some again he gave other animals as food. And some he made to have few young ones, while those who were their prey were very prolific; and in this manner the race was preserved. Thus did Epimetheus, who, not being very wise, forgot that he had distributed among the brute animals all the qualities which he had to give, — and when he came to man, who was still unprovided, he was terribly perplexed. Now while he was in this perplexity, Prometheus came to inspect the distribution, and he found that the other animals were suitably furnished, but man alone was naked and shoeless, and had neither bed nor arms of defence. The appointed hour was approaching when man in his turn was to go forth from underground into the light of day; and Prometheus, not knowing how else to devise man's salvation, stole the mechanical arts of Hephaestus and Athene, and fire with them (they could neither have been acquired nor used without fire), and gave them to man. Thus man had the wisdom necessary to the support of life, but political wisdom he had not; for that was in the keeping of Zeus, and the power of Prometheus did not extend to entering into the citadel of heaven, where Zeus dwelt, who moreover had terrible sentinels; but he did enter by stealth into the common workshop of Athene and Hephaestus, in which they used to practise their favourite arts, and carried off Hephaestus' art of working by fire, and also the art of Athene, and gave them to man. And in this way man was supplied with the means of life. But Prometheus is said to have been afterwards prosecuted for theft, owing to the blunder of Epimetheus.

Thus man, having a share of the divine attributes, was at first the only one of the animals who had any gods, because he alone was of their kindred; and he would raise altars and images of them. He was not long in inventing articulate speech and names; and he also constructed houses and clothes and shoes and beds, and drew sustenance from the earth. Thus provided, mankind at first lived dispersed, and there were no cities. But the consequence was that they were destroyed by the wild beasts, for they were utterly weak in comparison with them, and their art was only sufficient to provide them with the means of sustenance, and did not enable them to carry on war against the animals: food they had, but not as yet the art of government, of which the art of war is a part. After a while the desire of self-preservation gathered them into cities; but when they were gathered together, having no art of government, they evil entreated one another, and were again in process of dispersion and destruction. Zeus feared that the entire race would be exterminated, and so he sent Hermes to them, bearing reverence and justice to be the ordering principles of cities and the bonds of friendship and society. Hermes asked Zeus how he should impart justice and reverence among men: — Should he distribute them as the arts are distributed; that is to say, to a favoured few only, one skilled individual having enough of medicine or of any other art for many unskilled ones? 'Shall this be the manner in which I am to distribute justice and reverence among men, or shall I give them to all?' 'To all,' said Zeus; 'I should like them all to have a share; for cities cannot exist, if a few only share in the virtues, as in the arts. And further, make a law by my order, that he who has no part in reverence and justice shall be put to death, for he is a plague of the state.'

And this is the reason, Socrates, why the Athenians and mankind in general, when the question relates to carpentering or any other mechanical art, allow but a few to share in their deliberations; and when any one else interferes, then, as you say, they object, if he be not of the favoured few; which, as I reply, is very natural. But when they meet to deliberate about political virtue, which proceeds only by way of justice and wisdom, they are patient enough of any man who speaks of them, as is also natural, because they think that every man ought to share in this sort of virtue, and that states could not exist if this were otherwise. I have explained to you, Socrates, the reason of this phenomenon.[27]

In this passage the myth of Prometheus reappears. The reason for the bringing of fire to man is to provide him with an equipment in the struggle for racial survival suitable to his nature. The theme of man's inferiority to the animals in bodily endowment, which opens the seventh book of Pliny's *Natural History* and was to be so often elaborated in subsequent periods, is played upon. But the gifts of Prometheus were not sufficient; not until the political art was made possible by the divine impartation, not to some but to all men, of the fundamental moral ideas and virtues, was man's life made secure and distinctively human. City life is not degeneration but progress, and war, which was the abomination of all primitivists who thought about it, becomes a desirable means of defence. Government, which for the primitivist is usually an evil made necessary by man's lapse from the innocence of the Golden Age, is here a blessing. The only suggestion of primitivism in the speech is the insistence that all men have civic virtues — a democratic note often in modern times associated with the notion that democracy is a return to the natural goodness of man which

[27] Jowett's tr. with some changes; 3rd ed. Oxford, I, pp. 142-4.

has been corrupted by the very process of civilization which Protagoras eulogizes.[28]

CRITIAS

In Plato's dialogue bearing the name of Critias — "the most detested of Athenian names" (Jowett) — that brilliant but sinister figure in the politics and letters of the end of the fifth century is presented in a highly favorable light (as also in *Charmides* 154 b, 157 e) and is made the spokesman of a semi-primitivistic version of the early history of Athens and Atlantis (cf. Ch. V, Nos. 3, 4). But Plato's depiction of the views as well as of the character of this kinsman of his is of questionable historical value. For Xenophon (*Mem.* I, ii, 24 ff.) Critias is an insincere pupil of Socrates who, like his associate Alcibiades, was early corrupted by pride of birth, wealth, and political ambition; and as the leader of the oligarchy of 'the Thirty,' he was a Greek precursor of some contemporary dictators, who overthrew democratic institutions by the violence of armed bands and sought to establish a totalitarian state by the suppression of all freedom of speech (attempting this even in the case of Socrates). But aside from his stormy political career, he was also a lyric poet, dramatist (several of his plays being long attributed by later writers to Euripides), materialistic psychologist, and pioneer student of comparative constitutional law. His attitude towards the primitivism of his period was probably determined by his reactionary political temper and an aristocratic contempt for average human nature. Of the original condition of mankind his picture is of the usual anti-primitivistic type. What distinguishes the relevant passage is his view as to the means — the permanently necessary means — of man's escape from this condition. Not even the introduction of the civil state with penal laws was enough to tame man. Not until religion — the belief in a deity who "seeth in secret" and supplements the political with supernatural sanctions — was invented could the anti-social passions of men be effectually restrained. Critias thus anticipated Voltaire's argument for a 'police-God,' whom, if he did not exist, it would be necessary, in the interest of society, to invent. As the fragment is from a play, it is possible though improbable, that the passage does not express an opinion of Critias himself.[29]

---

[28] Protagoras was the author of a treatise *Concerning the Original Condition of Mankind* (Diog. Laert. IX, 55) which may be inferred to have been an attack upon chronological primitivism.

[29] Sextus Empiricus (cf. Diels, *Fragm.* 25, II, 319) says that Critias "seems to have been one of the band of atheists," citing this passage as evidence. Critias's play *Perithous*, on the other hand, contains a highly poetic apostrophe to the "self-created" deity, author of nature, about whom "light and darkness and the countless starry host forever circle in their choral dance" (*Fragm.* 19). Either passage may be purely dramatic, or they may belong to different periods in the author's life.

VII, 13. *Fragm.* 25, lines 1-21, 24-26, in Sextus Empir. *Adv. Math.* IX, 34.

ἦν χρόνος, ὅτ' ἦν ἄτακτος ἀνθρώπων βίος
καὶ θηριώδης ἰσχύος θ' ὑπηρέτης,
ὅτ' οὐδὲν ἆθλον οὔτε τοῖς ἐσθλοῖσιν ἦν
οὔτ' αὖ κόλασμα τοῖς κακοῖς ἐγίγνετο.
κἄπειτά μοι δοκοῦσιν ἄνθρωποι νόμους
θέσθαι κολαστάς, ἵνα δίκη τύραννος ἦι
⟨ὁμῶς ἁπάντων⟩ τήν θ' ὕβριν δούλην ἔχηι·
ἐζημιοῦτο δ' εἴ τις ἐξαμαρτάνοι.
ἔπειτ' ἐπειδὴ τἀμφανῆ μὲν οἱ νόμοι
ἀπεῖργον αὐτοὺς ἔργα μὴ πράσσειν βίαι,
λάθραι δ' ἔπρασσον, τηνικαῦτά μοι δοκεῖ
⟨πρῶτον⟩ πυκνός τις καὶ σοφὸς γνώμην ἀνήρ [γνῶναι]
⟨θεῶν⟩ δέος θνητοῖσιν ἐξευρεῖν, ὅπως
εἴη τι δεῖμα τοῖς κακοῖσι, κἂν λάθραι
πράσσωσιν ἢ λέγωσιν ἢ φρονῶσί ⟨τι⟩.
ἐντεῦθεν οὖν τὸ θεῖον εἰσηγήσατο,
ὡς ἔστι δαίμων ἀφθίτωι θάλλων· βίωι,
νόωι τ' ἀκούων καὶ βλέπων, φρονῶν τ' ἄγαν
προσέχων τε ταῦτα, καὶ φύσιν θείαν φορῶν,
ὃς πᾶν τὸ λεχθὲν ἐν βροτοῖς ἀκούσεται,
⟨τὸ⟩ δρώμενον δὲ πᾶν ἰδεῖν δυνήσεται.

.   .   .   .   .   .

.   .   .   .   τούσδε τοὺς λόγους λέγων
διδαγμάτων ἥδιστον εἰσηγήσατο
ψευδεῖ καλύψας τὴν ἀλήθειαν λόγωι.[30]

There was a time when the life of men was undisciplined and bestial, at the mercy of force, when there was neither reward for the good nor yet punishment for the wicked. And then men seem to me to have made punitive laws that justice might be lord alike for all and insolence be mastered; and that if any man should do wrong he might be punished. But then, when the laws prevented them from doing open misdeeds by violence, they did wrong in secret; and thereupon, I think, some clever and wise man first discovered the fear of gods for mortals, so that evil men might be afraid, should they do or say or think anything in secret. He therefore introduced the divine, as a spirit vigorous with imperishable life, and hearing and seeing with his mind, and of great wisdom, and attending to these things, and having a divine nature, who hears all that is said among men and can see all that is done on earth. . . . By means of such words he introduced the most beneficent of doctrines, concealing the truth by his delusive speech.

The writings of Plato and Aristotle include some important parts of the history of Greek anti-primitivism, which belong chronologically at this point; but the position of both writers being somewhat complex and in need of analysis, they have been dealt with separately. We here continue with briefer examples of the opposition to primitivism in less important writers.

[30] Diels, II, pp. 320-321.

PHILEMON

A fourth-century fragment of the comic poet Philemon seems to attribute human progress not to individual inventors or teachers of the arts, but to the gradual process of time itself. The context of the lines is undiscoverable and we do not know the comedy from which they were quoted. Stobaeus, who preserves them for us, indexes them under *Time*.

VII, 14. In Stobaeus, *Eclogae Physicae* I, viii, 34.

"Οσαι τέχναι γεγόνασι, ταύτας, ὦ Λάχης,
πάσας ἐδίδαξεν ὁ χρόνος, οὐχ ὁ διδάσκαλος.[31]

Whatsoever arts have come to be, all these, Laches, have been taught by time, not by the school-master.

By implication these lines suggest that at one time man was without the arts, but they contain no suggestion as to their value. Philemon, however, in some of his moods was no admirer of mankind. He bewailed in one fragment (Meineke, *Fab. Inc.* III) the diversity of human nature; in another (*ibid.* IV, 1-7) his inferiority to the beasts in regard to nature's bounty; and in a third (*ibid.* VIII) his inferiority to the beasts in his ability to reason. Unfortunately the context of these lines is lost, so that we have no means of knowing how seriously Philemon expressed what later became a commonplace.

ATHENIO

A fourth or third century comic writer, Athenio, plays humorously upon the same theme of human progress, maintaining that the art of cooking was the source of man's rise from cannibalism and non-social life to his present condition. The first step upward is accidental and the continued progress is stimulated by the pleasures to be found in it, not by the teaching of a god. The use of the theme in comedy is evidence of the vogue of speculations concerning the origin of civilization.

VII, 15. In Athenaeus, *Deipnos.* XIV, 660-661.

Οὐκ οἶσθ' ὅτι πάντων ἡ μαγειρικὴ τέχνη
πρὸς εὐσέβειαν πλεῖστα προσενήνεχθ' ὅλως;
Β. τοιοῦτόν ἐστι τοῦτο; Α. πάνυ γε, βάρβαρε.
τοῦ θηριώδους καὶ παρασπόνδου βίου
ἡμᾶς γὰρ ἀπολύσασα καὶ τῆς δυσχεροῦς
ἀλληλοφαγίας, ἤγαγ' εἰς τάξιν τινά,
καὶ τουτονὶ περιῆψεν ὃν νυνὶ βίον
ζῶμεν. Β. τίνα τρόπον; Α. πρόσεχε, κἀγώ σοι φράσω.
ἀλληλοφαγίας καὶ κακῶν ὄντων συχνῶν,
γενόμενος ἄνθρωπός τις οὐκ ἀβέλτερος
ἔθυσ' ἱερεῖον πρῶτος, ὤπτησεν κρέας.
ὡς δ' ἦν τὸ κρέας ἥδιον ἀνθρώπου κρεῶν,

---

[31] In Meineke, *Com. Graec.* IV, 54.

αὐτοὺς μὲν οὐκ ἐμασῶντο, τὰ δὲ βοσκήματα
θύοντες ὤπτων. ὡς δ' ἅπαξ τῆς ἡδονῆς
ἐμπειρίαν τιν' ἔλαβον, ἀρχῆς γενομένης,
ἐπὶ πλεῖον ηὖξον τὴν μαγειρικὴν τέχνην.
ὅθεν ἔτι καὶ νῦν τῶν πρότερον μεμνημένοι
τὰ σπλάγχνα τοῖς θεοῖσιν ὀπτῶσιν φλογὶ
ἅλας οὐ προσάγοντες· οὐ γὰρ ἦσαν οὐδέπω
εἰς τὴν τοιαύτην χρῆσιν ἐξευρημένοι.
ὡς δ' ἦρεσ' αὐτοῖς ὕστερον, καὶ τοὺς ἅλας
προσάγουσιν ἤδη, τῶν ἱερῶν γεγραμμένων,
τὰ πάτρια διατηροῦντες. ἅπερ ἡμῖν μόνα
ἅπασιν ἀρχὴ γέγονε τῆς σωτηρίας,
τὸ προσφιλοτεχνεῖν διά τε τῶν ἡδυσμάτων
ἐπὶ πλεῖον αὔξειν τὴν μαγειρικὴν τέχνην.
Β. καινὸς γάρ ἐστιν οὑτοσὶ Παλαίφατος.
Α. μετὰ ταῦτα γαστρίον τις ὠνθυλευμένον
προϊόντος εἰσηνέγκατ' ἤδη τοῦ χρόνου·
ἐρίφιον ἐτακέρωσε, πνικτῷ διέλαβεν
περικομματίῳ, διεγίγγρασ' ὑποκρούσας γλυκεῖ,
ἰχθῦν παρεισεκύκλησεν οὐδ' ὁρώμενον,
λάχανον, τάριχος πολυτελές, χόνδρον, μέλι.
ὡς πολὺ ⟨δὲ⟩ διὰ τὰς ἡδονὰς ἃς νῦν λέγω
ἀπεῖχ' ἕκαστος τοῦ φαγεῖν ἂν ἔτι νεκροῦ,
αὐτοῖς ἅπαντες ἠξίουν συζῆν, ὄχλος
ἠθροίζετ', ἐγένονθ' αἱ πόλεις οἰκούμεναι
διὰ τὴν τέχνην, ὅπερ εἶπα, τὴν μαγειρικήν.
Β. ἄνθρωπε χαῖρε, περὶ πόδ' εἶ τῷ δεσπότῃ.
Α. καταρχόμεθ' ἡμεῖς οἱ μάγειροι, θύομεν,
σπονδὰς ποιοῦμεν, τῷ μάλιστα τοὺς θεούς
ἡμῖν ὑπακούειν διὰ τὸ ταῦθ' εὑρηκέναι
τὰ μάλιστα συντείνοντα πρὸς τὸ ζῆν καλῶς.[32]

A. Don't you know that the art of cooking has contributed more than any other to piety?

B. Do you really mean this?

A. Absolutely, barbarian, for it has freed us from the bestial and uncontrolled life and the hateful devouring of one another; it has brought us to a certain order, and has fashioned for us this life which we now live.

B. In what way?

A. Give heed and I shall tell you. When cannibalism and many evils existed, there arose a certain man, no fool either, who first roasted the sacrificial meat as an offering. And as the meat was sweeter than the flesh of men, they did not chew each other up but they sacrificed and roasted cattle. As soon as they once experienced this pleasure, having once begun, they extended still further the art of cooking. Wherefore even now those mindful of the past roast the inwards for the gods in the flame and sprinkle no salt upon them. For they had not as yet discovered such a use for salt; but in accordance with a later taste, people now sprinkle salt also, maintaining faithfully that ancestral tradition of the sacred rites. From this

[32] Ed. Kaibel, Leipzig, 1890, III.

beginning comes the only salvation for us all — the further cultivation of art through the extension of the art of cooking by means of seasoning.

B. Why this fellow is a new Palaephatus!

A. After this someone, as time passed, introduced the stuffed sausage; he boiled a kid; he cut up the meat for a stew; with mincemeat he tuned it up, beating time with sweetening; he slyly introduced a disguised fish, greens, expensive smoked fish, cartilage, honey. And as every one of them abstained from eating (human flesh) even of the dead, then, because of the pleasures of which I am now speaking, they all desired to live together, a community was formed, and inhabited cities grew up because of the very art of cooking, as I have said.

B. Dear man, you are every inch a lord.

A. We cooks are the rulers, we are the sacrificers, we pour the libations, by reason of the fact that the gods listen to us more than to others, because of the discovery of the things which above all make for good living.

MOSCHION

The documents already cited in this chapter show the diversity of opinions, among anti-primitivistic writers, concerning the origin of civilization. A third-century fragment of Moschion somewhat vaguely distinguishes three theories on the subject: the inventiveness of a Prometheus, the gradual development of the arts as a necessity in man's struggle to survive, and the teaching of 'nature.' What the third theory means is not clear; it possibly is like that of Democritus, that man first learned the arts by imitating the animals. All of these theories are curiously subordinated to the proposition that " Time changed mortal life," as if the writer believed in a necessary process of development, whatever its specific cause. Agriculture is apparently conceived as the earliest of the arts.

VII, 16. In Stobaeus, *Ecl.* I, viii, 38 ff.

Πρῶτον δ' ἄνειμι καὶ διαπτύξω λόγῳ
ἀρχὴν βροτείου καὶ κατάστασιν βίου.
ἦν γάρ ποτ' αἰὼν κεῖνος, ἦν ποθ' ἡνίκα
θηρσὶν διαίτας εἶχον ἐμφερεῖς βροτοί,
ὀρειγενῆ σπήλαια καὶ δυσαυλίους
φάραγγας ἐνναίοντες· οὐδέπω γὰρ ἦν
οὔτε στεγήρης οἶκος οὔτε λαΐνοις
εὐρεῖα πύργοις ὠχυρωμένη πόλις·
οὐ μὴν ἀρότροις ἀγκύλοις ἐτέμνετο
μέλαινα καρποῦ βῶλος ὀμπνίου τροφός,
οὐδ' ἐργάτης σίδηρος εὐιώτιδος
θάλλοντας οἴνης ὀρχάτους ἐτημέλει,
ἀλλ' ἦν ἀκύμων κωφὰ χηρεύουσα γῆ·
βοραὶ δὲ σαρκοβρῶτες ἀλληλοκτόνους
παρεῖχον αὐτοῖς δαίτας· ἦν δ' ὁ μὲν νόμος
ταπεινός, ἡ βία δὲ σύνθρονος Διί,
ὁ δ' ἀσθενὴς ἦν τῶν ἀμεινόνων βορά.

ἐπεὶ δ' ὁ τίκτων πάντα καὶ τρέφων χρόνος
τὸν θνητὸν ἠλλοίωσεν ἔμπαλιν βίον,
εἴτ' οὖν μέριμναν τὴν Προμηθέως σπάσας,
εἴτ' οὖν ἀνάγκην, εἴτε τῇ μακρᾷ τριβῇ
αὐτὴν παρασχὼν τὴν φύσιν διδάσκαλον·
τόθ' εὑρέθη μὲν καρπὸς ἡμέρου τροφῆς
Δήμητρος ἁγνῆς, εὑρέθη δὲ Βακχίου
γλυκεῖα πηγή· γαῖα δ' ἡ πρὶν ἄσπορος
ἤδη ζυγουλκοῖς βουσὶν ἠροτρεύετο.
ἄστη δ' ἐπυργώσαντο καὶ περισκεπεῖς
ἔτευξαν οἴκους, καὶ τὸν ἠγριωμένον
εἰς ἥμερον ·δίαιταν ἤγαγον βίον·
κὰκ τοῦδε τοὺς θανόντας ὥρισεν νόμος
τύμβοις καλύπτειν κἀπιμοιρᾶσθαι κόνιν
νεκροῖς ἀθάπτοις, μηδ' ἐν ὀφθαλμοῖς ἐᾶν
τῆς πρόσθε θοίνης μνημόνευμα δυσσεβές.[33]

First I shall begin to unfold in my poem the original condition of human life. For there was once a time when men lived like beasts, dwelling in mountain caves and sunless ravines. For not yet was there either a roofed house or a wide city to be found fortified with stone towers. Nor with curved ploughs was the black earth cut to be a nurse of the ripening corn, nor did the pruning iron care for the exuberant rows of the Bacchic vineyards, but the sterile earth lay silent and solitary.[34] The flesh of their fellows was men's food. And Law was humble and Brute Strength was enthroned with Zeus, and the weak was food for his betters. And when Time, the father and nurturer of all things, changed mortal life again, either by the forethought of Prometheus, or through necessity, or again through long practice making nature herself their teacher, then were discovered cultivated fruits, the food given by chaste Demeter, and there was discovered the sweet stream of Bacchus. And earth, till then unsown, was now ploughed by yoked oxen; and cities were turretted and roofed houses built; and they changed their savage way of life for civilization. And law decreed that the dead be concealed in tombs, and that the unburied dead be buried and not be left before men's gaze as a reminder of their impious meals of earlier days.

POLYBIUS (*ca.* 204-122 B. C.).

Of an absolute beginning of human history Polybius does not attempt to tell; he adopts (probably from Plato) the assumption of recurrent natural catastrophes through which civilization has repeatedly been destroyed, though a few survivors have in each case been left. The condition of these he assumes to have been similar to that of the gregarious animals. His concern is, given this starting-point, to explain the psychological genesis of moral feelings and social standards, and of the earliest form of civil

---

[33] Ed. Meineke, Leipzig, 1860.

[34] The text here is very doubtful. Scholars are referred to the variant readings in Wachsmuth-Hense.

government. The explanation is of a type which foreshadows some eighteenth-century theories of the origin of judgments of approbation and disapproprobation. A disapproves those actions of B toward C which he would dislike or resent if he were in C's place; and as these reactions to the behavior of others are spontaneous and identical in all men, they result in the formulation of uniform and generally accepted moral codes, which are then enforced by public opinion. The difference between the earliest true kings and the primitive leaders of human herds is that the former owe their power, not to physical superiority, but to the support of public opinion.

VII, 17. *Histor.* VI, 4-6 (543-546).

Ποίας οὖν ἀρχὰς λέγω καὶ πόθεν φημὶ φύεσθαι τὰς πολιτείας πρῶτον; ὅταν ἢ διὰ κατακλυσμοὺς ἢ διὰ λοιμικὰς περιστάσεις ἢ δι' ἀφορίας καρπῶν ἢ δι' ἄλλας τοιαύτας αἰτίας φθορὰ γένηται τοῦ τῶν ἀνθρώπων γένους, οἵας ἤδη γεγονέναι παρειλήφαμεν καὶ πάλιν πολλάκις ἔσεσθ' ὁ λόγος αἱρεῖ, τότε δὴ συμφθειρομένων πάντων τῶν ἐπιτηδευμάτων καὶ τεχνῶν, ὅταν ἐκ τῶν περιλειφθέντων οἷον εἰ σπερμάτων αὖθις αὐξηθῇ σὺν χρόνῳ πλῆθος ἀνθρώπων, τότε δήπου, καθάπερ ἐπὶ τῶν ἄλλων ζῴων, καὶ ἐπὶ τούτων συναθροιζομένων — ὅπερ εἰκός, καὶ τούτους εἰς τὸ ὁμόφυλον συναγελάζεσθαι διὰ τὴν τῆς φύσεως ἀσθένειαν — ἀνάγκη τὸν τῇ σωματικῇ ῥώμῃ καὶ τῇ ψυχικῇ τόλμῃ διαφέροντα, τοῦτον ἡγεῖσθαι καὶ κρατεῖν, καθάπερ καὶ ἐπὶ τῶν ἄλλων γενῶν ἀδοξοποιήτων ζῴων θεωρούμενον τοῦτο χρὴ φύσεως ἔργον ἀληθινώτατον νομίζειν, παρ' οἷς ὁμολογουμένως τοὺς ἰσχυροτάτους ὁρῶμεν ἡγουμένους, λέγω δὲ ταύρους, κάπρους, ἀλεκτρυόνας, τὰ τούτοις παραπλήσια. τὰς μὲν οὖν ἀρχὰς εἰκὸς τοιούτους εἶναι καὶ τοὺς τῶν ἀνθρώπων βίους, ζῳηδὸν συναθροιζομένων καὶ τοῖς ἀλκιμωτάτοις καὶ δυναμικωτάτοις ἑπομένων· οἷς ὅρος μέν ἐστι τῆς ἀρχῆς ἰσχύς, ὄνομα δ' ἂν εἴποι τις μοναρχίαν. ἐπειδὰν δὲ τοῖς συστήμασι διὰ τὸν χρόνον ὑπογένηται συντροφία καὶ συνήθεια, τοῦτ' ἀρχὴ βασιλείας φύεται, καὶ τότε πρώτως ἔννοια γίνεται τοῦ καλοῦ καὶ δικαίου τοῖς ἀνθρώποις, ὁμοίως δὲ καὶ τῶν ἐναντίων τούτοις. ὁ δὲ τρόπος τῆς ἀρχῆς καὶ τῆς γενέσεως τῶν εἰρημένων τοιόσδε. πάντων γὰρ πρὸς τὰς συνουσίας ὁρμώντων κατὰ φύσιν, ἐκ δὲ τούτων παιδοποιίας ἀποτελουμένης, ὁπότε τις τῶν ἐκτραφέντων εἰς ἡλικίαν ἱκόμενος μὴ νέμοι χάριν μηδ' ἀμύναι τούτοις οἷς ἐκτρέφοιτ', ἀλλά που τἀναντία κακῶς λέγειν ἢ δρᾶν τούτους ἐγχειροίη, δῆλον ὡς δυσαρεστεῖν καὶ προσκόπτειν εἰκὸς τοὺς συνόντας καὶ συνιδόντας τὴν γεγενημένην ἐκ τῶν γεννησάντων ἐπιμέλειαν καὶ κακοπάθειαν περὶ τὰ τέκνα καὶ τὴν τούτων θεραπείαν καὶ τροφήν. τοῦ γὰρ γένους τῶν ἀνθρώπων ταύτῃ διαφέροντος τῶν ἄλλων ζῴων, ᾗ μόνοις αὐτοῖς μέτεστι νοῦ καὶ λογισμοῦ, φανερὸν ὡς οὐκ εἰκὸς παρατρέχειν αὐτοὺς τὴν προειρημένην διαφοράν, καθάπερ ἐπὶ τῶν ἄλλων ζῴων, ἀλλ' ἐπισημαίνεσθαι τὸ γινόμενον καὶ δυσαρεστεῖσθαι τοῖς παροῦσι, προορωμένους τὸ μέλλον καὶ συλλογιζομένους ὅτι τὸ παραπλήσιον ἑκάστοις αὐτῶν συγκυρήσει. καὶ μὴν ὅταν που πάλιν ἄτερος ὑπὸ θατέρου τυχὸν ἐπικουρίας ἢ βοηθείας ἐν τοῖς δεινοῖς μὴ νέμῃ τῷ σώσαντι χάριν, ἀλλά ποτε καὶ βλάπτειν ἐγχειρῇ τοῦτον, φανερὸν ὡς εἰκὸς τῷ τοιούτῳ δυσαρεστεῖσθαι καὶ προσκόπτειν τοὺς εἰδότας, συναγανακτοῦντας μὲν τῷ πέλας, ἀναφέροντας δ' ἐφ' αὑτοὺς τὸ παραπλήσιον. ἐξ ὧν ὑπογίνεταί τις ἔννοια παρ' ἑκάστῳ τῆς τοῦ καθήκοντος δυνάμεως καὶ θεωρίας· ὅπερ ἐστὶν ἀρχὴ καὶ τέλος δικαιοσύνης. ὁμοίως πάλιν ὅταν ἀμύνῃ μέν τις πρὸ πάντων ἐν τοῖς δεινοῖς, ὑφίσταται δὲ καὶ μένῃ τὰς ἐπιφορὰς τῶν ἀλκιμωτάτων ζῴων, εἰκὸς μὲν τὸν τοιοῦτον ὑπὸ τοῦ πλήθους ἐπισημασίας τυγχάνειν εὐνοϊκῆς καὶ προστατικῆς, τὸν δὲ τἀναντία

τούτῳ πράττοντα καταγνώσεως καὶ προσκοπῆς. ἐξ οὗ πάλιν εὔλογον ὑπο-
γίνεσθαί τινα θεωρίαν παρὰ τοῖς πολλοῖς αἰσχροῦ καὶ καλοῦ καὶ τῆς τούτων
πρὸς ἄλληλα διαφορᾶς, καὶ τὸ μὲν ζήλου καὶ μιμήσεως τυγχάνειν διὰ τὸ
συμφέρον, τὸ δὲ φυγῆς. ἐν οἷς ὅταν ὁ προεστὼς καὶ τὴν μεγίστην δύναμιν
ἔχων ἀεὶ συνεπισχύῃ τοῖς προειρημένοις κατὰ τὰς τῶν πολλῶν διαλήψεις, καὶ
δόξῃ τοῖς ὑποταττομένοις διανεμητικὸς εἶναι τοῦ κατ' ἀξίαν ἑκάστοις, οὐκέτι
τὴν βίαν δεδιότες, τῇ δὲ γνώμῃ τὸ πλεῖον εὐδοκοῦντες, ὑποτάττονται καὶ
συσσῴζουσι τὴν ἀρχὴν αὐτοῦ, κἂν ὅλως ᾖ γηραιός, ὁμοθυμαδὸν ἐπαμύνοντες
καὶ διαγωνιζόμενοι πρὸς τοὺς ἐπιβουλεύοντας αὐτοῦ τῇ δυναστείᾳ. καὶ δὴ
τῷ τοιούτῳ τρόπῳ βασιλεὺς ἐκ μονάρχου λανθάνει γενόμενος, ὅταν παρὰ τοῦ
θυμοῦ καὶ τῆς ἰσχύος μεταλάβῃ τὴν ἡγεμονίαν ὁ λογισμός.[35]

What beginnings shall I relate and whence shall I say states first
arose? When because of floods or pestilential conditions [36] or failure
of crops or other such cases the tribes of men have been destroyed —
which tradition tells us has already happened, and which will happen
often again, as stands to reason — and when all crafts and all arts
have perished, then from the survivors, as if from seeds, there
gradually grows up a new multitude of men, and at first, no doubt,
as is the case with the other animals, so when these had gathered
together (the truth being that these herd with those of their kind
because of the weakness of their nature) he who was preëminent in
bodily strength and courage was necessarily their leader and ruler —
just as among the other races of unreasoning creatures this must be
recognized to be the most genuine work of nature; for among them
the strongest we see to be by common consent the masters — I speak
of bulls, boars, cocks, and the like. Such then, probably, were the
primitive ways of human life; in the manner of the beasts they
herded together and followed the bravest and most powerful. When
the ruler's strength is the limit of his power, the form of government
should be monarchy. But when in the course of time there grows
up among such human herds a community of feeling and of customs,
then true kingship is born, and then first the notions of goodness
and justice and their opposites have their origin among men. The
manner of their origination was as follows. Since all men are by
nature given to sexual intercourse and since this results in the birth
of children, whenever one of these, after he has grown up, does not
show gratitude to those who have reared him, nor assist them, but
on the contrary takes to speaking ill of them or ill-treating them, it
is evident that he will offend and disgust those who are acquainted
with his parents and have observed with what care and sacrifice of
their own comfort they have nurtured and brought up their children.
For inasmuch as men differ from other animals in alone participating
in intellect and reason, it is evidently unlikely that such a difference
in conduct will escape their notice, as it does escape that of other
animals; they will disapprove and be displeased at such behavior,
looking to the future and reflecting that they may any one of them
suffer the same treatment. And again whenever a man who has been
assisted or rescued by another when in danger, does not show gratitude to his rescuer, but on the contrary actually tries to do him

[35] Ed. Dindorf-Büttner-Wobst. Leipzig, 1924, II.
[36] Liddell and Scott suggest " of the air."

injury, it is evident that those who observe this will be displeased and offended, sharing the resentment of their neighbor who has been wronged and imagining the same thing happening to themselves. In these ways there arises in every man a notion of the meaning and import of duty, which is the beginning and end of justice. Similarly again, when any man is foremost in defending his fellows from danger, and faces and withstands the attack of ferocious beasts, he will be likely to receive marks of favor and honor from the people, while the man who acts in the opposite way will be disliked and despised. From this again some conception of what is base and what is noble, and of the nature of the difference between them, will, it is reasonable to suppose, arise among the generality of men; and what is noble will be admired and imitated because it is advantageous, while what is base will be avoided. Now when the outstanding and most powerful man among the people always gives his support to the opinions on such matters that are generally accepted, and when he appears to his subjects to apportion rewards and punishments according to desert, then they no longer obey him through fear of his force, but because they consent to his judgment; and they accept and join in maintaining his rule even in his extreme old age, defending him by common consent and fighting against those who plot to deprive him of power. And thus a mere monarch insensibly becomes a genuine king whenever, in place of violence and force, reason takes command.

The second stage in political history is thus an advance upon the first. Polybius, however, is no believer in a general law of social progress. Human nature being what it is, these early kingships inevitably became corrupt and were overthrown. Government passes necessarily through a series of forms, each of which in turn — and each for the same reason — degenerates and becomes intolerable; and the end of the series is a return to the beginning. The children of the original kings do not inherit the wisdom and virtue of their parents; they arouse indignation in the hearts of their nobles and their subjects, who join forces, rebel, and supplant royalty with aristocracy. The first generation of aristocrats, like the early kings, are trustworthy, but again their children do not know the price of government, and therefore merely imitate the vices of tyrants, so that as royalty turns into tyranny, aristocracy turns into oligarchy. This once more leads to rebellion and gives way to democracy. But democracy in turn permits the rise of individuals who by corruption, bribery, gifts, attain to power. But hereupon, says Polybius, should some bold leader arise who is poor, he will attain power by violence, and democracy be shattered into anarchy, of which the disastrous results lead men to fall again under the rule of a despot and monarch. " Such," he concludes, " is the cycle of political organizations, such the economy of nature by which the forms of government are changed and brought back again to their original condition."

DIODORUS SICULUS

Diodorus thought it essential to prefix to his Universal History (second half of first century B. C.) both a brief account of the genesis of the world and of organisms and a description of the life of primeval men. His treatment of the latter two subjects was apparently influenced by the theories of the Epicureans, and, though much more summary, has a good deal in common with the passages of Lucretius dealing with the same topics.[37] While non-committal on the question at issue between the Peripatetics and other schools as to whether the universe and mankind have existed from all eternity or both had their beginning at a definite time (I, 6), Diodorus gives an exposition of the latter hypothesis. The embryos of the first animals were generated directly from the earth when it was still in a moist state, under the influence of extreme heat; these autochthonous ova when they reached the limit of their growth burst, and the various kinds of organisms emerged and betook themselves to their proper elements. The earth, however, since it has grown more solid, is no longer able to give birth to the larger animals, which are now generated solely by sexual reproduction (I, 7). Of the original state of mankind, also, Diodorus professes to report only the account given by some other unnamed writers.

VII, 18. *Bibliotheca historica,* I, 8.

> τοὺς δὲ ἐξ ἀρχῆς γεννηθέντας τῶν ἀνθρώπων φασὶν ἐν ἀτάκτῳ καὶ θηριώδει βίῳ καθεστῶτας σποράδην ἐπὶ τὰς νομὰς ἐξιέναι, καὶ προσφέρεσθαι τῆς τε βοτάνης τὴν προσηνεστάτην καὶ τοὺς αὐτομάτους ἀπὸ τῶν δένδρων καρπούς. καὶ πολεμουμένους μὲν ὑπὸ τῶν θηρίων ἀλλήλοις βοηθεῖν ὑπὸ τοῦ συμφέροντος διδασκομένους, ἀθροιζομένους δὲ διὰ τὸν φόβον ἐπιγινώσκειν ἐκ τοῦ κατὰ μικρὸν τοὺς ἀλλήλων τύπους. τῆς φωνῆς δ' ἀσήμου καὶ συγκεχυμένης οὔσης ἐκ τοῦ κατ' ὀλίγον διαρθροῦν τὰς λέξεις, καὶ πρὸς ἀλλήλους τιθέντας σύμβολα περὶ ἑκάστου τῶν ὑποκειμένων γνώριμον σφίσιν αὐτοῖς ποιῆσαι τὴν περὶ ἁπάντων ἑρμηνείαν. τοιούτων δὲ συστημάτων γινομένων καθ' ἅπασαν τὴν οἰκουμένην, οὐχ ὁμόφωνον πάντας ἔχειν τὴν διάλεκτον, ἑκάστων ὡς ἔτυχε συνταξάντων τὰς λέξεις· διὸ καὶ παντοίους τε ὑπάρξαι χαρακτῆρας διαλέκτων καὶ τὰ πρῶτα γενόμενα συστήματα τῶν ἁπάντων ἐθνῶν ἀρχέγονα γενέσθαι. τοὺς οὖν πρώτους τῶν ἀνθρώπων μηδενὸς τῶν πρὸς βίον χρησίμων εὑρημένου ἐπιπόνως διάγειν, γυμνοὺς μὲν ἐσθῆτος ὄντας, οἰκήσεως δὲ καὶ πυρὸς ἀήθεις, τροφῆς δ' ἡμέρου παντελῶς ἀνεννοήτους. καὶ γὰρ τὴν συγκομιδὴν τῆς ἀγρίας τροφῆς ἀγνοοῦντας μηδεμίαν τῶν καρπῶν εἰς τὰς ἐνδείας ποιεῖσθαι παράθεσιν· διὸ καὶ πολλοὺς αὐτῶν ἀπόλλυσθαι κατὰ τοὺς χειμῶνας διά τε τὸ ψῦχος καὶ τὴν σπάνιν τῆς τροφῆς. ἐκ δὲ τοῦ κατ' ὀλίγον ὑπὸ τῆς πείρας διδασκομένους εἴς τε τὰ σπήλαια καταφεύγειν ἐν τῷ χειμῶνι καὶ τῶν καρπῶν τοὺς φυλάττεσθαι δυναμένους ἀποτίθεσθαι. γνωσθέντος δὲ τοῦ πυρὸς καὶ τῶν ἄλλων τῶν χρησίμων κατὰ μικρὸν καὶ τὰς τέχνας εὑρεθῆναι καὶ τἆλλα τὰ δυνάμενα τὸν κοινὸν βίον

---

[37] It is uncertain whether the final version of Bk. I of the *Bibliotheca historica* was written before or after the publication of the *De rerum natura*; for a discussion of the question of the dates of the several parts of Diodorus's work *vide* Oldfather, *Diodorus of Sicily*, I, Loeb Classical Lib., 1933, pp. vii-xi.

ὠφελῆσαι. καθόλου γὰρ πάντων τὴν χρείαν αὐτὴν διδάσκαλον γενέσθαι τοῖς
ἀνθρώποις, ὑφηγουμένην οἰκείως τὴν ἑκάστου μάθησιν εὐφυεῖ ζώῳ καὶ συνεργοὺς
ἔχοντι πρὸς ἅπαντα χεῖρας καὶ λόγον καὶ ψυχῆς ἀγχίνοιαν.

Καὶ περὶ μὲν τῆς πρώτης γενέσεως τῶν ἀνθρώπων καὶ τοῦ παλαιοτάτου
βίου τοῖς ῥηθεῖσιν ἀρκεσθησόμεθα, στοχαζόμενοι τῆς συμμετρίας.[38]

The men who were born in the beginning lived, they say, an undisciplined and brutish life, each going off to feed by himself upon
the tenderest herbs and the fruits that grew wild upon the trees.
When they were attacked by wild beasts they, taught by self-interest,
came to one another's aid; and after they had thus been led by fear
to gather into groups, they presently came to understand the signs [39]
they made to one another. The sounds which they uttered to each
other were, indeed, at first obscure and confused; but they soon
developed articulate speech, and by agreeing with one another upon
symbols for the various objects they met with, they made the signification of these terms mutually intelligible. But since groups of this
kind arose in every part of the inhabited world, they did not all have
the same language; for each framed its own speech as chance
determined. This is the reason why there now exist all manner of
languages. And out of these first groups all the original peoples of
the world arose.

The first men, therefore, led a miserable existence, none of the
things which are useful for life having yet been discovered: they had
no clothing, were unacquainted with the use of fire and dwellings,
and knew nothing at all of the cultivation of food. And since they
were ignorant of the harvesting of wild foods, they made no provision
of fruits against their needs; consequently many of them perished
in the winters from cold and lack of food. But gradually they
learned from experience to take refuge in caves in the winter and to
store up such fruits as could be preserved. And when they had become acquainted with fire and other useful things, they gradually
discovered the arts and whatever else is serviceable to social life. For
in general it was necessity that was man's teacher, providing suitable
instruction in all things to an animal which was well endowed by
nature, and had hands and speech and an intelligent mind to assist
it in all its efforts. With respect to the genesis of men and the life
of the earliest times we shall let what has already been said suffice,
since we aim to preserve due proportion.

---

[38] Ed. F. Vogel, Lepzig, 1888.

[39] Or possibly "one another's characters"; but this rendering fits the context
poorly.

CHAPTER EIGHT

LUCRETIUS: PRIMITIVISM AND THE IDEA OF PROGRESS

The earliest considerable Roman document of the history of primitivism consists of the last 686 lines of Book V of the *De rerum natura* (ll. 771-1457).[1] It is also one of the most extensive; and it has a special importance as our principal source of evidence concerning the position of the Epicurean school. Lucretius gives a detailed account of what he conceives must have been the early phases of terrestrial history and of the development of human society. The poem, however, was left unfinished, or at all events unrevised, at its author's death; and, presumably for this reason, a good deal of the relevant part of the Fifth Book reads like a collection of passages written separately and not completely articulated. There are several manifest contradictions, and the chronological order of the origins of the several arts, and of the stages of 'social evolution,' remains in part obscure. It should be added that it is uncertain that the position of Lucretius — in spite of the Epicurean orthodoxy of his metaphysics and cosmology and of his attitude towards the popular religious beliefs of his time — is identical at all points with that of Epicurus on the questions here pertinent.[2] But he is, at all events, representative of the Epicurean method in connecting his version of man's beginnings with a cosmogonic hypothesis and with ideas about the general course of cosmical history. If the specific conception of this history in Lucretius is genuinely Epicurean, that philosophy, like his own, is much less thoroughly 'evolutionistic' than it has often been said to be.

THE PRIME OF MOTHER EARTH

Concerning the relative degree of productive energy possessed by the earth at its beginning and in later times Lucretius gives a curiously wavering account. For the most part he appears to follow the theory that the first age was that of Nature's greatest vigor and fecundity, and that with the lapse of time she has become exhausted and barren like an aged woman (V, 821-826). Her original offspring were more numerous in kind, larger, and physically more powerful (799-800, 925-930), this high primeval fertility being connected with the higher temperature and humidity of the

---

[1] The passage is nearly contemporaneous with Cicero's *De re publica*, but — assuming 55 B. C. as the year of Lucretius's death — is slightly earlier in date of composition.

[2] There is a brief passage of Epicurus referring to the origin of intelligence and language and their subsequent progress (Diog. Laert. X, 75-6), but it is vague and conventional.

earth at that time (806). The fecundity of Nature in her prime was so
excessive that all manner of monsters unviable or incapable of reproduction were born by spontaneous generation, the existing species being the
remnant that were adapted, in one way and another, to survival (837-877,
not cited). Yet other lines in the same passage imply that at the outset
the world and all things and forces in it were characterized by the weakness
of infancy; even heat and cold and the winds were young and, so to say, of
undeveloped powers (818-820). What is more, the world is even now but
in its childhood, and a long period of progress may be expected before its
inevitable disintegration begins; evidence of this Lucretius finds in the
recency of the discovery of the arts and sciences and the fact that many of
them are still in the early stages of their development (324-326). Later
partisans both of the theory of a cosmical degeneration already far advanced,
and of the belief in progress — in the past and during a long though not
unlimited future — could both find expressions of their doctrines in the
confused eclecticism of the Lucretian conception of early world history.

VIII, 1. *De rerum natura*, V, 780-792, 801-836 (Translation on p. 224).

> nunc redeo ad mundi novitatem et mollia terrae
> arva, novo fetu quid primum in luminis oras
> tollere et incertis credunt committere ventis.
>   Principio genus herbarum viridemque nitorem
> terra dedit circum collis camposque per omnis,
> florida fulserunt viridanti prata colore,
> arboribusque datumst variis exinde per auras
> crescendi magnum inmissis certamen habenis.
> ut pluma atque pili primum saetaeque creantur
> quadripedum membris et corpore pennipotentum,
> sic nova tum tellus herbas virgultaque primum
> sustulit, inde loci mortalia saecla creavit
> multa modis multis varia ratione coorta
>
> .   .   .   .
>
> principio genus alituum variaeque volucres
> ova relinquebant exclusae tempore verno,
> folliculos ut nunc teretis aestate cicadae
> lincunt sponte sua victum vitamque petentes.
> tum tibi terra dedit primum mortalia saecla.
> multus enim calor atque umor superabat in arvis.
> hoc ubi quaeque loci regio opportuna dabatur,
> crescebant uteri terram radicibus apti;
> quos ubi tempore maturo patefecerat aestus [3]
> infantum fugiens umorem aurasque petessens,
> convertebat ibi natura foramina terrae
> et sucum venis cogebat fundere apertis
> consimilem lactis; sicut nunc femina quaeque

[3] *Aestus* is retained in place of *aetas*, as Merrill in his 1917 ed., and other editors,
prefer.

cum peperit, dulci repletur lacte, quod omnis
impetus in mammas convertitur ille alimenti.
terra cibum pueris, vestem vapor, herba cubile
praebebat multa et molli lanugine abundans.
at novitas mundi nec frigora dura ciebat
nec nimios aestus nec magnis viribus auras.
omnia enim pariter crescunt et robora sumunt.

    Quare etiam atque etiam maternum nomen adepta
terra tenet merito, quoniam genus ipsa creavit
humanum atque animal prope certo tempore fudit
omne quod in magnis bacchatur montibu' passim,
aeriasque simul volucres variantibu' formis.
sed quia finem aliquam pariendi debet habere,
destitit, ut mulier spatio defessa vetusto.
mutat enim mundi naturam totius aetas
ex alioque alius status excipere omnia debet,
nec manet ulla sui similis res: omnia migrant,
omnia commutat natura et vertere cogit.
namque aliut putrescit et aevo debile languet,
porro aliut ⟨suc⟩crescit et ⟨e⟩ contemptibus exit.
sic igitur mundi naturam totius aetas
mutat et ex alio terram status excipit alter;
quod tulit ut nequeat, possit quod non tulit ante.[4]

I now return to the world's infancy, to tell what things first the fields of earth in their tender age and at their earliest parturition gained strength to bring forth to the regions of light and to commit to the fickle winds. In the beginning the earth produced the species of grasses and bright verdure about the hills and over all the plains, and the flowering meadows were bright with the color green; and then the various kinds of trees went through a mighty struggle as they raced unchecked to grow up into the air. As feathers and hair and bristles are the first growth on the bodies and limbs of quadrupeds or strong-winged birds, so the new-born earth first put forth herbage and trees,[5] and in the next place created the generations of mortal creatures [animals], which arose in many kinds and many ways through various causes. . . .

Then first, note you, the earth brought forth the generations of mortal creatures. For there was great abundance of heat and moisture in the fields; consequently, wherever there was a suitable place, wombs would grow, fastened to the earth with roots; when in due time these were burst apart by the movements[6] of the infants, fleeing from the fluid [within the womb] and seeking the air, then nature would at those places change the pores of the earth and compel it to exude from its open veins a liquid like milk; just as now a woman when she has brought forth is filled with sweet milk, because all the flow of nourishment is directed towards the breasts. Earth

---

[4] Ed. Merrill, 1907, with emendations.

[5] The theory that plants were produced before animals was probably Empedoclean; cf. *Fragm.* 21, 23 (Diels).

[6] The text is uncertain; see n. 3.

gave food to the young, the warm air clad them, the herbage furnished a bed well supplied with rich and soft down. But the infancy of the world produced neither severe cold nor excessive heat nor winds of great force; for all things grow and gain strength together. Wherefore the earth has again and again won the name of mother which has been given her, since of herself she created the human race, and almost at a fixed time produced every animal that ranges wild in the great mountains, and, at the same time, the birds of the air in all their varied forms. But because she must have some limit to her bearing, she has ceased, like a woman worn out with old age. For time changes the nature of the whole world, and all things must pass from one condition to another, and nothing remains like itself; all things are in process, all things nature transforms and compels to alter; for one thing crumbles away and becomes faint and enfeebled with age, another in its turn springs up from and rises above despised things. So therefore time changes the nature of the whole world, and one state of the earth gives place to another; so that what once she bore she can bear no longer, but can bear what she bore not before.

EARLY PHASES OF HUMAN HISTORY

In spite of the uncertainty of the chronological sequence of some of the episodes in the Lucretian account of man's early cultural history, four fairly well marked periods seem to be distinguishable in it.

Primeval man

Like other animals man was produced directly from the earth, and at the same time; nor did his manner of life at the outset, or for some indeterminate period thereafter, differ from that of his fellow-beasts.

VIII, 2. *De rerum natura*, V, 925-1010 (Translation on p. 227).

> At genus humanum multo fuit illud in arvis
> durius, ut decuit, tellus quod dura creasset,
> et maioribus et solidis magis ossibus intus
> fundatum, validis aptum per viscera nervis,
> nec facile ex aestu nec frigore quod caperetur
> nec novitate cibi nec labi corporis ulla.
> multaque per caelum solis volventia lustra
> volgivago vitam tractabant more ferarum.
> nec robustus erat curvi moderator aratri
> quisquam, nec scibat ferro molirier arva
> nec nova defodere in terram virgulta neque altis
> arboribus veteres decidere falcibu' ramos.
> quod sol atque imbres dederant, quod terra crearat
> sponte sua, satis id placabat pectora donum.
> glandiferas inter curabant corpora quercus
> plerumque; et quae nunc hiberno tempore cernis
> arbita puniceo fieri matura colore,
> plurima tum tellus etiam maiora ferebat.
> multaque praeterea novitas tum florida mundi

pabula dura tulit, miseris mortalibus ampla.
at sedare sitim fluvii fontesque vocabant,
ut nunc montibus e magnis decursus aquai
claru' citat late sitientia saecla ferarum.
denique nota vagi silvestria templa tenebant
nympharum, quibus e scibant umori' fluenta
lubrica proluvie larga lavere umida saxa,
umida saxa, super viridi stillantia musco,
et partim plano scatere atque erumpere campo.
necdum res igni scibant tractare neque uti
pellibus et spoliis corpus vestire ferarum,
sed nemora atque cavos montis silvasque colebant
et frutices inter condebant squalida membra
verbera ventorum vitare imbrisque coacti.
nec commune bonum poterant spectare neque ullis
moribus inter se scibant nec legibus uti.
quod cuique obtulerat praedae fortuna, ferebat
sponte sua sibi quisque valere et vivere doctus.
et Venus in silvis iungebat corpora amantum;
conciliabat enim vel mutua quamque cupido
vel violenta viri vis atque inpensa libido
vel pretium, glandes atque arbita vel pira lecta.
et manuum mira freti virtute pedumque
consectabantur silvestria saecla ferarum
missilibus saxis et magno pondere clavae;
multaque vincebant, vitabant pauca latebris;
saetigerisque pares subus silvestria membra
nuda ⟨da⟩bant terrae nocturno tempore capti,
circum se foliis ac frondibus involventes.
nec plangore diem magno solemque per agros
quaerebant pavidi palantes noctis in umbris,
sed taciti respectabant somnoque sepulti,
dum rosea face sol inferret lumina caelo.
a parvis quod enim consuerant cernere semper
alterno tenebras et lucem tempore gigni,
non erat ut fieri posset mirarier umquam
nec diffidere ne terras aeterna teneret
nox in perpetuum detracto lumine solis.
sed magis illud erat curae, quod saecla ferarum
infestam miseris faciebant saepe quietem.
eiectique domo fugiebant saxea tecta
spumigeri suis adventu validique leonis
atque intempesta cedebant nocte paventes
hospitibus saevis instrata cubilia fronde.

Nec nimio tum plus quam nunc mortalia saecla
dulcia linquebant lamentis lumina vitae.
unus enim tum quisque magis deprensus eorum
pabula viva feris praebebat, dentibus haustus,
et nemora ac montis gemitu silvasque replebat
viva videns vivo sepeliri viscera busto.
at quos effugium servarat corpore adeso,
posterius tremulas super ulcera taetra tenentes

palmas horriferis accibant vocibus Orcum,
donique eos vita privarant vermina saeva
expertis opis, ignaros quid volnera vellent.
at non multa virum sub signis milia ducta
una dies dabat exitio nec turbida ponti
aequora lidebant navis ad saxa virosque.
hic temere incassum frustra mare saepe coortum
saevibat leviterque minas ponebat inanis,
nec poterat quemquam palcidi pellacia ponti
subdola pellicere in fraudem ridentibus undis.
improba navigii ratio tum caeca iacebat.
tum penuria deinde cibi languentia leto
membra dabat, contra nunc rerum copia mersat.
illi ⟨in⟩prudentes ipsi sibi saepe venenum
vergebant, nunc dant ⟨aliis⟩ sollertius ipsi.[7]

But the human race was then much hardier on the land, as was fitting since hard earth had created it. It was built upon larger and more solid bones within, fitted with strong sinews throughout the flesh. Nor was it to be harmed easily by heat or cold, by unaccustomed foods, or any bodily illness. And while the sun revolved through the sky for many lustres, men lived their life after the roving fashion of the beasts. There was then none who sturdily guided the curved plough, or who knew how to work the fields with iron blade, or to plant young seedlings in the ground, or to prune old branches from the tall trees with pruning knives. What sun and showers bestowed, what earth produced spontaneously, that gift was sufficient to content their hearts. They fed their bodies from the acorn-bearing oaks for the most part, and those arbute berries, which you now see ripe in their scarlet in the winter, then were produced by the earth in greater quantity and larger. And besides these, many other kinds of food the flowering infancy of the world then bore — coarse but sufficient for [those] poor mortals. The streams and springs called to them to quench their thirst, as now the waters tumbling down the great mountains call clearly far and wide to the thirsty herds of wild beasts; at last, as they wandered, they would settle in well-known woodland sanctuaries of the nymphs, from which they knew that flowing streams washed the wet rocks with lavish waters, as they dript over the green moss and here and there bubbled up on the level plain.

Not yet did they know how to work things with fire nor to use skins and clothe the body with the pelts of wild beasts. But they dwelt in woods and forests and in caves in the mountains, and sheltered their filthy limbs in the thickets when forced to avoid the lashing of the winds and rains. They were unable to give heed to the common good, or to make use, in their dealings with one another, of settled customs and laws. Whatever booty chance gave to each, that each bore off at his own pleasure, taught to be strong and live for himself alone. And in the woods Venus united the bodies of lovers; for each woman was won either by mutual desire, or by the violence of a man and his vehement lust, or at a price in acorns,

[7] Ed. Merrill, 1907.

arbute berries or choice pears.   And trusting in the wonderful
strength of their hands and feet, men chased the woodland beasts
with stones and heavy clubs, capturing many, but losing some in
their hiding places.   When overtaken by night they laid their
naked bodies on the ground like bristly boars, rolling themselves
in leaves and foliage.   Nor did they go wailing through the fields
to seek the day and the sunlight, fearing the shadows of the night;
but quietly and buried in sleep they waited until the sun with red
torch should bring light to the sky.   For since from infancy they
had been used to seeing darkness and sunlight born in turn, it could
not occur to them ever to wonder or to doubt whether eternal night
might not hold the earth forever and the light of the sun be with-
drawn.   But they were troubled rather about the herds of beasts,
which often made rest dangerous to these unhappy beings.   Driven
from home they fled their rocky shelters at the coming of a foaming
boar or mighty lion, and at dead of night yielded in terror their
leaf-strewn beds to their savage guests.

Not less then than now did mortal generations leave the sweet
light of life with lamentations.   For more often in those days one
of them would be caught and furnish living food to the beasts,
mangled by their teeth, and would fill the groves and mountains
and forests with his groaning, as he saw his living flesh buried in a
living tomb.   But those whom flight had saved, though with body
half-devoured, holding trembling hands over their frightful wounds,
would call upon Orcus with horrible cries, until they died in wild
convulsions, helpless, not knowing how to care for their wounds.
But one day did not then see many thousands of men given to death
under the standards, nor did the stormy waters of the sea crush
ships and men upon the rocks.   Idly, to no end, in vain, the stormy
ocean raged, and then lightly dropped its empty threats; nor could
the treacherous cunning of the calm sea's smiling waves lure anyone
into its trap.   The wicked art of navigation was then hidden.   At
that time it was famine that brought their fainting limbs to death;
now, on the contrary, it is abundance that destroys us.   In those
days men often took poison in ignorance; now, better instructed,
they give it to others.

The beginnings of human society

VIII, 3. *De rerum natura*, V, 1011-1027.

> Inde casas postquam ac pellis ignemque pararunt,
> et mulier coniuncta viro concessit in unum
>
> .   .   .   .
>
> cognita sunt prolemque ex se videre creatam,
> tum genus humanum primum mollescere coepit.
> ignis enim curavit ut alsia corpora frigus
> non ita iam possent caeli sub tegmine ferre,
> et Venus inminuit viris puerique parentum
> blanditiis facile ingenium fregere superbum.
> tunc et amicitiem coeperunt iungere aventes
> finitimi inter se nec laedere nec violari,
> et pueros commendarunt muliebreque saeclum,

vocibus et gestu cum balbe significarent
imbecillorum esse aecum misererier omnis.
nec tamen omnimodis poterat concordia gigni,
sed bona magnaque pars servabat foedera caste;
aut genus humanum iam tum foret omne peremptum
nec potuisset adhuc perducere saecla propago.[8]

Next, after they had equipped themselves with huts and tents of hides, and with fire, and the woman in mating with man gave herself to one only, [a line is missing] . . . were known, and when they saw offspring born of them, then mankind began to grow soft. For fire made their shivering bodies less able to endure the cold under the open sky, and Venus sapped their strength, and children by their caresses easily broke the fierce spirit of their parents. And then neighbors began eagerly to unite in friendly agreement with one another neither to do nor to suffer violence, and they commended their children and their womankind to the protection of others, signifying stammeringly by speech and gesture that it is right for all to have pity on the weak. Nevertheless universal concord could not yet be brought about; but a good and great part kept their covenants inviolate. Else mankind would even then have been entirely destroyed and breeding could not have continued the race until our day.

Apparently early in this period man developed articulate speech from instinctive animal cries (1028-1090), and learned to keep alive fires started by lightning or the friction of trees.[9] In the course of time, observation of the softening effect of the sun's heat taught them the art of cooking (1091-1104); weaving was invented — by men, not women; animals were domesticated; and agriculture had its beginning [10] (1350-60, 1297-99, 1361-69 — none of these passages are here reproduced). Also, seemingly, in this age the art of song, the first musical instruments and the dance made their appearance; and with these the men of that time lived in a merry life.[11]

VIII, 4. *De rerum natura,* V, 1379-1435, omitting lines 1388-9 (Translation on p. 231).

At liquidas avium voces imitarier ore
ante fuit multo quam levia carmina cantu
concelebrare homines possent aurisque iuvare.

[8] Ed. Merrill.

[9] Lucretius curiously fails to say anything about the genesis of the art of fire-making, which in the Prometheus myth and other Greek accounts of man's emergence from his primeval wretchedness plays the primary part.

[10] That the invention of agriculture was a good thing for mankind is implied by VI, 1-2.

[11] It has been suggested by some scholars that in this passage Lucretius is influenced by a current theory of the origin of comedy in the harvest-festival; Professor Tenney Frank points out an analogous passage in Tibullus II, 1, 50. Whatever the force of this conjecture, the Lucretian scheme of the early stages of social developments remains unaffected.

et zephyri, cava per calamorum, sibila primum
agrestis docuere cavas inflare cicutas.
inde minutatim dulcis didicere querellas,
tibia quas fundit digitis pulsata canentum,
avia per nemora ac silvas saltusque reperta,
per loca pastorum deserta atque otia dia.
haec animos ollis mulcebant atque iuvabant
cum satiate cibi; nam tum sunt omnia cordi.
saepe itaque inter se prostrati in gramine molli
propter aquae rivom sub ramis arboris altae
non magnis opibus iucunde corpora habebant,
praesertim cum tempestas ridebat et anni
tempora pingebant viridantis floribus herbas.
tum ioca, tum sermo, tum dulces esse cachinni
consuerant. agrestis enim tum musa vigebat;
tum caput atque umeros plexis redimire coronis
floribus et foliis lascivia laeta monebat,
atque extra numerum procedere membra moventes
duriter et duro terram pede pellere matrem;
unde oriebantur risus dulcesque cachinni,
omnia quod nova tum magis haec et mira vigebant.
et vigilantibus hinc aderant solacia somno
ducere multimodis voces et flectere cantus
et supera calamos unco percurrere labro.
unde etiam vigiles nunc haec accepta tuentur
et numerum servare genus didicere, neque hilo
maiorem interea capiunt dulcedini' fructum
quam silvestre genus capiebat terrigenarum.
nam quod adest praesto, nisi quid cognovimus ante
suavius, in primis placet et pollere videtur,
posteriorque fere melior res illa reperta
perdit et immutat sensus ad pristina quaeque.
sic odium coepit glandis, sic illa relicta
strata cubilia sunt herbis et frondibus aucta.
pellis item cecidit vestis contempta ferinae;
quam reor invidia tali tunc esse repertam,
ut letum insidiis qui gessit primus obiret,
et tamen inter eos distractam sanguine multo
disperiisse neque in fructum convertere quisse.
tunc igitur pelles, nunc aurum et purpura curis
exercent hominum vitam belloque fatigant;
quo magis in nobis, ut opinor, culpa resedit.
frigus enim nudos sine pellibus excruciabat
terrigenas; at nos nil laedit veste carere
purpurea atque auro signisque ingentibus apta,
dum plebeia tamen sit quae defendere possit.
ergo hominum genus in cassum frustraque laborat
semper et ⟨in⟩ curis consumit inanibus aevom,
nimirum quia non cognovit quae sit habendi
finis et omnino quoad crescat vera voluptas.
idque minutatim vitam provexit in altum
et belli magnos commovit funditus aestus.[12]

[12] Ed. Merrill, 1907.

The imitation of the liquid notes of birds with the mouth began long before men could delight their ears by singing smooth carols together; and it was the zephyrs whistling through hollow reeds that first taught these rustic folk to blow into hollow hemlock-stalks. Next, little by little, they learned the sweet notes the reed-pipe gives forth when tapped by the player's fingers — the pipe that is heard in the deep forests and the woodland pastures, in the solitary haunts of shepherds and the quiet of the open air. These delighted their minds and gave them pleasure when they had their fill of food; for it is then that song is grateful. Often, therefore, stretched out together on the soft grass beside a stream of water under the branches of a tall tree, they made merry at small cost, above all when the weather smiled and the season of the year painted the green herbage with flowers. Then would they rejoice in jests and talk and pleasant bursts of laughter. For then the rustic muse was in its prime; then with head and shoulders wreathed with plaited leaves and flowers they would give themselves to jollity, and march with limbs moving rudely out of time, beating mother earth with their hard feet; from which mirth and pleasant bursts of laughter would arise, because all these things, then new and wonderful, were in their prime. And when they were wakeful their consolation for sleep was to sing many a long-drawn note and turn a tune and run along the tops of their reed-pipes with curved lip. And thus it is that even now those who keep late hours follow these customs and know how to observe the various kinds of rhythm. Nevertheless they get from them not a whit more pleasure than the earth-born woodland people did. For what lies ready to hand pleases us most and seems to have the advantage, unless we have formerly known something more agreeable; and then the better thing discovered afterward spoils it, and changes our taste for anything old. So it was that men grew to dislike acorns, and to desert those beds spread with herbage and piled-up leaves. The garment, also, of wild-beasts' pelts fell into contempt — which at the time when it was discovered, I imagine, aroused such envy that its first wearer was killed from ambush, and even the garment was torn to pieces among them with much bloodshed and was destroyed and could not be turned to use. Thus in that day pelts, in our own gold and purple, fill men's life with cares and weary it with war; in which I think the greater fault rests with us. For the earth-born men, naked and without coats of fur, were racked with cold; but it does us no harm to go without a robe of purple or embroidered with gold and great figures, so long as there is the plain man's cloak to cover us. Therefore mankind labor always in vain and to no purpose and consume their days in empty cares, plainly because they do not know the limit of possession nor at what point true pleasure ceases to increase. And this little by little has carried life into deep waters and has stirred up from the depths the great billows of war.

Between the beginning and end of this period various other advances in the arts took place; and at the same time the earliest form of government developed — chiefship of the men of superior ability.

VIII, 5. *De rerum natura*, V, 1105-1112.

Inque dies magis hi victum vitamque priorem

commutare novis monstrabant rebu' benigni [13]
ingenio qui praestabant et corde vigebant.
condere coeperunt urbis arcemque locare
praesidium reges ipsi sibi perfugiumque,
et pecus atque agros divisere atque dedere
pro facie cuiusque et viribus ingenioque;
nam facies multum valuit viresque vigebant.

More and more daily the men of good will who excelled in mind
and judgment taught them to change their former mode of life
and subsistence for new ways. Kings began to found cities and to
build themselves citadels as a protection and refuge; and they
divided cattle and lands, giving to each man his share in proportion
to his strength and looks; for good looks counted for much and
strength was held in great esteem in those days.

Man's lapse from primitive simplicity: its causes and consequences

VIII, 6. *De rerum natura*, V, 1113-1142.

Posterius res inventast aurumque repertum,
quod facile et validis et pulchris dempsit honorem;
divitioris enim sectam plerumque secuntur
quamlubet et fortes et pulchro corpore creti.
quod siquis vera vitam ratione gubernet,
divitiae grandes homini sunt vivere parce
aequo animo; neque enim est umquam penuria parvi.
at claros homines voluerunt se atque potentes,
ut fundamento stabili fortuna maneret
et placidam possent opulenti degere vitam,
nequiquam, quoniam ad summum succedere honorem
certantes iter infestum fecere viai,
et tamen e summo, quasi fulmen, deicit ictos
invidia interdum contemptim in Tartara taetra;
invidia quoniam, ceu fulmine, summa vaporant
plerumque et quae sunt aliis magis edita cumque;
ut satius multo iam sit parere quietum
quam regere imperio res velle et regna tenere.
proinde sine incassum defessi sanguine sudent,
angustum per iter luctantes ambitionis;
quandoquidem sapiunt alieno ex ore petuntque
res ex auditis potius quam sensibus ipsis,
nec magis id nunc est neque erit mox quam fuit ante.
    Ergo regibus occisis subversa iacebat
pristina maiestas soliorum et sceptra superba,
et capitis summi praeclarum insigne cruentum
sub pedibus volgi magnum lugebat honorem;
nam cupide conculcatur nimis ante metutum.
res itaque ad summam faecem turbasque redibat,
imperium sibi cum ac summatum quisque petebat.[14]

[13] Munro's reading of *rebu' benigni* is here preferred to Merrill's *rebus et igni*.
[14] Ed. Merrill, 1907.

After this, property was invented and gold was discovered,[15] which easily robbed those who are strong and handsome of their honor; for the majority follow the party of the richer, however powerful and handsome men may be by birth. But if anyone should govern his life by true reason, man's greatest riches is to live on little with contented mind; for of little there is never lack. Men, however, desired to become distinguished and powerful, so that their fortunes might remain established upon a firm foundation, and that through wealth they might live a quiet life — in vain, since in the struggle to attain to the highest honor they caused their path to be beset with dangers, and even from the summit of it envy, like a thunderbolt, contemptuously cast them down into loathsome Tartarus, since envy, like the thunderbolt, usually strikes the highest places and whatever things are raised up above others. So that it is far better to be a subject and live in peace than to seek dominion in the state and to rule kingdoms. Let those, then, who struggle along the narrow path of ambition sweat blood and weary themselves in vain, since for them things have savor only through the mouths of other men [16] and they pursue objects only because of what they have heard others say, rather than from their own feelings. And this is no different now, nor will it be hereafter, from what it was before. The kings, therefore, were slain, and the primitive majesty of thrones and proud sceptres lay overthrown, and the glorious dignity of the sovereign head, bleeding beneath the feet of the mob, bewailed its lost honor; for men eagerly tread underfoot what they have too much feared. And so the rule of things came back to the last dregs of mankind and to the unruly mobs,[17] when each man sought power and supremacy for himself.

Beginning of the reign of law

This state of chaos and violence became intolerable to everyone, and,

---

[15] A fuller and somewhat different account of the beginnings of metallurgy is given by Lucretius in lines 1281-1296; here gold is the last of the metals to come into use.

[16] Previous English translators seem to us to have at least partially missed the point of lines 1134-5, and consequently to have misrendered *sapiunt*. The primary meaning of *sapere*, to taste, or feel the savor of a thing, is still to be found in authors of the classical period, e. g. Plautus, Juvenal, Seneca, Pliny; and the sense requires it here. The usual translation, "they get their knowledge from others' lips" (Munro; similar versions in Rouse and Leonard) does not fit the context. Lucretius is describing the psychology of the "ambitious" man, who seeks distinction and preëminence. It is not to the point to characterize such men as "getting knowledge from others' lips," which is no peculiarity of theirs; it is very much to the point to say that the end which they pursue gets its savor, i. e. value, from what other men say. The factitiousness of the desire for distinction or 'honor' is a characteristic primitivistic theme, of which there are suggestions elsewhere in Lucretius, e. g. lines 1426-1433.

[17] The ambiguity of *res* and *faeces* makes the translation uncertain; Rouse in the *Loeb Classical Library* edition renders: "so things came to the uttermost dregs of confusion."

again under the leadership of superior men, the political state and positive law were introduced as the only remedy.

VIII, 7. *De rerum natura*, V, 1143-1160.

> inde magistratum partim docuere creare
> iuraque constituere, ut vellent legibus uti.
> nam genus humanum, defessum vi colere aevom,
> ex inimicitiis languebat; quo magis ipsum
> sponte sua cecidit sub leges artaque iura.
> acrius ex ira quod enim se quisque parabat
> ulcisci quam nunc concessumst legibus aequis,
> hanc ob rem est homines pertaesum vi colere aevom.
> inde metus maculat poenarum praemia vitae.
> circumretit enim vis atque iniuria quemque
> atque, unde exortast, ad eum plerumque revertit,
> nec facilest placidam ac pacatam degere vitam
> qui violat factis communia foedera pacis.
> etsi fallit enim divom genus humanumque,
> perpetuo tamen id fore clam diffidere debet;
> quippe ubi se multi per somnia saepe loquentes
> aut morbo delirantes protraxe ferantur
> et celata ⟨diu⟩ in medium et peccata dedisse.[18]

In consequence there arose some who taught them to create magistracies and to establish laws, so that they might be willing to obey statutes. For mankind, weary of violence, was grown weak from its feuds, so that it was the more ready of its own accord to subject itself to the restraint of laws. For because each man would in his wrath seek to avenge himself more cruelly than is now permitted by just laws, for this reason men were utterly weary of living in violence. Hence the fear of punishment robs the spoils of life of their glitter; for violence and injury catch in their net those who practice them and oftenest return upon him who began them; nor is it easy for him to lead a quiet and peaceful life whose deeds violate the common compacts of peace. Even if he hide his deed from gods and men, he must yet be uncertain that it will remain forever hidden, since it is said often to have happened to many men that when talking in their dreams, or delirious in sickness, they have betrayed themselves and have revealed long hidden sins and misdeeds to public knowledge.

WAR: ITS BEGINNING AND PROGRESS

The discovery of the art of metallurgy brought with it not only the curse of gold, but also made feuds and wars far more terrible. Lucretius deals with the tragic progress of the art of war as a separate topic, and does not very clearly indicate the chronological relation of its genesis to the other early stages of cultural history; the history of it, in outline, is traced down to so recent an episode as the introduction of war-elephants by the Carthaginians (1132-34). Its beginning, at all events, was coincident with the

---

[18] Ed. Merrill, 1907.

introduction of bronze agricultural instruments. Upon the persistent and
suicidal pugnacity of men and nations since the discovery of the arts which
have made war effective and increasingly destructive Lucretius dilates in
the spirit of the primitivistic pacifist.

VIII, 8. *De rerum natura,* V, 1289-1296, 1305-1307, 1347-1349.

> aere solum terrae tractabant, aereque belli
> miscebant fluctus et vulnera vasta serebant
> et pecus atque agros adimebant; nam facile ollis
> omnia cedebant armatis nuda et inerma.
> inde minutatim processit ferreus ensis
> versaque in obprobrium species est falcis ahenae,
> et ferro coepere solum proscindere terrae
> exaequataque sunt creperi certamina belli.
>
> .   .   .   .
>
> sic alit ex alio peperit discordia tristis,
> horribile humanis quod gentibus esset in armis,
> inque dies belli terroribus addidit augmen.
>
> .   .   .   .
>
> sed facere id non tam vincendi spe voluerunt,
> quam dare quod gemerent hostes, ipsique perire,
> qui numero diffidebant armisque vacabant.[19]

With bronze men tilled the soil of the earth, and with bronze they
stirred up the waves of war and dealt monstrous wounds and seized
herds and fields; for to those who were armed all that was naked
and unarmed easily yielded. Then little by little the sword of iron
gained ground, and the bronze scythe became an object of contempt;
and with iron they began to break the soil of the earth, and the
struggles of war were now fought on equal terms. . . . Thus gloomy
discord gave birth to one thing after another which should be horrible
to the nations of men in battle, and added new terrors to warfare
day by day. . . . But they wished to do these things not so much in
the hope to conquer, as with the desire to cause their enemies to
mourn; and they perished themselves if they were weak in numbers
or lacking in arms.

The Present and Future Progress of Knowledge

Despite his gloomy picture of human motives and behavior since the
second age, and of the increasingly evil effects of many of man's inventions,
Lucretius was no consistent disparager of the arts and no primitivistic
anti-intellectualist; equally characteristic of him is an enthusiasm over the
progress of knowledge and technology, and the improvement of the conditions of life thereby. The world, after all, is young and the arts are new
and still advancing.

[19] Ed. Merrill, 1907.

VIII, 9. *De rerum natura*, V, 324-337.

> Praeterea si nulla fuit genitalis origo
> terrarum et caeli semperque aeterna fuere,
> cur supera bellum Thebanum et funera Troiae
> non alias alii quoque res cecinere poetae?
> quo tot facta virum totiens cecidere neque usquam
> aeternis famae monimentis insita florent?
> verum, ut opinor, habet novitatem summa recensque
> naturast mundi neque pridem exordia cepit.
> quare etiam quaedam nunc artes expoliuntur,
> nunc etiam augescunt; nunc addita navigiis sunt
> multa, modo organici melicos peperere sonores.
> denique natura haec rerum ratioque repertast
> nuper, et hanc primus cum primis ipse repertus
> nunc ego sum in patrias qui possim vertere voces.[20]

If there never was a time when earth and heaven first had their birth, if they have existed always and from everlasting, why have not other poets also sung of other things before the Theban war and the fall of Troy? Why have so many deeds of men so often fallen into oblivion, and nowhere shine among the eternal monuments of fame? But, as I think, the world is new and nature is young, and it is not long since the beginning. Wherefore even now some arts are being improved, even now are still in growth; many new devices are being added to ships; and it was but a little time ago when musicians invented melodious tunes. And finally, the nature and system of the world has been but lately discovered, and I myself, among the first who have learned this, am now the first who has been able to set it forth in our mother tongue.

And it is in the same strain that the Fifth Book concludes:

VIII, 10. *De rerum natura*, V, 1448-57.

> Navigia atque agri culturas moenia leges
> arma vias vestes et cetera de genere horum,
> praemia, delicias quoque vitae funditus omnis,
> carmina picturas, et daedala signa polire,
> usus et impigrae simul experientia mentis
> paulatim docuit pedetemtim progredientis.
> sic unumquicquid paulatim protrahit aetas
> in medium ratioque in luminis erigit oras.
> namque alid ex alio clarescere et ordine debet
> artibus, ad summum donec venere cacumen.[21]

Navigation and agriculture, fortifications and laws, arms, roads, clothing and all else of this kind, all the prizes of life and its deepest delights also, poetry and pictures and sculpture, these slowly, step by step, were taught by practice and the experience of man's mind as it progressed. Thus by degrees time draws forth everything before us and reason raises it to the realm of light. For things must be

---

[20] Ed. Merrill.

[21] Ed. Merrill. Last two lines Munro's reading.

brought to light one after another and in due order in the arts, until they have reached their highest point.[22]

The same strain continues in the opening passage of the concluding book of *De rerum natura* (VI, 1-41). From Athens came three great boons for mankind — agriculture, a new order of social life based upon established laws, and lastly, the teaching of Epicurus, who, by making clear the true nature of things, freed men from supernatural terrors, " set bounds to both desire and fear " (*finem statuit cuppedinis atque timoris*), and showed the nature of the chief good which we all seek (*exposuit bonum summum quo tendimus omnes*).

THE SENESCENCE AND DEATH OF EARTH

Whatever temporary improvement may be looked for in the future of mankind, the Epicurean cosmology followed by Lucretius permitted no belief in an indefinite progress of the world as a whole; the theory of a necessary senescence and eventual collapse, expressed in Book II, determines the general conception of the course of terrestrial history. Every body, great or small, comes to the end of its development when the specific limit of its capacity for absorbing additional atoms is reached; from that point on the process is reversed and a continuous decline begins, ending in the disintegration which awaits all composite things. In so far as Lucretius represents the earth as already old and worn out the passage is in manifest contradiction with V, 324 ff., already cited.

VIII, 11. *De rerum natura,* II, 1122-1174, omitting lines 1146-49 and 1153-63.

> nam quaecumque vides hilaro grandescere adauctu
> paulatimque gradus aetatis scandere adultae,
> plura sibi adsumunt quam de se corpora mittunt,
> dum facile in venas cibus omnis inditur et dum
> non ita sunt late dispessa ut multa remittant
> et plus dispendi faciant quam vescitur aetas.
> nam certe fluere atque recedere corpora rebus
> multa manus dandum est; sed plura accedere debent,
> donec alescendi summum tetigere cacumen.
> inde minutatim vires et robur adultum
> frangit et in partem peiorem liquitur aetas.
> quippe etenim quanto est res amplior, augmine adempto,
> et quo latior est, in cunctas undique partis
> plura modo dispargit et a se corpora mittit,
> nec facile in venas cibus omnis diditur ei
> nec satis est, proquam largos exaestuat aestus,
> unde queat tantum suboriri ac subpeditare.
> iure igitur pereunt, cum rarefacta fluendo

---

[22] If the MS. reading of the end of line 1456, accepted by Giussani, Merrill and Rouse, *corde videbant*, is adopted, the translation should be: " [men's] intellects saw one thing after another brought to light," etc.

sunt et cum externis succumbunt omnia plagis;
quandoquidem grandi cibus aevo denique defit,
nec tuditantia rem cessant extrinsecus ullam
corpora conficere et plagis infesta domare.
　Sic igitur magni quoque circum moenia mundi
expugnata dabunt labem putris⟨que⟩ ruinas.

.　　.　　.　　.　　.　　.　　.

iamque adeo fracta est aetas effetaque tellus
vix animalia parva creat quae cuncta creavit
saecla deditque ferarum ingentia corpora partu.

.　　.　　.　　.　　.　　.　　.

iamque caput quassans grandis suspirat arator
crebrius, incassum magnos cecidisse labores,
et cum tempora temporibus praesentia confert
praeteritis, laudat fortunas saepe parentis.
tristis item vetulae vitis sator atque ⟨vietae⟩
temporis incusat momen caelumque fatigat,
et crepat, anticum genus ut pietate repletum
perfacile angustis tolerarit finibus aevom,
cum minor esset agri multo modus ante viritim;
nec tenet omnia paulatim tabescere et ire
ad capulum spatio aetatis defessa vetusto.[23]

Whatever you see growing with joyous increase and little by little
mounting the steps that lead to adult life, absorbs more bodies than
it discharges, so long as food is easily absorbed into all its veins and
so long as they are not so widely dilated that they let go much that
enters them and do not lose more than their age ingests.　For
certainly it must be granted that much matter flows away and passes
out from things; but still more must pass in, until they have reached
the climax of their growth.　After that by minute degrees age
breaks the strength and vigor of maturity and lapses into decay.
For the larger and broader a thing is, the more, when it ceases to
grow, it ejects matter from itself and scatters it on all sides; and
food is not easily absorbed into its veins, nor is it sufficient, in
proportion to the copious streams that flow out, to enable an equivalent amount of substance to be formed in their place.　Rightly therefore all things perish when they have become attenuated by this
flux, and succumb to blows from without; since in great age nourishment at last is lacking, while external bodies, incessantly beating
upon everything, disintegrate and overwhelm it with their blows.
　So it is that the walls of the mighty universe shall be overthrown
through all their circuit and collapse into crumbling ruins. . . .
(1150)　And even now the force of life is broken and the worn-out
earth scarce produces tiny creatures — she who once produced all
animals of every kind and gave birth to the huge bodies of wild
beasts. . . . (1164)　And now the ancient ploughman often shakes
his head and sighs that the labors of his hands have come to nought,
and when he compares times present with times past, often praises
the good fortune of his forebears.　And the cultivator of an old and

---

[23] Ed. Merrill, 1907, with emendations from later editions.

withering vineyard rails at the work of time and importunes heaven
and grumbles that the men of former days, rich in piety, easily
supported life upon a scant domain — for in the olden time one
man's portion of land was much smaller than it is now. He does
not see that all things little by little wear away and, exhausted by
the long-drawn span of time, approach their tomb.

General Position of Lucretius

It is evident from the foregoing texts and summaries that the position
of Lucretius in the history of primitivism is not a simple nor an unequivocal
one.   Strict chronological primitivism he definitely rejects; as man first
came from the womb of nature he was a squalid beast, without social ties
or even the rudiments of morality, living in terror of the bigger beasts
around him. Some advantages, indeed, he even then had which he has since
lost; he was physically stronger and healthier, and was less harmful to his
own kind than civilized man has become. But the first age was for Lucretius clearly no ideal state of nature. Towards cultural primitivism, on the
other hand, his attitude was wavering. The condition of mankind in what
has been above distinguished as the second period corresponds in the main
to that of savages in the pastoral or early agricultural stage of culture.
Only the simplest arts were practised. Towards (apparently) the end of
this period social groups were ruled by chiefs by virtue of natural superiority; but there seem to have been no coercive political institutions and no
positive law; and though private property in flocks and herds already
existed, differences in wealth were not extreme. Now it is implied, though
not expressly said, by Lucretius that this condition, if it could have endured,
would have been the happiest for man; certainly he draws *con amore* an
idyllic picture of it. Though there had already been some loss of the
physical vigor of the primeval *bête humaine* and though individual feuds
and violence were not unknown, men for the most part dwelt at peace with
one another and through mutual aid lived in comparative security; while
they were free from the great evils of civilized life, on which Lucretius
expatiates with especial earnestness and eloquence — wars ever more horrible and destructive, the corroding cares that attend both the pursuit and
the possession of riches, political rivalries and the civil disorders which
result from them, and the boundless multiplication of men's desires, especially for things which have no utility in themselves but are valued only
because they gratify the craving to appear distinguished above one's fellows.
And Lucretius is in accord with the main primitivistic tradition also in so
far as he sees in the " invention of wealth " the cause of man's lapse from a
state of comparative innocence and happiness; though he identifies this
disastrous innovation not with the establishment of private property in
land but with the introduction of money, made possible by the beginning of
the crafts of mining and metallurgy. There are strains that accord with the

moralizing of the Cynic primitivists — the identification of "true riches" with the ability to be content with that little which need never be lacking to the poorest man (1117 ff.), and the special scorn for fine clothes (1425 ff.).[24] But it is, at the same time, implied by Lucretius that the early idyllic mode of life could not have endured; the ingenious mind of man, which had already progressively devised numerous harmless or beneficent arts, inevitably went on to discover others which, because of weaknesses implicit in human nature from the outset, were turned to evil uses, became the occasions or the instruments of a general mutual conflict between individuals, and resulted, for a time, in a condition of intolerable anarchy — Hobbes's *bellum omnium contra omnes*. In great part, then, Lucretius is at one with the cultural primitivism of his own day; and primitivistic writers of modern times could, and probably did, get in part from the *De rerum natura* many of the themes which they elaborated in their own fashion. On the other hand, he is no believer in a juristic state of nature; man being what he is, and the advances of the arts having placed in his hands powers which, when unrestrained, he is prone to use in anti-social and self-destructive ways, his salvation lay in the establishment of the organized civil state, with formulated and recognized laws effectively enforced by severe penalties. This has its own disadvantages, but they are far outweighed by its benefits; Lucretius perhaps regarded the political state — in comparison with the irrecoverable second phase of man's history — as a *pis aller*, but it was for him at all events a necessary one. And finally there is the strain in Lucretius in which he appears as an *Aufklärer* of the first century B. C. and even a precursor of the enthusiasts for the idea of progress in the seventeenth and eighteenth centuries. This was at bottom irreconcilable with the well-marked strain of cultural primitivism in him; but in the combination of these two incongruous moods Lucretius most of all resembles many writers of that later age.[25]

Though it is a partial anticipation of a much later episode in this history, it is pertinent to point out here how much of Lucretius's version of man's early development turns up again in Rousseau, especially in the *Second Discourse*.[26] The ancient and the modern writer agree in combining the rejection of chronological with the acceptance of a large measure of cultural

---

[24] L. Robin, "Sur la conception du progrès des épicuréens" (*Rev. de Mét. et de Morale*, XXIII, 1916, pp. 697-719) has excellently presented the evidence for the primitivism of Lucretius, without, however, fully bringing out the poet's waverings and inconsistencies in his utterances on the subject. Cf. especially *op. cit.* pp. 704-5, 711, 716.

[25] For eighteenth-century examples, cf. R. D. Havens, "Primitivism and the Idea of Progress in Thomson," *Studies in Philology*, XXIX, No. 1, January, 1932, and Lois Whitney, *Primitivism and the Idea of Progress in the Eighteenth Century*, 1934.

[26] Cf. A. O. Lovejoy, "The Supposed Primitivism of Rousseau's *Discourse on Inequality*," *Mod. Philology*, XXI, 1923, pp. 185-186.

primitivism. For Rousseau also primeval man was but a solitary, roving, stupid and unmoral beast (in fact, an orang-outang or chimpanzee), though healthier and stronger than his civilized progeny, and less dangerous to his fellows; and the same picture is drawn of his squalid mode of existence, of his casual matings, and of his struggles with animals of other species. For Rousseau also the happiest state of mankind was not the earliest, but that of *la société naissante*, intermediate between the primitive and the civilized, similar to the condition of most contemporary savage peoples — a state which was reached only after the development of language and the family and the discovery of a number of simple arts, not yet become noxious to their inventor. And the beginning of the end of this idyllic, though not perfect, phase of human life, for Rousseau also, came with the invention of metallurgy or of agriculture; *pour le poëte* [Lucretius?], *c'est l'or et l'argent, mais pour le philosophe, ce sont le fer et le blé qui ont civilisé les hommes et perdu le genre humain.* For these, giving an incitement and an opportunity previously lacking to an originally latent but characteristic impulse in human nature, led increasingly to economic inequality and also to private feuds and to wars: *l'ambition dévorante, l'ardeur d'élever sa fortune relative, moins par un véritable besoin que pour se mettre au-dessus des autres, inspire à tous les hommes un noir penchant à se nuire mutuellement; . . . en un mot, concurrence et rivalité d'une part, de l'autre l'opposition d'intérêts, et toujours le désir caché de faire son profit aux dépens de l'autrui: tous ces maux sont le premier effet de la propriété et le cortège inséparable de l'inégalité naissante.* Most noteworthy of all is the adumbration by Lucretius of Rousseau's account of the inner psychological causes of this 'fall': man's *amour-propre* or *fureur de se distinguer*, and his strangely factitious desires, his tendency to crave things, not because they of themselves give him pleasure or serve his real needs, but because, under the corrupting influence of social suggestion, they seem to him necessary for the gratification of his self-esteem. *Le sauvage vit en lui-même; l'homme sociable, toujours hors de lui, ne sait que vivre dans l'opinion des autres, et c'est pour ainsi dire de leur seul jugement qu'il tire le sentiment de sa propre existence:* this is a fuller and clearer rephrasing of Lucretius's description of the victims of " ambition," who *sapiunt ex ore alieno petuntque res ex auditis quam sensibus ipsis* (1133-4; see translation above). Lucretius's third period of general social anarchy, resulting from these causes (1136 ff.), has also its counterpart in Rousseau: *une situation qui les armoit tous contre les autres, qui leur rendoit leurs possessions aussi onéreuses que leurs besoins, et où nul ne trouvoit sa sûreté ni dans la pauvreté ni dans la richesse.* In his deep conviction of the *méchanceté naturelle* of man — after his cultural ' progress ' was once well started, and therefore potentially from the beginning — Rousseau's appraisal of human nature in the *Second Discourse* is essentially similar to that of Lucretius (cf. lines 1135, 1305 ff., 1423 ff.).

Nor are the other aspects of Lucretius's attitude wholly without their analogues in Rousseau. In later writings — especially in the first draft of the *Contrat Social* — he too sees in the *état civil*, the régime of law, the only possible and the permanently necessary means of avoiding that state of universal conflict and social chaos into which mankind once fell and into which it would otherwise inevitably revert.[27]   And, even in the *Discourse on the Origin of Inequality*, there are occasional moments of dilatation over the *perfectibilité* of man resulting from his inventiveness and capacity for intellectual progress, which recall analogous passages of Lucretius, as they also foreshadow the increasing progressivist enthusiasms of the later eighteenth and the nineteenth century. The themes which Rousseau sounds in unison with Lucretius are enriched and elaborated by him, and he has, of course, others foreign to the Roman poet; but, with respect to the issues pertinent to the controversy over primitivism, Lucretius may on the whole be said to stand nearer to Rousseau's position than any other classical writer.[28]

---

[27] Cf. Lovejoy, *op. cit.* in *Mod. Philology*, XXI, 1923, pp. 182-3.

[28] Rousseau used a motto from Lucretius (incorrectly cited as *immutat animus ad pristina*) in the frontispiece of his *Projet . . . pour la Musique*, 1742; cf. also *Corresp. générale*, I, p. 183. M. Reichenburg, *Essai sur les lectures de Rousseau*, 1932, has noted six passages in Rousseau indicating a familiarity with the *De rerum natura*. For possible actual borrowings from Lucretius in the *Disc. on the Origin of Inequality* see further the article of J. Morel, *Ann. de la Soc. J.-J. Rousseau*, V, pp. 163 ff. L. Robin (*op. cit.* p. 717) concludes that " les emprunts de Rousseau sont très probables."

CHAPTER NINE

CICERO

Cicero's significance in the history of the ideas with which we are concerned lies, it need hardly be said, less in any original contribution of his own than in his services as a philosophical middle-man — as the first and chief interpreter of a considerable part of Greek philosophy to his countrymen in their own tongue, as one of the principal sources of our knowledge of certain phases of that philosophy from the third to the first century, for which original texts are scanty, and as the classical writer in whom every person having any knowledge of the humanities from the Renaissance to the eighteenth century was probably best read. As will be seen, he transmitted formulas and conceptions which both the spokesmen and the opponents of primitivistic strains in later literature utilized. Yet he held a fairly distinctive, though not entirely consistent, eclectic position of his own; and he at least adumbrated one idea which was to have great importance in a much later period.

Anti-Primitivism

Cicero [1] was intimately acquainted from the beginning of his literary career with Lucretius's outline of man's cultural history, and he accepted one important feature of it. Man at the outset was, in his actual character and condition, not superior to the other animals. Cicero's earliest account of the state of nature and of the beginnings of civilization differs from that of Lucretius chiefly in a partial fusion of the latter writer's first and third periods, and the omission of the second — the idyllic interlude between them. The men of the first age were brutes without social bonds, morals or laws, and followed only " the simple plan that he should get who has the power and he should keep who can." Salvation from this reign of violence was found (as in Lucretius) by the establishment (under the leadership of men of superior ability) of the first political societies with definite laws.

IX, 1. *Pro Sestio* (56 B. C.), xlii, 91-92.

> Quis enim nostrum, iudices, ignorat ita naturam rerum tulisse, ut quodam tempore homines nondum neque naturali neque civili jure descripto, fusi per agros ac dispersi vagarentur, tantumque haberent, quantum manu ac viribus per caedem ac vulnera aut eripere aut retinere potuissent? qui igitur primi virtute et consilio praestanti extiterunt, ii perspecto genere humanae docilitatis atque ingenii dissupatos unum in locum congregarunt eosque ex feritate illa

---

[1] See Cicero's letter to his brother Quintus, *Ep.* 132, ed. Tyrrell, 1886, II, p. 106. That Cicero was actually the redactor of the poem of Lucretius cannot be considered certain; cf. *loc. cit.* n. 4.

ad justitiam atque ad mansuetudinem transduxerunt. tum res ad
communem utilitatem, quas publicas appellamus, tum conventi-
cula hominum, quae postea civitates nominatae sunt, tum domicilia
conjuncta, quas urbes dicimus, invento et divino jure et humano-
⟨ut⟩ moenibus saepserunt. atque inter hanc vitam perpolitam
humanitate et illam immanem nihil tam interest quam jus atque
vis.[2]

For who does not know the condition of nature to have been once
such that men, in the days before either natural or civil law had
been drawn up, wandered dispersed and scattered about the fields,
and that each possessed no more than he could seize or keep by his
own strength, through killing or wounding others? But those who
first arose endowed with superior virtue and prudence, having
recognized a kind of intelligence and teachableness in man, gathered
these scattered individuals together in one place and converted them
from wildness to justice and gentleness. Establishing first political
societies for the common advantage, then the small associations of
men which were afterwards named towns, then those groupings of
domiciles which we call cities, they fortified all these with law,
human and divine, as with walls. And between our present mode
of life, refined through humanity, and that wretched one, the
principal difference is the difference between law and force.

In the *Republic*, which was composed in the four or five years after the
delivery of the *Pro Sestio*, the same anti-primitivistic strain continues.[3]
The opening of the third book exists only in a paraphrase by St. Augustine
in which the language used is so close to that of Pliny in the opening of
the seventh book of the *Natural History* that we must believe either that
Pliny copied Cicero, or that St. Augustine used in his paraphrase words that
had already become a literary cliché. The uniqueness and superiority of man,
in his possession of reason, is insisted upon; but this was at first merely
latent. There is thus an emphasis, lacking in Lucretius, upon the differentiation of man by a trait approximating what in the eighteenth century
was to be called his ' perfectibility '; the peculiarity of the species lies, not
in any attribute which has been apparent throughout its history, but in a
potentiality which inevitably but gradually manifested itself in the course
of time. The conception was doubtless a development of a characteristically
Aristotelian idea (cf. Chap. VI, pp. 188, 190).

IX, 2. *De re publica* (55-51 B. C.), III, i, 1; in Augustine, *Contra
Julianum*, IV, 12, 60.

In libro tertio de re publica idem Tullius hominem dicit non ut
a matre sed ut a noverca natura editum in vitam, corpore nudo,

---

[2] Ed. A. Klotz and F. Schoell, Leipzig, 1919, with some changes in punctuation.
[3] It should be borne in mind that, except for the passages quoted by Augustine,
Lactantius and others, the text of the *Republic* was not known to modern writers
before the last century, the palimpsest containing it having been published in 1822.

fragili et infirmo, animo autem anxio ad molestias, humili ad timores, molli ad labores, prono ad libidines, in quo tamen inesset tamquam obrutus quidam divinus ignis ingenii et mentis.[4]

In the third book of the *Republic* Tullius says that man has been produced by nature not as if she were a mother but a stepmother — with a body naked, frail and weak, with a mind fearful of dangers, timid, indolent, prone to lusts; in which however there is as it were hidden a certain divine fire of intelligence and reason.

A passage from Lactantius is traditionally inserted here enlarging upon the power of reason to overcome the handicap of bodily infirmity — a theme played upon at great length by Plutarch (*On Fortune* iv, v), and in imitation of him by such writers of the Renaissance as Gelli, Montaigne, and their imitators. We then have a fragment of Cicero's text again illustrating the growth of civilization through the use of reason.

IX, 3. *De re publica*, III, ii, 3.

... et vehiculis tarditati, eademque cum accepisset homines inconditis vocibus inchoatum quiddam et confusum sonantes, incidit has et distinxit in partis, et ut signa quaedam sic verba rebus inpressit, hominesque antea dissociatos iucundissimo inter se sermonis vinculo conligavit. a simili etiam mente vocis qui videbantur infiniti soni paucis notis inventis sunt omnes signati et expressi, quibus et conloquia cum absentibus et indicia voluntatum et monumenta rerum praeteritarum tenerentur. accessit eo numerus, res cum ad vitam necessaria tum una inmutabilis et aeterna; quae prima inpulit etiam ut suspiceremus in caelum nec frustra siderum motus intueremur, dinumerationibusque noctium ac die⟨rum⟩ [5]

... [overcoming] their slowness with wagons. And when she found men with stammering voices uttering unformed and confused sounds, she set to work on these sounds and sorted them into classes, and certain words were given to things as their symbols, and men who had not previously been associated she thus united by the delightful bond of speech. By a similar act of the mind, vocal sounds, which had seemed innumerable, were all symbolized and expressed by a few invented characters, by which one might speak with the absent, write one's will, and preserve the records of history. Number was next discovered, a thing not only necessary to life, but also unique in its immutability and eternity. Number it was that first directed our gaze to the heavens that we might not stare to no purpose at the motion of the stars, and by the counting of nights and days ...

The origin of the state, as one of the steps in human progress, is discussed in a passage in Lactantius, usually inserted as part of the twenty-fifth chapter of the first book of the *De re publica*; whether it is Ciceronian

[4] Ed. K. Ziegler, Leipzig, 1915.
[5] Ed. K. Ziegler.

is not altogether certain. The beginning of the passage, in any case, is obviously an abridgment of Lucretius's description of the life of the primeval earth-born men; and he is doubtless the writer chiefly attacked in the concluding sentence. The contention that men have come to live in society, not merely for security, but by virtue of an inherent social instinct, distinguishes the Stoic from the Epicurean theory, but was doubtless derived by the Stoics from Aristotle.

IX, 4. *De re publica,* I, xxv, 40; Lactantius, *Inst.* VI, 10, 13-15. 18.

> Urbis condendae originem atque causam non unam intulerunt, sed alii eos homines, qui sint ex terra primitus nati, cum per silvas et campos erraticam degerent vitam, nec ullo inter se sermonis aut iuris vinculo cohaererent, sed frondes et herbam pro cubilibus, speluncas et antra pro domibus haberent, bestiis et fortioribus animalibus praedae fuisse commemorant. tum eos qui aut laniati effugerant, aut laniari proximos viderant, admonitos periculi sui ad alios homines decucurrisse, praesidium implorasse et primo nutibus voluntatem suam significasse, deinde sermonis initia temptasse, ac singulis quibusque rebus nomina inprimendo paulatim loquendi perfecisse rationem. cum autem multitudinem ipsam viderent contra bestias esse tutandam, oppida etiam coepisse munire, ut vel quietem noctis tutam sibi facerent, vel ut incursiones atque impetus bestiarum non pugnando, sed obiectis aggeribus arcerent. . . . (18) Haec aliis delira visa sunt ut fuerunt, dixeruntque non ferarum laniatus causam fuisse coëundi, sed ipsam potius humanitatem, itaque inter se congregatos, quod natura hominum solitudinis fugiens et communionis ac societatis adpetens esset.[6]

> For the original founding of cities more than one explanation has been offered. Some say that those men who were first born from earth, when they led a wandering life through woods and fields and had no common bond of speech or law, had leaves and grasses for their beds, grottoes and caves for houses, and were a prey to the beasts and stronger animals. Then they who had fled wounded, or had seen their fellows wounded, warned by their peril, ran off to other men, implored their aid, and signified their wishes first with gestures, then attempted the beginnings of speech, and, by giving names to each thing in turn, little by little perfected the art of speech. Then when they saw that not even their numbers were proof against the beasts, they began to fortify their towns, either to make their sleep secure or to ward off the onsets and attacks of beasts not by fighting but by erecting barriers. To others these views seem absurd, and they have said that the attacks of wild beasts were not the cause of human association but rather humanity itself; thus men came together because it was the nature of man to flee solitude and seek intercourse and company.

In his favorite conception of the originally merely germinal rationality of man Cicero found what seemed to him a way of resolving the traditional

---

[6] Ed. K. Ziegler.

antithesis of nature and art. From the Peripatetics, the Old Academy and the Stoics he had learned to distinguish the *prima naturae* or *prima naturalia*,[7] the primitive impulses of nature in the individual, from those which are later unfolded; and the latter, being expressions of man's latent reason and of the special kind of sociability which is connected with this, manifest themselves in the arts. These are thus a necessary supplement to nature, i. e. to the *prima naturae*, but are also themselves "natural," in the senses that (a) their development is a part of the purpose of cosmic "nature," and that (b) it is also inherent in the specific "nature" of man, as distinguished from that of other animals by the potentiality of wisdom, or intelligence (*sapientia*). The influence of the analogy of individual and racial development is apparent throughout; it is here turned against primitivism.

IX, 5. *De finibus*, IV, vi, 15-17.

15. Itaque ab iis constitutio illa prima naturae, a qua tu quoque ordiebare,[8] his prope verbis exponitur:

16. ' Omnis natura vult esse conservatrix sui, ut et salva sit et in genere conservaretur suo. Ad hanc rem aiunt artis quoque requisitas quae naturam adjuvarent, in quibus ea numeretur in primis quae est vivendi ars, ut tueatur quod a natura datum sit, quod desit adquirat. . . .

17. Sed cum sapientiam totius hominis custodem et procuratricem esse vellent, quae esset naturae comes et adiutrix, hoc sapientiae munus esse dicebant ut ⟨cum⟩ eum tueretur, qui constaret ex animo et corpore, in utroque iuvaret eum ac contineret.[9]

They [Xenocrates and Aristotle] therefore describe the primary constitution of nature, which you also took as your starting point, approximately as follows: "Every 'nature' [i. e. the nature of any being] desires its own preservation, so that it may continue unimpaired and be conserved in accordance with its own specific type. To this end, they say, the arts also were called in to assist nature — first among which must be numbered the art of living, of which the function is to safeguard what nature has already bestowed and to obtain what is lacking. . . . But since they considered that wisdom, as the companion and helper of nature, is the guardian and protectress of the *whole* man, they said that the task of wisdom — inasmuch as it is the protectress of a being consisting of mind and body — was to assist and conserve him in both respects.

[7] Cf. *De finibus*, II, 34, 35, 38; III, 17, 21, 22, 30; IV, 18, 25, 39; V, 17, 18, 19, 24, 45, 58. On the history of the conception and its place in the ethics of various schools, cf. Dümmler, *Academica*, II, 42. It does not appear necessary to enumerate here the diverse denotations of the term in the doctrines of these schools.

[8] Cicero, speaking in his own person, is addressing Marcus Cato as the expositor of the Stoic ethics.

[9] Ed. Th. Schiche, Leipzig, 1915; punctuation changed.

IX, 6. *De finibus*, IV, xiii, 34.

> . . . non enim ipsa genuit hominem, sed accepit a natura inchoa-
> tum. hanc ergo intuens debet institutum illud quasi signum
> absolvere.[10]

> Wisdom did not herself create man, but took him over in the
> rough from Nature; it is her task, keeping her eye on Nature, to
> complete the statue which Nature began.

IX, 7. *De finibus*, IV, xv, 41.

> . . . ipsa hominis institutio si loqueretur, hoc diceret, primos suos
> quasi coeptus appetendi fuisse, ut se conservaret in ea natura, in
> qua ortus esset. nondum autem explanatum satis erat, quid maxime
> natura vellet.[11]

> Man's constitution itself, if it should speak, would tell us that
> his, so to say, first beginnings of desire were to preserve himself in
> that natural condition in which he originated. But the chief
> purpose of Nature had not yet been sufficiently disclosed.

In the sympathetic exposition which Cicero gives of the doctrine of
Antiochus of the Old Academy in Book V of the *De finibus*, there appears
the same conception of man as the one animal left by nature at birth with
powers peculiarly undeveloped, requiring to be completed by his own conscious art. The passage refers primarily to the development of the individual, but the analogy with that of the race is fairly evident.

IX, 8. *De finibus*, V, xxi, 58-60.

> 58. Omnium . . . rerum principia parva sunt, sed suis progres-
> sionibus usa augentur, nec sine causa; in primo enim ortu inest
> teneritas ac mollitia quaedam, ut nec res videre optimas nec agere
> possint. . . . Quare, quoniam de primis naturae commodis satis dic-
> tum est, nunc de maioribus consequentibusque videamus. 59. Natura
> igitur corpus quidem hominis sic et genuit et formavit, ut alia in
> primo ortu perficeret, alia progrediente aetate fingeret, neque sane
> multum adiumentis externis et adventiciis uteretur. Animum autem
> reliquis rebus ita perfecit, ut corpus; sensibus enim ornavit ad res
> percipiendas idoneis, ut nihil aut non multum adiumento ullo ad
> suam confirmationem indigeret; quod autem in homine praestantis-
> simum atque optimum est, id deseruit. Etsi dedit talem mentem,
> quae omnem virtutem accipere posset, ingenuitque sine doctrina
> notitias parvas rerum maximarum et quasi instituit docere et induxit
> in ea, quae inerant, tamquam elementa virtutis. sed virtutem
> ipsam inchoavit, nihil amplius. 60. itaque nostrum est (quod nos-
> trum dico, artis est) ad ea principia, quae accepimus, consequentia
> exquirere, quoad sit id, quod volumus, effectum.[12]

> 58. All things are small in their beginnings, but increase as
> they gain the advantages of the stages of progress through which

---

[10] Ed. Th. Schiche.   [11] Ed. Th. Schiche.   [12] Ed. Th. Schiche.

they pass; and not without reason; for in their original state there is a certain weakness and softness, so that they can neither perceive nor do the best things [of which they are capable]. . . . But since enough has been said of the primary goods of nature, let us now consider those that are subsequent and more important. . . . 59. Nature, then, has generated and fashioned man's body in such a way that some parts [or faculties] of it were perfect at birth, others were formed as its age increased, without much use of external and adventitious aids. Now in other respects she made the mind as perfect as the body, endowing it with senses capable of perceiving things, so that little or no assistance of any sort was needful to supplement them. But that faculty which is highest and most excellent in man she left lacking. It is true that she gave him a mind capable of receiving every virtue, and implanted at birth and without instruction some small intimations of the greatest truths, and thus, as it were, laid the foundation for education and instilled into those faculties which the mind already had what may be called the germs of virtue. But of virtue itself she merely furnished the rudiments; nothing more. 60. Therefore it is our task (and when I say 'our' I mean that it is the task of art) to supplement those mere beginnings by searching out the further developments which were implicit in them, until what we seek is fully attained.

The general thesis that reason and its products are the manifestation of " nature " in man is elaborated in the *De officiis*, though without emphasis upon their absence in his primitive state.

IX, 9. *De officiis*, I, iv, 11-14 (Translation on p. 250).

11. Principio generi animantium omni est a natura tributum, ut se, vitam corpusque tueatur, declinet ea, quae nocitura videantur, omniaque, quae sint ad vivendum necessaria, anquirat et paret, ut pastum, ut latibula, ut alia generis eiusdem. Commune item animantium omnium est coniunctionis adpetitus procreandi causa et cura quaedam eorum, quae procreata sint; sed inter hominem et beluam hoc maxime interest, quod haec tantum, quantum sensu movetur, ad id solum, quod adest quodque praesens est, se accomodat paulum admodum sentiens praeteritum aut futurum; homo autem, quod rationis est particeps, per quam consequentia cernit, causas rerum videt earumque praegressus et quasi antecessiones non ignorat, similitudines comparat rebusque praesentibus adiungit atque adnectit futuras, facile totius vitae cursum videt ad eamque degendam praeparat res necessarias. 12. Eademque natura vi rationis hominem conciliat homini et ad orationis et ad vitae societatem ingeneratque in primis praecipuum quendam amorem in eos, qui procreati sunt, impellitque, ut hominum coetus et celebrationes et esse et a se obiri velit ob easque causas studeat parare ea, quae suppeditent ad cultum et ad victum, nec sibi soli, sed coniugi, liberis ceterisque, quos caros habeat tuerique debeat; quae cura exsuscitat etiam animos et maiores ad rem gerendam facit. 13. In primisque hominis est propria veri inquisitio atque investigatio. Itaque cum sumus necessariis negotiis curisque vacui, tum avemus aliquid videre,

audire, addiscere cognitionemque rerum aut occultarum aut admirabilium ad beate vivendum necessariam ducimus. Ex quo intellegitur, quod verum, simplex sincerumque sit, id esse naturae hominis aptissimum. Huic veri videndi cupiditati adiuncta est adpetitio quaedam principatus, ut nemini parere animus bene informatus a natura velit nisi praecipienti aut docenti aut utilitatis causa iuste et legitime imperanti; ex quo magnitudo animi existit humanarumque rerum contemptio. 14. Nec vero illa parva vis naturae est rationisque, quod unum hoc animal sentit, quid sit ordo, quid sit quod deceat, in factis dictisque qui modus. Itaque eorum ipsorum, quae aspectu sentiuntur, nullum aliud animal pulchritudinem, venustatem, convenientiam partium sentit; quam similitudinem natura ratioque ab oculis ad animum transferens multo etiam magis pulchritudinem, constantiam, ordinem in consiliis factisque conservandam putat cavetque, ne quid indecore effeminateve faciat, tum in omnibus et opinionibus et factis ne quid lubidinose aut faciat aut cogitet.[13]

11. In the first place Nature has endowed every species of animal with a propensity to preserve its own life and limb, to avoid whatever seems injurious to it, and to seek and to procure everything needful for its existence, such as food, shelter, and the like. Common to all animals, also, is the mating instinct, of which the object is the propagation of its kind and a certain degree of care for the offspring. But between man and beast the chief difference is this, that the beast, inasmuch as it is moved only by the senses and has little thought of past or future, adapts itself only to that which is present at the moment; whereas man — because he participates in reason, whereby he comprehends causes and effects, is not ignorant of the sequences and successions of events, recognizes similarities in things, and connects and binds together present and future — easily surveys the course of his whole life and prepares whatever is necessary for the conduct of it.

12. Nature, too, by the power of reason unites man with man and, that there may be the bond of common speech and social life, first of all implants in him an especially strong love of his offspring. She also prompts men to desire that there should be gatherings and assemblages and to attend them themselves; and in consequence of all this she likewise leads man to endeavor to provide himself with the means of subsistence and of refinement — and not for himself alone, but for his wife and children and the others whom he holds dear and of whom he should take care; and this responsibility also stimulates his mental powers and makes them more adequate for the business of life.

13. Above all peculiar to man is the search and inquiry after truth. And so when we have leisure from our necessary business and ordinary concerns, we are eager to see, to hear, to learn something new, and we regard a knowledge of things hidden or wonderful as itself necessary to a happy life. Thus it can be seen that what is true, simple and genuine is what is most suitable to the nature of man. To this craving to know truth is added as it were a hunger to be one's own master, so that a mind well-formed by nature is

[13] Ed. G. Segre, Torino, 1902.

unwilling to be subject to any man, except to a teacher or preceptor, or to one who rules for the general good in accordance with justice and law. From this quality comes greatness of mind and a disdain for human affairs.

14. Nor is it a slight evidence of the force of Nature and Reason that this animal alone understands what order is, and what is moderate and becoming in word and deed. And so no other animal has a sense of the beauty and loveliness and harmony of the visible world; and Nature and Reason, transferring the likeness of these qualities from the eyes to the mind, judges and admonishes us that beauty, constancy and order are far more to be maintained in our thoughts and actions, so that nothing shall be done in an effeminate or unbecoming manner, and that there shall be nothing licentious in our opinions or our conduct.

Cicero is therefore so far removed from the temper of cultural primitivism — and so oblivious of any of the evils which have attended technological progress — that he writes of the advance of the arts in a tone of unqualified enthusiasm, and declares that life would not be worth living without them. It is noteworthy, however, that it is their past achievements and not their possible greater triumphs in the future that evoke this rhapsodic strain.

IX, 10. *De officiis,* II, iv, 15.

Quid enumerem artium multitudinem, sine quibus vita omnino nulla esse potuisset? Qui enim aegris subveniretur, quae esset oblectatio valentium, qui victus aut cultus, nisi tam multae nobis artes ministrarent? quibus rebus exculta hominum vita tantum distat a victu et cultu bestiarum. Urbes vero sine hominum coetu non potuissent nec aedificari nec frequentari; ex quo leges moresque constituti, tum iuris aequa discriptio certaque vivendi disciplina; quas res et mansuetudo animorum consecuta et verecundia est; effectumque, ut esset vita munitior, atque ut dando et accipiendo mutuandisque facultatibus et commodandis nulla re egeremus.[14]

Why should I recount the multitude of arts, without which life would be a thing of no value? For how would the sick be healed, what pleasure would there be in health, how should we obtain either the necessaries or the refinements of life, if there were not so many arts to minister to us? In all these respects the civilized life of men is far removed from the level of subsistence and comfort of the animals. And without the association of men, cities could neither have been built nor peopled, as a result of which laws and customs were established, and then the equitable determination of rights, and a settled discipline of life. When these were assured there followed a more humane spirit and the sense of what is morally becoming, so that life was more secure, and that, by giving and receiving, by mutual exchange of goods and services, we were able to satisfy all our needs.

[14] Ed. Mueller, Pt. IV, vol. III, p. 61. A similar passage in *De nat. deor.* II, lx, 151-2; men, adds Cicero, through the arts create "a second nature," *altera natura.*

Primitivistic Elements

Despite his predominant anti-primitivistic tone, Cicero's writings were among the classical sources from which modern primitivists in the Renaissance and the Enlightenment could, and pretty certainly did, draw some of their inspiration.

'Nature' as catchword

Aside from the influence of specific ideas, Cicero afforded copious examples of a practice which, in innumerable eighteenth-century writers especially, became a fixed habit — the incessant use of the word 'nature' in a reverential tone and with some manifestly normative implications, yet often without any clear discrimination of meanings, or even with no determinable meaning.[15] *Natura* is frequently interchangeable with *deus*,[16] though sometimes antithetic;[17] it connotes, at all events, numerous attributes of deity: it is the creator of all things and the universal providence (*omnium rerum quas et creat natura et tuetur*: *De fin.* V, xiii, 38); it is the *communis parens omnium* (*Tusc. disp.* V, xiii, 37) or 'Mother Nature,' *mater, ut ita dicam, rerum omnium natura* (*Paradoxa*, 14); it is said to have will or purposes;[18] it is the guide and teacher of man.[19] These pious uses of the term, it is plain, usually had behind them no definite philosophical reflection; they were *façons de parler* which vaguely satisfied the desire to refer in a devout way to some general cause of natural phenomena — *omnia subiecta esse naturae eaque ab ea pulcherrime geri* (*De nat. deor.* II, xxxii, 81) — without specification of the character or *modus operandi* of that cause. But just for that reason it was easy to read into them ideas associated with various other uses of the term, including the primitivistic; and this was especially the case because the word thus obscurely synonymous with 'deity' served also as the designation of certain elements in human nature or of some — often not less vague — normative principle. While sometimes, in passages already given, *natura* is distinguished from *ratio*, or is a name for the mere rudiments of the latter, the two are sometimes equivalent, or "nature" is the source of reason; it is "nature which *through* the force of reason reconciles man with man."[20] To the phrase-

---

[15] In Merguet's *Lexikon zu den Schriften Cicero's*, 1892, the citations (including repetitions) for *natura* and *naturalis* fill 33 columns, those for *deus* about the same number. *Ars* requires only eight columns.

[16] *Academica*, II, 61; *De nat. deor.*, II, xii, 33; *Tusc. disp.* V, i, 3, and numerous other passages. Uses cited are often those of Stoic interlocutors.

[17] E. g. *Acad.* II, 61; *De leg.* I, vii, 21.

[18] E. g. *De nat. deor.* III, iv, 9; *De fin.* IV, xv, 41.

[19] E. g. *De leg.* I, viii, 26; *Tusc. disp.* V, xiii, 38; *De fin.* V, xii, 59.

[20] *De off.* I, iv, 12 and 14. For the antithesis, cf. also *De nat. deor.* III, 26 and I, 46; in the latter passage, however, *natura* signifies the primary notions implanted in every rational mind and *ratio* the processes of deliberate reasoning by which these are amplified and completed.

ology in which nature is described as guide or model or standard Cicero probably did more than any other Latin author to give currency and sanctity; e. g. *in hoc sumus sapientes, quod naturam optimam ducem tamquam deum sequimur eique paremus. . . . Quid est enim aliud Gigantum modo bellare cum dis nisi naturae repugnare?* (*De Sen.* II, 5); "the first thing that wisdom will look to when she undertakes any action is that it be *naturae accommodatum*" (*Ac.* II, 24); the true conception of good and bad is "that all the things which Nature rejects are among the evils, all that she approves are to be reckoned goods," *omnia, quae natura aspernetur in malis esse, quae asciscat in bonis* (*Tusc. disp.* II, xiii, 30). For Cicero himself such phrases did not ordinarily carry either primitivistic or ethically 'naturalistic' implications; but they easily lent themselves to such interpretations.

Aside, however, from his part in familiarizing classically educated moderns — especially those who had more Latin than Greek — from their schooldays with the chief primitivistic catchword, Cicero gave expression to certain conceptions which were destined to play a great rôle in the primitivistic thought of later centuries.

Epistemological primitivism

Notably in the seventeenth and eighteenth centuries it was to become a commonplace that men's minds as nature made them, i. e., illuminated with the 'pure light of nature' undimmed by the sophistications arising from intellectual vanity, priestcraft, and the long accretion of tradition and convention, saw most clearly the simple and fundamental truths which man most needs to know. In the thought of most of the deists from Herbert of Cherbury to Tindal and Voltaire this assumption was fundamental; but it was also a common and characteristic part of the dominant popular philosophy of the Enlightenment.[21] While Cicero cannot be said to have accepted this 'epistemological primitivism' consistently or usually, he nevertheless, following Plato, furnished the chief classical text for it, using it as the primary premise in his argument for the immortality of the soul.

IX, 11. Cicero, *Tusc. disp.* I, xii, 26-27.

> Auctoribus quidem ad istam sententiam, quam vis obtineri, uti optimis possumus, . . . primum quidem omni antiquitate, quae quo propius aberat ab ortu et divina progenie, hoc melius ea fortasse, quae erant vera, cernebat. Itaque unum illud erat insitum priscis illis, quos *cascos* appellat Ennius, esse in morte sensum neque excessu vitae sic deleri hominem, ut funditus interiret.[22]

In support of the view which you wish to see established, we can

---

[21] Cf. Lovejoy, "The Parallel of Deism and Classicism," *Mod. Philology*, 1932, pp. 281 ff.

[22] Ed. M. Pohlenz, Leipzig, 1918.

make use of the best of authorities: . . . namely, first of all, the whole of antiquity; for it probably perceived the truth more clearly in proportion to its nearness to its origin and divine ancestry. Thus it was a belief implanted in those men of early times whom Ennius calls 'the old ones' that the dead have sensation, and that when man departs from life he is not annihilated so as to perish utterly.

Similarly Cicero says (*De legibus*, II, x, 27) that religious rites which have come down by-tradition from remote antiquity ought to be observed, *quoniam antiquitas proxume accedit ad deos*. The contradiction of the view expressed in *Pro Sestio* (No. 1, above) is complete.

From an early stage in the history of the sanctity of the word 'nature,' moreover, certain implications of the term tended to suggest that the 'natural,' and therefore the normal, could best be observed in the child; *teste* Cicero's expositor of the ethics of the Old Academy:

IX, 12. *De finibus*, V, xx, 55:

> Omnes veteres philosophi, maxime nostri, ad incunabula accedunt, quod in pueritia facillime se arbitrantur naturae voluntatem posse cognoscere.[23]

> All the older philosophers, those of our own school especially, have been accustomed to go to the cradle [for instruction], because they believed that nature's purpose can be most easily discerned in child-hood.[24]

This tended to suggest that the same was true of the race. But in the *Republic* precisely the opposite presumption had been emphatically laid down. In the earlier ages men were peculiarly liable to error and childishly credulous; it is only with the progress of learning and civilization that they become competent judges of what is true. The speaker is the chief interlocutor in the dialogue, Scipio Africanus Minor.

IX, 13. *De re publica*, II, x, 18-19.

> . . . hoc eo magis est in Romulo admirandum, quod ceteri, qui dii ex hominibus facti esse dicuntur, minus eruditis hominum saeculis fuerunt, ut fingendi proclivis esset ratio, cum imperiti facile ad credendum inpellerentur, Romuli autem aetatem minus his sescentis annis iam inveteratis litteris atque doctrinis omnique illo antiquo ex inculta hominum vita errore sublato fuisse cernimus. . . . antiquitas enim recepit fabulas fictas etiam non numqu⟨am incondite, haec aetas autem iam exculta, praesertim eludens omne, quod fieri non potest, respuit⟩.[25]

[23] Ed. Th. Schiche.

[24] The speaker, however, was no primitivist and he alsewhere expresses almost precisely the contrary view (*ibid.* V, xxi, 58).

[25] Ed. K. Ziegler, Leipzig, 1915. Cf. *De nat. deor.* II, ii, 5, for the same view.

[The apotheosis of Romulus] is the more remarkable because all other men who have been deified lived in ruder ages, when there was a strong inclination to invent fabulous tales, and men with their limited experience were readily induced to believe them. But we know that Romulus lived less than six hundred years ago, at a time when letters and education had long been in existence and all those ancient errors which arise in the uncivilized state of human life had disappeared. . . . For antiquity accepted fictitious fables, even of the crudest sort sometimes, whereas the age [of Romulus], being already a highly civilized one, rejected all impossible tales with derision.

So elsewhere in the same dialogue, the defender of monarchy insists that he is *not* relying upon the witness of primeval or savage races:

IX, 14. *De re publica*, I, xxxvii, 58.

Si enim et prudentes homines et non veteres reges habere voluerunt, utor neque perantiquis neque inhumanis ac feris testibus.[26]

If sensible men living not very long ago wished to have kings, then the witnesses [in favor of kingship] whom I am citing are neither of remote antiquity nor uncivilized and savage.

In the *Tusculan Disputations* an intermediate view is suggested; the light of nature is implanted in every man from the outset, but it is a dim light and it it is soon obscured. The last theme, at least, was the foreshadowing of a favorite one of later primitivistic rationalists: the suppression of 'nature's light' by 'prejudices' due to early education.

IX, 15. *Tusc. disp.* III, i, 2.

Quod si talis nos natura genuisset, ut eam ipsam intueri et perspicere eademque optima duce cursum vitae conficere possemus, haut erat sane quod quisquam rationem ac doctrinam requireret. nunc parvulos nobis dedit igniculos, quos celeriter malis moribus opinionibusque depravati sic restinguimus, ut nusquam naturae lumen appareat.[27]

If Nature had brought us into existence capable from the beginning of understanding her and perceiving her as she is, and of going through life with her as our best guide, no one, assuredly, would ever need reasoning or instruction. But in fact she has given us some small glimmerings of light, which we so speedily quench under the depraving influence of bad habits and opinions that nothing of the light of nature is left.

Primitive beliefs and the consensus gentium

As the light of nature (whatever its power) was assumed to be a universal endowment of man, the argument for, e. g., the belief in immortality, or in the existence of gods, drawn from the assumption of early man's greater

[26] Ed. K. Ziegler.   [27] Ed. M. Pohlenz, Leipzig, 1918.

knowledge of the truth was connected with the proof from the *consensus gentium*. In modern writers the two were often to be related in such a way that the supposed primitiveness of a belief was the crucial test of its true universality, and therefore of its validity: that must be presumed true which all men everywhere accept, *provided* the natural light of reason has not been corrupted in them; but as this light is least corrupted in primeval men and savages, what these believe may be taken as 'naturally' universal. Cicero gave no such superior weight to the witness of savages to the existence of gods; he only insists that even they are not wholly destitute of that belief. The concluding sentence of the passage is the *locus classicus* in Latin literature for the identification — common in so many 16th-18th century writings — of the universally accepted with the 'law of nature.'

IX, 16. *Tusc. disp.* I, xiii, 30.

> . . . firmissimum hoc adferri videtur cur deos esse credamus, quod nulla gens tam fera, nemo omnium tam sit inmanis, cuius mentem non imbuerit deorum opinio (multi de diis prava sentiunt — id enim vitioso more effici solet — omnes tamen esse vim et naturam divinam arbitrantur, nec vero id conlocutio hominum aut consessus efficit, non institutis opinio est confirmata, non legibus; omni autem in re consensio omnium gentium lex naturae putanda est). . . .[28]

> This seems to be put forward as the strongest reason why we should believe in the existence of gods: that there is no people so uncivilized, no one in all the world so barbarous, that his mind has not at least some tincture of a belief in gods. Many, it is true, have wrong notions about the gods, for that is the usual effect of moral corruption; nevertheless, all men believe that a divine power and a divine nature exist. Nor is this due to any human convention or verbal agreement; it is not a belief which has its basis in laws or decrees. But on every matter the consensus of all peoples is to be regarded as the law of nature.

The same proposition reappears in a later dialogue as an Epicurean thesis — quoted apparently approvingly — connected with the doctrine of innate ideas. All men — by implication, irrespective of their culture — have some primary truths implanted by nature in their minds.

IX, 17. *De nat. deorum*, I, xvii, 44.

> Cum enim non instituto aliquo aut more aut lege sit opinio constituta maneatque ad unum omnium firma consensio, intellegi necesse est esse deos, quoniam insitas eorum vel potius innatas cognitiones habemus; de quo autem omnium natura consentit, id verum esse necesse est. . . .[29]

---

[28] Ed. M. Pohlenz.

[29] Ed. O. Plasberg, Leipzig, 1933. This "innate idea" Cicero also calls an *anticipatio* or *praenotio*, which he coins as Latin equivalents of Epicurus's *prolepsis*.

For since it is not an opinion resting upon any institution or custom or law, and since there remains upon one point a firm and universal consensus, the gods must necessarily be recognized to exist, since we actually have an implanted or rather innate knowledge of them [the gods]; and any [belief] in which the nature of all men consents must necessarily be true. . . .

On the other hand, the representative of the Academic School in *De natura deorum* (I, xxiii, 62) attacks the argument from the *consensus gentium* as "both intrinsically weak and untrue" (*leve per se, tum etiam falsum*); i. e. the supposed universal agreement is not established, and if it were, it would prove nothing. In the *De officiis* I, 14, the actual acceptance or non-acceptance of moral principles is said to have no bearing on their validity. "What is morally right, even if it should be praised by no man, is by nature deserving of praise" (*honestum . . . etiamsi a nullo laudetur, natura esse laudabile*).

Perhaps the view most congenial to Cicero as to the universality of the reason implanted in men by nature, and therefore as to its possession by primitive men, is that expressed in the *Laws*: reason is simply a universal and equal capacity of learning.

IX, 18. *De leg.* I, x, 30.

ratio . . . certe est communis, doctrina differens, discendi quidem facultate par. Nam et sensibus eadem omnia conprehenduntur, et ea, quae movent sensus, itidem movent omnium, quaeque in animis inprimuntur, de quibus ante dixi, inchoatae intellegentiae similiter in omnibus inprimuntur. . . .[30]

Reason certainly is a common possession [of men]; there are differences in [the amount of acquired] knowledge, but an equality in the faculty of learning. For all things are apprehended by the senses in the same way, and those things which act upon the senses likewise act upon whatever faculties are implanted in the minds of all men; wherefore I have already said that the rudiments of intelligence [or rudimentary concepts] are implanted in a similar way in all men.

Communism

Cicero in two passages also characteristically furnished the Latin text of the favorite premise of the discourses of later primitivistic (and other) communists, while himself avoiding its application. That private property does not exist "by nature" is admitted; nevertheless it came to be established, in one way or another. Whether these were legitimate ways, or what the ethical basis is for the existing division of property, Cicero avoids discussing.

[30] Ed. C. W. Keyes, 1928.

IX, 19. *De officiis*, I, vii, 21.

Sunt autem privata nulla natura, sed aut vetere occupatione, ut qui quondam in vacua venerunt, aut victoria, ut qui bello potiti sunt, aut lege, pactione, condicione, sorte; ex quo fit, ut ager Arpinas Arpinatium dicatur, Tusculanus Tusculanorum; similisque est privatarum possessionum discriptio. Ex quo, quia suum cuiusque fit eorum, quae natura fuerant communia, quod cuique obtigit, id quisque teneat; e quo si quis sibi appetet, violabit ius humanae societatis.[31]

There is, however, nothing that is private property by nature; private property arises either through prior occupancy, as in the case of those who in some early time settled in unoccupied lands, or through conquest, as in the case of those who gained possession by war, or by law, agreement or contract, or by drawing lots. Thus it came about that the lands of Arpinum are said to belong to the Arpinates, those of Tusculum to the Tusculans; and the apportionment of private possessions is similar. Therefore, inasmuch as in each case some of the things which by nature were common became the property of an individual, let each one retain that which has fallen to his lot; and if any one covets any part of this, he will be violating the law of human society.

IX, 20. *De officiis*, I, xvi, 51.

. . . in qua [societate] omnium rerum, quas ad communem hominum usum natura genuit, est servanda communitas, ut, quae discripta sunt legibus et iure civili, haec ita teneantur, ut sit constitutum legibus ipsis, cetera sic observentur, ut in Graecorum proverbio est, *amicorum esse communia omnia.*[32]

[In human society] community of rights to all things which nature has produced for the common use of all men is to be maintained in such wise that whatever is assigned as private property by statutes and the civil law shall be held as the laws themselves prescribe, but that all other things shall — as the Greek proverb says [33] — be the common property of friends.

The corruption by man of the law of nature

It is in speaking of the vitiation of the law of nature by human customs and legislation that Cicero comes nearest to the vehemence of the primitivists' denunciations of the corruption of the original natural order by man's misguided ingenuity. Nature is the *fons iuris* (*De off.* III, xvii, 72); but it is from other fountains that men have largely drawn their laws.

IX, 21. *De leg.* II, v, 13.

Quid, quod multa perniciose, multa pestifere sciscuntur in populis? quae non magis legis nomen adtingunt, quam si latrones aliquas

---

[31] Ed. Mueller, Leipzig, 1879, p. 9. The passage is probably derived from Panaetius of Rhodes or some other Stoic philosopher (cf. *De off.* I, 6, 7 and III, 7).

[32] Ed. Mueller.   [33] Plato, *Phaedrus*, 279 c.

consessu suo sanxerint. Nam neque medicorum praecepta dici vere possunt, si quae inscii inperitique pro salutaribus mortifera conscripserunt, neque in populo lex, cuicuimodi fuerit illa, etiamsi perniciosum aliquid populus acceperit. ergo est lex iustorum iniustorumque distinctio ad illam antiquissimam et rerum omnium principem expressa naturam. . . .[34]

What of the many pernicious and pestiferous statutes which have been enacted by various nations? These do not deserve to be called laws any more than the rules which a band of robbers might adopt. For if ignorant and inexpert men have prescribed deadly drugs supposing them to be beneficial, you cannot properly call these physicians' prescriptions; and likewise in the case of a people, you cannot call a thing a law regardless of its character, even though it may, however pernicious, have been accepted by the people. Law, therefore, is the distinction between things just and things unjust which is expressed in accordance with that first and most ancient of all things, Nature.

Cicero, again, reflects the fundamental moral temper of the hard primitivists in passages in which he indicates his accord with this strain in Epicureanism, e. g. *Tusc. Disp.* V, xxxiii, 89, already cited.[35]

The old idea that the arts were acquired through the 'imitation of nature' is expressed, though whether this refers to imitation of the animals is not clear.

X, 22. *De leg.* I, viii, 26.

Artes vero innumerabiles repertae sunt docente natura: quam imitata ratio res ad vitam necessarias sollerter consecuta est.[36]

Innumerable arts have been discovered through Nature's teaching; for it is by imitating her that reason has sagaciously acquired the things necessary for life.

Elsewhere a spokesman of the Academy says, *à propos* of " speech, and the knowledge of numbers, and singing ":

X, 23. *De nat. deor.* III, xi, 27.

Naturae ista sunt, . . . naturae non artificiose ambulantis, ut ait Zeno . . . sed omnia cientis et agitantis motibus et mutationibus suis.[37]

These things are [processes] of nature — not nature proceeding with deliberate art, as Zeno says, but nature moving and agitating all things with her own motions and mutations.

---

[34] Ed. C. W. Keyes, 1928.
[35] Ch. IV, no. 26.
[36] Ed. cit.
[37] Ed. O. Plasberg.

CHAPTER TEN

STOIC PRIMITIVISM

It is in the writings of the Roman Stoics, and especially in Seneca, that the cultural and chronological primitivism of the school is most fully and zealously expressed; and our texts are therefore taken from that author, some of whose *Epistulae morales* and tragedies were probably the most important classical sources of hard primitivism in the sixteenth and seventeenth centuries. Though comparable passages cannot be cited from the extant fragments of the writings of the third-century Greek founders of the school, there is sufficient scattered evidence of the continuance in their ethical doctrines of much of the Cynic temper and a number of specific Cynic tenets. Cleanthes, as well as Zeno, apparently emulated the Cynics in coarseness and frugality of diet and rudeness of apparel;[1] and he both taught and practised the gospel of work so strenuously that he was called "the second Hercules."[2] Zeno's teaching, if a satirist's report is to be trusted, appealed especially to the poorest classes.[3] The first and third heads of the school — one or both — are said to have held the following moral opinions also characteristic of Cynic moralists: that wives should be in common (Zeno, Chrysippus);[4] that incest is permissible (Zeno, Chrysippus);[5] that anthropophagy, at least "in certain circumstances," is not immoral (Zeno);[6] that the use of money "should not be regarded as necessary either for exchange or for foreign travel" (Zeno);[7] that reputa-

---

[1] Diog. Laert. VII, 27, 169. But elsewhere Zeno is described as possessing considerable wealth, living in a modest but by no means ascetic manner, and occasionally employing servants (*ibid.* VII, 13).

[2] *Ibid.* VII, 170, 172.

[3] *Ibid.* VII, 16, quotation from Timon.

[4] *Ibid.* VII, 33 and 34; Sextus Empir. *Hyp.* III, 205.

[5] For Zeno, cf. Sextus Empir. in Arnim, *Stoicorum veterum fragmenta*, I, *Fragm.* 256; for Chrysippus, Diog. Laert. VII, 188. The specific ground for this seems for Chrysippus, as for the Cynics, to have been the supposed existence of the practice in early ages, and among some existing peoples; i. e. the prohibition was not supported by a *consensus gentium* (cf. Sextus Empir. *Hyp.* III, 246). Sextus also declares that both "the adherents of the Cynic philosophy and the disciples of Zeno and Cleanthes and Chrysippus" classed sodomy among "the things morally indifferent" (*ibid.* 200). This assertion of a writer of the 2nd-3rd c. A. D. is scarcely in accord with the account of Zeno's attitude towards paederasty given by Diogenes Laertius (VII, 17, 18), unquestionably on the authority of earlier writers, and cannot be regarded as conclusive evidence. But cf. also Sextus, *op. cit.* III, 245.

[6] Diog. Laert. VII, 121.

[7] *Ibid.* VII, 33. Zeno also would have "prohibited the building of temples, law-courts and gymnasia in cities" (*ibid.*).

tion and the esteem of others are not goods (Zeno).[8] Beneath this agreement in particular traits and theses lay a broad identity in fundamental principles. The Stoic ethics, like the Cynic, was in the main, the product of a fusion of the Socratic ideal of self-sufficiency[9] with the maxim of 'conformity to nature';[10] and the logical implications of these premises (when 'nature' was taken in certain of its common senses) we have already seen:[11] in so far as such premises were consistently carried out, they entailed the primitivistic scheme of values.

Of the points in which Stoicism diverged from Cynicism, some tended to strengthen the primitivistic tendency. From an early period in the history of the school the use of 'nature'—in the formula 'to live conformably to nature'—as equivalent to 'the cosmos' or 'the cosmic order' pantheistically conceived, was emphasized to a degree not apparent in the extant Cynic fragments;[12] and the result (or, psychologically considered, perhaps the cause) was an especially intense cosmical piety, a religion of not only "accepting the universe" but adoring all its works and ways—illustrated best, in the case of the Greek Stoics, by Cleanthes's Hymn to Zeus. But the more the cosmical substance was apotheosized and regarded as permeated with intelligence and rational purpose, the more the blame for the evils in human life fell upon man: all things are perfectly and divinely ordered "except the works that evil men do in their folly."[13] And even men, as Nature made them, must have been perfect; thus there was implicit in the Stoic piety the assumption of a fall of mankind from its primeval and natural excellence. This was reënforced by the adoption by most of the Stoics of the theory of world-cycles,[14] in which "God . . . indestructible and ingenerable, the artificer of the cosmic order, at certain regular periods absorbs into himself the whole of substance and again generates it from himself."[15] The phases of the cycle nearest to this regeneration of the world from its divine source, or (which for the Stoic meant the same thing) from the cosmic fire in its purest form, were necessarily the best, and henceforward the process was one of gradual weakening and deterioration. Thus chronological primitivism had in the Stoic theology and cosmology additional motivations not, so far as the surviving evidence goes, to be found in Cynicism.

[8] *Ibid.* VII, 115, 117.

[9] Cf. Diog. Laert. VII, 27, and the lines of Zenodotus on Zeno, *ibid.* 30: he "established self-sufficiency" (as the rule of life) and "eschewed the vainglory of wealth."

[10] E. g. Diog. Laert. VII, 85, 87-89, 148.   [11] Cf. Ch. IV, p. 120.

[12] It is uncertain, and for our purpose unimportant, by which of the first three scholarchs this emphasis was introduced. Cf. Diog. Laert. VII, 89; Cicero, *De nat. deor.* II, 57.

[13] Cf. Cleanthes, *Hymn*, in Arnim, I, *op. cit.* Fragm. 537, 8.

[14] On this feature of the Stoic doctrine, see Ch. II, sect. C, p. 83, and No. 6, below.

[15] Diog. Laert. VII, 137.

On the other hand, two of the deviations of Greek Stoicism from its Cynic antecedents had a tendency adverse to the more extreme sort of cultural primitivism. The rigor of the Cynic program of life was, in the first place, weakened by the Stoics' recognition of a class of " things indifferent " or " neutral," i. e. neither good nor bad, which included " life, health, pleasure, beauty, wealth, fair fame, good birth, and their opposites," and by the admission that these are further divisible into " things to be preferred " and " things to be avoided." [16]   Value having been first denied to all external goods, was then equivocally and illicitly restored to many of them under another name. The Stoic should be emotionally indifferent to the " preferable things," and capable of losing them without the least disturbance of his " apathy," yet he was to appraise certain external circumstances and possessions more highly than others — an obvious psychological impossibility; and he need not dispense with the " things indifferent but preferable," but should, by implication, endeavor so far as possible to obtain them. The stricter Stoics of the fourth century seem to have been averse to recognizing this implication in practice; but it is said to have been frankly drawn by Posidonius (1st c. B. C.).[17]   In those Stoics, then, who were disposed to make the most of this incongruous qualification of the principles common to Stoicism and Cynicism, the spirit of cultural primitivism was, at the least, considerably relaxed; thus Posidonius pronounced " the arts of which use is made in daily life " a benign discovery of " philosophy." [18]   A Stoic, in short, could, if he wished, find among the formulas of his philosophy a justification for living, in external respects, much as other men lived in the civilized society in which he found himself, and even for regarding the refinements and conveniences of such a society as among the " things to be preferred " — provided he kept his inner imperturbability unbroken.

Finally, some at least of the early Stoics could not, with consistency, carry the disparagement of merely intellectual or ' theoretical ' interests and inquiries to the pitch to which it was apparently carried by some Cynics. For they conceived that a logical theory, a theory of the constitution of matter, and a theology were a necessary propaedeutic or supplement to

[16] Diog. Laert. VII, 102-7. These distinctions are attributed by Diogenes Laertius to Chrysippus, Hecato and Apollodorus, but are said by Cicero (De finibus, III, 51) and Stobaeus (Ecl. II, 156) to have been introduced by Zeno; cf. Arnim, I, Fragm. 190-194.

[17] Diog. Laert. VII, 103: " Posidonius maintains that these things too are among the goods "; the immediate reference is to wealth and health. According to Seneca, however, even Posidonius held that riches, though not evils in themselves, tend to engender in those who possess them evil feelings, such as envy and pride, and " in the end to produce a kind of madness " (Ep. mor. LXXXVII, 31).

[18] Cf. Seneca's polemic against Posidonius for this aberration from strict primitivism, Ep. mor. XC, 7-26, cited below, pp. 265, 269.

ethics;[19] some of them advanced hypotheses upon questions of astronomy; and they sometimes became involved in controversies amongst themselves on essentially speculative questions. There was not, however, agreement in the Early and Middle Stoa as to the indispensability of these theoretical inquiries; almost from the beginning of the school there were, with respect to this and other matters, two wings of Stoicism, one diverging but little from Cynicism, the other more widely.[20] Even the latter would probably have accepted the saying of a Stoic of the second century B. C., that " Cynicism is a short-cut to virtue ";[21] and for some, especially among the Roman Stoics, the short road was the best. And Antisthenes's disparagement of the ἐγκύκλιος παιδεία, the course of recognized liberal studies, was repeated by Zeno,[22] of whose utterances on the subject the passage of Seneca cited below (No. 2) may be supposed to be an elaboration.

SENECA

The primitivism of Seneca — both cultural and chronological — is extreme, but it is not unwavering. Most of the usual elements of the eulogy of the state of nature are present, and receive from him their most rhetorical elaboration in ancient literature: the emphasis on the physical superiority of primitive men, on the advantages they gained from having no arts, on their communism. Both the soft and hard aspects of their life are dwelt upon; it was at once easy and austere. Of their sexual relations, however, Seneca has little that is definite to say.

But though the primitives, early or contemporary, could be said to live as Stoic philosophers should live, it could not be denied that they were *not* Stoic philosophers; and to Seneca philosophy, resulting from conscious reflection and issuing in a conscious discipline of the emotions and of conduct, was indispensable to the best life. Primitive men are, so to say, Stoics *sans le savoir*; but the *savoir* is essential. The virtue which comes through insight and inner conflict is both more complete, and of greater intrinsic moral value, than the innocence of man in his natural state. Seneca, therefore, after seeming to go the whole way with the primitivists,

---

[19] Chrysippus is credited by Diogenes Laertius with the authorship of " 705 writings," of which 311 were on logical questions (VII, 180, 198). He " thought that young men should first attend lectures on logic, then on ethics, then on physics, in order that their instruction may conclude with the doctrine concerning the gods " (Plutarch, *De stoic. repugn.* 9, 1035a, in Arnim, *op. cit.* II, *Fragm.* 42). Chrysippus pretty certainly increased, though he did not originate, the theoretical content of Stoicism, and " provided the school with a learned and copious dialectical apparatus," as Dümmler has remarked (*Antisthenica*, p. 64), this phase of the movement, as he contends, being followed considerably later by a reversion towards the Cynic attitude.

[20] Cf. Diog. Laert (VII, 160) on Ariston, pupil of Zeno (*ca.* 320-250 B. C.).

[21] Apollodorus of Seleucia in his *Ethics*; Diog. Laert. VII, 121.

[22] Diog. Laert. VII, 32.

draws back at the end, as is especially apparent in the first of the texts cited: for the technological and economic state of nature his preference is apparently unqualified, but what we have called the ethical state of nature he regards as a condition almost less than human. In so far as men have developed moral philosophy, and in so far as some of them have learned the right philosophy, there has been progress, and a good unknown to early man or to savage races is now attainable. But even this is not progressive; the essential moral truths were discovered by the Greek masters of the Cynic and Stoic schools, and stand in no need of further investigation.[23]

X, 1. Seneca: *Epist. mor.* XC (Translation on p. 268).

1. Quis dubitare, mi Lucili, potest, quin deorum immortalium munus sit quod vivimus, philosophiae quod bene vivimus? itaque tanto plus huic nos debere quam dis, quanto maius beneficium est bona vita quam vita, pro certo haberetur, nisi ipsam philosophiam distribuissent. cuius scientiam nulli dederunt, facultatem omnibus. nam si hanc quoque bonum vulgare fecissent et prudentes nasceremur, sapientia quod in se optimum habet, perdidisset, inter fortuita non esse. nunc enim hoc in illa pretiosum atque magnificum est, quod non obvenit, quod illam sibi quisque debet, quod non ab alio petitur. quid haberes quod in philosophia suspiceres, si beneficiaria res esset? huius opus unum est de divinis humanisque verum invenire. ab hac numquam recedit religio, pietas, iustitia et omnis alius comitatus virtutum consertarum et inter se cohaerentium. haec docuit colere divina, humana diligere, et penes deos imperium esse, inter homines consortium. quod aliquandiu inviolatum mansit, antequam societatem avaritia distraxit et paupertatis causa etiam is, quos fecit locupletissimos, fuit. desiderant[24] enim omnia possidere, dum volunt propria. sed primi mortalium quique ex his geniti naturam incorrupti sequebantur, eundem habebant et ducem et legem, commissi melioris arbitrio. naturae est enim potioribus deteriora summittere. mutis quidem gregibus aut maxima corpora praesunt aut vehementissima. non praecedit armenta degener taurus, sed qui magnitudine ac toris ceteros mares vicit. elephantorum gregem excelsissimus ducit: inter homines pro summo est optimum. animo itaque rector eligebatur, ideoque summa felicitas erat gentium, in quibus non poterat potentior esse nisi melior. tuto enim quantum vult potest, qui se nisi quod debet non putat posse. illo ergo saeculo, quod aureum perhibent, penes sapientes fuisse regnum Posidonius iudicat. hi continebant manus et infirmiorem a validioribus tuebantur, suadebant dissuadebantque et utilia atque inutilia monstrabant. horum prudentia ne quid deesset suis providebat, fortitudo pericula arcebat, beneficentia augebat ornabatque subiectos. officium erat imperare, non regnum. nemo quantum posset, adversus eos experiebatur, per quos coeperat posse, nec erat cuiquam aut animus in iniuriam aut causa, cum bene imperanti bene pareretur nihilque rex maius minari male parentibus posset, quam ut abirent e regno. sed postquam

---

[23] For Seneca on the "noble savage," see Ch. XI, pp. 364-365.
[24] The text is uncertain; but *desiderant* seems preferable to *desierunt*.

subrepentibus vitiis in tyrannidem regna conversa sunt, opus esse legibus coepit, quas et ipsas inter initia tulere sapientes. Solon qui Athenas aequo iure fundavit, inter septem fuit sapientia notos. Lycurgum si eadem aetas tulisset, sacro illi numero accessisset octavus . . . 7. hactenus Posidonio adsentior: artes quidem a philosophia inventas, quibus in cotidiano vita utitur, non concesserim nec illi fabricae adseram gloriam: 'illa' inquit 'sparsos et aut cavis tectos aut aliqua rupe suffossa aut exesae arboris trunco docuit tecta moliri.' ego vero philosophiam iudico non magis excogitasse has machinationes tectorum supra tecta surgentium et urbium urbes prementium quam vivaria piscium in hoc clausa, ut tempestatum periculum non adiret gula et quamvis acerrime pelago saeviente haberet luxuria portus suos, in quibus distinctos piscium greges saginaret. quid ais ? philosophia homines docuit habere clavem et seram ? quid[quid] aliud erat avaritiae signum dare ? philosophia haec cum tanto habitantium periculo inminentia tecta suspendit ? parum enim erat fortuitis tegi et sine arte et sine difficultate naturale invenire sibi aliquod receptaculum. mihi crede, felix illud saeculum ante architectos fuit, ante tectores. ista nata sunt iam nascente luxuria, in quadratum tigna decidere et serra per designata currente certa manu trabem scindere, 'nam primi cuneis scindebant fissile lignum.' . . . 10. in illo quoque dissentio a Posidonio, quod ferramenta fabrilia excogitata a sapientibus viris iudicat. isto enim modo dicat licet sapientes fuisse, per quos 'tunc laqueis captare feras et fallere visco inventum et magnos canibus circumdare saltus.' omnia enim ista sagacitas hominum, non sapientia invenit. in hoc quoque dissentio, sapientes fuisse qui ferri metalla et aeris invenerint, cum incendio silvarum adusta tellus in summo venas iacentis liquefactas fudisset: ista tales inveniunt, quales colunt. ne illa quidem tam suptilis mihi quaestio videtur quam Posidonio, utrum malleus in usu esse prius an forcipes coeperint. utraque invenit aliquis excitati ingenii, acuti, non magni nec elati, et quicquid aliud corpore incurvato et animo humum spectante quaerendum est. sapiens facilis victu fuit, quidni? cum hoc quoque saeculo esse quam expeditissimus cupiat. quomodo, oro te, convenit, ut et Diogenen mireris et Daedalum? uter ex his sapiens tibi videtur? qui serram commentus est, an ille qui cum vidisset puerum cava manu bibentem aquam, fregit protinus exemptum e perula calicem *cum* hac obiurgatione sui: 'quamdiu homo stultus supervacuas sarcinas habui? ,' qui se conplicuit in dolio et in eo cubitavit? hodie utrum tandem sapientiorem putas, qui invenit quemadmodum in inmensam altitudinem crocum latentibus fistulis exprimat, qui euripos subito aquarum impetu implet aut siccat et versatilia cenationum laquearia ita coagmentat, ut subinde alia facies atque alia succedat et totiens tecta quotiens fericula mutentur, an eum, qui et aliis et sibi hoc monstrat, quam nihil nobis natura durum ac difficile imperaverit, posse nos habitare sine marmorario ac fabro, posse nos vestitos esse sine commercio sericorum, posse nos habere usibus nostris necessaria, si contenti fuerimus iis quae terra posuit in summo? quem si audire humanum genus voluerit, tam supervacuum sciet sibi cocum esse quam militem. illi sapientes fuerunt aut certe sapientibus similes, quibus expedita erat tutela corporis. simplici cura constant necessaria: in delicias laboratur. non desiderabis artifices: sequere

naturam. illa noluit esse districtos. ad quaecumque nos cogebat,
instruxit. ' frigus intolerabilest corpori nudo.' quid ergo? non pelles
ferarum et aliorum animalium a frigore satis abundeque defendere
queunt? non corticibus arborum pleraeque gentes tegunt corpora?
non avium plumae in usum vestis conseruntur? non hodieque magna
Scytharum pars tergis vulpium induitur ac murum, quae tactu
mollia et inpenetrabilia ventis sunt? ' opus est tamen calorem solis
aestivi umbra crassiore propellere.' quid ergo? non vetustas multa
abdidit loca, quae vel iniuria temporis vel alio quolibet casu excavata
in specum recesserunt? quid ergo? non quilibet virgeam cratem
texuerunt manu et vili obliverunt luto, deinde [de] stipula aliisque
silvestribus operuere fastigium, et pluviis per devexa labentibus hie-
mem transiere securi? quid ergo? non in defosso latent Syrticae
gentes quibusque propter nimios solis ardores nullum tegimentum
satis repellendis caloribus solidum est nisi ipsa arens humus? non
fuit tam inimica natura, ut, cum omnibus aliis animalibus facilem
actum vitae daret, homo solus non posset sine tot artibus vivere.
nihil horum ab illa nobis imperatum est, nihil aegre quaerendum, ut
possit vita produci. ad parata nati sumus: nos omnia nobis diffi-
cilia facilium fastidio fecimus. tecta tegimentaque et fomenta cor-
porum et cibi et quae nunc ingens negotium facta sunt, obvia erant
et gratuita et opera levi parabilia: modus enim omnium prout
necessitas erat: nos ista pretiosa, nos mira, nos magnis multisque
conquirenda artibus fecimus. sufficit ad id natura, quod poscit. a
natura luxuria descivit, quae cotidie se ipsa incitat et tot saeculis
crescit et ingenio adiuvat vitia. primo supervacua coepit concupiscere,
inde contraria, novissime animum corpori addixit et illius deservire
libidini iussit. omnes istae artes, quibus aut circitatur civitas aut
strepit, corporis negotium gerunt, cui omnia olim tamquam servo
praestabantur, nunc tamquam domino parantur. itaque hinc texto-
rum, hinc fabrorum officinae sunt, hinc odores coquentium, hinc
molles corporis motus docentium mollesque cantus et infractos.
recessit enim ille naturalis modus desideria ope necessaria finiens:
iam rusticitatis et miseriae est velle, quantum sat est . . . 24. omnia
ista ratio quidem, sed non recta ratio commenta est. hominis enim,
non sapientis inventa sunt, tam mehercules quam navigia, quibus
amnes quibusque maria transimus aptatis ad excipiendum ventorum
impetum velis et additis a tergo gubernaculis, quae huc atque illuc
cursum navigii torqueant. exemplum a piscibus tractum est, qui
cauda reguntur et levi eius in utrumque momento velocitatem suam
flectunt. ' omnia ' inquit ' haec sapiens quidem invenit: sed minora
quam ut ipse tractaret, sordidioribus ministris dedit.' immo non aliis
excogitata ista sunt quam quibus hodieque curantur. quaedam nostra
demum prodisse memoria scimus, ut speculariorum usum perlucente
testa clarum transmittentium lumen, ut suspensuras balneorum et
inpressos parietibus tubos, per quos circumfunderetur calor, qui ima
simul ac summa foveret aequaliter. quid loquar marmora, quibus
templa, quibus domus fulgent? quid lapideas moles in rotundum
ac leve formatas, quibus porticus et capacia populorum tecta sus-
cipimus ? quid verborum notas, quibus quamvis citata excipitur
oratio et celeritatem linguae manus sequitur? vilissimorum manci-
piorum ista commenta sunt: sapientia altius sedet nec manus
edocet, animorum magistra est . . . 34. quid sapiens investigaverit,

quid in lucem protraxerit, quaeris? primum verum naturamque,
quam non ut cetera animalia oculis secutus est tardis ad divina.
deinde vitae legem, quam ad universa derexit, nec nosse tantum sed
sequi deos docuit et accidentia non aliter excipere quam imperata.
vetuit parere opinionibus falsis et quanti quidque esset, vera aestima-
tione perpendit. damnavit mixtas paenitentia voluptates et bona
semper placitura laudavit et palam fecit felicissimum esse cui
felicitate non opus est, potentissimum esse qui se habet in potestate.
non de ea philosophia loquor, quae civem extra patriam posuit, extra
mundum deos, quae virtutem donavit voluptati, sed ⟨de⟩ illa, quae
nullum bonum putat nisi quod honestum est, quae nec hominis nec
fortunae muneribus deleniri potest, cuius hoc pretium est, non posse
pretio capi. hanc philosophiam fuisse illo rudi saeculo, quo adhuc
artificia deerant et ipso usu discebantur utilia, non credo. secutast
fortunata tempora, cum in medio iacerent beneficia naturae promiscue utenda, antequam avaritia atque luxuria dissociavere mortales et
ad rapinam ex consortio discurrere. non erant illi sapientes viri, etiam
si faciebant facienda sapientibus. statum quidem generis humani non
alium quisquam suspexerit magis, nec si cui permittat deus terrena
formare et dare gentibus mores, aliud probaverit quam quod apud
illos fuisse memoratur, apud quos ' nulli subigebant arva coloni, ne
signare quidem aut partiri limite campum fas erat: in medium
quaerebant, ipsaque tellus omnia liberius nullo poscente ferebat.'
quid hominum illo genere felicius? in commune rerum natura
fruebantur. sufficiebat illa ut parens ita tutela omnium, haec erat
publicarum opum secura possessio. quidni ego illud locupletissimum
mortalium genus dixerim, in quo pauperem invenire non posses?
inrupit in res optime positas avaritia et, dum seducere aliquid cupit
atque in suum vertere, omnia fecit aliena et in angustum se ex
inmenso redegit. avaritia paupertatem intulit et multa concupis-
cendo omnia amisit. licet itaque nunc conetur reparare quod per-
didit, licet agros agris adiciat vicinum vel pretio pellens vel iniuria,
licet in provinciarum spatium rura dilatet et possessionem vocet per
sua longam peregrinationem: nulla nos finium propagatio eo reducet
unde discessimus. cum omnia fecerimus, multum habebimus: uni-
versum habebamus. terra ipsa fertilior erat inlaborata et in usus
populorum non diripientium larga. quidquid natura protulerat, id
non minus invenisse quam inventum monstrare alteri voluptas erat.
nec ulli aut superesse poterat aut deesse, inter concordes divide-
batur. nondum valentior inposuerat infirmiori manum, nondum
avarus abscondendo quod sibi iaceret, alium necessariis quoque
excluserat: par erat alterius ac sui cura. arma cessabant incruen-
taeque humano sanguine manus odium omne in feras verterant. illi
quos aliquod nemus densum a sole protexerat, qui adversus saevitiam
hiemis aut imbris vili receptaculo tuti sub fronde vivebant, placidas
transigebant sine suspirio noctis. sollicitudo nos in nostra purpura
versat et acerrimis excitat stimulis: at quam mollem somnum
illis dura tellus dabat! non inpendebant caelata laquearia, sed in
aperto iacentes sidera superlabebantur et insigne spectaculum
noctium mundus in praeceps agebatur silentio tantum opus ducens.
tam interdiu illis quam nocte patebant prospectus huius pulcherri-
mae domus. libebat intueri signa ex media caeli parte vergentia,
rursus ex occulto alia surgentia. quidni iuvaret vagari inter tam

late sparsa miracula? at vos ad omnem tectorum pavetis sonum et
inter picturas vestras, si quid increpuit, fugitis adtoniti. non habebant domos instar urbium. spiritus ac liber inter aperta perflatus
et levis umbra rupis aut arboris et perlucidi fontes rivique non opere
nec fistula nec ullo coacto itinere obsolefacti, sed sponte currentes
et prata sine arte formosa, inter haec agreste domicilium rustica
politum manu: haec erat secundum naturam domus, in qua libebat
habitare nec ipsam nec pro ipsa timentem: nunc magna pars nostri
metus tecta sunt. sed quamvis egregia illis vita fuerit et carens
fraude, non fuere sapientes, quando hoc iam in opere maximo nomen
est. non tamen negaverim fuisse alti spiritus viros et, ut ita dicam,
a dis recentes. neque enim dubium est, quin meliora mundus nondum
effetus ediderit. quemadmodum autem omnibus indoles fortior fuit
et ad labores paratior, ita non erant ingenia omnibus consummata.
non enim dat natura virtutem: ars est bonum fieri. illi quidem
non aurum nec argentum nec perlucidos ⟨lapides⟩ *in* ima terrarum
faece quaerebant parcebantque adhuc etiam mutis animalibus: tantum aberat ⟨ut⟩ homo hominem non iratus, non timens, tantum
spectaturus occideret. nondum vestis illis erat picta, nondum texe-
batur aurum, adhuc nec eruebatur. quid ergo *est*? ignorantia
rerum innocentes erant. multum autem interest, utrum peccare
aliquis nolit an nesciat. deerat illis iustitia, deerat prudentia, deerat
temperantia ac fortitudo. omnibus his virtutibus habebat similia
quaedam rudis vita: virtus non contingit animo nisi instituto et
edocto et ad summum adsidua exercitatione perducto. ad hoc quidem, sed sine hoc nascimur et in optimis quoque, antequam erudias,
virtutis materia, non virtus est.[24]

1. Who, my dear Lucilius, can doubt that life is a gift of the immortal gods, but that a good life is the gift of philosophy? From
this it would follow that we should owe as much more to philosophy
than to the gods as a good life is a greater benefit than life — were
it not that philosophy itself has been bestowed upon us by the gods.
The knowledge of it they have, indeed, given to none; but the
possibility of acquiring it to all. For if they had made it a gift
common to all men, and if we were born wise, wisdom would lack
what is best in it — that it is not among the gifts of fortune. For,
as it is, its most precious and noble characteristic is that it is not
allotted to us without effort on our part, that every man must win
it for himself, that it is not to be had from another for the asking.
What would there be in philosophy worthy of your reverence if she
were a free gift ? She has one task, to discover the truth about
things human and divine. From her side religion never departs,
nor piety, nor justice, nor any of the whole company of the virtues,
which are inseparably conjoined and interconnected. She has taught
us to worship what is divine and to love what is human, and that
dominion belongs to the gods, to men, fellowship. This fellowship
long remained inviolate among them, until greed tore society
asunder, and impoverished even those whom it most enriched. For
when men begin to wish to have things for their own, their desire
does not stop short of the possession of all things.

[25] Ed. Otto Hense, Leipzig, 1914.

But the first men and those who sprang from them, being still uncorrupted, followed nature. They had one man as their leader and their law, submitting themselves to the judgment of the better. For it is the way of nature to make the inferior subject to the superior. Even among the dumb beasts, those that are largest or fiercest dominate the others. It is not the weakling bull that has the first place in the herd, but the one that surpasses the others in size and brawn. It is the largest elephant that leads the herd. Among men too, the best was regarded as the greatest; the leader, however, was chosen for the qualities of his mind. Thus it was that the happiest of mankind were those peoples among whom a man could not be the more powerful unless he were the better. For a man who holds it impossible for him to do the things he ought not may safely be allowed to do whatever he will. Therefore in that age which we call golden Posidonius holds that rulership was confided to the wise. They restrained the hands of their fellows, and protected the weaker from the stronger. They persuaded and dissuaded, and showed what things were useful and what useless. Their prudence saw to it that their fellows lacked nothing; their courage warded off dangers; their beneficence brought increase and honor to their subjects. For them ruling was a public duty, not a mere exercise of kingly power. None of them tried to use his power against those from whom he derived it; nor had any man either inclination or excuse for evil-doing, since a good ruler has good subjects; and a king could utter no greater threat against the disobedient than that they should be exiled from the kingdom.

But afterwards, when vices crept in and these kingships were converted into tyrannies, the need of laws began to be felt; and at the beginning the laws themselves were framed by the wise men; Solon, who established Athens on a basis of just laws, was one of seven who were renowned for their wisdom. If Lycurgus had lived in the same age, an eighth would have been added to this sacred number . . .

7. So far I agree with Posidonius. But that philosophy discovered the arts which are of use in our daily life I cannot admit; I will not ascribe to her the reputation of an artisan. Posidonius says: "When men were scattered over the earth, finding their shelter in caves or holes in the rocks or hollow trees, it was philosophy that taught them to build houses." But for my part, I do not hold that philosophy devised these artificial contrivances of houses rising story above story, and of cities crowding against cities — any more than I hold that she invented the fishponds which were enclosed for the purpose of saving gluttons from having to go out in bad weather and of assuring to luxury, no matter how the seas might rage, safe havens in which to fatten fancy breeds of fish. What! was it philosophy that taught the use of locks and keys? What did this accomplish except to give a hint to greed? Was it philosophy that built all these towering tenements, so dangerous to those who live in them? But men were not content to dwell in chance shelters and find for themselves some natural refuge, without the help of art and without trouble. Believe me, that was a happy age when there were no architects and no builders! All this sort of thing was

born when luxury was born – – this squaring-off of timbers and saw-
ing of beams with saws that must follow with nice precision the
line marked out.

The first of men with wedges split their wood.

. . . .

10. On another point also I differ with Posidonius — in that he
thinks iron tools were invented by wise men. For on the same
grounds one could say that those were wise who found out how

To capture beasts with traps and birds with lime,
Or compass woodlands round with hunting-dogs.
[Virgil, *Georgics*, I, 140 f.; cf. Ch. XII, 3].

It was the cunning of men, not their wisdom, that devised all these
things. I differ with him also when he says that it was wise men
who discovered mines of iron and copper, when the soil scorched by
forest fires melted the veins of ore which lay near the surface and
caused the metal to pour forth. The sort of men who discovered
such things are the sort of men whose heart is set upon them. Nor
do I think that the question whether the hammer or the tongs
came first into use is so subtle a one as Posidonius deems it. They
were both invented by some man of active and keen but not of great
or elevated mind; and the same is true of all other things which
must be sought out with body bent and mind fixed upon the ground.

The wise man was not fastidious about his food. And why
should he have been? Even in our own'time he will wish to be as
little cumbered as possible. How, I ask you, can you consistently
admire both Daedalus and Diogenes? Which of the two seems to
you to be the wise man — he who devised the saw, or he who, seeing
a boy drink water from the hollow of his hand, forthwith took his
cup from his wallet and broke it, saying " What a fool I have been
to carry superfluous baggage all this time " — and then curled himself up in his tub and went to sleep? In our own day, which man,
think you, is the wiser — the one who invents a device for spraying
perfumes at great heights from hidden pipes, who fills or empties
canals by a sudden rush of water, who so cleverly constructs a dining-
room with movable ceilings that the roof changes as often as the
courses — or the one who makes plain to others, and to himself,
that nature has laid upon us no hard and difficult command, that
we can live without the marble-mason and the smith, that we can
be clothed without the silk-merchant, that we can have everything
that is needful for our use, if only we will be content with those
things which the earth has placed upon its surface? If the human
race were willing to listen to such a man as this, they would know
that a cook is as superfluous to them as a soldier. Those were wise
men or, surely, like the wise, for whom the care of the body was a
simple matter. Necessities are procured with little pains; it is the
luxuries that require labor. Seek not out the makers of artificial
things, but follow Nature. Nature did not wish us to be distracted
over many things. She equipped us for whatever she forced upon
us. " But cold is intolerable to the naked body." What then?
Are there not skins of wild beasts and other animals, which are sufficient, and more than sufficient, to protect us from the cold? Do not

many peoples cover their bodies with the bark of trees? Are not the feathers of birds sewn together to serve as clothing? Even at this day, do not a great part of the Scythians wear the skins of foxes and mice, soft to the touch and impervious to the winds? " But men must have some thicker shelter than the skin to keep off heat in summer." What then? Has there not been produced in the lapse of ages many a cavern, hollowed out either through the damage wrought by time itself or through some accident or other? What then? Did not some men weave wicker mats by hand, coat them with common mud, and then with branches and other products of the forest construct pitched roofs, and so pass their winters in security while the rain ran down the slating coverings? What then? Do not the Syrtian people dwell in dug-outs, and, indeed, all others who, because of the too fierce blaze of the sun, have no sufficient protection against the heat except in the parched soil itself?

Nature was not so unkind to man that, when she made it easy for all the other animals to maintain life, she made it impossible for him to do so without so many arts. In none of these has she commanded us to engage; none of them needed to be painfully sought out in order that our lives might be prolonged. We were born with everything made ready for us; we have made everything difficult for ourselves, through our disdain of what is easy. Houses, clothes, food and bodily comforts, and all that has now been converted into an immensely troublesome business, lay ready to hand, and free, and obtainable with but trifling pains. For the supply of all things was in proportion to the need of them; but we have made those other needless things precious and wonderful, and have caused them to be sought after with many and great devices. Nature suffices for what she demands. Luxury has abandoned nature; day by day she grows greater, age after age she has been gathering strength and making intellect the minister of vice. She began by desiring superfluities, then things contrary to nature; finally she has made the mind the servant of the body and bidden it devote itself to satisfying the body's lusts. All those arts by which the bustle or the uproar of the city are kept up, are engaged in the body's business. Once the body was treated as a slave, now as a master. From this have come the workshops of the weavers and the carpenters, the savory odors which the cooks produce, the effeminate movements taught by the dancing-masters and the soft and sickly airs taught by the singing-masters. For the moderation of nature which limits our desires to our needs is gone; it is now a mark of boorishness or of poverty to want only what is enough.

.   .   .   .

24. All these things were devised by reason, it is true, but not by right reason. It was man, but not the wise man, that discovered them. The same is true, by Hercules, of the invention of ships fitted with sails for catching the force of the wind and with rudders for steering, whereby we are enabled to cross rivers and seas. The model for them was taken from the fish, which steers itself by its tail, and by a slight movement of it to one side or another alters its rapid course. " But," says Posidonius, " the wise man did indeed discover these things; but they were too trivial for

him to deal with himself, so he gave them over to his meaner assistants." But in truth the sort of men who first devised these things were the sort who today concern themselves with them. We know certain inventions that have appeared within our own memory — such as window-panes which transmit the light clearly through transparent shells, and vaulted baths with pipes built into the walls to distribute the heat, which is thus kept at an even temperature at the upper as well as the lower levels. What shall I say of the marbles with which temples and houses gleam? Or of the rounded and polished masses of stone by means of which we erect porticos and buildings spacious enough to contain whole nations? What of shorthand, by which a speech is taken down while it is being uttered and the speed of tongue is matched by the speed of hand? All these things were contrived by the lowest sort of slaves. Wisdom has a higher seat; she is not the trainer of our hands but the mistress of our minds.

$\cdot \quad \cdot \quad \cdot \quad \cdot \quad \cdot \quad \cdot \quad \cdot$

34. Do you ask what it is that the wise man *has* sought out and brought to light? First of all, the true, and the nature of things, which he, unlike the other animals, has not looked for with the eyes, which are too slow to perceive things divine. Then the law of life, which he directs in accordance with universal principles. And he has taught us not merely to know the gods but to follow them, and to accept what fortune brings as a divine command. He has forbidden us to receive false opinions and has weighed the worth of everything by a true standard. He has condemned those pleasures with which remorse is mingled; has extolled those goods which always please; and has made it known that the happiest man is he who has no need of happiness, and the most powerful, he who has power over himself.

I am not speaking of that philosophy which [26] places the citizen outside his country and the gods outside the world, which makes a virtue of enjoyment — but of that which considers nothing good except what is honorable, which cannot be cozened by the gifts either of man or of fortune, which is of so great price that it cannot be bought for a price. That this philosophy existed in that rude age in which artificial things were still unknown, and when men learned what things were useful by use, I do not believe. These followed [27] that happy time when the bounties of nature lay open for the use of all alike, before avarice and luxury had dissolved the ties which bind men into a society, and they turned from mutual fellowship to mutual plunder. The men of that age were not wise men, even though they did what wise men should do. There is indeed no other condition of the human race which any one would esteem more highly than this, and if one should receive from God authority to fashion earthly creatures and to prescribe customs for peoples, one would choose no other condition than that which is reported of the men of the age when

> No ploughman tilled the ground,
> No fence dividing field from field was found;

---

[26] I. e., *Epicureanism.*   [27] The text here is somewhat doubtful.

> When to the common store all gains were brought,
> And earth gave freely goods which none had sought.[28]

What race of men was ever happier than these? They enjoyed all
Nature in common. She sufficed for them as mother and defender
of all. Their defence was the secure possession of the common
resources. Why, indeed, should I not call that the richest race of
mortals, since no poor man could be found among them? But
Avarice broke in upon this best of all conditions and, seeking to
possess something not shared by others and to claim it for her own,
made all things the property of others, and thus passed from boundless wealth to meagerest poverty. It was greed that begot need, and,
by craving much, lost all. And so, though she now tries to recover
what she has lost, though she adds field to field, evicting her neighbors either by purchase or by violence, though she extends her
country-seats to the size of provinces and calls walking through her
vast estates possessing them — in spite of all this, no enlargement of
our boundaries can bring us back to the state from which we have
departed. When we shall have done all we can, we shall possess
much; but we once possessed the whole world. The earth itself was
more fertile when unploughed, and it provided abundance for peoples
who did not rob one another. Whatever nature produced, men took
no more pleasure in finding it than in showing it, when found, to
their fellows. It was impossible for any man to have more or less
than another; all things were divided amongst them without discord. The stronger had not yet laid hands upon the weaker; not
yet had the miser, by hiding his wealth away unused, deprived others
of the very necessities of life. Each cared as much for his neighbor as
himself, weapons were unknown, and the hand unstained by human
blood turned all its hatred against wild beasts. The men who found
shelter from the sun in some thick wood, and protection against cold
or rain in some lowly refuge beneath the leaves, passed tranquil
nights without a sigh. Care disturbs us in our purple and arouses
us with sharpest goads; but what sweet sleep the hard earth gave
them! No panelled ceilings hung over them; but as they lay beneath
the open sky the stars swept noiseless above them and — wondrous
spectacle of the night — the world moved through the heights of
heaven, performing silently its mighty task. To them by day as well
as by night the prospect of this most lovely dwelling-place of ours
lay open. They took delight in watching the constellations as they
moved, some sinking from the zenith while others rose out of their
hiding-places. What joy to wander among marvels so widely strewn!
But you of the present age tremble every time your roof creaks,
and if you hear something crack in your frescoed walls, you flee in
terror. But the men of those days had no houses as big as cities.
The air, the breezes blowing free through the open spaces, the light
shade of rock or tree, crystal fountains, streams running at will
unspoiled by any confinement of their waters in pipes or canals,
and meadows beautiful without the aid of art — amongst these they
made their rude homes adorned with rustic hand. This was a house
according to nature, in which it was a joy to live, having no fear

---

[28] Virgil, *Georgics*, I, 125 ff.; cf. Chap. XII, 3, p. 370.

either of it or for it; whereas in these days our houses cause a great part of our fears.

But however excellent and guileless their life, the men of that time were not wise men, since that name is reserved for the highest of man's achievements. Yet I would not deny that they were men of lofty spirit and — if I may put it so — fresh from the gods. For there is no doubt that the world brought forth better things when it was not yet worn out. But while the native powers of all of them were greater than ours and more fitted for labors, nevertheless these powers had not in all of them been brought to their highest development. For virtue is not bestowed by nature; it is an art to become good. For all that, they did not grub for gold and silver and transparent stones in the lowest dregs of the earth; and they still were merciful even to dumb animals — so far were they from killing men, not in anger or in fear, but merely for a spectacle. Not yet were their garments dyed, not yet was gold wrought; it had not yet been mined. What follows, then? They were innocent through ignorance. But it makes a great difference whether a man is unwilling to sin or does not know how to sin. Justice was still unknown to them, and prudence, and self-control, and fortitude. Their rude life had in it certain qualities resembling all these virtues; but virtue itself is attained by the soul only when it has been taught and trained, and by unremitting practice has been brought to perfection. For this, but without it, we were born; and even in the best of men, without instruction, there is but the stuff of virtue, not virtue itself.

The question proposed by the Academy of Dijon in 1749 for the competition in which Rousseau carried off the prize with his *First Discourse* had, in substance, been raised by Stoic writers and answered by some of them in the negative. The study of the arts and sciences does not contribute *à épurer les moeurs,*[29] and therefore it is of minimal value, and often actually harmful. Not only has the progress of the mechanical arts been conducive to luxury, and therefore pernicious; the researches of specialists in the so-called liberal arts are at best a waste of time upon questions both trivial and useless. Some instruction in letters and in elementary science has a proper place in the education of the young; but *inquiry* into these subjects is an unworthy employment for grown men. The motivation of this disparagement of both humanistic and scientific studies lay chiefly in the ultra-moralism of the Stoics, especially of the Roman Stoics; but it was akin to the anti-intellectualist temper of primitivism and tended to the same conclusion; the continual advancement of learning which is the aim of the investigator is not *progress* in any eulogistic sense of the term; on the whole, it is the reverse. A single example of this attitude, taken from Seneca, will suffice.

Having first disposed summarily of the studies which aim at money-

---

[29] In the specific form given it by the Academy the question was whether the Revival of Learning had had this effect.

making as "mercenary employments," useful only as elementary exercises for the mind, which should not long detain it, Seneca proceeds to attack also the *liberalia studia*, as commonly understood. Under his condemnation of these as "petty and puerile" fall linguistics, poetics, Homeric philology, history, music, mathematics, astronomy, painting. The passage rings the changes tediously, not only upon the same theme, but also upon the same rhetorical device; it is therefore given with some abridgement.

X, 2. Seneca: *Epist. mor.* LXXXVIII, 2-12, 20, 31-2 (Translation on p. 276).

2. ... unum studium vere liberale est, quod liberum facit. hoc est sapientiae, sublime, forte, magnanimum. cetera pusilla et puerilia sunt: an tu quicquam in istis esse credis boni, quorum professores turpissimos omnium ac flagitiosissimos cernis? non discere debemus ista, sed didicisse. quidam illud de liberalibus studiis quaerendum iudicaverunt, an virum bonum facerent: ne promittunt quidem nec huius rei scientiam adfectant. grammaticus circa curam sermonis versatur et, si latius evagari vult, circa historias, iam ut longissime fines suos proferat, circa carmina. quid horum ad virtutem viam sternit? syllabarum enarratio et verborum diligentia et fabularum memoria et versuum lex ac modificatio? quid ex his metum demit, cupiditatem eximit, libidinem frenat? [ad geometriam transeamus et ad musicen: nihil apud illas invenies, quod vetet timere, vetet cupere. quisquis ignorat, alia frustra scit.] ... utrum doceant isti virtutem an non: si non docent, ne tradunt quidem. si docent, philosophi sunt. vis scire, quam non ad docendam virtutem consederint? aspice, quam dissimilia inter se omnium studia sint: atqui similitudo esset idem docentium. nisi forte tibi Homerum philosophum fuisse persuadent, cum his ipsis, quibus colligunt, negent: nam modo Stoicum illum faciunt, virtutem solam probantem et voluptates refugientem et ab honesto ne inmortalitatis quidem pretio recedentem, modo Epicureum, laudantem statum quietae civitatis et inter convivia cantusque vitam exigentis, modo Peripateticum, tria bonorum genera inducentem, modo Academicum, omnia incerta dicentem: adparet nihil horum esse in illo, quia omnia sunt. ista enim inter se dissident. demus illis Homerum philosophum fuisse, nempe sapiens factus est, antequam carmina ulla cognosceret: ergo illa discamus, quae Homerum fecere sapientem. hoc quidem me quaerere, uter maior aetate fuerit, Homerus an Hesiodus, non magis ad rem pertinet quam scire, cum minor Hecuba fuerit quam Helena, quare tam male tulerit aetatem. quid? inquam, annos Patrocli et Achillis inquirere ad rem existimas pertinere? quaeris, Ulixes ubi erraverit, potius quam efficias, ne nos semper erremus? non vacat audire, utrum inter Italiam et Siciliam iactatus sit an extra notum nobis orbem, neque enim potuit in tam angusto error esse tam longus: tempestates nos animi cotidie iactant et nequitia in omnia Ulixis mala inpellit. non deest forma, quae sollicitet oculos, non hostis; hinc monstra effera et humano cruore gaudentia, hinc insidiosa blandimenta aurium, hinc naufragia et tot varietates malorum. hoc me doce, quomodo patriam amem, quomodo uxorem, quomodo patrem, quomodo ad haec tam honesta vel

naufragus navigem. quid inquiris, an Penelopa [in]pudica fuerit, an
verba saeculo suo dederit? an Ulixem illum esse, quem videbat,
antequam sciret, suspicata sit? doce me, quid sit pudicitia et
quantum in ea bonum, in corpore an in animo posita sit. ad musicum
transeo: doces me, quomodo inter se acutae ac graves consonent,
quomodo nervorum disparem reddentium sonum fiat concordia: fac
potius, quomodo animus secum meus consonet nec consilia mea
discrepent. monstras mihi, qui sint modi flebiles: monstra potius,
quomodo inter adversa non emittam flebilem vocem. metiri me
geometres docet latifundia potius quam doceat, quomodo metiar,
quantum homini satis sit. numerare docet me et avaritiae commodat
digitos potius quam doceat nihil ad rem pertinere istas conputa-
tiones, non esse feliciorem, cuius patrimonium tabularios lassat,
immo quam supervacua possideat, qui infelicissimus futurus est, si
quantum habeat per se conputare cogetur. quid mihi prodest scire
agellum in partes dividere, si nescio cum fratre dividere? quid
prodest colligere subtiliter pedes iugeri et conprendere etiam si quid
decempedam effugit, si tristem me facit vicinus inpotens et aliquid
ex meo abradens? docet quomodo nihil perdam ex finibus meis: at
ego discere volo, quomodo totos hilaris amittam. 'paterno agro et
avito' inquit 'expellor.' quid? ante avum tuum quis istum agrum
tenuit? cuius, non dico hominis, sed populi fuerit, expedire potes?
non dominus isto, sed colonus intrasti. cuius colonus es? si bene
tecum agitur, heredis. negant iurisconsulti quicquam usu capi
⟨publicum: hoc, quod tenes, quod tuum dicis,⟩ publicum est et
quidem generis humani . . . 20. 'quid ergo? nihil nobis liberalia
conferunt studia?' ad alia multum, ad virtutem nihil. nam et hae
viles ex professo artes, quae manu constant, ad instrumenta vitae
plurimum conferunt, tamen ad virtutem non pertinent. 'quare ergo
liberalibus studiis filios erudimus?' non quia virtutem dare possunt, sed quia animum ad accipiendam virtutem praeparant.
quemadmodum prima illa, ut antiqui vocabant, litteratura, per quam
pueris elementa traduntur, non docet liberales artes, sed mox per-
cipiendis locum parat, sic liberales artes non perducunt animum
ad virtutem, sed expediunt . . . 31. 'cum dicatis' inquit 'sine
liberalibus studiis ad virtutem non perveniri, quemadmodum negatis
illa nihil conferre virtuti?' quia nec sine cibo ad virtutem perveni-
tur, cibus tamen ad virtutem non pertinet. ligna navi nihil conferunt, quamvis non fiat navis nisi ex lignis: non est, inquam, cur
aliquid putes eius adiutorio fieri, sine quo non potest fieri. potest
quidem etiam illud dici, sine liberalibus studiis veniri ad sapientiam
posse. quamvis enim virtus discenda sit, tamen non per haec
discitur.[30]

One study is truly liberal: that which makes a man free. This is
the study of wisdom, a study sublime, strong, characteristic of a
great soul; the others are petty and puerile. Can you believe that
there is good in any of those studies whose teachers you perceive to
be the most base and ignoble of all? We ought not to be learning
these things, but to have learned them.

There are those who think we should ask about liberal studies

[30] Ed. Otto Hense.

whether they can make a man good; but they do not even promise this, nor aim at it. The student of literature is concerned with language, and if he seeks to proceed farther, with history, or, to give his study its farthest reach, with poetry. But which of these paves the way to virtue? The explanation of syllables, the investigation of words, the memorizing of stories, the rules and measures of verse — which of these dispels fear or drives out covetousness or bridles passion? Pass to geometry and music: in them, too, you will find nothing that forbids fear and desire. Anyone who does not know this, knows nothing else to any purpose. Look to it [with respect to any teachers] whether they teach virtue or not; if they do not teach it, then neither do they impart it. If they do teach it, then they are philosophers. Do you wish proof that they do not occupy their chairs for the purpose of teaching virtue? Then observe how dissimilar to one another are the studies in which they engage; whereas, if they taught the same thing, their studies would be similar.

Perhaps, however, they persuade you that Homer is a philosopher, even though they deny this by the very arguments from which they infer it. For sometimes they make him a Stoic who approves nothing but virtue, avoids pleasures, and does not depart from rectitude even at the price of immortality; sometimes an Epicurean, praising the city in which life is placid and is spent in feasting and song; sometimes a Peripatetic, who holds goods to be of three kinds; sometimes an Academic, who declares everything to be uncertain. It is clear that none of these doctrines are to be found in Homer, because all of them can be found in him; for they are inconsistent with one another. But let us grant to these people that Homer was a philosopher; yet surely he became a wise man before he knew anything of poetry. Let us then learn what it was that made Homer wise.

To this question it is no more pertinent to ask me whether he was older than Hesiod than to ask why Hecuba, though younger than Helen, bore her age so badly. Or again, what, I ask, has an inquiry concerning the ages of Achilles and Patroclus to do with the case? Do you seek to know through what lands Ulysses strayed, rather than to enable us to avoid going astray always? We have no time to hear whether he was storm-tost to and fro between Italy and Sicily, or beyond the limits of the world known to us (for in truth so long a wandering would not have been possible in so narrow a space): the tempests of the soul toss us to and fro every day, and our vices involve us in all the misfortunes of Ulysses. The beauty that tempts the eye, the enemy that assails us, is not wanting; here are savage monsters delighting in human blood, here insidious enchantments of the ear, here shipwrecks and how many other ills. Teach me this, rather: how I should love my country, my wife, my father; how, even though I have suffered shipwreck, I may steer my course towards these so worthy ends. Why do you ask whether Penelope was chaste or only deceived the folk of her time with words; or whether she suspected the man she saw was Ulysses before she knew it? Teach me, rather, what chastity is, and how great a good it is, whether it be of the body or the soul.

I turn to the musician. You instruct me how to harmonize high and low voices, how I may produce a concord from differing strings; instruct me, rather, how my soul may be in harmony with itself and my purposes not be discordant. You show me what sorts of music make men weep; show me, rather, how, in the midst of adversity, I may never cry aloud. The mathematician teaches me to measure the area of my lands, instead of teaching me what its measure ought to be, how much is sufficient for a man. He teaches me to count, and trains my fingers for avarice, instead of teaching me that these computations are to no purpose, that a man is not happier for tiring out the book-keepers with his possessions — nay, that any man possesses a superfluity who would be most unhappy if he were compelled to compute for himself how much he owns. What does it profit me to know how to divide a field into parts, if I do not know how to share it with my brother? What does it profit me to figure out with precision the number of feet in an acre and to know whether any bit of it has escaped my measuring rod, if I take it hard when a poor neighbor has scraped off a little of my land? The mathematician shows me how I may lose none of my boundaries; but I desire to learn how I may lose all of them with a light heart. But, one says, " I am being driven from the land which my father and grandfather owned." Well, who owned the land before your father and grandfather? Can you tell to what people — I do not say, to what man — it originally belonged? You have occupied it not as owner but as tenant. Whose tenant are you? If all goes well with you, of your heir. The lawyers say that public property cannot become a private possession merely by undisturbed occupancy; now the property which you call yours is public — it belongs, indeed, to all mankind.

. . . .

" What, then," you say, " do we gain no advantage at all from liberal studies? " In other respects, much advantage; but with respect to virtue, none. For even those admittedly low manual arts are very useful as aids to mere living, but they have nothing to do with virtue. " Why, then, should we educate our children in liberal studies? " Not because they can produce virtue, but because they prepare the mind for the reception of virtue. Just as that primary course in " letters " (as the ancients called it), which gives boys their elementary knowledge, does not teach the liberal arts, but prepares the ground so that they may presently be acquired, so the liberal arts do not lead the mind all the way to virtue, but only furnish a preparation for it.

. . . .

" But," someone says, " since you admit that virtue cannot be attained without liberal studies, how can you deny that they lend assistance to virtue? " Because you cannot attain virtue without food, either; nevertheless food has nothing to do with virtue. Wood does not lend assistance to a ship, though a ship cannot be built except of wood. There is no reason, I say, why you should think that a thing is assisted by that without which it cannot be made. It may even be said that it is possible to attain to virtue without liberal studies; for although virtue must be learned, yet it cannot be learned through them.[31]

A passage in the *Medea* lays emphasis chiefly upon the happiness of primeval man in being ignorant of navigation. The chorus speaks.

X, 3. *Medea*, 301-339, 364-379 (Translation on p. 280).

> Audax nimium qui freta primus
> rate tam fragili perfida rupit
> terrasque suas posterga videns
> animam levibus credidit auris,
> dubioque secans aequora cursu
> potuit tenui fidere ligno
> inter vitae mortisque vias
> nimium gracili limite ducto.
> nondum quisquam sidera norat,
> stellisque quibus pingitur aether
> non erat usus, nondum pluvias
> Hyadas poterat vitare ratis,
> non Oleniae lumina caprae,
> nec quae sequitur flectitque senex
> Attica tardus plaustra Bootes,
> nondum Boreas,
> nondum Zephyrus nomen habebant.
> Ausus Tiphys pandere vasto
> carbasa ponto
> legesque novas scribere ventis:
> nunc lina sinu tendere toto,
> nunc prolato pede transversos
> captare notos, nunc antemnas
> medio tutas ponere malo,
> nunc in summo religare loco,
> cum iam totos avidus nimium
> navita flatus optat et alto
> rubicunda tremunt sipara velo.
> Candida nostri saecula patres
> videre, procul fraude remota.
> sua quisque piger litora tangens
> patrioque senex factus in arvo,
> parvo dives, nisi quas tulerat
> natale solum, non norat opes:
> bene dissaepti foedera mundi
> traxit in unum Thessala pinus
> iussitque pati verbera pontum
> partemque metus fieri nostri
> mare sepositum.
>
> . . . .
>
> Nunc iam cessit pontus et omnes
> patitur leges: non Palladia
> compacta manu regum referens
> inclita remos quaeritur Argo —

---

[31] For Seneca in a very different mood, cf. p. 378.

> quaelibet altum cumba pererrat;
> terminus omnis motus et urbes
> muros terra posuere nova,
> nil qua fuerat sede reliquit
> pervius orbis:
> Indus gelidum potat Araxen,
> Albin Persae Rhenumque bibunt.
> venient annis saecula seris,
> quibus Oceanus vincula rerum
> laxet et ingens pateat tellus
> Tethysque novos detegat orbes
> nec sit terris ultima Thule.[32]

Too bold was he who first in fragile ship broke through the treacherous seas, and looking behind him at his lands trusted his life to the fickle blasts, and cutting the water with uncertain course put his faith in thin wood — too slim a boundary laid down between the ways of life and death. Not yet did anyone know the constellations nor use the stars with which the aether is adorned, not yet could a vessel avoid the rainy Hyades, not yet did the lights of the Olenian goat nor the Attic Wain which slow old Bootes follows and drives, not yet did Boreas, not yet did Zephyr, have a name.

Tiphys dared to spread his sails over the wide sea and to write new laws for the winds: now to stretch the full breasted sail, now swinging round to catch the cross breezes, now to set the sail-yards safely in mid-mast, now to tie them at the top, when the sailor too eager prays for all the winds and the ruddy topsails flap above the high sail.

Our fathers knew an age of honesty, far removed from deceit. Each man sluggishly clung to his own shores and grew old on his paternal fields, rich with little, unknowing other wealth than what his native soil produced. The Thessalian pine drew together into one the communities of a well divided world, and ordered the sea to suffer blows, and made the distant seas one of the terrors that affright us.

After mentioning the perils of the deep, Scylla and the Sirens, the Chorus continues:

Now the sea has yielded and is subject to all men's bidding. No famous Argo made by the hand of Pallas and bearing the oars of kings is sought for; any ship may now wander over the deep. Every boundary has been moved, and cities have placed their walls in new lands: the globe, accessible in every part, has left nothing in the place where it was. The Indian drinks the frozen Araxes, the Persians imbibe the Elbe and the Rhine. An age will come in future years when Ocean shall loosen the chains of things and the huge earth lie open and Tethys shall uncover new worlds, nor will Thule then be the uttermost part of the earth.

The passage in the *Phaedra* (or *Hippolytus*) is significant because it brings

---

[32] Ed. Peiper-Richter, Leipzig, 1921. But we preserve the traditional order of the text, not the order of Leo.

into dramatic opposition two interpretations of the conception of 'following Nature.' The first, expressed in the speech of the Nurse (446-482), is at once anti-primitivistic, hedonistic and antinomian; he who takes Nature as his guide will live in cities and seek the society of men, for the savage denizens of the wood know naught of life; and he will 'let himself go,' lay hold on all attainable pleasures, knowing that to endure hardship is not a duty that has been imposed upon men. But the Nurse's speech also introduces a theme which was to recur repeatedly in late medieval and early modern literature: the praise of Venus Genetrix as the renewer of life, and the consequent denunciation of celibacy as inimical to life and contrary to Nature's plan for the maintenance of the world. Of this strain the echo is to be found in the thirteenth century both in the *De planctu naturae* of Alain de Lille and in the *Roman de la Rose*; and it is in part with the arguments and rhetoric of Phaedra's Nurse that sacerdotal and monachal celibacy was assailed by its medieval critics. Both elements of her tirade reappear in the speech in which Milton's Comus warns the Lady against "those budge doctors of the Stoic fur", and bids her

" be not cosen'd
With that same vaunted name, Virginity."

X, 4. *Phaedra,* 446-454, 461-482.

aetate fruere: mobili cursu fugit.	446
nunc facile pectus, grata nunc iuveni Venus:	
exultet animus. cur toro viduo iaces?	
tristem iuventam solve; nunc cursus rape,	
effunde habenas, optimos vitae dies	
effluere prohibe. propria descripsit deus	
officia et aevum per suos duxit gradus:	
laetitia iuvenem, frons decet tristis senem.	
quid te coherces et necas rectam indolem? . . .	
truculentus et silvester ac vitae inscius	461
tristem iuventam solve; nunc luxus rape,	
hoc esse munus credis indictum viris,	
ut dura tolerent, cursibus domitent equos	
et saeva bella Marte sanguineo gerant?	465
quam varia leti genera mortalem trahunt	475
carpuntque turbam, pontus et ferrum et doli!	
sed ista credas desse: sic atram Styga	
iam petimus ultro. caelibem vitam probet	
sterilis iuventus: hoc erit, quicquid vides,	
unius aevi turba et in semet ruet.	480
providit ille maximus mundi parens,	466
cum tam rapaces cerneret Fati manus,	
ut damna semper subole repararet nova.	
excedat agedum rebus humanis Venus,	
quae supplet ac restituit exhaustum genus:	
orbis iacebit squalido turpis situ,	
vacuum sine ullis piscibus stabit mare,	

> alesque caelo derit et silvis fera
> solis et aer pervius ventis erit.   474
> proinde vitae sequere naturam ducem: 481
> urbem frequenta, civium coetum cole.[33]

Enjoy thy youth; it fast takes flight. Now feeling is easily aroused, now love to youth is pleasing. Make merry. Why lie on a lonely couch? Have done with this cheerless youth; lay hold on pleasures; let go the reins; let not life's best days slip from thee. God has drawn out this life of ours through several stages and assigned to each its proper duties; joy befits the young, a solemn face the old. Why dost thou hold thyself in check and stifle the powers that are within thee? . . . Wilt thou like a rude fellow of the woods, ignorant of life, spend thy youth in melancholy and let Venus be deserted? Is it, thinkest thou, a task laid upon men to endure hardships, tame horses in their course, and wage fierce strife in bloody battle? How various are the forms of death that seize and feed upon the mortal throng — the sea, the sword, and guile. Yet suppose these lacking; still, by such a course of life as thine we should press on of ourselves towards the shades of death. The unwedded life let barren youth applaud; its end will be that all thou beholdest will be the throng of one generation only, and with its end will come ruin. The almighty father of the universe, when he saw how greedy are the hands of fate, took care ever by fresh progeny to make losses good. Come now, let Venus be excluded from human affairs, Venus who supplies and renews the worn-out race, and the whole globe will lie in foul decay; the sea will stand empty of fish; there will be no birds in the heavens nor beasts in the woods; and the paths of air will know no travellers but the winds. Follow, then, Nature as the guide of life; frequent the city, cultivate the society of men.

To this the austere youth replies with a long and eloquent eulogy of the state of nature, which is not to be found in cities nor among men in whom greed has bred both luxury and cruelty, but in the simple life of the primitive age.

X, 5. *Phaedra*, 483-558 (Translation on p. 284).

> Non alia magis est libera et vitio carens
> ritusque melius vita quae priscos colat,
> quam quae relictis moenibus silvas amat.
> non illum avarae mentis inflammat furor
> qui se dicavit montium insontem iugis,
> non aura populi et vulgus infidum bonis,
> non pestilens invidia, non fragilis favor;
> non ille regno servit aut regno imminens
> vanos honores sequitur aut fluxas opes,
> spei metusque liber, haud illum niger
> edaxque livor dente degeneri petit;
> nec scelera populos inter atque urbes sata

---

[33] Ed. Peiper-Richter. But F. J. Miller (*Loeb Class. Lib.*) is here followed in the order of lines and in reading *luxus* instead of *cursus* in line 449 and *ista* instead of *fata* in line 477.

novit nec omnes conscius strepitus pavet
aut verba fingit; mille non quaerit tegi
dives columnis nec trabes multo insolens
suffigit auro; non cruor largus pias
inundat aras, fruge nec sparsi sacra
centena nivei colla summittunt boves:
sed rure vacuo potitur et aperto aethere
innocuus errat. callidas tantum feris
struxisse fraudes novit et fessus gravi
labore niveo corpus Iliso fovet:
nunc ille ripam celeris Alphei legit,
nunc nemoris alti densa metatur loca,
ubi Lerna puro gelida perlucet vado,
sedesque mutas: hinc aves querulae fremunt
ornique ventis lene percussae tremunt
veteresque fagi. iuvit aut amnis vagi
pressisse ripas, caespite aut nudo leves
duxisse somnos, sive fons largus citas
defundit undas sive per flores novos
fugiente dulcis murmurat rivo sonus.
excussa silvis poma compescunt famem
et fraga parvis vulsa dumetis cibos
faciles ministrant. regios luxus procul
est impetus fugisse: sollicito bibunt
auro superbi; quam iuvat nuda manu
captasse fontem! certior somnus premit
secura duro membra versantem toro.
non in recessu furta et obscuro improbus
quaerit cubili seque multiplici timens
domo recondit: aethera ac lucem petit
et teste caelo vivit. hoc equidem reor
vixisse ritu prima quos mixtos deis
profudit aetas. nullus his auri fuit
caecus cupido, nullus in campo sacer
divisit agros arbiter populis lapis;
nondum secabant credulae pontum rates:
sua quisque norat maria; non vasto aggere
crebraque turre cinxerant urbes latus;
non arma saeva miles aptabat manu
nec torta clausas fregerat saxo gravi
ballista portas, iussa nec dominum pati
iuncto ferebat terra servitium bove:
sed arva per se feta poscentes nihil
pavere gentes, silva nativas opes
et opaca dederant antra nativas domos.
rupere foedus impius lucri furor
et ira praeceps quaeque succensas agit
libido mentes; venit imperii sitis
cruenta, factus praeda maiori minor:
pro iure vires esse. tum primum manu
bellare nuda saxaque et ramos rudes
vertere in arma: non erat gracili levis
armata ferro cornus aut longo latus

mucrone cingens ensis aut crista procul
galeae comantes: tela faciebat dolor.
invenit artes bellicus Mavors novas
et mille formas mortis. hinc terras cruor
infecit omnis fusus et rubuit mare.
tum scelera dempto fine per cunctas domos
iere, nullum caruit exemplo nefas:
a fratre frater, dextera gnati parens
cecidit, maritus coniugis ferro iacet
perimuntque fetus impiae matres suos;
[taceo novercas. mitius nil est feris] [34]

There is no life freer and more innocent, none which better
cherishes the ancient ways, than that which, leaving city walls
behind, loves the woods. His mind is inflamed by no mad greed of
gain who gives himself up to a harmless existence on the mountain
heights; no breath of popular applause is there, no mob faithless to
good men, no poisonous envy and no fickle favor. He serves no
ruler nor, seeking himself to rule, does he pursue empty honors or
fleeting wealth. Since he is free alike from hope and fear, black
devouring envy does not attack him with its ignoble tooth; unknown
to him are the crimes that spawn in teeming cities; nor does he,
conscious of guilt, tremble at every sound, or fashion lies. He does
not seek shelter beneath a roof reared upon a thousand costly columns, nor does he in pride overlay his rafter-beams with gold. No
streaming blood drenches his pious altars, no hecatombs of snow-
white bulls sprinkled with sacred meal bend their necks to the knife;
but he is master of the empty countryside and wanders harmless
beneath the open sky.

His only skill is to set cunning traps for the wild beasts, till,
wearied with heavy toil, he refreshes his body in the snowy waters of
Illissus. Now he wanders by the bank of swift Alpheus, now seeks
out the silent depths of lofty woods, where chill Lerna gleams
through her pure shallows, where plaintive birds murmur, and the
ash-trees and the ancient beeches quiver in the gentle breeze. Sweet
is it to lie upon the bare turf beside a wandering stream and dream
untroubled dreams, whether it be where some copious spring pours
down its rushing waters or where through new-sprung flowers some
rivulet gently murmurs as it slips along. Fruits shaken from the
trees appease his hunger and berries plucked from the low bushes
offer easy food. Far from the luxury of kings he has pushed his
flight. The proud drink water from uneasy cups of gold; how
pleasant to catch with bare hand the water from the spring. A
surer slumber falls upon him as, with quiet mind, he lays himself
down upon his hard bed. He does not seek furtive loves in hidden
chamber or on secret couch, fearfully hiding himself from sight
within some intricate abode. He seeks the air and light, and lives
under the eye of heaven.

In this way, I think, lived, mingling with the gods, those whom the
first age brought forth. They had no blind love of gold. No sacred
boundary stone stood as a witness to the peoples, dividing field from

<hr>

[34] Ed. Peiper-Richter.

field; not yet did rash ships plough the sea; each man knew only his native waters. Cities had not girt themselves with mighty walls thick-set with towers; no soldier set his hand to cruel weapons; nor did the twisted ballista shatter the closed gates with heavy rocks. Not yet did earth, compelled to submit to a master's rule, endure the labor of the yoked ox; but the fields, fruitful of themselves, fed peoples who demanded nothing more; the woods gave men their natural wealth and dim caves their natural shelter. Impious love of gain broke up this harmony, and headlong wrath, and lust that sets men's hearts aflame. Then came the ruthless thirst for power; the weaker was made the stronger's prey, and might came to pass for right. At first men fought with bare fists, then turned stones and rude clubs to the use of arms. As yet there was no light javelin made from cornel-wood and tipped with iron; no long sharp-pointed sword hung at the side; no helmets adorned with tufts of hair gleamed from afar. But wrath furnished weapons. Warlike Mars invented new arts and a thousand forms of death. And so bloodshed spread through all lands, and the seas grew red. Then crime that knew no limit stalked through every home, and no kind of wickedness lacked example: brother fell by the hand of brother, parent by the hand of child, husband was slain by the dagger of his wife, and impious mothers destroyed their own offspring. Of stepmothers I do not speak; they are no whit gentler than the beasts.[35]

From the tone of some of these passages, taken alone, it might be supposed that Seneca was a primitivist of the more hopeful type, who conceived it possible that men might be persuaded eventually to return to the simplicity and austerity of the state of nature, while substituting for its mere innocence the conscious and disciplined virtue of the Stoic wise man. But his philosophy as a whole permitted no such cheerful outlook. The Stoic cosmology implied that the preaching of the Stoic moralist must in the end prove futile. In each cycle the earth must pass through a succession of changes rigorously determined *ab initio* by the constitution of nature; the first morning of creation wrote what the last dawn shall read: *a primo die mundi, . . . quando mergerentur terrena decretum est.*[36] Not only will man and all his works be finally destroyed (*erit terminus rebus humanis*),[37] but, as earth grows old and worn out, man, with all her offspring, will

---

[35] For an analogous passage in the pseudo-Senecan Octavia, in which the philosophic primitivism of the Stoic is fused with the legend of the Ages, *vide*, Ch. II, 19. For further illustration of the denunciation of luxury in Seneca, see *Dialogi: De vita beata*, xi, 3-4 (Tr. J. W. Basore, Loeb Class. Lib. II, 1932). But in the same essay (xvii-xxviii) Seneca, in order to meet the charge that he does not practise what he preaches, virtually recants his praise of poverty and the simple life. The wise man knows the right use of wealth, and finds in it ampler scope for the exercise of virtue: *maior materia sapienti viro [est] animum explicandi suum in divitiis quam in paupertate* (xxii, 1).

[36] *Quaestiones naturales*, III, xxx, 1.

[37] *Ibid.* III, xxix, 5.

gradually deteriorate, so that in the latter days his life will be like that of
the beasts. Of the final catastrophe, as Seneca sometimes conceives it,
there will be two stages. A deluge will first cover the whole earth and sweep
away all living things; then will come the cosmical conflagration: *omnia
sternet abducetque secum vetustas, . . . et inundationibus quicquid habitatur obducet necabitque omne animal orbe submerso, et ignibus vastis
torrebit incendetque mortalia.*[38] Thereafter, it is true, another cycle will
begin with another age of innocence; but the old and melancholy story
will be repeated: man's goodness and happiness will not outlast the infancy
of earth and of the race.

X, 6. *Quaestiones naturales,* III, xxx, 7-8.

> . . . peracto exitio generis humani extinctisque pariter feris, in
> quarum homines ingenia transierant, iterum aquas terra sorbebit,
> terra pelagus stare aut intra terminos suos furere coget, et reiectus
> e nostris sedibus in sua secreta pelletur oceanus, et antiquus ordo
> revocabitur.   8. Omne ex integro animal generabitur dabiturque
> terris homo inscius scelerum et melioribus auspiciis natus. Sed
> illis quoque innocentia non durabit, nisi dum novi sunt. Cito
> nequitia subrepit.[39]

When the annihilation of the human race has been completed, and
the wild beasts — into whose way of life men will have already
lapsed — have likewise been destroyed, the earth will absorb the
waters again into itself, and will compel the seas to stand fast or to
rage only within their appointed bounds. Ocean then, banished
from our place of habitation, will be driven back to his own secret
abode, and the former order of the world will be restored. Every
species of animal will be created afresh, and the earth will once
more be inhabited by men — men born under happier auspices,
knowing naught of evil. But their innocence will endure only so
long as they are new. Wickedness creeps in swiftly.

---

[38] *Dial.* VI (*Consolatio ad Marciam*, xxvi, 6; in Basore's ed., II, p. 94).

[39] Ed. P. Oltramare, 1929, I, p. 159. The *ecpyrosis*, it will be noted, is here
omitted by Seneca.

CHAPTER ELEVEN

THE NOBLE SAVAGE IN ANTIQUITY

The idealization of savages is, of course, cultural primitivism isolated from chronological primitivism. It is, it is true, often combined with the belief that there was an original ideal state of all mankind which now persists only among the savages; but even this implies that a considerable part of the human race has thus far been exempt from degeneration. That they will continue to be so is not necessarily implied, for it was despondently recognized by some ancient and many modern writers that the disease of civilization could not be prevented from spreading — that it must eventually infect even those who had thus far, through a fortunate isolation, escaped it. What part, then, did this mode of primitivism play in ancient thought and what form did it chiefly assume?

In dealing with this subject it is essential to distinguish the real noble savages of antiquity from the inhabitants of the mythic Elysiums which the Greeks placed on the several margins of the world, e. g. the Aethiopians to the south, the Hyperboreans in the farthest north, the dwellers in the Islands of the Blest at the edge of the western sea. Even these, it is true, were not wholly unreal. The Isles of the Blest are — in Hesiod and Pindar — simply the equivalents of heaven with a (nominally) definite geographical location on earth. In Hesiod they are the abode only of some of the Heroes, of his Fourth Age, to whom immortality had been granted; in Pindar they are the final home of all purified souls. But in either case, they are wholly inaccessible to living men, and the life in them is carried on under conditions impossible to mortals here. The Aethiopians, proverbially the happiest of mortal men, were, in a sense, an idealization of an actual race; but the descriptions of them were almost wholly the product of the mythopoeic imagination. This is even more manifestly true of the Hyperboreans, in whose reality so late and learned, if uncritical, a writer as the elder Pliny at least half-believed.

But all of these "happy lands, far, far away" were simply, so to say, bits of the Golden Age surviving in various odd corners of the world; and there was little of the spirit of cultural primitivism in them — hardly more than in the popular Christian idea of heaven — and nothing at all of the temper of hard primitivism. It is, therefore, probably a mistake to connect these beliefs closely — as Eichoff tends to do — with the genesis of the sort of glorification of the savage life which is to be described below. Eichoff, remarking that " the pictures of the Hyperboreans lingered long in the Greek imagination," suggests that the ideas and feelings which had grown up with reference to them were simply transferred later to an actual and not wholly unknown race, the Scythians; and this transfer he believes to have been made first by the historian Ephorus, who flourished in the early fourth century B. C. and was a pupil of the rhetorician Isocrates. This theory of the origin of the idealization of the savage does not seem very probable, especially in so far as it relates to the Hyperboreans, for, unlike that mythical people, the Scythians were essentially 'hard' savages, and the usual pictures of the two are highly dissimilar. The idealization of the Scythians seems to have had earlier and deeper roots in Greek tradition; in fact, the primitivistic form of exoticism may be said to start with the author of the *Iliad* or with the state of mind that he reflects. He is manifestly inclined to believe that the most remote peoples must be the best. The epithet for the Ethiopians, for example, is "blameless," and the Ethiopians were the inhabitants of Homer's farthest south. But there was another distant folk upon whom he bestowed a still more eulogistic epithet. In *Iliad*, XIII, 3 f., Zeus, turning his weary eyes from the scenes of violence upon the plains of Troy, beholds, far to the north, the land of "the noble mare-milkers and the milk-drinking Abioi, the most righteous of men." The general region suggested, and the epithets, seem early to have led to the identification of these Hippemolgi and Galactophagi with the nomadic horse-breeding Scythians of the steppes between the Carpathians and the Don. This identification already appears in Hesiodic writings cited by Strabo (VII, 300 and 302); and·in Aeschylus, *Prometheus Unbound* (*Fragm.* 196).

Thus, as Riese was seemingly the first to point out, these lines of the *Iliad* appear to be the probable "source of the later romantic glorification of the Scythians and of the northern primitive peoples (*Naturvölker*) in general." It is apparently because of the remoteness of the antiquity to which we can thus trace the cult of the northern, if not exactly of the Nordic, that this fact seems significant to Riese; in relation to our theme it is of interest as showing that a 'hard' and rather extreme type of cultural primitivism had behind it, for the Greeks of the classical period, the authority of Homer. For the life of the Scythians was at least known to be quite unlike the life of Hesiod's Golden Race. Ephorus, however, though probably not the originator, was evidently recognized by subsequent Greek and Roman writers as one of the principal literary representatives of the belief in the exemplary virtues of the Scythians, and as one who spoke with especial authority on the subject because he had himself visited (or, at all events, was believed to have visited) that people. This is indicated by the passage in Strabo's *Geography*, VII, 302 (3, § 9), where "the fourth book of the *Europa* of Ephorus," who had "made a circuit of Europe even to the Scythians," is quoted as the principal source of Strabo's account of that race. Ephorus described the Scythians as vegetarians and (following Homer) as distinguished above other peoples for their justice; and he finds the reason for their virtues in the fact that they live a simple life and are free from cupidity, since they have all things in common, including wives and children. At the same time, they are immune against attacks by neighboring peoples, because they possess nothing which could arouse anyone's covetousness. This last seems a little unconvincing, since they possessed herds of horses, a very precious form of wealth among nomadic peoples.[1]

At least from the fourth century B. C. on, then, the Scythians apparently were to the ancients very much what the North American Indians were to the primitivists of the sixteenth to the eighteenth centuries in modern Europe — except that, if anything, they were somewhat more realistically depicted than the American aborigines were. In an ironic form, the theme appears in the comic writers, e. g. in Antiphanes, a poet of the Middle Comedy: " Are not the Scythians very wise, who give to new-born babes the milk of horses and cows to drink, but admit among them no evil-minded wet-nurses or schoolmasters? " [2] The same writer in a fragment, perhaps from a comedy about drunken wives: " Ill-starred the man who marries a wife — except among the Scythians. For there alone the vine grows not." [3]

The tendency to merge or confuse the Scythians with the Thracian Getae, and to ascribe to the latter many of the characteristics of the former (which is manifest in familiar passages of Horace and Virgil) appears first, Riese observes, in Posidonius; [4] and in this Stoic writer the contrast between the virtues of these savages and the degeneracy of the Greeks is first (so far as the evidence goes) pointedly drawn — though it is surely implicit in the passage from Ephorus.

The rôle of the Scythians in ancient cultural primitivism is, however, especially clear in writers of the late first century B. C. and the early first century A. D. Strabo, for example, does more than report the primitivism of Ephorus, over three centuries earlier; he makes it his own, and bears testimony to its prevalence among his contemporaries. Strabo is arguing on his own account that Homer (whose geographical attainments he always is eager to magnify) knew of the Scythians and that they *were* the " mare-milkers and milk-drinkers " to whom the poet referred. He continues: " And wherein is it to be wondered at that, because of the prevalence of injustice with respect to contracts among us, Homer called ' most just ' and ' proud ' those who live wholly without contracts and money-getting — who, rather, possess all things in common except sword and drinking-cup, and, above all, have their wives and children in common, after the Platonic

---

[1] What is probably the same passage of Ephorus is also cited by Nicolaus of Damascus (Müller, *Fragm. hist. graec.* III, 460, *Fragm.* 123) as Riese points out: *Die Idealisierung der Naturvölker des Nordens in der griechischen und römischen Literatur*, 1875.

[2] Cited by Riese, p. 21.

[3] Meineke-Bothe, *Poetarum comicorum fragmenta*, Paris 1855, p. 359.

[4] Cited in Strabo, VII, 296; p. 96.

manner? . . . And this assumption (of the goodness of the Scythians) still prevails among the Greeks; for we look upon them as the simplest (or most honest, ἁπλούστατοι) and least deceitful of men, far more frugal and self-sufficing (αὐταρκέστεροι) than we. For our mode of life has caused the deterioration of nearly all peoples, introducing among them softness (τρυφή) and the love of pleasure and evil arts (κακοτεχνίαι) and greed in its myriad forms. Much of this corruption has now reached even some of the nomadic barbarians; those who live near the sea (i. e. who can be reached by voyagers from civilized lands) have degenerated; they kill and rob strangers, have acquired through commerce with others desires for costly luxuries, and have become dishonest in their dealings. These things seem to contribute to more humane living, but they corrupt morals and introduce ποικιλία (complexity or subtlety) in place of the simplicity of which we have spoken." [5] Strabo adds, however, a shrewd comment on the roots in human nature of the general tendency which is now called exoticism, and on its relation to primitivism. " This belief about the nomads fits in with a certain common opinion amongst those of both earlier and later times — that the peoples who are most remote from other men are the milk-drinkers, the Abioi, the justest of mankind. It was no invention of Homer's." [6]

Though the Scythians were the commonest, they were not the only example cited by ancient writers of the superiority of the culturally primitive state. There was evidently a tendency to describe all savages as noble, even when there was abundant evidence to the contrary. But the various peoples who were held up as models to the ancient world and the various attitudes which writers took towards them will be shown in detail.

ISLANDS OF THE BLEST

The legend of the Islands of the Blest is of interest to us only in so far as it strengthened the belief that the life of the Golden Age continued to be lived in some part of the world. Its eschatological implications do not concern us. The accounts which we have of these islands are not based entirely upon mythology. The reports of voyagers to the Canary Islands, and possibly the Madeiras seem to have contributed certain details, as is apparent in the passage from Pliny quoted below (XI, 7). (Cf. Cary and Warmington, *The Ancient Explorers,* 1929, pp. 52-54.)

The Hesiodic version of the Golden Age legend (see No. II, 2, above) tells us that when Cronus was overthrown by Zeus, he was exiled to rule over the heroes in Elysium. This gave at least a literary reason for believing that if the Islands of the Blest could be found, one would find there the same conditions as prevailed on earth during the Age of Cronus.

The Elysian Fields in Homer are the dwelling place of heroes who are

[5] *Geogr.* 300-301.   [6] *Ibid.* 303.

preserved there in immortal life — that is, they are *translated* [7] there while still alive. Their dwelling is at the ends of the earth by the stream of Ocean. It is to the West. The life led there is peculiarly easy.

XI, 1. *Odyssey,* IV, 561-568.

> σοὶ δ' οὐ θέσφατόν ἐστι, διοτρεφὲς ὦ Μενέλαε,
> Ἄργει ἐν ἱπποβότῳ θανέειν καὶ πότμον ἐπισπεῖν,
> ἀλλά σ' ἐς Ἠλύσιον πεδίον καὶ πείρατα γαίης
> ἀθάνατοι πέμψουσιν, ὅθι ξανθὸς Ῥαδάμανθυς,
> τῇ περ ῥηίστη βιοτὴ πέλει ἀνθρώποισιν·
> οὐ νιφετός, οὔτ' ἂρ χειμὼν πολὺς οὔτε ποτ' ὄμβρος,
> ἀλλ' αἰεὶ Ζεφύροιο λιγὺ πνείοντος ἀήτας
> Ὠκεανὸς ἀνίησιν ἀναψύχειν ἀνθρώπους· [8]

O noble Menelaus, it is not your allotted fate to die and meet your end in horse-pasturing Argos; but the immortals will send you to the Elysian Field, to the boundaries of the earth, where is yellow-haired Rhadamanthus. There in truth is the easiest life for men. There is neither snow there nor long winter nor even rain, but Ocean ever sends forth the gently blowing breezes of Zephyr to refresh men. [9]

This is repeated by Pindar (*ca.* 520-*ca.* 440 B. C.).

XI, 2. Pindar, *Olymp.* II, 68-76.

> Ὅσοι δ' ἐτόλμασαν ἐστρὶς
> ἑκατέρωθι μείναντες ἀπὸ πάμπαν ἀδίκων ἔχειν
> ψυχάν, ἔτειλαν Διὸς ὁδὸν παρὰ Κρόνου τύρσιν·
> ἔνθα μακάρων
> νᾶσος ὠκεανίδες
> αὖραι περιπνέοισιν, ἄνθεμα δὲ χρυσοῦ φλέγει,
> τὰ μὲν χερσόθεν ἀπ' ἀγλαῶν δενδρέων, ὕδωρ
> δ' ἄλλα φέρβει,
> ὅρμοισι τῶν χέρας ἀναπλέκοντι καὶ στεφάνοις
> βουλαῖς ἐν ὀρθαῖσι Ῥαδαμάνθυος,
> ὃν πατὴρ ἔχει ⟨μέ⟩γας ἑτοῖμον αὐτῷ πάρεδρον. [10]

[7] On translation, see Rohde's *Psyche* (Eng. trans. by W. B. Hillis), New York and London, 1925, Ch. II. See the fate of Achilles in Plato's *Symp.* 179e, where translation is clearly opposed to death. For a humorous reference to translation, see the Platonic *Menexenus* 235c.

[8] Ed. Dindorf-Hentze, Leipzig, 1899.

[9] Rohde in his notes to the passage in which he quotes these lines justly compares them to the description of Olympus in *Od.* VI, 41-46. Compare this passage with a *Skolion* in Bergk's *Poet. lyr. graec.* III, 646-647.

> Φίλταθ' Ἁρμόδι', οὔ τί που τέθνηκας,
> νήσοις δ' ἐν μακάρων σέ φασιν εἶναι,
> ἵνα περ ποδώκης Ἀχιλεύς,
> Τυδεΐδην τέ φασιν ἐσθλὸν Διομήδεα.

Dearest Harmodius, you are not dead, but they say that you are in the Islands of the Blessed, where is Achilles fleet of foot, and noble Diomed, son of Tydeus.

[10] Ed. Sir J. Sandys, London, Loeb Lib. 1915.

But all those who, while remaining three times in either world, have had the endurance to keep their souls free from all sin, have completed the road of Zeus to the tower of Cronus, where the ocean breezes blow about the Islands of the Blest and flowers of gold are gleaming, some from landward on the glorious trees, and others the water nourishes, and they wreathe their hands with garlands and wear crowns of them in the righteous councils of Rhadamanthus, the ready counsellor of the great father.[11]

Pindar, however, makes no use of the idea of translation, and in other passages he speaks in similar terms of the life in the nether world, presumably the Elysian Fields.[12] So in later literature it is not uncommon to read of the Islands of the Blessed in terms like those used of the Christian Heaven. Thus Regilla, the wife of Herodes Atticus, in poetic fashion, is said to be dwelling there, nor is there any doubt of her death.

XI, 3. Marcellus, *Epigr. ad Regillam.*

$$αὐτὴ δὲ μεθ' ἡρῴνῃσι νένασται$$
$$ἐν μακάρων νήσοισιν, ἵνα Κρόνος ἐνβασιλεύει.^{13}$$

She dwells among the heroines in the Islands of the Blessed where Cronus is king.

Still later the idea of translation was forgotten, at least by some writers, for Servius in the fourth century of our own era, commenting on the words of Anchises to his son, to the effect that he does not live in Tartarus but in Elysium (*Aen.* V, 735), says that Elysium is where the souls of the virtuous live *post corporis animaeque discretionem*, and adds that, according to the philosophers, Elysium is the Fortunate Islands. And in *Aeneid,* VI, 637 ff. there is no suggestion of the *sedes beatae* being in the stream of Ocean. They are in the lower world.

Yet the belief that the Islands of the Blessed were real islands [14] is brought out by the story of Sertorius. He was reported by Plutarch to have thought of escaping to them after his military disappointments. But years before Plutarch, the same note is sounded in the sixteenth epode of Horace.

XI, 4. Horace, *Epod.* XVI, 40-end.

Nos manet Oceanus circumvagus; arva beata
Petamus, arva divites et insulas,
Reddit ubi cererem tellus inarata quotannis
Et imputata floret usque vinea,

[11] Cf. *Pyth.* II, 25; III, 94. It will be noted that the righteous go to the Islands of the Blessed in this passage. No moral prerequisites are mentioned by Homer.

[12] See *Fragm.* 129, 130, in the edition of Sandys (Loeb Lib.), p. 587 f.

[13] Kaibel, *Epigr. graeca* 1046, 8-9, Berlin, 1878.

[14] Heroes could be translated to other real islands. Thus Achilles, according to some legends, although translated, was not living in the Elysian Field but in Leuke, a shining island in the northern part of the Aegean. (For the classical references see Pauly-Wissowa, *Achilleus.*)

Germinat et numquam fallentis termes olivae,
  Suamque pulla ficus ornat arborem,
Mella cava manant ex ilice, montibus altis
  Levis crepante lympha desilit pede.
Illic iniussae veniunt ad mulctra capellae,
  Refertque tenta grex amicus ubera,
Nec vespertinus circumgemit ursus ovile,
  Neque intumescit alta viperis humus.
Pluraque felices mirabimur, ut neque largis
  Aquosus Eurus arva radat imbribus,
Pinguia nec siccis urantur semina glaebis,
  Utrumque rege temperante caelitum.
Non huc Argoo contendit remige pinus,
  Neque impudica Colchis intulit pedem;
Non huc Sidonii torserunt cornua nautae;
  Laboriosa nec cohors Ulixei.
Nulla nocent pecori contagia, nullius astri
  Gregem aestuosa torret impotentia.
Iuppiter illa piae secrevit litora genti,
  Ut inquinavit aere tempus aureum;
Aere, dehinc ferro duravit secula, quorum
  Piis secunda vate me datur fuga.[15]

The encircling stream of Ocean awaits us. Let us seek those fields, those blessed fields, and the Fortunate Islands, where the unplowed earth distributes the gifts of Ceres year by year, where the vine blooms untouched by the pruning knife; where the olive buds always ripen, and the dark fig adorns its tree, honey drips from the hollow oak, and from the high mountains the smooth stream trips down with plashing foot. There the goats unbidden come to be milked and the friendly ewe offers her heavy teats. The bear at evening never growls about the sheep-pen nor does the earth heave with vipers. Many other wonders we shall happily behold: watery Eurus never tears up the fields with his downpours nor are the rich seeds burned in the dry glebe; both rain and sun are tempered by the king of the gods. Thither the ship Argo never sailed, nor did the shameless Colchian set her feet there. Thither the Sidonian sailors never turned their prows nor the toiling companions of Ulysses. Disease never harms the flocks; no burning star ever ravages the herds. Jupiter hid those shores for virtuous folk, when he alloyed the golden age with bronze; with bronze, and then he hardened the ages with iron, but, as I prophesy, escape from them both is open to the virtuous.

According to this passage the Islands of the Blessed are identified with the Fortunate Islands. They are no longer miraculous but still provide a comfortable and easy life. Occasionally it rains but generally the weather is fair, and though the soil apparently is tilled, men live chiefly on spontaneous productions of earth, a kind of production practically the rule in the Golden Age.

---

[15] Ed. Paul Shorey, Boston, 1910.

That there was a more or less common belief in fertile lands in the Ocean is shown by the elder Seneca's first *Suasoria,* which is entitled: " Alexander considers whether he should sail the Ocean." This dates presumably from the early first century A. D. No indication is given of the authority for this belief nor are any reasons given in its support. In fact the text runs in part, *Facile ista finguntur quia Oceanus navigari non potest,* which shows that Seneca, or the person whom he is representing as the proponent of this part of the speech, did not hold with the current belief.

An account much like that of Horace is given by Plutarch in the *Life of Sertorius,* with the same emphasis upon the climatic features and the productivity of the soil.

XI, 5. Plutarch, *Sertorius,* VIII-IX, 571-572.

Ἐνταῦθα ναῦταί τινες ἐντυγχάνουσιν αὐτῷ, νέον ἐκ τῶν Ἀτλαντικῶν νήσων ἀναπεπλευκότες, αἳ δύο μέν εἰσι, λεπτῷ παντάπασι πορθμῷ διαιρούμεναι, μυρίους δ' ἀπέχουσι Λιβύης σταδίους, καὶ ὀνομάζονται Μακάρων. ὄμβροις δὲ χρώμεναι μετρίοις σπανίως, τὰ δὲ πλεῖστα πνεύμασι μαλακοῖς καὶ δροσοβόλοις, οὐ μόνον ἀροῦν καὶ φυτεύειν παρέχουσιν ἀγαθὴν καὶ πίονα χώραν, ἀλλὰ καὶ καρπὸν αὐτοφυῆ φέρουσιν, ἀποχρῶντα πλήθει καὶ γλυκύτητι βόσκειν ἄνευ πόνων καὶ πραγματείας σχολάζοντα δῆμον. ἀὴρ δ' ἄλυπος ὡρῶν τε κράσει καὶ μεταβολῆς μετριότητι κατέχει τὰς νήσους. οἱ μὲν γὰρ ἐνθένδε τῆς γῆς ἀποπνέοντες ἔξω βορέαι καὶ ἀπηλιῶται διὰ μῆκος ἐκπεσόντες εἰς τόπον ἀχανῆ διασπείρονται καὶ προαπολείπουσι, πελάγιοι δὲ περιρρέοντες ἀργέσται καὶ ζέφυροι, βληχροὺς μὲν ὑετοὺς καὶ σποράδας ἐκ θαλάττης ἐπάγοντες, τὰ δὲ πολλὰ νοτεραῖς αἰθρίαις ἐπιψύχοντες, ἡσυχῇ τρέφουσιν· ὥστε μέχρι τῶν βαρβάρων διῖχθαι πίστιν ἰσχυράν, αὐτόθι τὸ Ἠλύσιον εἶναι πεδίον καὶ τὴν τῶν εὐδαιμόνων οἴκησιν, ἣν Ὅμηρος ὕμνησε.

IX. Ταῦθ' ὁ Σερτώριος ἀκούσας, ἔρωτα θαυμαστὸν ἔσχεν οἰκῆσαι τὰς νήσους καὶ ζῆν ἐν ἡσυχίᾳ, τυραννίδος ἀπαλλαγεὶς καὶ πολέμων ἀπαύστων.[16]

[On the Iberian coast] some mariners newly arrived from the Atlantic Islands met him. These islands are two in number separated entirely by a narrow strait, and they are ten thousand stadia distant from Libya and are called the Islands of the Blessed. And even moderate showers fall there only rarely. For the most part they have gentle and dew-bringing winds, which not only render the soil good and rich for plowing and planting but make the islands bear spontaneously fruits in such abundance, and such sweetness as to feed the people in leisure without any toil on their part or trouble. And the air, which is never sharp, keeps the seasons temperate and preserves the islands from excessive change. For the north and east winds, blowing from off the land, become exhausted because of the distance they have travelled and are scattered over a wide extent and dispersed before arriving. And the north-west winds and west winds blowing from the deep bring slight periodic showers from the sea. They refresh the land with moist weather and gently nourish it, so that even among the barbarians it is an article of firm faith that there are the Elysian Fields and the abode of the blessed which Homer hymns.

When Sertorius heard these things he had a wonderful desire to

[16] *Vitae,* ed. Lindskog-Ziegler, Leipzig, vol. II, fasc. I, 1932.

inhabit the islands and to live in peace free from tyranny and never-ending wars.

When we return to the geographers we find Strabo (*ca.* 63 B. C.-*ca.* 19 A. D.) describing the Fortunate Islands in comments on the speech of Proteus to Menelaus as if identical with Elysium, whereas Pliny, plainly speaking of the same region, gives us an account which is far from attractive. In Strabo we read that the Islands of the Blest are still pointed out to us not far distant from the shores of Mauretania lying opposite Gades (Strabo, III, ii, 13).

Similarly we find the following passage:

XI, 6. Strabo, *Geogr.* I, i, 4-5.

Τῶν δ' ἑσπερίων ἀνδρῶν καὶ τὴν εὐδαιμονίαν ἐμφανίζει καὶ τὴν εὐκρασίαν τοῦ περιέχοντος, πεπυσμένος, ὡς ἔοικε, τὸν Ἰβηρικὸν πλοῦτον, ἐφ' ὃν καὶ Ἡρακλῆς ἐστράτευσε καὶ οἱ Φοίνικες ὕστερον . . . ἐνταῦθα γὰρ αἱ τοῦ ζεφύρου πνοαί, ἐνταῦθα δὲ καὶ τὸ Ἠλύσιον ποιεῖ πεδίον ὁ ποιητής, εἰς ὃ πεμφθήσεσθαί φησι τὸν Μενέλαον ὑπὸ τῶν θεῶν . . .

Καὶ αἱ τῶν μακάρων δὲ νῆσοι πρὸ τῆς Μαυρουσίας εἰσὶ τῆς ἐσχάτης πρὸς δύσιν, καθ' ὃ μέρος συντρέχει καὶ τῆς Ἰβηρίας τὸ ταύτῃ πέρας· ἐκ δὲ τοῦ ὀνόματος δῆλον ὅτι καὶ ταύτας ἐνόμιζον εὐδαίμονας διὰ τὸ πλησιάζειν τοιούτοις χωρίοις.[17]

And [Homer] brings out clearly the happiness of western men and the temperateness of the climate, having heard, it would seem, of the wealth of Iberia, for which Hercules made an expedition, as the Phoenicians did later, . . . For there are the breezes of Zephyr, and there the poet places the Elysium Fields, whither, he says, Menelaus will be sent by the gods. . . . And the Islands of the Blest are to the west of the most western parts of Mauretania, where the coast approaches that of Iberia. And from their name it is clear that they were called 'happy' because they were near to happy countries.

In Pliny (*ca.* 23-79 A. D.) the following description is given of the Fortunate Islands:

XI, 7. Pliny, *Nat. hist.* VI (202-205), 32 (37).

32. (37.) Sunt qui ultra eas Fortunatas putent esse quasdamque alias, quarum e numero idem Sebosus etiam spatia conplexus Iunoniam abesse a Gadibus DCCL p. tradit, ab ea tantundem ad ocasum versus Pluvialiam Caprariamque, in Pluvialia non esse aquam nisi ex imbribus; ab iis CCL Fortunatas contra laevam Mauretaniae in VIII horam solis, vocari Invallem a convexitate et Planasiam a specie, Invallis circuitu CCC p.; arborum ibi proceritatem ad CXL pedes adolescere. Iuba de Fortunatis ita inquisivit: sub meridiem positas esse prope occasum, a Purpurariis DCXXV p., sic ut CCL supra occasum navigetur, dein per CCCLXXV ortus petatur; primam vocari Ombrion nullis aedificiorum vestigiis, habere in montibus stagnum, arbores similes ferulae, ex quibus aqua exprima-

---

[17] Ed. Meineke, Leipzig, 1921, I.

tur, e nigris amara, ex candidioribus potui iucunda; alteram insulam Iunoniam appellari, in ea aediculam esse tantum lapide exstructam; ab ea in vicino eodem nomine minorem, deinde Caprariam lacertis grandibus refertam; in conspectu earum esse Ninguariam, quae hoc nomen acceperit a perpetua nive, nebulosam; proximam ei Canariam vocari a multitudine canum ingentis magnitudinis — ex quibus perducti sunt Iubae duo; apparent ibi vestigia aedificiorum — cum omnes autem copia pomorum et avium omnis generis abundent, hanc et palmetis caryotas ferentibus ac nuce pinea abundare, esse copiam et mellis, papyrum quoque et siluros in amnibus gigni; infestari eas beluis quae expellantur adsidue putescentibus.[18]

There are some who may think that beyond these [i. e. the Purple Islands] are the Fortunate Islands, and certain others, the number of which Sebosus relates as well as the distances, stating that Junonia is distant from Gades 750 miles. The same distance from it to the west lie Pluvialia and Capraria. In Pluvialia there is no water except from showers. Two hundred and fifty miles from these are the Fortunate Islands, opposite the left of Mauretania where the sun is in the eighth hour.[19] One is called Invallis from its convexity, and one Planasia from its appearance. Invallis has a circumference of three hundred miles. The trees grow there to a height of one hundred and forty feet. Juba has found out the following concerning the Fortunate Islands. They are situated in a nearly westerly direction 625 miles from the Purple Islands, so that one must sail west 250 miles, then they should be sought for 375 miles to the east.[20] The first is called Ombrios and has no trace of buildings: it has a lake in the mountains, trees like a tall cane from which water is pressed out, bitter from the black ones, from the whiter pleasant to drink. The other island is called Junonia, on which there is only a little temple built of stone. Near this is another island of the same name, then Capraria, full of great lizards. Within sight is Ninguaria, which takes this name from its perpetual snow, a foggy land. Next to it is Canaria, so called from the multitude of dogs of huge size, from which two were brought back to Juba. And there appear there traces of buildings. Although all the islands abound in many fruits and birds of all kinds, this one has an abundance of palms bearing caryotas as well as of pine nuts. And there is much honey there. And there are also papyrus in the rivers and the silurus [a fish]. They are also infested by decaying monsters which are continually cast up [on their shores].

There is surely little in this description which would lead one to identify the Fortunate Islands with Elysium or with any other place in which the life of the Golden Age survived. With the exception of the abundance of fruit trees, most of the details are repulsive — fog, snow, monstrous dogs,

---

[18] Ed. D. Detlefsen, Berlin, 1904, in the *Quellen und Forschungen zur alten Geschichte und Geographie*, ed. by W. Sieglin.

[19] This probably means " in the general direction of the position of the sun at two o'clock."

[20] This is obviously absurd. But there is no alternative reading to help us.

and decaying marine animals. Pliny's account, while retaining the eulogistic name of the islands, omits their utopian features. His point of view, however, is in general lost,[21] in spite of the fact that the medieval geographers follow him closely in most of their opinions. And when we turn to Isidore of Seville (ca. 570-636 A. D.) we find an account of the Islands which, although it denies that they are Paradise, yet asserts that they " produce all good things," *quasi felices et beatae fructum ubertate.*

XI, 8. Isidore, *Etymol.* XIV, vi, 8.

> Fortunatae insulae vocabulo suo significant omnia ferre bona, quasi felices, et beatae fructum ubertate. Suapte enim natura pretiosarum poma silvarum parturiunt. Fortuitis vitibus juga collium vestiuntur, ad herbarum vicem messis et olus vulgo est; unde gentilium error, et saecularium carmina poetarum, propter soli fecunditatem, easdem esse Paradisum putaverunt. Sitae sunt autem in Oceano contra laevam Mauritaniae, Occiduo proximae, et inter se interjecto mari discretae.[22]

The name of the Fortunate Islands signifies that they produce all good things, as if one should say Happy Isles, and are blest in the wealth of their fruits. For by their own nature they produce fruits of the most precious trees. The slopes of their hills are clothed in untended vines. Instead of weeds, there are crops and garden vegetables, whence the error of the Gentiles and of the pagan poets who in their songs identified them, because of the fecundity of the soil, with Paradise. Be that as it may, they are situated in the stream of Ocean to the left of Mauretania, nearest to the west, and are separated from one another by the sea.

In Plutarch Cronus is still dwelling in a mysterious island west of Britain near Calypso's Isle, Ogygia. This is not the land of the dead heroes, nor the dwelling place of noble savages, but a peculiarly marvelous place, in that the ruler of the Golden Age is still to be found there, and in the traditional softness of its life.

XI, 9. *De fac. in orb. lun.* XXVI, 26, a-c, e.

> ' Ὠγυγίη τις νῆσος ἀπόπροθεν εἰν ἁλὶ κεῖται,'
> δρόμον ἡμερῶν πέντε Βρεττανίας ἀπέχουσα πλέοντι πρὸς ἑσπέραν· ἕτεραι
> δὲ τρεῖς ἴσον ἐκείνης ἀφεστῶσαι καὶ ἀλλήλων πρόκεινται μάλιστα κατὰ δυσμὰς
> ἡλίου θερινάς· ὧν ἐν μιᾷ τὸν Κρόνον οἱ βάρβαροι καθεῖρχθαι μυθολογοῦσιν
> ὑπὸ τοῦ Διός, τὸν δ' ὡς υἱὸν ἔχοντα φρουρὸν τῶν τε νήσων ἐκείνων καὶ τῆς
> θαλάττης, ἣν Κρόνιον πέλαγος ὀνομάζουσι, πέραν κατῳκίσθαι. τὴν δὲ μεγάλην
> ἤπειρον, ὑφ' ἧς ἡ μεγάλη περιέχεται κύκλῳ θάλαττα, τῶν μὲν ἄλλων ἔλαττον
> ἀπέχειν, τῆς δ' Ὠγυγίας περὶ πεντακισχιλίους σταδίους κωπήρεσι πλοίοις
> κομιζομένῳ· βραδύπορον γὰρ εἶναι καὶ πηλῶδες ὑπὸ πλήθους ῥευμάτων τὸ
> πέλαγος· τὰ δὲ ῥεύματα τὴν μεγάλην ἐξιέναι γῆν καὶ γίγνεσθαι προσχώσεις

---

[21] It is retained by Ptolemy who notes the existence of the Fortunate Islands but does not describe them. *Vide Geogr.* I, xi, 1; xii, 10; xiv, 7; IV, vi, 14 where he names six of them out of Pliny's seven—giving them the same names as in Pliny.

[22] Migne, *Patrologia Latina* (hereafter *MPL*), LXXII, 514.

ἀπ' αὐτῶν καὶ βαρεῖαν εἶναι καὶ γεώδη τὴν θάλατταν, ᾗ καὶ πεπηγέναι δόξαν
ἔσχε. τῆς δ' ἠπείρου τὰ πρὸς τῇ θαλάττῃ κατοικεῖν Ἕλληνας περὶ κόλπον
οὐκ ἐλάττονα τῆς Μαιώτιδος, οὗ τὸ στόμα τῷ στόματι τοῦ Κασπίου πελάγους
μάλιστα κατ' εὐθεῖαν κεῖσθαι· λαλεῖν δὲ καὶ νομίζειν ἐκείνους ἠπειρώτας μὲν
αὑτούς νησιώτας δὲ τοὺς ταύτην τὴν γῆν κατοικοῦντας, ὡς καὶ κύκλῳ περίρρυτον
οὖσαν ὑπὸ τῆς θαλάσσης· οἴεσθαι δὲ τοῖς Κρόνου λαοῖς ἀναμιχθέντας ὕστερον
τοὺς μεθ' Ἡρακλέους παραγενομένους καὶ ὑπολειφθέντας ἤδη σβεννύμενον
τὸ Ἑλληνικὸν ἐκεῖ καὶ κρατούμενον γλώττῃ τε βαρβαρικῇ καὶ νόμοις καὶ
διαίταις οἷον ἀναζωπυρῆσαι πάλιν ἰσχυρὸν καὶ πολὺ γενόμενον· διὸ τιμὰς
ἔχειν πρώτας τὸν Ἡρακλέα, δευτέρας δὲ τὸν Κρόνον. . . . ἐξεῖναι μὲν γὰρ
ἀποπλεῖν οἴκαδε τοὺς τῷ θεῷ τὰ τρὶς δέκ' ἔτη συλλατρεύσαντας, αἱρεῖσθαι
δὲ τοὺς πλείστους ἐπιεικῶς αὐτόθι κατοικεῖν, τοὺς μὲν ὑπὸ συνηθείας, τοὺς
δ' ὅτι πόνου δίχα καὶ πραγμάτων ἄφθονα πάρεστι πάντα, πρὸς θυσίαις καὶ
χορηγίαις ἢ περὶ λόγους τινὰς ἀεὶ καὶ φιλοσοφίαν διατρίβουσι. θαυμαστὴν
γὰρ εἶναι τῆς τε νήσου τὴν φύσιν καὶ τὴν πραότητα τοῦ περιέχοντος ἀέρος,
ἐνίοις δὲ καὶ τὸ θεῖον ἐμποδὼν γίγνεσθαι διανοηθεῖσιν ἀποπλεῖν ὥσπερ συνήθεσι
καὶ φίλοις ἐπιδεικνύμενον· οὐκ ὄναρ γὰρ μόνον οὐδὲ διὰ συμβόλων, ἀλλὰ
καὶ φανερῶς ἐντυγχάνειν πολλοὺς ὄψεσι δαιμόνων καὶ φωναῖς. αὐτὸν μὲν γὰρ
τὸν Κρόνον ἐν ἄντρῳ βαθεῖ περιέχεσθαι πέτρας χρυσοειδοῦς καθεύδοντα, τὸν
γὰρ ὕπνον αὐτῷ μεμηχανῆσθαι δεσμὸν ὑπὸ τοῦ Διός, ὄρνιθας δὲ τῆς πέτρας
κατὰ κορυφὴν εἰσπετομένους ἀμβροσίαν ἐπιφέρειν αὐτῷ, καὶ τὴν νῆσον εὐωδίᾳ
κατέχεσθαι πᾶσαν, ὥσπερ ἐκ πηγῆς σκιδναμένη τῆς πέτρας.[23]

" A certain island, Ogygia, lies far off in the sea," distant about
five days from Britain sailing to the west. And three others placed
at equal distance from it and from one another, lie rather towards
the spot where the sun sets in summer. In one of these the barbarians relate that Cronus was imprisoned by Zeus, and that he
[Zeus], as his son who has the guardianship both of these islands
and of the sea, which they name the Cronian sea, dwells opposite.
And the great continent, by which the great sea is surrounded in a
circle, is less distant from the others, but from Ogygia about five
thousand stadia to one journeying in a boat with oars. For the sea
is slow to pass and muddy from the multitude of streams. And the
streams come down from the great continent and banks of mud are
produced from them, and the sea is thick and earthy, and this gave
rise to the opinion that it was frozen. Now the part of the continent towards the sea is inhabited by Greeks about a bay not smaller
than the Maeotic, the mouth of which lies in a fairly straight line
from the mouth of the Caspian Sea. And they call and name themselves the inhabitants of the continent, and the inhabitants of this
land, "islanders," as though they lived in a land which the sea
encircled. And they think that, mingling with the people of Cronus,
the people who came earlier with Hercules and were left behind by
him, revived the Greek people there well-nigh extinct and oppressed
by barbarian tongue and laws and ways of living, so that it was
revived again and was strong and numerous. Therefore they give
first honors to Hercules and second to Cronus.

(Here follows a description of their ritualistic voyages to the island of
Cronus.)

[23] Ed. G. N. Bernardakis, Leipzig, 1893, vol. V.

Though they may sail homeward after having served the god thirty years, most of them prefer to dwell there quietly, some from habit, but some because without toil there is an abundance of things both for sacrifices and festivals, to permit them to pass their time in discourse and philosophizing. For the nature of the island is wonderful, as well as the mildness of the climate, and to some wishing to set sail the god has intervened, appearing as to companions and friends. Not only in dreams and symbols, but also many have met him openly before their eyes and ears through *daimones*. For Cronus himself is there in a deep cave of a gold-like rock sleeping, for sleep has been devised as his fetters by Zeus; and there are birds upon the rock which fly down to bring him ambrosia, and the whole island is pervaded with fragrance, rising from the rock as from a fountain.

Like many another legend, this one of the Fortunate Islands suffered ridicule at the hands of Lucian. The vagabond adventurers of his *True History* touch upon the Island of the Blest — one island rather than many. It is bathed in atmospheric perfume compounded of the scent of many flowers.[24] It has many calm harbors and calm rivers. Soft breezes blow there and the inhabitants dance and sing to flutes and harps.

XI, 10. Lucian, *Verae narrationes,* II, 4-16 (Translation on p. 301).

μετ' ὀλίγον δὲ πολλαὶ νῆσοι ἐφαίνοντο, πλησίον μὲν ἐξ ἀριστερῶν ἡ Φελλώ, ἐς ἣν ἐκεῖνοι ἔσπευδον, πόλις ἐπὶ μεγάλου καὶ στρογγύλου φελλοῦ κατοικου-μένη· πόρρωθεν δὲ καὶ μᾶλλον ἐν δεξιᾷ πέντε μέγισται καὶ ὑψηλόταται, καὶ πῦρ πολὺ ἀπ' αὐτῶν ἀνεκαίετο, κατὰ δὲ τὴν πρῷραν μία πλατεῖα καὶ ταπεινή, σταδίους ἀπέχουσα οὐκ ἐλάττους πεντακοσίων. ἤδη δὲ πλησίον ἦμεν, καὶ θαυμαστή τις αὔρα περιέπνευσεν ἡμᾶς, ἡδεῖα καὶ εὐώδης, οἵαν φησὶν ὁ συγ-γραφεὺς Ἡρόδοτος ἀπόζειν τῆς εὐδαίμονος Ἀραβίας. οἷον γὰρ ἀπὸ ῥόδων καὶ ναρκίσσων καὶ ὑακίνθων καὶ κρίνων καὶ ἴων, ἔτι δὲ μυρρίνης καὶ δάφνης καὶ ἀμπελάνθης, τοιοῦτον ἡμῖν τὸ ἡδὺ προσέβαλλεν. ἡσθέντες δὲ τῇ ὀσμῇ καὶ χρηστὰ ἐκ μακρῶν πόνων ἐλπίσαντες κατ' ὀλίγον ἤδη πλησίον τῆς νήσου ἐγινόμεθα. ἔνθα δὴ καὶ καθεωρῶμεν λιμένας τε πολλοὺς περὶ πᾶσαν ἀκλύστους καὶ μεγάλους, ποταμούς τε διαυγεῖς ἐξιέντας ἠρέμα εἰς τὴν θάλασσαν, ἔτι δὲ λειμῶνας καὶ ὕλας καὶ ὄρνεα μουσικά, τὰ μὲν ἐπὶ τῶν ἠόνων ᾄδοντα, πολλὰ δὲ καὶ ἐπὶ τῶν κλάδων· ἀήρ τε κοῦφος καὶ εὔπνους περιεκέχυτο τὴν χώραν· καὶ αὖραι δέ τινες ἡδεῖαι πνέουσαι ἠρέμα τὴν ὕλην διεσάλευον, ὥστε καὶ ἀπὸ τῶν κλάδων κινουμένων τερπνὰ καὶ συνεχῆ μέλη ἀπεσυρίζετο, ἐοικότα τοῖς ἐπ' ἐρημίας αὐλήμασι τῶν πλαγίων αὐλῶν. καὶ μὴν καὶ βοὴ σύμμικτος ἠκούετο ἄθρους, οὐ θορυβώδης, ἀλλ' οἵα γένοιτ' ἂν ἐν συμποσίῳ, τῶν μὲν αὐλούντων, τῶν δὲ ἐπαδόντων, ἐνίων δὲ κροτούντων πρὸς αὐλὸν ἢ κιθάραν. τούτοις ἅπασι κηλούμενοι κατήχθημεν, ὁρμίσαντες δὲ τὴν ναῦν ἀπεβαίνομεν, τὸν Σκίνθαρον ἐν αὐτῇ καὶ δύο τῶν ἑταίρων ἀπολιπόντες. προϊόντες δὲ διὰ λειμῶνος εὐανθοῦς ἐντυγχάνομεν τοῖς φρουροῖς καὶ περιπόλοις, οἱ δὲ δήσαντες ἡμᾶς ῥοδίνοις στεφάνοις — οὗτος γὰρ μέγιστος παρ' αὐτοῖς δεσμός ἐστιν — ἀνῆγον ὡς τὸν ἄρχοντα, παρ' ὧν δὴ καθ' ὁδὸν ἠκούσαμεν ὡς ἡ μὲν νῆσος εἴη τῶν Μακάρων προσαγορευομένη, ἄρχος δὲ ὁ Κρὴς Ῥαδάμανθυς. . . . τέταρτοι δὲ ἡμεῖς προσήχθημεν· καὶ ὁ μέν ἤρετο τί παθόντες ἔτι ζῶντες ἱεροῦ χωρίου ἐπι-

---

[24] Cf. selection from Pindar, No. XI, 2, above, and the description of the Isle of Cronus, from Plutarch, No. XI, 9.

βαίημεν· ἡμεῖς δὲ πάντα ἑξῆς διηγησάμεθα. οὕτω δὴ μεταστησάμενος ἡμᾶς
ἐπὶ πολὺν χρόνον ἐσκέπτετο καὶ τοῖς συνέδροις ἐκοινοῦτο περὶ ἡμῶν. συν-
ήδρευον δὲ ἄλλοι τε πολλοὶ καὶ Ἀριστείδης ὁ δίκαιος ὁ Ἀθηναῖος. ὡς δὲ
ἔδοξεν αὐτῷ, ἀπεφήναντο, τῆς μὲν φιλοπραγμοσύνης καὶ τῆς ἀποδημίας,
ἐπειδὰν ἀποθάνωμεν, δοῦναι τὰς εὐθύνας, τὸ δὲ νῦν ῥητὸν χρόνον μείναντας
ἐν τῇ νήσῳ καὶ συνδιαιτηθέντας τοῖς ἥρωσιν ἀπελθεῖν. ἔταξαν δὲ καὶ τὴν προ-
θεσμίαν τῆς ἐπιδημίας μὴ πλέον μηνῶν ἑπτά.

τοὐντεῦθεν αὐτομάτων ἡμῖν τῶν στεφάνων περιρρυέντων ἐλελύμεθα καὶ εἰς
τὴν πόλιν ἠγόμεθα καὶ εἰς τὸ τῶν Μακάρων συμπόσιον. αὐτὴ μὲν οὖν ἡ πόλις
πᾶσα χρυσῆ, τὸ δὲ τεῖχος περίκειται σμαράγδινον· πύλαι δέ εἰσιν ἑπτά, πᾶσαι
μονόξυλοι κινναμώμιναι· τὸ μέντοι ἔδαφος τὸ τῆς πόλεως καὶ ἡ ἐντὸς τοῦ
τείχους γῆ ἐλεφαντίνη· ναοὶ δὲ πάντων θεῶν βηρύλλου λίθου ᾠκοδομημένοι,
καὶ βωμοὶ ἐν αὐτοῖς μέγιστοι μονόλιθοι ἀμεθύστινοι, ἐφ' ὧν ποιοῦσι τὰς
ἑκατόμβας. περὶ δὲ τὴν πόλιν ῥεῖ ποταμὸς μύρου τοῦ καλλίστου, τὸ πλάτος
πήχεων ἑκατὸν βασιλικῶν, βάθος δὲ ⟨πέντε⟩, ὥστε νεῖν εὐμαρῶς. λουτρὰ
δέ ἐστιν αὐτοῖς οἶκοι μεγάλοι ὑάλινοι, τῷ κινναμώμῳ ἐγκαιόμενοι· ἀντὶ μέντοι
τοῦ ὕδατος ἐν ταῖς πυέλοις δρόσος θερμή ἐστιν. ἐσθῆτι δὲ χρῶνται ἀραχνίοις
λεπτοῖς, πορφυροῖς. αὐτοὶ δὲ σώματα μὲν οὐκ ἔχουσιν, ἀλλ' ἀναφεῖς καὶ
ἄσαρκοί εἰσιν, μορφὴν δὲ καὶ ἰδέαν μόνην ἐμφαίνουσιν, καὶ ἀσώματοι ὄντες
ὅμως συνεστᾶσιν καὶ κινοῦνται καὶ φρονοῦσι καὶ φωνὴν ἀφιᾶσιν, καὶ ὅλως
ἔοικε γυμνή τις ἡ ψυχὴ αὐτῶν περιπολεῖν τὴν τοῦ σώματος ὁμοιότητα περι-
κειμένη· εἰ γοῦν μὴ ἅψαιτό τις, οὐκ ἂν ἐξελέγξειε μὴ εἶναι σῶμα τὸ ὁρώμενον·
εἰσὶ γὰρ ὥσπερ σκιαὶ ὀρθαί, οὐ μέλαιναι. γηράσκει δὲ οὐδείς, ἀλλ' ἐφ' ἧς
ἂν ἡλικίας ἔλθῃ παραμένει. οὐ μὴν οὐδὲ νὺξ παρ' αὐτοῖς γίνεται, οὐδὲ ἡμέρα
πάνυ λαμπρά· καθάπερ δὲ τὸ λυκαυγὲς ἤδη πρὸς ἕω, μηδέπω ἀνατείλαντος
ἡλίου, τοιοῦτο φῶς ἐπέχει τὴν γῆν. καὶ μέντοι καὶ ὥραν μίαν ἴσασιν τοῦ
ἔτους· αἰεὶ γὰρ παρ' αὐτοῖς ἔαρ ἐστὶ καὶ εἷς ἄνεμος πνεῖ παρ' αὐτοῖς ὁ ζέφυρος.
ἡ δὲ χώρα πᾶσι μὲν ἄνθεσιν, πᾶσι δὲ φυτοῖς ἡμέροις τε καὶ σκιεροῖς τέθηλεν·
αἱ μὲν γὰρ ἄμπελοι δωδεκάφοροί εἰσιν καὶ κατὰ μῆνα ἕκαστον καρποφοροῦσιν·
τὰς δὲ ῥοιὰς καὶ τὰς μηλέας καὶ τὴν ἄλλην ὀπώραν ἔλεγον εἶναι τρισκαι-
δεκάφορον· ἑνὸς γὰρ μηνὸς τοῦ παρ' αὐτοῖς Μινῴου δὶς καρποφορεῖν· ἀντὶ
δὲ πυροῦ οἱ στάχυες ἄρτον ἕτοιμον ἐπ' ἄκρων φύουσιν ὥσπερ μύκητας. πηγαὶ
δὲ περὶ τὴν πόλιν ὕδατος μὲν πέντε καὶ ἑξήκοντα καὶ τριακόσιαι, μέλιτος δὲ
ἄλλαι τοσαῦται, μύρου δὲ πεντακόσιαι, μικρότεραι μέντοι αὗται, καὶ ποταμοὶ
γάλακτος ἑπτὰ καὶ οἴνου ὀκτώ.

τὸ δὲ συμπόσιον ἔξω τῆς πόλεως πεποίηνται ἐν τῷ Ἠλυσίῳ καλουμένῳ
πεδίῳ· λειμὼν δέ ἐστιν κάλλιστος καὶ περὶ αὐτὸν ὕλη παντοία πυκνή, ἐπι-
σκιάζουσα τοὺς κατακειμένους. καὶ στρωμνὴν μὲν ἐκ τῶν ἀνθῶν ὑποβέβληνται,
διακονοῦνται δὲ καὶ παραφέρουσιν ἕκαστα οἱ ἄνεμοι πλήν γε τοῦ οἰνοχοεῖν·
τούτου γὰρ οὐδὲν δέονται, ἀλλ' ἔστι δένδρα περὶ τὸ συμπόσιον ὑάλινα μεγάλα
τῆς διαυγεστάτης ὑάλου, καὶ καρπός ἐστι τῶν δένδρων τούτων ποτήρια παντοῖα
καὶ τὰς κατασκευὰς καὶ τὰ μεγέθη. ἐπειδὰν οὖν παρίῃ τις ἐς τὸ συμπόσιον,
τρυγήσας ἓν ἢ καὶ δύο τῶν ἐκπωμάτων παρατίθεται, τὰ δὲ αὐτίκα οἴνου πλήρη
γίνεται. οὕτω μὲν πίνουσιν, ἀντὶ δὲ τῶν στεφάνων αἱ ἀηδόνες καὶ τὰ ἄλλα
τὰ μουσικὰ ὄρνεα ἐκ τῶν πλησίον λειμώνων τοῖς στόμασιν ἀνθολογοῦντα
καταψιφεῖ αὐτοὺς μετ' ᾠδῆς ὑπερπετόμενα. καὶ μὴν καὶ μυρίζονται ὧδε·
νεφέλαι πυκναὶ ἀναπάσασαι μύρον ἐκ τῶν πηγῶν καὶ τοῦ ποταμοῦ καὶ
ἐπιστᾶσαι ὑπὲρ τὸ συμπόσιον ἠρέμα τῶν ἀνέμων ὑποθλιβόντων ὕουσι λεπτὸν
ὥσπερ δρόσον. ἐπὶ δὲ τῷ δείπνῳ μουσικῇ τε καὶ ᾠδαῖς σχολάζουσιν· ᾄδεται
δὲ αὐτοῖς τὰ Ὁμήρου ἔπη μάλιστα· καὶ αὐτὸς δὲ πάρεστι καὶ συνευωχεῖται
αὐτοῖς ὑπὲρ τὸν Ὀδυσσέα κατακείμενος. οἱ μὲν οὖν χοροὶ ἐκ παίδων εἰσὶν
καὶ παρθένων· ἐξάρχουσι δὲ καὶ συνᾴδουσιν Εὔνομός τε ὁ Λοκρὸς καὶ Ἀρίων
ὁ Λέσβιος καὶ Ἀνακρέων καὶ Στησίχορος· καὶ γὰρ τοῦτον παρ' αὐτοῖς

ἐθεασάμην, ἤδη τῆς Ἑλένης αὐτῷ διηλλαγμένης. ἐπειδὰν δὲ οὗτοι παύσωνται
ᾄδοντες, δεύτερος χορὸς παρέρχεται ἐκ κύκνων καὶ χελιδόνων καὶ ἀηδόνων.
ἐπειδὰν δὲ καὶ οὗτοι ᾄσωσιν, τότε ἤδη πᾶσα ἡ ὕλη ἐπαυλεῖ τῶν ἀνέμων
καταρχόντων. μέγιστον δὲ δὴ πρὸς εὐφροσύνην ἐκεῖνο ἔχουσιν· πηγαί εἰσι
δύο παρὰ τὸ συμπόσιον, ἡ μὲν γέλωτος, ἡ δὲ ἡδονῆς· ἐκ τούτων ἑκατέρας
πάντες ἐν ἀρχῇ τῆς εὐωχίας πίνουσιν καὶ τὸ λοιπὸν ἡδόμενοι καὶ γελῶντες
διάγουσιν.[25]

A little further several islands appeared; close to us on the left
was Cork-land, to which they [the companions of the writer] were
hastening, a city founded on a great round cork. Farther on and
more to the right were five very large and lofty islands, and a great
fire was spouting up from them. And straight ahead lay one which
was broad and low, stretching out not less than sixty stadia. And
as we approached it a sort of wonderful breeze blew round us, sweet
and fragrant, such as the historian Herodotus says comes from
Arabia Felix. For as if it were the fragrance of roses and narcissi
and hyacinths and lilies and violets, even myrtle and laurel and the
wild vine, such was the sweetness that encompassed us. Delighted
with the perfume and hoping for a happy issue to our great labors,
we drew near to the island. Then we beheld many harbors, sheltered all around from the waves and very great, and clear rivers
flowing gently to the sea, and meadows also and groves and tuneful
birds, some singing on the shore, others on the branches of the
trees. And a light and fragrant air pervaded the countryside, and
sweet breezes blowing gently bent the trees, so that from the moving branches came the murmuring of joyful and unbroken song, like
the pipings in the wilderness of slanting flutes. And along with it
was heard mingled voices of a crowd, not tumultuous, but such as
would arise in a banquet, of flute players and of singers, and of some
who were applauding the flute players and the harpist. Charmed by
all this we approached the land and mooring the ship we landed,
leaving Scintharus in her and two companions.

Advancing through the flowery meadows we came upon the sentinels and patrols, and they, binding us with festoons of roses —
for these are their strongest chains — led us to the ruler, and from
them as we went along the road we heard that the island was called
the Island of the Blest, and its ruler the Cretan Rhadamanthus. . . .

We next were brought up. And he asked us what had happened
to us that we should enter upon the holy place while still alive. And
we straightway set forth all our adventures. And so, ordering us to
one side, he considered our case for a long time and communicated
with the council about us. And there were many councillors and
among them the Athenian, Aristides the Just. And it was his
opinion, and he so declared, it, that because of our curiosity and
travelling we should be punished when we died, but that now for a
specified time we should remain on the island and after dwelling for
a while with the heroes, we should go away. And he set the limit of
our stay at no more than seven months.

All at once our garlands fell off from us spontaneously and we were
freed, and we went into the city and to the banquet of the Blest.

[25] Ed. Nils Nilén, Leipzig, 1906.

Now the whole city is of gold and is surrounded by a wall of emerald.
And it has seven gates, each made of single planks of cinnamon wood.
The pavement of the city and the ground within the wall are of ivory.
The temples of all the gods are built of beryl stone, and the altars
in them are huge amethyst monoliths, on which they offer hecatombs.
Around the city flows a river of the finest perfume, a hundred royal
cubits broad and five deep, so that swimming is easy. The baths are
in great glass buildings heated with cinnamon wood. And instead
of water there is warm dew in the tubs. For garments they use fine
purple gossamer. They do not have bodies, but are intangible and
incorporeal, and they exhibit form and idea alone, and though
bodiless yet they stand and move and think and give voice, and their
naked souls seem to walk about wearing the likeness of a body.
Unless one should touch them, he would not know that what he saw
was not a body. For they are, as it were, shadows, upright and not
black. Nor does anyone of them grow old, but remains at the age at
which he came there. Nor have they any night nor bright day. But
the gray twilight just before dawn, when the sun is not yet up,
gives some such light on earth. They know, moreover, but one season
of the year. For it is always spring there. And one wind blows
among them, Zephyr. The country abounds in every flower and in
every cultivated shade tree. And the vines bear twelve times a year,
and each month they gather in the fruit. And they said that they
harvested the pomegranates and apples and the other fruits thirteen
times. For in one of their months, Minous, the fruit trees bear
twice. Instead of grain the wheat produces bread all made from the
ears, like mushrooms. And the springs of water about the city are
three hundred and sixty five, and the same number of springs of
honey, and five hundred of perfume, though less copious, and there
are seven rivers of milk and eight of wine.

The banquet place was situated outside the city in the plain called
Elysium. It is a very beautiful field, and every sort of tree grows
thickly around it, shading the reclining banqueters. And they lie
on couches of flowers, and they are served and waited upon by the
winds, except for the wine. For this they need no service; but
there are great trees about the banquet hall of the clearest crystal,
and the fruit of these trees is drinking cups of every type of shape
and size. And when anyone comes to the banquet place, he picks
one or two of the cups and sets them down and immediately they
become full of wine. Thus they drink. And instead of crowns the
nightingales and other singing birds, picking flowers with their beaks
from the surrounding meadows, as they fly about singing, send down
a snowfall of petals upon them. And they are perfumed in this way:
thick clouds draw up perfume from the springs and the river, and
standing over the banquet place let fall a gentle dew when lightly
pressed by the winds. During the meal they have leisure for music
and song. They especially like to hear the epics of Homer. And he
himself is present and dines with them, reclining at the place next
to Odysseus. The choruses are of boys and girls. And they are
trained and directed by Eunomus the Lochrian, Arion the Lesbian,
and Anacreon and Stesichorus. For he was seen among them, since
Helen had become reconciled with him. When these ceased singing,
a second chorus appeared, of swans and swallows and nightingales.

And when these had sung, then the whole wood began to murmur songs, conducted by the winds. And then they have the greatest source of merriment. There are two springs by the banquet place, one of laughter and one of pleasure. All drink from both of these in the beginning of the festivities, and the rest of the time they pass in pleasure and laughter.[26]

The Islands of the Blessed are peculiarly interesting because of the stimulus which they gave men in the late Middle Ages and early Renaissance to seek them. But there were other lands whose fertility was believed to be as miraculous and whose people as happy. When we omit from our discussion admittedly fictitious lands — like the Merope of Theopompus, where some of the features of the Golden Age survived — there is still a distinction to be made between the real and the imaginary peoples. In general we may say that in antiquity the imaginary lands and peoples were characterized by the features of soft primitivism, the real of hard.

IMAGINARY AND SEMI-IMAGINARY LANDS AND PEOPLES

The Land of the Cyclôpes

The earliest document to contribute to the legend of the *arva beata* peoples a miraculously fertile country with a race of bloodthirsty monsters. This is the land of the Cyclôpes in the *Odyssey*. The life of these monsters is undeservedly like life in the Hesiodic Golden Age — that is, it is a technological, juristic, and economic state of nature.

XI, 11. *Odyssey*, IX, 106-115, 125-135.

Κυκλώπων δ' ἐς γαῖαν ὑπερφιάλων ἀθεμίστων
ἱκόμεθ', οἳ ῥα θεοῖσι πεποιθότες ἀθανάτοισιν
οὔτε φυτεύουσιν χερσὶν φυτὸν οὔτ' ἀρόωσιν,
ἀλλὰ τά γ' ἄσπαρτα καὶ ἀνήροτα πάντα φύονται,
πυροὶ καὶ κριθαὶ ἠδ' ἄμπελοι, αἵ τε φέρουσιν
οἶνον ἐρισταφυλον, καί σφιν Διὸς ὄμβρος ἀέξει.
τοῖσιν δ' οὔτ' ἀγοραὶ βουληφόροι οὔτε θέμιστες,
ἀλλ' οἵ γ' ὑψηλῶν ὀρέων ναίουσι κάρηνα
ἐν σπέσσι γλαφυροῖσι, θεμιστεύει δὲ ἕκαστος
παίδων ἠδ' ἀλόχων, οὐδ' ἀλλήλων ἀλέγουσιν.

. . . .

οὐ γὰρ Κυκλώπεσσι νέες πάρα μιλτοπάρηοι,
οὐδ' ἄνδρες νηῶν ἔνι τέκτονες, οἵ κε κάμοιεν
νῆας ἐυσσέλμους, αἵ κεν τελέοιεν ἕκαστα
ἄστε' ἐπ' ἀνθρώπων ἱκνεύμεναι, οἷά τε πολλὰ
ἄνδρες ἐπ' ἀλλήλους νηυσὶν περόωσι θάλασσαν·
οἵ κέ σφιν καὶ νῆσον ἐυκτιμένην ἐκάμοντο.
οὐ μὲν γάρ τι κακή γε, φέροι δέ κεν ὥρια πάντα·
ἐν μὲν γὰρ λειμῶνες ἁλὸς πολιοῖο παρ' ὄχθας
ὑδρηλοὶ μαλακοί· μάλα κ' ἄφθιτοι ἄμπελοι εἶεν·

---

[26] This burlesque description should be compared with the comic fragments given above, Nos. II, 10, 11, 12, 13.

ἐν δ᾽ ἄροσις λείη· μάλα κεν βαθὺ λήιον αἰεὶ
εἰς ὥρας ἀμῷεν, ἐπεὶ μάλα πῖαρ ὑπ᾽ οὖδας.[27]

　　And we came to the land of the Cyclôpes, a froward and a lawless folk, who trusting to the deathless gods plant not aught with their hands, neither plough; but, behold, all these things spring for them in plenty, unsown and untilled, wheat, and barley, and vines, which bear great clusters of the juice of the grape, and the rain of Zeus gives them increase. These have neither gatherings for council nor oracles of law, but they dwell in hollow caves on the crests of the high hills, and each one utters the law to his children and his wives, and they reck not one of another. . . . The Cyclôpes have by them no ships of vermillion cheek, not yet are there shipwrights in the island who might fashion decked barques which should accomplish all their desire, voyaging to the towns of men (as oft times men cross the sea to one another in ships), who might likewise have made of their isle a goodly settlement. Yea, it is in no wise a sorry land, but would bear all things in their season; for therein are soft water-meadows by the shores of the grey salt sea, and there the vines know no decay, and the land is level to plough; thence might they reap a crop exceeding deep in due season, for verily there is fatness beneath the soil.[28]

　　In Plutarch (*Gryllus* 986 F) the land of the Cyclôpes is compared to Ithaca, as Nature is to Art, with preference given to the former.[29] This literary device enters Renaissance letters through the *Circe* of G.-B. Gelli, first published in 1549, a book frequently imitated in 16th and 17th century French literature.

The Hyperboreans

　　The legend of the Hyperboreans is almost as old as that of the Cyclôpes. We find them mentioned in the Homeric *Hymn to Dionysus* (*Hymns*, VII, 29) and they are reported by Herodotus (IV, 32) to have been dealt with by Hesiod and the author of the *Epigoni*.

　　The earliest document we have of any length on their customs comes to us from Pindar (*Pyth.* x), though we know from Himerius that Alcaeus (7th-6th c. B. C.) also mentioned them.[30] This passage shows that at the beginning of the fifth century this people was supposed to worship Apollo, to be fond of and gifted in music and the dance, free from disease, old age,

[27] Ed. Dindorf-Hentze, Leipzig, 1899.

[28] Tr. by Butcher and Lang.

[29] Cf. Strabo on the Albanians, XI, iv, 3, quoted below, No. XI, 52. Cf. XIII, 17, below.

[30] See Bergk, *Poet. lyr. graec.* III, 147 (ed. of 1914). It is worth observing that the Homeric *Hymn to Apollo* does not mention the god's relations with the Hyperboreans, though a great part of it deals with his fondness for Delos. The land of the Hyperboreans is used by Bacchylides (III, 58, ed. Jebb) as the Elysian Fields are used by others, an earthly Paradise to which deserving mortals are translated. This is a unique instance, according to Jebb.

toil and battle, and relatively inaccessible to ordinary means of transport. In other words, they enjoy the traditional blessings of the Golden Race.

XI, 12. Pindar, *Pythians*, X, 29-43.

> ναυσὶ δ' οὔτε πεζὸς ἰὼν ⟨κεν⟩ εὕροις
> ἐς Ὑπερβορέων ἀγῶνα θαυματὰν ὁδόν.
> παρ' οἷς ποτε Περσεὺς ἐδαίσατο λαγέτας,
> δώματ' ἐσελθών,
> κλειτὰς ὄνων ἑκατόμβας ἐπιτόσσαις θεῷ
> ῥέζοντας· ὧν θαλίαις ἔμπεδον
> εὐφαμίαις τε μάλιστ' Ἀπόλλων
> χαίρει, γελᾷ θ' ὁρῶν ὕβριν ὀρθίαν κνωδάλων.
> Μοῖσα δ' οὐκ ἀποδαμεῖ
> τρόποις ἐπὶ σφετέροισι· παντᾷ δὲ χοροὶ παρθένων
> λυρᾶν τε βοαὶ καναχαί τ' αὐλῶν δονέονται·
> δάφνᾳ τε χρυσέᾳ κόμας ἀναδήσαντες εἰλαπινάζοισιν εὐφρόνως.
> νόσοι δ' οὔτε γῆρας οὐλόμενον κέκραται
> ἱερᾷ γενεᾷ· πόνων δὲ καὶ μαχᾶν ἄτερ
> οἰκέοισι φυγόντες
> ὑπέρδικον Νέμεσιν.[31]

Going neither by ships nor on foot could you find the wonderful road to the councils of the Hyperboreans. Among them once Perseus, leader of the people, feasted, entering their dwellings, being there while they were sacrificing noble hecatombs of asses to the god.[32] Apollo never fails to enjoy their auspicious festivals and laughs as he sees the prancing restiveness of the beasts.

But the Muse is not absent from their lives; but on all sides choruses of maidens and the sound of lyres and the shrill voices of the flutes are heard. And with golden laurel they bind their hair and merrily make good cheer. Neither diseases nor destructive old age touch the sacred race, but far from toil and battle they dwell, fleeing severe Nemesis.[33]

The Hyperboreans are discussed by both Hellanicus and Herodotus in the fifth century. Hellanicus (450 B. C.) kept alive the tradition of their righteousness and certain other of their traits which were analogous to the traits of the Golden Race. He situates them beyond the Rhiphaean Mountains.

XI, 13. Hellanicus, *Fragm.* 96.

> Ἑλλάνικος ἐν ταῖς Ἱστορίαις ἔφη, τοὺς Ὑπερβορέους οἰκεῖν μὲν ὑπὲρ τὰ Ῥίπαια ὄρη, ἀσκεῖν δὲ δικαιοσύνην, μὴ κρεοφαγοῦντας, ἀλλ' ἀκροδρύοις χρωμένους.[34]

---

[31] Ed. Sir John Sandys, London, Loeb Lib. 1915.

[32] In the second century A. D. we find Antoninus Liberalis in the story of Cleinis maintaining that Apollo would not tolerate this sacrifice elsewhere. The story apparently goes back at least to Simnias, the Alexandrian poet. See Powell's *Collectanea alexandrina*, Oxford, 1925, p. 110, *sub* Simnias, *Fragm.* 2.

[33] For the happiness of the Hyperboreans as merely a literary figure, cf. Aeschylus, *Choephoroe*, 373.

[34] In Müller, *Fr. hist. graec.* I, 58.

Hellanicus in his *Histories* says that the Hyperboreans live beyond the Rhiphaean Mountains, and practice justice, eating no meat but living on acorns.[35]

Herodotus puts more information at our disposal. His account is peculiarly interesting in that it shows that even in his day the existence of this people could be doubted.

XI, 14. Herodotus, *Historiae*, IV, 32-36.

Ὑπερβορέων δὲ πέρι ἀνθρώπων οὔτε τι Σκύθαι λέγουσι, οὔτε τινὲς ἄλλοι τῶν ταύτῃ οἰκημένων, εἰ μὴ ἄρα Ἰσσηδόνες· ὡς δ' ἐγὼ δοκέω, οὐδ' οὗτοι λέγουσιν οὐδέν· ἔλεγον γὰρ ἂν καὶ Σκύθαι, ὃς περὶ τῶν μουνοφθάλμων λέγουσι. ἀλλ' Ἡσιόδῳ μέν ἐστι περὶ Ὑπερβορέων εἰρημένα, ἔστι δὲ καὶ Ὁμήρῳ ἐν Ἐπιγόνοισι, εἰ δὴ τῷ ἐόντι γε Ὅμηρος ταῦτα τὰ ἔπεα ἐποίησε· Πολλῷ δέ τι πλεῖστα περὶ αὐτῶν Δήλιοι λέγουσι, φάμενοι ἱρὰ ἐνδεδεμένα ἐν καλάμῃ πυρῶν, ἐξ Ὑπερβορέων φερόμενα ἀπικνέεσθαι ἐς Σκύθας. ἀπὸ δὲ Σκυθέων ἤδη δεκομένους αἰεὶ τοὺς πλησιοχώρους ἑκάστους, κομίζειν αὐτὰ τὸ πρὸς ἑσπέρης ἑκαστάτω ἐπὶ τὸν Ἀδρίην· ἐνθεῦτεν δὲ πρὸς μεσαμβρίην προπεμπόμενα πρώτους Δωδωναίους Ἑλλήνων δέκεσθαι· ἀπὸ δὲ τούτων καταβαίνειν ἐπὶ τὸν Μηλιέα κόλπον, καὶ διαπορεύεσθαι ἐς Εὔβοιαν· πόλιν τε ἐς πόλιν πέμπειν, μέχρι Καρύστου· τὸ δ' ἀπὸ ταύτης, ἐκλιπεῖν Ἄνδρον· Καρυστίους γὰρ εἶναι τοὺς κομίζοντας ἐς Τῆνον, Τηνίους δὲ ἐς Δῆλον· ἀπικνέεσθαι μέν νυν ταῦτα τὰ ἱρὰ οὕτω λέγουσι 'ἐς Δῆλον· πρῶτον δὲ τοὺς Ὑπερβορέους πέμψαι φερούσας τὰ ἱρὰ δύο κόρας, τὰς οὐνομάζουσι Δήλιοι εἶναι Ὑπερόχην τε καὶ Λαοδίκην· ἅμα δὲ αὐτῇσι ἀσφαλίης εἵνεκεν πέμψαι τοὺς Ὑπερβορέους τῶν ἀστῶν ἄνδρας πέντε πομπούς, τούτους οἳ νῦν Περφερέες καλέονται τιμὰς μεγάλας ἐν Δήλῳ ἔχοντες· ἐπεὶ δὲ τοῖσι Ὑπερβορέοισι τοὺς ἀποπεμφθέντας ὀπίσω οὐκ ἀπονοστέειν, δεινὰ ποιευμένους εἰ σφέας αἰεὶ καταλάμψεται ἀποστέλλοντας μὴ ἀποδέκεσθαι, οὕτω δὴ φέροντας ἐς τοὺς οὔρους τὰ ἱρὰ ἐνδεδεμένα ἐν πυρῶν καλάμῃ τοῖς πλησιοχώροις ἐπισκήπτειν κελεύοντας προπέμπειν σφέα ἀπὸ ἑωυτῶν ἐς ἄλλο ἔθνος· καὶ ταῦτα μὲν οὕτω προπεμπόμενα ἀπικνέεσθαι λέγουσι ἐς Δῆλον· . . . τὸν γὰρ περὶ Ἀβάριος λόγον τοῦ λεγομένου εἶναι Ὑπερβορέω οὐ λέγω, λέγων ὡς τὸν ὀϊστὸν περιέφερε κατὰ πᾶσαν τὴν γῆν οὐδὲν σιτεόμενος. εἰ δέ εἰσί τινες Ὑπερβόρεοι ἄνθρωποι, εἰσὶ καὶ ὑπερνότιοι ἄλλοι.[36]

Neither the Scythians nor any of the other tribes inhabiting these parts say anything about the Hyperboreans, except possibly the Issedonians. But I believe that not even they say anything. For the Scythians would have spoken of it, if they did, as they speak of the one-eyed men. But there is mention of the Hyperboreans in Hesiod and also in Homer in the *Epigoni,* if to be sure Homer really wrote them.[37]

The Delians have by far the most to say about them, relating that offerings wrapped in wheat straw were carried from the Hyperboreans and brought into Scythia. When they were received by the Scythians they were handed over to their immediate neighbors to be

---

[35] For justification of this rendering, see Hesiod, *Op. et d.* 230; Plato, *Rep.* II, 363 b. The diet of acorns is usually attributed to peoples exemplifying hard primitivism. See Juvenal, II, 39, and the section on the Arcadians below.

[36] Ed. J. W. Blakesley, London, 1854.

[37] The passages referred to are no longer extant.

passed westward until they reached the Adriatic. Thence they were sent southward, and the first Greeks to receive them were the Dodoneans. From them they descended to the Maliac Gulf and were brought over into Euboea. They were passed on from city to city, until they reached Carystos. The people of this city forwarded them, passing over Andros. For the Carystians brought them to Tenos and the Tenians to Delos. In such a manner, they say, these offerings reach Delos.

In the beginning the Hyperboreans used to send two maidens to bear the offerings, who the Delians say were named Hyperoche and Laodice. And along with them, to protect them, they sent five of their male citizens as escorts, and these are now called Perpherees and have great honors in Delos. And when they who had been sent out by the Hyperboreans failed to return, thinking that it would be terrible to be always liable to lose their envoys, the Hyperboreans wrapped their offerings in wheat straw and bore them to their frontiers and bade their neighbors forward them to another nation. And they say that when they were forwarded in this way they reached Delos. . . . I do not speak of the tale which is told of Abaris, who is said to have been a Hyperborean and to have gone round the whole earth on his arrow without food. But if there are Hyperborean men, there are others too who are Hypernotians.

His mild skepticism regarding the existence of the Hyperboreans did not encourage Herodotus to recount their manners and customs and the story of the passage of gifts to Delos is repeated with easily recognizable variations in later writers.

Hecataeus of Abdera is reported to have written a book entirely devoted to the Hyperboreans. Of this book we have only a few fragments, of which the following are the most important. It is questionable whether these should be called " fragments," since they are not quotations from this author but later accounts in indirect discourse of what he and " certain others " had to say.

It will be noted that the seat of this happy people was a matter of dispute. This passage locates it on an island — a favorite device of writers of imaginary and semi-imaginary voyages — an island which might be Great Britain or Iceland.[38] One of the usual features of the Golden Race is preserved, the fertility of the land and the favor of a god.

XI, 15. Diodorus Siculus, *Bibl. hist.* II, 47 (1st c. B. C.).

Ἡμεῖς δ' ἐπεὶ τὰ πρὸς ἄρκτους κεκλιμένα μέρη τῆς Ἀσίας ἠξιώσαμεν ἀναγραφῆς, οὐκ ἀνοίκειον εἶναι νομίζομεν τὰ περὶ τῶν Ὑπερβορέων μυθολογούμενα διελθεῖν. τῶν γὰρ τὰς παλαιὰς μυθολογίας ἀναγεγραφότων Ἑκαταῖος καί τινες ἕτεροί φασιν ἐν τοῖς ἀντιπέρας τῆς Κελτικῆς τόποις κατὰ τὸν ὠκεανὸν εἶναι νῆσον οὐκ ἐλάττω τῆς Σικελίας. ταύτην ὑπάρχειν μὲν κατὰ τὰς ἄρκτους, κατοικεῖσθαι δὲ ὑπὸ τῶν ὀνομαζομένων Ὑπερβορέων ἀπὸ τοῦ

---

[38] As will appear, most writers locate the Hyperboreans in the Far North—beyond the North Wind (Boreas). Posidonius Apamensis (*Fragm.* 90), however, puts them near the Italian Alps! See Müller's *Fr. hist. graec.* III, 290.

πορρωτέρω κεῖσθαι τῆς βορείου πνοῆς· οὖσαν δ' αὐτὴν εὔγειόν τε καὶ πάμφορον,
ἔτι δ' εὐκρασίᾳ διαφέρουσαν, διττοὺς κατ' ἔτος ἐκφέρειν καρπούς. μυθολογοῦσι
δ' ἐν αὐτῇ τὴν Λητὼ γεγονέναι· διὸ καὶ τὸν Ἀπόλλω μάλιστα τῶν ἄλλων
θεῶν παρ' αὐτοῖς τιμᾶσθαι· εἶναι δ' αὐτοὺς ὥσπερ ἱερεῖς τινας Ἀπόλλωνος
διὰ τὸ τὸν θεὸν τοῦτον καθ' ἡμέραν ὑπ' αὐτῶν ὑμνεῖσθαι μετ' ᾠδῆς συνεχῶς
καὶ τιμᾶσθαι διαφερόντως. ὑπάρχειν δὲ καὶ κατὰ τὴν νῆσον τέμενός τε
Ἀπόλλωνος μεγαλοπρεπὲς καὶ ναὸν ἀξιόλογον ἀναθήμασι πολλοῖς κεκοσ-
μημένον, σφαιροειδῆ τῷ σχήματι. καὶ πόλιν μὲν ὑπάρχειν ἱερὰν τοῦ θεοῦ τούτου,
τῶν δὲ κατοικούντων αὐτὴν τοὺς πλείστους εἶναι κιθαριστάς, καὶ συνεχῶς
ἐν τῷ ναῷ κιθαρίζοντας ὕμνους λέγειν τῷ θεῷ μετ' ᾠδῆς, ἀποσεμνύνοντας
αὐτοῦ τὰς πράξεις. ἔχειν δὲ τοὺς Ὑπερβορέους ἰδίαν τινὰ διάλεκτον, καὶ
πρὸς τοὺς Ἕλληνας οἰκειότατα διακεῖσθαι, καὶ μάλιστα πρὸς τοὺς Ἀθηναίους
καὶ Δηλίους, ἐκ παλαιῶν χρόνων παρειληφότας τὴν εὔνοιαν ταύτην. καὶ τῶν
Ἑλλήνων τινὰς μυθολογοῦσι παραβαλεῖν εἰς Ὑπερβορέους, καὶ ἀναθήματα
πολυτελῆ καταλιπεῖν γράμμασιν Ἑλληνικοῖς ἐπιγεγραμμένα. ὡσαύτως δὲ
καὶ ἐκ τῶν Ὑπερβορέων Ἄβαριν εἰς τὴν Ἑλλάδα καταντήσαντα τὸ παλαιὸν
ἀνασῶσαι τὴν πρὸς Δηλίους εὔνοιάν τε καὶ συγγένειαν. φασὶ δὲ καὶ τὴν
σελήνην ἐκ ταύτης τῆς νήσου φαίνεσθαι παντελῶς ὀλίγον ἀπέχουσαν τῆς γῆς
καί τινας ἐξοχὰς γεώδεις ἔχουσαν ἐν αὐτῇ φανεράς. λέγεται δὲ καὶ τὸν θεὸν
δι' ἐτῶν ἐννεακαίδεκα καταντᾶν εἰς τὴν νῆσον, ἐν οἷς αἱ τῶν ἄστρων ἀπο-
καταστάσεις ἐπὶ τέλος ἄγονται· καὶ διὰ τοῦτο τὸν ἐννεακαιδεκαετῆ χρόνον
ὑπὸ τῶν Ἑλλήνων Μέτωνος ἐνιαυτὸν ὀνομάζεσθαι. κατὰ δὲ τὴν ἐπιφάνειαν
ταύτην τὸν θεὸν κιθαρίζειν τε καὶ χορεύειν συνεχῶς τὰς νύκτας ἀπὸ ἰσημερίας
ἐαρινῆς ἕως πλειάδος ἀνατολῆς ἐπὶ τοῖς ἰδίοις εὐημερήμασι τερπόμενον.
βασιλεύειν δὲ τῆς πόλεως ταύτης καὶ τοῦ τεμένους ἐπάρχειν τοὺς ὀνομαζο-
μένους Βορεάδας, ἀπογόνους ὄντας Βορέου, καὶ κατὰ γένος ἀεὶ διαδέχεσθαι
τὰς ἀρχάς.[39]

Since we deemed the parts of Asia lying to the north worthy of
description, we do not think it unseemly to record what is said about
the Hyperboreans. For of those who have written about historical
legends [mythology], Hecataeus and certain others say that in the
regions beyond the Celtic territory is an island no smaller than
Sicily. This island lies towards the north and is inhabited by the
Hyperboreans, so-called from the fact that they live beyond the
North Wind. This island is fertile and all-productive and has so
excellent a climate that it produces two crops yearly. And they
relate how Leto was born there. Wherefore Apollo is held in honor
among them more than all the other gods. And they are, as it were,
priests of Apollo, because this god is hymned all day long by them
with song and highly honored. There are also on this island a magnificent precinct of Apollo and a temple worth mentioning, decorated
with many offerings and spherical in shape. And the city is sacred
to this god; and of those who inhabit it, most play the lyre and continually celebrate the god with hymn and song, glorifying his deeds.
And the Hyperboreans have their own peculiar dialect, and they are
well disposed to the Greeks, especially to the Athenians and Delians,
having inherited this feeling of good-will from olden times. For
they tell how certain Greeks landed among the Hyperboreans and
left rich offerings inscribed with Greek letters. Likewise Abaris,
coming down to Greece a long time ago, confirmed the good-will of

[39] Ed. Dindorf-Vogel, Leipzig, 1888, I, 244 f.

the Delians and their kinship (συγγένεια). They also say that the moon is clearly seen from this island very close to the earth, having earthy prominences plainly visible. And it is said that the god comes down to the island every nineteen years at the time when the revolution of the stars is completed, and on this account this nineteen year period is called the Metonic year by the Greeks. At the time of this epiphany the god plays the lyre and dances through the nights from the vernal equinox until the rising of the Pleiades,[40] rejoicing in the good times he has brought. And there reign over the city and tend the shrine the so-called Boreades, descendants of Boreas, who on account of their descent have always had the ruling power.

The musical gifts of the Hyperboreans are also emphasized in a passage from Aelian which reports Hecataeus as relating " many noble things " about them.

XI, 16. Aelian, *Historiae animalium,* XI, 1.

ἱερεῖς εἰσι τῷδε τῷ δαίμονι Βορέου καὶ Χιόνης υἱεῖς, τρεῖς τὸν ἀριθμόν, ἀδελφοὶ τὴν φύσιν, ἑξαπήχεις τὸ μῆκος. ὅταν οὖν οὗτοι τὴν νενομισμένην ἱερουργίαν κατὰ τὸν συνήθη καιρὸν τῷ προειρημένῳ ἐπιτελῶσιν, ἐκ τῶν 'Ριπαίων οὕτω καλουμένων παρ' αὐτοῖς ὀρῶν καταπέτεται κύκνων ἄμαχα τῷ πλήθει νέφη, καὶ περιελθόντες τὸν νεὼν καὶ οἱονεὶ καθήραντες αὐτὸν τῇ πτήσει, εἶτα μέντοι κατίασιν ἐς τὸν τοῦ νεὼ περίβολον, μέγιστόν τε τὸ μέγεθος καὶ τὸ κάλλος ὡραιότατον ὄντα. ὅταν οὖν οἵ τε ᾠδοὶ τῇ σφετέρᾳ μούσῃ τῷ θεῷ προσᾴδωσι καὶ μέντοι καὶ οἱ κιθαρισταὶ συγκρέκωσι τῷ χορῷ παναρμόνιον μέλος, ἐνταῦθά τοι καὶ οἱ κύκνοι συναναμέλπουσιν ὁμορροθοῦντες καὶ οὐδαμῶς οὐδαμῇ ἀπηχὲς καὶ ἀπῳδὸν ἐκεῖνοι μελῳδοῦντες, ἀλλὰ ὥσπερ οὖν ἐκ τοῦ χορολέκτου τὸ ἐνδόσιμον λαβόντες καὶ τοῖς σοφισταῖς τῶν ἱερῶν μελῶν τοῖς ἐπιχωρίοις συνᾴσαντες. εἶτα τοῦ ὕμνου τελεσθέντος οἱ δὲ ἀναχωροῦσι τῇ πρὸς τὸν δαίμονα τιμῇ τὰ εἰθισμένα λατρεύσαντες καὶ τὸν θεὸν ἀνὰ πᾶσαν τὴν ἡμέραν οἱ προειρημένοι ὡς εἰπεῖν χορευταὶ πτηνοὶ μέλψαντές τε ἅμα καὶ ᾄσαντες.[41]

The priests of this god are the sons of Boreas and Chione, three brothers, six cubits tall. Whenever they perform their customary religious ceremony at the usual time to the aforesaid god, clouds of swans fly down from the Rhiphaean Mountains, as they call them, without resistance into the throngs of people, circling round the temple, as if they were purifying it by their flight. Then they descend into the court-yard of the temple, which is very large and very beautiful to the eye. When the singers hymn the god in their song and the lute-players sing together in chorus their harmonious melodies, then the swans join with them in harmony, and they sing not discordantly nor unmelodiously but as if they were taking the pitch from the chorus-leader, and singing in tune with those of the natives most skilled in sacred melodies. Then when the hymn is over, they withdraw, having performed the customary rites in honor

---

[40] This probably refers to nothing more than that the sun shines all day for six months and disappears for six months in the Far North. See selection from Mela below.

[41] Ed. R. Hercher, Leipzig, 1864.

of the god, those winged choristers of whom we have spoken, who
have hymned and chanted the god all day long.[42]

Callimachus in his *Hymn to Delos* (280-299) tells the story of the
Hyperboreans sending gifts to Apollo in Delos wrapt in corn-stalks. His
route — from the Hyperboreans to Dodona, to Malis, to Euboea, to Delos —
differs from that of Herodotus, which is to Scythia, to the Adriatic, to
Dodona, to Malis, to Carystus in Euboea, to Andros, to Tenos, to Delos.
This route in Pausanias (I, 31, 2) is Arimaspi, Issedones, Sinope, through
Greece to Prasiae (in Attica), to Delos by the Athenians.[43]

The Hyperboreans were a long-lived race ($\pi o \lambda v \chi \rho o \nu \omega \tau a \tau o \nu$ $a l \mu a$) according to Callimachus (*Hymn to Delos,* 282), but their other admirable
features are omitted.

More details are given by Pomponius Mela (1st c. A. D.), who not only
re-emphasizes their goodness but adds their joyful suicide when they have
lived long enough.

XI, 17. Mela, *Chorographia*, III, 36-37.

Inde Asiae confinia nisi ubi perpetuae hiemes sedent et intole-
rabilis rigor. Scythici populi incolunt, fere omnes et in unum
Belcae adpellati. in Asiatico litore primi Hyperborei super aquilonem
Riphaeosque montes sub ipso siderum cardine iacent; ubi sol non
cotidie ut nobis sed primum verno aequinoctio exortus autumnali
demum occidit; ideo sex mensibus dies et totidem aliis nox usque
continua est. terra angusta aprica per se fertilis. cultores iustissimi
et diutius quam ulli mortalium et beatius vivunt. quippe festo
semper otio laeti non bella novere non iurgia, sacris operati maxime
Apollinis, quorum primitias Delon misisse initio per virgines suas,
deinde per populos subinde tradentes ulterioribus, moremque eum
diu et donec vitio gentium temeratus est servasse referuntur. habi-
tant lucos silvasque, et ubi eos vivendi satietas magis quam taedium
cepit, hilares redimiti sertis semet ipsi in pelagus ex certa rupe praecipites dant. id eis funus eximium est.[44]

In the confines of Asia there is nothing but unending winter and
unbearable cold. The Scythian peoples dwell there, almost all called
by the one name of Belcae. On the Asiatic shore the Hyperboreans
are first found, lying beyond the Northwind and beyond the
Rhiphaean mountains and under the very pole. There the sun does
not rise every day as among us, but having arisen first at the time
of the vernal equinox, it does not sink until the autumnal. Thus
there is a continuous day of six months and a night of another six.

---

[42] The singing of the swans in honor of Apollo reminds one of a poem by Alcaeus
(7th c. B. C.) recorded by Himerius (4th c. A. D.) in which nightingales and
swallows are the winged choristers. See Bergk, *Lyr. graec.* III, 147 (ed. of 1914).
This poem also associated Apollo with the Hyperboreans but in the account given of
it by Himerius says nothing of their life and customs.

[43] For the question of the diversities of route, see Frazer, *Pausanias's Description
of Greece*, London, 1898, II, 405 f.

[44] Ed. C. Frick, Leipzig, 1880.

The narrow sunny land is spontaneously fertile. The inhabitants are very just and live longer than any other mortals and more happily. In fact, always happy with festive leisure, they know neither wars nor altercation. They bestow particular pains upon the rites of Apollo. Their first fruits [45] they sent to Delos, in the beginning by their maidens, then by peoples who would deliver them over to more distant peoples, and this custom they are recorded as having observed until it was violated by human wickedness. They inhabit woods and groves; and when sufficiency of living rather than boredom has come upon them, laughingly they wreath their heads with garlands and throw themselves headlong into the sea from a certain rock. This is their strange funeral rite.

As time went on and the limits of the world were pushed back, the Hyperboreans were placed at a remoter distance. Nevertheless they were still believed to be a real people, and Pliny includes them in his geographical chapters along with known tribes. He adds nothing to the legends already in circulation, except to soften still more the condition of their life.

XI, 18. Pliny, *Nat. hist.* IV (89-91), 12 (26).

Pone eos montes ultraque Aquilonem gens felix (si credimus), quos Hyperboreos appellavere, annoso degit aevo, fabulosis celebrata miraculis. Ibi creduntur esse cardines mundi extremique siderum ambitus semenstri luce et una die solis aversi, non, ut imperiti dixere, ab aequinoctio verno in autumnum. semel in anno solstitio oriuntur iis soles, brumaque semel occidunt. regio aprica, felici temperie, omni adflatu noxio carens. domus iis nemora lucique, et deorum cultus viritim gregatimque, discordia ignota et aegritudo omnis. mors non nisi satietate vitae epulatis delibutoque senia luxu e quadam rupe in mare salientium. hoc genus sepulturae beatissimum. Quidam eos in prima parte Asiae litorum posuere, non in Europa, quia sunt ibi similitudine et situus Attacorum nomine. alii medios fecere eos inter utrumque solem, antipodum occasus exorientemque nostrum, quod fieri nullo modo potest tam vasto mari interveniente. qui alibi quam in semenstri luce constituere eos, serere matutinis, meridie metere, occidente fetus arborum decerpere, noctibus in specus condi tradiderunt. Nec licet dubitare de gente ea, tot auctores produnt frugum primitias solitos Delum mittere Apollini quem praecipue colunt. virgines ferebant eas hospitiis gentium per annos aliquot venerabiles, donec violata fide in proximis accolarum finibus deponere sacra ea instituere, hique ad conterminos deferre, atque ita Delum usque. mox et hoc ipsum exolevit. [46]

Beyond the mountains and on the other side of the North Wind [lives] a happy people, if we may believe [what we are told], called Hyperboreans. They live to an old age full of years, [47] famous for

---

[45] This is the first mention we find of the nature of their offerings. That they bore fruits is used by Porphyry (*De abstinentia*, II, 19) to indicate that in ancient times there were no blood sacrifices, though *primitiae* need not be confined to fruits.

[46] Ed. Detlefsen, Berlin, 1904.

[47] This apparently by Pliny's time had become a stock epithet. See Callimachus *Hymn to Delos*, 282.

legendary marvels. There are believed to be the hinges of the world.
and the farthest limits of the orbits of the stars. The sun there is
up for one day of six months' length, not, as the experts say, from
the vernal equinox to the autumn, but in the summer solstice their
sun rises and sets in the winter solstice. The region is sunny, of
happy climate, lacking all noxious winds. Their homes are groves
and woods, and the worship of the gods is carried on singly and in
groups. Discord is unknown as well as all forms of illness. When
they have had enough of life and their old age is weakened by high
living, they meet death by leaping from a certain rock into the sea.
This kind of sepulture is the most blessed.

Some place this people on the edge of Asia, not in Europe,
because there is a people there like them (and whose country is like
theirs) the Attaci by name. Others put them midway between both
suns, where the antipodal sun sets and ours rises. This is untenable,
so wide a sea lies in between. Those who place them elsewhere [48]
than in the six-months' day, relate that they sow in the morning,
reap at noon, gather the fruit of their trees at evening, and during
the night hide in caves. We may not entertain doubts about this
people, so many authors tell how they used to send their first fruits
to Delos to Apollo, whom they especially worship. Maidens brought
them — venerated as the guests of the peoples [along the route],
for many, many years, until, because of broken faith, the Hyperboreans began to lay their sacred offerings on the frontiers of their
nearest neighbors and these carried them to their neighbors and so
on to Delos. But soon this custom too was dropped.

The Hyperborean cult of Apollo was perhaps responsible for the legend
related by Pausanias that this people inaugurated the Delphic oracle.

XI, 19. Pausanias, *Graec. descr.* X, 5, 7-9.

ἤκουσα δὲ καὶ ὡς ἄνδρες ποιμαίνοντες ἐπιτύχοιεν τῷ μαντείῳ, καὶ ἔνθεοί τε
ἐγένοντο ὑπὸ τοῦ ἀτμοῦ καὶ ἐμαντεύσαντο ἐξ Ἀπόλλωνος. μεγίστη δὲ καὶ
παρὰ πλείστων ἐς Φημονόην δόξα ἐστίν, ὡς πρόμαντις γένοιτο ἡ Φημονόη
τοῦ θεοῦ πρώτη καὶ πρώτη τὸ ἑξάμετρον ᾖσεν. Βοιὼ δὲ ἐπιχωρία γυνὴ
ποιήσασα ὕμνον Δελφοῖς ἔφη κατασκευάσασθαι τὸ μαντεῖον τῷ θεῷ τοὺς
ἀφικομένους ἐξ Ὑπερβορέων τούς τε ἄλλους καὶ Ὠλῆνα· τοῦτον δὲ καὶ
μαντεύσασθαι πρῶτον καὶ ᾆσαι πρῶτον τὸ ἑξάμετρον. πεποίηκε δὲ ἡ Βοιὼ
τοιάδε·

ἔνθα τοι εὔμνηστον χρηστήριον ἐκτελέσαντο
παῖδες Ὑπερβορέων Παγασὸς καὶ δῖος Ἀγυιεύς.

ἐπαριθμοῦσα δὲ καὶ ἄλλους τῶν Ὑπερβορέων, ἐπὶ τελευτῇ τοῦ ὕμνου τὸν
Ὠλῆνα ὠνόμασεν·

Ὠλήν θ', ὃς γένετο πρῶτος Φοίβοιο προφάτας,
πρῶτος δ' ἀρχαίων ἐπέων τεκτάνατ' ἀοιδάν.

[48] We translate this as the latest editors give it. At the same time it should
be noted that this does not make sense. It would be better to read " qui non,"
" those who do not place them elsewhere than in the six-months' day," with Johan-
nes Cesarius in his edition of 1524, Cologne.

οὐ μέντοι τά γε ἥκοντα ἐς μνήμην ἐς ἄλλον τινά, ἐς δὲ γυναικῶν μαντείαν
ἀνήκει μόνων. ποιηθῆναι δὲ τὸν ναὸν τῷ Ἀπόλλωνι τὸ ἀρχαιότατον δάφνης
φασί, κομισθῆναι δὲ τοὺς κλάδους ἀπὸ τῆς δάφνης τῆς ἐν τοῖς Τέμπεσι·
καλύβης δ' ἂν σχῆμα οὗτός γε ἂν εἴη παρεσχηματισμένος ὁ ναός. δεύτερα
δὲ λέγουσιν οἱ Δελφοὶ γενέσθαι ὑπὸ μελισσῶν τὸν ναὸν ἀπό τε τοῦ κηροῦ
τῶν μελισσῶν καὶ ἐκ πτερῶν· πεμφθῆναι δὲ ἐς Ὑπερβορέους φασὶν αὐτὸν
ὑπὸ τοῦ Ἀπόλλωνος.[49]

And I have heard that men leading their flocks happened upon the
oracle, and were inspired by the smoke and began prophesying at
the inspiration of Apollo. But the usual opinion was about Phemonoe, that Phemonoe was the first prophetess of the god and the
first to speak in hexameters. But Boeo, a native woman, having
made a hymn for the Delphians, said that the oracle of the god was
inaugurated by those coming from the Hyperboreans, and among
others Olen. And he first prophesied and first sang in hexameters.
And Boeo made these verses,

" Here they constructed the well remembered oracle,
  Children of the Hyperboreans, Pagasus and godlike Aguieus."

And having enumerated others of the Hyperboreans, at the end of
the hymn she named Olen.

" And Olen, who was the first prophet of Phoebus
  And first of the ancients devised the singing of songs."

Yet legends recall to memory no other man, but know oracles of
women alone. And they say the most ancient shrine of Apollo was
made of laurel, and the branches of the laurel were cut down in the
Vale of Tempe. And the temple would be built in form like a hut.
And the Delphians say the next temple was made by the bees from
beeswax and their wings. And they say it was sent to the Hyperboreans by Apollo.

The story of the Hyperboreans now passes into medieval literature without change. The two following quotations from Solinus (3rd c. A. D.)
and Martianus Capella (5th c. A. D.) respectively, illustrate this.

XI, 20. Solinus, *Collect. rerum memor.* xxvi.

Fabulae erant Hyperborei et rumor irritus, si quae illinc ad nos
usque fluxerunt, temere forent credita: sed cum probissimi auctores
et satis vero idonei sententias pares faciant, nullus falsum reformidet.
de Hyperboreis rem loquemur. incolunt pone Pterophoron, quem
ultra aquilonem accepimus iacere. gens beatissima. eam Asiae
quidam magis quam Europae dederunt. alii statuunt mediam inter
utrumque solem, antipodum occidentem et nostrum renascentem:
quod aspernatur ratio, tam vasto mari duos orbes interfluente. sunt
igitur in Europa. apud quos mundi cardines esse credunt et extimos
siderum ambitus, semestrem lucem, aversum una tantum die solem:
quamquam existant qui putent non cotidie ibi solem ut nobis, sed
vernali aequinoctio exoriri, autumnali occidere: ita sex mensibus
infinitum diem, sex aliis continuam esse noctem. de caelo magna
clementia: aurae spirant salubriter: nihil noxium flatus habent.

domus sunt nemora vel luci : in diem victum arbores sumministrant.
discordiam nesciunt: aegritudine non inquietantur: ad innocentiam
omnibus aequale votum. mortem accersunt et voluntario interitu
castigant obeundi tarditatem: quos satias vitae tenet, epulati deli-
butique de rupe nota praecipitem casum in maria destinant: hoc
sepulturae genus optimum arbitrantur. aiunt etiam solitos per virgines probatissimas primitiva frugum Apollini Delio missitare:
verum hae quoniam perfidia hospitum non inlibatae revenissent,
devotionis quam peregre prosequebantur pontificium mox intra fines
suos receperunt.

The Hyperboreans were fables and vain rumor, if the things
that have come down to us about them should be rashly believed.
But since the most trustworthy and honest authors make similar
statements about them, no one need fear them to be false. We shall
discuss the Hyperboreans. They live beyond Pterophoron, which we
believe to lie beyond the North Wind. They are a very happy people.
Some locate them in Asia rather than in Europe. Others put them
midway between both suns, the antipodal on the west and ours on
the east: which is repugnant to reason, so vast a sea lies between
the two worlds. Therefore they are in Europe. Among these people
are believed to be the pole of the world and the limits of the orbits
of the stars, a six-months' day, the sun removed for one day only,
although there exist those who would think that the sun up there
does not rise daily as with us, but in the vernal equinox, to sink in
the autumnal ; thus the day lasts for six months and the night is continuous for six months. The climate is very clement; salubrious
breezes blow; there are no noxious blasts. Their homes are groves
or thickets; from day to day the trees provide food. They know
not discord; they are not disturbed by illness; to innocence all alike
are vowed. They summon death and punish its tardiness by suicide.
Those who have had enough of living, after feasting and drinking,
leap into the sea from a known rock. They consider this the best
form of burial.

It is said that they used to send their first fruits to Delian Apollo
by their purest virgins. But since these maids did not return
uninjured, because of the perfidy of their hosts, they performed their
devout exercises at home rather than abroad.

XI, 21. Martianus Capella, *De nuptiis Philologiae et Mercurii*, VI, 664.

Post eosdem montes [i. e. Riphaeos] trans Aquilonem Hyperborei, apud quos mundi axis continua rotatione torquetur, gens
moribus, prolixitate vitae, deorum cultu, aëris clementia, semenstri
die, fine etiam habitationis humanae praedicanda.[51]

Beyond these mountains (i. e. the Rhiphaean) beyond the North
Wind live the Hyperboreans, among whom the axis of the world
turns in continual rotation, a people to be praised for their way of
living, their longevity, their worship of the gods, the clemency of
their climate, their six-months' day, yet at the limits of human
habitation.

---

[50] Ed. Th. Mommsen, Berlin, 1864.   [51] Ed. Adolph Dick, Leipzig, 1925.

REAL LANDS AND PEOPLES

Scythians

When one turns to the real savage peoples, one finds a very different picture; it is they who provide the models for the hard primitivist. The most important of these peoples are the Scythians, one of whose legendary figures, Anacharsis, was listed among the Seven Wise Men.[52]

XI, 22. Homer, *Iliad*, XIII, 1-6.

> Ζεὺς δ' ἐπεὶ οὖν Τρῶάς τε καὶ Ἕκτορα νηυσὶ πέλασσε,
> τοὺς μὲν ἔα παρὰ τῇσι πόνον τ' ἐχέμεν καὶ ὀϊζὺν
> νωλεμέως, αὐτὸς δὲ πάλιν τρέπεν ὄσσε φαεινώ,
> νόσφιν ἐφ' ἱπποπόλων Θρῃκῶν καθορώμενος αἶαν
> Μυσῶν τ' ἀγχεμάχων καὶ ἀγαυῶν Ἱππημολγῶν
> γλακτοφάγων, Ἀβίων τε, δικαιοτάτων ἀνθρώπων.[53]

When now Zeus had brought the Trojans and Hector to the ships, he held them fast to their toil and suffering there, and he himself again turned his shining eyes away to the land of the horsebreeding Thracians and the Mysians, hand-to-hand fighters, and the noble Mare-milkers, milk drinkers, and the Abioi, the most righteous of men.[54]

That the Abioi were righteous because they were more 'natural' than other men is not stated here. But in Aeschylus, the Gabioi, who, if we may trust Stephanus Byzantinus,[55] were the Abioi of Homer, were characterized by a righteousness and kindness to strangers which won them a spontaneous crop from earth, i. e. they lived in a technological state of nature like the Golden Race.

XI, 23. Aeschylus, *Fragm.* 196.

> ἔπειτα δ' ἥξεις δῆμον ἐνδικώτατον
> ⟨βροτῶν⟩ ἁπάντων καὶ φιλοξενώτατον,
> Γαβίους, ἵν' οὔτ' ἄροτρον οὔτε γατόμος
> τέμνει δίκελλ' ἄρουραν, ἀλλ' αὐτόσποροι
> γύαι φέρουσι βίοτον ἄφθονον βροτοῖς.[56]

---

[52] According to Diogenes Laertius (I, 40 f.) this was done as early as Ephorus (4th c. B. C.). These lists of Wise Men, however, varied greatly and we have no certain method of dating the beginning of the Scythian's reputation as a sage.

[53] Ed. Dindorf-Hentze, Leipzig, 1890, II.

[54] Lang, Leaf and Meyer translation.

[55] See under Ἄβιοι. Not to be confused with Γάβιοι, a Latin city whose inhabitants were called Γαβῖται. Cf. Scholia, *Iliad* N 6. Nicolaus of Damascus (1st c. B. C.) is quoted by Stobaeus (*Floril.* V, 73) as identifying the Milk-drinkers and the Abioi. They are very just, and live in an economical and marital state of nature. All seniors are called fathers, all juniors, children, all coevals, brothers. Anacharsis was from this tribe. They are called Abioi, ἢ διὰ τὸ γῆν μὴ γεωρεῖν ἢ διὰ τὸ ἀοίκους εἶναι ἢ διὰ τὸ χρῆσθαι τούτους μόνους τόξοις. βιὸν γὰρ λέγει τὸ τόξον, "either because they do not work the land or because they have no houses or because they alone do not use bows. For the bow is called *bios*".

[56] Nauck, *Trag. graec. fragm.* Leipzig, 1889, p. 66.

And afterwards you will come to the most righteous of all men and the kindest to strangers, the Gabioi, amongst whom neither the plough nor the earth-clearing mattock cuts the ground, but self-sown soils bear food unstinted for men.

The epithet of " well-ordered " as applied to the Scythians was apparently common in fifth century Greece. Thus Aeschylus again refers to them:

XI, 24. Aeschylus, *Fragm.* 198.

ἀλλ᾽ ἱππάκης βρωτῆρες εὔνομοι Σκύθαι.[57]

The well-ordered Scythians, drinkers of mare's milk.

Sophocles, the younger contemporary of Aeschylus, however, shows us that during the same period the Scythians were not held in universal high esteem. For we already find a phrase indicating their savagery in his fragment, Σκυθιστὶ χειρόμακτρον ἐκκεκαρμένος, " shaved to make a towel [58] in the Scythian manner " (*Fragm.* 429, Nauck), quoted by Athenaeus (IX, 410 C) from the *Oenomaus*. A Scythian towel, we learn from Hesychius, is a scalp. We shall see below a later comment on scalping. So Choerilus (*ca.* 450 B. C.), the epic poet of Samos:

XI, 25. In Strabo, *Geogr.* VII, 3, 9 (303):

μηλονόμοι τε Σάκαι, γενεῇ Σκύθαι· αὐτὰρ ἔναιον Ἀσίδα πυροφόρον· νομάδων γε μὲν ἦσαν ἄποικοι, ἀνθρώπων νομίμων.[59]

The sheep-tending Sacae, of Scythian race. But they lived in wheat-bearing Asia. Yet they were colonists from the Nomads, law-abiding men.

The Scythians as a group are given several paragraphs in the Hippocratic " Airs, Waters, and Places." [60] This treatise discusses them, however, from the medical point of view, as an example of the influence of climate upon temperament. It describes their nomadic life, their diet of meat and mare's milk, and mare's-milk cheese. The writer definitely establishes the tradition of their hardihood. They are essentially a timid people and slow, and therefore little inclined to eroticism. Their perpetual riding is supposed to render many of the men impotent; their fatness and indolence, the women. Impotent men are given women's clothes and do women's work, and are worshipped by the tribes because they are afflicted with a divine visitation. As a matter of fact, says the author of this treatise, this malady is no more supernatural than any other.

XI, 26. Hippocrates, *De aere, aquis, locis,* 18-23 (Translation on p. 319).

18. Περὶ δὲ τῶν λοιπῶν Σκυθέων τῆς μορφῆς, ὅτι αὐτοὶ αὐτοῖσιν ἐοίκασι καὶ οὐδαμοῖς ἄλλοις, ωὑτὸς λόγος καὶ περὶ τῶν Αἰγυπτίων, πλὴν ὅτι οἱ μὲν

---

[57] Nauck, *Op. cit.*

[58] We translate χειρόμακτρον in the traditional manner. For another use of the term see D. M. Robinson's *Sappho and her Influence*, p. 256, n. 79.

[59] Ed. Meineke, Leipzig, 1915.   [60] Ch. 18-22, inc.

ὑπὸ τοῦ θερμοῦ εἰσι βεβιασμένοι, οἱ δὲ ὑπὸ τοῦ ψυχροῦ. ἡ δὲ Σκυθέων ἐρημίη
καλευμένη πεδιάς ἐστι καὶ λειμακώδης καὶ ψιλὴ καὶ ἔνυδρος μετρίως. ποταμοὶ
γάρ εἰσι μεγάλοι, οἳ ἐξοχετεύουσι τὸ ὕδωρ ἐκ τῶν πεδίων. ἐνταῦθα καὶ οἱ
Σκύθαι διαιτεῦνται, Νομάδες δὲ καλεῦνται, ὅτι οὐκ ἔστιν οἰκήματα, ἀλλ' ἐν
ἁμάξῃσιν οἰκεῦσιν. αἱ δὲ ἅμαξαί εἰσιν αἱ μὲν ἐλάχισται τετράκυκλοι, αἱ δὲ
ἑξάκυκλοι· αὗται δὲ πίλοις περιπεφραγμέναι· εἰσὶ δὲ καὶ τετεχνασμέναι ὥσπερ
οἰκήματα τὰ μὲν διπλᾶ, τὰ δὲ τριπλᾶ. ταῦτα δὲ καὶ στεγνὰ πρὸς ὕδωρ καὶ
πρὸς χιόνα καὶ πρὸς τὰ πνεύματα. τὰς δὲ ἁμάξας ἕλκουσι ζεύγεα τὰς μὲν
δύο, τὰς δὲ τρία βοῶν κέρως ἄτερ. οὐ γὰρ ἔχουσι κέρατα ὑπὸ τοῦ ψύχεος.
ἐν ταύτῃσι μὲν οὖν τῇσιν ἁμάξῃσιν ⟨αἱ⟩ γυναῖκες διαιτεῦνται. αὐτοὶ δ' ἐφ'
ἵππων ὀχεῦνται [οἱ ἄνδρες]. ἕπονται δὲ αὐτοῖς καὶ τὰ πρόβατα ⟨τὰ⟩ ἐόντα
καὶ αἱ βόες καὶ οἱ ἵπποι. μένουσι δ' ἐν τῷ αὐτῷ τοσοῦτον χρόνον, ὅσον ἂν
ἀποχρῇ αὐτοῖσι τοῖς κτήνεσιν ὁ χόρτος· ὁκόταν δὲ μηκέτι, ἐς ἑτέρην χώρην
ἔρχονται. αὐτοὶ δ' ἐσθίουσι κρέα ἑφθὰ καὶ πίνουσι γάλα ἵππων. καὶ ἱππάκην
τρώγουσι· τοῦτο δ' ἐστὶ τυρὸς ἵππων.

19. Τὰ μὲν ἐς τὴν δίαιταν αὐτῶν οὕτως ἔχει καὶ τοὺς νόμους· περὶ δὲ τῶν
ὡρέων καὶ τῆς μορφῆς, ὅτι πολὺ ἀπήλλακται τῶν λοιπῶν ἀνθρώπων τὸ
Σκυθικὸν γένος καὶ ἔοικεν αὐτὸ ἑωυτῷ ὥσπερ τὸ Αἰγύπτιον καὶ ἥκιστα
πολύγονόν ἐστι καὶ ἡ χώρη ἐλάχιστα θηρία τρέφει κατὰ μέγεθος καὶ πλῆθος.
κεῖται γὰρ ὑπ' αὐτῇσι τῇσιν ἄρκτοις καὶ τοῖς ὄρεσι τοῖς Ῥιπαίοισιν, ὅθεν
ὁ βορέης πνεῖ. ὅ τε ἥλιος τελευτῶν ἐγγύτατα γίνεται, ὁκόταν ἐπὶ τὰς θερινὰς
ἔλθῃ περιόδους, καὶ τότε ὀλίγον χρόνον θερμαίνει καὶ οὐ σφόδρα· τὰ δὲ
πνεύματα τὰ ἀπὸ τῶν θερμῶν πνέοντα ⟨οὐκ⟩ ἀφικνεῖται, ἢν μὴ ὀλιγάκις καὶ
ἀσθενέα, ἀλλ' ἀπὸ τῶν ἄρκτων αἰεὶ πνέουσι πνεύματα ψυχρὰ ἀπό τε χιόνος
καὶ κρυστάλλου καὶ ὑδάτων πολλῶν. οὐδέποτε δὲ τὰ ὄρεα ἐκλείπει· ἀπὸ
τούτων δὲ δυσοίκητά ἐστι. ἠήρ τε κατέχει πολὺς τῆς ἡμέρης τὰ πεδία, καὶ
ἐν τούτοισι διαιτεῦνται· ὥστε τὸν μὲν χειμῶνα αἰεὶ εἶναι, τὸ δὲ θέρος ὀλίγας
ἡμέρας καὶ ταύτας μὴ λίην. μετέωρα γὰρ τὰ πεδία καὶ ψιλὰ καὶ οὐκ ἐστεφάνω-
ται ὄρεσιν, ἀλλ' ἢ ἀνάντεα ἀπὸ τῶν ἄρκτων· αὐτόθι καὶ τὰ θηρία οὐ γίνεται
μεγάλα, ἀλλ' οἷά τέ ἐστιν ὑπὸ γῆν σκεπάζεσθαι. ὁ γὰρ χειμὼν κωλύει καὶ
τῆς γῆς ἡ ψιλότης, ὅτι οὐκ ἔστιν ἀλέη οὐδὲ σκέπη. αἱ γὰρ μεταβολαὶ τῶν
ὡρέων οὐκ εἰσι μεγάλαι οὐδὲ ἰσχυραί, ἀλλ' ὅμοιαι καὶ ὀλίγον μεταλλάσσουσαι·
διότι καὶ τὰ εἴδεα ὅμοιοι αὐτοὶ ἑωυτοῖς εἰσι σίτῳ τε χρεώμενοι αἰεὶ ὁμοίῳ
ἐσθῆτί τε τῇ αὐτῇ καὶ θέρεος καὶ χειμῶνος τόν τε ἠέρα ὑδατεινὸν ἕλκοντες
καὶ παχὺν τά τε ὕδατα πίνοντες ἀπὸ χιόνος καὶ παγετῶν τοῦ τε ταλαιπώρου
ἀπεόντες. οὐ γὰρ οἷόν τε τὸ σῶμα ταλαιπωρεῖσθαι οὐδὲ τὴν ψυχήν, ὅκου
μεταβολαὶ μὴ γίνονται ἰσχυραί. διὰ ταύτας τὰς ἀνάγκας τὰ εἴδεα αὐτῶν
παχέα ἐστὶ καὶ σαρκώδεα καὶ ἄναρθρα καὶ ὑγρὰ καὶ ἄτονα, αἵ τε κοιλίαι
ὑγρόταται πασέων κοιλιῶν αἱ κάτω. οὐ γὰρ οἷόν τε νηδὺν ἀναξηραίνεσθαι
ἐν τοιαύτῃ χώρῃ καὶ φύσει καὶ ὥρης καταστάσει, ἀλλὰ διὰ πιμελήν τε καὶ
ψιλὴν τὴν σάρκα τά [τε] εἴδεα ἔοικεν ἀλλήλοισι τά τε ἄρσενα τοῖς ἄρσεσι
καὶ τὰ θήλεα τοῖς θήλεσι. τῶν γὰρ ὡρέων παραπλησίων ἐουσέων φθοραὶ οὐκ
ἐγγίνονται οὐδὲ κακώσιες ἐν τῇ τοῦ γόνου συμπήξει, ἢν μή τινος ἀνάγκης
βιαίου τύχῃ ἢ νούσου.

20. Μέγα δὲ τεκμήριον ἐς τὴν ὑγρότητα παρέξομαι. Σκυθέων γὰρ τοὺς
πολλούς, μάλιστα ὅσοι Νομάδες, εὑρήσεις κεκαυμένους τούς τε ὤμους καὶ
τοὺς βραχίονας καὶ τοὺς καρποὺς τῶν χειρῶν καὶ τὰ στήθεα ⟨καὶ τὰ⟩ ἰσχία
καὶ τὴν ὀσφὺν δι' ἄλλ' οὐδὲν ἢ διὰ τὴν ὑγρότητα τῆς φύσιος καὶ τὴν μαλακίην.
οὐ γὰρ δύνανται οὔτε τοῖς τόξοις συντείνειν οὔτε τῷ ἀκοντίῳ ἐμπίπτειν τῷ
ὤμῳ ὑπὸ ὑγρότητος καὶ ἀτονίης. ὁκόταν δὲ κανθέωσιν, ἀναξηραίνεται ἐκ τῶν
ἄρθρων τὸ πολὺ τοῦ ὑγροῦ, καὶ ἐντονώτερα μᾶλλον γίνεται καὶ τροφιμώτερα
καὶ ἠρθρωμένα τὰ σώματα μᾶλλον. ῥοϊκὰ δὲ γίνεται καὶ πλατέα, πρῶτον μὲν

ὅτι οὐ σπαργανοῦνται ὥσπερ ἐν Αἰγύπτῳ οὐδὲ νομίζουσι διὰ τὴν ἱππασίην, ὅκως ἂν εὔεδροι ἔωσιν· ἔπειτα δὲ διὰ τὴν ἕδρην· τά τε γὰρ ἄρσενα, ἕως ἂν οὐχ οἷά τε ἐφ' ἵππου ὀχεῖσθαι, τὸ πολὺ τοῦ χρόνου κάθηνται ἐν τῇ ἁμάξῃ καὶ βραχὺ τῇ βαδίσει χρέονται διὰ τὰς μεταναστάσιας καὶ περιελάσιας· τὰ δὲ θήλεα θαυμαστὸν οἷον ῥοϊκά ἐστι καὶ βλαδέα τὰ εἴδεα. πυρρὸν δὲ τὸ γένος ἐστὶ τὸ Σκυθικὸν διὰ τὸ ψῦχος, οὐκ ἐπιγινομένου ὀξέος τοῦ ἡλίου. ὑπὸ δὲ τοῦ ψύχεος ἡ λευκότης ἐπικαίεται καὶ γίνεται πυρρή.

21. Πολύγονον δὲ οὐχ οἷόν τε εἶναι φύσιν τοιαύτην. οὔτε γὰρ τῷ ἀνδρὶ ἡ ἐπιθυμίη τῆς μείξιος γίνεται πολλὴ διὰ τὴν ὑγρότητα τῆς φύσιος καὶ τῆς κοιλίης τὴν μαλθακότητά τε καὶ [τὴν] ψυχρότητα, ἀφ' ὅτων ἥκιστα εἰκὸς ἄνδρα οἷόν τε λαγνεύειν· καὶ ἔτι ὑπὸ τῶν ἵππων αἰεὶ κοπτόμενοι ἀσθενέες γίνονται ἐς τὴν μεῖξιν. τοῖσι μὲν ἀνδράσιν αὗται αἱ προφάσιες γίνονται, τῇσι δὲ γυναιξὶν ἥ τε πιότης τῆς σαρκὸς καὶ ὑγρότης· οὐ γὰρ δύνανται ἔτι συναρπάζειν αἱ μῆτραι τὸν γόνον· οὔτε γὰρ ἐπιμήνιος κάθαρσις αὐτῇσι γίνεται ὡς χρεών ἐστιν, ἀλλ' ὀλίγον καὶ διὰ χρόνου, τό τε στόμα τῶν μητρέων ὑπὸ πιμελῆς συγκλείεται καὶ οὐχ ὑποδέχεται τὸν γόνον· αὐταί τε ἀταλαίπωροι καὶ πίεραι καὶ αἱ κοιλίαι ψυχραὶ καὶ μαλθακαί. [καὶ] ὑπὸ τούτων τῶν ἀναγκέων οὐ πολύγονόν ἐστι τὸ γένος τὸ Σκυθικόν. μέγα δὲ τεκμήριον αἱ οἰκέτιδες ποιέουσιν· οὐ γὰρ φθάνουσι παρὰ ἄνδρα ἀφικνεύμεναι καὶ ἐν γαστρὶ ἴσχουσιν διὰ τὴν ταλαιπωρίην καὶ ἰσχνότητα τῆς σαρκός.

22. Ἔτι τε πρὸς τούτοισιν εὐνουχίαι γίνονται οἱ πλεῖστοι ἐν Σκύθῃσι καὶ γυναικεῖα ἐργάζονται καὶ ὡς αἱ γυναῖκες ⟨διαιτεῦνται⟩ διαλέγονταί τε ὁμοίως· καλεῦνταί [τε] οἱ τοιοῦτοι Ἀναριεῖς. οἱ μὲν οὖν ἐπιχώριοι τὴν αἰτίην προστιθέασι θεῷ καὶ σέβονται τούτους τοὺς ἀνθρώπους καὶ προσκυνέουσι, δεδοικότες περὶ ἑωυτῶν ἕκαστοι. ἐμοὶ δὲ καὶ αὐτῷ δοκεῖ ταῦτα τὰ πάθεα θεῖα εἶναι καὶ τἆλλα πάντα καὶ οὐδὲν ἕτερον ἑτέρου θειότερον οὐδὲ ἀνθρωπινώτερον, ἀλλὰ πάντα ὁμοῖα καὶ πάντα θεῖα. ἕκαστον δὲ αὐτῶν ἔχει φύσιν τὴν ἑωυτοῦ καὶ οὐδὲν ἄνευ φύσιος γίνεται. καὶ τοῦτο τὸ πάθος ὥς μοι δοκεῖ γίνεσθαι φράσω· ὑπὸ τῆς ἱππασίης αὐτοὺς κέδματα λαμβάνει, ἅτε αἰεὶ κρεμαμένων ἀπὸ τῶν ἵππων τοῖς ποσίν· ἔπειτα ἀποχωλοῦνται καὶ ἑλκοῦνται τὰ ἰσχία, οἳ ἂν σφόδρα νοσήσωσιν. ἰῶνται δὲ σφᾶς αὐτοὺς τρόπῳ τοιῷδε. ὁκόταν γὰρ ἄρχηται ἡ νοῦσος, ὄπισθεν τοῦ ὠτὸς ἑκατέρου φλέβα τάμνουσιν. ὁκόταν δὲ ἀπορρυῇ τὸ αἷμα, ὕπνος ὑπολαμβάνει ὑπὸ ἀσθενείης καὶ καθεύδουσιν. ἔπειτα ἀνεγείρονται, οἱ μέν τινες ὑγιέες ἐόντες, οἱ δ' οὔ. ἐμοὶ μὲν οὖν δοκεῖ ἐν ταύτῃ τῇ ἰήσει διαφθείρεσθαι ὁ γόνος. εἰσὶ γὰρ παρὰ τὰ ὦτα φλέβες, ἃς ἐάν τις ἐπιτάμῃ, ἄγονοι γίνονται οἱ ἐπιτμηθέντες. ταύτας τοίνυν μοι δοκέουσι τὰς φλέβας ἐπιτάμνειν. οἱ δὲ μετὰ ταῦτα ἐπειδὰν ἀφίκωνται παρὰ γυναῖκας καὶ μὴ οἷοί τ' ἔωσι χρῆσθαί σφισιν [αὐταῖς], τὸ πρῶτον οὐκ ἐνθυμεῦνται, ἀλλ' ἡσυχίην ἔχουσι. ὁκόταν δὲ δὶς καὶ τρὶς καὶ πλεονάκις αὐτοῖσι πειρωμένοισι μηδὲν ἀλλοιότερον ἀποβαίνῃ, νομίσαντές τι ἡμαρτηκέναι τῷ θεῷ, ὃν ἐπαιτιῶνται, ἐνδύονται στολὴν γυναικείην καταγνόντες ἑωυτῶν ἀνανδρείην. γυναικίζουσί τε καὶ ἐργάζονται μετὰ τῶν γυναικῶν ἃ καὶ ἐκεῖναι.

23. Τοῦτο δὲ πάσχουσι Σκυθέων [οἱ πλούσιοι,] οὐχ οἱ κάκιστοι, ἀλλ' οἱ εὐγενέστατοι καὶ ἰσχὺν πλείστην κεκτημένοι διὰ τὴν ἱππασίην, οἱ δὲ πένητες ἧσσον· οὐ γὰρ ἱππάζονται. καίτοι ἐχρῆν, ἐπεὶ θειότερον τοῦτο τὸ νόσευμα τῶν λοιπῶν ἐστιν, οὐ τοῖς γενναιοτάτοις τῶν Σκυθέων καὶ τοῖς πλουσιωτάτοις προσπίπτειν μούνοις, ἀλλὰ τοῖς ἅπασιν ὁμοίως, καὶ μᾶλλον τοῖσιν ὀλίγα κεκτημένοισιν, εἰ δὴ τιμώμενοι χαίρουσιν οἱ θεοὶ καὶ θαυμαζόμενοι ὑπ' ἀνθρώπων καὶ ἀντὶ τούτων χάριτας ἀποδιδόασιν. εἰκὸς γὰρ τοὺς μὲν πλουσίους θύειν πολλὰ τοῖς θεοῖς καὶ ἀνατιθέναι ἀναθήματα ἐόντων χρημάτων πολλῶν καὶ τιμᾶν, τοὺς δὲ πένητας ἧσσον διὰ τὸ μὴ ἔχειν, ἔπειτα καὶ ἐπιμεμφομένους, ὅτι οὐ διδόασι χρήματα αὐτοῖσιν, ὥστε τῶν τοιούτων ἁμαρτιῶν τὰς ζημίας

τοὺς ὀλίγα κεκτημένους φέρειν μᾶλλον ἢ τοὺς πλουσίους. ἀλλὰ γάρ, ὥσπερ
καὶ πρότερον ἔλεξα, θεῖα μὲν καὶ ταῦτά ἐστιν ὁμοίως τοῖς ἄλλοις· γίνεται
δὲ κατὰ φύσιν ἕκαστα. καὶ ἡ τοιαύτη νοῦσος ἀπὸ τοιαύτης προφάσιος τοῖς
Σκύθῃσι γίνεται οἵην εἴρηκα. ἔχει δὲ καὶ κατὰ τοὺς λοιποὺς ἀνθρώπους
ὁμοίως. ὅκου γὰρ ἱππάζονται μάλιστα καὶ πυκνότατα, ἐκεῖ πλεῖστοι ὑπὸ
κεδμάτων καὶ ἰσχιάδων καὶ ποδαγριῶν ἁλίσκονται καὶ λαγνεύειν κάκιστοί εἰσι.
ταῦτα δὲ τοῖσι [τε] Σκύθῃσι πρόσεστι, καὶ εὐνουχοειδέστατοί εἰσιν ἀνθρώπων
διὰ ταύτας ⟨τε⟩ τὰς προφάσιας καὶ ὅτι ἀναξυρίδας ἔχουσιν αἰεὶ καί εἰσιν
ἐπὶ τῶν ἵππων τὸ πλεῖστον τοῦ χρόνου, ὥστε μήτε χειρὶ ἅπτεσθαι τοῦ αἰδοίου
ὑπό τε τοῦ ψύχεος καὶ τοῦ κόπου ἐπιλήθεσθαι τοῦ ἱμέρου καὶ τῆς μείξιος καὶ
μηδὲν παρακινεῖν πρότερον ἢ ἀνανδρωθῆναι.[61]

18. As to the physique of the other Scythians, in that they
are like one another and not at all like others, the same remark
applies to them as to the Egyptians, only the latter are distressed
by the heat, the former by the cold. What is called the Scythian
desert is level grassland, without trees, and fairly well-watered. For
there are large rivers which drain the water from the plains. There
too live the Scythians, who are called Nomads because they have no
houses but live in wagons. The smallest have four wheels, others
six wheels. They are covered over with felt and are constructed
like houses, sometimes in two compartments and sometimes in three,
which are proof against rain, snow and wind. The wagons are
drawn by two or by three yoke of hornless oxen. They have no horns
because of the cold. Now in these wagons live the women, while the
men ride alone on horseback, followed by the sheep they have, their
cattle and their horses. They remain in the same place just as long
as there is sufficient fodder for the animals; when it gives out they
migrate. They themselves eat boiled meats and mares' milk. They
have a sweetmeat called *hippace*, which is a cheese from the milk of
mares (*hippoi*).

19. So much for their mode of living and their customs. As
to their seasons and their physique, the Scythians are very different
from all other men, and, like the Egyptians, are homogeneous; they
are the reverse of prolific, and Scythia breeds the smallest and the
fewest wild animals. For it lies right close to the north and the
Rhiphaean mountains, from which blows the north wind. The sun
comes nearest to them only at the end of its course, when it reaches
the summer solstice, and then it warms them but slightly and for a
short time. The winds blowing from hot regions do not reach them,
save rarely, and with little force; but from the north there are constantly blowing winds that are chilled by snow, ice, and many waters,
which, never leaving the mountains, render them uninhabitable. A
thick fog envelopes by day the plains upon which they live, so that
winter is perennial, while summer, which is but feeble, lasts only a
few days. For the plains are high and bare, and are not encircled
with mountains, though they slope from the north. The wild animals, too, that are found there are not large, but such as can find
shelter under ground. They are stunted owing to the severe climate
and the bareness of the land, where there is neither warmth nor
shelter. And the changes of the seasons are neither great nor vio-

[61] Ed. Kuehlewein, Leipzig, 1894, vol. I.

lent, the seasons being uniform and altering but little. Wherefore the men also are like one another in physique, since summer and winter they always use similar food and the same clothing, breathing a moist, thick atmosphere, drinking water from ice and snow, and abstaining from hard labor. For neither bodily nor mental endurance is possible where the changes are not violent. For these causes their physiques are gross, fleshy, showing no joints, moist and flabby, and the lower bowels are as moist as bowels can be. For the belly cannot possibly dry up in a land like this, with such a nature and such a climate, but because of their fat and the smoothness of their flesh their physiques are similar, men's to men's and women's to women's. For as the seasons are alike, there takes place no corruption or deterioration in the coagulation of the seed, except through the blow of some violent cause or of some disease.

20. I will give clear testimony to their moistness. The majority of the Scythians, all that are Nomads, you will find have their shoulders cauterized, as well as their arms, wrists, breast, hips and loins, simply because of the moistness and softness of their constitution. For owing to their moistness and flabbiness they have not the strength either to draw a bow or to throw a javelin from the shoulder. But when they have been cauterized the excess of moisture dries up from their joints, and their bodies become more braced, more nourished and better articulated. Their bodies grow relaxed and squat, firstly because, unlike the Egyptians, they do not use swaddling clothes, of which they have not the habit, for the sake of their riding, that they may sit a horse well; secondly, through their sedentary lives. For the boys, until they can ride, sit the greater part of the time in the wagon, and because of the migrations and wanderings rarely walk on foot; while the girls are wonderfully flabby and torpid in physique. The Scythians are a ruddy race because of the cold, not through any fierceness in the sun's heat. It is the cold that burns their white skin and turns it ruddy.

21. A constitution of this kind prevents fertility. The men have no great desire for intercourse because of the moistness of their constitution and the softness and chill of their abdomen, which are the greatest checks on venery. Moreover, the constant jolting on their horses unfits them for intercourse. Such are the causes of barrenness in the men; in the women they are the fatness and moistness of their flesh, which are such that the womb cannot absorb the seed. For neither is their monthly purging as it should be, but scanty and late, while the mouth of the womb is closed by fat and does not admit the seed. They are personally fat and lazy, and their abdomen is cold and soft. These are the causes which make the Scythian race unfertile. A clear proof is afforded by their slave-girls. These, because of their activity and leanness of body, no sooner go to a man than they are with child.

22. Moreover, the great majority among the Scythians become impotent, do women's work, live like women and converse accordingly. Such men they call Anaries. Now the natives put the blame upon Heaven, and respect and worship these creatures, each fearing for himself. I too think that these diseases are divine, and so are all others, no one being more divine or more human than any other; all are alike, and all divine. Each of them has a nature of its own,

and none arises without its natural cause. How, in my opinion, this disease arises I will explain. The habit of riding causes swellings at the joints, because they are always astride their horses; in severe cases follow lameness and sores on the hips. They cure themselves in the following way. At the beginning of the disease they cut the vein behind each ear. When the blood has ceased to flow faintness comes over them and they sleep. Afterwards they get up, some cured and some not. Now, in my opinion, by this treatment the seed is destroyed. For by the side of the ear are veins, to cut which causes impotence, and I believe that these are the veins which they cut. After this treatment, when the Scythians approach a woman but cannot have intercourse, at first they take no notice and think no more about it. But when two, three or even more attempts are attended with no better success, thinking that they have sinned against Heaven they attribute thereto the cause, and put on women's clothes, holding that they have lost their manhood. So they play the woman, and with the women do the same work as women do.

This affliction affects the rich Scythians because of their riding, not the lower classes but the upper, who possess the most strength; the poor, who do not ride, suffer less. But, if we suppose this disease to be more divine than any other, it ought to have attacked, not the highest and richest classes only of the Scythians, but all classes equally — or rather the poor especially, if indeed the gods are pleased to receive from men respect and worship, and repay these with favors. For naturally the rich, having great wealth, make many sacrifices to the gods, and offer many votive offerings, and honor them, all of which things the poor, owing to their poverty, are less able to do; besides, they blame the gods for not giving them wealth, so that the penalties for such sins are likely to be paid by the poor rather than by the rich. But the truth is, as I said above, these affections are neither more nor less divine than any others, and all and one are natural. Such a disease arises among the Scythians for such a reason as I have stated, and other men too are equally liable to it, for wherever men ride very much and very frequently, there the majority are attacked by swellings at the joints, sciatica and gout, and are sexually very weak. These complaints come upon the Scythians, and they are the most impotent of men, for the reasons I have given, and also because they always wear trousers and spend most of their time on their horses, so that they do not handle the parts, but owing to cold and fatigue forget about sexual passion, losing their virility before any impulse is felt.[62]

Such a discussion of the Scythians contains nothing eulogistic. It is a simple statement of the supposed effects of their environment upon this people.

In Herodotus, however, the attitude is different. Though they still have many undesirable traits, yet they have produced one wise man, Anacharsis, and have thereby excelled all other trans-Pontine peoples. They have, moreover, in the simplicity of their life many of the ways of the Golden

---

[62] Tr. W. H. S. Jones, *Loeb Class. Lib.* London, 1923, vol. I, with slight changes.

Race; no cities, no fortifications, no agriculture. But it is noteworthy that Herodotus does not make this comparison.

XI, 27. Herodotus, *Historiae*, IV, 19; 46-47.

19. τὸ δέ πρὸς τὴν ἠῶ γεωργῶν τούτων Σκυθέων, διαβάντι τόν Παντικάπην ποταμὸν, νομάδες ἤδη Σκύθαι νέμονται, οὔτε τι σπείροντες οὐδὲν, οὔτε ἀροῦντες· (ψιλὴ δὲ δενδρέων πᾶσα αὕτη γῆ, πλὴν τῆς Ὑλαίης.) οἱ δὲ νομάδες οὗτοι τό πρός τήν ἠῶ, ἡμερέων τεσσέρων καί δέκα ὁδὸν, νέμονται χώρην κατατείνουσαν ἐπὶ ποταμὸν Γέρρον. . . .

46. Ὁ δὲ Πόντος ὁ Εὔξεινος, ἐπ' ὃν ἐστρατεύετο Δαρεῖος, χωρέων πασέων παρέχεται, ἔξω τοῦ Σκυθικοῦ ἔθνεα ἀμαθέστατα· οὔτε γὰρ ἔθνος τῶν ἐντὸς τοῦ Πόντου οὐδὲν ἔχομεν προβαλέσθαι σοφίης πέρι, οὔτε ἄνδρα λόγιον οἴδαμεν γενόμενον, πάρεξ τοῦ Σκυθικοῦ ἔθνεος καὶ Ἀναχάρσιος. τῷ δὲ Σκυθικῷ γένεϊ ἓν μὲν τὸ μέγιστον τῶν ἀνθρωπηΐων πρηγμάτων σοφώτατα πάντων ἐξεύρηται τῶν ἡμεῖς ἴδμεν· τὰ μέντοι ἄλλα οὐκ ἄγαμαι. τὸ δὲ μέγιστον οὕτω σφι ἀνεύρηται, ὥστε ἀποφυγέειν τε μηδένα ἐπελθόντα ἐπὶ σφέας, μὴ βουλομένους τε ἐξευρεθῆναι καταλαβεῖν μὴ οἷόν τε εἶναι· τοῖσι γὰρ μήτε ἄστεα μήτε τείχεα ᾖ ἐκτισμένα, ἀλλὰ φερέοικοι ἐόντες πάντες ἔωσι ἱπποτοξόται, ζῶντες μὴ ἀπ' ἀρότου ἀλλ' ἀπὸ κτηνέων, οἰκήματά τέ σφι ᾖ ἐπὶ ζευγέων, κῶς οὐκ ἂν εἴησαν οὗτοι ἄμαχοί τε καὶ ἄποροι προσμίσγειν; ἐξεύρηται δέ σφι ταῦτα, τῆς τε γῆς ἐούσης ἐπιτηδέης καὶ τῶν ποταμῶν ἐόντων σφι συμμάχων· ἥ τε γὰρ γῆ ἐοῦσα πεδιὰς αὕτη, ποιώδης τε καὶ εὔυδρός ἐστι· ποταμοί τε δι' αὐτῆς ῥέουσι οὐ πολλῷ τεῳ ἀριθμὸν ἐλάσσονες τῶν ἐν Αἰγύπτῳ διωρύχων.[63]

But to the east of these land-working Scythians, crossing the Panticapes River, dwell the nomad Scythians, who neither sow nor plough. And all this country is bare of trees except the Hylea [the Bush]. And these nomads inhabit the country which stretches fourteen days' journey to the Gerrus River. . . .

And the Euxine Pontus, against which Darius led his army, of all countries except the Scythian, furnishes the most ignorant nations. For of those across the Pontus we have no nation which exhibits any wisdom nor do we know of any learned man born there, except in the Scythian nation, Anacharsis. And the Scythian race has discovered regarding the greatest of human problems the wisest thing we know, though I do not admire them in other respects. But as regards this greatest problem they have discovered a means of preventing anyone attacking them from escaping and anyone wishing to capture them from finding them. For since they have neither cities nor fortifications, but all carry their houses with them and are mounted archers living not by agriculture but from their cattle, having their dwellings on wagons, why should they not be invincible and impossible to find? This was, moreover, discovered in a land which is accommodated to it and with rivers which fight along with the inhabitants. For the land is flat, grassy, and well-watered, and rivers flow through it not much fewer in number than the canals of Egypt.

The unfavorable view of the Scythians is developed by Aristotle's pupil, Clearchus of Soli, also of the fourth century. This writer explains their fall as the result primarily of wealth.

[63] Ed. Blakesley, London, 1854, I.

XI, 28. Clearchus Solensis, in Athenaeus, *Deipn.* XII, 524c.

Καὶ περὶ Σκυθῶν δ' ἑξῆς ὁ Κλέαρχος τάδε ἱστορεῖ· "Μόνον δὲ νόμοις κοινοῖς πρῶτον ἔθνος ἐχρήσατο τὸ Σκυθῶν· εἶτα πάλιν ἐγένοντο πάντων ἀθλιώτατοι βροτῶν διὰ τὴν ὕβριν. Ἐτρύφησαν μὲν γὰρ ὡς οὐδένες ἕτεροι, τῶν πάντων εὐροίας καὶ πλούτου καὶ τῆς λοιπῆς αὐτοὺς χορηγίας κατασχούσης. Τοῦτο δὲ δῆλον ἐκ τῆς ἔτι καὶ νῦν ὑπολειπούσης περὶ τοὺς ἡγεμόνας αὐτῶν ἐσθῆτός τε καὶ διαίτης. Τρυφήσαντες δὲ, καὶ μάλιστα δὴ καὶ πρῶτοι πάντων τῶν ἀνθρώπων ἐπὶ τὸ τρυφᾶν ὁρμήσαντες, εἰς τοῦτο προῆλθον ὕβρεως, ὥστε πάντων τῶν ἀνθρώπων, εἰς οὓς ἀφίκοιντο, ἠκρωτηρίαζον τὰς ῥῖνας· [ἀφ'] ὧν οἱ ἀπόγονοι μεταστάντες, ἔτι καὶ νῦν ἀπὸ τοῦ πάθους ἔχουσι τὴν ἐπωνυμίαν. Αἱ δὲ γυναῖκες αὐτῶν τὰς Θρᾳκῶν τῶν πρὸς ἑσπέραν καὶ ἄρκτον [τῶν] περιοίκων γυναῖκας ἐποίκιλλον τὰ σώματα, περόναις γραφὴν ἐνεῖσαι. Ὅθεν πολλοῖς ἔτεσιν ὕστερον αἱ ὑβρισθεῖσαι τῶν Θρᾳκῶν γυναῖκες ἰδίως ἐξηλείψαντο τὴν συμφοράν, προσκαταγραψάμεναι τὰ λοιπὰ τοῦ χρωτός, ἵν' ὁ τῆς ὕβρεως καὶ τῆς αἰσχύνης ἐπ' αὐταῖς χαρακτὴρ εἰς ποικιλίαν καταριθμηθεὶς κόσμου προσηγορίᾳ τοὔνειδος ἐξαλείψῃ. Πάντων δὲ οὕτως ὑπερηφάνως προέστησαν, ὥστε οὐδένων ἄδακρυς ἡ τῆς δουλείας ὑπουργία γιγνομένη, διήγγειλεν εἰς τοὺς ἐπιγιγνομένους τὴν ἀπὸ Σκυθῶν ῥῆσιν, οἷα τις ἦν. Διὰ τὸ πλῆθος οὖν τῶν κατασχουσῶν αὐτοὺς συμφορῶν, ἐπεὶ διὰ τὸ πένθος ἅμα τόν τε τῶν βίων ὄλβον καὶ τὰς κόμας περιεσπάσθησαν παντὸς ἔθνους, οἱ ἔξω τὴν ἐφ' ὕβρει κουρὰν ἀπεσκυθίσθαι προσηγόρευσαν." [64]

And concerning the Scythians Clearchus relates these things: The Scythian people first had one set of laws in common. Then, in turn, they became the most degraded of all men by reason of insolence. For they sank into luxury beyond all others, once they had been involved in abundance of all things and of money and of other forms of wealth. And this is plain from the clothing and habit of life of their leaders which has persisted even to our time. In their pursuit of luxury they went to such an extent of insolence that they amputated the noses of all the men they came upon. Even though their descendants have abandoned the practices of their forebears, their name still to-day signifies that character. Their wives tattooed the bodies of the women of their Thracian neighbors to the west and north, injecting the markings with pins. Consequently many years later the Thracian women who had been maltreated obliterated these in a peculiar way, by marking up the rest of their skin also, in order that the badge they bore of insolence and shame, by being reckoned a decoration, might under the name of ornament wipe out the disgrace.

[The Scythians] lorded it over everyone so arrogantly that since none served them in slavery without tears, this circumstance handed down to posterity the meaning of the phrase "Scythian speech," whatever that may have been. [65]

[64] Ed. Kaibel, Leipzig, 1890, III, with minor changes in punctuation. For Aristotle's opinion of the Scythians, which no doubt influenced Clearchus's, see VI, 7.

[65] This proverbial expression goes back at least to Herodotus, IV, 127. Although the sentence containing the words ἡ ἀπὸ Σκυθέων ῥῆσις is bracketed by many editors, Macan points out in his note on this section that they occur in all the MSS. See R. W. Macan, *Herodotus—the Fourth, Fifth and Sixth Books*, vol. I, Lond. 1895. In Demetrius (d. 283 B.C.) *De elocutione*, § 216, ἡ ἀπὸ Σκυθῶν ῥῆσις means "a brutal expression." Cf. 297 where it is contrasted with ἠθικῶς and ἐμμελῶς. Diogenes

So by reason of the multitude of the vicissitudes which befell them, since through their misfortunes they had been shorn at once of the happiness of their lives and the hair of the whole race, foreigners called the shearing of the head as a punishment for insolence, " Scythification." [66]

In the fourth century we find the Scythians praised, perhaps not seriously, by the comic poet Antiphanes (4th c. B. C.).

XI, 29. Antiphanes, in Athenaeus, *Deipnosoph.* VI, 226 d.

Εἶτα οὐ σοφοὶ δῆτ' εἰσὶν οἱ Σκύθαι σφόδρα,
οἱ γενομένοισιν εὐθέως τοῖς παιδίοις
διδόασιν ἵππων καὶ βοῶν πίνειν γάλα;
Β. οὐ μὰ Δία τιτθὰς εἰσάγουσι βασκάνους,
καὶ παιδαγωγούς. . . .[67]

Are not the Scythians very wise who give their new born babes the milk of mares and cows to drink? It is not they who admit among them malicious wet-nurses and pedagogues.

In the geographical writings of the pseudo-Scymnus (2d c. B. C.) there is a definite eulogy of the Scythians, which emphasizes their piety and communism.

XI, 30. Pseudo-Scymnus, *Orbis descriptio*, 850-859.

Τόν Παντικάπην διαβάντι Λιμναίων ἔθνος
ἕτερά τε πλείον' οὐ διωνομασμένα,
Νομαδικά δ' ἐπικαλούμεν', εὐσεβῆ πάνυ,
ὦν οὐδὲ εἷς ἔμψυχον ἀδικῆσαι ποτ' ἄν·
οἰκοφόρα δ', ὡς εἴρηκε, καὶ σιτούμενα
γαλάκτι ταῖς Σκυθικαῖσί θ' ἱππομολγίαις·
ζῶσιν δὲ τήν τε κτῆσιν ἀναδεδειχότες
κοινὴν ἁπάντων τήν θ' ὅλην συνουσίαν.
Καὶ τὸν σοφὸν δ' Ἀνάχαρσιν ἐκ τῶν Νομαδικῶν
φησὶν γενέσθαι τῶν σφόδρ' εὐσεβεστάτων.[68]

When the Panticapes is crossed, one meets the tribe of Limnaei, and others not more well-known. And those called Nomads are very pious, and none of them would do an injury to a living thing. And they are house-bearing [i. e. live in wagons], as is said, and feed on the milk of Scythian mares. And they live in common, having their property and whole social life on a communal basis. And the sage Anacharsis is said to have come from the Nomads, the most pious of men.[69]

Laertius, I, 101 (Ch. 8) says that the outspokenness of Anacharsis was the occasion of the proverb's being coined. In Aelian, *Rusticae epistolae*, *Ep.* XIV (Hercher) it is used of an angry retort. In Aristaenetus, *Ep.* II, xx (Hercher) to Aristobulus, it is used of the heartless reply of a girl to her beseeching suitor.

[66] In Aeschines, an older contemporary of Clearchus, the Scythian ancestry of Demosthenes is used to prejudice the Greeks against him. See *De fals. legat.* 78 and 180; *In Ctesiph.* 172.

[67] Ed. Kaibel, Leipzig, 1887, II.   [68] In Müller, *Georg. graec. min.* I, 232.

[69] Cf. the anonymous *Periplus ponti euxini*, Ch. 49, a paraphrase of the Pseudo-Scymnus.

The eulogistic attitude of the Pseudo-Scymnus is reflected in Strabo (a century later). Quoting Homer and Aeschylus,[70] he points out that the Scythians do not engage in business and have all things, except sword and drinking-cup, in common; and he continues:

XI, 31. Strabo, *Geogr.* VII, 301-303 (Translation on p. 326).

αὕτη δ' ἡ ὑπόληψις καὶ νῦν ἔτι συμμένει παρὰ τοῖς Ἕλλησιν· ἁπλουσ-
τάτους τε γὰρ αὐτοὺς νομίζομεν καὶ ἥκιστα κακεντρεχεῖς εὐτελεστέρους τε
πολὺ ἡμῶν καὶ αὐταρκεστέρους· καίτοι ὅ γε καθ' ἡμᾶς βίος εἰς πάντας
σχεδόν τι διατέτακε τὴν πρὸς τὸ χεῖρον μεταβολήν, τρυφὴν καὶ ἡδονὰς καὶ
κακοτεχνίας καὶ πλεονεξίας μυρίας πρὸς ταῦτ' εἰσάγων. πολὺ οὖν τῆς τοιαύτης
κακίας καὶ εἰς τοὺς βαρβάρους ἐμπέπτωκε τούς τε ἄλλους καὶ τοὺς νομάδας·
καὶ γὰρ θαλάττης ἁψάμενοι χείρους γεγόνασι λῃστεύοντες καὶ ξενοκτονοῦντες,
καὶ ἐπιπλεκόμενοι πολλοῖς μεταλαμβάνουσι τῆς ἐκείνων πολυτελείας καὶ
καπηλείας· ἃ δοκεῖ μὲν εἰς ἡμερότητα συντείνειν, διαφθείρει δὲ τὰ ἤθη καὶ
ποικιλίαν ἀντὶ τῆς ἁπλότητος τῆς ἄρτι λεχθείσης εἰσάγει.

Οἱ μέντοι πρὸ ἡμῶν καὶ μάλιστα οἱ ἐγγὺς τοῖς Ὁμήρου χρόνοις τοιοῦτοί
τινες ἦσαν καὶ ὑπελαμβάνοντο παρὰ τοῖς Ἕλλησιν ὁποίους Ὅμηρός φησιν.
ὅρα δὲ ἃ λέγει Ἡρόδοτος περὶ τοῦ τῶν Σκυθῶν βασιλέως, ἐφ' ὃν ἐστράτευσε
Δαρεῖος, καὶ τὰ ἐπεσταλμένα παρ' αὐτοῦ. ὅρα δὲ καὶ ἃ λέγει Χρύσιππος περὶ
τῶν τοῦ Βοσπόρου βασιλέων τῶν περὶ Λεύκωνα. πλήρεις δὲ καὶ αἱ Περσικαὶ
ἐπιστολαὶ τῆς ἁπλότητος ἧς λέγω, καὶ τὰ ὑπὸ τῶν Αἰγυπτίων καὶ Βαβυλωνίων
καὶ Ἰνδῶν ἀπομνημονευόμενα. διὰ τοῦτο δὲ καὶ ὁ Ἀνάχαρσις καὶ Ἄβαρις
καί τινες ἄλλοι τοιοῦτοι παρὰ τοῖς Ἕλλησιν εὐδοκίμουν, ὅτι ἐθνικόν τινα
χαρακτῆρα ἐπέφαινον εὐκολίας καὶ λιτότητος καὶ δικαιοσύνης. καὶ τί δεῖ τοὺς
πάλαι λέγειν; Ἀλέξανδρος γὰρ ὁ Φιλίππου κατὰ τὴν ἐπὶ Θρᾷκας τοὺς ὑπὲρ
τοῦ Αἵμου στρατείαν ἐμβαλὼν εἰς Τριβαλλούς, ὁρῶν μέχρι τοῦ Ἴστρου
καθήκοντας καὶ τῆς ἐν αὐτῷ νήσου Πεύκης, τὰ πέραν δὲ Γέτας ἔχοντας,
ἀφῖχθαι λέγεται μέχρι δεῦρο, καὶ εἰς μὲν τὴν νῆσον ἀποβῆναι μὴ δύνασθαι
σπάνει πλοίων (ἐκεῖσε γὰρ καταφυγόντα τὸν τῶν Τριβαλλῶν βασιλέα Σύρμον
ἀντισχεῖν πρὸς τὴν ἐπιχείρησιν), εἰς δὲ τοὺς Γέτας διαβάντα ἑλεῖν αὐτῶν
πόλιν καὶ ἀναστρέψαι διὰ ταχέων εἰς τὴν οἰκείαν, λαβόντα δῶρα [παρὰ] τῶν
ἐθνῶν καὶ παρὰ τοῦ Σύρμου. φησὶ δὲ Πτολεμαῖος ὁ Λάγου κατὰ ταύτην τὴν
στρατείαν συμμῖξαι τῷ Ἀλεξάνδρῳ Κελτοὺς τοὺς περὶ τὸν Ἀδρίαν φιλίας
καὶ ξενίας χάριν, δεξάμενον δὲ αὐτοὺς φιλοφρόνως τὸν βασιλέα ἐρέσθαι παρὰ
πότον, τί μάλιστα εἴη ὃ φοβοῖντο, νομίζοντα αὐτὸν ἐρεῖν· αὐτοὺς δ' ἀπο-
κρίνασθαι ὅτι οὐδὲν πλὴν εἰ ἄρα μὴ ὁ οὐρανὸς αὐτοῖς ἐπιπέσοι, φιλίαν γε
μὴν ἀνδρὸς τοιούτου περὶ παντὸς τίθεσθαι. ταῦτα δὲ ἁπλότητος τῆς τῶν
βαρβάρων ἐστὶ σημεῖα, τοῦ τε μὴ συγχωρήσαντος μὲν τὴν ἀπόβασιν τὴν εἰς
τὴν νῆσον, δῶρα δὲ πέμψαντος καὶ συνθεμένου φιλίαν, καὶ τῶν φοβεῖσθαι
μὲν οὐδένα φαμένων, φιλίαν δὲ περὶ παντὸς τίθεσθαι μεγάλων ἀνδρῶν. ὅ τε
Δρομιχαίτης κατὰ τοὺς διαδόχους ἦν Γετῶν βασιλεύς· ἐκεῖνος τοίνυν λαβὼν
ζωγρίᾳ Λυσίμαχον ἐπιστρατεύσαντα αὐτῷ, δείξας τὴν πενίαν τήν τε ἑαυτοῦ
καὶ τοῦ ἔθνους, ὁμοίως δὲ καὶ τὴν αὐτάρκειαν, ἐκέλευσε τοῖς τοιούτοις μὴ
πολεμεῖν, ἀλλὰ φίλοις χρῆσθαι· ταῦτα δ' εἰπών, ξενίσας καὶ συνθέμενος
φιλίαν ἀπέλυσεν αὐτόν.

Ἔφορος δ' ἐν τῇ τετάρτῃ μὲν τῆς ἱστορίας Εὐρώπη δ' ἐπιγραφομένῃ βίβλῳ,
περιοδεύσας τὴν Εὐρώπην μέχρι Σκυθῶν ἐπὶ τέλει φησὶν εἶναι τῶν τε ἄλλων
Σκυθῶν καὶ τῶν Σαυρομάτων τοὺς βίους ἀνομοίους· τοὺς μὲν γὰρ εἶναι
χαλεποὺς ὥστε καὶ ἀνθρωποφαγεῖν, τοὺς δὲ καὶ τῶν ἄλλων ζῴων ἀπέχεσθαι.

[70] See Nos. XI, 22, 23, 24.

οἱ μὲν οὖν ἄλλοι, φησί, τὰ περὶ τῆς ὠμότητος αὐτῶν λέγουσιν, εἰδότες τὸ
δεινόν τε καὶ τὸ θαυμαστὸν ἐκπληκτικὸν ὄν· δεῖν δὲ τἀναντία καὶ λέγειν καὶ
παραδείγματα ποιεῖσθαι· καὶ αὐτὸς οὖν περὶ τῶν δικαιοτάτοις ἤθεσι χρωμένων
ποιήσεσθαι τοὺς λόγους· εἶναι γάρ τινας τῶν νομάδων Σκυθῶν γάλακτι τρεφο-
μένους ἵππων τῇ τε δικαιοσύνῃ πάντων διαφέρειν· μεμνῆσθαι δ᾽ αὐτῶν τοὺς
ποιητάς, Ὅμηρον μὲν " γλακτοφάγων ἀβίων τε, δικαιοτάτων ἀνθρώπων "
φήσαντα τὴν γῆν καθορᾶν τὸν Δία, Ἡσίοδον δ᾽ ἐν τῇ καλουμένῃ γῆς περιόδῳ
τὸν Φινέα ὑπὸ τῶν Ἁρπυιῶν ἄγεσθαι " γλακτοφάγων εἰς γαῖαν ἀπήναις οἰκί᾽
ἐχόντων." εἶτ᾽ αἰτιολογεῖ διότι ταῖς διαίταις εὐτελεῖς ὄντες καὶ οὐ χρηματισταὶ
πρός τε ἀλλήλους εὐνομοῦνται, κοινὰ πάντα ἔχοντες τά τε ἄλλα καὶ τὰς
γυναῖκας καὶ τέκνα καὶ τὴν ὅλην συγγένειαν, πρός τε τοὺς ἐκτὸς ἄμαχοί εἰσι
καὶ ἀνίκητοι, οὐδὲν ἔχοντες ὑπὲρ οὗ δουλεύσουσι.[71]

And this opinion still exists among the Greeks, for we consider
them the simplest and the least crafty, and more thrifty and self-
sufficient than we. And yet life in our manner has spread to almost
all peoples a change for the worse, introducing luxury among them,
and pleasures and evil practices and countless selfish acts. Hence
much of this type of evil has penetrated to the Barbarians, to others
as well as to the Nomads. For having taken to the sea, they have
deteriorated, engaging in piracy and murdering strangers. And
having mingled with many peoples, they have shared their extravagance and trading habits. These things seem to lead to greater
civility, but they corrupt morals and introduce craft instead of the
simplicity mentioned above.

Those before our time and especially those near the time of
Homer, were such, and were supposed among the Greeks to be such
as Homer says. See, too, what Herodotus says about the king of
the Scythians against whom Darius led an expedition and his
messages. And see what Chrysippus says about the kings of the
Bosphorus of the dynasty of Leuco.[72] And the Persian letters, too,
are full of the simplicity of which I am speaking, and also the
memoirs of the Egyptians and Babylonians and Indians. Wherefore
Anacharsis and Abaris and certain others of this type were well
thought of among the Greeks, because they showed the national
character of good temper, plain-living, and justice. But why need
I speak of those of old? For Alexander, the son of Philip, on the
expedition against the trans-Haeman Thracians, penetrated among
the Triballians, and seeing the land extend to the Danube and the
island of Peuce in it, and the district beyond held by the Getae, is
said to have gone that far, and not to have been able to land on
the island for lack of boats. For then the king of the Triballians,
Syrmus, had fled there and held out against his attack. But crossing
over to the Getae, he took their city and returned speedily home,
after receiving presents from the people and from Syrmus. And
Ptolemy, the son of Lagus, says that on this expedition the Celts
about the Adriatic associated themselves with Alexander to win his
friendship and hospitality and that the king, receiving them,
amicably asked them over the cups what they feared most, thinking

[71] Ed. Meineke, Leipzig, 1866, 1915.

[72] Jones in his translation of Strabo (Loeb Lib.) refers to Plutarch's *De stoic.*
repugnant, 1043 B for some idea of what Chrysippus said on this subject.

they would say himself. But they answered that they feared nothing unless it were that Heaven might fall upon them, while putting the friendship of such a man (as Alexander) above all. And these things are signs of the simplicity of the barbarians; not permitting the landing on the island, yet sending gifts and writing in friendship, and saying that they feared no one, but putting the friendship of great men above all. Dromichaetes in the time of the Diadochi [73] was king of the Getae. When he took prisoner Lysimachus, who was making an expedition against him, he pointed out his poverty and that of his people, as well as their self-dependence, and bade him not to make war on such folk but to treat them as friends. And so saying, he entertained him and bound himself to him in friendship and freed him.

Ephorus in the fourth book of his history, entitled *Europe*, after having travelled around Europe as far as the Scythians, says towards the end that the lives of the Sauromatae and the other Scythians are unlike. For the former are cruel to the point of cannibalism and the latter refrain from eating animals at all. Other writers, he says speak of their cruelty because they know that the fearful and wonderful is startling. But they ought to tell the opposite sort of thing and hold them up as models, and he himself will accordingly speak of those who have the most just morals. For there are some of the Scythian Nomads who feed on mare's milk and in their justice surpass all, and the poets recall them to mind. Homer says, " The milk-drinking Abioi, the most righteous of men," speaking of Zeus looking down upon the land, and Hesiod in the so-called *Circuit of the Earth* says that Phineas was driven by the Harpies " into the land of the milk-drinkers who have houses on wagons." And he explains this on the ground that being thrifty and not business men, they are well-behaved towards one another, and have all things in common, their wives and children and their whole kin. Yet they are unconquerable by foreigners, for they have nothing for which they might be enslaved.[74]

The ground of Strabo's admiration for the Scythians is their non-commercial and communistic life — in which by inference the *amor habendi* must perforce be absent, — their general simplicity and lack of luxury, in short the rude austerity of their regimen. It will be observed that he notes the debilitating effect of civilization upon the noble savage much in the manner of writers of to-day upon the Polynesians. This theme appears later in Greek literature, as we shall see below.

A similar eulogy of Scythians as hard primitives is found in another writer of the first century B. C.

XI, 32. Pompeius Trogus, in Justin, *Hist. Phil. epit.* II, ii.

Scythia autem in orientem porrecta includitur ab uno latere Ponto, ab altero montibus Riphaeis, a tergo Asia et Phasi flumine. Multum in longitudinem et latitudinem patet. Hominibus inter se

---

[73] Roughly the last quarter of the 4th c. B. C.
[74] This account is repeated abridged in the *Chrestomathia straboniana*, VII, 14.

nulli fines. Neque enim agrum exercent, nec domus illis ulla aut
tectum aut sedes est, armenta et pecora semper pascentibus et per
incultas solitudines errare solitis. Uxores liberosque secum in plaustris vehunt, quibus coriis imbrium hiemisque causa tectis pro domibus utuntur. Iustitia gentis ingeniis culta, non legibus. Nullum
scelus apud eos furto gravius: quippe sine tecto munimentoque
pecora et armenta habentibus quid inter silvas superesset, si furari
liceret? Aurum et argentum perinde aspernantur ac reliqui mortales
adpetunt. Lacte et melle vescuntur. Lanae his usus ac vestium
ignotus, [et] quamquam continuis frigoribus urantur; pellibus tamen
ferinis ac murinis utuntur. Haec continentia illis morum quoque
iustitiam dedit, nihil alienum concupiscentibus; quippe ibi divi-
tiarum cupido est, ubi et usus. Atque utinam reliquis mortalibus
similis moderatio abstinentiaque alieni foret; profecto non tantum
bellorum per omnia saecula terris omnibus continuaretur, neque
plus hominum ferrum et arma quam naturalis fatorum condicio
raperet, prorsus ut admirabile videatur, hoc illis naturam dare, quod
Graeci longa sapientium doctrina praeceptisque philosophorum con-
sequi nequeunt, cultosque mores incultae barbariae conlatione super-
ari. Tanto plus in illis proficit vitiorum ignoratio quam in his
cognitio virtutis.[75]

The Scythia, however, which stretches towards the east, is bounded
on one side by the Pontus, on the other by the Rhiphaean Mountains,
in the rear by Asia and the Phasus River. It stretches far in length
and breadth. The people of that country recognize no boundaries
[i. e. they hold their land in common], for they do not work the
land. Nor have they any houses nor shelters nor fixed habitations,
but, feeding their flocks and herds, they are accustomed to wander
through uncultivated solitudes. They carry their wives and children
with them in wagons, which, covered with hides to keep out the rain
and cold, they use for houses. Justice is served by the tribe's inherent respect for it, not by laws. Theft is the most serious crime
in their eyes, since, if it were permitted to steal, what would men
whose flocks and herds are in the woods unprotected by a roof have
left? They shun gold and silver just as the rest of mortals seek it.
They live on milk and honey. The use of woolen clothing is unknown to them, although they are nipped by unceasing cold; yet
they use the skins of wild animals and rodents. This moderation
shows the justice of their way of life, for they desire nothing they
do not possess. Indeed the desire for riches exists only where there
is a use for them. Would that the rest of mortals had similar
moderation and regard for others' property! There would not have
been waged so many wars throughout the ages in all lands, nor
would martial weapons destroy more men than the natural course
of fate. How wonderful indeed it would seem that Nature gave to
them what the Greeks by the long teaching of their sages and the
precepts of their philosophers were unable to attain—that civilization
should be surpassed by comparison with barbarism. So much more
does ignorance of vice accomplish for the latter than knowledge of
virtue for the former.

[75] Ed. F. Ruehl, Leipzig, 1886, pp. 15-16.

In this passage there is a definite philosophic thesis. The superiority of the Scythians rests on their greater "naturalness" and the contrast between nature and art, inborn and acquired wisdom, comes out clearly. "Nature" has given the Scythians, moreover, many of the characteristics of the Golden Race. They are communistic; they live in a juristic state of nature; their life is simple and virtuous. But no detail — except possibly their diet of milk and honey — suggests soft primitivism. They are on the contrary almost as hard as the primitive men of Juvenal.

A similar point of view is expressed in the spurious *Letters* of Anacharsis.[76] These letters, which date at least from the first century B. C., are typical forgeries which use the Scythian Sage as the critic of civilization, much as Voltaire later used the Huron. They are too long to be quoted in full. Internal evidence suggests a Cynic origin. The first letter, addressed to the Athenians, begins by chiding the writer's hosts for laughing at his foreign accent. They — were they speaking Scythian — would make as poor a showing. It is not one's pronunciation but one's opinions which should be judged. "Scythians judge a speech bad when its thoughts are bad." [77]

The second letter, to Solon, plays upon the theme of the universality of the right, the third upon the necessity of sobriety. The fourth letter, to Medocus, repeats the Cynic commonplace that envy and disturbance of mind are signs of inner depravity; the Scythians rejoice in another's good fortune, they do not envy it. The fifth letter, to Hanno, has a peculiar interest in that it may be the source of a passage in Cicero.

XI, 33.   Pseudo-Anacharsis, *Epist.* V.

> Ἐμοὶ μὲν περίβλημα χλαῖνα σκυθική, ὑπόδημα δέρμα ποδῶν, κοίτη δὲ πᾶσα γῆ, δεῖπνον καὶ ἄριστον γάλα καὶ τυρὸς καὶ κρέας ὀπτόν, πιεῖν ὕδωρ. ὡς οὖν ἄγοντός μου σχολὴν ὧν οἱ πλεῖστοι ἕνεκεν ἀσχολοῦνται, παραγενοῦ πρός με, εἴ τινά μου χρείαν ἔχεις. δῶρα δ' οἷς ἐντρυφᾶτε ἀντιδωροῦμαί σοι, ὑμεῖς δ' ὅσοι Καρχηδονίων εἰς χάριν σὴν ἀνέθεσθε θεοῖς.[78]

My wrap is a Scythian cloak, my sandal the soles of my feet, my bed is the whole earth, and my dinner and breakfast milk and cheese and roasted meats, my drink is water.   Wherefore since I have respite from those things for which most men are busied, come to me if you have need of me.   But the gifts in which you revel I return to you, and do you offer them as a thank offering to the gods of the Carthaginians.

This letter is slightly modified in Cicero's version.[79]

---

[76] Published in Hercher's *Epistolographi graeci*, Paris, 1873, pp. 102 ff.

[77] Cf. Socrates's criticism of rhetorical devices in the *Phaedrus*.

[78] Hercher, *Epistolographi graeci*, Paris, 1873.

[79] K. Praechter, in "Die Berner Handschrift der Anacharsisbriefe," *Philologus*, lviii (1899), p. 256 f. seems to admit that Cicero translated this letter. The words *pulpamentum fames* are not in the Greek, nor is there anything in Cicero to correspond to the drinking of water. The MS which Praechter is discussing has the words πᾶν ὄψον πεῖνα in place of ὀπτόν, πιεῖν ὕδωρ, which would seem to account for Cicero's rendering.

XI, 34. Cicero, *Tusc. disp.* V, xxxii, 90.

An Scythes Anacharsis potuit pro nihilo pecuniam ducere, nostrates philosophi facere non potuerunt? Illius epistola fertur his verbis: " Anacharsis Hannoni salutem. Mihi amictui est Scythicum tegimen, calciamentum solorum callum, cubile terra, pulpamentum fames; lacte, caseo, carne vescor. Quare ut ad quietum me licet venias; munera autem ista, quibus es delectatus, vel civibus tuis vel dis immortalibus dona." Omnes fere philosophi omnium disciplinarum, nisi quos a recta ratione natura vitiosa detorsisset, eodem hoc animo esse potuerunt.[80]

Could the Scythian Anacharsis hold money in no esteem, while our own philosophers have been unable to do so? A letter of his was expressed in these words: " Anacharsis to Hanno, greetings. My clothing is a Scythian cloak, my footgear the calluses of my soles, my bed the earth, my appetizer hunger. I live on milk, cheese, meat. Wherefore you may come to me as to one at rest. Those gifts of yours, however, in which you delight, give either to your fellow citizens or to the immortal gods." Virtually all the philosophers of all the schools, except those whom a vicious nature has misled from right reason, might be of the same mind.

The simplicity of Scythian life and its attendant moral freedom are again indicated in the sixth letter, addressed " To the King's Son." " You," says the Scythian, " have flutes and purses; I have javelins and a bow. Therefore it is not strange that you are a slave and I a free man, and that you have many enemies, I none. But should you wish to throw away your money and to carry the bow and arrow and live with the Scythians, the same fortune will attend you." The seventh and eighth letters are without interest to us (the seventh is indeed almost meaningless in the text given by Hercher), but in the ninth, to Croesus, the familiar note of primitive communism is struck. The Greeks, says the writer, by dividing the heavens, the sea, and the land among the sons of Cronus, attributed their own weaknesses to the gods. For the Greeks have nothing in common. Expanding on the evils of private ownership, the writer extols by contrast the communistic life of the Scythians, in which there is no love of gain and no warfare.[81]

It was also to the Scythians that Horace turned when he wished to satirize his degenerate fellows. They hold exactly the same position in his satire as the men of the Golden Age in other poets.

---

[80] Ed. M. Pohlenz, Leipzig, 1918.

[81] The supposed attitude of Anacharsis towards wealth is interestingly brought out on an *ostrakon* which dates from the second century A. D. (140/1), the inscription of which was published by Jouguet and Lefebvre in *Bull. de Correspondance Hellénique* XXVIII (1904), pp. 201 ff. This *ostrakon* tells the story of the wealthy son who gave but little to his father. He was brought before Anacharsis for judgment. The son exclaims, " But has he not a house, possessions, heaps of gold? What tyrant then or what judge or ancient lawgiver would speak rightly ⟨against me⟩? " The answer of Anacharsis is not given, but may be guessed.

XI, 35. Horace, *Odes*, III, 24, 1-32.

> Intactis opulentior
>   Thesauris Arabum et divitis Indiae
> Caementis licet occupes
>   Tyrrhenum omne tuis et mare Apulicum,
> Si figit adamantinos
>   Summis verticibus dira Necessitas
> Clavos, non animum metu,
>   Non mortis laqueis expedies caput.
> Campestres melius Scythae,
>   Quorum plaustra vagas rite trahunt domos,
> Vivunt et rigidi Getae,
>   Immetata quibus iugera liberas
> Fruges et Cererem ferunt,
>   Nec cultura placet longior annua,
> Defunctumque laboribus
>   Aequali recreat sorte vicarius.
> Illic matre carentibus
>   Privignis mulier temperat innocens,
> Nec dotata regit virum
>   Coniunx nec nitido fidit adultero;
> Dos est magna parentium
>   Virtus et metuens alterius viri
> Certo foedere castitas,
>   Et peccare nefas aut pretiumst mori.
> O quisquis volet impias
>   Caedis et rabiem tollere civicam,
> Si quaeret pater urbium
>   Subscribi statuis, indomitam audeat
> Refrenare licentiam,
>   Clarus post genitis: quatenus, heu nefas!
> Virtutem incolumem odimus,
>   Sublatam ex oculis quaerimus invidi.[82]

Though you be richer than the untouched treasuries of the Arabs and the wealth of India, though you fill the whole Tyrrhenian and Apulian seas with your concrete foundations, if dire Necessity fastens her iron nails in your forehead, you will not free your soul from fear nor your body from the snares of death. Better live the Scythians of the plains, whose wagons drag their homes awandering after their manner, and the frozen Getae. Their unfenced [lit. unmeasured] acres bear free grains and corn, nor do they care to plant for longer than a year.[83] A proxy with his labor relieves the man who has already done his share. There the kindly wife is forbearing with her motherless stepchildren; the dowered spouse does not rule her husband nor turn to a spruce lover. The great dowry is the virtue of one's parents and chastity which, contract unbroken, dreads the husband of another. There it is wrong to sin and the price is death. You who wish to abolish impious murders and civic madness, if you seek to have " the Father of Cities " inscribed on

---

[82] Ed. P. Shorey and G. Laing, Chicago, 1919.

[83] Shorey notes a similar custom reported by Caesar of the Suevi (*B. G.* 4, 1) and by Tacitus of the Germans (*Germ.* 19).

your statues, dare to check unbridled licence and you will be famous
to posterity. For, alas! we hate virtue when she is alive, and we
seek her regretfully when she is snatched from our eyes.[84]

The rigor of Scythian life became almost proverbial and we find in Virgil
an extended account of it. He believes, however, that the Scythians are a
merry lot in spite of their simple ways of living.[85]

XI, 36. Virgil, *Georgics*, III, 349-383 (37-30 B. C.).

At non qua Scythiae gentes Maeotiaque unda,
turbidus et torquens flaventis Hister harenas,
quaque redit medium Rhodope porrecta sub axem.
illic clausa tenent stabulis armenta, neque ullae
aut herbae campo apparent aut arbore frondes;
sed iacet aggeribus niveis informis et alto
terra gelu late septemque adsurgit in ulnas.
semper hiemps, semper spirantes frigora cauri.
tum sol pallentis haut umquam discutit umbras,
nec cum invectus equis altum petit aethera, nec cum
praecipitem Oceani rubro lavit aequore currum.
concrescunt subitae currenti in flumine crustae,
undaque iam tergo ferratos sustinet orbis,
puppibus illa prius, patulis nunc hospita plaustris;
aeraque dissiliunt volgo, vestesque rigescunt
indutae, caeduntque securibus umida vina,
et totae solidam in glaciem vertere lacunae,
stiriaque impexis induruit horrida barbis.
interea toto non setius aëre ninguit:
intereunt pecudes, stant circumfusa pruinis
corpora magna boum, confertoque agmine cervi
torpent mole nova et summis vix cornibus extant.
hos non immissis canibus, non cassibus ullis
puniceaeve agitant pavidos formidine pinnae,
sed frustra oppositum trudentis pectore montem
comminus obtruncant ferro graviterque rudentis
caedunt et magno laeti clamore reportant.
ipsi in defossis specubus secura sub alta
otia agunt terra congestaque robora totasque
advolvere focis ulmos ignique dedere.
hic noctem ludo ducunt at pocula laeti
fermento atque acidis imitantur vitea sorbis.
talis hyperboreo septem subiecta trioni
gens effrena virum Riphaeo tunditur euro,
et pecudum fulvis velatur corpora saetis.[86]

But things are not thus where dwell the tribes of Scythia and the
Maeotian waters flow, where the Danube turbidly rolls its yellow
sand and Rhodope turns and stretches towards the pole. There the

---

[84] This *Ode* should be compared with III, vi, esp. lines 21-48, in which the ancient—
but not primitive—Romans take the place of the Scythians.

[85] That Virgil's sympathies were not, on the whole, with the idyllic sort of primitivism seems clear from another passage in the *Georgics*, II, 121 ff.

[86] Ed. O. Ribbeck, Leipzig, 1894.

herds are kept closed in stables and no grass appears in the fields nor
leaves upon the trees. But earth lies shapeless under the drifted
snow and deep frost, and rises in hillocks seven ells high. It is
always winter, the north winds are always breathing cold. The sun
never scatters the pallid shadows, neither when he seeks the high
aether borne along by his horses nor when he plunges his chariot
headlong into the ruddy stream of ocean. Sudden films now gather
in the running river and the water now holds iron wheels on its back;
the water that once welcomed ships now welcomes broad wagons.
Bronze [vessels] commonly fly apart and clothing stiffens on the
back. The liquid wine is cut with axes and all the pools turn to solid
ice. Bristling icicles stiffen on uncombed beards. Meanwhile the air
too is full of snow. The herds perish, the huge bodies of oxen stand
buried in snow, and huddled together the deer are numb under the
unwonted mass and scarcely do the tips of their antlers show. These
timid creatures cannot be moved by letting dogs loose upon them nor
with snares, nor with the " scare " of scarlet feather. But pressing
in vain on the weight against their chests, they are killed by the
sword and, falling with deep roaring cries, they are joyfully carried
off by the loudly shouting [huntsmen]. The men in dugouts lead a
life of safe idleness deep under the earth, and roll piles of oak logs
and whole elms upon the hearth and give them to the fire. Here they
pass the night in sport, and joyfully drink, in place of wine, beer and
the sour juice of the sorb-apple. Such is the race, unbridled in force,
which lives under the northern constellation (Orion), buffeted by the
Rhiphaean blasts, their bodies covered with the tawny hides of their
flocks.

Virgil's knowledge of Scythia was of course entirely at second hand, but
his younger contemporary, Ovid, had a direct acquaintance with at least a
limited part of the country and its inhabitants. It is interesting that
though he detested, as any Italian would, the climate, he yet learned to
admit the existence of some admirable traits in the Scythians themselves.
His knowledge of Scythia was gained, to be sure, under adverse conditions,
for he spent the last ten years of his life there in exile.

The Scythians whom Ovid knew were the Getae, later to be identified
with the Goths. The most poignant description of the country and its
people is to be found in *Tristia,* III, x. Here he complains primarily of the
cold, in a passage which cannot fail to suggest that of Virgil just quoted,
of the constant threat of barbarian invasion, and of the soil which lies
barren and neglected.

XI, 37. Ovid, *Tristia,* III, x (Translation on p. 335).

> Si quis adhuc istic meminit Nasonis adempti,
>   et superest sine me nomen in urbe meum,
> suppositum stellis numquam tangentibus aequor
>   me sciat in media vivere barbarie.
> Sauromatae cingunt, fera gens, Bessique Getaeque,
>   quam non ingenio nomina digna meo!
> dum tamen aura tepet, medio defendimur Histro:
>   ille suis liquidus bella repellit aquis.

at cum tristis Hiems squalentia protulit ora,
   terraque marmoreo candida facta gelu est,
dum vetat et boreas et nix habitare sub Arcto,
   tum liquet, has gentes axe tremente premi.
nix iacet, et iactam ne sol pluviaeque resolvunt,
   indurat Boreas perpetuamque facit.
ergo ubi delicuit nondum prior, altera venit,
   et solet in multis bima manere locis;
tantaque commoti vis est aquilonis, ut altas
   aequet humo turres tectaque rapta ferat.
pellibus et sutis arcent mala frigora bracis,
   oraque de toto corpore sola patent.
saepe sonant moti glacie pendente capilli,
   et nitet inducto candida barba gelu;
nudaque consistunt, formam servantia testae,
   vina, nec hausta meri, sed data frusta bibunt.
quid loquar, ut vincti concrescant frigore rivi,
   deque lacu fragiles effodiantur aquae:
ipse, papyrifero qui non angustior amne
   miscetur vasto multa per ora freto,
caeruleos ventis latices durantibus, Hister
   congelat et tectis in mare serpit aquis;
quaque rates ierant, pedibus nunc itur, et undas
   frigore concretas ungula pulsat equi;
perque novos pontes, subter labentibus undis,
   ducunt Sarmatici barbara plaustra boves.
vix equidem credar — sed, cum sint praemia falsi
   nulla, ratam debet testis habere fidem — :
vidimus ingentem glacie consistere pontum,
   lubricaque inmotas testa premebat aquas.
nec vidisse sat est. durum calcavimus aequor,
   undaque non udo sub pede summa fuit.
si tibi tale fretum quondam, Leandre, fuisset,
   non foret angustae mors tua crimen aquae.
tum neque se pandi possunt delphines in auras
   tollere; conantes dura coërcet hiems;
et quamvis Boreas iactatis insonet alis,
   fluctus in obsesso gurgite nullus erit;
inclusaeque gelu stabunt in marmore puppes,
   nec poterit rigidas findere remus aquas.
vidimus in glacie pisces haerere ligatos,
   sed pars ex illis tunc quoque viva fuit.
sive igitur Boreae nimii vis saeva marinas,
   sive redundatas flumine cogit aquas;
protinus aequato siccis Aquilonibus Histro
   invehitur celeri barbarus hostis equo;
hostis equo pollens longeque volante sagitta
   vicinam late depopulatur humum.
diffugiunt alii, nullisque tuentibus agros
   incustoditae diripiuntur opes;
ruris opes parvae, pecus et stridentia plaustra,
   et quas divitias incola pauper habet.

pars agitur vinctis post tergum capta lacertis,
    respiciens frustra rura Laremque suum:
pars cadit hamatis misere confixa sagittis:
    nam volucri ferro tinctile virus inest.
quae nequeunt secum ferre aut abducere, perdunt,
    et cremat insontes hostica flamma casas.
tunc quoque, cum pax est, trepidant formidine belli,
    nec quisquam presso vomere sulcat humum.
aut videt, aut metuit locus hic, quem non videt, hostem;
    cessat iners rigido terra relicta situ.
non hic pampinea dulcis latet uva sub umbra,
    nec cumulant altos fervida musta lacus.
poma negat regio: nec haberet Acontius, in quo
    scriberet hic dominae verba legenda suae.
aspiceres nudos sine fronde, sine arbore, campos:
    heu loca felici non adeunda viro!
ergo tam late pateat cum maximus orbis,
    haec est in poenam terra reperta meam? [87]

If there be anyone who still remembers banished Naso, if my name still survives in the city in my absence, be it known that I am living in the midst of barbarism, beneath stars which never touch the sea. I am surrounded by Sauromatae, a savage tribe, by Bessi and by Getae, names how little worthy of my genius! Still, while breezes blow warm, we are defended by the Danube; he repels wars with his flowing waters. But when gloomy winter thrusts out his squalid jaws, and earth shines white with frost like marble, when Boreas and the snow prevent one from living under the Bear, then it is clear that these peoples are hard pressed by the quivering pole. Snow lies over the land, and neither sun or shower melt it, but Boreas hardens it and makes it enduring. Before one fall of snow has melted another has come, and often in many places remains on the ground for two years. So great is the force of Aquilo once aroused that he razes high towers and blows buildings away. The natives ward off the evil cold with skins and stitched trousers, and of their whole body the face alone is exposed. Often their hair tinkles with pendant icicles and their beards shine white with a frosty covering. Wine unsheltered stands stiff, preserving the shape of the wine jar, nor does one drink draughts of wine, but pieces.

Why speak of streams bound fast with cold or of brittle water dug out of pools? Danube itself, no more narrow than the papyrus-bearing stream, mingles with the vast deep through many mouths, and as the winds stiffen its blue waters, freezes, and worms its way into the sea under ice. Where ships once went, now feet go, and horses' hooves beat upon frozen waters. Over the new bridges above the gliding stream, Sarmatian oxen draw the barbarian wagons. I shall hardly be believed, but, since there are no rewards for falsehood, the witness ought to be trusted — we have seen the huge sea rigid with ice, and a slippery shell [of ice] pressing upon the immobile waters. It is not enough to have seen it; we have walked upon the hard sea, and the water's surface was dry under our feet. If such

[87] Ed. A. Riese, Leipzig, 1874, with minor changes in punctuation.

a sea had once been yours, Leander, your death would not have been charged against the strait. Now the curved dolphins cannot leap into the air; harsh winter frustrates their attempts. Though Boreas thunder with beating wings, no wave leaps up from the stricken flood. Locked in ice the ships will stand like stone nor will the oar cleave the stiffened waters. We have seen fish bound fast in ice, but some of them also still alive. Whether the savage force of too great Boreas freezes the sea or the abundant waters of the river, when Danube has been leveled by dry Aquilo, the barbarian enemy dashes onward with swift horse; an enemy strong in horse and in far flying arrow plunders the neighboring land far and wide. Some take flight, and with none protecting the fields, the unguarded wealth is looted, the scant wealth of the country, flocks and creaking wagons, and what riches the poor farmer has. Some with arms bound behind their backs are led off looking back in vain upon their homesteads and Lares: some fall in pain pierced by barbed arrows, for poison has stained the winged steel. What they cannot carry off or lead away they destroy, and burn with hostile flame the harmless cabins. But even when there is peace one trembles at the threat of war, nor does anyone cleave the soil with pressing plow. This place either sees an enemy or fears one it does not see. The land inert lies idle, utterly abandoned. Not here does the sweet grape hide under the shade of its leaves, nor does the bubbling must fill deep vats to the brim. This region refuses to bear the apple, nor would Acontius have wherewith to write words for his mistress to read. You may see fields stript of leaf or tree, places, alas! no happy man would enter! When the great earth lies so wide about us, is this the land for my punishment? [88]

Ovid's horror of his place of exile allowed him to appreciate some of the moral qualities of the *duri Getae*, but to no great degree. Writing to his friend, Cotta (*Ex Ponto*, III, ii, 39-100), he relates how they are moved by tales of friendship. But in general his companions leave him cold. They are "filthy Getae" (*Ex P.* I, ii, 106); they are *inhumani* (*id.* I, v, 66); "wild" (*trux*) (*id.* I, vii, 12); savage (*ferus*) (*id.* I, viii, 15; II, i, 66 (*ferox*)). They laugh at his Latin and talk maliciously about him in his presence (*Tristia*, V, x, 38 f.); so that their sensitivity to tales of friendly devotion does not weigh heavily in the poet's appraisal of them. Moreover, the detail is introduced to show that *even* the Getae were moved by friendship, not to credit them with an unusual virtue.

The reputation of the Scythians as philosophers is carried on in a passage from Quintus Curtius which reproduces an oration made by one of their nobles to Alexander the Great. It is presumably this to which Voltaire refers in his *Essai sur les Moeurs* [89] as a *harangue philosophique*. The speech, full of proverbial philosophy, resembles those ascribed to Indian chiefs in the eighteenth and nineteenth centuries.

[88] This whole poem reproduces most of the sentiment of *Tristia*, V, x.

[89] Introduction, Ch. XIV, ed. Beuchot, rev. by Moland, Paris, 1878 (*Oeuvres Complètes*, XI, 42).

XI, 38. Quintus Curtius. *De gestis Alexandri Magni*, VII, xxxiv-xxxv
(Translation on p. 338).

Si dii habitum corporis tui aviditati animi parem esse voluissent,
orbis te non caperet; altera manu orientem, altera occidentem con-
tingeres, et hoc assequutus scire velles, ubi tanti numinis fulgor
conderetur. Sic quoque concupiscis, quae non capis. Ab Europa
petis Asiam: ex Asia transis in Europam; deinde si humanum
genus omne superaveris, cum silvis et nivibus et fluminibus ferisque
bestiis gesturus es bellum. Quid? tu ignoras arbores magnas diu
crescere, una hora extirpari? Stultus est, qui fructus earum spectat,
altitudinem non metitur. Vide, ne dum ad cacumen pervenire con-
tendis, cum ipsis ramis, quos comprehenderis, decidas. Leo quoque
aliquando minimarum avium pabulum fuit; et ferrum rubigo consumit. Nihil tam firmum est, cui periculum non sit etiam ab
invalido. Quid nobis tecum est? Nunquam terram tuam attigimus.
Qui sis, unde venias, licetne ignorare in vastis silvis viventibus?
Nec servire ulli possumus, nec imperare desideramus. Dona nobis
data sunt, ne Scytharum gentem ignores, iugum, aratrum, hasta,
sagitta, patera. His utimur et cum amicis et adversus inimicos.
Fruges amicis damus boum labore quaesitas; patera cum his vinum
diis libamus; inimicos sagitta eminus, hasta cominus petimus. Sic
Syriae regem et postea Persarum Medorumque superavimus, pa-
tuitque nobis iter usque in Aegyptum. At tu, qui te gloriaris ad
latrones persequendos venire, omnium gentium, quas adisti, latro es.
Lydiam cepisti; Syriam occupasti; Persidem tenes; Bactrianos
habes in potestate; Indos petisti; iam etiam ad pecora nostra avaras
et insatiabiles manus porrigis. Quid tibi divitiis opus est, quae
esurire cogunt? Primus omnium satietate parasti famem; ut quo
plura haberes, acrius, quae non habes, cuperes. Non succurrit tibi,
quamdiu circum Bactra haereas? dum illos subigis, Sogdiani bellare
coeperunt. Bellum tibi ex victoria nascitur. Nam ut maior for-
tiorque sis, quam quisquam, tamen alienigenam dominum pati nemo
vult.
XXXV. Transi modo Tanaim: scies, quam late pateant, nunquam tamen consequeris Scythas. Paupertas nostra velocior erit,
quam exercitus tuus, qui praedam tot nationum vehit. Rursus quum
procul abesse nos credes, videbis in tuis castris. Eadem enim veloci-
tate et sequimur, et fugimus. Scytharum solitudines graecis etiam
proverbiis audio eludi. At nos deserta et humano cultu vacua magis,
quam urbes et opulentos agros sequimur. Proinde fortunam tuam
pressis manibus tene. Lubrica est, nec invita teneri potest. Salubre
consilium sequens, quam praesens tempus ostendit melius. Impone
felicitati tuae frenos: facilius illam reges. Nostri sine pedibus
dicunt esse fortunam, quae manus et pinnas tantum habet; quum
manus porrigit, pinnas quoque comprehendere non sinit. Denique
si deus es, tribuere mortalibus beneficia debes, non sua eripere; sin
autem homo es, id quod es, semper esse te cogita. Stultum est eorum
meminisse, propter quae tui oblivisceris. Quibus bellum non intu-
leris, bonis amicis poteris uti. Nam et firmissima est inter pares
amicitia, et videntur pares, qui non fecerunt inter se periculum
virium. Quos viceris, amicos tibi esse cave credas: inter dominum et
servum nulla amicitia est; etiam in pace belli tamen iura servantur.
Iurando gratiam Scythas sancire ne credideris: colendo fidem iurant.

Graecorum ista cautio est, qui pacta consignant, et deos invocant:
nos religionem in ipsa fide novimus. Qui non reverentur homines,
fallunt deos. Nec tibi amico opus est, de cuius benivolentia dubites.
Ceterum nos et Asiae et Europae custodes habebis: Bactra, nisi
dividat Tanais, contingimus: ultra Tanaim usque ad Thraciam
colimus: Thraciae Macedoniam coniunctam esse fama est. Utrique
imperio tuo finitimos hostes an amicos velis esse considera.[90]

If the gods had wished the disposition of your body to be equal
to the avidity of your mind, the world would not have held you.
With one hand you would touch the orient, with the other the occident, and having reached these limits, you would wish to know where
the brilliance of so great a god [the Sun] is established. Thus
you desire also what you do not possess. From Europe you set
out to seize Asia. From Asia you pass over into Europe. Then
if you should have conquered the whole human race, you would begin
to wage war on the forests and snowbanks, the rivers and the wild
beasts. What, do you not know that trees which reach their height
after years of growth are cut down in an hour? He is a fool who
looks upon their fruit and does not measure their height. Look to it
that while you strive to reach the top, you do not fall with the very
branches which you have grasped. The lion too has been sometimes
the food of tiny birds, and rust has consumed iron. Nothing is so
strong that it is not in danger from the weak. What is your business
in this land of ours? We have never touched the borders of yours.
May we who live in the vast forests not be ignorant of who you are,
of whence you come? We can serve no man nor do we desire to
command any. That you may not be ignorant of the Scythian
people, know that we have our gifts, the yoke, the plow, the spear,
the arrow, the cup. We use these both with our friends and against
our enemies. We give to our friends the grain grown with the labor
of our oxen; we pour libations of wine from the cup to these gods;
we seek our distant enemies with the arrows, those close at hand with
the spear. Thus have we conquered the king of Syria and afterwards
the king of the Medes and Persians. The road has lain open before
us as far as Egypt. But you, who boast about coming in pursuit of
plunderers, have been the plunderer of all the peoples into whose
country you have entered. You have taken Lydia; you have occupied Syria; you hold Persia; you have Bactrians in your power;
you have sought the Indies; even now you stretch out your greedy
and insatiable hands towards our flocks. What need have you of
riches, which stir up your hunger? You are the first to whet your
appetite by a satiety of everything, so that the more you have, the
more sharply do you desire what you do not have. Does it not occur
to you how long you lingered about Bactria? While you were sub-
jugating it, the Sogdiani began to fight. Your wars are the children
of your victories. For although you may be greater and stronger
than anyone else, yet no one wishes to suffer foreign dominion.

Cross now the Tanais. You will know that though their country
stretches far and wide, you will none the less never capture the
Scythians.[91] Our poverty will be swifter than your army which car-

---

[90] Ed. Julius Mützell, Berlin, 1841, p. 694 ff.

[91] Replacing Mützell's semicolon after *pateant* with a comma.

ries the booty of so many peoples. Again, when you believe we are far away, you will see us in your camp. For we pursue and flee with equal speed. I have heard that the Scythian wastes are ridiculed in Greek proverbs.[92] But we seek deserted tracts devoid of human cultivation rather than cities and rich fields. Henceforth hold to fortune with clenched fists. Fortune is slippery, and cannot be held against her will. Good counsel appears better in the future than in the present. Check your felicity; it is more easily ruled. Our sages tell us that fortune has no feet but has only hands and wings. When she stretches out her hands, she does not let her wings be grasped as well. Finally, if you are a god, you ought to confer blessings on mortals, not to snatch theirs away. But if you are a man, always think of what you are. It is foolish to remember those things because of which you forget yourself. Those upon whom you will not wage war, you may always enjoy as good friends. For friendship is strongest among equals and they appear equal who have not made a test of their strength against each other. Guard against believing that your victims are your friends. Between master and slave there is no friendship. Even in peace the laws of war will be retained. Do not think that the Scythians sanctify an obligation by swearing; they swear good faith by observing it. Swearing is a precaution of the Greeks, who seal treaties and invoke the gods. We have learned religion in good faith itself. They who do not reverence men, deceive the gods. Nor have you any need of a friend whose good will you may doubt. But us you will have as guardians of Asia and Europe. We touch the borders of Bactria except where the Tanais divides it; our lands run beyond the Tanais to Thrace; rumor has it that Macedonia lies next to Thrace. Consider whether you wish the neighbors of your two empires to be enemies or friends.

Ovid's bad impression of the Scythians was derived from direct personal acquaintance with them. And indeed as the Greeks and Romans came into closer contact with this savage people, the romantic notion of their nobility began to fade. Fronto, however, in a preamble to a history of the Parthian war which he planned to write from materials supplied him by Lucius (165 A. D.),[93] admits that the poverty of the Scythians kept them free, since there is no reward for conquering the poor; but of all the plundering nomads he selects only the Parthians as fit to be called "enemies" rather than "brigands," since they fought successfully against Roman emperors. We find, indeed, that their reputation steadily sank as the civilized world locked horns with them. Thus when we come to Julian, we find him writing [94] of becoming worse to strangers than the Scythians (Σκυθῶν κακοξενώτεροι),[95] as if the phrase

[92] Mützell quotes two of these proverbs in a note.

[93] See C. R. Haines in his translation of Fronto (Loeb Lib. 1920, vol. II, 203).

[94] *Fragm. Epist.* 291 B.

[95] There was a legend that the Scythians sacrificed strangers to Artemis, which is probably the foundation of this. See Herodotus IV, 103; Sext. Emp. *Hyp.* III, 208, etc.

would carry its own force regardless of the long literary tradition in their favor. This seems to have been a subject for wonder by Julian's contemporaries and "the Scythians" became a stock topic for sophistic eloquence, if we may judge from Philostratus.[96] Just what the orators said about them is largely a matter of conjecture except in one case, which is very revealing. This is a reference by Philostratus to a speech of Alexander the Sophist which pretends — for of course these speeches were only pretense — to recall the Scythians to their earlier nomadic life, on the ground that they are losing their health by living in cities.

It is obvious that both the unfavorable and favorable views of Scythians were early, and we find them both lingering on side by side in later writers.

The interest in savages in the second century A. D. is further illustrated by the fact that Dio Chrysostom wrote a work, now lost, on the Getae, among whom he had travelled during his exile.[97] In his extant works we find the following.

XI, 39. Dio Chrysostom, *De virtute*, Orat. LXIX, 1-6.

Ἄπορόν μοι δοκεῖ εἶναι ὅτι οἱ ἄνθρωποι ἄλλα μὲν ἐπαινοῦσι καὶ θαυμάζουσιν, ἄλλων δὲ ἐφίενται καὶ περὶ ἄλλα ἐσπουδάκασιν. ἐπαινοῦσι μὲν γάρ, ὡς ἔπος εἰπεῖν, πάντες καὶ θεῖα καὶ σεμνά φασιν ἀνδρείαν καὶ δικαιοσύνην καὶ φρόνησιν καὶ συλλήβδην ἀρετὴν πᾶσαν. καὶ οὓς ἂν ἡγῶνται τοιούτους εἶναι ἢ γεγονέναι ἢ ἐγγύς, θαυμάζουσι καὶ ὑμνοῦσι· καὶ τοὺς μέν τινας θεούς, τοὺς δὲ ἥρωας ἀποφαίνουσιν, οἷον Ἡρακλέα καὶ Διοσκούρους καὶ Θησέα καὶ Ἀχιλλέα καὶ πάντας τοὺς ἡμιθέους λεγομένους. ⟨οἷς⟩ ὃν ἂν ὅμοιον ὑπολαμβάνωσιν, ἕτοιμοί εἰσιν ἅπαντες ἐκείνῳ πείθεσθαι καὶ ὑπηρετεῖν, ὅ τι ἂν προστάττῃ, καὶ βασιλέα καὶ ἄρχοντα ἀποδεικνύναι ἑαυτῶν καὶ τὰ σφέτερα ἐπιτρέπειν, ὃν ἂν σώφρονα καὶ δίκαιον καὶ φρόνιμον ὄντως ὑπολαμβάνωσι καὶ ἁπλῶς ἄνδρα ἀγαθόν. ὥστε ταύτῃ μὲν οὐκ ἄν τις αὐτοῖς μέμψαιτο ὡς οὐκ αἰσθανομένοις ὅτι σεμνόν τι καὶ τίμιον καὶ τοῦ παντὸς ἄξιον χρῆμα ἀρετή· ἐπιθυμοῦσί γε μὴν πάντων μᾶλλον ἢ ἀγαθοὶ γενέσθαι καὶ πράττουσι πάντα πρότερον ἢ ὅπως σωφρονήσουσι καὶ φρόνιμοι ἔσονται καὶ δίκαιοι καὶ ἄνδρες σπουδαῖοι, καλῶς μὲν αὐτῶν δυνάμενοι προΐστασθαι, καλῶς δὲ οἶκον οἰκῆσαι, καλῶς δὲ ἄρξαι πόλεως, εὖ δὲ πλοῦτον ἐνεγκεῖν, εὖ δὲ πενίαν, εὖ δὲ προσενεχθῆναι φίλοις, εὖ δὲ συγγενέσι, δικαίως δ' ἐπιμεληθῆναι γονέων, ὁσίως δὲ θεραπεῦσαι θεούς. ἀλλ' οἱ μέν τινες περὶ γεωργίαν πραγματεύονται, οἱ δὲ περὶ ἐμπορίαν, οἱ δ' ἐπὶ στρατείαν ὁρμῶσιν, οἱ δ' ἐπ' ἰατρικήν, οἱ δὲ οἰκοδομικὴν ἢ ναυπηγικὴν ἐκμανθάνουσιν, οἱ δὲ κιθαρίζειν ἢ αὐλεῖν ἢ σκυτοτομεῖν ἢ παλαίειν, οἱ δὲ ὅπως δεινοὶ δόξουσι περὶ τὸ εἰπεῖν ἐν δήμῳ ἢ δικαστηρίῳ τὴν πᾶσαν σπουδὴν ἔχουσιν, οἱ δὲ ὅπως ἰσχυροὶ ἔσονται τὰ σώματα. καίτοι τοὺς ἐμπόρους μὲν καὶ γεωργοὺς καὶ στρατιώτας καὶ ἰατροὺς καὶ οἰκοδόμους καὶ κιθαριστὰς καὶ αὐλητὰς καὶ παιδοτρίβας, ἔτι δὲ τοὺς λεγομένους ῥήτορας καὶ τοὺς πάνυ ἰσχύοντας τοῖς σώμασιν, ἀθλίους καὶ δυστυχεῖς ⟨τοὺς⟩ πολλοὺς ἂν εὕροι τις ἢ μικροῦ δεῖν ἅπαντας. ἂν δὲ ἡ ψυχὴ ἔμφρων γένηται καὶ ὁ νοῦς ἀγαθὸς καὶ ἱκανοὶ ὦσι τά τε αὐτῶν πράγματα ὀρθῶς πράττειν καὶ τὰ τῶν ἄλλων, τούτους ἀνάγκη καὶ εὐδαιμόνως ζῆν, νομίμους ἄνδρας γενομένους καὶ ἀγαθοῦ δαίμονος τυχόντας καὶ φίλους ὄντας τοῖς θεοῖς. οὐ γὰρ ἄλλους μὲν φρονίμους εἰκὸς

[96] *Lives of the Sophists*, 572, 575, 620.

[97] Cf. Dio, ed. Arnim, vol. II, pp. iv-ix. Also in Budé, *Dionis Chrys. Orat.* II, pp. 396 f.

εἶναι, ἄλλους δὲ ἐμπείρους τῶν ἀνθρωπίνων πραγμάτων, οὐδὲ ἄλλους μὲν
τἀνθρώπεια ἐπίστασθαι, ἄλλους δὲ τὰ θεῖα, οὐδὲ ἄλλους μὲν εἶναι τῶν θείων
ἐπιστήμονας, ἄλλους δὲ ὁσίους, οὐδὲ ἄλλους μὲν ὁσίους, ἄλλους δὲ θεοφιλεῖς·
οὐδὲ ἕτεροι μὲν ἔσονται θεοφιλεῖς, ἕτεροι δὲ εὐδαίμονες. οὐδὲ ἕτεροι μέν εἰσιν
ἄνθρωποι ἄφρονες, ἕτεροι δ᾽ ἀγνοοῦσι τὰ καθ᾽ αὑτοὺς πράγματα· οὐδὲ οἱ τὰ
σφέτερα πράγματα ἀγνοοῦσι, τὰ θεῖα ἴσασιν· οὐδὲ οἱ φαύλως περὶ τῶν θείων
ὑπειληφότες οὐκ ἀνόσιοί εἰσιν. οὐδέ γε τοὺς ἀνοσίους οἷόν τε φίλους εἶναι
θεοῖς, οὐδὲ τοὺς μὴ φίλους θεοῖς μὴ δυστυχεῖς εἶναι. διὰ τί ποτ᾽ οὖν οἱ [μὲν]
ὀρεγόμενοι ὅπως εὐδαιμονήσουσιν οὐ προθυμοῦνται τοιούτους παρέχειν σφᾶς
αὑτούς; ἃ δὲ πράττοντας οὐδὲν αὑτοὺς κωλύει κακῶς καὶ ἀθλίως ζῆν, πᾶσαν
τούτων ἐπιμέλειαν ποιοῦνται; καίτοι ἄνευ μὲν αὐλητῶν καὶ κιθαριστῶν καὶ
σκυτοτόμων καὶ παιδοτριβῶν καὶ ῥητόρων καὶ ἰατρῶν οὐκ ἀδύνατον ἀνθρώποις
βιοῦν πάνυ καλῶς καὶ νομίμως, οἶμαι δ᾽ ἐγὼ καὶ δίχα γεωργῶν καὶ οἰκοδόμων·
Σκύθαι γοῦν οὐδὲν κωλύονται οἱ νομάδες μήτε οἰκίας ἔχοντες μήτε γῆν
σπείροντες ἢ φυτεύοντες δικαίως καὶ κατὰ νόμους πολιτεύεσθαι· ἄνευ δὲ
νόμου καὶ δικαίου μὴ κακῶς ζῆν ἀνθρώπους καὶ πολὺ τῶν θηρίων ὠμότερον
οὐ δυνατόν.[98]

It seems to me hard to understand that, while men praise and
admire certain things, they desire and strive after quite different
things. For almost all praise, and call holy and divine, courage and
justice and prudence and, in short, all virtue. And they admire and
hymn those whom they believe to have or to have had these virtues,
and declare some of them to be gods and others heroes, such as
Hercules and the Dioscuri and Theseus and Achilles and all the so-
called demigods. And him whom they suppose to be like these men
they all are ready to obey and to serve in whatever he commands
and to appoint him their king and ruler and to turn over their possessions to him whom they suppose to be wise and just and truly
prudent and in all ways a good man. So that no one, in this particular, could blame them as not perceiving that virtue is a thing holy
and honorable, and the most precious of possessions. Yet they desire
anything rather than to become good, and there is nothing in the
world they will not busy themselves about in preference to practising
temperance and endeavoring to make themselves just and dutiful
men, able to conduct their own affairs properly, build a good house,
rule a city properly, bear well either riches or poverty, treat their
friends and kinsmen well, care duly for their parents, and serve the
gods reverently. But some busy themselves with farming, some with
commerce, some spend their energies on warfare, some on medicine,
some on the study of housebuilding or shipbuilding, some on playing
the lyre or flute or cobbling or wrestling; some devote their attention
to making a good appearance as orators or pleaders in the courts,
some to becoming stout and strong in body. And yet the merchants
and farmers and soldiers and doctors and carpenters and lyre-players
and flute-players and wrestling masters, even the so-called orators,
and those who have great bodily strength — one would find many, if
not nearly all of them, miserable and unfortunate. But if the soul
is prudent and the intellect good, and men are capable of conducting
their own and other people's affairs aright, they will necessarily also
live happily, as men do who are law-abiding and upright and god-

fearing. For it is not reasonable that there be a contrast between prudent men and men experienced in human affairs, nor between those acquainted with human affairs and those with divine, nor between those acquainted with divine and those who are holy, nor between the holy and the god-fearing, nor between the god-fearing and the really happy. Nor are these imprudent men and those ignorant of their own affairs; nor do those who are ignorant of their own affairs understand divine matters, nor are those holy who have wrong ideas about religion. Nor is it possible for the unholy to be friends of the gods, nor for those who are not friends of the gods to be happy. Why, then, do not those who earnestly strive to be happy strive to make themselves such men as these? But do they not spend all their care on those things the doing of which will in no way keep them from leading an evil and miserable life? And yet it is not impossible for men to live nobly and lawfully without flute-players and lyre-players and cobblers and wrestling masters and orators and doctors, yes, and even, I suppose, without farmers and housebuilders. At least the nomadic Scythians, though they neither have houses nor plant nor cultivate the soil, conduct their government justly and according to law. But without law and justice men cannot but live evilly and more savagely than beasts.

Here the hard, uncivilized life of the Scythians with its absence not only of luxury but of many things commonly considered necessities, is held up to a luxury-loving gentleman as an example of the virtuous life which he ought to emulate.

One might have expected the Christians to be influenced by this legend and to hold up the savages as examples to the Greeks and Romans. Tertullian, however, like most early Christian writers, speaks of them with horror.[99]

XI, 40. Tertullian, *Adversus Marcionem*, I, 1.

Pontus igitur, qui Euxinus natura negatur, nomine inluditur. ceterum hospitalem Pontum nec de situ aestimes; ita ab humanioribus fretis nostris quasi quodam barbariae suae pudore secessit. gentes ferocissimae inhabitant; si tamen habitatur in plaustro. sedes incerta, vita cruda, libido promiscua et plurimum nuda; etiam cum abscondunt, suspensis de iugo pharetris ut indicibus notantur, ne qui intercedat. ita nec armis suis erubescunt. parentum cadavera cum pecudibus caesa convivio convorant. qui non ita decesserint, ut escatiles fuerint, maledicta mors est. nec feminae sexu mitigantur secundum pudorem; ubera excludunt, pensum securibus faciunt, malunt militare quam nubere. duritia de caelo quoque. dies numquam patens, sol numquam ridens, unus aër nebula, totus annus hibernum, omne quod flaverit aquilo est. liquores ignibus [100] redeunt, amnes glacie negantur, montes pruina exaggerantur. omnia torpent, omnia rigent; nihil illic nisi feritas calet, illa scilicet, quae fabulas

---

[99] St. Basil (4th c.) speaks of the Σκυθῶν τινῶν ἢ Μασσαγετῶν ἀμουσία as replacing the politeness of earlier days. See Letter lxxiv.

[100] Restoring the MS reading.

scaenis dedit de sacrificiis Taurorum et amoribus Colchorum et crucibus Caucasorum.[101]

The Pontus [Black Sea], which its nature denies to be Euxine (i. e. hospitable), is mocked at by its name. Nor should you believe the Pontus to be friendly even from its location, so far removed is it from our more humane seas, as if it were ashamed of its barbarity. The most savage tribes dwell in it, if, indeed, one can be said to dwell in a wagon. Their domicile is unsettled, their life is rude, their lust is promiscuous and for the most part open. Even when they hide it, they give notice of it with quivers hung from the yoke as a warning that no one intrude. They do not blush even at their weapons. They devour the bodies of their parents slaughtered with their cattle at their feasts. Those who have not died to be eaten meet an accursed death. Nor are the women softened by their sex as modesty dictates: they cut off their breasts, their distaff is the ax; they would rather wage war than wed. The climate, too, is hard: the day is never clear; the sun never smiles; the air is but one cloud; the whole year is winter; all that blows is the North Wind. Water is obtained only by fire [i. e. by melting snow], rivers are frustrated by ice, mountains heightened by frost. All is torpid, all is stiff. Nothing there is hot except savagery, which has furnished plots for the theatre: the sacrifices of the Tauri, the loves of the Colchi and the tortures of the Caucasus.[102]

We shall close this section with a quotation from Claudian (4th-5th c. A. D.) which takes such primitive traits of the Scythians as a Juvenal would have found ennobling and uses them as evidence of barbarism. This passage occurs in his poem against Rufinus and may have been dictated in part by the desire to make Stilicho's war against this people appear the more difficult and hence the more praiseworthy.

XI, 41. Claudian, *In Rufinum*, I, 323-331.

> Est genus extremos Scythiae vergentis in ortus
> Trans gelidum Tanain, quo non famosius ullum
> Arctos alit. Turpes habitus obscenaque visu
> Corpora, mens duro nunquam cessura labori.
> Praeda cibus, vitanda Ceres frontemque secare
> Lusus et occisos pulchrum jurare parentes.
> Nec plus nubigenas duplex natura biformes
> Cognatis aptavit equis. Acerrima nullo
> Ordine mobilitas insperatique recursus.[103]

There is a people living where Scythia turns towards the far east across the frozen Tanais, than whom the North nourishes none of worse fame. They have a shameful appearance and bodies hideous to behold; and their minds never relax from hard toil. Plunder is their food, Ceres is to be avoided; scarring their foreheads is their sport, and they think it comely to swear by their slaughtered parents. A double nature has not more closely fitted the two-formed children

---

[101] *Opera*, Ed. Kroymann, Leipzig, 1906, III.
[102] The opinions of other Christian writers on savages will be given in Volume II.
[103] Ed. L. Jeep, Leipzig, 1876.

of the clouds [Centaurs] to their kindred steeds. Their speedy onset is without order and their return unexpected.

The Arcadians

The Arcadians are peculiarly interesting in that they lived not on the outskirts of the world but in Greece itself. Their legendary character may be accounted for by their geographical isolation, their relative racial purity, and their pastoral life.

The age of the Arcadians was a matter of comment in very early times. This is illustrated by the peculiar adjective " proselenic " which was sometimes used of them. Hippys Rheginus (early 5th c. B. C.) is said by Stephanus of Byzantium (v. 'Αρκάς) to have first called them that. Aristophanes in the *Clouds* (397) used the form βεκκεσέληνε, which according to the Scholiast [104] was appropriate because the Arcadians claimed to have been born before the moon. Their pride of age is given in a story told by the Scholiast of an argument they had with the Phrygians and Persians as to which people was the oldest. This argument was settled by Psammetichos of Egypt. Psammetichos took two new-born children who were either given to goats to be suckled or to their mothers after their mothers' tongues had been cut out. They thus could have no linguistic training from their nurses. Yet when a stranger saw them three years later, they called out, " Bek," which is the Phrygian for " bread." This settled the question of which race was the oldest. (It is, moreover, interesting evidence of the antiquity of the opinion that children represent man's primitive condition.)

The *proselenic* appearance of the Arcadians occurs also in Apollonius Rhodius (IV, 264) with the addition of the note that — like Juvenal's primitive men — they lived on acorns in the mountains.

This fabulous legend, which is found as late as Plutarch (*Quaest. rom.* 76), is ridiculed by Lucian (*Astrol.* 26), but the antiquity of the race does not seem to have been questioned. So hard-headed a writer as Xenophon (*Hellenica*, VII, i, 22 f.), maintains, perhaps after Hellanicus,[105] that they alone were indigenous inhabitants of the Peloponnesus and adds a word, repeated by Demosthenes (*De fals. leg.* 261), on their bravery and outstanding physique.

In Theopompus (4th c. B. C.) their social equalitarianism is mentioned. The 64th book of his *Histories* is quoted as saying,

XI, 42. Theopompus, in Athenaeus, *Deipn.* IV, 149 D.

Οἱ 'Αρκάδες . . . ἐν ταῖς ἑστιάσεσιν ὑποδέχονται τοὺς δεσπότας καὶ τοὺς

---

[104] See Dindorf's ed. of Aristophanes, Oxford, 1838, IV, 455 f. esp. n. 21.

[105] Hellanicus (middle 5th c. B. C.), according to Harpocrates (v. Αὐτόχθονες) maintained that they, the Aeginetans, and the Thebans were autochthonous. They were said to have descended from Arcas, a son of either Apollo or Zeus, a genealogy attributed to Charon (late 6th c. B. C.) according to Tzetzes (*Ad Lycoph.* v. 480). We find this as late as Pausanias (2d c. A. D.). See Bk. I, i.

δούλους καὶ μίαν πᾶσι τράπεζαν παρασκευάζουσι καὶ τὰ σιτία πᾶσιν εἰς τὸ
μέσον παρατιθέασι καὶ κρατῆρα τὸν αὐτὸν πᾶσι κιρνᾶσι.[106]

The Arcadians receive both masters and slaves at their feasts and
they lay one table for all and place food for all in the middle and use
the same mixing bowl for all.

Legend attributes other features of primitive life to this people. Thus
an oracle cited by Herodotus (I, 66) calls them " eaters of acorns," [107] and
Pausanias, six hundred years later, adds that they wore clothes of skin, at
least in battle (IV, vi, 3).

The nobility of this people and their peculiar skill in music is first
described by Polybius (2nd c. B. C.). The passage also is an early expression of the " theory of climates " which was to have vogue in the eighteenth
century.

XI, 43. Polybius, Hist. IV, 19-21 (Translation on p. 346).

Κυναιθεῖς δὲ μεγάλοις ἀτυχήμασιν ὑπ' Αἰτωλῶν καὶ μεγάλαις συμφοραῖς
περιπεσόντες ὅμως πάντων ἀνθρώπων ἔδοξαν ἠτυχηκέναι δικαιότατα.
Ἐπειδὴ δὲ κοινῇ τὸ τῶν Ἀρκάδων ἔθνος ἔχει τινὰ παρὰ πᾶσι τοῖς Ἕλλησιν
ἐπ' ἀρετῇ φήμην, οὐ μόνον διὰ τὴν ἐν τοῖς ἤθεσι καὶ βίοις φιλοξενίαν καὶ
φιλανθρωπίαν, μάλιστα δὲ διὰ τὴν εἰς τὸ θεῖον εὐσέβειαν, ἄξιον βραχὺ δια-
πορῆσαι περὶ τῆς Κυναιθέων ἀγριότητος, πῶς ὄντες ὁμολογουμένως Ἀρκάδες
τοσοῦτο κατ' ἐκείνους τοὺς καιροὺς διήνεγκαν τῶν ἄλλων Ἑλλήνων ὠμότητι
καὶ παρανομίᾳ. δοκοῦσι δέ μοι, διότι τὰ καλῶς ὑπὸ τῶν ἀρχαίων ἐπινενοημένα
καὶ φυσικῶς συντεθεωρημένα περὶ πάντας τοὺς κατοικοῦντας τὴν Ἀρκαδίαν,
ταῦτα δὴ πρῶτοι καὶ μόνοι Ἀρκάδων ἐγκατέλιπον. μουσικὴν γάρ, τήν γ'
ἀληθῶς μουσικήν, πᾶσι μὲν ἀνθρώποις ὄφελος ἀσκεῖν, Ἀρκάσι δὲ καὶ ἀναγκαῖον. οὐ γὰρ ἡγητέον μουσικήν, ὡς Ἔφορός φησιν ἐν τῷ προοιμίῳ τῆς
ὅλης πραγματείας, οὐδαμῶς ἁρμόζοντα λόγον αὑτῷ ῥίψας, ἐπ' ἀπάτῃ καὶ
γοητείᾳ παρεισῆχθαι τοῖς ἀνθρώποις, οὐδὲ τοὺς παλαιοὺς Κρητῶν καὶ Λακε-
δαιμονίων αὐλὸν καὶ ῥυθμὸν εἰς τὸν πόλεμον ἀντὶ σάλπιγγος εἰκῇ νομιστέον
εἰσαγαγεῖν, οὐδὲ τοὺς πρώτους Ἀρκάδων εἰς τὴν ὅλην πολιτείαν τὴν μουσικὴν
παραλαβεῖν ἐπὶ τοσοῦτον ὥστε μὴ μόνον παισὶν οὖσιν, ἀλλὰ καὶ νεανίσκοις
γενομένοις ἕως τριάκοντ' ἐτῶν κατ' ἀνάγκην σύντροφον ποιεῖν αὐτήν, τἄλλα
τοῖς βίοις ὄντας αὐστηροτάτους. ταῦτα γὰρ πᾶσίν ἐστι γνώριμα καὶ συνήθη,
διότι σχεδὸν παρὰ μόνοις Ἀρκάσι πρῶτον μὲν οἱ παῖδες ἐκ νηπίων ᾄδειν
ἐθίζονται κατὰ νόμους τοὺς ὕμνους καὶ παιᾶνας, οἷς ἕκαστοι κατὰ τὰ πάτρια
τοὺς ἐπιχωρίους ἥρωας καὶ θεοὺς ὑμνοῦσι· μετὰ δὲ ταῦτα τοὺς Φιλοξένου καὶ
Τιμοθέου νόμους μανθάνοντες πολλῇ φιλοτιμίᾳ χορεύουσι κατ' ἐνιαυτὸν τοῖς
Διονυσιακοῖς αὐληταῖς ἐν τοῖς θεάτροις, οἱ μὲν παῖδες τοὺς παιδικοὺς ἀγῶνας,
οἱ δὲ νεανίσκοι τοὺς τῶν ἀνδρῶν λεγομένους. ὁμοίως γε μὴν καὶ παρ' ὅλον
τὸν βίον τὰς ἀγωγὰς τὰς ἐν ταῖς συνουσίαις οὐχ οὕτως ποιοῦνται διὰ τῶν
ἐπεισάκτων ἀκροαμάτων ὡς δι' αὑτῶν, ἀνὰ μέρος ᾄδειν ἀλλήλοις προστάττοντες.
καὶ τῶν μὲν ἄλλων μαθημάτων ἀρνηθῆναί τι μὴ γινώσκειν οὐδὲν αἰσχρὸν
ἡγοῦνται, τήν γε μὴν ᾠδὴν οὔτ' ἀρνηθῆναι δύνανται διὰ τὸ κατ' ἀνάγκην πάντας
μανθάνειν, οὔθ' ὁμολογοῦντες ἀποτρίβεσθαι διὰ τὸ τῶν αἰσχρῶν παρ' αὑτοῖς
νομίζεσθαι τοῦτο. καὶ μὴν ἐμβατήρια μετ' αὐλοῦ καὶ τάξεως ἀσκοῦντες, ἔτι
δ' ὀρχήσεις ἐκπονοῦντες μετὰ κοινῆς ἐπιστροφῆς καὶ δαπάνης κατ' ἐνιαυτὸν

[106] Ed. Kaibel, Leipzig, 1887, I.
[107] So too Pausanias, VIII, i, 6; VIII, xlii, 6.

ἐν τοῖς θεάτροις ἐπιδείκνυνται τοῖς αὐτῶν πολίταις οἱ νέοι. ταῦτά τέ μοι
δοκοῦσιν οἱ πάλαι παρεισαγαγεῖν οὐ τρυφῆς καὶ περιουσίας χάριν, ἀλλὰ θεωροῦντες μὲν τὴν ἑκάστων αὐτουργίαν καὶ συλλήβδην τὸ τῶν βίων ἐπίπονον
καὶ σκληρόν, θεωροῦντες δὲ τὴν τῶν ἠθῶν αὐστηρίαν, ἥτις αὐτοῖς παρέπεται
διὰ τὴν τοῦ περιέχοντος ψυχρότητα καὶ στυγνότητα τὴν κατὰ τὸ πλεῖστον
ἐν τοῖς τόποις ὑπάρχουσαν, ᾧ συνεξομοιοῦσθαι πεφύκαμεν πάντες ἄνθρωποι
κατ' ἀνάγκην· οὐ γὰρ δι' ἄλλην, διὰ δὲ ταύτην τὴν αἰτίαν κατὰ τὰς ἐθνικὰς
καὶ τὰς ὁλοσχερεῖς διαστάσεις πλεῖστον ἀλλήλων διαφέρομεν ἤθεσί τε καὶ
μορφαῖς καὶ χρώμασιν, ἔτι δὲ τῶν ἐπιτηδευμάτων τοῖς πλείστοις. βουλόμενοι
δὲ μαλάττειν καὶ κιρνᾶν τὸ τῆς φύσεως αὔθαδες καὶ σκληρόν, τά τε προειρη-
μένα πάντα παρεισήγαγον, καὶ πρὸς τούτοις συνόδους κοινὰς καὶ θυσίας
πλείστας ὁμοίως ἀνδράσι καὶ γυναιξὶ κατείθισαν, ἔτι δὲ χοροὺς παρθένων ὁμοῦ
καὶ παίδων, καὶ συλλήβδην πᾶν ἐμηχανήσαντο, σπεύδοντες τὸ τῆς ψυχῆς
ἀτέραμνον διὰ τῆς τῶν ἐθισμῶν κατασκευῆς ἐξημεροῦν καὶ πραΰνειν. ὧν
Κυναιθεῖς ὀλιγωρήσαντες εἰς τέλος, καὶ ταῦτα πλείστης δεόμενοι τῆς τοιαύτης
ἐπικουρίας διὰ τὸ σκληρότατον παρὰ πολὺ τῆς Ἀρκαδίας ἔχειν ἀέρα καὶ
τόπον, πρὸς αὐτὰς δὲ τὰς ἐν ἀλλήλοις διατριβὰς καὶ φιλοτιμίας ὁρμήσαντες,
τέλος ἀπεθηριώθησαν οὕτως ὥστε μηδ' ἐν ὁποίᾳ γεγονέναι τῶν Ἑλληνίδων
πόλεων ἀσεβήματα μείζονα καὶ συνεχέστερα. σημεῖον δὲ τῆς Κυναιθέων
ἀτυχίας περὶ τοῦτο τὸ μέρος καὶ τῆς τῶν ἄλλων Ἀρκάδων τοῖς τοιούτοις
τῶν ἐπιτηδευμάτων δυσαρεστήσεως· καθ' οὓς γὰρ καιροὺς τὴν μεγάλην σφαγὴν
ποιήσαντες Κυναιθεῖς ἐπρέσβευσαν πρὸς Λακεδαιμονίους, εἰς ἃς πόλεις ποτ'
Ἀρκαδικὰς εἰσῆλθον κατὰ τὴν ὁδόν, οἱ μὲν ἄλλοι παραχρῆμα πάντες αὐτοὺς
ἐξεκήρυξαν, Μαντινεῖς δὲ μετὰ τὴν ἀπαλλαγὴν αὐτῶν καὶ καθαρμὸν ἐποιήσαντο
καὶ σφάγια περιήνεγκαν τῆς τε πόλεως κύκλῳ καὶ τῆς χώρας πάσης.

Ταῦτα μὲν οὖν ἡμῖν εἰρήσθω χάριν τοῦ μὴ διὰ μίαν πόλιν τὸ κοινὸν ἦθος
διαβάλλεσθαι τῶν Ἀρκάδων, ὁμοίως δὲ καὶ τοῦ μὴ νομίσαντας ἐνίους τῶν
κατοικούντων τὴν Ἀρκαδίαν περιουσίας χάριν τὰ κατὰ μουσικὴν ἐπὶ πλεῖον
ἀσκεῖσθαι παρ' αὐτοῖς ὀλιγωρεῖν ἐγχειρῆσαι τούτου τοῦ μέρους, ἔτι δὲ καὶ
Κυναιθέων ἕνεκεν, ἵν' ἄν ποτ' αὐτοῖς ὁ θεὸς εὖ δῷ, τραπέντες πρὸς παιδείαν
ἡμερῶσιν αὐτούς, καὶ μάλιστα ταύτης πρὸς μουσικήν· οὕτως γὰρ μόνως ἂν
λήξαιεν τῆς τότε περὶ αὐτοὺς γενομένης ἀγριότητος.[108]

Though the Cynaetheans suffered great misfortunes and reverses
at the hand of the Aetolians, yet they seemed to have been of all men
the most justly punished. Since in general the Arcadians had a
certain reputation among all the Greeks for virtue, not only because
of their friendliness to strangers and kindliness in life and deeds,
but above all because of their religious piety, it is worth while asking briefly about the savagery of the Cynaetheans, how, being con-
fessedly Arcadians, they surpassed to such an extent the other Greeks
of those times in cruelty and lawlessness. They seem to me [to have
met this fate] because they were the first and only Arcadians to
abandon the institutions obtaining among all the inhabitants of
Arcadia, institutions well contrived by the ancients and thought out
in accordance with nature. For it is important for all to practise
music, that is, music in the true sense of the word, but for the
Arcadians it is a matter of necessity. For one must not suppose
that music, as Ephorus says in the preface to his General History,
was invented as a trick and cheat for men, nor must it be thought
that the ancient Cretans and Lacedemonians heedlessly introduced

[108] Ed. Dindorf-Büttner-Wobst, Leipzig, 1889, II.

flutes and rhythm into battle instead of trumpets, nor that the primitive Arcadians welded music into their whole political structure to such a degree that it was necessary not only for children but also for youths up to the age of thirty years to make it an integral part of their lives, though they lived most austerely in other respects. For this is knowledge common to all, that virtually only among the Arcadians are children accustomed from infancy to sing in measure the hymns and paeans in which each, as his fathers before him, celebrates the heroes and gods of his country. And after this, while they are learning the measures of Philoxenus and Timotheus, they dance in great rivalry every year at the flute-festivals of Dionysus in the theatres, the boys in children's games, the youths in those called manly. Likewise throughout their whole life they conduct their festivals not so much through hired entertainers as by themselves, each bidding the other sing in turn. And as to other fields of knowledge, they do not consider it shameful to admit that they do not know them, yet singing they are not able to reject because all learn it of necessity, nor do they admit that they are injured by it, because this would be considered shameful by them. And practising military marches accompanied by the flute and according to set steps, and elaborating dances, each year the young men give a demonstration in the theatres to their fellow citizens under the general supervision and at the general expense of the city. Now it seems to me that the men of old did not introduce these things for the sake of luxury or superfluity, but because they saw the necessity of personal labor and the painful and hard course of their life, and because they considered the austerity of their manners, which was the consequence of the chilly and gloomy climate which prevailed for the most part in that region. To our climate all of us become adapted by necessity. For it is not from any other cause but from this that we differ from one another in our racial and all our peculiarities — in character and form and complexion, and still more in most of our customs. But [the Arcadians], wishing to smooth and soften the stubborness and hardness of nature, introduced all the above mentioned things and instituted, besides these, common assemblies and sacrifices, and most of the sacrifices in common for men and women, and choruses of girls and boys together, and in short devised all manner of measures to tame and soften the hardness of the soul through education. But the Cynaetheans, taking small account of these things — though they most of all needed such aids, since they had the harshest air and site of any in Arcadia — engaged instead in warfare and conflict with one another, to such a degree that they became so bestial that nowhere in the Greek cities were there impieties worse or more continuous. There is evidence of the evil estate of the Cynaetheans in this respect and of the detestation of the other Arcadians for their behaviour. For when the Cynaetheans after a great massacre sent an embassy to the Lacedemonians, into whatever city of Arcadia they came along the way, all ordered them begone forthwith, and the Mantineans after their departure even purified the city and carried sacrificial victims round it and the whole country.

Let these facts be recognized by us as sufficient reasons not to attack the general customs of the Arcadians because of one city, and

not to consider that some of the inhabitants of Arcadia practise
music so extensively for luxury's sake, nor to try to belittle it. But
with regard to the Cynaetheans, may God in his goodness grant that
they may civilize themselves and turn to education and especially
music; for thus only would they free themselves of the savagery
which has grown up amongst them.

This passage is of interest not only as a document illustrating the literary
fortunes of the Arcadians but also for its curious picture of a noble savage
who lives in accordance with nature and yet improves his natural condition
by practising one of the arts, music. The Arcadians of Polybius are not, in
general, less ignorant than other savages, but they seek to ameliorate the
character which their environment would normally produce — in accordance
with good Hippocratic theory, be it noted — by a peculiar type of aesthetic
education.

The legend of their musical skill and pastoral life is developed by the
Alexandrians. The Arcadian shepherds of Theocritus are by no means
those of Polybius. Nor are those of Virgil, *soli cantare periti* (*Ecl.* X, 32).
They have, by a course which we can no longer trace, lost their vigor and
become mere literary figures.

The Aethiopians and the other " holy " peoples

The Aethiopians were not an entirely imaginary people, but their traits
are those to be found in fiction rather than in fact. The geographical
position of their country varies. They are first mentioned in Homer, where
they are " divided in two, some near the setting sun, some near its rise "
(*Odys.* I, 22-3).

XI, 44. *Iliad*, I, 423-4.

> Ζεὺς γὰρ ἐς Ὠκεανὸν μετ' ἀμύμονας Αἰθιοπῆας
> χθιζὸς ἔβη κατὰ δαῖτα. . . .[109]

Zeus went yesterday to Ocean to the blameless Aethiopians for
a feast.[110]

Their remoteness was evidently legendary, as is suggested by a line in
Pindar (*Nem.* VI, 51 f.).

In Hanno [111] their blamelessness is omitted, and they or another people
of the name are described as inhospitable and living in a land infested with
wild beasts.

Their beauty and unusual height are recorded by what has remained of
Scylax of Carymander (6th-5th c. B. C.), who, like Homer, distinguishes
between the eastern and western Aethiopians. The western group is
described as follows:

---

[109] Ed. Dindorf-Hentze, Leipzig, 1886.

[110] " Blameless " was presumably a fairly colorless adjective of praise, for Liddell
and Scott point out that it was used even of Aegisthus.

[111] *Periplus* vii, in Müller's *Geog. graec. min.* I, 6.

XI, 45. Scylax, *Periplus,* 112.

Εἰσὶ δὲ οὗτοι οἱ Αἰθίοπες μέγιστοι ἀνθρώπων πάντων ὧν ἡμεῖς ἴσμεν, μείζους ἢ τετραπήχεις· εἰσὶ δέ τινες αὐτῶν καὶ πενταπήχεις· καὶ πωγωνοφόροι εἰσὶ καὶ κομῆται, καὶ κάλλιστοι πάντων ἀνθρώπων οὗτοί εἰσι. Καὶ βασιλεύει αὐτῶν οὗτος, ὃς ἂν ᾖ μέγιστος. Εἰσὶ καὶ ἱππηλάται καὶ ἀκοντισταὶ καὶ τοξόται, καὶ χρῶνται τοῖς βέλεσι πεπυρακτωμένοις.[112]

And these Aethiopians are the tallest of all the men we know, taller than four cubits. And some of them are five cubits tall.[113] And they are bearded and have long hair and are the most beautiful of all men. And he rules over them who is the tallest.[114] And they are horsemen and javelin-throwers and archers, and they use darts hardened in the fire.

The peculiar height and beauty of these people is also mentioned by Herodotus (III, 20), with no added details as to their customs. But when we come to Agatharchides in, the late second century B. C. we find that the Aethiopians [115] have taken on most of the traits of the men of the Golden Age. They have all the necessities and desire none of the luxuries; they follow nature, not custom; they are peaceful; they do not engage in maritime commerce, and they have no law-suits.

XI, 46. Agatharchides, *De mari erythraeo,* 49.

Ὅτι τῆς ζωῆς ἡμῶν ἡμῖν ἐφεστώσης ἔν τε τοῖς περιττοῖς καὶ τοῖς ἀναγκαίοις, τὰ εἰρημένα γένη τῶν Ἰχθυοφάγων τὰ μὲν ἄχρηστα περιγεγράφασιν ἅπαντα, φησί, τῶν δὲ καθηκόντων οὐδὲν ἐλλείπουσι, τῇ θείᾳ πρὸς τὸ ζῆν ὁδῷ βραβευόμενοι πάντες, οὐ τῇ παρασοφιζομένῃ ταῖς δόξαις τὴν φύσιν· οὐ γὰρ ἀρχῆς ἱμειρόμενοι τυχεῖν ἀγωνίᾳ φιλονείκῳ καὶ δυστυχεῖ συνέχονται· οὐδὲ πλεονεξίας ἐρῶντες πολλὰ μὲν ἄλλους δρῶσι, πολλὰ δὲ πάσχουσι τῶν οὐκ ἀναγκαίων· οὐδ' ἔχθρας ἐνιστάμενοι μείζους ἐπὶ βλάβῃ σώματος πολεμίου σφάλλονται ἐν ἀτυχίαις οἰκείων, οὐδὲ ναυτιλλόμενοι, κέρδους ἕνεκα τὸ ζῆν ὑπερτείναντες, προσπταίσμασι τοῦ βίου μετροῦσι τὴν λύπην· ἀλλὰ μικρῶν δεόμενοι μικρὰ καὶ πενθοῦσι, τὸ μὲν ἀρκοῦν κτώμενοι, τὸ δὲ πλέον οὐ ζητοῦντες. Ἐνοχλεῖ δ' ἕκαστον οὐ τὸ ἀγνοούμενον, εἰ μὴ πάρεστιν, ἀλλὰ τὸ βουλητόν, ὅταν ὑστερίζῃ τοῦ καιροῦ τῆς ἐπιθυμίας σπευδούσης. Οὐκοῦν ἐκεῖνος πάντ' ἔχων ἃ θέλει, εὐτυχήσει κατὰ τὸν τῆς φύσεως λογισμόν, οὐ κατὰ τὸν τῆς δόξης. Νόμοις δὲ οὐ δικαιοῦνται· τί γὰρ δεῖ προστάγματι δουλεύειν τὸν χωρὶς γράμματος εὐγνωμονεῖν δυνάμενον; [116]

While the life which we pursue is divided between superfluities and necessities, the tribes of the Ichthyophagi, already mentioned, are said to have limited all useless things and lack nothing which is fitting [for a proper way of living], all endeavoring to follow the

[112] In Müller's *Geog. graec. min.* I, 94. Though the date of Scylax was the sixth century B. C., the *Periplus* as we have it is of the fourth.

[113] In Pliny they are eight cubits tall, *Nat Hist.* VI, 30 (35).

[114] This legend was treated with suspicion as early as Aristotle's time. See *Politics,* 1290 b 5.

[115] These are the Fish-eaters, who would be of the eastern branch of the Aethiopians. See map in Cary and Warmington: *The Ancient Explorers,* opp. p. 66.

[116] In Müller: *Geog. graec. min.* I, 140-1.

divine way of life and not the way which tries to surpass nature by false opinions. For since they do not crave power, they are not involved in contentious and unhappy strife. And since they do not love superfluity, they do not do many things to others nor suffer many things from others which are unnecessary. And since they do not start great feuds so as to do bodily injury to their enemies, they are not undone by the misfortunes of their kinsmen. They do not endanger their lives by navigation for the sake of gain, thereby meting out pain through fatal shipwrecks. But needing little, they have few griefs. Gaining a sufficiency, they do not demand super-fluities. None is troubled by the absence of what is beyond his ken, but only of that for which he wishes when he falls short of the satisfaction of some urgent desire. Therefore, having all that he wants, he is happy according to the logic of nature, not according to that of opinion. These people, moreover, are not governed by laws. For why need one be subservient to ordinances who is able to be honest without instruction?

Nicolaus of Damascus (1st c. B. C.) continues these legends. According to Stobaeus (*Floril.* XLIV, 41), he says that they hold sisters in greatest honor and that succession passes from the king, not to his sons, but to his sister's sons. Then if none of these survive — this is new with Nicolaus — they choose the most beautiful of all and the most warlike.

XI, 47. Nicolaus of Damascus in Stobaeus, *Floril.* XLIV, 25 (41 Meineke).

[Αἰθίοπες] τὸν κάλλιστον ἐκ πάντων καὶ μαχιμώτατον αἱροῦνται βασιλέα. ἀσκοῦσι δὲ εὐσέβειαν καὶ δικαιοσύνην. ἄθυροι δ' αὐτῶν αἱ οἰκίαι, καὶ ἐν ταῖς ὁδοῖς κειμένων πολλῶν οὐδὲ εἷς κλέπτει.[117]

[The Aethiopians] choose as their king the most handsome of all and the most warlike. They are pious and just, and their houses are without doors, and though many things lie about on their streets, nothing is ever stolen.

The Aethiopians are given a further mark of nobility by Favorinus of Arles (2d c. A. D.). Stephanus of Byzantium cites him as saying that their land was the first to be formed and that they were the first to worship gods and have laws.

XI, 48. Favorinus in Stephanus, *Ethnica,* sub. Αἰθίοψ.

Τὴν γὰρ Αἰθιοπίαν γῆν πρώτην φασὶ παγῆναι· πρῶτοι καὶ θεοὺς ἐτίμησαν καὶ νόμοις ἐχρήσαντο.[118]

The legend of the Aethiopians, as a peculiarly holy and god-fearing people, is introduced into the Middle Ages by the *Periegesis* of Dionysius [119]

---

[117] Ed. Otto Hense, Berlin, 1909, IV.   [118] Ed. A. Westermann, Leipzig, 1839.

[119] The date of Dionysius is uncertain, the latest given being the end of the third century A. D. E. H. Bunbury, *Ancient Geography*, II, 480 ff., puts his *floruit* from the reign of Nero to that of Trajan, i. e., 54-98.

(lines 558-561), translated into Latin in the late fourth century by Rufus Festus Avienus in his *Descriptio orbis terrae* (lines 738 f.), and paraphrased by Priscian in the beginning of the sixth century.[120] That it continued to seem an important book is illustrated by the fact that in the twelfth century Eustathius published a commentary on it and in the sixteenth (1572) T. Twine translated it into English.

Agatharchides, who gave us our most extended account of the Aethiopians, seems to have specialized in exotic peoples. Thus the Sabaeans (*De mari eryth.* 97-102)[121] live in divine happiness. The Hylophagi and Spermatophagi live in trees and leap from branch to branch; they go unclothed and have wives and children in common (*Id.* 51). They are not, however, praised. The most extraordinary of these eastern peoples is the people of Eden, the Camarini, described in the *Liber junioris philosophi* (ch. 4 ff.). They are exceedingly pious and good, suffering no evil either of soul or body. They do not use our food and drink, but eat bread that rains down on them. They are without government but are self-ruled, and live without weakness or fatigue to the age of one hundred and twenty years.[122]

The Essenes

Closely related to the Camarini are the Essenes. Although not an imaginary people but a pre-Christian monastic order of Jews, they seem to have been thought of as a race by Pliny and his followers. They are first mentioned in Greek literature by Philo Judaeus.

XI, 49. Philo, *Quod omnis probus*, XII.

12. Ἔστι δὲ καὶ ἡ Παλαιστίνη Συρία καλοκαγαθίας οὐκ ἄγονος, ἣν πολυανθρωποτάτου ἔθνους τῶν Ἰουδαίων οὐκ ὀλίγη μοῖρα νέμεται. λέγονταί τινες παρ᾽ αὐτοῖς ὄνομα Ἐσσαῖοι, πλῆθος ὑπερτετρακισχίλιοι, κατ᾽ ἐμὴν δόξαν — οὐκ ἀκριβεῖ τύπῳ διαλέκτου Ἑλληνικῆς — παρώνυμοι ὁσιότητος, ἐπειδὴ κἀν τοῖς μάλιστα θεραπευταὶ θεοῦ γεγόνασιν, οὐ ζῷα καταθύοντες, ἀλλ᾽ ἱεροπρεπεῖς τὰς ἑαυτῶν διανοίας κατασκευάζειν ἀξιοῦντες. οὗτοι τὸ μὲν πρῶτον κωμηδὸν οἰκοῦσι τὰς πόλεις ἐκτρεπόμενοι διὰ τὰς τῶν πολιτευομένων χειροήθεις ἀνομίας, εἰδότες ἐκ τῶν συνόντων ὡς ἀπ᾽ ἀέρος φθοροποιοῦ νόσον ἐγγινομένην προσβολὴν ψυχαῖς ἀνίατον· ὧν οἱ μὲν γεωπονοῦντες, οἱ δὲ τέχνας μετιόντες ὅσαι συνεργάτιδες εἰρήνης, ἑαυτούς τε καὶ τοὺς πλησιάζοντας ὠφελοῦσιν, οὐκ ἄργυρον καὶ χρυσὸν θησαυροφυλακοῦντες οὐδ᾽ ἀποτομὰς γῆς μεγάλας κτώμενοι δι᾽ ἐπιθυμίαν προσόδων, ἀλλ᾽ ὅσα πρὸς τὰς ἀναγκαίας τοῦ βίου χρείας ἐκπορίζοντες. μόνοι γὰρ ἐξ ἁπάντων σχεδὸν ἀνθρώπων ἀχρήματοι καὶ ἀκτήμονες γεγονότες ἐπιτηδεύσει τὸ πλέον ἢ ἐνδείᾳ εὐτυχίας πλουσιώτατοι νομίζονται, τὴν ὀλιγοδείαν καὶ εὐκολίαν, ὅπερ ἐστί, κρίνοντες περιουσίαν. βελῶν ἢ ἀκόντων ἢ ξιφιδίων ἢ κράνους ἢ θώρακος ἢ ἀσπίδος

---

[120] See *Periegesis*, lines 570-573.

[121] Müller, *Geog. graec. min.* I, 186-190.

[122] The *Liber junioris philosophi* seems to be a translation of a lost Greek work, influenced by Jewish or Christian legends, composed at Antioch or Alexandria *ca.* 350 A. D. See Müller's *Geog. graec. min.* II, 513. This passage belongs properly to the medieval section of this work, where it will be found in full.

οὐδένα παρ' αὐτοῖς ἂν εὕροις δημιουργὸν οὐδὲ συνόλως ὁπλοποιὸν ἢ μηχανο-
ποιὸν ἤ τι τῶν κατὰ πόλεμον ἐπιτηδεύοντα· ἀλλ' οὐδὲ ὅσα τῶν κατ' εἰρήνην
εὐόλισθα εἰς κακίαν· ἐμπορίας γὰρ ἢ καπηλείας ἢ ναυκληρίας οὐδ' ὄναρ ἴσασι,
τὰς εἰς πλεονεξίαν ἀφορμὰς ἀποδιοπομπούμενοι. δοῦλός τε παρ' αὐτοῖς οὐδὲ
εἷς ἐστιν, ἀλλ' ἐλεύθεροι πάντες ἀνθυπουργοῦντες ἀλλήλοις· καταγινώσκουσί
τε τῶν δεσποτῶν, οὐ μόνον ὡς ἀδίκων, ἰσότητα λυμαινομένων, ἀλλὰ καὶ ὡς
ἀσεβῶν, θεσμὸν φύσεως ἀναιρούντων, ἢ πάντας ὁμοίως γεννήσασα καὶ θρεψα-
μένη μητρὸς δίκην ἀδελφοὺς γνησίους, οὐ λεγομένους ἀλλ' ὄντας ὄντως,
ἀπειργάσατο· ὧν τὴν συγγένειαν ἡ ἐπίβουλος πλεονεξία παρευημερήσασα
διέσεισεν, ἀντ' οἰκειότητος ἀλλοτριότητα καὶ ἀντὶ φιλίας ἔχθραν ἐργασαμένη.
φιλοσοφίας τε τὸ μὲν λογικὸν ὡς οὐκ ἀναγκαῖον εἰς κτῆσιν ἀρετῆς λογοθήραις,
τὸ δὲ φυσικὸν ὡς μεῖζον ἢ κατὰ ἀνθρωπίνην φύσιν μετεωρολέσχαις ἀπολιπόντες, πλὴν ὅσον αὐτοῦ περὶ ὑπάρξεως θεοῦ καὶ τῆς τοῦ παντὸς γενέσεως
φιλοσοφεῖται, τὸ ἠθικὸν εὖ μάλα διαπονοῦσιν ἀλείπταις χρώμενοι τοῖς πατρίοις
νόμοις, οὓς ἀμήχανον ἀνθρωπίνην ἐπινοῆσαι ψυχὴν ἄνευ κατοκωχῆς ἐνθέου.
τούτους ἀναδιδάσκονται μὲν καὶ παρὰ τὸν ἄλλον χρόνον, ἐν δὲ ταῖς ἑβδόμαις
διαφερόντως. ἱερὰ γὰρ ἡ ἑβδόμη νενόμισται, καθ' ἣν τῶν ἄλλων ἀνέχοντες
ἔργων, εἰς ἱεροὺς ἀφικνούμενοι τόπους, οἳ καλοῦνται συναγωγαί, καθ' ἡλικίας
ἐν τάξεσιν ὑπὸ πρεσβυτέροις νέοι καθέζονται, μετὰ κόσμου τοῦ προσήκοντος
ἔχοντες ἀκροατικῶς. εἶθ' εἷς μέν τις τὰς βίβλους ἀναγινώσκει λαβών, ἕτερος
δὲ τῶν ἐμπειροτάτων ὅσα μὴ γνώριμα παρελθὼν ἀναδιδάσκει· τὰ γὰρ πλεῖστα
διὰ συμβόλων ἀρχαιοτρόπῳ ζηλώσει παρ' αὐτοῖς φιλοσοφεῖται. παιδεύονται
δὲ εὐσέβειαν, ὁσιότητα, δικαιοσύνην, οἰκονομίαν, πολιτείαν, ἐπιστήμην τῶν
πρὸς ἀλήθειαν ἀγαθῶν καὶ κακῶν καὶ ἀδιαφόρων, αἱρέσεις ὧν χρὴ καὶ φυγὰς
τῶν ἐναντίων, ὅροις καὶ κανόσι τριττοῖς χρώμενοι, τῷ τε φιλοθέῳ καὶ φιλαρέτῳ
καὶ φιλανθρώπῳ. τοῦ μὲν οὖν φιλοθέου δείγματα παρέχονται μυρία· τὴν παρ'
ὅλον τὸν βίον συνεχῆ καὶ ἐπάλληλον ἁγνείαν, τὸ ἀνώμοτον, τὸ ἀψευδές, τὸ
πάντων μὲν ἀγαθῶν αἴτιον, κακοῦ δὲ μηδενὸς νομίζειν εἶναι τὸ θεῖον· τοῦ δὲ
φιλαρέτου τὸ ἀφιλοχρήματον, τὸ ἀφιλόδοξον, τὸ ἀφιλήδονον, τὸ ἐγκρατές,
τὸ καρτερικόν, ἔτι δὲ ὀλιγοδείαν, ἀφέλειαν, εὐκολίαν, τὸ ἄτυφον, τὸ νόμιμον,
τὸ εὐσταθές, καὶ ὅσα τούτοις ὁμοιότροπα· τοῦ δὲ φιλανθρώπου εὔνοιαν,
ἰσότητα, τὴν παντὸς λόγου κρείττονα κοινωνίαν, περὶ ἧς οὐκ ἄκαιρον βραχέα
εἰπεῖν. πρῶτον μὲν τοίνυν οὐδενὸς οἰκία τίς ἐστιν ἰδία, ἣν οὐχὶ πάντων εἶναι
κοινὴν συμβέβηκε· πρὸς γὰρ τῷ κατὰ θιάσους συνοικεῖν ἀναπέπταται καὶ τοῖς
ἑτέρωθεν ἀφικνουμένοις τῶν ὁμοζήλων. εἶτ' ἐστὶ ταμεῖον ἓν πάντων καὶ
δαπάναι ⟨κοιναί⟩, καὶ κοιναὶ μὲν ἐσθῆτες, κοιναὶ δὲ τροφαὶ συσσίτια πεποιη-
μένων· τὸ γὰρ ὁμωρόφιον ἢ ὁμοδίαιτον ἢ ὁμοτράπεζον οὐκ ἄν τις εὕροι παρ'
ἑτέροις μᾶλλον ἔργῳ βεβαιούμενον· καὶ μήποτ' εἰκότως· ὅσα γὰρ ἂν μεθ'
ἡμέραν ἐργασάμενοι λάβωσιν ἐπὶ μισθῷ, ταῦτ' οὐκ ἴδια φυλάττουσιν, ἀλλ' εἰς
μέσον προτιθέντες κοινὴν τοῖς ἐθέλουσι χρῆσθαι τὴν ἀπ' αὐτῶν παρασκευάζουσιν
ὠφέλειαν. οἵ τε νοσοῦντες οὐχ ὅτι πορίζειν ἀδυνατοῦσιν ἀμελοῦνται, τὰ πρὸς
τὰς νοσηλείας ἐκ τῶν κοινῶν ἔχοντες ἐν ἑτοίμῳ, ὡς μετὰ πάσης ἀδείας ἐξ
ἀφθονωτέρων ἀναλίσκειν. αἰδὼς δ' ἐστὶ πρεσβυτέρων καὶ φροντίς, οἷα γονέων
ὑπὸ γνησίων παίδων χερσὶ καὶ διανοίαις μυρίαις ἐν ἀφθονίᾳ τῇ πάσῃ
γηροτροφουμένων.[123]

Moreover Palestine is not barren of moral excellence. It is inhabited by no small portion of that very populous nation of the Jews.
Some among them are called Essenes, in number something over
four thousand in my opinion, who derive their name from their piety

[123] *Opera*, ed. L. Cohn and P. Wendland, VI, Berlin, 1915. Cf. *De vita contempla-
tiva, passim*; Eusebius, *Praep. evan.* viii (379).

(ὁσιότης) (though not according to any accurate form of the Greek language) because they are men especially devoted to the service of God, not sacrificing animals, but deeming it proper to prepare their own minds for holiness. These men live in villages, avoiding cities on account of the habitual lawlessness of urban dwellers, knowing that the soul will be attacked by a fatal disease from association with them, as from a corrupting climate. Some of them cultivate the earth, and others practise the peaceful arts and benefit both themselves and all those who come in contact with them, not storing up silver and gold, nor procuring for themselves great tracts of land out of a desire for revenue, but providing all things which are needed for the necessities of life. For alone of nearly all men who have been born without possessions and in poverty, from custom rather than from any lack of good luck, they consider themselves very rich, judging contentment with little, and good health, to be more than enough, which they are.

Among these men you would find no makers of arrows nor of javelins nor of swords nor of helmets nor of breastplates nor of shields; nor any armorer nor maker of military machines nor anyone who makes things related to war. Nor would you find any of those things done in times of peace which might be turned to evil use; for they never dream of trade or commerce or navigation, rejecting with abhorrence the causes of greed. There is not a single slave among them, but all are free, helping one another. And they condemn masters, not only as unjust, since they ruin equality, but also as impious, since they destroy the institutions of nature which gave birth to them all as equals and nursed them like a mother, brothers born in rightful wedlock, not in name only but in very reality. Treacherous greed which brings about inequality of wealth has disrupted human kinship, creating estrangement in the place of intimacy, hatred in the place of friendship. (The Essenes) abandon logic, as not necessary to the attainment of virtue, to the word-catchers; and physics, as beyond the powers of human nature, to those who speculate — except so much of this as studies the existence of God and the creation of the universe; but ethics they toil over diligently, using as their teachers the laws of their fathers which, they believe, the human mind could not have contrived without divine inspiration.

These laws they are taught at all times, but most especially on on the seventh day, for the seventh day is considered sacred. On it they abstain from other works and go to the holy places which are called synagogues, and they sit according to their age in rows, the younger below the elders, listening with fitting decorum. Then someone taking the Bible reads it aloud, and another of the most skilled men comes forward and expounds whatever is not familiar. For most things are studied among them through the interpretation of symbols in the ancient manner. Thus they are taught piety, holiness, justice, economics, political science, and the knowledge of such things as are in truth good, bad, or indifferent, the choice of what is right and the flight from the opposite, using triple definitions and canons, namely, the love of God, the love of virtue, and the love of man.

Accordingly, they furnish thousands of instances of the love of God, purity continued through the whole of life and uninterrupted, considering the divine to be the unbound by oaths, the true, the cause of all good and of no evil. They also furnish us with instances of the indifference to wealth of the lover of virtue, of his indifference to reputation and to pleasure, his temperance, his endurance, and also his contentment with little, his simplicity, healthfulness, his lack of pride, his conformity to law, his steadfastness, and everything of that sort. And last, they furnish instances of the love of man, goodwill, equality, and fellowship beyond all words, about which it is not unreasonable to speak briefly.

In the first place, no one's house is his own, for it also belongs to everyone in common; for besides the fact that they all live together in groups, they also welcome others of the same faith who come to them from elsewhere. Then there is one storehouse for them all, and common expenditures and common garments and common food, since they all eat together. You could not find among others a common use of the same house, a common mode of life, and a common table more thoroughly established in practice, and this is perhaps to be expected. For whatever they have earned after a day's work they do not keep as their own, but, putting in into the common store for those who wish to use it, they make it of service to them. They who are sick are not neglected because they cannot produce, since they have at hand what is needed for their care in the common property, so that in all security they spend lavishly. And they respect their elders and honor them, just as parents are supported by their lawful children, both by the work of their hands and by great thoughtfulness, with full readiness.

The Essenes in this account approach the conditions of life in the Golden Age in their great virtue, their rural felicity, their pacifism, their economic primitivism, and their communism. They were brought to the attention of the Western world not only by the reports of Philo but by those of another hellenizing Jew, Josephus (1st century A. D.), in his *Jewish War* (II, viii, 2-13).

The Essenes of Josephus, like those of Philo, do not marry, are communistic, and practise the virtues of humility and obedience. They are also described simply as a monastic order.[124] Yet when we come to Pliny, we find them described as if they were a race or tribe. They are not mentioned in what we have of Mela.

XI, 50. Pliny, *Nat. hist.* V, xvii, 73.

Ab occidente litora Esseni fugiunt, usque qua nocent, gens sola — et in toto orbe praeter ceteras mira — sine ulla femina, omni venere abdicata, sine pecunia, socia palmarum. In diem ex aequo convenarum turba renascitur, large frequentantibus, quos vita fessos ad mores eorum fortunae fluctibus agitat. Ita per saeculorum milia (incredibile dictu) gens aeterna est, in qua nemo nascitur; tam fecunda illis aliorum vitae paenitentia est.[125]

---

[124] Josephus has another account of the Essenes in a much shorter form in *Ant. jud.* XVIII, 11-12. Porphyry paraphrases this in *De abstinentia*, IV, 11.

[125] Ed. Detlefsen, Berlin, 1904.

To the west [of the Asphalt Lake] . . . and where it is no longer harmful the Essenes have taken flight, a people unique and wonderful beyond all others in the world, living without women, having abandoned all sexual desire, without money, with palms alone as their fellows. Daily their group is kept at the same number by the large crowd of those whom, wearied by life, the waves of fortune have driven to this way of living. Thus through thousands of years, incredible to relate, a race is kept alive in which no one is born; so fruitful to it is the weariness of life felt by others.

This account by Pliny is the source of medieval accounts of the Essenes, of which we cite here only that of Solinus (3rd c. A. D.).

XI, 51. Solinus, *Collectanea rerum memorabilium*, xxxv, 9-11.

Interiora Iudaeae occidentem quae contuentur Esseni tenent, qui memorabili disciplina recesserunt a ritu gentium universarum, maiestatis ut reor providentia ad hunc morem destinati. nulla ibi femina: venere se penitus abdicaverunt. pecuniam nesciunt. palmis victitant. nemo ibi nascitur nec tamen deficit hominum multitudo. locus ipsi addictus pudicitiae est: ad quem plurimi licet undique gentium properent, nullus admittitur, nisi quem castitatis fides et innocentiae meritum prosequatur: nam qui reus est vel levis culpae, quamvis summa ope adipisci ingressum velit, divinitus submovetur. ita per immensum spatium saeculorum, incredibile dictu, aeterna gens est cessantibus puerperiis.[126]

The western part of Judea is occupied by the Essenes, who by a memorable way of life have cut themselves off from the general customs of men, destined, I believe, by divine providence to this manner of living. No woman is to be found there; they have denied themselves lust. They have no money. They live on palms. No one is born there, yet there never lacks a host of men. The place is given over to virtue. Many enter there from all sides; none is admitted unless he has been deemed worthy by a reputation for chastity and innocence. For he who is accused of even a mild sin, although he should wish to effect his entrance by a great sum of money, is removed by divine law. Thus for many centuries, incredible to relate, a people is kept eternal without childbirth.

The Aremphaei

Similarly holy people are the Aremphaei. Our first notice of them is from Mela (1st c. A. D.).

XI, 52. Pomponius Mela, *Chorographia,* I, 117.

Tum continuis rupibus late aspera et deserta regio ad Aremphaeos usque permittitur. his iustissimi mores, nemora pro domibus, alimenta bacae, et feminis et maribus nuda sunt capita. sacri itaque habentur, adeoque ipsos nemo de tam feris gentibus violat, ut aliis quoque ad eos confugisse pro asylo sit. ultra surgit mons Riphaeus ultraque eum iacet ora quae spectat oceanum.[127]

---

[126] Ed. Mommsen, Berlin, 1864, pp. 172-173.   [127] Ed. C. Frick, Leipzig, 1880.

A rough and desert region of unending rocks stretches broadly to the Aremphaei. They have the justest manners, groves for dwellings, for food berries. Both men and women go bareheaded. They are held for sacred, and therefore no one of so many savage peoples harms them, in order that it may be possible for others to flee to them for asylum. Beyond rises Mount Rhiphaeus, and beyond it lies the shore which faces the Ocean.

The version of Pliny is more detailed as to their geographical location, but reproduces most of Mela's account.

XI, 53. Pliny, *Nat. hist.* VI, 13 (14).

Nunc omnibus quae sunt Asiae interiora dictis Ripaeos montes transcendat animus dextraque litore oceani incedat. Tribus hic partibus caeli adluens Asiam Scythicus a septentrione, ab oriente Eous, a meridie Indicus vocatur, varieque per sinus et accolas in conplura nomina dividitur. verum Asiae quoque magna portio, apposita septentrioni iniuria sideris rigens vastas solitudines habet. Ab extremo aquilone ad initium orientis aestivi Scythae sunt. extra eos ultraque aquilonis initia Hyperboreos aliqui posuere, pluribus in Europa dictos. Primum inde noscitur promunturium Scythiae Lytharmis, fluvius Carambucis. ubi lassata cum siderum vi Ripaeorum montium deficiunt iuga, ibique Arimphaeos quosdam accepimus, haut dissimilem Hyperboreis gentem. sedes illis nemora, alimenta bacae, capillus iuxta feminis virisque in probro existimatus, ritus clementes. itaque sacros haberi narrant inviolatosque esse etiam feris accolarum populis, nec ipsos modo sed illos quoque qui ad eos profugerint.[128]

Since all things about the interior of Asia have now been said, let our minds cross the Rhiphaean mountains, and land upon the shores of Ocean to the right. Ocean washes Asia with three of its parts, called the Scythian on the north, on the east the Eastern, on the south the Indic, and is variously divided by many names according to its bays and peoples. Indeed a great part of Asia towards the north has vast solitudes caused by the freezing climate. From the extreme north to the place where the summer sun rises are the Scythians. Beyond these and beyond the beginnings of the North, some have placed the Hyperboreans, said by more to be in Europe. The first place known after this is the promontory of Scythian Lytharmis, the river Carambux, where the slopes of the Rhiphaean mountains fall away, as the rigor of the climate diminishes. There we believe to be a people called Arimphaei, not unlike the Hyperboreans. Their dwellings are groves, their food berries; [long] hair of both men and women is held in disrepute; they are kindly in their manners. And so they are said to be held sacred, and are unharmed even by the wild people who are their neighbors, and this applies not only to themselves, but to those also who have fled to them for refuge.[129]

[128] Ed. Detlefsen, Berlin, 1904.

[129] Pliny's account is reproduced by Solinus, ch. xvii, and Martianus Capella, Bk. VI, p. 214.

The Albanians and Tibareni

The Albanians (of Asia), a Scythian tribe, are not among the more famous noble savages of antiquity. They owe their reputation to Strabo. They reproduce the following features of the Golden Age: abstention from navigation, possession of an almost spontaneously fertile earth, childlike simplicity and guilelessness, absence of government. They are, however, not wholly innocent of war.

XI, 54. Strabo, *Geogr.* XI, iv, 1; 3-5 (501-502).

1. Ἀλβανοὶ δὲ ποιμενικώτεροι καὶ τοῦ νομαδικοῦ γένους ἐγγυτέρω, πλὴν ἀλλ' οὐκ ἄγριοι· ταύτῃ δὲ καὶ πολεμικοὶ μετρίως. οἰκοῦσι δὲ μεταξὺ τῶν Ἰβήρων καὶ τῆς Κασπίας θαλάττης. . . .

3. Τάχα μὲν οὖν τῷ τοιούτῳ γένει τῶν ἀνθρώπων οὐδὲν δεῖ θαλάττης· οὐδὲ γὰρ τῇ γῇ χρῶνται κατ' ἀξίαν, πάντα μὲν ἐκφερούσῃ καρπὸν καὶ τὸν ἡμερώτατον, πᾶν δὲ φυτόν· καὶ γὰρ τὰ ἀειθαλῆ φέρει· τυγχάνει δ' ἐπιμελείας οὐδὲ μικρᾶς "ἀλλὰ τάγ' ἄσπαρτα καὶ ἀνήροτα πάντα φύονται," καθάπερ οἱ στρατεύσαντές φασι, Κυκλώπειόν τινα διηγούμενοι βίον· πολλαχοῦ γὰρ σπαρεῖσαν ἅπαξ δὶς ἐκφέρειν καρπὸν ἢ καὶ τρίς, τὸν δὲ πρῶτον καὶ πεντηκοντάχουν, ἀνέαστον καὶ ταῦτα οὐδὲ σιδήρῳ τμηθεῖσαν ἀλλ' αὐτοξύλῳ ἀρότρῳ. ποτίζεται δὲ πᾶν τὸ πεδίον τοῦ Βαβυλωνίου καὶ τοῦ Αἰγυπτίου μᾶλλον τοῖς ποταμοῖς καὶ τοῖς ἄλλοις ὕδασιν ὥστ' ἀεὶ ποώδη φυλάττειν τὴν ὄψιν· διὰ δὲ τοῦτο καὶ εὔβοτόν ἐστι· πρόσεστι δὲ καὶ τὸ εὐάερον ἐκείνων μᾶλλον. ἄσκαφοι δ' αἱ ἄμπελοι μένουσαι διὰ τέλους, τεμνόμεναι δὲ διὰ πενταετηρίδος, νέαι μὲν διετεῖς ἐκφέρουσιν ἤδη καρπόν, τέλειαι δ' ἀποδιδόασι τοσοῦτον ὥστ' ἀφιᾶσιν ἐν τοῖς κλήμασι πολὺ μέρος. εὐερνῆ δ' ἐστὶ καὶ τὰ βοσκήματα παρ' αὐτοῖς τά τε ἥμερα καὶ τὰ ἄγρια.

Καὶ οἱ ἄνθρωποι κάλλει καὶ μεγέθει διαφέροντες, ἁπλοῖ δὲ καὶ οὐ καπηλικοί· οὐδὲ γὰρ νομίσματι τὰ πολλὰ χρῶνται, οὐδὲ ἀριθμὸν ἴσασι μείζω τῶν ἑκατόν, ἀλλὰ φορτίοις τὰς ἀμοιβὰς ποιοῦνται· καὶ πρὸς τἆλλα δὲ τὰ τοῦ βίου ῥαθύμως ἔχουσιν. ἄπειροι δ' εἰσὶ καὶ μέτρων τῶν ἐπ' ἀκριβὲς καὶ σταθμῶν, καὶ πολέμου δὲ καὶ πολιτείας καὶ γεωργίας ἀπρονοήτως ἔχουσιν· ὅμως δὲ καὶ πεζοὶ καὶ ἀφ' ἵππων ἀγωνίζονται, ψιλοί τε καὶ κατάφρακτοι, καθάπερ Ἀρμένιοι. στέλλουσι δὲ μείζω τῆς Ἰβήρων στρατιάν. ὁπλίζουσι γὰρ καὶ ἐξ μυριάδας πεζῶν, ἱππέας δὲ μυρίους καὶ δισχιλίους, ὅσοις πρὸς Πομπήιον διεκινδύνευσαν. καὶ τούτοις δὲ συμπολεμοῦσιν οἱ νομάδες πρὸς τοὺς ἔξωθεν, ὥσπερ τοῖς Ἴβηρσι, κατὰ τὰς αὐτὰς αἰτίας. ἄλλως δ' ἐπιχειροῦσι τοῖς ἀνθρώποις πολλάκις ὥστε καὶ γεωργεῖν κωλύουσιν. ἀκοντισταὶ δέ εἰσι καὶ τοξόται, θώρακας ἔχοντες καὶ θυρεούς, περίκρανα δὲ θήρεια παραπλησίως τοῖς Ἴβηρσιν.[130]

1. The Albanians are more pastoral and more like the nomadic tribes except that they are not savage. And therefore they are only moderately warlike. And they live between the Iberians [131] and the Caspian Sea. . . .

3. Now a people of this kind has no need of the sea. Nor do they use the land to the full extent of its value, the land which bears every kind of fruit, even the cultivated, and every kind of plant. For it bears ever-blooming plants. Nor does it require the slightest attention, "but all things grow there untilled and unsowed," as the

[130] Ed. Meineke, Leipzig, 1915, II.
[131] The Asiatic, not the European Iberians (Spaniards).

soldiers say, living a sort of Cyclopean life. For in many places after they have sowed once, they reap two or three times, and the first sowing multiplies itself fifty fold, and these crops are not raised by cutting the land with iron but with a wooden plow. And the whole plain is watered even more than those of Babylonia and Egypt by rivers and other streams, so that it always keeps its grassy appearance; it is therefore excellent pasture land. And besides the Albanians enjoy a better climate. The vines remain unhoed forever, and are pruned every fifth year; for when young, at two years, they give fruit and when old they return so much that the people leave a large part of it unpicked. And their cattle are very sleek, both domesticated and wild.

4. The men themselves are distinguished in beauty and height, and are simple and not tricky. Nor do they even use currency for the most part, nor can they count above one hundred, but they barter their goods. And in other respects they take life easily. They are indefinite about exact measures and weights. And they give no thought to war and government and farming. However they fight on foot and horseback, both unprotected and in armor, like Armenians. And they mobilize an army bigger than that of the Iberians. For they have 60,000 light armed foot soldiers, and 12,000 horsemen, with which they made a desperate attempt against Pompey. And the nomads fought with them against the invaders as they did with the Iberians, for the same cause. And otherwise they make attacks on other men often so that they prevent them from working their land. And they are javelin throwers and archers, having breastplates and shields and helmets in the shape of animal heads like the Iberians.

This account is repeated in the *Chrestomathia straboniana*, XI, 21, with emphasis upon the " Cyclopean " character of the land (cf. ch. XI, 11, above).

XI, 55. *Chrestomathia straboniana*, XI, 21.

"Οτι οἱ ᾿Αλβανοὶ γῆν νέμονται, δίκην τῆς Κυκλώπων, ἀγαθωτάτην, οἵαν φησὶν ἐκεῖνος· " ἀλλ᾿ ἥγ᾿ ἄσπαρτος καὶ ἀνήροτος " καρποφορεῖ. Καὶ αἱ ἄμπελοι αὐτοῖς ἄσκαφοι καὶ διὰ πενταετίας κλαδευόμεναι φέρουσι τὸν καρπόν. Ἡ δὲ χώρα οὐδὲ σιδήρῳ τέμνεται, ἀλλὰ τῷ τοῦ ἀρότρου ξύλῳ, καὶ ἅπαξ σπαρεῖσα ἐπὶ διετίαν ἢ καὶ τριετίαν καρποφορεῖ. Οἵ τε ποταμοὶ αὐτοῖς τὴν γῆν ποτίζουσιν, ὥσπερ ὁ Νεῖλος καὶ ὁ Εὐφράτης, καὶ ἁπλῶς ὑπερβολὴν οὐκ ἀπολείπει ἡ χοῦς τῆς ᾿Αλβανίας εἰς ἀρετὴν καρπογονίας (οὕτως δὲ δεῖ λέγειν καὶ θηλυκῶς ἡ χοῦς). Εἰσὶ δὲ αὐτοῖς καὶ τὰ κτήνη πολυτόκα. Καὶ αὐτοὶ καλοί τε τὰς ὄψεις καὶ μεγάλοι καὶ ἁπλοῖ τοῖς ἤθεσι· καὶ διὰ τὴν εὐηθίαν οὐκ ἴσασί τινες αὐτῶν ἀριπμεῖν, οἱ δὲ εἰδότες οὐ πλείω τῶν ἑκατὸν μετροῦσιν.[132]

The Albanians cultivate a land like that of the Cyclôpes, very good, as [Homer] says, and " unsowed and untilled " it bears fruit (*Od.* IX, 109). And their vines are unhoed, and, pruned in the fifth year, they bear fruit. And the land is not cut by iron but by a plow of wood, and when once sowed with seed it bears fruit for

---

[132] Müller, *Geog. graec. min.* II, 595.

two or three years. And the rivers give drink to the land, like the Nile and the Euphrates, and in all ways the alluvial earth of Albania lacks nothing in the excellence of its fertility — and thus one ought to say " the alluvial earth " in the feminine. And those people have very prolific cattle. And they themselves are also beautiful of face and tall and simple in their way of living. And because of their guilelessness, some of them do not know how to count, and those who do know do not count beyond 100.

Another Scythian tribe of noble manners was the Tibareni. They are represented by Ephorus (4th c. B. C.) as a happy people.

XI, 56. Ephorus, in Stephanus Byzantinus, *Ethnica*, sub Τιβαρηνία.

> Ἔφορος ἐν πέμπτῳ φησίν, ὅτι Τιβαρηνοὶ καὶ τὸ παίζειν καὶ τὸ γελᾶν εἰσιν ἐζηλωκότες καὶ μεγίστην εὐδαιμονίαν τοῦτο νομίζουσιν.[133]

Ephorus in the fifth book says that the Tibareni are very fond of laughter and play and consider them the greatest happiness.

They are also mentioned eulogistically by Nymphodorus of Syracuse (date uncertain).

XI, 57. Nymphodorus, in *Schol. Apoll. Rhod.* II, 1010.

> Τιβαρηνοί, ἔθνος Σκυθίας. Οὗτοι δικαιότατοι λέγονται· καὶ οὐδέποτε μάχην τινὶ συνέβαλον, εἰ μὴ πρότερον καταγγείλειαν καὶ ἡμέραν καὶ τόπον καὶ ὥραν τῆς μάχης. Ἐν δὲ τῇ τῶν Τιβαρηνῶν γῇ αἱ γυναῖκες, ὅταν τέκωσι, τημελοῦσι τοὺς ἄνδρας, ὥσπερ λεχούς.[134]

The Tibareni, a Scythian people. These are said to be the most just of men. And never do they give battle without first announcing the day and the place and the hour. And in the land of the Tibareni the women, when they bring forth their young, care for their husbands as if they [the husbands] were in childbirth.

The Illyrians

XI, 58. Ps. Scymnus, *Orb. descr.* 415-425. (2d c. B. C.)

> Ἡ δ' Ἰλλυρὶς μετὰ ταῦτα παρατείνουσα γῆ
> ἔθνη περιέχει πολλά· πλήθη γὰρ συχνά
> τῶν Ἰλλυριῶν λέγουσιν εἶναι καὶ τὰ μέν
> αὐτῶν κατοικεῖν τὴν μεσόγειον νεμόμενα
> ἃ δὲ τὴν παράλιον ἐντὸς ἐπέχειν Ἀδρίου,
> καί τινα μὲν αὐτῶν βασιλικαῖς ἐξουσίαις
> ὑπήκο' εἶναι, τινὰ δὲ καὶ μοναρχίαις,
> ἃ δ' αὐτονομεῖσθαι· θεοσεβεῖς δ' αὐτοὺς ἄγαν
> καὶ σφόδρα δικαίους φασὶ καὶ φιλοξένους.
> κοινωνικὴν διάθεσιν ἠγαπηκότας
> εἶναι, βίον ζηλοῦν τε κοσμιώτατον.[135]

After these lands is that of Illyria, containing many nations. For they say there is a great multitude of Illyrians and some of them

---

[133] Ed. A. Westermann, Leipzig, 1839. Also Müller *F. H. G.*, I, 259.
[134] *Fragm.* 15, Müller, *F. G. H.* II, 379.   [135] Müller, *Geog. graec. min.* I, 213.

inhabit and cultivate the inland regions and others possess the maritime district along the Adriatic. And some of them are obedient to royal authority and some to monarchical, while others are self-ruled. And they are said to be god-fearing and exceedingly just, and kindly to strangers, and delight in social fellowship, and admire a well-ordered life.[136]

The Argippeans

XI, 59. Herodotus, *Hist.* IV, 23.

Μέχρι μὲν δὴ τῆς τούτων τῶν Σκυθέων χώρης, ἔστι ἡ καταλεχθεῖσα πᾶσα πεδιάς τε γῆ καὶ βαθύγεος· τὸ δ' ἀπὸ τούτου, λιθώδης τ' ἐστὶ καὶ τρηχέη. διεξελθόντι δὲ καὶ τῆς τρηχέης χῶρον πολλὸν, οἰκέουσι ὑπώρεαν οὐρέων ὑψηλῶν ἄνθρωποι λεγόμενοι εἶναι πάντες φαλακροὶ ἐκ γενεῆς γινόμενοι, καὶ ἔρσενες καὶ θήλεαι ὁμοίως, καὶ σιμοὶ καὶ γένεια ἔχοντες μεγάλα, φωνὴν δὲ ἰδίην ἱέντες ἐσθῆτι δὲ χρεώμενοι Σκυθικῇ, ζῶντες δὲ ἀπὸ δενδρέων· ποντικὸν μὲν οὔνομα τῷ δενδρέῳ ἀπὸ τοῦ ζῶσι, μέγαθος δὲ κατὰ συκέην μάλιστά κη· καρπὸν δὲ φορέει κυάμῳ ἴσον, πυρῆνα δὲ ἔχει· τοῦτο ἐπεὰν γένηται πέπον, σακκέουσι ἱματίοισι· ἀπορρέει δ' ἀπ' αὐτοῦ παχὺ καὶ μέλαν· οὔνομα δὲ τῷ ἀπορρέοντί ἐστι ἄσχυ· τοῦτο καὶ λείχουσι καὶ γάλακτι συμμίσγοντες πίνουσι, καὶ ἀπὸ τῆς παχύτητος αὐτοῦ τῆς τρυγὸς παλάθας συντιθέασι, καὶ ταύτας σιτέονται· πρόβατα γάρ σφι οὐ πολλά ἐστι, οὐ γάρ τι σπουδαῖαι νομαὶ αὐτόθι εἰσί· ὑπὸ δενδρέῳ δὲ ἕκαστος κατοίκηται· τὸν μὲν χειμῶνα, ἐπεὰν τὸ δένδρεον περικαλύψῃ πίλῳ στεγνῷ λευκῷ· τὸ δὲ θέρος, ἄνευ πίλου. τούτους οὐδεὶς ἀδικέει ἀνθρώπων· ἱροὶ γὰρ λέγονται εἶναι· οὐδέ τι ἀρήϊον ὅπλον ἐκτέαται· καὶ τοῦτο μὲν τοῖσι περιοικέουσι οὗτοί εἰσι οἱ τὰς διαφορὰς διαιρέοντες· τοῦτο δὲ ὃς ἂν φεύγων καταφύγῃ ἐς τούτους, ὑπ' οὐδενὸς ἀδικέεται· οὔνομα δέ σφί ἐστι Ἀργιππαῖοι.[137]

As far as the country of these Scythians, the land above mentioned is all flat and deep-soiled, but beyond it is rocky and rough. And when one goes along through the rough country there are living on the slopes of the high mountains men said to be all bald from birth, both men and women alike, and snub-nosed and having great beards, and speaking their own language, but wearing Scythian garments, and living from trees. " Pontic " is the name of the tree from which they live, and its size is about that of a fig-tree. And it bears a fruit the size of a bean and has a pit. When this is ripe, they strain it through cloths, and there flows from it something thick and black And the name of what flows off is *aschu*. And they lick this up, or mixing it with milk they drink it, and from the thickest of its lees they fashion cakes and eat them. They have not many small cattle, for the pasturage there is not very good. Under a tree each man lives; as soon as it is winter he covers the tree with a white waterproof felt, but in summerheat they live without the felt. No man does wrong to these people, for they are said to be

---

[136] It is difficult to believe that these are the Illyrians spoken of by Theopompus (4th c. B. C.) according to Athenaeus, X, 443, who were such gluttons that they were enticed by their enemies, the Celts, into eating a huge meal into the dishes of which a strong purgative had been mixed. The Illyrians could not stand the pain and were thus captured by the Celts.

[137] Ed. Blakesley, Lond. 1854.

sacred; nor do they possess any martial weapons. And it is they who settle differences for those who dwell about them, and whatever fugitive has fled among them is wronged by none. And their name is Argippeans.

The accounts of most of the peoples which we have quoted are obviously colored by legend, even when the peoples themselves are real. In Tacitus we are given savages who are a mixture of nobility and barbarism.

The Fenni

XI, 60. Tacitus, *Germania,* XLVI.

Peucinorum Venedorumque et Fennorum nationes Germanis an Sarmatis adscribam dubito, quamquam Peucini, quos quidam Bastarnas vocant, sermone cultu, sede ac domiciliis ut Germani agunt. sordes omnium ac torpor: ora procerum conubiis mixtis non-nihil in Sarmatarum habitum foedantur. Venedi multum ex mori-bus traxerunt; nam quidquid inter Peucinos Fennosque silvarum ac montium erigitur latrociniis pererrant. hi tamen inter Germanos potius referunter, quia et domos figunt et scuta gestant et pedum usu ac pernicitate gaudent: quae omnia diversa Sarmatis sunt in plaustro equoque viventibus. Fennis mira feritas, foeda paupertas: non arma, non equi, non penates; victui herba, vestitui pelles, cubili humus: sola in sagittis spes, quas inopia ferri ossibus asperant. idemque venatus viros pariter ac feminas alit; passim enim comi-tantur partemque praedae petunt. nec aliud infantibus ferarum imbriumque suffugium quam ut in aliquo ramorum nexu conte-gantur: huc redeunt iuvenes, hoc senum receptaculum. sed beatius arbitrantur quam ingemere agris, inlaborare domibus, suas alienasque fortunas spe metuque versare: securi adversus homines, securi ad-versus deos rem difficillimam adsecuti sunt, ut illis ne voto quidem opus sit.[138]

I am in doubt whether the tribes of the Peucini, Venedi, and Fenni are to be classified among the Germans or the Sarmatians, though the Peucini, whom some call Bastarnae, are like the Ger-mans in speech, clothing, and in having a fixed domicile. They are generally dirty and lazy. The features of their chiefs have been defiled by intermarriage into an appearance much like that of the Sarmatians. The Venedi have taken over many of their customs. For whatever woods and mountains there are between the Peucini and the Fenni, they wander through for pillage. Yet they should rather be classified with the Germans, both because they build houses and carry shields and take pleasure in the use and speed of their feet, all of which traits are different from the Sarmatians, who live in wagons and on horseback. The savagery of the Fenni is wonderful, their poverty loathsome. They have neither arms nor horses nor household goods. Their food is herbs, their clothing skins, their bed the ground. Their sole hope is in their arrows, which, lacking iron, they sharpen out of bone. The same hunt feeds both men and women alike; they accompany each other, they seek

[138] Ed. C. Halm, Leipzig, 1911.

each his part of the prey. The children have no other refuge from the wild beasts and rains than to be concealed in some woven branches. Hither the young come home, this is a shelter for the old. But they think this a happier lot than to groan in the fields, to labor over houses, to worry about their own and others' fortune in hope and fear. They are without concern for men or for the gods; they have achieved the most difficult thing — to have no need even of prayers.

Though Tacitus clearly is repelled by the sordidness of the lives of this people, he as clearly admires their self-sufficiency, approximating that of the Cynic wise man.

The Germans

The Germans first appear as noble savages in Caesar's *De bello gallico* (51 B. C.). Caesar's description, with that of Tacitus, is probably the source of all that is said by medieval [139] and later writers on this people. The Germans, according to Caesar, are without priests and do not engage in sacrifice; their life is spent in hunting and war-making; they are extremely chaste; they have no agriculture nor privately owned land, partly because of the supposed immoral effect of the *amor habendi*; they rob their neighbors but not their own citizens; they are hospitable.

We have here a picture which combines features of the ideal of cultural primitivism — absence of agriculture; that of hard primitivism — fortitude and simplicity of diet; the economic state of nature — absence of private property; and two of the usual traits of the ancient noble savage, sexual continence and hospitality. At the same time Caesar does not omit less pleasing traits, their belligerency and fierce destructiveness, and their predatory attitude towards neighbors. Caesar, however, is not engaged in either praising or belittling the Germans; he is attempting to describe them.

XI, 61. Julius Caesar, *De bello gallico,* VI, 21-23.

Germani multum ab hac consuetudine differunt. Nam neque druides habent, qui rebus divinis praesint, neque sacrificiis student. Deorum numero eos solos ducunt, quos cernunt et quorum aperte opibus iuvantur, Solem et Vulcanum et Lunam, reliquos ne fama quidem acceperunt. Vita omnis in venationibus atque in studiis rei militaris consistit: a parvis labori ac duritiae student. Qui diutissime impuberes permanserunt, maximam inter suos ferunt laudem; hoc ali staturam, ali vires nervosque confirmari putant. Intra annum vero vicesimum feminae notitiam habuisse in turpissimis habent rebus; cuius rei nulla est occultatio, quod et promiscue in fluminibus perluuntur et pellibus aut parvis renonum tegimentis utuntur magna corporis parte nuda.

[139] Caesar's account of the Germans, not that of Tacitus, was quoted *in extenso* in the eleventh century by Aimoin of Fleury in his *Historia francorum*, Migne, *Pat. Lat.* 139, p. 630.

22. Agriculturae non student, maiorque pars eorum victus in lacte, caseo, carne consistit. Neque quisquam agri modum certum aut fines habet proprios; sed magistratus ac principes in annos singulos gentibus cognationibusque hominum, qui una coierunt, quantum et quo loco visum est agri, adtribuunt atque anno post alio transire cogunt. Eius rei multas adferunt causas: ne adsidua consuetudine capti studium belli gerendi agricultura commutent; ne latos fines parare studeant, potentioresque humiliores possessionibus expellant; ne accuratius ad frigora atque aestus vitandos aedificent; nequa oriatur pecuniae cupiditas, qua ex re factiones dissensionesque nascuntur; ut animi aequitate plebem contineant, cum suas quisque opes cum potentissimis aequari videat.

23. Civitatibus maxima laus est quam latissime circum se vastatis finibus solitudines habere. Hoc proprium virtutis existimant, expulsos agris finitimos cedere, neque quemquam prope se audere consistere; simul hoc se fore tutiores arbitrantur, repentinae incursionis timore sublato. Cum bellum civitas aut inlatum defendit aut infert, magistratus, qui ei bello praesint, et vitae necisque habeant potestatem, deliguntur. In pace nullus est communis magistratus, sed principes regionum atque pagorum inter suos ius dicunt controversiasque minuunt. Latrocinia nullam habent infamiam, quae extra fines cuiusque civitatis fiunt, atque ea iuventutis exercendae ac desidiae minuendae causa fieri praedicant. Atque ubi quis ex principibus in concilio dixit, se ducem fore, qui sequi velint, profiteantur, consurgunt ii, qui et causam et hominem probant, suumque auxilium pollicentur atque a multitudine conlaudantur; qui ex his secuti non sunt, in desertorum ac proditorum numero ducuntur, omniumque his rerum postea fides derogatur. Hospitem violare fas non putant; qui quacunque de causa ad eos venerunt, ab iniuria prohibent, sanctosque habent, hisque omnium domus patent victusque communicatur.[140]

The Germans differ greatly from this way of living [i. e., the way of the Gauls]. For they have neither Druids, who preside over religious matters, nor do they engage in sacrifice. They consider only those to be of the number of the gods whom they perceive and by whose powers they are obviously aided, the Sun and Vulcan and the Moon; the rest they have not received even by legend. Their whole life is spent in hunting and in military pursuits; from childhood they strive in toil and hardship. They who remain chaste for the longest period, bear the highest honors among them; some believe that this increases their stature, others the strength of their sinews. To have knowledge of woman before the twentieth year they hold among the most shameful of deeds: of this thing there is no concealment, for they bathe openly in the rivers and they use pelts or small coverings of reindeer with a great part of the body naked.

22. They do not engage in agriculture, and the greater part of their food consists of milk, cheese, and meat. Nor has anyone a fixed length of field nor his own boundaries; but the magistrates and leaders each year assign to the families and kinsmen of the men, who meet together, a certain quantity and position of land, and the

[140] Ed. A. Klotz, Leipzig, 1921, with minor changes in punctuation.

following year they must change. They give many reasons for this:
that snared by steady habit they may not change their zeal for wag-
ing war into agriculture; that they may not strive to broaden their
acres and the more powerful expel the humbler from their possessions; that they may not build houses too elaborately to ward off
cold and heat; that a certain love of money may not arise from
which factions and dissensions are born; that they may keep the
people in equanimity by having each see that his possessions equal
those of the most powerful.

23. Those states are most greatly praised whose borders are surrounded by waste lands. They think this the mark of virtue, that
their neighbors expelled from their fields withdraw and no one dare
to remain near; at the same time they believe they will be safer
thus, with the fear of sudden invasion removed. When the state is
engaged in either defensive or offensive war, magistrates are chosen
to preside over the war, and they have the power of life and death.
In peace there is no common magistrate, but the chiefs of the regions
and districts make law among their followers and settle disputes.
They hold robbery in no disrepute so long as it goes on beyond the
borders of each state, and they extol its performance for the sake
of training the youth and reducing slothfulness. And when any
one of their chiefs says in council that he will be leader, calling upon
those who wish to follow him to say so, they spring up who approve
both the cause and the man, and promise their aid, and are applauded
by the multitude; they who of this number have not followed, are
considered as deserters and traitors, and no trust is put in their
word afterwards in any matter. They do not think it right to harm
a guest; those who have come to them, for any cause whatsoever,
they shield from injury, hold as sacred, and the houses of all are
open to them and food is given them.

In Seneca one finds the beginning of the tradition which idealizes the
Germans. In the manner of Dio Chrysostom he uses the hard life of the
savage to point a moral to his luxury-loving fellow citizens. They become in
his *De providentia* an exemplary people, happy in spite of, or perhaps
because of, the hardships of their existence — which Seneca considerably
exaggerates.

XI, 62. Seneca (1st c. A. D.), *De providentia,* IV, 14-15.

Omnes considera gentes, in quibus Romana pax desinit, Germanos dico et quicquid circa Istrum vagarum gentium occursat.
perpetua illos hiems, triste coelum premit, maligne solum sterile
sustentat, imbrem culmo aut fronde defendunt, super durata glacie
stagna persultant, in alimentum feras captant. Miseri tibi videntur?
nihil miserum est quod in naturam consuetudo perduxit.[141]

Consider all the tribes whom the *pax Romana* does not reach; I
mean the Germans and all the nomad tribes in conflict with us along
the Danube. Unending winter and a gloomy sky oppress them; the
barren soil grudgingly supports them; they keep off the rain with
thatch or leaves. They range over ice-bound swamps, and hunt wild

[141] Ed. Haase, Leipzig, 1898.

beasts for food. Do they seem to you unhappy? No one is unhappy whom custom has led in the path of nature.

Seneca, however, on occasion criticizes the reasoning of those who praised the Nordic savage.

XI, 63. Seneca, *De ira,* II, xv.

'Vt scias' inquit 'iram habere in se generosi aliquid, liberas videbis gentes, quae iracundissimae sunt, ut Germanos et Scythas.' quod evenit, quia fortia solidaque natura ingenia, antequam disciplina molliantur, prona in iram sunt. quaedam enim non nisi melioribus innascuntur ingeniis, sicut valida arbusta laeta quamvis neglecta tellus creat, et alto fecundi soli silva est: itaque et ingenia natura fortia iracundiam ferunt nihilque tenue et exile capiunt ignea et fervida, sed inperfectus illis vigor est ut omnibus, quae sine arte ipsius tantum naturae bono exurgunt, sed nisi cito domita sunt, quae fortitudini apta erant, audaciae temeritatique consuescunt. quid? non mitioribus animis vitia leniora contuncta sunt, ut misericordia et amor et verecundia? itaque saepe tibi bonam indolem malis quoque suis ostendam; sed non ideo vitia non sunt, si naturae melioris indicia sunt. deinde omnes istae feritate liberae gentes leonum luporumque ritu ut servire non possunt, ita nec imperare; non enim humani vim ingenii, sed feri et intractabilis habent; nemo autem regere potest nisi qui et regi. fere itaque imperia penes eos fuere populos, qui mitiore caelo utuntur. in frigora septemtrionemque vergentibus inmansueta ingenia sunt, ut ait poeta, suoque simillima caelo.[142]

"That you may be convinced," an opponent may say, "that anger has in it something noble, observe that free peoples, such as the Germans and the Scythians, are those that are most given to anger." This comes about because minds that are by nature strong and sturdy are prone to anger before they have been softened by discipline. For there are some qualities which are inborn only in better natures, just as rich ground, even though neglected, produces vigorous trees and a lofty forest springs from a fertile soil. And so characters that are by nature strong produce anger, and, being fiery and impetuous, do not take things mildly and meekly. But their vigor is imperfect, as is that of anything which grows up without art, merely as a gift of nature. And unless it is quickly tamed, a quality which might have become fortitude usually shows itself as mere recklessness and audacity. Nay, are not the milder faults, such as pity and love and bashfulness, combined with gentler natures? It is because these things are so that I can often show you by the very faults which a man has that his innate disposition is good; but they are none the less faults because they are evidences of a superior nature. And as for all those peoples who, after the manner of lions and wolves, are free by reason of their wildness — just as they cannot submit themselves to governance, so they are incapable of governing; for the force that they possess is not that of a human being, but of something wild and intractable. But no man is able to rule unless he can also be ruled. Those who are situ-

142 Ed. E. Hermes, Leipzig, 1917, pp. 86-87.

ated in the frozen north have tempers savage "like their skies," as the poet says.

The Germans, according to Tacitus [143] (*Germ.* iv), are probably a pure strain, so that all have a family resemblance. They are capable of great effort, and though they support cold and hunger, cannot resist thirst and heat. They are a cattle raising people and do not know the use of money (*id.* v) or precious metals. They dress simply and have no pride of adornment. They are particularly brave and honor bravery in others (*id.* vii). Unlike many noble savages, they are belligerent, even seeking war when peace has been of long duration (*id.* xiv). Nor do they cultivate the fields in time of peace, but pass their time eating and drinking (*id.* xv). They have no cities and but the roughest habitations (*id.* xvi). Their clothing is scanty and rough (*id.* xvii). They are chaste and in general monogamous, except when several families seek a martial alliance with one of them (*id.* xviii). They have no corrupting spectacles, nor passion-stirring banquets. Adultery is very little known. "*Nemo enim illic vitia ridet; nec corrumpere et corrumpi seculum vocatur*" (*id.* xix): "no one laughs at vice, nor is it called up-to-date to corrupt and be corrupted." All are reared in the same simple fashion, preserving their vigor until marriage. The Germans (like the Argippeans and the Illyrians) are extremely hospitable; *Notum ignotumque, quantum ad jus hospitii, nemo discernit* (*id.* xxi): "no one discriminates between known and unknown so far as the right to hospitality is concerned." One gives his guests whatever they demand. Though they are prone to drunkenness, they rid their minds in drunkenness of hypocritical secrets. Their games are athletic, and no prizes are awarded, except the applause of the onlookers. At the same time they are inveterate gamblers (*id.* xxiv). They have no private property but each cultivates the land assigned him and cultivates it for use not for beauty (*id.* xxvi). Finally they have no lavish funerals and no ostentatious grief.

It is easy to see that this account has no other purpose than to depict a people as it is. It would appear to be based upon observation rather than upon preconceived ideas, and the usual extravagant accounts of the noble savage do not seem to have colored it. The Germans as a whole have both admirable and regrettable traits, and Tacitus, like Caesar, includes both.

The noblest of the German tribes, according to Tacitus, are the Chauci.

XI, 64. Tacitus, *German.* XXXV.

> . . . populus inter Germanos nobilissimus, quique magnitudinem suam malit iustitia tueri. sine cupiditate, sine impotentia, quieti secretique nulla provocant bella, nullis raptibus aut latrociniis populantur. id praecipuum virtutis ac virium argumentum est, quod, ut

---

[143] To do full justice to Tacitus, the *De moribus germanorum* would have to be reprinted in its entirety. As that is impracticable, even in a work of the scope of the present one, we must violate our rule of direct quotation and paraphrase for the most part.

superiores agant, non per iniurias adsequuntur; prompta tamen omnibus arma ac, si res poscat, [exercitus], plurimum virorum equorumque; et quiescentibus eadem fama.[144]

[The Chauci are] the noblest people among the Germans, a people which prefers that its greatness be sustained by justice. Without greed, without poverty, peaceful and reserved, they never provoke war, nor are they busied with rapine and pillage. The most conspicuous proof of their courage and their strength is that in order to be victors they do not employ wrongful means. Yet their arms are always ready and, if affairs demand it, their armies as well, with a large number of men and horses. And their renown is undiminished when they are at peace.

The Hebrideans

The Hebrideans are not eulogized by any writer before Solinus, although the islands themselves are known to Pliny. Nevertheless the account given by Solinus of their manner of living is such a clear combination of various accounts of the good life in his predecessors that it is incredible that he should have invented it. The Hebrideans are so primitive techologically that they do not even practise agriculture. Their king is singled out to exemplify the life of a noble savage, being without property and without family. This might be held to be a reminiscence of Plato, were it not for the fact that a people near the Scythians, the Agathyrses, are spoken of by Herodotus (IV, 104) as practising conjugal communism so that all may be related by blood and thus friendly. So Nicolaus of Damascus, as we have seen above, describes the Milk-drinkers as communistic both in goods and wives. It is therefore possible that Solinus in view of the supposed diet of the Hebrideans is attributing to them traits of other noble savages.

XI, 65. Solinus, *Collectanea, App.* xxii, 12-15.

. . . Ebudes insulae quinque numero, quarum incolae nesciunt fruges, piscibus tantum et lacte vivunt. rex unus est universis, nam quotquot sunt, omnes angusta interluvie dividuntur. rex nihil suum habet, omnia universorum. ad aequitatem certis legibus stringitur ac ne avaritia devertat a vero, discit paupertate iustitiam, utpote cui nihil sit rei familiaris, verum alitur e publico. nulla illi femina datur propria, sed per vicissitudines, in quamcunque commotus sit, usurariam sumit. unde ei nec votum nec spes conceditur liberorum.[145]

. . . The Islands of the Hebrides, five in number, whose inhabitants have no knowledge of grains, but live only on fish and milk. There is one king of them all, for though there are many islands, all are separated only by narrow straits. The king has nothing of his own, all things are owned in common. He is bound to equity by definite laws, and lest avarice turn him from the true path, he learns justice through poverty, since he has no private property but is maintained by the public. He has no wife of his own, but from time to time he takes to himself as a loan her towards whom he may be drawn. Wherefore he has neither the promise nor hope of children.

[144] Ed. C. Halm, Leipzig, 1911.   [145] Ed. Mommsen, 1864.

CHAPTER TWELVE

ANTI-PRIMITIVISM AND THE IDEA OF PROGRESS IN LATER CLASSICAL LITERATURE

VARRO

In Varro we apparently find the not unusual combination of a tendency towards cultural primitivism with chronological anti-primitivism. His *De re rustica* is of course a panegyric of country life, and the famous phrase, " divina natura dedit agros, ars humana aedificavit urbes,"[1] suggests, as does the general tone of the work, that he regarded the agricultural stage as the best. If so, the following passage must be construed as anti-primitivistic; for in tracing the gradual sequence of stages of culture, he places two of them before the agricultural; while agriculture itself is an ' art' which has been improved by technical knowledge, *scientia* (I, 3, 1). But the beginning of urban life was a degeneration: *neque solum antiquior cultura agri, sed melior* (III, 1, 4).

XII, 1. *De re rustica* (37 B. C.), II, 1, 3 ff.

> . . . Igitur, inquam, et homines et pecudes cum semper fuisse sit necesse natura — sive enim aliquod fuit principium generandi animalium, ut putavit Thales Milesius et Zeno Citieus, sive contra principium horum extitit nullum, ut credidit Pythagoras Samius et Aristoteles Stagirites, necesse est humanae vitae ab summa memoria gradatim descendisse ad hanc aetatem, ut scribit Dicaearchus, et summum gradum fuisse naturalem, cum viverent homines ex iis rebus, quae inviolata ultro ferret terra, ex hac vita in secundam descendisse pastoriciam, e feris atque agrestibus ut arboribus ac virgultis [ac] decarpendo glandem, arbutum, mora, poma colligerent ad usum, sic ex animalibus cum propter eandem utilitatem, quae possent, silvestria deprenderent ac concluderent et mansuescerent. in quis primum non sine causa putant oves adsumptas et propter utilitatem et propter placiditatem. maxime enim hae natura quietae et aptissimae ad vitam hominum. ad cibum enim lacte et caseum adhibitum, ad corpus vestitum et pelles adtulerunt. tertio denique gradu a vita pastorali ad agri culturam descenderunt, in qua ex duobus gradibus superioribus retinuerunt multa, et quo descenderant, ibi processerunt longe, dum ad nos perveniret.[2]

> Therefore, I say, that since it is necessary in the nature of things that men and flocks have always existed — whether there was a first cause of the generation of animals, as Thales of Miletus

---

[1] *Op. cit.* III, 4. Verrall points out in the *Companion to Latin Studies* (p. 650) that this is the ancestor of Cowper's " God made the country and man made the town."

[2] Ed. H. Keil, Leipzig, 1889. For the passage of Dicaearchus cited, cf. Ch. II, 57. It is to be noted that Varro omits Dicaearchus's eulogy of the earliest stage.

and Zeno of Citium thought, or on the contrary no first cause of them ever existed, as Pythagoras of Samos or Aristotle the Stagirite, believed, it must be true that step by step from the most remote period human life has come down to this age, as Dicaearchus writes,[3] and that the earliest stage was a state of nature, when men lived on those things which the virgin earth bore; from this life they passed into a second, a pastoral life, and as they plucked from the wild and untrimmed trees and bushes acorns, arbute-berries, blackberries, apples and gathered them for their use, in like manner they caught such wild animals as they could and shut them up and tamed them. Among these, it is reasonable to think, the first to be caught were sheep, both because of their utility and their placidity. For they are by nature especially tame and most useful for human life. For food they supply milk and cheese, for clothing the body they furnish skins. Finally in the third stage, from the pastoral life they attained the agricultural, in which they retained many of the features of the two earlier periods, and from which they continued for a long time in the condition which they had reached until that in which we live was attained.

Nevertheless this apparent anti-primitivistic implication seems contradicted in the following passage.

XII, 2. *De re rustica,* I, 2, 16.

. . . Et quidem licet adicias, inquam, pastorum vitam esse incentivam, agricolarum succentivam auctore doctissimo homine Dicaearcho, qui Greciae vita qualis fuerit ab initio nobis ita ostendit, ut superioribus temporibus fuisse doceat, cum homines pastoriciam vitam agerent neque scirent etiam arare terram aut serere arbores aut putare; ab iis inferiore gradu aetatis susceptam agri culturam. quocirca ea succinit pastorali, quod est inferior, ut tibia sinistra a dextrae foraminibus.[4]

And indeed you might add that the pastoral life is like the first and main tune, and the agricultural life like an accompaniment which is struck up later,[5] according to the learned author Dicaearchus, who has shown us the character of primeval Greek life.[6]

VIRGIL

Virgil is engaged in the *Georgics* in promoting a 'back-to-the-farm' movement; in other words, he is expressing a mild form of cultural semi-primitivism. But for this purpose, the traditional pictures of the Golden Age, when your food dropped into your lap, were anything but serviceable. Though the opening lines are in the traditional vein, it is on the whole a

---

[3] For the passage from Dicaearchus, see II, 57.

[4] Ed. H. Keil.

[5] The pun on *inferiore* cannot be translated in English. It here apparently means at once "lower" in tone, "subordinate" to the main theme, and "later" in time.

[6] The question of the priority of agriculture to other modes of life is echoed in the pseudo-Plutarchan *Pro nobilitate,* xx.

Gospel of Work that Virgil is apparently here preaching; and it takes form in a significant reversal of the original valuation of the Age of Saturn and that of Jupiter, respectively. In the former, man's life, it is still assumed, was easy, carefree, spontaneous; and when Jove succeeded Saturn it became arduous, dangerous and laborious. But this was a gain, not a loss; it was, Virgil seems to suggest, for man's good that Jove made it necessary for him to seek his subsistence through conscious and painful effort. The immediate divine originator of agriculture was Ceres, but only in its rudiments; it is still an imperfectly understood art — hence the practical details of the successful practice of it in which the poet seeks to give instruction in the *Georgics*.[7]

XII, 3. *Georgics (ca.* 35 B. C.), I, 125-155.

> ante Iovem nulli subigebant arva coloni;
> ne signare quidem aut partiri limite campum
> fas erat: in medium quaerebant, ipsaque tellus
> omnia liberius nullo poscente ferebat.
> ille malum virus serpentibus addidit atris,
> praedarique lupos iussit pontumque moveri,
> mellaque decussit foliis, ignemque removit,
> et passim rivis currentia vina repressit,
> ut varias usus meditando extunderet artes
> paulatim, et sulcis frumenti quaereret herbam.
> [ut silicis venis abstrusum excuderet ignem.]
> tunc alnos primum fluvii sensere cavatas;
> navita tum stellis numeros et nomina fecit,
> Pleïadas, Hyadas, claramque Lycaonis Arcton;
> tum laqueis captare feras et fallere visco
> inventum, et magnos canibus circumdare saltus;
> atque alius latum funda iam verberat amnem
> alta petens, alius pelago trahit umida lina;
> tum ferri rigor atque argutae lamina serrae
> [nam primi cuneis scindebant fissile lignum]
> tum variae venere artes. labor omnia vicit
> improbus, et duris urguens in rebus egestas.
> prima Ceres ferro mortalis vertere terram
> instituit, cum iam glandes atque arbuta sacrae
> deficerent silvae et victum Dodona negaret.
> mox et frumentis labor additus, ut mala culmos
> esset robigo, segnisque horreret in arvis
> carduos: intereunt segetes, subit aspera silva,
> lappaeque tribolique, interque nitentia culta
> infelix lolium et steriles dominantur avenae.[8]

Before the time of Jupiter no farmer worked the fields: it was not even right to mark off or to divide the land with boundaries: they toiled for the common good, and earth herself bore all things

---

[7] The Golden Age, the "spring of the world," is again referred to in *Georgics*, II, 336-345, in a more primitivistic tone.

[8] Ed. Otto Ribbeck, Leipzig, 1898.

the more freely since no one asked for them. It was he who added evil poison to the dark serpents, and bade the wolves to prey and the sea to be stirred up; and he stripped the leaves of their honey, and withheld fire, and stifled the vines which ran hither and thither along the ground; so that by reflecting on his needs he (man) might little by little fashion various arts, and cut the ears of wheat with sickles, and strike a spark hidden in the veins of flint. Then first the rivers felt the hollow ships; then the sailor gave names to the stars and counted them; the Pleiades, the Hyades, and bright Arctos, daughter of Lycaon. Then man discovered how to capture wild beasts in nets and to trap birds with birdlime, and to surround broad woodlands with hunting dogs. And one man whips the wide river with his drag-net seeking the depths, and another draws his wet lines through the sea. Then the hard iron and the blade of the gleaming saw — for primitive man used to split the fissile wood with wedges — then the various arts arose. Persistent labor conquered all things, and need pressing on against hardships.

Ceres first showed mortals how to turn back the earth with iron blade, after acorns and the arbute berries began to fail in the sacred wood and Dodona withheld food. Soon more labor was added in the care of growing grain, as evil mildew began to consume the stalks and the unfruitful thistle bristled in the fields. The cornfields perished, rough scrub sprang up, and burdocks and thorn-bushes, and amongst the blooming tillage the unhappy tares and sterile wild oat reigned.

HORACE

The Epicurean or Lucretian account of man's rise from a beastlike condition, with caves for shelter and acorns for food, is repeated by Horace, with the addition of the somewhat equivocal moral observation that 'nature,' while it distinguishes what is desirable and what is undesirable (presumably from the egoistic point of view), does not distinguish the just from the unjust. Horace may have meant by this no more than that men in a state of nature were ignorant of moral distinctions; he could, however, have been taken by his contemporaries — in view of the current normative implications of 'nature' — to mean either (a) that 'just' and 'unjust' are valid conceptions only in so far as they are derived from the idea of *petenda* and *fugienda* — a sort of egoistic utilitarianism — or (b) that the rules of justice are determined by positive law, and would have neither validity nor meaning before the establishment of civil society. The last two lines of the first passage following could, certainly, have been adopted by Hobbes as a motto for his ethical and political doctrine.

XII, 4. *Satires* (*ca.* 35 B. C.), I, iii, 99-114.

> cum prorepserunt primis animalia terris,
> mutum et turpe pecus, glandem atque cubilia propter
> unguibus et pugnis, dein fustibus, atque ita porro
> pugnabant armis quae post fabricaverat usus,
> donec verba quibus voces sensusque notarent
> nominaque invenere; dehinc absistere bello,

oppida coeperunt munire, et ponere leges,
ne quis fur esset, neu latro, neu quis adulter.
nam fuit ante Helenam cunnus taeterrima belli
causa, sed ignotis perierunt mortibus illi,
quos venerem incertam rapientis more ferarum
viribus editior caedebat ut in grege taurus.
iura inventa metu iniusti fateare necesse est,
tempora si fastosque velis evolvere mundi.
nec natura potest iusto secernere iniquum,
dividit ut bona diversis, fugienda petendis.[9]

When, as beasts, they sprang from the earth in its beginning, a dumb and squalid herd, they fought for acorns and for dens with claw and fist; later with clubs, and so on step by step until they fought with arms, which experience had fashioned for them. Finally they invented words and names whereby to express meaning and sense. Thereupon they began to desist from warfare, to build towns, and to lay down laws that no man should be a thief or robber or adulterer. For even before Helen woman had been a shameful cause of war; but those who snatched a fickle love, in the manner of beasts, perished by unknown deaths, slain by a stronger rival, as a bull in a herd. It must be granted, if you will unfold the pages of the world's history, that laws were invented from fear of injustice. Nor can Nature discriminate what is just from what is unjust in the way in which she distinguishes good things from their opposites, the things which are to be shunned from those which are to be sought after.

XII, 5. *Ars poetica*, 391-393.

silvestris homines sacer interpresque deorum
caedibus et victu foedo deterruit Orpheus,
dictus ob hoc lenire tigris rapidosque leones.[10]

Orpheus, the holy, interpreter of the gods, turned the men of the forests from slaughter and loathsome food; whence he was said to have tamed tigers and raging lions.

OVID

While the famous passage in *Metamorphoses* (cf. II, 17, p. 43) was one of the principal Latin texts of primitivism, with a thousand modern echoes, Ovid in his *carmina iuvenilia* had (though not without some grumbling at the restrictions imposed during the Cerealia) devoutly celebrated the goddess of agriculture, whose intervention is, in the later poem, set down among

---

[9] Ed. E. C. Wickham, Oxford, 1900. Horace in another mood writes in the vein of a *laudator temporis acti*, if not, perhaps, a chronological primitivist, as in the famous lines in *Odes*, III, vi, 46-8: *Aetas parentum, peior avis tulit, Nos nequiores, mox daturos Progeniem vitiosiorem.* The description of the *prisca gens mortalium* in Epode II contains features of the usual picture of the Golden Age, but the moral here also is merely 'back to the farm!'

[10] Ed. E. C. Wickham.

the evils which marked the lapse from the Golden to the Silver Age. In the passage from the *Ars amatoria* he is obviously reproducing in an abridged form the Lucretian picture of the purely animal existence of primitive man. As noted in Chapter XI, Ovid later, during his exile, became acquainted with certain actual savage peoples and found he did not care for the primitive as in them exemplified.

XII, 6. *Amores,* III, x, 1-15.

> Annua venerunt Cerealis tempora sacri:
>   secubat in vacuo sola puella toro.
> flava Ceres, tenues spicis redimita capillos,
>   cur inhibes sacris commoda nostra tuis?
> te, dea, munificam gentes ubiquaque loquuntur:
>   nec minus humanis invidet ulla bonis.
> ante nec hirsuti torrebant farra coloni,
>   nec notum terris area nomen erat:
> sed glandem quercus, oracula prima, ferebant;
>   haec erat, et teneri caespitis herba, cibus.
> prima Ceres docuit turgescere semen in agris
>   falce coloratas subsecuitque comas:
> prima iugis tauros supponere colla coegit,
>   et veterem curvo dente revellit humum.[11]

The season of the sacred festival of Ceres comes again; the maiden lies upon her bed alone. Oh golden haired Ceres, whose silken locks are wreathed with ears of wheat, why do you stop our pleasures with your sacred rites? Goddess, men everywhere call you munificent, nor does any goddess less envy human fortune. Before you came the hairy rustics parched no corn, nor was the word " threshing-floor " known on earth, but the oak, man's first oracle, bore acorns; these and the tender shoots of grass were man's food. Ceres first taught the seed to swell in the fields and with the sickle cut the colored tresses (of the grain). She first forced bulls to bow their necks beneath the yoke and turned back the ancient earth with the plough's curved tooth.

This passage obviously was not intended to be a serious discussion of man's rise. The same may be said of the following from *Ars amatoria.* Both are simply poetic utilizations of a form of anti-primitivism and are important for us as indications of its popularity.

XII, 7. *Ars amatoria,* II, 467-480.

> Prima fuit rerum confusa sine ordine moles,
>   unaque erat facies sidera, terra, fretum;
> mox caelum impositum terris, humus aequore cincta est
>   inque suas partes cessit inane chaos;
> silva feras, volucres aër accepit habendas,
>   in liquida pisces delituistis aqua.
> tum genus humanum solis errabat in agris,
>   idque merae vires et rude corpus erat:

---

[11] Ed. A. Riese, Leipzig, 1871.

> silva domus fuerat, cibus herba, cubilia frondes,
>   iamque diu nulli cognitus alter erat:
> blanda truces animos fertur mollisse voluptas.
>   constiterant uno femina virque loco;
> quid facerent, ipsi nullo didicere magistro:
>   arte Venus nulla dulce peregit opus.[12]

First there was a confused mass of things without order, and stars, earth and sea looked all alike. Soon sky was set above the earth, land was girt by sea, and empty chaos withdrew to its own place. The woods received wild beasts to keep, the air the birds; you fishes hid in the flowing waters. Then man wandered in the lonely fields; his strength was unabated, his body rough. The woods were his home, his food was herbs, his bed leaves. And still for a long time none knew his fellow. Alluring pleasure is said to have softened their savage minds; a man and woman came together in one place. What they should do, they learned by themselves with no teacher. Venus accomplished her sweet work without art.

VITRUVIUS

The commonplaces of the Lucretian theory of the rise of primitive man are repeated by Vitruvius. He is interested, naturally, mainly in the origin of architecture, but the picture he gives of primitive life includes more general features of a technological state of nature.

XII, 8. Vitruvius, *De architectura*, II, 1.

Homines veteri more ut ferae in silvis et speluncis et nemoribus nascebantur ciboque agresti vescendo vitam exigebant. Interea quodam in loco ab tempestatibus et ventis densae crebritatibus arbores agitatae et inter se terentes ramos ignem excitaverunt, et eo flamma vehementi perterriti qui circa eum locum fuerunt sunt fugati. Post ea requieta propius accedentes cum animadvertissent commoditatem esse magnam corporibus ad ignis teporem, ligna adicientes et ita conservantes alios adducebant et nutu monstrantes ostendebant quas haberent ex eo utilitates. In eo hominum congressu cum profunderentur aliter spiritu voces, cotidiana consuetudine vocabula ut obtigerant constituerunt, deinde significando res saepius in usu ex eventu fari fortuito coeperunt et ita sermones inter se procreaverunt. Ergo cum propter ignis inventionem conventus initio apud homines et concilium et convictus esset natus, et in unum locum plures convenirent habentes ab natura praemium praeter reliqua animalia ut non proni sed erecti ambularent mundique et astrorum magnificentiam aspicerent, item manibus et articulis quam vellent rem faciliter tractarent, coeperunt in eo coetu alii de fronde facere tecta, alii speluncas fodere sub montibus, nonnulli hirundinum nidos et aedificationes earum imitantes de luto et virgulis facere loca quae subirent. Tunc observantes aliena tecta et adicientes suis cogitationibus res novas, efficiebant in dies meliora genera casarum. Cum essent autem homines imitabili docilique natura, cotidie inventionibus gloriantes alius alii ostendebant aedi-

---

[12] Ed. A. Riese.

ficiorum effectus, et ita exercentes ingenia certationibus in dies melioribus iudiciis efficiebantur.[13]

In the olden days men were born like wild beasts in woods and caves and groves and kept alive by eating rough food. Somewhere meanwhile the close grown trees, tossed by storms and winds and rubbing their branches together, caught fire. Terrified by the flames, those who were near the spot fled. When the storm subsided they drew near, and since they noticed how pleasant to their bodies was the warmth of the fire, they laid on wood, and thus keeping it alive they brought up some of their fellows and indicating the fire with a gesture they showed them the use which they might make of it. When in this meeting of men sounds were breathed forth with differing intensity, they made customary by daily use these chance syllables. Then giving names to things more frequently used, they began to speak because of this fortuitous event, and so they held conversation among themselves. Since therefore from the discovery of fire a beginning of human association was made and of union and intercourse, and since many now came together in one place, being endowed by nature with a gift beyond that of the other animals, so that they walked not looking down, but erect, and saw the magnificence of the universe and the stars and, moreover, did easily with their fingers whatever they wished, some in that society began to make roofs of leaves, others to dig out caves under the hills; some, imitating the nests and constructions of the swallows, made places into which they might go out of mud and twigs. Finding then other shelters and inventing new things by their power of thought, they built in time better dwellings. Since, however, men were of an imitative and docile nature, rejoicing in their daily inventions they showed one another the results of their building, and so, exercising their talents in competition, they gradually improved their power of judgment.

GRATIUS FALISCUS

The Aristotelian and Ciceronian conception of reason as the necessary complement of 'nature,' and the radically anti-primitivistic thesis of the divine origin of the arts, are repeated by this writer of the first century B. C.

XII, 9. *Cynegeticon*, 2-12.

> prius omnis in armis
> spes fuit et nuda silvas virtute movebant
> inconsulti homines vitaque erat error in omni.
> post alia propiore via meliusque profecti
> te sociam, Ratio, rebus sumpsere gerendis:
> hinc omne auxilium vitae rectusque reluxit
> ordo et contiguas didicere ex artibus artis
> proserere, hinc demens cecidit violentia retro.
> sed primum auspicium deus artibus altaque circa
> firmamenta dedit; tum partis quisque secutus
> exegere suas tetigitque industria finem.[14]

[13] Ed. V. Rose, Leipzig, 1899.

[14] Ed. P. J. Enk, Zutphen, 1918. The *Cynegeticon* must have been written between 30 B. C. and 8 A. D. See Enk's edition, pp. 26 ff.

In the olden days man's one hope lay in his weapons. Untaught, men roamed through the woods with naked courage, and their life in every way was random wandering. Later they followed a shorter and a better path, and took thee, Reason, as their companion in the conduct of their affairs. Through this came every aid of life; order shone forth, and they learned to derive new arts from kindred arts; through this mad violence gave way. But God gave the first sanction to the arts and set about them lofty safeguards. Then each man sought and found his proper place and industry came to its perfection.

MANILIUS

The benefits resulting to mankind from the discovery of number and its application in astronomy had impressed most anti-primitivists. Manilius (early 1st c. A. D.) in his poem upon astronomy makes the most of this. In the passage which concerns us progress comes, not through the aid of a culture-hero, but by need and skill. Primitive times are, indeed, like the Golden Age in their technological ignorance, their lack of gold and navigation. But Manilius naturally cannot admire them for these traits.

XII, 10. *Astronomicon*, I, 66-98.

> nam rudis ante illos nullo discrimine vita
> in speciem conversa operum ratione carebat
> et stupefacta novo pendebat lumine mundi,
> tum velut amissis maerens, tum laeta renatis
> sideribus, variosque dies incertaque noctis
> tempora nec similis umbras, iam sole regresso
> iam propiore, suis discernere *nescia* causis.
> necdum etiam doctas sollertia fecerat artes,
> terraque sub rudibus cessabat vasta colonis;
> tumque in desertis habitabat montibus aurum,
> immotusque novos pontus subduxerat orbes,
> nec vitam pelago nec ventis credere vota
> audebant; se quisque satis novisse putabant.
> sed cum longa dies acuit mortalia corda
> et labor ingenium miseris dedit et sua quemque
> advigilare sibi iussit fortuna premendo,
> seducta in varias certarunt pectora curas
> et quodcumque sagax temptando repperit usus
> in commune bonum commenta elata dederunt.
> tunc et lingua suas accepit barbara leges,
> et fera diversis exercita frugibus arva,
> et vagus in caecum penetravit navita pontum,
> fecit et ignotis linter commercia terris.
> tum belli pacisque artes commenta vetustas;
> semper enim ex aliis alias proseminat usus.
> ne vulgata canam, linguas didicere volucrum,
> consultare fibras et rumpere vocibus angues,
> sollicitare umbras imumque Acheronta movere,
> in noctemque dies, in lucem vertere noctes.
> omnia conando docilis sollertia vicit.

nec prius imposuit rebus finemque manumque
quam caelum ascendit ratio cepitque profundam
naturam rerum causis viditque quod usquam est.[15]

For before the time of those men life was uniformly rough and, entirely occupied with the appearance of things, lacked reason. Men hung spellbound upon the new dawn, now mourning as if the stars had been lost, now joyful at their rebirth, and ignorant how to explain by their true causes the varying length of day and shifting time of night and the shadows changing as the sun is now far, now near. Not yet had they the skill to produce the learned arts, and the great earth lay sterile beneath its rude inhabitants. Gold lay in the uninhabited mountains, and the unsailed sea cut men off from new worlds; they did not dare trust their lives to the waves and their hopes to the winds; each thought he knew enough. But when long ages had sharpened human minds, and labor had given wit to those poor wretches, and the pressure of adversity had bidden each watch over his own welfare, their minds were led to struggle against various troubles, and whatsoever invention wise practice had discovered by trial they published abroad and contributed to the common good. And then their barbarous tongue submitted to appropriate laws and the wild fields when ploughed produced divers grains, and wandering sailors penetrated the blind sea and boats made trade with hitherto unknown lands. Then continued practice produced the arts of war and peace, for use has always found the seeds of new things in old. But let me not write of things already known. They learned the tongues of the birds, to interpret the meaning of entrails, to charm serpents, to invoke the shades and move the depths of Acheron, to turn day to night and night to day. By effort man's ingenuity learned to conquer all. Nor did it end its labors until reason had scaled the heavens and pierced through to the deepest nature of things and seen the causes of all existence.

PLINY THE ELDER

A passage of the first century A. D., most interesting and tantalizing in its brevity, suggests the doctrine of infinite perfectibility, usually associated with the eighteenth century. Pliny the Elder in mentioning changes in astronomical theory says:

XII, 11. *Nat. hist.* II, 15, 62:

modo ne quis desperet saecula proficere semper.

Let no one lose hope that the ages will always grow better.

Just how much is implied in this phrase it is impossible to determine. No passage of earlier date so definitely projects the notion of boundless progress into the future.

[15] A. E. Housman, London, 1903. Lines 68-71 express a theory about primitive man which had been attacked by Lucretius, V, 973 ff.; cf. Ch. VIII, 2.

SENECA

At about the same time Seneca, along with his sometimes extreme chronological primitivism (cf. Chap. X, 1, 2, pp. 264, 275) and disparagement of the arts, expresses a similar — though not explicitly an equally unlimited — faith in the future progress of knowledge.

XII, 12. *Naturales quaestiones*, VII, 25.

> multae hodieque sunt gentes, quae tantum facie noverunt coelum, quae nondum sciunt, cur luna deficiat, quare obumbretur. haec apud nos quoque nuper ratio ad certum perduxit.[16] Veniet tempus, quo ista, quae nunc latent, in lucem dies extrahat et longioris aevi diligentia. ad inquisitionem tantorum aetas una non sufficit, ut tota coelo vacet. quid, quod tam paucos annos inter studia ac vitia non aequa portione dividimus? itaque per successiones ista longas explicabuntur. Veniet tempus, quo posteri nostri tam aperta nos nescisse mirentur.[17]

There are many people to-day who know only the appearance of the heavens, but do not yet know why the moon wanes, why it is eclipsed. It is but lately that reason has made these things known to us. The day will come when those matters which now lie hidden will be brought to light by longer study. One age is not enough for the discovery of such great matters, even though it devoted itself entirely to the sky. How could it be otherwise, since we divide our so few years unequally between studies and vices? Those things too will be explained through a long series of years. The day will come when our children will wonder at our ignorance of such obvious things.

XII, 13. *Ad Lucilium, Epist.* LXIV, 6-9.

> . . . mihi certe multum auferre temporis solet contemplatio ipsa sapientiae: non aliter illam intueor obstupefactus quam ipsum interim mundum, quem saepe tamquam spectator novus video. veneror itaque inventa sapientiae inventoresque: adire tamquam multorum hereditatem iuvat. mihi ista adquisita, mihi laborata sunt. sed agamus bonum patrem familiae: faciamus ampliora, quae accepimus. maior ista hereditas a me ad posteros transeat. multum adhuc restat operis multumque restabit, nec ulli nato post mille saecula praecludetur occasio aliquid adhuc adiciendi. sed etiam si omnia a veteribus inventa sunt, hoc semper novum erit, usus et inventorum ab aliis scientia ac dispositio. puta relicta nobis medicamenta, quibus sanarentur oculi: non opus est mihi alia quaerere, sed haec tamen morbis et temporibus aptanda sunt. hoc asperitas oculorum conlevatur; hoc palpebrarum crassitudo tenuatur; hoc vis subita et umor avertitur; hoc acuetur visus: teras ista oportet et eligas tempus, adhibeas singulis modum. animi remedia inventa sunt ab antiquis: quomodo autem admoveantur aut quando, nostri operis

---

[16] For the same idea that knowledge is in its infancy, cf. Lucretius, above (*De rer. nat.* V, 324-337, Chap. VIII, 9, p. 236, n. 16).

[17] Ed. Haase, *Opera*, II, 312, Leipzig, 1898.

est quaerere. multum egerunt, qui ante nos fuerunt, sed non peregerunt.[18]

I certainly give much of my time to the contemplation of science. I look upon it amazed, as I look upon the world itself, which I often see with the eyes of one beholding it for the first time. And so I venerate the discoveries and discoverers of science. I like to approach it as the legacy of many. These things belong to me; this toil was carried on for me. But let us act as good fathers, let us increase the patrimony we have inherited. Let us leave a greater legacy to our descendants. Much work remains to be done and will always remain. The children to be born a thousand centuries from now will lack no opportunity for continuing our labors. Even if all things had been discovered by the ancients, this would always be new: to know how to use and apply the discoveries of others. Suppose that someone has left us medicines for curing diseases of the eye; I need not seek other cures, but I must know how to apply this to the disease according to the season. This medicine relieves smarting in the eyes; this helps the thickness of the eyelids; this strengthens the sight and alleviates watering; this sharpens vision; you must prepare the drugs and choose the right time for their application, you must administer each in its proper fashion. The ancients found cures for diseases of the mind: how and when they are to be used, it is our function to discover. Our predecessors did much but they did not do everything.

PLINY THE YOUNGER

The *laus temporis acti* which Horace satirized grew rather than declined, and was met apparently by an opposition which also found its sacred bard. Tacitus (if the *De oratoribus* be his) gives evidence of the Roman Battle between the Ancients and the Moderns, and Pliny the Younger (2nd c. A. D.) in his *Letters* shows that he was not unaware of the debate. The battle in itself is of concern to us only as its participants based their arguments on primitivistic or anti-primitivistic foundations. The passage is of interest because it seems to indicate a belief held by his contemporaries that the creative force of Nature was capable of increase; there is a scarcely questionable reference to the expressions of the contrary view by Lucretius and Seneca.

XII, 14. *Epist.* VI, 21.

Sum ego is, qui mirer antiquos, non tamen ut quidam temporum nostrorum ingenia despicio. Neque enim quasi lassa et effeta natura nihil jam laudabile parit.[19]

I am the kind of man who admires the ancients, yet, unlike some, I do not despise the talents of our times. For it is not as if Nature were tired and worn out so that she can no longer produce anything worthy of praise.

[18] Ed. O. Hense, Leipzig, 1914. Seneca here seems to have forgotten his Stoic cosmology with its theory of progressive degeneration (cf. Ch. X, 6).

[19] Ed. R. C. Kukula, 2d. ed. Leipzig, 1912.

STATIUS

The survival of the poetic legends of primitive times appears in Statius. Here we have in the late first century A. D. a number of already well-worn literary *clichés*.

XII, 15. *Thebaid*, IV, 275-284.

> Arcades huic veteres astris lunaque priores,
> agmina fida datis, nemorum quos stirpe regenti
> fama satos, cum prima pedum vestigia tellus
> admirata tulit; nondum arva domusque nec urbes
> conubiisve modus; quercus laurique ferebant
> cruda puerperia, ac populos umbrosa creavit
> fraxinus, et feta viridis puer excidit orno.
> hi lucis stupuisse vices noctisque feruntur
> nubila et occiduum longe Titana secuti
> desperasse diem.[20]

The ancient Arcadians followed, born before the stars and moon, a people faithful to what was given them, who, according to legend, were born from the hard stock of trees, when earth in wonder felt the first foot-steps of man. There were not yet ploughed fields, nor horses, nor cities, nor regulated wedlock. The oak and laurel bore rude offspring, and the shady beech created a people, and the child stepped forth like a green shoot from the pregnant ash. These men saw alternate night and day and followed with their eyes the Titan as he sank, in despair of ever seeing day again.

PAUSANIAS

In Pausanias (late 2d c. A. D.) we see Prometheanism surviving with a primitive king taking the place of a god. This culture hero, Pelasgus, devises houses and clothing. He departs from the hoary custom of eating acorns which, as we have seen, were the earliest food according to most legends.

XII, 16. *Descr. graec.* VIII, 1, 4-6.

> φασὶ δὲ Ἀρκάδες ὡς Πελασγὸς γένοιτο ἐν τῇ γῇ ταύτῃ πρῶτος. εἰκὸς δὲ ἔχει τοῦ λόγου καὶ ἄλλους ὁμοῦ τῷ Πελασγῷ μηδὲ αὐτὸν Πελασγὸν γενέσθαι μόνον· ποίων γὰρ ἂν καὶ ἦρχεν ὁ Πελασγὸς ἀνθρώπων; μεγέθει μέντοι καὶ κατὰ ἀλκὴν καὶ κάλλος προεῖχεν ὁ Πελασγὸς καὶ γνώμην ὑπὲρ τοὺς ἄλλους ἦν, καὶ τούτων ἕνεκα αἱρεθῆναί μοι δοκεῖ βασιλεύειν ὑπ' αὐτῶν. πεποίηται δὲ καὶ Ἀσίῳ τοιάδε ἐς αὐτόν·
>
>> Ἀντίθεον δὲ Πελασγὸν ἐν ὑψικόμοισιν ὄρεσσι
>> γαῖα μέλαιν' ἀνέδωκεν, ἵνα θνητῶν γένος εἴη.
>
> Πελασγὸς δὲ βασιλεύσας τοῦτο μὲν ποιήσασθαι καλύβας ἐπενόησεν, ὡς μὴ ῥιγοῦν τε καὶ ὕεσθαι τοὺς ἀνθρώπους μηδὲ ὑπὸ τοῦ καύματος ταλαιπωρεῖν· τοῦτο δὲ τοὺς χιτῶνας τοὺς ἐκ τῶν δερμάτων τῶν οἰῶν, οἷς καὶ νῦν περί τε Εὔβοιαν ἔτι χρῶνται καὶ ἐν τῇ Φωκίδι ὁπόσοι βίου σπανίζουσιν, οὗτός ἐστιν

[20] Ed. P. Kohlmann, Leipzig, 1884.

ὁ ἐξευρών. καὶ δὴ καὶ τῶν φύλλων τὰ ἔτι χλωρὰ καὶ πόας τε καὶ ῥίζας οὐδὲ
ἐδωδίμους, ἀλλὰ καὶ ὀλεθρίους ἐνίας σιτουμένους τοὺς ἀνθρώπους τούτων μὲν
ἔπαυσεν ὁ Πελασγός· ὁ δὲ τὸν καρπὸν τῶν δρυῶν οὔτι που πασῶν, ἀλλὰ
τὰς βαλάνους τῆς φηγοῦ τροφὴν ἐξεῦρεν εἶναι. παρέμεινέ τε ἐνίοις ἐς τοσοῦτο
ἀπὸ Πελασγοῦ τούτου ἡ δίαιτα, ὡς καὶ τὴν Πυθίαν, ἡνίκα Λακεδαιμονίοις
γῆς τῆς Ἀρκάδων ἀπηγόρευεν ἅπτεσθαι, καὶ τάδε εἰπεῖν τὰ ἔπη·

> πολλοὶ ἐν Ἀρκαδίῃ βαλανηφάγοι ἄνδρες ἔασιν,
> οἵ σ' ἀποκωλύσουσιν· ἐγὼ δέ τοι οὔ τι μεγαίρω.

Πελασγοῦ δὲ βασιλεύοντος γενέσθαι καὶ τῇ χώρᾳ Πελασγίαν φασὶν ὄνομα.[21]

The Arcadians say that Pelasgus was the first man to be in this
country. But it is more reasonable to believe that there were others
along with Pelasgus and that he did not live there alone. For of
what men would he have been king? In size and courage and
beauty Pelasgus excelled and in intelligence he was above the
others, and because of these things he was chosen by them to be their
king, I believe. And these lines were composed about him by Asius.

> Black earth bore godlike Pelasgus on the hills covered with
> lofty foliage, that humankind might be.

Pelasgus as king devised the making of huts, that men might not
shiver from cold nor be drenched with rain nor be weary from the
heat. And he invented pigskin smocks, such as are still used in
Euboea and in Phocis; whatever they needed for their life, this he
invented. And Pelasgus made men cease eating green leaves and
grass and roots which were unfit for food, some to the point of being
even poisonous. And he discovered the fruit of the oak to be good
food — not all oaks, but the acorns of the *Phegos*. This diet has
lingered on among some people from the time of Pelasgus, so that
the Pythian priestess when she forbade the Lacedemonians to touch
the land of the Arcadians said these lines:

> There are many acorn-eating men in Arcadia who will prevent
> you. But I do not withhold it from you.

And when Pelasgus was king, they say that the name of the
country was Pelasgia.

MACROBIUS

In spite of the impetus given to a form of primitivism by the Christian
story of the Fall, the opposing view was still urged as late as the late fourth
century. In Macrobius the anti-primitivistic arguments are supported by
the evidence of inventions as well as by legends. The passage seems to be
another echo of Lucretius, V, 324 ff.

XII, 17. *Somn. Scip.* II, x, 6.

nam quis facile mundum semper fuisse consentiat, cum et ipsa
historiarum fides multarum rerum cultum emendationemque vel
ipsam inventionem recentem esse fateatur, cumque rudes primum
homines et incuria silvestri non multum a ferarum asperitate dissi-

---

[21] Ed. Fr. Spiro, Leipzig, 1903, II, 258-9.

miles meminerit vel fabuletur antiquitas, tradatque, nec hunc eis quo nunc utimur, victum fuisse sed glande prius et bacis altos sero sperasse de sulcis alimoniam, cumque ita exordium rerum et ipsius humanae nationis opinemur, ut aurea primum saecula fuisse credamus, et inde natura per metalla viliora degenerans ferro saecula postrema foedaverit? [22]

Who would readily admit that the world has always existed, when credible histories show that the cultivation and improvement and even the invention itself of many things are recent, and when antiquity remembers or relates that men were originally rough and in their wild carelessness not much different from the savagery of the beasts, and when there is a tradition that they did not eat the same food as we, but first were nourished by acorns and berries, and only later hoped to derive sustenance from the furrows? And since we think this to have been the beginning of things and of the human race itself, how can we believe the ages first to have been golden, and that then nature, degenerating through the baser metals, debased the later ages with iron?

LEGENDS OF INVENTORS

Legends of human inventors of specific arts or tools concern us here only in so far as their reporters believe inventions to have been an improvement of man's lot. Yet the fact that the catalogues of inventors include many names of culture-heroes, demi-gods, and gods, along with those of mortals, would seem to indicate that they were compiled to do honor rather than dishonor.

A. Kleingünther's study of this subject [23] concludes that Greek investigations into the origins of the specific arts began in the period following that of the intellectual and artistic revolutions and innovations of the seventh and sixth centuries. At that time there arose, according to this author, both a belief in the personal origin and production of the arts and crafts and a definite experience of their growth. It was not until the time of Herodotus, though he was to a certain extent anticipated by Xenophanes and Hecataeus, that we begin to have definite names attributed to the authors of the great deeds which interested him. Xenophanes had suggested man's ability to improve the god-given lot; Hecataeus had suggested rational explanations of traditional customs; but Herodotus with his ethnographic researches found many Greek customs and arts in the possession of what he conceived to be " older " peoples, and laid the foundations for later heurematography.

Greek catalogues of inventors of the fifth century B. C. remain only in fragments.[24] The first list which is of any length is that of Hyginus, the

---

[22] Ed. Fr. Eyssenhardt, Leipzig, 1893.

[23] ΠΡΩΤΟΣ ΕΥΡΕΤΗΣ (*Philologus*, Supplementband XXVI, Heft 1), Leipzig, 1933.

[24] See Müller's *Frag. hist. graec.* II, 181 ff. Cf. M. Kremmer's *De catalogis heurematum*, Leipzig, 1890.

date of which is uncertain.[25] We reproduce only one document, Pliny's long account of the benefactors of mankind, which is typical of the *genre* and the source of most of the later accounts. The passage is preceded by the famous lament over nature's indifference to man (Chap. XIII, 14, p. 383). After this preamble Pliny continues with a long disquisition upon man's diversity of traits, social customs, physical characteristics. And then, as if to offset this emphasis on man's natural bad fortune, he gives a list of his benefactors and their inventions.

XII, 18. Pliny, *Nat. hist.* VII, lvi, 57 (Translation on p. 401).

Consentaneum videtur, priusquam digrediamur a natura hominum, indicare quae cuiusque inventa sint. Emere ac vendere instituit Liber pater, idem diadema, regium insigne, et triumphum invenit, Ceres frumenta, cum antea glande vescerentur, eadem molere et conficere in Attica, et ali in Sicilia, ob id dea iudicata, eadem prima leges dedit, ut alii putavere, Rhadamanthus. Litteras semper arbitror Assyriis fuisse, sed alii apud Aegyptios a Mercurio, ut Gellius, alii apud Syros repertas volunt. utique in Graeciam attulisse e Phoenice Cadmum sedecim numero, quibus Troiano bello Palameden adiecisse quattuor hac figura ZΨΦX, totidem post eum Simoniden melicum, YΞΩΘ, quarum omnium vis in nostris recognoscitur. Aristoteles decem et octo priscas fuisse et duas ab Epicharmo additas ΨZ quam a Palamede mavolt. Anticlides in Aegypto invenisse quendam nomine Menon tradit xv annorum ante Phoronea antiquissimum Graeciae regem, idque monumentis adprobare conatur. E diverso Epigenes apud Babylonios dccxx annorum observationes siderum coctilibus laterculis inscriptas docet, gravis auctor in primis, qui minimum, Berosus et Critodemus, ccccxc ex quo apparet aeternus litterarum usus. in Latium eas attulerunt Pelasgi. Laterarias ac domos constituerunt primi Euryalus et Hyperbius fratres Athenis. antea specus erant pro domibus. Gellio Toxius Caeli filius lutei aedificii inventor placet, exemplo sumpto ab hirundinum nidis. Oppidum Cecrops a se appellavit Cecropiam quae nunc est arx Athenis. Aliqui Argos a Phoroneo rege ante conditum volunt, quidam et Sicyonem, Aegypti vero multo ante apud ipsos Diospolin. Tegulas invenit Cinyra Agriopae filius et metalla aeris, utrumque in insula Cypro, item forcipem, martulum, vectem, incudem; puteos Danaus ex Aegypto advectus in Graeciam quae vocabatur Argos Dipsion; lapicidinas Cadmus Thebis, aut ut Theophrastus, in Phoenice; turres ut Aristoteles Cyclopes, Tirynthii ut Theophrastus; Aegyptii textilia, inficere lanas Sardibus Lydi, fusos in lanificio Closter filius Arachnae, linum et retia Arachne, fulloniam artem Nicias Megarensis, sutrinam Tychius Boeotius. Medicinam Aegyptii apud ipsos volunt repertam, alii per Arabum Babylonis et Apollinis filium, herbariam et medi-

---

[25] The traditional date of this writer is the first century B. C. but Kremmer (*op. cit.* p. 89) believes that the catalogue as we have it is partly taken from the *Fabulae* of the authentic Hyginus, partly from the commentaries of Servius, partly from the catalogue of Pliny. We know, he maintains, merely the date before which it must have been written, 207 A. D.

camentariam a Chirone Saturni et Philyrae filio. Aes conflare et temperare Aristoteles Lydum Scythen monstrasse, Theophrastus Delam Phrygem putat, aerariam fabricam alii Chalybas alii Cyclopas, ferrum Hesiodus in Creta eos qui vocati sunt Dactyli Idaei. Argentum invenit Erichthonius Atheniensis, ut alii Aeacus, auri metalla et flaturam Cadmus Phoenix ad Pangaeum montem, ut alii Thoas aut Aeacus in Panchaia aut Sol Oceani filius cui Gellius medicinae quoque inventionem ex metallis assignat. plumbum ex Cassiteride insula primus adportavit Midacritus. Fabricam ferream invenerunt Cyclopes, figlinas Coroebus Atheniensis, in iis orbem Anacharsis Scythes, ut alii Hyperbius Corinthius; fabricam materiariam Daedalus, et in ea serram, asciam, perpendiculum, terebram, glutinum, ichthyocollam, normam autem et libellam et tornum et clavem Theodorus Samius, mensuras et pondera Phidon Argivus, aut Palamedes ut maluit Gellius; ignem e silice Pyrodes Cilicis filius, eundem adservare ferula Prometheus, vehiculum cum quattuor rotis Phryges, mercaturas Poeni, culturam vitium et arborum Eumolpus Atheniensis, vinum aquae misceri Staphylus Sileni filius, oleum et trapetas Aristaeus Atheniensis, idem mella; bovem et aratrum Buzyges Atheniensis, ut alii Triptolemus, regiam civitatem Aegyptii, popularem Attici post Theseum. Tyrannus primus fuit Phalaris Agraganti. servitium invenere Lacedaemonii. iudicium capitis in Areopago primum actum est. Proelium Afri contra Aegyptios primi fecere fustibus, quos vocant phalangas. Clupeos invenerunt Proetus et Acrisius inter se bellantes, sive Chalcus Athamantis filius, loricam Midias Messenius, galeam, gladium, hastam Lacedaemonii, ocreas et cristas Cares. Arcum et sagittam Scythem Iovis filium, alii sagittas Persen Persei filium invenisse dicunt, lanceas Aetolos, iaculum cum ammento Aetolum Martis filium, hastas velitares Tyrrenum, pilum Penthesileam Amazonem, securim Pisaeum, venabula et in tormentis scorpionem Cretas, catapultam Syrophoenicas, ballistam et fundam, aeneam tubam Pisaeum Tyrreni, testudines Artemonem Clazomenium, equom (qui nunc aries appellatur) in muralibus machinis Epium ad Troiam, equo vehi Bellorophontem, frenos et strata equorum Pelethronium, pugnare ex equo Thessalos qui Centauri appellati sunt habitantes secundum Pelium montem. Bigas prima iunxit Phrygum natio, quadrigas Erichthonius. ordinem exercitus, signi dationem, tesseras, vigilias Palamedes invenit Troiano bello, specularum significationem eodem Sinon, inducias Lycaon, foedera Theseus, auguria ex avibus Car a quo Caria appellata; adiecit ex ceteris animalibus Orpheus, aruspicia Delphus, ignispicia Amphiaraus, extispicia avium Tiresias Thebanus, interpretationem ostentorum et somniorum Amphictyon, astrologiam Atlans Libyae filius, ut alii Aegyptii, ut alii Assyrii; sphaeram in ea Milesius Anaximander, ventorum rationem Aeolus Hellenis filius; musicam Amphion, fistulam et monaulum Pan Mercuri, obliquam tibiam Midas in Phrygia, geminas tibias Marsyas in eadem gente, Lydios modulos Amphion, Dorios Thamyris Thrax, Phrygios Marsyas Phryx, citharam Amphion, ut alii Orpheus, ut alii Linus. septem chordis primum cecinit III ad IIII primas additis Terpander, octavam Simonides addidit, nonam Timotheus. Cithara sine voce cecinit Thamyris primus, cum cantu Amphion, ut alii Linus. citharoedica carmina conposuit Terpander, cum tibiis canere voce Troezenius Ardalus instituit. Saltationem armatam Curetes docuere, pyrrichen Pyrrus, utramque in Creta. Versum heroum Pythio oraculo debemus. De poematum origine magna quaestio. ante Troianum bellum probantur fuisse. Prosam orationem condere Pherecydes Syrius instituit Cyri regis aetate, historiam Cadmus Milesius, ludos gymnicos in Arcadia Lycaon, funebres Acastus in Iolco, post eum Theseus in Isthmo, Hercules Olympiae, athleticam Pythus, pilam lusoriam Gyges Lydus, picturam Aegypti et in Graecia Euchir Daedali cognatus ut Aristoteli placet, ut Theophrasto Polygnotus Atheniensis. Nave primus in Graeciam ex Aegypto Danaus advenit. antea ratibus navigabatur inventis in mari Rubro inter insulas a rege Erythra. Reperiuntur qui Mysos et Troianos priores excogitasse in Hellesponto putent, cum transirent adversus Thracas. Etiamnunc in Britannico oceano vitilis corio circumsutae fiunt, in Nilo ex papyro ac scirpo et harundine. Longa nave Iasonem primum navigasse Philostephanus auctor est, Hegesias Parhalum, Ctesias Semiramin, Archemachus Aegaeonem, biremem Damastes Erythraeos fecisse, triremem Thucydides Aminoclen Corinthium, quadriremem Aristoteles Carthaginiensis, quinqueremem Mnesigiton Salaminios, sex ordinum Xenagoras Syracusios, ab ea ad decemremem Mnesigiton Alexandrum magnum, ad duodecim ordines Philostephanus Ptolemaeum Soterem, ad quindecim Demetrium Antigoni, ad triginta Ptolemaeum Philadelphum, ad XL Petolemaeum Philopatorem qui Tryphon cognominatus est. Onerariam Hippus Tyrius invenit, lembum Cyrenenses, cumbam Phoenices, celetem Rhodii, cercyrum Cyprii, siderum observationem in navigando Phoenices, remum Copae, latitudinem eius Plataeae, vela Icarus, malum et antennam Daedalus, hippegum Samii aut Pericles Atheniensis, tectas longas Thasii, antea ex prora tantum et puppi pugnabatur. Rostra addidit Pisaeus Tyrreni, ancoram Eupalamus, eandem bidentem Anacharsis, harpagones et manus Pericles Atheniensis, adminicula gubernandi Tiphys. Classe princeps depugnavit Minos. Animal occidit primus Hyperbius Martis filius. Prometheus bovem.[26]

It seems proper before we leave man's nature to point out what were the inventions of various individuals. Father Bacchus introduced buying and selling; he also invented the shining diadem of kings and triumphal processions; Ceres gave men grain, before which they ate acorns; she also taught them to mill and prepare it for baking in Attica, as others say, in Sicily, wherefore she was deemed a goddess; she also first gave laws, or, as some think, Rhadamanthus. I have always thought letters came from the Assyrians, but some, like Gellius, believe them to have been introduced among the Aegyptians by Mercury, others among the Syrians; in any event they were introduced into Greece from Phoenicia by Cadmus, to the number of sixteen, to which during the Trojan War Palamedes added these four, ZΨΦX, after which Simonides, the melic poet, invented the same number, ΥΞΩΘ, the import of all which is recognized by us. Aristotle prefers to believe that the most ancient letters were eighteen in number, and that two, ΨZ, were added by Epicharmus rather

---

[26] Ed. D. Detlefsen, Berlin, 1866, with minor changes in punctuation.

than Palamedes. Anticlides relates that a certain man in Egypt
named Meno invented them fifteen thousand years before Phoroneus,
the most ancient king of Greece, and he tries to prove this from the
monuments. On the other hand Epigenes declares that among the
Babylonians for seven hundred and twenty thousand years observations of the heavenly bodies were inscribed on baked tiles, and he is
a weighty author among the best, such as Berosus and Critodemus,
who give as a minimum four hundred and ninety thousand years.
From which the use of letters appears to be eternal. The Pelasgians
introduced them into Latium. Beams and houses were first instituted by Euryalus and Hyperbius, brothers of Athene; before this
men used caves for houses. Gellius believes that Toxius, son of
Caelus, was the inventor of building clay, by following the example
of swallows building their nests. Cecrops called the city which is
now the citadel of Athena Cecropia, after himself. Some prefer to
believe that Argos was founded before this by King Phoroneus and
others by Sicyon, and indeed the Egyptians much earlier had
founded in their own country Diospolis. Cinyras, son of Agriopa,
invented tiles and bronze, both in the island of Cyprus, as well as
tongs, hammer, lever, and mallet; Danaus brought cisterns from
Egypt into Greece, which was called Argos Dipsion. Cadmus discovered the use of stone quarries either in Thebes or, as Theophrastus says, in Phoenicia. Thrason invented walls, the Cyclôpes towers,
according to Aristotle, the Tirynthians according to Theophrastus. The Egyptians first made textiles; the Lydians in Sardis first
spun wool; Closter, son of Arachne, made spindles; Arachne invented ropes and nets; Nicias of Megara, the fuller's art; Tychius,
the Beotian, cobbling. The Egyptians like to believe that medicine
was discovered among them, others by Arabus, son of Babylo
and Apollo, the use of herbs and drugs by Chiron, son of Saturn
and Philyra. The melting and tempering of bronze Aristotle says
was first taught by Lydus the Scythian; Theophrastus thinks [27]
it was Delas the Phrygian; some say the Chalybes invented metallurgy, others the Cyclôpes; Hesiod says that iron was discovered in
Crete by them who are called the "Dactyli Idaei." Erichthonius,
the Athenian, discovered silver, but, as others say, Aeacus; gold-
mining and smelting Cadmus, the Phoenician, invented near Mount
Pangaeus, but, as others say, Thoas or Eacus in Panchaia or Sol,
son of Ocean, to whom Gellius also ascribes the invention of a medical remedy from metals. Midacritus first brought lead from the
Cassiterides islands [the Scilly Isles?]. The Cyclôpes invented iron-
smithing, Coroebus, the Athenian, the art of pottery, Anacharsis,
the Scythian, the potter's wheel, or, as others say, Hyperbius the
Corinthian; Daedalus invented carpentry, and the saw, the ax, the
plumb-line, the awl, vegetable and fish glue; the square, however,
and balance and lathe and key were invented by Theodorus, the
Samian, weights and measures by Phidon the Argive, or Palamedes,
as Gellius prefers, fire and flint by Pyrodes, son of Cilex. Prometheus preserved the same in a fennel stalk. The Phrygians invented
four wheeled vehicles, the Carthaginians commerce, Eumolpus, the
Athenian, viticulture and arboriculture. Staphylus, son of Silenus,

[27] Reading *putat*.

first mixed wine and water; Aristaeus, the Athenian, invented oil
and oil-mills; the same first prepared honey. Bouzyges, the Athenian, first trained cattle and invented the plough,[28] or, as others say,
Triptolemus. The Egyptian formed the first monarchy, the Atti-
cans, after Theseus, the first popular state. The first tyrant was
Phalaris of Agrigentum; the Lacedemonians invented slavery;
capital punishment was first decreed on the Areopagus. The Afri-
cans first made war upon the Egyptians with cudgels which they
called "phalanges." Proetus and Acrisius invented round shields
when they fought together or else it was Chalus, son of Athamas.
Midias, the Messenian, invented the leather cuirass; the Lacedemonians the helmet, sword, and spear, the Carians greaves and plumes.
Scythes, son of Jupiter, invented the bow and arrow, though some
say that Perses, son of Perseus, invented arrows, the Aetolians
lances, Aetolus, son of Mars, the thonged javelin, Tyrrenus the
spears of the *velites,* Penthesilea, the Amazon, the heavy javelin,
Pisaeus the battle-ax, the Cretans hunting spears and the scorpions we
hurl, the Syrophoenicians the catapult, Pisaeus, the son of Tyrrenus,
the ballista and sling, the bronze trumpet, Artemones, the Clazomen-
ian, the *testudo.* The "horse," which is now called a "ram," for
battering down walls, was invented by Epeus against Troy. Bellero-
phon invented horsemanship, Pelethronius reins and saddles. The
Thessalians, who are called Centaurs, living near Mount Pelium,
invented cavalry fighting. The nation of the Phrygians first made
use of two-horse chariots, Erichthonius of four-horse. Palamedes
invented during the Trojan War battle-order, the giving of signals;
Sinon in the same war signaling from watch-towers; Lycaon truces;
Theseus treaties. Car, after whom Caria was named, invented
augury from birds; Orpheus from other animals; Delphus oracles;
Amphiaraus divination by fire; Tiresias, the Theban, inspection of
entrails; Amphictyon the interpretation of visions and dreams;
Atlas, son of Libya, astrology, but as others say, the Egyptians, and
still others, the Assyrians. The Milesian Anaximander invented the
celestial globe; Aeolus, son of Helen, discovered why the winds blow;
Amphion discovered music; Pan, son of Mercury, the pipe and flute,
Midas in Phrygia the slanting pipes; Marsyas, of the same people,
the double pipes; Amphion invented the Lydian mode; Thamyris,
the Thracian, the Dorian; Marsyas, the Phrygian, the Phrygian
mode. Amphion invented the cithara, but as others say, Orpheus,
and still others, Linus. Terpander sang to seven strings by adding
three to the original four; Simonides added an eighth; Timotheus
a ninth. Thamyris first played the cithara without singing; Amphion, or as others say Linus, first with song. Terpander first composed music for it. The Troezenian Ardalus introduced singing to
pipes. The Curetes taught dancing with arms; Pyrrhus the Pyrrhic
dance, both in Crete. Heroic poetry we owe to the Pythian oracle.
Concerning the origin of poetry there is a great debate; it is proved
to have existed before the Trojan War. Pherecydes the Syrian began
to write prose speech in the reign of King Cyrus; the Milesian Cadmus history; Lycaon in Arcadia instituted gymnastic games;

[28] Cf. Ch. VII, p. 194.

Acastus in Iolchus funeral games; after him Theseus in the Isthmus, Hercules in Olympia, athletics, Pythus ball-playing; Gyges, the Lydian, invented painting in Egypt, and in Greece Euchir, a kinsman of Daedalus, as Aristotle believes, but according to Theophrastus, Polygnotus the Athenian. Danaus first came to Greece from Egypt in a ship; before this men sailed from island to island on the Red Sea on rafts invented by the king Erythras. There are some who think that the Mysians and Trojans first devised them on the Hellespont when they crossed over to Thrace. Even now in the British Ocean wicker rafts bound together with leather straps are made, and on the Nile one finds them made of papyrus and rushes and cane. Philostephanus is authority for the statement that Jason first sailed in a long boat, Hegesias says Parhalus, Ctesias Semiramis, Archemachus Aegaeones, Damastes that the Erythraeans made the first bireme, Thucydides that Aminocles of Corinth made the first trireme, Aristotle that the Carthaginians made the first quadrireme, Mnesigiton that the Salaminians made the first quinquereme; Xenagoras said the Syracusans put in six rows of oars; this was developed into a decemreme by Alexander the Great, according to Mnesigiton; it was extended to twelve rows by Ptolemy Soter according to Philostephanus, to fifteen by Demetrius son of Antigonus, to thirty by Ptolemy Philadelphus, to forty by Ptolemy Philopator who was surnamed Tryphon. Hippus of Tyre invented merchant-vessels, the people of Cyrene the pinnace, the Phoenicians the skiff, the Rhodians the swift *celes,* the Cyprians the light *cercyrus.* The Phoenicians first used stellar observations in navigation, the people of Copae the oar, the Plataeans [increased] its width, Icarus devised the sail, Daedalus the mast and sailyard, either the Samians or Pericles, the Athenian, the cavalry transport, the Thasians long covered [ships]; before this people fought from the prow and poop of a vessel only. Pisaeus, the Tyrian, added the beak, Eupalamus the anchor, Anacharsis the double anchor, Pericles, the Athenian, the grapple and iron hooks, Tiphys the rudder. Minos first fought in fleet-formation. Hyperbius, son of Mars, first killed an animal, Prometheus an ox.

This long account of human inventions and discoveries is clear evidence not only of Pliny's belief that most of our arts and sciences did not exist in a state of nature, but of a general belief to that effect. For Pliny, as we have seen, was no innovator. Although there is no explicit praise of these inventions, there is no dispraise of them as in Seneca. Pliny accepts them all without comment.

It is also interesting that he has gone beyond the belief that any one individual, Prometheus or Ceres, is responsible for man's acquisition of the arts and sciences. In euhemeristic fashion he makes no distinction between divine and mortal culture-heroes.

The interest in inventors did not die out. The early Christian writers, Tatianus, Clement of Alexandria, and Gregory Nazianzenus, and later in the Western world Cassiodorus, all helped preserve these legends. Since their lists are largely repetition, we shall omit them here.

CHAPTER THIRTEEN

THE SUPERIORITY OF THE ANIMALS

Xenophon's *Memorabilia*[1] appears to contain the earliest extended discussion of the possible superiority of animals to men.[2] The first relevant passage is a conversation between Socrates and Aristodemus who "neither sacrificed to the gods nor practised divination" (*Mem.* I, iv. 2). It is supposed to refute the opinion of those who maintained that Socrates was incapable of making his companions better. Its burden is an anthropocentric teleology and emphasizes the utility of human organs. The comparison between animals and men is introduced to show that God is more interested in human welfare than in other things. Socrates is represented as maintaining that corporeally man is unique in possessing erect posture, hands, speech, sexual appetite "unbroken to old age"; he is psychically unique in his knowledge of the gods, ability to anticipate and therefore provide against hunger and thirst, cold and heat, and in his ability to learn. Socrates, it should be noted, is not answering animalitarian arguments of his interlocutor; he is simply listing reasons for believing in man's superiority to the beasts.

Similar remarks should be made about a second passage in the *Memorabilia* (IV, iii, 9-12), in which Socrates is trying to persuade Euthydemus that the gods have a special love for man, by arguing that although they confer certain benefits, such as food from the earth and warmth from the sun, on beasts as well as upon mankind, yet the beasts are born and bred for man's sake.

Whether the historical Aristodemus and Euthydemus held that the gods were kinder to the beasts than to men, we have no way of knowing. Yet we do know that the nature and degree of the difference between man and animals was discussed as early as the time of Alcmaeon and Anaxagoras. The former, according to Theophrastus (*De sens.* 25), was the first to attempt formally to define this, putting it in man's power of understanding or comprehension, in distinction to the animal power of merely feeling or having sensation. The latter, according to Aristotle (*De anima*, 404 b, 1), attributed intelligence to all animals, "both large and small, worthy and unworthy," as indeed his metaphysics would seem to have implied. In keeping with his habit of not "chopping things off as with a hatchet," Anaxagoras recognized degrees of intelligence in the animals and ranked man before all other living beings in sagacity (*De part. anim.* 687 a, 7).

---

[1] See N. G. Dakyns, *The Works of Xenophon*, London, 1897, III, xxiii.

[2] The history of the idea of the physical superiority of animals is exhaustively studied in S. O. Dickerman's *De argumentis quibusdam e structura hominis et animalium petitis*, Halle, 1909.

This rank, says Aristotle, he attributed to man's possession of hands, whereas he ought to have attributed man's hands to his superior intellect. Archelaus, another fifth century writer, agreed with Anaxagoras that all animals possessed intelligence, but maintained that some used it more sluggishly (βραδυτέρως), others more nimbly (ταχυτέρως). Our real difference from the beasts is our possession of leaders and laws and arts and cities (*Fragm.* A 4).[3]

The passages which we have make no comparative evaluation of reason and instinct, but it is not likely that philosophers before the Sophists would have thought of depreciating reason. We know, however, that innate knowledge was praised by at least one poet, Pindar, at the expense of learning, a commonplace which was allied to the question of the relative merits of art and nature. We cannot, therefore, date with finality the origin of animalitarianism.

There is a possibility that the use of animal behavior as a model for human was in vogue in the fifth century, if that be the object of Aristophanes's satire in *Clouds*, 1427-1429. In that passage Pheidippides justifies himself for beating his father by the examples of the " cocks and other beasts." It is scarcely likely that Socrates would have maintained such an opinion, and it is always possible that Aristophanes invented the argument. But on the other hand his joke would have had little point if there were not some Sophists who, in more edifying ways, invoked animal examples.

By the fourth century the question was apparently widely discussed. It seems to have centered about the problem of the relative happiness of man and beast. It was, of course, obvious that the human infant was defenceless against his enemies and incapable of surviving if left to his own devices. Tradition, indeed, bases Anaximander's theory of man's derivation from earlier animal forms on this very observation. Protagoras, in Plato's dialogue of that name (321 d), relates that Prometheus gave his first men the mechanical arts to atone for their corporeal inferiority to the rest of nature. In later years human helplessness was to furnish the occasion for numerous complaints and consolations.

That there were contemporaries of Aristotle who dwelt upon the superior physical endowment of the beasts is shown in *De partibus animalium* (687 a). Aristotle says there that such writers base their contention on the fact that man is born barefooted, naked and defenceless. His reply, which obviously does not meet the point, is that the human hand is a better means of defence than horns, claws, and hooves, for it can vary the weapon it wishes to use, whereas each beast is forever condemned to use whatever weapon it was given at birth.

Aristotle is himself the authority usually cited by philosophers of the classical and medieval periods for defining the differentia of man as the

---

[3] This opinion is echoed by Isocrates, in his *Nicocles* 27b, the date of which was probably between 372-365.

possession of reason. At the same time he is used to prove the opposite
thesis, and the stories of the technological abilities of the beasts which he
relates were to appear as evidence that they are more intelligent than we,
or at least not less intelligent. The nest-building of the swallow and its
child-rearing as related in the *Historia animalium* (612 b), the military
organization of the cranes, from the same treatise (614 b), the medicinal
knowledge of the Cretan goats (612 a), the singing lessons given by the
mother nightingale to her young (538 b 18), appear again and again in
animalitarians of later times. It would be difficult, if not impossible, to
make such stories fit into the scheme of nature given in the *De anima,*
with its sharp divisions between vegetable, animal, and human life. But
in the *Historia animalium* (588 a) Aristotle opens the eighth book with a
discussion of the similarity between human and animal life. Here he
assumes a principle of continuity in nature and suggests that the animals
have *in potentia* the rational powers which man has *in actu.*[4] He compares
them to children, who psychologically hardly differ from the beasts (a thesis
which he utilizes also in the *Nichomachean Ethics*) but who have the seeds
of what will later be full-fledged human traits.[5]

DEMOCRITUS (5th c.)

Perhaps the most significant anticipation of later animalitarianism is to
be found in a fragment of Democritus in which the beasts are praised for
their knowledge of the extent of their needs. The wisdom of reducing one's
desires to one's needs is of course a steady refrain of later moralists.

XIII, 1. *Fragm.* 198.

Τὸ χρῆιζον οἶδεν, ὁκόσον χρήιζει, ὁ δὲ χρήιζων οὐ γινώσκει.[6]

[How much wiser the animals are than man]; they, when they
have need of anything, know how much they need; but when he
needs something, he does not know how much of it he needs.

THE CYNICS

The note struck by this fragment of Democritus is continued in the writings and reported saying of the Cynics. In extant Greek literature it is
they who first fuse animalitarianism with primitivism by sometimes substituting animals for primitive men in their depreciation of civilized man.
The Cynics, as hard primitivists who attributed man's unhappiness to his
desire for superfluities, held up the beasts as superior to men because they
are wholly free from such desires and from the softness which has resulted
from this indulgence.[7]

---

[4] Cf. Porphyry, *De abstinentia,* III, 9 f. and *passim.*

[5] In *Hist. anim.* 612b 18, he expressly identifies the technological ability of the
nest-building swallow with that of man.

[6] Diels, 4th ed., II, 102.

[7] For a late survival of this in the writings of an eclectic, see Plutarch's *Gryllus,*
no. XIII, 16, p. 411, below.

XIII, 2.   Diogenes (?) in Dio Chrysostom, *Disc.* VI, 21-23, 26-28.

ἔλεγε δὲ διὰ τὴν μαλακίαν τοὺς ἀνθρώπους ἀθλιώτερον ζῆν τῶν θηρίων. ἐκεῖνα γὰρ ὕδατι μὲν ποτῷ χρώμενα, τροφῇ δὲ βοτάνῃ, τὰ πολλὰ δὲ αὐτῶν γυμνὰ ὄντα δι᾽ ἔτους, εἰς οἰκίαν δὲ οὐδέποτε εἰσιόντα, πυρὶ δὲ οὐδὲν χρώμενα, ζῆν μὲν ὁπόσον ἡ φύσις ἑκάστοις ἔταξε χρόνον, ἐὰν μηδεὶς ἀναιρῇ· ἰσχυρὰ δὲ καὶ ὑγιαίνοντα διάγειν ὁμοίως ἅπαντα, δεῖσθαι δὲ μηδὲν ἰατρῶν μηδὲ φαρμάκων. τοὺς δὲ ἀνθρώπους οὕτως μὲν πάνυ φιλοζώους ὄντας, τοσαῦτα δὲ μηχανωμένους πρὸς ἀναβολὴν τοῦ θανάτου, τοὺς μὲν πολλοὺς αὐτῶν μηδὲ εἰς γῆρας ἀφικνεῖσθαι, ζῆν δὲ νοσημάτων γέμοντας, ἃ μηδὲ ὀνομάσαι ῥᾴδιον, τὴν δὲ γῆν αὐτοῖς μὴ ἐξαρκεῖν παρέχουσαν φάρμακα, δεῖσθαι δὲ καὶ σιδήρου καὶ πυρός. . . . 26. ἐπεὶ δὲ ἔλεγόν τινες οὐ δυνατὸν εἶναι ζῆν τὸν ἄνθρωπον ὁμοίως τοῖς ἄλλοις ζῴοις διὰ τὴν ἀπαλότητα τῶν σαρκῶν καὶ διότι ψιλός ἐστιν, οὔτε θριξὶ σκεπόμενος, ὥσπερ τὰ πολλὰ τῶν θηρίων, οὔτε πτεροῖς, οὐδὲ δέρμα ἰσχυρὸν ἐπαμπέχεται, πρὸς ταῦτα ἀντέλεγεν, οὕτως μὲν σφόδρα ἀπαλοὺς εἶναι διὰ τὴν δίαιταν· φεύγειν μὲν γὰρ ὡς τὸ πολὺ τὸν ἥλιον, φεύγειν δὲ τὸ ψῦχος. τὴν δὲ ψιλότητα τοῦ σώματος μηδὲν ἐνοχλεῖν. ἐπεδείκνυε δὲ τούς τε βατράχους καὶ ἄλλα οὐκ ὀλίγα ζῷα πολὺ μὲν ἀπαλώτερα ἀνθρώπου, πολὺ δὲ ψιλότερα, καὶ ἔνια τούτων ἀνεχόμενα οὐ τὸν ἀέρα μόνον, ἀλλὰ καὶ ἐν τῷ ψυχροτάτῳ ὕδατι ζῆν δυνάμενα τοῦ χειμῶνος. ἐπεδείκνυε δὲ τῶν ἀνθρώπων αὐτῶν τούς τε ὀφθαλμοὺς καὶ τὸ πρόσωπον οὐδὲν δεόμενα σκέπης. καθόλου δὲ ἐν μηδενὶ τόπῳ γίγνεσθαι ζῷον, ὃ μὴ δύναται ζῆν ἐν αὐτῷ· ἢ πῶς ἂν ἐσώθησαν οἱ πρῶτοι ἄνθρωποι γενόμενοι, μήτε πυρὸς ὄντος μήτε οἰκιῶν μήτε ἐσθῆτος μήτε ἄλλης τροφῆς ἢ τῆς αὐτομάτου; [8]

[21] [Diogenes] used to say that men because of their softness live more wretched lives than the beasts. For these have water for their drink and grass for their food; most of them go naked the year round; they never enter a house, and make no use of fire. Yet, unless some one kills them, they live out the full span that nature has allotted to each of them; and all alike go through life strong and healthy, with no need of doctors or of drugs. Men, however, though they are exceedingly fond of life and invent so many devices for postponing death, for the most part do not in fact even reach old age; and their life is passed under a burden of ailments so numerous that it is not easy to name them all. Nor do the drugs which the earth produces suffice them; they must needs resort to knife and cautery as well. . . . [26] To the objection that it is impossible for man to live like the animals, by reason of the tenderness of his flesh and because he is naked, being unprotected by fur, as most animals are, or by feathers, or by a tough hide, [Diogenes] would reply that the reason for men's extreme tenderness lies in their manner of life — in the fact that they avoid both sunlight and cold. It is not the bareness of their bodies that causes the trouble. And he would point to the frogs and many other animals much more delicate and less protected than man, some of which nevertheless not only withstand cold air but are even able to live through the winter in the coldest water. He pointed out also that in man himself the eyes and face need no covering; and that in general no animal is born in a place in which it cannot live. If this were not so, how

8 Ed. J. von Arnim, 1893, I, 88-89.

could the first human beings to be born have survived, without fire or houses or clothes or any food except what grew wild? [9]

XIII, 3. Diogenes Laertius, VI, 22.

Μῦν θεασάμενος διατρέχοντα, . . . καὶ μήτε κοίτην ἐπιζητοῦντα μήτε σκότος εὐλαβούμενον ἢ ποθοῦντά τι τῶν δοκούντων ἀπολαυστῶν, πόρον ἐξεῦρε τῆς περιστάσεως.[10]

Through watching a mouse running about and not looking for a place to lie down, not avoiding the dark, not seeking for any of the things that mice enjoy, he [Diogenes] discovered the way to be superior to circumstances.

These passages say nothing about the one great deficiency which was generally regarded as the mark of the inferiority of the animals — the lack of reason. But Diogenes, according to tradition, thought even that compensated by their " one supreme good," their lack of possessions.

XIII, 4. Diogenes (?) in Dio Chrysostom, *Disc.* X, 16.

οὐχ ὁρᾷς τὰ θηρία ταῦτα καὶ τὰ ὄρνεα, ὅσῳ ζῇ τῶν ἀνθρώπων ἀλυπότερον, πρὸς δὲ καὶ ἥδιον, καὶ μᾶλλον ὑγιαίνει καὶ πλέον ἰσχύει καὶ ζῇ χρόνον ἕκαστον αὐτῶν ὅσον πλεῖστον δύναται, καίτοι οὔτε χεῖρας ἔχοντα οὔτε ἀνθρώπου διάνοιαν; ἀλλ' ὅμως ἀντὶ πάντων αὐτοῖς τῶν ἄλλων [κακῶν] ὑπάρχει μέγιστον ἀγαθόν, ὅτι ἀκτήμονά ἐστιν.[11]

Do you not see these beasts and birds? how much more free from trouble they live than men and how much more happily, too; and how much healthier and stronger they are, and how each of them lives as long as is possible for it. Yet they have neither hands nor human intelligence; but they enjoy one supreme good which overbalances all their disadvantages: they possess no property.

THE NEW COMEDY

In the New Comedy it was not unusual to find the life of animals used as a basis of comparison with that of man to the disadvantage of the latter. Man is an unnatural creature; and his two principal differentiae — his reason and his concern about the opinions of others — are a curse rather than a blessing. He does not by taking thought become happier, but the reverse; and where instinct is sure and straightforward, intellect is hesitant, troubled, fumbling, and unstable.

Philemon

XIII, 5. *Fragm.* 88.

πολύ γ' ἐστὶ πάντων ζῷον ἀθλιώτατον

[9] It has been conjectured by some modern historians that the book which Antisthenes is reported to have written *On the Nature of Animals* was an elaboration of the same theme of the superior health and happiness of animals and of the advantages of animal instinct over ' art.' Cf. Diogenes Laertius, VI, 15, and Gomperz, *Greek Thinkers*, tr. II, p. 144.

[10] Ed. R. D. Hicks, *Loeb Class. Library*, 1925.

[11] Ed. J. von Arnim, Berlin, 1893, I, 111.

ἄνθρωπος, εἴ τις ἐξετάζοι κατὰ τρόπον·
τὸν γὰρ βίον περίεργον εἰς τὰ πάντ' ἔχων
ἀπορεῖ τὰ πλεῖστα διὰ τέλους πονεῖ τ' ἀεί.
καὶ τοῖς μὲν ἄλλοις πᾶσιν ἡ γῆ θηρίοις
ἑκοῦσα παρέχει τὴν καθ' ἡμέραν τροφήν,
αὐτὴ πορίζουσ', οὐ λαβοῦσα . . .
 . . . .   πάνυ μόλις
ὥσπερ τὸ κατὰ χρέος κεφάλαιον ἐκτίνει
τὸ σπέρμα, τοὺς τόκους δ' ἀνευρίσκουσ' ἀεὶ
πρόφασίν τιν' αὐχμὸν ἢ πάχνην ἀποστερεῖ.
καὶ δὴ τυχὸν μὲν διὰ τὸ παρέχειν πράγματα
μόνους ἑαυτῇ καὶ ποιεῖν τἄνω κάτω
ταύτην παρ' ἡμῶν λαμβάνει τιμωρίαν.[12]

Much the most wretched of all animals is man, should anyone examine into his way of life. For he lives a life over-careful in all things and he is usually wholly at a loss about things and always toiling. And to all the other beasts earth has freely given their daily bread, providing them herself, not taking, . . . but for men she grudgingly pays back the seed, as though returning the capital alone, and finding in drought or frost a pretext, withholds the interest. And perhaps because we alone give her trouble and turn her topsy-turvy, she takes this vengeance upon us.

XIII, 6. *Fragm.* 93.

῍Ω τρισμακάρια πάντα καὶ τρισόλβια
τὰ θηρί', οἷς οὐκ ἔστι περὶ τούτων λόγος·
οὔτ' εἰς ἔλεγχον οὐδὲν αὐτῶν ἔρχεται,
οὔτ' ἄλλο τοιοῦτ' οὐδέν ἐστ' αὐτοῖς κακὸν
ἔπακτον, ἣν δ' ἂν εἰσενέγκηται φύσιν
ἕκαστον, εὐθὺς καὶ νόμον ταύτην ἔχει.
ἡμεῖς δ' ἀβίωτον ζῶμεν ἄνθρωποι βίον·
δουλεύομεν δόξαισιν, εὑρόντες νόμους,
προγόνοισιν, ἐγγόνοισιν. οὐκ ἔστ' ἀποτυχεῖν
κακοῦ, πρόφασιν δ' ἀεί τιν' ἐξευρίσκομεν.[13]

Oh thrice blessed and thrice happy in all things are the beasts who do not reason! None of them are ever put to the necessity of arguing, nor is any other such evil thing imposed upon them, but whatever nature each one bears, this he has as his law. But we men live an unlivable life. We are slaves to opinions in our law-making, slaves to our ancestors, slaves to our descendants. It is not possible to avoid evil, but we always find some excuse for not avoiding it.

The beasts, moreover, are represented in the following fragment as always being true to type, whereas each man has his own way of life. This in itself is not animalitarianism, but it was a commonplace of Greek thought that aberration from type is a deviation from the good,[14] for the individual of any given species.

---

[12] Th. Kock, *Com. att. fragm.* Leipzig, 1884, II, part I, pp. 503-504.

[13] Ed. Th. Kock, *Com. att. fragm.* II, pt. 1, 507.

[14] This idea is used in disparagement of man as late as Maximus of Tyre, *Diss.* XXIX, 7.

XIII, 7. *Fragm.* 89.

Τί ποτε Προμηθεύς, ὃν λέγουσ' ἡμᾶς πλάσαι
καὶ τἄλλα πάντα ζῷα, τοῖς μὲν θηρίοις
ἔδωχ' ἑκάστῳ κατὰ γένος μίαν φύσιν;
ἅπαντες οἱ λέοντές εἰσιν ἄλκιμοι,
δειλοὶ πάλιν ἑξῆς πάντες εἰσὶν οἱ λαγώ.
ουκ ἔστ' ἀλώπηξ ἡ μὲν εἴρων τῇ φύσει
ἡ δ' αὐθέκαστος, ἀλλ' ἐὰν τρισμυρίας
ἀλώπεκάς τις συναγάγῃ, μίαν φύσιν
ἀπαξαπασῶν ὄψεται τρόπον θ' ἕνα.
ἡμῶν δ' ὅσα καὶ τὰ σώματ' ἐστὶ τὸν ἀριθμὸν
καθ' ἑνός, τοσούτους ἔστι καὶ τρόπους ἰδεῖν.[15]

Why in the world did Prometheus, who they say made us and all the other living beings, give to the beasts each a single nature according to its kind? All lions are brave; all hares, again, are timid. One fox is not a dissembler by nature and another sincere, but if one should collect thousands of foxes, he would see one nature in each and every one of them and one way of life. But as great as is the number of human individuals and of their bodies, so great is the spectacle of their ways of life.

Menander

The following passage further develops the idea of man's unnaturalness. The other animals have to suffer evils, but they are such evils as Nature causes; man, on the contrary, is so out of harmony with Nature that his mind has produced fears and other evils from which the beasts, because of their lack of intelligence, are free.

XIII, 8. *Fragm.* 534.

ἅπαντα τὰ ζῷ' ἐστὶ μακαριώτατα
καὶ νοῦν ἔχοντα μᾶλλον ἀνθρώπου πολύ.
τὸν ὄνον ὁρᾶν ἔξεστι πρῶτα τουτονί,
οὗτος κακοδαίμων ἐστὶν ὁμολογουμένως·
τούτῳ κακὸν δι' αὑτὸν οὐδὲν γίνεται,
ἃ δ' ἡ φύσις δέδωκεν αὐτῷ ταῦτ' ἔχει.
ἡμεῖς δὲ χωρὶς τῶν ἀναγκαίων κακῶν
αὐτοὶ παρ' αὑτῶν ἕτερα προσπορίζομεν.
[λυπούμεθ' ἂν πτάρῃ τις, ἂν εἴπῃ κακῶς
ὀργιζόμεθ', ἂν ἴδῃ τις ἐνύπνιον σφόδρα
φοβούμεθ', ἂν γλαὺξ ἀνακράγῃ δεδοίκαμεν.]
ἀγωνίαι, δόξαι, φιλοτιμίαι, νόμοι,
ἅπαντα ταῦτ' ἐπίθετα τῇ φύσει κακά.[16]

All the animals are most blessed and have much more intelligence than man. Look first at this ass. He is admittedly born under an unlucky star. No evil comes to him through himself, but whatsoever evils Nature has given him, these he has. But we, aside from the necessary evils, invent others by ourselves. We are pained if

---

[15] Th. Kock, *Com. att. fragm.* II, pt. I, 504.
[16] Th. Kock, *Com. att. fragm.* III, 158.

someone sneezes; if someone speaks ill, we are angry; if someone has a dream, we are frightened; if an owl hoots, we are terrified. Struggles, opinions, contests, laws, all these evils are added to those in nature.

We have another fragment of Menander in which men, at least of his generation, are shown to be inferior to the beasts because of their injustice. In the fragment the higher morality of animal life is asserted in a more specific form than by the Cynics.

XIII, 9. *Fragm. 223.*

> εἴ τις προσελθών μοι θεῶν λέγοι ' Κράτων,
> ἐπὰν ἀποθάνῃς, αὖθις ἐξ ἀρχῆς ἔσει·
> ἔσει δ' ὅ τι ἂν βούλῃ, κύων, πρόβατον, τράγος,
> ἄνθρωπος, ἵππος· δὶς βιῶναι γάρ σε δεῖ·
> εἱμαρμένον τοῦτ' ἐστίν, ὅ τι βούλει δ' ἑλοῦ '·
> ἅπαντα μᾶλλον, εὐθὺς εἰπεῖν ἂν δοκῶ,
> ποίει με πλὴν ἄνθρωπον· ἀδίκως εὐτυχεῖ
> κακῶς τε πράττει τοῦτο τὸ ζῷον μόνον.
> ὁ κράτιστος ἵππος ἐπιμελεστέραν ἔχει
> ἑτέρου θεραπείαν· ἀγαθὸς ἂν γένῃ κύων,
> ἐντιμότερος εἶ τοῦ κακοῦ κυνὸς πολύ.
> ἀλεκτρυὼν γενναῖος ἐν ἑτέρᾳ τροφῇ
> ἔστιν, ὁ δ' ἀγεννὴς καὶ δέδιε τὸν κρείττονα·
> ἄνθρωπος ἂν ᾖ χρηστός, εὐγενής, σφόδρα
> γενναῖος, οὐδὲν ὄφελος ἐν τῷ νῦν γένει.
> πράττει δ' ὁ κόλαξ ἄριστα πάντων, δεύτερα
> ὁ συκοφάντης, ὁ κακοήθης τρίτα λέγει.
> ὄνον γενέσθαι κρεῖττον ἢ τοὺς χείρονας
> ὁρᾶν ἑαυτοῦ ζῶντας ἐπιφανέστερον.[17]

If one of the gods should say to me, " Crato, when you die, you shall immediately be reborn, and you shall be whatever you wish, a dog, a sheep, a goat, a man, a horse; for you must live twice. This is your destiny. Choose whatever you wish." " Anything," I think I should immediately say, " make me anything rather than a man. This animal alone wins success unjustly and does ill. The best horse has better care than the others. If you are a good dog, you are much more highly honored than a bad dog. A well-born cock lives on a particular kind of food, the low-born fears his better. A man even if he is good, well-born, well-bred, has no advantage among the present generation. The flatterer does best of all, the sycophant comes next, and the malignant man is third. To be born an ass would be better than to see one's inferiors living more splendidly than oneself.

PHILO JUDAEUS

The greater kindness of nature to the beasts became a commonplace, as we have said, in later writers, many of whom were not, in spite of their agreement with this thesis, animalitarians. Thus Philo (1st c. B. C.-1st c.

---

[17] Th. Kock, *Com. att. fragm.* III, 63-64.

A. D.), discussing the question whether bodily goods are the appropriate end of man, admits the bodily superiority of the animals, and attributes what had become a famous phrase, "Nature is a step-mother rather than a mother to man," to the ancients. Yet he does not agree with animalitarians that the bodily superiority of animals overbalances man's mental superiority.

XIII, 10. *De posteritate Caini,* 160-162.

160. νυνὶ δὲ καὶ τῶν θηρίων τὰ ἀτιθασώτατα μᾶλλον τοῖς ἀγαθοῖς τούτοις, εἰ δὴ ἀγαθὰ πρὸς ἀλήθειάν ἐστιν, ἢ οἱ λογικοὶ κέχρηνται. 161. τίς γὰρ ἂν ἀθλητὴς πρὸς ταύρου δύναμιν ἢ ἐλέφαντος ἀλκὴν ἐξισωθείη; τίς δ' ἂν δρομεὺς πρὸς σκύλακος ἢ λαγωδαρίου ποδώκειαν; ὁ μὲν γὰρ ἀνθρώπων ὀξυδερκέστατος πρὸς ἱεράκων ἢ ἀετῶν ὄψιν ἀμβλυωπέστατος. ἀκοαῖς γε μὴν ἢ ὀσμαῖς πολλῷ τῷ περιόντι τὰ ἄλογα κεκράτηκεν, ὡς καὶ ὄνος μέν, τὸ δοκοῦν ἐν ζῴοις εἶναι νωθέστατον, κωφὴν ἂν ἀποδείξαι τὴν ἡμετέραν ἀκοὴν ἐλθὼν εἰς ἐπίκρισιν, κύων δὲ περιττὸν ἐν ἀνθρώπῳ μυκτῆρας μέρος δι' ὑπερβολὴν τοῦ περὶ τὰς ὀσμὰς τάχους· ἐξικνοῦνται γὰρ ἐπὶ μήκιστον, ὡς ὀφθαλμῶν ἁμιλλᾶσθαι φορᾷ. 162. καὶ τί δεῖ περὶ ἑκάστου διεξιόντα μακρηγορεῖν; ἤδη γὰρ τοῦτο παρὰ τοῖς δοκιμωτάτοις τῶν πάλαι λογίων ὡμολόγηται, οἳ τῶν μὲν ἀλόγων μητέρα τὴν φύσιν, ἀνθρώπων δὲ μητρυιὰν ἔφασαν εἶναι, τὴν κατὰ σῶμα τῶν μὲν ἀσθένειαν, τῶν δὲ ὑπερβάλλουσαν ἐν ἅπασιν ἰσχὺν κατανοήσαντες.[18]

160. But now even the most savage of the wild beasts enjoy these goods, if they are in truth goods, more than rational beings. 161. For what athlete would be equal to the bull in power or to the elephant in strength? And what runner could equal the hunting dog or hare in fleetness of foot? The most keen-sighted of men is most dim-sighted in comparison with the vision of hawks or eagles. In hearing, moreover, and scent the irrational animals far and away surpass us, as the ass, thought to be the stupidest of the beasts, would make our hearing seem like deafness, if he were to enter a contest with us. And a dog would make the human nose seem a superfluous organ in comparison with his swift scent, for it reaches to the farthest distances, so that it rivals the eyes in range. 162. But why must we speak in great detail about each? For this was agreed upon by the most esteemed of ancient wise men, who used to say that Nature was the mother of the irrational animals but the step-mother of men, when they considered the bodily weakness of the latter and the surpassing strength of the former in all respects.

Arguments to the same end are found in Seneca (*Epist. mor.* XX, vii, 124), and the play upon the words *natura non mater, sed noverca* is attributed to Cicero by St. Augustine.[19] Cicero also admitted (*De finibus,* II, xxxiv, 111) that if the hedonistic premise of Epicurean ethics were admitted, the beasts would excel man in happiness. But he was far from admitting that premise, and indeed in one place (*De finibus,* II, xiii, 40) accuses the Cyrenaics of making "this divine animal," man, into a sort of "slow and languid ox, born for eating and the pleasures of procreation." Again,

[18] Ed. P. Wendland, Berlin, 1897, II.
[19] *Contra Jul.* 4, 12, 60, usually printed as *De re pub.* III, i, 1.

in one of his extreme expressions of anthropocentric teleology (*De nat. deor.* II, xlvii, 120-153), he lists what were by his time well known examples of animal intelligence, but argues that no matter how well-equipped the beasts may be for the continuation of their individual lives and those of the species, they exist for the sake of man, like the rest of the natural order.[20]

DIODORUS SICULUS

The *Bibliotheca historica* of Diodorus Siculus is largely a collection of anecdotes made towards the end of the first century B. C. and existing now only in fragmentary form. One of these anecdotes relates the visit of the Seven Sages to Croesus and makes a definite contrast between the naturalness of the animal way of life and the conventionality of the human, with, as tradition demanded, the implication that therefore the animals were better than men.

The legend of the visit of at least one of the Sages, Solon, to Croesus is old as Herodotus,[21] and a study of the sources of Diodorus made during the last century concludes that the relevant portion of his book derives from Ephorus (middle fourth century B. C.),[22] which would make it contemporary with the New Comedy.

XIII, 11. *Bibl. hist.* IX, 26.

... Κροῖσος μετεπέμπετο ἐκ τῆς Ἑλλάδος τοὺς ἐπὶ σοφίᾳ πρωτεύοντας, ἐπιδεικνύμενος τὸ μέγεθος τῆς εὐδαιμονίας, καὶ τοὺς ἐξυμνοῦντας τὴν εὐτυχίαν αὐτοῦ ἐτίμα μεγάλαις δωρεαῖς. μετεπέμψατο δὲ καὶ Σόλωνα, ὁμοίως δὲ καὶ τῶν ἄλλων τῶν ἐπὶ φιλοσοφίᾳ μεγίστην δόξαν ἐχόντων, τὴν ἰδίαν εὐδαιμονίαν διὰ τῆς τούτων τῶν ἀνδρῶν μαρτυρίας ἐπισφραγίζεσθαι βουλόμενος. παρεγενήθη δὲ πρὸς αὐτὸν Ἀνάχαρσις ὁ Σκύθης καὶ Βίας καὶ Σόλων καὶ Πιττακός, οὓς ἐπὶ τὰς ἑστιάσεις κατὰ τὸ συνέδριον εἶχεν ἐν μεγίστῃ τιμῇ, τόν τε πλοῦτον αὐτοῖς ἐπιδεικνύμενος καὶ τὸ μέγεθος τῆς τούτου δυναστείας. παρὰ δὲ τοῖς πεπαιδευμένοις τῆς βραχυλογίας τότε ζηλουμένης, ὁ [δὲ] Κροῖσος ἐπιδειξάμενος τὴν τῆς βασιλείας εὐδαιμονίαν τοῖς ἀνδράσι καὶ τὸ πλῆθος τῶν κεχειρωμένων ἐθνῶν, ἠρώτησεν Ἀνάχαρσιν, ὄντα πρεσβύτατον τῶν σοφιστῶν, τίνα νομίζει τῶν ὄντων ἀνδρειότατον. ὁ δὲ τὰ ἀγριώτατα τῶν ζώων ἔφησε· μόνα γὰρ προθύμως ἀποθνήσκειν ὑπὲρ τῆς ἐλευθερίας. ὁ δὲ Κροῖσος νομίσας ἡμαρτηκέναι αὐτόν, ἐν τῷ δευτέρῳ πρὸς χάριν αὐτῷ ποιήσεσθαι τὴν ἀπόκρισιν ὑπολαβών, ἠρώτησε τίνα δικαιότατον κρίνει τῶν ὄντων. ὁ δὲ πάλιν ἀπεφαίνετο τὰ ἀγριώτατα τῶν θηρίων· μόνα γὰρ κατὰ φύσιν ζῆν, οὐ κατὰ νόμους· εἶναι γὰρ τὴν μὲν φύσιν θεοῦ ποίησιν, τὸν δὲ νόμον ἀνθρώπου θέσιν, καὶ δικαιότερον εἶναι χρῆσθαι τοῖς τοῦ θεοῦ ἢ τοῖς τῶν ἀνθρώπων εὑρήμασιν. ὁ δὲ διασῦραι βουλόμενος Ἀνάχαρσιν ἠρώτησεν εἰ καὶ σοφώτατα τὰ θηρία. ὁ δὲ συγκαταθέμενος ἐδίδασκεν ὅτι τὴν τῆς φύσεως ἀλήθειαν τῆς τοῦ νόμου θέσεως προτιμᾶν ἰδιώτατον ὑπάρχειν σοφίας. ὁ δὲ τούτου κατεγέλασεν ὡς ἐκ τῆς Σκυθίας καὶ θηριώδους διαγωγῆς πεποιημένου τὰς ἀποκρίσεις.[23]

---

[20] Cf. *De nat. deor.* II, lxii, 156, and *De legibus*, I, vii, 22 —I, ix, 27.

[21] See *Hist.* I, 29.

[22] See R. Klüber, *Ueber die Quellen des Diodor von Sicilien, im IX Buch*, Würzburg, 1868.

[23] Ed. L. Dindorf, Leipzig, 1867.

Croesus summoned from Greece those pre-eminent in wisdom, exhibiting the height of his own happiness, and rewarding those lauding his good fortune with great gifts. He had sent for Solon as well as for the others who had the greatest reputation in philosophy, wishing his own happiness to be marked by the testimony of these men. And Anacharsis the Scythian appeared before him and Bias and Solon and Pittacus, whom he held in the highest honor at the tables of his counsellors, and he showed them his riches and the might of his rule. But since brevity of speech is esteemed among men of education, Croesus, after exhibiting his royal happiness to them, and the hosts of nations which he had conquered, asked Anacharsis, since he was the oldest of the sages, whom he considered the most courageous of beings. He replied, " The wildest of the beasts.²⁴ For they alone die willingly for freedom." But Croesus, thinking that he had missed the point and assuming that in a second attempt the reply would be in his favor, asked whom he judged to be the justest of beings. But once more he was told the wildest of the beasts, for they alone live in accordance with nature, not law. Nature, said Anacharsis, was the work of God, but law a convention of man, and it is more just to employ the devices of God than those of man. But Croesus, wishing to demolish Anacharsis, asked him whether the beasts were also the wisest. Anacharsis answered in the affirmative, saying that to reverence the truth of nature above the conventions of law was the most characteristic possession of wisdom. But Croesus laughed at him as a Scythian, who had therefore given the answers of one used to a bestial way of living.²⁵

OVID

Ovid carries into literature the Cynic fashion of using animal behavior as a criterion of what is right for human beings. The animals are here again presented as more natural than man and for that reason better. The behavior which has to be justified is Myrrha's incestuous love for her father.

XIII, 12. *Metamorphoses*, X, 319-331.

> illa quidem sentit foedoque repugnat amori
> et secum " quo mente feror? quid molior? " inquit
> " di, precor, et pietas sacrataque iura parentum,
> hoc prohibete nefas scelerique resistite nostro;
> si tamen hoc scelus est. sed enim damnare negatur
> hanc Venerem pietas: coeuntque animalia nullo
> cetera delectu, nec habetur turpe iuvencae
> ferre patrem tergo, fit equo sua filia coniunx;
> quasque creavit, init pecudes caper; ipsaque, cuius
> semine concepta est, ex illo concipit ales.

²⁴ The paradox is stronger in Greek, for the word translated " courageous " also signifies " manly."

²⁵ Athenaeus (XIV, 613d) attributes to Anacharsis the observation that apes are funny by nature, men by training. Whether the contrast between nature and art here implies the superiority of the natural is questionable.

felices, quibus ista licent! humana malignas
cura dedit leges, et quod natura remittit,
invida iura negant." [26]

(Myrrha) indeed is aware of her unseemly love and fights against it, and says to herself, "Whither does my mind carry me? What is my purpose? Ye gods, and piety, and the sacred rights of parents, I pray, ward off this sin and defend me against this crime, if crime it be. Yet piety refuses to condemn such love. The other animals mate without distinction, nor is it thought shameful for the heifer to be covered by her sire nor for the filly to be mate to hers.[27] The buck goes in among the herd he has begotten, and the bird herself conceives from the seed of him from whom she was conceived. Oh happy beasts, to whom such things are permitted! Human thought has produced spiteful laws, and what nature pardons, the envious laws forbid."

SENECA

Though we find few later examples in extant Latin literature of this mode of appeal to the example of the beasts, the practice must have been somewhat current, for we find Seneca deprecating it in his *De ira* (II, 16), some fifty years after.

XIII, 13. *De ira,* II, 16.

" Animalia," inquit, "generosissima habentur, quibus multum inest irae." Errat qui ea in exemplum hominis adducit, quibus pro ratione est impetus: homini pro impetu ratio est. Sed ne illis quidem omnibus idem prodest: iracundia leones adiuvat, pavor cervos, accipitrem impetus, columbam fuga. Quid, quod ne illud quidem verum est, optima animalia esse iracundissima? feras putem, quibus ex raptu alimenta sunt, meliores quo iratiores; patientiam laudaverim boum et equorum frenos sequentium. Quid est autem cur hominem ad tam infelicia exempla revoces, cum habeas mundum deumque, quem ex omnibus animalibus, ut solus imitetur, solus intellegit? [28]

" The animals," he says, " are held to be most noble, yet they are greatly given to anger."

He errs who adduces them as an example for man, for in them impulse takes the place of reason. In man reason takes the place of impulse. But not even all the beasts benefit by the same impulse. Anger is an advantage to lions, timidity to the stag, attack to the hawk, flight to the dove. Why, since not even that is true, are the best animals the most wrathful? Then I should think the wild beasts which feed upon prey better because they are the more wrathful. I should myself have praised the patience of the ox and the obedience of horses to the bit. But why should you propose to man such infelicitous examples, when you have the world and God, whom man, alone of all the animals understands, so that he alone may imitate him?

---

[26] Ed. A. Riese, Leipzig, 1872.
[27] But see the story of the King of Scythia's mare in Aristotle's *Hist. anim.* 631a.
[28] Ed. E. Hermes, Leipzig, 1917.

PLINY

The one Latin writer of the later period whose influence in favor of animalitarianism was greatest was Pliny. His *Natural History* not only passed on most of the classic stories of animal intelligence and goodness,[29] but also contained the most celebrated diatribe upon man's misery. He concedes that, as Cicero and others had said, nature has given man the highest place in creation, but maintains that she has done so at an exorbitant price. Man alone of animals has no instinctive knowledge; all his knowledge is laboriously acquired; he alone is subject to grief, inordinate desire, ambition, avarice and other evil passions. Finally, he alone makes war upon his kind.

XIII, 14. *Historia naturalis*, VII, Proem. Sect. 1 (Translation on p. 402).

> Mundus et in eo terrae, gentes, maria, insignes insulae, urbes ad hunc modum se habent. animantium in eodem natura nullius prope partis contemplatione minor est, etsi omnia quidem exsequi humanus animus nequeat. principium iure tribuetur homini, cuius causa videtur cuncta alia genuisse natura magna, saeva mercede contra tanta sua munera, ut non sit satis aestimare, parens melior homini an tristior noverca fuerit. Ante omnia unum animantium cunctorum alienis velat opibus, ceteris varie tegimenta tribuit, testas, cortices, spinas, coria, villos, saetas, pilos, plumam, pinnas, squamas, vellera. truncos etiam arboresque cortice, interdum gemino, a frigoribus et calore tutata est. hominem tantum nudum et in nuda humo natali die abicit ad vagituus statim et ploratum, nullumque tot animalium aliud ad lacrimas, et has protinus vitae principio. at, Hercule, risus praecox ille et celerrimus ante XL diem nulli datur. Ab hoc lucis rudimento, quae ne feras quidem inter nos genitas, vincula excipiunt et omnium membrorum nexus, itaque feliciter natus iacet manibus pedibusque devinctis, flens, animal ceteris imperaturum, et a suppliciis vitam auspicatur unam tantum ob culpam, qua natum est. heu dementiam ab his initiis existimantium ad superbiam se genitos! Prima roboris spes primumque temporis munus quadrupedi similem facit. quando homini incessus! quando vox! quando firmum cibis os! quamdiu palpitans vertex, summae inter cuncta animalia inbecillitatis indicium! iam morbi tot atque medicinae tot contra mala excogitatae, et hae quoque subinde novitatibus victae! et cetera sentire naturam suam, alia pernicitatem usurpare, alia praepetes volatus, alia nare, hominem nihil scire, nisi doctrina, non fari, non ingredi, non vesci, breviterque non aliud naturae sponte quam flere. itaque multi extitere qui non nasci optimum censerent aut quam ocissime aboleri. uni animantium luctus est datus, uni luxuria, et quidem innumerabilibus modis ac per singula membra, uni ambitio, uni avaritia, uni inmensa vivendi cupido, uni superstitio, uni sepulturae cura atque etiam post se de

---

[29] See VIII, i, 1, for the intellectual superiority of the elephant; VIII, v, 5, for their sense of shame; VIII, xxvii, 41, for the medical knowledge of certain beasts; X, xxxiv, 52, for the marital fidelity of the dove.

futuro. nulli vita fragilior, nulli rerum omnium libido maior, nulli pavor confusior, nulli rabies acrior. denique cetera animantia in suo genere probe degunt. congregari videmus et stare contra dissimilia. leonum feritas inter se non dimicat, serpentium morsus non petit serpentis, ne maris quidem beluae ac pisces nisi in diversa genera saeviunt. at, Hercule, homini plurima ex homine sunt mala.[30]

The world and the lands thereon, its peoples, its seas, its great islands, its cities, are such as has been shown; and the nature of the living things in it would be treated in the same way, with each of its divisions no less carefully studied, if only the human mind were able to investigate everything. The first place by right is given to man, for whose sake nature seems to have brought forth all else, selling her great favors at so high and cruel a price that it is not sufficient to think her a kindly mother to man. She is rather a cruel stepmother. In the first place she covers but one of all the animate creation with the aid of others; to the others she gave varied covering, shells, hulls, spines, hides, shaggy hair, bristles, fur, feathers, quills, scales, fleeces; even the trunks of trees are covered with bark, protected in a twofold manner, now from the heat, now from the cold; man only she casts forth on his natal day naked upon a naked soil, casts him forth at once to weep and beg; and no other of all the animals weeps from the moment of its birth. But laughter, by Hercules, even when precociously early, is given to none before the fortieth day. From the very dawn of life, he is bound by chains which not even the wild beasts born in captivity suffer, and all his limbs are tied; thus happily born he lies with hands and feet bound, a weeping animal who will be the master of the other animals, and enters upon life under punishment only for the crime of having been born. Alas, the folly of those who, having such a beginning, think they have been begotten to high estate. The first hope of strength and the first gift of time make man like a quadruped. When does man walk? when speak? when does he become capable of eating solid food? How long does his head wobble, a sign among all animals of the greatest weakness? how many remedies have been thought of against the evils of disease, only to be supplanted immediately by new ones? The other animals are conscious of their own nature; some exhibit speed, others winged flight, still others swim. Man knows nothing, nothing without instruction — either to talk, or walk, or eat; in short he can do nothing by his own inborn nature but weep. Therefore there have been many who thought it best not to have been born, or then to die as quickly as possible after birth.[31] To one alone of living beings has grief been given; to one alone the desire of luxury [or excess], luxury in numberless modes, luxury for each member; to one alone ambition, to one alone avarice, to one alone an immoderate desire of living, to one alone superstition, to one alone worry about sepulture and even about what is to be after he is gone. None has a more fragile life, a greater craving for all things, a more confused fear, a more violent rage. Finally, the other animals live properly among their own species; we see them assemble and take their stand against their dissimilars; the

[30] Ed. D. Detlefsen, Berlin, 1867, vol. II.   [31] Sophocles, *Oed. Col.* 1225.

ferocity of lions is not turned upon their fellows, the bite of serpents does not seek serpents, not even the monsters of the sea and the fishes war upon their own kind. But, by Hercules, most of man's evils come from man.[32]

Another passage from Pliny criticises man's sexual life as uniquely vicious.

XIII, 15. *Nat. hist.* X, lxiii, 83.

> Bipedum solus homo animal gignit. homini tantum primi coitus paenitentia, augurium scilicet vitae a paenitenda origine. ceteris animalibus stati per tempora anni concubitus, homini, ut dictum est, omnibus horis dierum noctiumque. ceteris satias in coitu, homini prope nulla. Messalina Claudii Caesaris coniunx regalem hanc existimans palmam elegit in id certamen nobilissimam e prostitutis ancillam mercenariae stipis, eamque nocte ac die superavit quinto atque vicensimo concubitu. in hominum genere maribus deverticula veneris excogitata, omnia scelere naturae, feminis vero abortus. quantum in hac parte multo nocentiores quam ferae sumus![33]

> Alone of the bipeds man is viviparous. Only man regrets his first coitus, a sign that life has a regrettable origin. The other animals unite at fixed periods of the year; man, as the saying is, at all hours of the day and night. The others find satiation in coitus, man virtually none. Messalina, wife of Claudius Caesar, thinking this a mark of royalty, invited to an erotic contest a notorious slave-girl who lived by prostitution, and outdid her night and day even to the twenty-fifth union. In the race of man there are sexual perversions among the males, abortions among the females, in fact every kind of crime against nature has been devised. How much more wicked are we in this matter than the wild beasts![34]

PLUTARCH

The reproach of man's defencelessness was answered by Galen in his *De usu partium,* the first book of which reproduces the Aristotelian argument that man's hands are the best of weapons. But the most influential texts germane to our subject are found in Plutarch. His *De sollertia animalium* repeated the Democritic thesis that we derived our arts from the beasts, and gave the usual examples of animal intelligence from Pliny and Aristotle. The *De amore prolis* is a further illustration of the frequency of appeals to animals for models. The treatise now exists only in a fragmentary condition, but it appears to have the peculiarity of accepting the proposition that the animals are more in accord with nature than man, while rejecting the disparagement of man often deduced from this.

---

[32] For an earlier example of this remark, cf. Dicaearchus, in Chap. I, section D, p. 96, above.

[33] Ed. D. Detlefsen, Berlin, 1867.

[34] These passages which berate man and lament nature's indifference to him, should be compared with *Nat. hist.* II, 154-159, which is an eloquent defence of natural teleology and Stoic organicism.

XIII, 16.   *De amore prolis* (Translation on p. 407).

1. Ἔκκλητοι κρίσεις καὶ ξενικῶν δικαστηρίων ἀγωγαὶ τοῖς Ἕλλησι τὸ
πρῶτον ἀπιστίᾳ τῇ πρὸς ἀλλήλους ἐπενοήθησαν, ἀλλοτρίας δικαιοσύνης ὥσπερ
ἑτέρου τινὸς τῶν ἀναγκαίων μὴ φυομένου παρ' αὐτοῖς δεηθεῖσιν. ἆρ' οὖν καὶ
οἱ φιλόσοφοι τῶν προβλημάτων ἔνια διὰ τὰς πρὸς ἀλλήλους διαφορὰς ἐπὶ
τὴν τῶν ἀλόγων φύσιν ζῴων ὥσπερ ἀλλοδαπὴν πόλιν ἐκκαλοῦνται καὶ τοῖς
ἐκείνων πάθεσι καὶ ἤθεσιν ὡς ἀνεντεύκτοις καὶ ἀδεκάστοις ἐφιᾶσι τὴν κρίσιν;
ἢ καὶ τοῦτο τῆς ἀνθρωπίνης κακίας ἔγκλημα κοινόν ἐστι, τὸ περὶ τῶν ἀναγ-
καιοτάτων καὶ μεγίστων ἀμφιδοξοῦντας ἡμᾶς ζητεῖν ἐν ἵπποις καὶ κυσὶ καὶ
ὄρνισι, πῶς γαμοῦμεν αὐτοὶ καὶ γεννῶμεν καὶ τεκνοτροφοῦμεν, ὡς μηδὲν ἐν
ἑαυτοῖς δήλωμα τῆς φύσεως ὄν, τὰ ⟨δὲ⟩ τῶν θηρίων ἤθη καὶ πάθη προ-
αγορεῦσαι καὶ καταμαρτυρῆσαι τοῦ βίου ἡμῶν πολλὴν τοῦ κατὰ φύσιν
ἐκδιαίτησιν καὶ παράβασιν, εὐθὺς ἐν ἀρχῇ καὶ περὶ τὰ πρῶτα συγχεομένων
καὶ ταραττομένων; ἄκρατον γὰρ ἐν ἐκείνοις ἡ φύσις καὶ ἀμιγὲς καὶ ἁπλοῦν
φυλάττει τὸ ἴδιον, ἐν δ' ἀνθρώποις ὑπὸ τοῦ λόγου καὶ τῆς συνηθείας, ὃ τοὔλαιον
ὑπὸ τῶν μυρεψῶν πέπονθε, πρὸς πολλὰ μιγνυμένη δόγματα καὶ κρίσεις ἐπι-
θέτους ποικίλη γέγονε καὶ ἡδεῖα, τὸ δ' οἰκεῖον οὐ τετήρηκε. καὶ μὴ θαυμάζωμεν,
εἰ τὰ ἄλογα ζῷα τῶν λογικῶν μᾶλλον ἕπεται τῇ φύσει· καὶ γὰρ τὰ φυτὰ
τῶν ζῴων· οἷς οὔτε φαντασίαν οὔθ' ὁρμὴν ἔδωκε ⟨δι'⟩ ἑτέρων ὄρεξιν τοῦ κατὰ
φύσιν ἀποσαλεύουσαν, ἀλλ' ὥσπερ ἐν δεσμῷ συνειργμένα μένει καὶ κεκράτηται,
μίαν ἀεὶ πορείαν ἣν ἡ φύσις ἄγει πορευόμενα. τοῖς δὲ θηρίοις τὸ μὲν πολύτροπον
τοῦ λόγου καὶ περιττὸν καὶ φιλελεύθερον ἄγαν οὐκ ἔστιν, ἀλόγους δ' ὁρμὰς
καὶ ὀρέξεις ἔχοντα καὶ χρώμενα πλάναις καὶ περιδρομαῖς πολλάκις ἀλλ' οὐ
μακρὰν ὡς ἐπ' ἀγκύρας τῆς φύσεως σαλεύει, καθάπερ οὖν ὁδὸν ὑφ' ἡνία καὶ
χαλινῷ βαδίζοντα δείκνυσιν εὐθεῖαν ὁ δεσπότης. ⟨ὁ δ' ἀδέσποτος⟩ ἐν ἀνθρώπῳ
καὶ αὐτοκρατὴς λόγος ἄλλας ἄλλοτε παρεκβάσεις καὶ καινοτομίας ἀνευρίσκων
οὐδὲν ἴχνος ἐμφανὲς οὐδ' ἐναργὲς ἀπολέλοιπε τῆς φύσεως.

2. Ὅρα περὶ τοὺς γάμους ὅσον ἐστὶν ἐν τοῖς ζῴοις τὸ κατὰ φύσιν. πρῶτον
οὐκ ἀναμένει νόμους ἀγαμίου καὶ ὀψιγαμίου, καθάπερ οἱ Λυκούργου πολῖται
καὶ Σόλωνος, οὐδ' ἀτιμίας ἀτέκνων δέδοικεν, οὐδὲ τιμὰς διώκει τριπαιδίας,
ὡς Ῥωμαίων πολλοὶ γαμοῦσι καὶ γεννῶσιν, οὐχ ἵνα κληρονόμους ἔχωσιν ἀλλ'
ἵνα κληρονομεῖν δύνωνται. ἔπειτα μίγνυται τῷ θήλει τὸ ἄρρεν οὐχ ἅπαντα
χρόνον· ἡδονὴν γὰρ οὐκ ἔχει τέλος ἀλλὰ γέννησιν καὶ τέκνωσιν· διὰ τοῦτ'
ἔτους ὥρᾳ, ἣ πνοάς τε γονίμους ἔχει καὶ πρόσφορον ὀχευομένοις κρᾶσιν,
ἦλθεν εἰς τὸ αὐτὸ τῷ ἄρρενι τὸ θῆλυ χειρόηθες καὶ ποθεινόν, ἡδείᾳ μὲν ὀσμῇ
χρωτὸς ἰδίῳ δὲ κόσμῳ σώματος ἀγαλλόμενον, δρόσου καὶ βοτάνης ἀνάπλεων
καθαρᾶς· αἰσθόμενον δ' ὅτι κύει καὶ πεπλήρωται, κοσμίως ἄπεισι καὶ προνοεῖ
περὶ τὴν κύησιν καὶ σωτηρίαν τοῦ ἀποτεχθέντος. ἀξίως δ' οὐκ ἔστιν εἰπεῖν
τὰ δρώμενα, πλὴν ὅτι γίνεται ἕκαστον αὐτῶν ἐν τῷ φιλοστόργῳ ταῖς προνοίαις
ταῖς καρτερίαις ταῖς ἐγκρατείαις. ἀλλὰ τὴν ⟨μὲν⟩ μέλιτταν ἡμεῖς σοφὴν
καλοῦμεν καὶ νομίζομεν ' ξανθὸν μέλι μηδομέναν ' (Simon. *Fragm.* 47 B),
κολακεύοντες τὸ ἡδὺ καὶ γαργαλίζον ἡμᾶς τῆς γλυκύτητος, τὴν δὲ τῶν ἄλλων
περὶ τὰς λοχείας καὶ τὰς ἀνατροφὰς σοφίαν καὶ τέχνην παρορῶμεν. οἷον
εὐθύς, ἡ ἀλκυὼν κύουσα τὴν νεοττιὰν συντίθησι συλλαμβάνουσα τὰς ἀκάνθας
τῆς θαλαττίας βελόνης καὶ ταύτας δι' ἀλλήλων ἐγκαταπλέκουσα καὶ συνείρουσα
τὸ μὲν σχῆμα περιαγὲς ὡς ἁλιευτικοῦ κύρτου καὶ πρόμηκες ἀπεργάζεται, τῇ
δ' ἁρμονίᾳ καὶ πυκνότητι συμφράξασα τὰς ἀκάνθας ἀκριβῶς ὑπέθηκε τῷ
κλύσματι τοῦ κύματος, ὡς τυπτόμενον ἡσυχῇ καὶ πηγνύμενον τὸ πίλημα τῆς
ἐπιφανείας στεγανὸν γένηται· γίγνεται δὲ σιδήρῳ καὶ λίθῳ δυσδιαίρετον.
ὃ δ' ἐστὶ θαυμασιώτερον, οὕτω τὸ στόμα τῆς νεοττιᾶς συμμέτρως πεπλάσθαι
πρὸς τὸ μέγεθος καὶ τὸ μέτρον τῆς ἀλκυόνος, ὥστε μήτε μεῖζον ἄλλο μήτε
μικρότερον ἐνδύεσθαι ζῷον, ὡς δέ φασι, μηδὲ θαλάττης παραδέχεσθαι μηδὲ

τὰ ἐλάχιστα. μάλιστα δ' οἱ γαλεοὶ ζῳογονοῦσι μὲν ἐν ἑαυτοῖς, ἐκβαίνειν
δὲ παρέχουσιν ἐκτὸς καὶ νέμεσθαι τοῖς σκυμνίοις, εἶτα πάλιν ἀναλαμβάνουσι
καὶ περιπτύσσουσιν ἐγκοιμώμενα τοῖς σπλάγχνοις. ἡ δ' ἄρκτος, ἀγριώτατον
καὶ σκυθρωπότατον θηρίον, ἄμορφα καὶ ἄναρθρα τίκτει, τῇ δὲ γλώττῃ καθάπερ
ἐργαλείῳ διατυποῦσα τοὺς ὑμένας οὐ δοκεῖ γεννᾶν μόνον ἀλλὰ καὶ δημιουργεῖν
τὸ τέκνον. . . . εἶτα ταῦτ' οἰόμεθα ⟨τὰ⟩ πάθη τούτοις ἐνειργάσθαι τὴν φύσιν
ἀλεκτορίδων ἐπιγονῆς καὶ κυνῶν καὶ ἄρκτων προνοοῦσαν, ἀλλ' οὐχ ἡμᾶς
δυσωποῦσαν καὶ τιτρώσκουσαν ἐπιλογιζομένους ὅτι ταῦτα παραδείγματα τοῖς
ἑπομένοις, τοῖς δ' ἀναλγήτοις ὀνείδη περίεστι τῆς ἀπαθείας, δι' ὧν κατηγοροῦσι
τῆς ἀνθρωπίνης φύσεως μόνης μὴ προῖκα τὸ στέργειν ἐχούσης μηδ' ἐπιστα-
μένης φιλεῖν ἄνευ χρείας; θαυμάζεται γὰρ ἐν τοῖς θεάτροις ὁ εἰπών

'μισθοῦ γὰρ ἄνθρωπον τίς ἀνθρώπων φιλεῖ;' (Com. adesp. 218),

⟨καίτοι⟩ κατ' Ἐπίκουρον (fr. 527) ὁ πατὴρ τὸν υἱόν, ⟨ἡ⟩ μήτηρ τὸ τέκνον,
οἱ παῖδες τοὺς τεκόντας· ἀλλ' εἰ λόγου γένοιτο τοῖς θηρίοις σύνεσις καὶ τοῦτό
τις εἰς κοινὸν θέατρον συναγαγὼν ἵππους καὶ βόας καὶ κύνας καὶ ὄρνιθας
ἀναφθέγξαιτο μεταγράψας, ὡς 'οὔτε κύνες ἐπὶ μισθῷ σκύλακας φιλοῦσιν
οὔθ' ἵπποι πώλους οὔτ' ὄρνιθες νεοττοὺς ἀλλὰ προῖκα καὶ φυσικῶς,' ἐπι-
γνωσθήσεται τοῖς ἁπάντων πάθεσιν ὡς εὖ καὶ ἀληθῶς λεγόμενον. αἰσχρὸν
γάρ, ὦ Ζεῦ, τὰς θηρίων γενέσεις καὶ λοχείας καὶ ὠδῖνας καὶ τεκνοτροφίας
φύσιν εἶναι καὶ χάριν, τὰς δ' ἀνθρώπων δάνεια καὶ μισθοὺς καὶ ἀρραβῶνας
ἐπὶ χρείαις διδομένους.

3. Ἀλλ' οὔτ' ἀληθὴς ὁ λόγος οὔτ' ἄξιος ἀκούειν. ἡ γὰρ φύσις ὥσπερ
ἐν φυτοῖς ἀγρίοις οἷον οἰνάνθαις ἐρινεοῖς κοτίνοις ἀρχὰς ἀπέπτους καὶ ἀτελεῖς
ἡμέρων καρπῶν ἐνέφυσεν, οὕτω τοῖς μὲν ἀλόγοις τὸ πρὸς τὰ ἔγγονα φιλόστοργον ἀτελὲς καὶ οὐ διαρκὲς πρὸς δικαιοσύνην οὐδὲ τῆς χρείας πορρωτέρω
προερχόμενον ἔδωκεν, ἄνθρωπον δέ, λογικὸν καὶ πολιτικὸν ζῷον, ἐπὶ δίκην
καὶ νόμον εἰσάγουσα καὶ θεῶν τιμὰς καὶ πόλεων ἱδρύσεις καὶ φιλοφροσύνην,
γενναῖα καὶ καλὰ καὶ φερέκαρπα τούτων σπέρματα παρέσχε τὴν πρὸς τὰ
ἔγγονα χάριν καὶ ἀγάπησιν, ἀκολουθοῦσαν ταῖς πρώταις ἀρχαῖς· αὗται δ'
ἦσαν ἐν ταῖς τῶν σωμάτων κατασκευαῖς. πανταχοῦ μὲν γὰρ ἡ φύσις ἀκριβὴς
καὶ φιλότεχνος καὶ ἀνελλιπὴς καὶ ἀπέριττος, 'οὐδέν' ὡς ἔφησεν Ἐρασίστρατος
'ἔχουσα ῥωπικόν,' τὰ δὲ περὶ τὴν γένεσιν ἀξίως οὐκ ἔστιν εἰπεῖν οὐδ' εὐπρεπὲς
ἴσως λίαν ἀκριβῶς τῶν ἀπορρήτων ἐμφύεσθαι τοῖς ὀνόμασι καὶ τοῖς ῥήμασιν,
ἀλλ' ἀποκειμένων καὶ κεκρυμμένων ἐπινοεῖν τὴν πρὸς τὸ γεννᾶν καὶ λοχεύεσθαι
τῶν μορίων ἐκείνων εὐφυΐαν. ἀρκεῖ δ' ἡ τοῦ γάλακτος ἐργασία καὶ οἰκονομία
τὴν πρόνοιαν αὐτῆς ἐμφῆναι καὶ ἐπιμέλειαν. . . . ἀλλὰ τούτων γε τῶν
τοσούτων ἐπὶ τὴν γένεσιν ἐργαλείων καὶ τοιούτων οἰκονομιῶν καὶ φιλοτιμίας
καὶ προνοίας οὐδὲν ἦν ὄφελος, εἰ μὴ τὸ φιλόστοργον ἡ φύσις καὶ κηδεμονικὸν
ἐνειργάσατο ταῖς τεκούσαις.

'οὐ μὲν γάρ τί πού ἐστιν ὀιζυρώτερον ἀνδρός,
πάντων ὅσσα τε γαῖαν ἔπι πνείει τε καὶ ἕρπει (P. 446)'—

τοῦτ' οὐ ψεύδεται λέγων ἐπὶ νηπίου καὶ ἀρτιγενοῦς. οὐδὲν γάρ ἐστιν οὕτως
ἀτελὲς οὐδ' ἄπορον οὐδὲ γυμνὸν οὐδ' ἄμορφον οὐδὲ μιαρὸν ὡς ἄνθρωπος ἐν
γοναῖς ὁρώμενος· ᾧ μόνῳ σχεδὸν οὐδὲ καθαρὰν ἔδωκεν εἰς φῶς ὁδὸν ἡ φύσις,
ἀλλ' αἵματι πεφυρμένος καὶ λύθρου περίπλεως καὶ φονευομένῳ μᾶλλον ἢ
γεννωμένῳ ἐοικὼς οὐδενός ἐστιν ἅψασθαι καὶ ἀνελέσθαι καὶ ἀσπάσασθαι καὶ
περιλαβεῖν ἢ τοῦ φύσει φιλοῦντος. διὸ τῶν μὲν ἄλλων ζῴων ὑπὸ τὴν γαστέρα
τὰ οὔθατα χαλᾷ [τοὺς μαστοὺς], ταῖς δὲ γυναιξὶν ἄνω γεγόνασιν περὶ τὸ
στέρνον ἐν ἐφικτῷ τοῦ φιλῆσαι καὶ περιπτύξαι καὶ κατασπάσασθαι τὸ νήπιον,
ὡς τοῦ τεκεῖν καὶ θρέψαι τέλος οὐ χρείαν ἀλλὰ φιλίαν ἔχοντος.

4. Ἐπὶ τοὺς παλαιοὺς ἀνάγαγε τὸν λόγον, ὧν ταῖς μὲν τεκεῖν πρώταις,

τοῖς δ' ἰδεῖν συνέβη τικτόμενον βρέφος· οὔτε νόμος ἦν ἐκείνοις τεκνοτροφεῖν προστάττων οὔτε προσδοκία χάριτος ἢ τροφείων ' ἐπὶ νέοις δανειζομένων ' (Plato Legg. 717 c). χαλεπὰς δὲ μᾶλλον εἴποιμ' ἂν εἶναι καὶ μνησικάκους τὰς τεκούσας τοῖς βρέφεσι, κινδύνων τε μεγάλων καὶ πόνων αὐταῖς γινομένων·

> ' ὡς δ' ὅταν ὠδίνουσαν ἔχῃ βέλος ὀξὺ γυναῖκα
> δριμύ, τό τε προϊᾶσι μογοστόκοι Εἰλείθυιαι,
> Ἥρης θυγατέρες, πικρὰς ὠδῖνας ἔχουσαι ' (Λ 269) —

ταῦτ' οὐχ Ὅμηρον αἱ γυναῖκες ἀλλ' Ὁμηρίδα γράψαι λέγουσι τεκοῦσαν ἢ τίκτουσαν ἔτι καὶ τὸ νύγμα τῆς ἀλγηδόνος ὁμοῦ πικρὸν καὶ ὀξὺ γινόμενον ἐν τοῖς σπλάγχνοις ἔχουσαν. ἀλλὰ τὸ φύσει φιλόστοργον ἔκαμπτε καὶ ἦγεν· ἔτι θερμὴ καὶ διαλγὴς καὶ κραδαινομένη τοῖς πόνοις οὐχ ὑπερέβη τὸ νήπιον οὐδ' ἔφυγεν, ἀλλ' ἐπεστράφη καὶ προσεμειδίασε καὶ ἀνείλετο καὶ ἠσπάσατο, μηδὲν ἡδὺ καρπουμένη μηδὲ χρήσιμον ἀλλ' ἐπιπόνως καὶ ταλαιπώρως ἀναδεχομένη, τῶν σπαργάνων ' ἐρειπίοις

> θάλπουσα καὶ ψήχουσα, καὶ πόνῳ πόνον
> ἐκ νυκτὸς ἀλλάσσουσα τὸν μεθ' ἡμέραν ' (Tr. adesp. 7).

τίνων ταῦτα μισθῶν ἢ χρειῶν ἐκείνοις; ἀλλ' οὐδὲ τοῖς νῦν· αἱ γὰρ ἐλπίδες ἄδηλοι καὶ μακραί. ἀμπελῶν ἰσημερίας ἐαρινῆς σκάψας μετοπωρινῆς ἐτρύγησε, πυρὸν ἔσπειρε δυομένης Πλειάδος εἶτ' ἀνατελλούσης θερίζει, βόες καὶ ἵπποι καὶ ὄρνιθες ἕτοιμα τίκτουσιν ἐπὶ τὰς χρείας· ἀνθρώπου δ' ἡ μὲν ἐκτροφὴ πολύπονος ἡ δ' αὔξησις βραδεῖα, τῆς δ' ἀρετῆς μακρὰν οὔσης προαποθνῄσκουσιν οἱ πλεῖστοι πατέρες. οὐκ ἐπεῖδε τὴν Σαλαμῖνα Νεοκλῆς τὴν Θεμιστοκλέους οὐδὲ τὸν Εὐρυμέδοντα Μιλτιάδης τὸν Κίμωνος, οὐδ' ἤκουσε Περικλέους Ξάνθιππος δημηγοροῦντος οὐδ' Ἀρίστων Πλάτωνος φιλοσοφοῦντος, οὐδ' Εὐριπίδου καὶ Σοφοκλέους νίκας οἱ πατέρες ἔγνωσαν· ψελλιζόντων καὶ συλλαβιζόντων ἠκροῶντο καὶ κώμους καὶ πότους καὶ ἔρωτας αὐτῶν οἷα νέοι πλημμελούντων ἐπεῖδον· ὥστ' ἐπαινεῖσθαι καὶ μνημονεύεσθαι τοῦ Εὐήνου τοῦτο μόνον, ὡς ἐπέγραψεν

> ' ἢ δέος ἢ λύπη παῖς πατρὶ πάντα χρόνον· ' (PL. II 270).

ἀλλ' ὅμως οὐ παύονται παῖδας τρέφοντες μάλιστα δ' οἱ παίδων ἥκιστα δεόμενοι. γελοῖον γάρ, εἴ τις οἴεται τοὺς πλουσίους θύειν καὶ χαίρειν γενομένων αὐτοῖς τέκνων, ὅτι τοὺς θρέψοντας ἕξουσι καὶ τοὺς θάψοντας· εἰ μὴ νὴ Δία κληρονόμων ἀπορίᾳ παῖδας τρέφουσιν· οὐ γὰρ ἔστιν εὑρεῖν οὐδ' ἐπιτυχεῖν τοῦ τἀλλότρια βουλομένου λαμβάνειν;

> ' ⟨οὐ⟩ ψάμμος ἢ κόνις ἢ πτερὰ ποικιλοθρόων οἰωνῶν
> τόσσον ἂν χεύαιτ' ἀριθμόν ' (Lyr. adesp. II p. 162 D),

ὅσος ἐστὶν ὁ τῶν κληρονομούντων.

> ' Δαναὸς ὁ πεντήκοντα θυγατέρων πατήρ ' (Eur. fr. 228),

εἰ δ' ἄτεκνος ἦν, πλείονας ἂν εἶχε κληρονομοῦντας, καὶ οὐχ ὁμοίους. οἱ μὲν γὰρ παῖδες χάριν οὐδεμίαν ἔχουσιν οὐδ' ἕνεκα τούτου θεραπεύουσιν οὐδὲ τιμῶσιν, ὡς ὀφείλημα τὸν κλῆρον ἐκδεχόμενοι· τῶν δ' ἀλλοτρίων περὶ τὸν ἄτεκνον φωνὰς ἀκούεις ταῖς κωμικαῖς ἐκείναις ὁμοίας,

> ' ὦ Δῆμε, λοῦσαι πρῶτον ἐκδικάσας μίαν,
> ἔνθου ῥόφησον ἔντραγ' ἔχε τριώβολον ' (Arist. Eq. 50)

τὸ δ' ὑπὸ τοῦ Εὐριπίδου λεγόμενον (Phoen. 439 sq.), ' τὰ χρήματ' ἀνθρώποισιν εὑρίσκειν φίλους δύναμίν τε πλείστην τῶν ἐν ἀνθρώποις ἔχειν,' οὐχ ἁπλῶς ἀληθές, ἀλλ' ἐπὶ τῶν ἀτέκνων· τούτους οἱ πλούσιοι δειπνίζουσιν,

οἱ ἡγεμόνες θεραπεύουσιν, οἱ ῥήτορες μόνοις τούτοις προῖκα συνηγοροῦσιν.
᾽ἰσχυρόν ἐστι πλούσιος ἀγνοούμενον ἔχων κληρονόμον᾽ (Com. adesp. 404).
πολλοὺς γοῦν πολυφίλους καὶ πολυτιμήτους ὄντας ἓν παιδίον γενόμενον
ἀφίλους καὶ ἀδυνάτους ἐποίησεν. ὅθεν οὐδὲ πρὸς δύναμιν οὐδέν ἐστιν ὠφέλιμον
ἀπὸ τῶν τέκνων, ἀλλὰ τῆς φύσεως τὸ πᾶν κράτος οὐχ ἧττον ἐν ἀνθρώποις
ἢ θηρίοις.

5. Ἐξαμαυροῦται γὰρ καὶ ταῦτα καὶ πολλὰ τῶν ἄλλων ὑπὸ τῆς κακίας,
ὥσπερ λόχμης ἡμέροις σπέρμασι παραβλαστανούσης· ἢ μηδ᾽ ἑαυτὸν φύσει
στέργειν τὸν ἄνθρωπον λέγωμεν, ὅτι πολλοὶ σφάττουσιν ἑαυτοὺς καὶ κατα-
κρημνίζουσιν. ὁ δ᾽ Οἰδίπους

᾽ἤρασσ᾽ ἐπαίρων βλέφαρα· φοίνιαι δ᾽ ὁμοῦ
γλῆναι γένει᾽ ἔτεγγον᾽ (Soph. O. R. 1276),

Ἡγησίας ⟨δὲ⟩ διαλεγόμενος πολλοὺς ἔπεισεν ἀποκαρτερῆσαι τῶν ἀκρωμένων.
᾽πολλαὶ μορφαὶ τῶν δαιμονίων᾽ (Eur. in fine Alc. al.)· ταῦτα δ᾽ ἐστὶν
ὥσπερ ἐκεῖνα νοσήματα καὶ πάθη ψυχῆς τοῦ κατὰ φύσιν ἐξιστάντα τὸν ἄνθρωπον, ὡς αὐτοὶ καταμαρτυροῦσιν ἑαυτῶν. ἂν γὰρ ὗς τεκοῦσα δελφάκιον
ἢ κωνύ διασπαράξῃ σκυλάκιον, ἀθυμοῦσι καὶ ταράττονται καὶ θεοῖς ἀποτρόπαια
θύουσι καὶ τέρας νομίζουσιν, ὡς πᾶσι καὶ παρὰ φύσιν στέργειν τὰ τικτόμενα
καὶ τρέφειν οὐκ ἀναιρεῖν προσῆκον. οὐ μὴν ἀλλ᾽ ὥσπερ ἐν τοῖς μετάλλοις
πολλῇ συμπεφυρμένον γῇ καὶ κατακεχωσμένον ὅμως διαστίλβει τὸ χρυσίον,
οὕτως ἡ φύσις ἐν αὐτοῖς τοῖς ἡμαρτημένοις ἤθεσι καὶ πάθεσιν ἐκφαίνει τὸ πρὸς
τὰ ἔγγονα φιλόστοργον. οἱ μὲν γὰρ πένητες οὐ τρέφουσι τέκνα, φοβούμενοι
μὴ χεῖρον ἢ προσήκει τραφέντα δουλοπρεπῆ καὶ ἀπαίδευτα καὶ τῶν καλῶν
πάντων ἐνδεᾶ γένηται·᾽ τὴν γὰρ πενίαν ἔσχατον ἡγούμενοι κακὸν οὐχ ὑπο-
μένουσι μεταδοῦναι τέκνοις ὥσπερ τινὸς χαλεποῦ καὶ μεγάλου νοσήματος.[35]

1. The Greeks first thought of appealing to the decisions and
procedure of foreign courts when they began to distrust one another,
for they felt the need of alien justice as something necessary not
found among themselves. Is this not also the case when philosophers, disputing about some of their problems because of mutual
differences, appeal to the nature of the irrational animals as if to a
foreign city, and determine their judgment by means of the passions
and actions of the animals, as if they were incorruptible and im-
partial? Is this not a general indictment of human weakness, to
seek the answer to our most urgent and greatest questions among
horses and dogs and birds: how we should marry and beget children
and educate them, as if we had no evidence from nature concerning
these things in ourselves, but the customs and feelings of the brutes
could declare and testify that our life deviated from nature, since we
erred and went astray in the very beginning concerning primary
matters? For in them nature is unmixed and pure and retains its
own simplicity, but in men, through reason and social life, just as
the olive is acted upon by the oil-press, so it has become many-
colored and strange by many mixed teachings and adventitious
opinions, and has not preserved its own character. Let us not,
moreover, wonder if the irrational animals, rather than the rational,
follow nature. For even the plants in this excel the animals. Things
which have neither imagination nor desire are secured by the force
of nature from the yearning for other things, and as if bound in

[35] Ed. Paton-Pohlenz, Sieveking, Leipzig, 1929, III.

fetters stand fast and are held firm, always travelling one road which nature prescribes. And the beasts have not subtle and extravagant and too liberal reason, but having irrational desires and yearnings and indulging in frequent but not extensive wanderings and runnings about, they ride as it were at nature's anchor, just as the rider indicates the right road to his horse as it proceeds under rein and bridle. But the free and self-ruled reason in man, though it discovers various deviations here and there and innovations, has not lost all clear and evident trace of nature.

2. Observe that regarding marriage whatsoever occurs among the beasts is in accordance with nature. First, they do not legislate against celibacy and too late marriage, as the fellow-citizens of Lycurgus and Solon did, nor have they had to fear the disgrace of childlessness, nor do they sue for the rewards for having three children, as many of the Romans marry and beget children, not that they may have heirs, but that they may be able to inherit. Furthermore the male does not unite with the female at all times. For he does not have pleasure as his end, but begetting and child-bearing, In the proper season which has fruitful breezes and temperature suitable for impregnation, the female, submissive and desired, unites with the male, attractive because of the sweet odor of flesh and the beauty of body, replenished with dew and pure grass. And when she feels that she has conceived and is full, she decorously withdraws and takes thought for the development and delivery of her young. It is not possible to describe their behavior fittingly, except that in each of them is tender care in their forethought, in their patience, in their continence. We call the honey-bee wise and hold in honor the " yellow maker of honey," flattering her for the sweet taste which tickles our palate. But the wisdom and art of the other animals concerning child-birth and education we overlook. For an obvious example, the halcyon, having conceived, puts together a nest by gathering the thorny sea-spines [36] and weaving these in and out and joining them together she gives them the round and long appearance of a fisherman's net, and when she has made the spines tight by fitting them closely together she places them high on the sea beach, so that, softly stroked by the waves and solidified, the surface becomes watertight, and it becomes harder than iron and stone. But what is more wonderful, so symmetrically fashioned to the size and measure of the halcyon is the opening of the nest that no other animal larger or smaller can enter it, and, as they say, it does not let in the sea even to the slightest degree. And again the sharks generate their young in themselves and permit them to go out of their bodies and to feed, after which they take them up and enfold them sleeping in their bowels. And the bear, the most savage and sullen of beasts, gives birth to a shapeless cub without joints, but shaping its sinews with the tongue as with a tool, she seems not only to have given birth to her young but to have created it. [He proceeds to give other instances of parental devotion among the beasts.] Are we therefore to believe that Nature has produced these feelings in these animals out of forethought for the offspring of

---

[36] An unidentified plant. The Greek word means literally a " needle " and is used of fir-needles.

hens and bitches and bears, and not to put us to shame and wound our pride, when we consider that she furnishes these as examples for those who follow her and as a reproach to the hard-hearted for their apathy, because of which they accuse human nature alone of not having the gift of parental affection or the understanding of disinterested love? For he is amazed who says in the play, "What man loves a man for pay?"; and yet, according to Epicurus, it is thus that a father loves his son, a mother her children, children their parents. But if there were comprehension of speech in the beasts, and some one were to assemble into a common theatre horses and cattle and dogs and birds, and, translating into their language, were to call out that "neither dogs love their puppies for pay nor horses their colts nor birds their chicks, but as a gift of nature," it would be recognized by the feelings of all that it was well and truly spoken. For it is a disgrace, O Zeus, that the procreation of the beasts and their child-bearing and their labor-pains and rearing of their young should be natural and free, whereas those of men are loans and hire and deposits made from self-interest.

3. But this argument is neither true nor worth listening to; for Nature, just as in wild plants, such as the grape, the fig, the wild olive, she has implanted immature and imperfect beginnings of cultivated fruits, so in the irrational animals she has placed care for offspring of an imperfect sort and insufficient for righteousness, and not greater than needed; but man, a rational and social animal, made for justice and law and reverence to the gods and the building of cities and kindliness, she has provided with noble and beautiful and fruitful seeds of these things, love for offspring and affection, following after the first rudiments, which were incorporated into the constitution of man's body. For in all ways Nature is exact and ingenious and unfailing and unadorned, "having no clap-trap about her," as Erasistratus said; but it is not possible to speak fittingly about birth, nor decent perhaps to put with great precision in words and phrases the secrets involved; but in reserved and obscure speech one must consider the natural adaptation of the members of generation and child-bearing. The preparation and economy of lactation suffice to illustrate Nature's forethought and care. . . . [He gives an account of this process of lactation.] But there would be no use for such organs of generation and for such arrangement and liberality and forethought if nature did not instil affection and watchfulness in mothers. "For what is more miserable than man of all the things that live and crawl on earth?"[37] This would be true if it referred to newborn infants. For there is nothing so incomplete or helpless or naked or shapeless or foul as man when seen at birth. To him almost alone Nature has given an impure road into the light of day; smeared all over with blood and filth, and more like one who has been slaughtered than one who has been born, he can be handled and carried and kissed and hugged by no one except one who loves him by nature. Wherefore the teats of the other animals hang down from the belly, but on woman they grow up on the breast within reach of the child, so that she may love and embrace him and pull

[37] *Iliad*, XVII, 446.

them down to him, as if the end of child-bearing and rearing were not self-interest but love.

4. Turn now the discussion upon the ancients, of whose wives it was the lot first to bear children and who first saw a child born. They had no law prescribing child-feeding, nor expectation of reward, nor had they nurses " lending themselves to babies." But I should rather say that the mothers would be angry and revengeful towards the children they had borne, since they were a great danger and labor to them. " And as when a sharp arrow pierces a woman in labor, and the Ilithyiai, daughters of Hera, helpers of women in childbirth, draw it out, for they know bitter pain " — these verses, women say, were written not by Homer but by some daughter of Homer who had borne children or was still bearing them, and knew the sting of pain when it shot piercing and swift in the womb. But the natural love of offspring guided and controlled the mother. Even while still hot and suffering and shaken with labor she did not transgress against the child or flee from it, but turned to it and smiled upon it and caught it up to her and embraced it, though experiencing nothing agreeable or to her advantage, but suffering painfully and in toil, and she " made it warm in its swaddling clothes and soothed it, turning from the labor of the night to the labor of the day." Were such things done for pay or for self-interest? But this is true of our own mothers. For their hopes are vague and for the distant future. He who has planted his vines at the vernal equinox gathers his fruit in the autumn; he who has sown wheat when the Pleiades are setting, reaps it when they rise; cattle and horses and birds bear young which are equipped for the satisfaction of their needs. But the education of man is full of toil and his growth is slow, and most fathers die before their children have attained much excellence. Neocles did not see the victory of Themistocles at Salamis, nor did Miltiades see that of Cimon at the Eurymedon, nor did Xanthippus hear Pericles addressing the people, nor did Ariston hear Plato philosophizing, nor did their fathers know of the triumphs of Euripides and Sophocles. They heard them babbling their first syllables, and they saw their games and carousals and love-affairs and whatever mistakes young men make. So that this verse alone of Evenus is praised and remembered, in which he wrote, " A boy is fear and grief for his father during his whole life."

But nevertheless men do not cease to educate their sons, especially they who need sons the least. For it would be laughable to think that the rich make sacrifices and rejoice when children are born to them, because they will have someone to care for them in their old age and to bury them. Unless, by Zeus, they raise children for lack of heirs. For is it not possible to find or meet anyone willing to receive the patrimony of another? " Neither sand nor ashes nor the feathers of the birds of varied song would make up so great a number " as that of heirs. " Danaus the father of fifty daughters," if he had been childless, would have had more heirs, and not like those he had. For children do not thank nor honor their parents, because they expect a legacy as their due. But you may hear strangers who hang about the childless man talking after the fashion of the comic verses: " O Demos, when you have decided a single suit, wash first, then eat, drink, gobble, take your juryman's pay." And this saying of Euripides, " Money has found friends for men and has the greatest power in human affairs," is not absolutely true, but is true in the case of the childless. The rich give them banquets, the leaders show them every attention, the orators plead only their causes gratis — " a rich man whose heir is unknown has the greatest power." Therefore the birth of one child has made many who had numbers of friends and were highly honored, friendless and powerless. Thus nothing conducive to power comes from children. But the whole force of nature is not less in men than in beasts.

5. For both these and many other feelings are obscured by vices, like shrubs growing amongst wild seeds. Or should we say that man does not even love himself by nature, because many cut their throats and throw themselves off heights? And Oedipus " raising his head tore out his eyes, and straightway his bloody sockets stained his cheeks." And Hegesias by argument persuaded many of his auditors to starve themselves to death. " Many are the forms of fate." But these things are like those diseases and passions of the soul which turn man away from that which is according to nature, as men themselves testify against themselves. For should a sow tear to pieces her young or a bitch her puppy, men become alarmed and troubled and make sacrifices to the gods to avert the portent, and consider it an evil omen, since for all creatures it is in accordance with nature and befitting to love their offspring and nurture them, not to do away with them. But just as in metals gold, though mixed with much earth and covered over, nevertheless shines through, so nature in the midst of sinful deeds and passions causes parental love to shine forth. For paupers do not rear their children from fear that they, if reared, will become worse than is becoming, slavish, ignorant, and lacking all that is excellent. For poverty they consider the worst of evils, and resolve not to hand it on to their children, as if it were a severe and great disease. . . .[38]

It was Plutarch's *Gryllus*, however, which had the greatest influence in later times, for it was imitated in the sixteenth century by G.-B. Gelli, who was read by Montaigne and imitated by a host of lesser writers.[39] The defender of animalitarianism, one of the companions of Ulysses, speaks from experience, having been transformed by Circe into a pig.

XIII, 17. *Bruta animalia ratione uti* (Translation on p. 415).

3. ΓΡ. Καὶ ἡμεῖς τοίνυν λέγειν. ἀρκτέον δὲ πρῶτον ἀπὸ τῶν ἀρετῶν, ἐφ' αἷς ὁρῶμεν ὑμᾶς μέγα φρονοῦντας, ὡς τῶν θηρίων πολὺ καὶ δικαιοσύνῃ καὶ φρονήσει καὶ ἀνδρείᾳ καὶ ταῖς ἄλλαις ἀρεταῖς διαφέροντας. ἀπόκριναι δή μοι, σοφώτατ' ἀνδρῶν· ἤκουσα γάρ σου ποτὲ διηγουμένου τῇ Κίρκῃ περὶ τῆς τῶν Κυκλώπων γῆς, ὡς οὔτ' ἀρουμένη τὸ παράπαν, οὔτε τινὸς εἰς αὐτὴν φυτεύοντος οὐδέν, οὕτως ἐστὶν ἀγαθὴ καὶ γενναία τὴν φύσιν, ὥσθ' ἅπαντας

---

[38] The rest is lacking. The sources of the quotations are not given in the translation, except in one case, since they are quoted with the Greek text.

[39] For a list of the better known of these imitations, see G. Boas, *The Happy Beast*, Baltimore, 1933, p. 35 f. The central idea of the dialogue is anticipated by Menander. See XIII, 9, p. 395, above.

ἐκφέρειν τοὺς καρποὺς ἀπ᾿ αὐτῆς· πότερον οὖν ταύτην ἐπαινεῖς μᾶλλον ἢ τὴν
αἰγίβοτον Ἰθάκην καὶ τραχεῖαν, ἢ μόλις ἀπ᾿ ἔργων τε πολλῶν καὶ διὰ πόνων
μεγάλων μικρὰ καὶ γλίσχρα καὶ μηδενὸς ἄξια τοῖς γεωργοῦσιν ἀναδίδωσι;
καὶ ὅπως οὐ χαλεπῶς οἴσεις, παρὰ τὸ φαινόμενον εὐνοίᾳ τῆς πατρίδος ἀπο-
κρινόμενος.

ΟΔ. Ἀλλ᾿ οὐ δεῖ ψεύδεσθαι· φιλῶ μὲν γὰρ καὶ ἀσπάζομαι τὴν ἐμαυτοῦ
πατρίδα καὶ χώραν μᾶλλον, ἐπαινῶ δὲ καὶ θαυμάζω τὴν ἐκείνων.

ΓΡ. Οὐκοῦν τοῦτο μὲν οὕτως ἔχειν φήσομεν, ὡς ὁ φρονιμώτατος ἀνθρώπων
ἄλλα μὲν οἴεται δεῖν ἐπαινεῖν καὶ δοκιμάζειν ἄλλα δ᾿ αἱρεῖσθαι καὶ ἀγαπᾶν,
ἐκεῖνο δ᾿ οἶμαί σε καὶ περὶ τῆς ψυχῆς ἀποκεκρίσθαι· ταὐτὸν γάρ ἐστι τῷ περὶ
τῆς χώρας, ὡς ἀμείνων ἥτις ἄνευ πόνου τὴν ἀρετὴν ὥσπερ αὐτοφυῆ καρπὸν
ἀναδίδωσιν.

ΟΔ. Ἔστω σοι καὶ τοῦθ᾿ οὕτως.

ΓΡ. Ἤδη οὖν ὁμολογεῖς τὴν τῶν θηρίων ψυχὴν εὐφυεστέραν εἶναι πρὸς
γένεσιν ἀρετῆς καὶ τελειοτέραν· ἀνεπίτακτος γὰρ καὶ ἀδίδακτος ὥσπερ ἄσπορος
καὶ ἀνήροτος ἐκφέρει καὶ αὔξει κατὰ φύσιν τὴν ἑκάστῳ προσήκουσαν ἀρετήν.

ΟΔ. Καὶ τίνος ποτ᾿ ἀρετῆς, ὦ Γρύλλε, μέτεστι τοῖς θηρίοις;

4. ΓΡ. Τίνος μὲν οὖν οὐχὶ μᾶλλον ἢ τῷ σοφωτάτῳ τῶν ἀνθρώπων; σκόπει
δὲ πρῶτον, εἰ βούλει, τὴν ἀνδρείαν, ἐφ᾿ ᾗ σὺ φρονεῖς μέγα καὶ οὐκ ἐγκαλύπτῃ
'θρασύς' καὶ 'πτολίπορθος' ἀποκαλούμενος, ὅστις, ὦ σχετλιώτατε, δόλοις
καὶ μηχαναῖς ἀνθρώπους ἁπλοῦς καὶ γενναῖον εἰδότας πολέμου τρόπον ἀπάτης
δὲ καὶ ψευδῶν ἀπείρους παρακρουσάμενος, ὄνομα τῇ πανουργίᾳ προστίθης τῆς
ἀρετῆς ἥκιστα πανουργίαν προσιεμένης. ἀλλὰ τῶν γε θηρίων τοὺς πρὸς
ἄλληλα καὶ πρὸς ὑμᾶς ἀγῶνας ὁρᾷς ὡς ἄδολοι καὶ ἄτεχνοι καὶ μετ᾿ ἐμφανοῦς
γυμνοῦ τε τοῦ θαρρεῖν πρὸς ἀληθινῆς ἀλκῆς ποιοῦνται τὰς ἀμύνας· καὶ οὔτε
νόμου καλοῦντος οὔτ᾿ ἀστρατείας δεδοικότα γραφὴν ἀλλὰ φύσει φεύγοντα τὸ
κρατεῖσθαι μέχρι τῶν ἐσχάτων ἐγκαρτερεῖ καὶ διαφυλάττει τὸ ἀήττητον· οὐ
γὰρ ἡττᾶται κρατούμενα τοῖς σώμασιν οὐδ᾿ ἀπαγορεύει ταῖς ψυχαῖς ἀλλὰ ταῖς
μάχαις ἐναποθνήσκει. πολλῶν δὲ θνησκόντων ἡ ἀλκὴ μετὰ τοῦ θυμοειδοῦς
ἀποχωρήσασά ποι καὶ συναθροισθεῖσα περὶ ἕν τι τοῦ σώματος μόριον ἀν-
θίσταται τῷ κτείνοντι καὶ πηδᾷ καὶ ἀγανακτεῖ, μέχρι ἂν ὥσπερ πῦρ ἐγ-
κατασβεσθῇ παντάπασι καὶ ἀπόληται. δέησις δ᾿ οὐκ ἔστιν οὐδ᾿ οἴκτου
παραίτησις οὐδ᾿ ἐξομολόγησις ἥττης, οὐδὲ δουλεύει λέων λέοντι καὶ ἵππος
ἵππῳ δι᾿ ἀνανδρίαν, ὥσπερ ἄνθρωπος ἀνθρώπῳ. . . . οἷς δὴ μάλιστα δῆλον
ὅτι τὰ θηρία πρὸς τὸ θαρρεῖν εὖ πέφυκε. τοῖς δ᾿ ἀνθρώποις ἡ παρρησία καὶ
παρὰ φύσιν ἐστίν· ἐκεῖθεν δ᾿ ἄν, ὦ βέλτιστ᾿ Ὀδυσσεῦ, μάλιστα καταμάθοις·
ἐν γὰρ τοῖς θηρίοις ἰσορροπεῖ πρὸς ἀλκὴν ἡ φύσις καὶ τὸ θῆλυ τοῦ ἄρρενος
οὐδὲν ἀποδεῖ, πονεῖν τε τοὺς ἐπὶ τοῖς ἀναγκαίοις πόνους ἀγωνίζεσθαί τε τοὺς
ὑπὲρ τῶν τέκνων ἀγῶνας. . . . ἀλλ᾿ ἐκ τούτων γε δῆλόν ἐστιν, ὅτι τοῖς
ἀνδράσιν οὐ φύσει μέτεστι τῆς ἀνδρείας· μετῆν γὰρ ἂν ὁμοίως καὶ ταῖς
γυναιξὶν ἀλκῆς. ὥσθ᾿ ὑμεῖς, κατὰ νόμων ἀνάγκην οὐχ ἑκούσιον οὐδὲ βουλο-
μένην ἀλλὰ δουλεύουσαν ἔθεσι καὶ ψόγοις καὶ δόξαις ἐπήλυσι καὶ λόγοις
πλαττομένην, μελετᾶτε ἀνδρείαν· καὶ τοὺς πόνους ὑφίστασθε καὶ τοὺς
κινδύνους, οὐ πρὸς ταῦτα θαρροῦντες ἀλλὰ τῷ ἕτερα μᾶλλον τούτων δεδιέναι.
ὥσπερ οὖν τῶν σῶν ἑταίρων ὁ φθάσας πρῶτος ἐπὶ τὴν ἐλαφρὰν ἀνίσταται
κώπην, οὐ καταφρονῶν ἐκείνης ἀλλὰ δεδιὼς καὶ φεύγων τὴν βαρυτέραν· οὕτως
ὁ πληγὴν ὑπομένων, ἵνα μὴ λάβῃ τραύματα, καὶ πρὸ αἰκίας τινὸς ἢ θανάτου
πολέμιόν τινα ἀμυνόμενος οὐ πρὸς ταῦτα θαρραλέος ἀλλὰ πρὸς ἐκεῖνα δειλός
ἐστιν. οὕτω δ᾿ ἀνεφάνη ὑμῖν ἡ μὲν ἀνδρεία δειλία φρόνιμος οὖσα, τὸ δὲ
θάρσος φόβος ἐπιστήμην ἔχων τοῦ δι᾿ ἑτέρων ἕτερα φεύγειν. ὅλως δέ, εἰ πρὸς
ἀνδρείαν οἴεσθε βελτίους εἶναι τῶν θηρίων, τί ποθ᾿ ὑμῶν οἱ ποιηταὶ τοὺς
κράτιστα τοῖς πολεμίοις μαχομένους 'λυκόφρονας' καὶ 'θυμολέοντας' καὶ
'συῒ εἰκέλους ἀλκήν' προσαγορεύουσιν, ἀλλ᾿ οὐ λέοντά τις αὐτῶν 'ἀνθρω-

πόθυμον᾿ οὐ σὺν ʻἀνδρὶ εἴκελον ἀλκήν᾿ προσαγορεύει· ἀλλ᾿ ὥσπερ οἶμαι τοὺς
ταχεῖς ʻποδηνέμους᾿ καὶ τοὺς καλοὺς ʻθεοειδεῖς᾿ ὑπερβαλλόμενοι ταῖς εἰκόσιν
ὀνομάζουσιν, οὕτω τῶν δεινῶν μάχεσθαι πρὸς τὰ κρείττονα ποιοῦνται τὰς
ἀφομοιώσεις. αἴτιον δέ, ὅτι τῆς μὲν ἀνδρείας οἷον βαφή τις ὁ θυμός ἐστι
καὶ στόμωμα· τούτῳ δ᾿ ἀκράτῳ τὰ θηρία χρῆται πρὸς τοὺς ἀγῶνας, ὑμῖν δὲ
προσμιγνύμενος πρὸς τὸν λογισμὸν ὥσπερ οἶνος πρὸς ὕδωρ ἐξίσταται παρὰ
τὰ δεινὰ καὶ ἀπολείπει τὸν καιρόν. ἔνιοι δ᾿ ὑμῶν οὐδ᾿ ὅλως φασὶ χρῆναι παρα-
λαμβάνειν ἐν ταῖς μάχαις τὸν θυμὸν ἀλλ᾿ ἐκποδὼν θεμένους νήφοντι χρῆσθαι
τῷ λογισμῷ, πρὸς μὲν σωτηρίας ἀσφάλειαν ὀρθῶς πρὸς δ᾿ ἀλκὴν καὶ ἄμυναν
αἴσχιστα λέγοντες. πῶς γὰρ οὐκ ἄτοπον αἰτιᾶσθαι μὲν ὑμᾶς τὴν φύσιν,
ὅτι μὴ κέντρα προσέφυσε τοῖς σώμασι μηδ᾿ ἀμυντηρίους ὀδόντας μηδ᾿ ἀγκύλους
ὄνυχας, αὐτοὺς δὲ τῆς ψυχῆς τὸ σύμφυτον ἀφαιρεῖν ὅπλον καὶ κολούειν;

5. ΟΔ. Παπαί, ὦ Γρύλλε, δεινός μοι δοκεῖς γεγονέναι σοφιστής, ὅς γε
καὶ νῦν ἐκ τῆς συηνίας φθεγγόμενος οὕτω νεανικῶς πρὸς τὴν ὑπόθεσιν ἐπι-
κεχείρηκας. ἀλλὰ τί οὐ περὶ τῆς σωφροσύνης ἐφεξῆς διεξῆλθες;

ΓΡ. Ὅτι ᾤμην σε τῶν εἰρημένων πρότερον ἐπιλήψεσθαι· σὺ δὲ σπεύδεις
ἀκοῦσαι τὸ περὶ τῆς σωφροσύνης, ἐπεὶ σωφρονεστάτης μὲν ἀνὴρ εἶ γυναικός,
ἀπόδειξιν δὲ σωφροσύνης αὐτὸς οἴει δεδωκέναι, τῶν Κίρκης ἀφροδισίων περι-
φρονήσας. καὶ τούτῳ μὲν οὐδενὸς τῶν θηρίων διαφέρεις πρὸς ἐγκράτειαν·
οὐδὲ γὰρ ἐκεῖνα τοῖς κρείττοσιν ἐπιθυμεῖ πλησιάζειν ἀλλὰ καὶ τὰς ἡδονὰς καὶ
τοὺς ἔρωτας πρὸς τὰ ὁμόφυλα ποιεῖται. οὐ θαυμαστὸν μὲν οὖν ἐστιν, εἰ
καθάπερ ὁ Μενδήσιος ἐν Αἰγύπτῳ τράγος λέγεται πολλαῖς καὶ καλαῖς συν-
ειργνύμενος γυναιξὶν οὐκ εἶναι μίγνυσθαι πρόθυμος ἀλλὰ πρὸς τὰς αἶγας
ἐπτόηται μᾶλλον, οὕτω σὺ χαίρων ἀφροδισίοις συνήθεσιν οὐ θέλεις ἄνθρωπος
ὢν θεᾷ συγκαθεύδειν. τὴν δὲ Πηνελόπης σωφροσύνην μυρίαι κορῶναι κρώζουσαι
γέλωτα θήσονται καὶ καταφρονήσουσιν, ὧν ἑκάστη, ἂν ἀποθάνῃ ὁ ἄρρην, οὐκ
ὀλίγον χρόνον ἀλλ᾿ ἐννέα χηρεύει γενεὰς ἀνθρώπων· ὥστε σοι τὴν καλὴν
Πηνελόπην ἐννάκις ἀπολείπεσθαι τῷ σωφρονεῖν ἧς βούλει κορώνης.

6. ᾿Αλλ᾿ ἐπεί σε μὴ λέληθα σοφιστὴς ὤν, φέρε χρήσωμαι τάξει τινὶ τοῦ
λόγου, τῆς μὲν σωφροσύνης ὅρον θέμενος κατὰ γένος δὲ τὰς ἐπιθυμίας
διελόμενος. ἡ μὲν οὖν σωφροσύνη βραχύτης τίς ἐστιν ἐπιθυμιῶν καὶ τάξις,
ἀναιροῦσα μὲν τὰς ἐπεισάκτους καὶ περιττὰς καιρῷ δὲ καὶ μετριότητι κοσμοῦσα
τὰς ἀναγκαίας. ταῖς δ᾿ ἐπιθυμίαις ἐνορᾷς που μυρίαν διαφοράν, καὶ τὴν μὲν
περὶ τὴν βρῶσιν καὶ τὴν πόσιν ἅμα τῷ φυσικῷ καὶ τὸ ἀναγκαῖον ἔχουσαν·
αἱ δὲ τῶν ἀφροδισίων αἷς ἀρχὰς ἡ φύσις ἐνδίδωσιν, ἔστι δέ που καὶ μὴ
χρώμενον ἔχειν ἱκανῶς ἀπαλλαγέντα, φυσικαὶ μὲν οὐκ ἀναγκαῖαι δ᾿ ἐκλήθησαν.
τὸ δὲ τῶν μήτ᾿ ἀναγκαίων μήτε φυσικῶν ἀλλ᾿ ἔξωθεν ὑπὸ δόξης κενῆς δι᾿
ἀπειροκαλίαν ἐπικεχυμένων γένος ὑμῶν μὲν ὀλίγου δεῖν τὰς φυσικὰς ἀπέκρυψεν
ὑπὸ πλήθους ἁπάσας, ἔχει δὲ καθάπερ ξένος ὄχλος ἔπηλυς ἐν δήμῳ κατα-
βιαζόμενος πρὸς τοὺς ἐγγενεῖς πολίτας. τὰ δὲ θηρία παντάπασιν ἀβάτους
καὶ ἀνεπιμίκτους ἔχοντα τοῖς ἐπεισάκτοις πάθεσι τὰς ψυχὰς καὶ τοῖς βίοις
πόρρω τῆς κενῆς δόξης ὥσπερ θαλάσσης ἀπῳκισμένα τῷ γλαφυρῶς καὶ περιττῶς
διάγειν ἀπολείπεται· τὸ δὲ σωφρονεῖν καὶ μᾶλλον εὐνομεῖσθαι ταῖς ἐπιθυμίαις,
οὔτε πολλαῖς συνοικούσαις οὔτ᾿ ἀλλοτρίαις, σφόδρα διαφυλάττεται. ἐμὲ γοῦν
ποτε καὶ αὐτὸν οὐχ ἧττον ἢ σὲ νῦν ἐξέπληττε μὲν χρυσὸς ὡς κτῆμα τῶν ἄλλων
οὐδενὶ παραβλητὸν ᾕρει δ᾿ ἄργυρος καὶ ἐλέφας. . . . ἀλλὰ νῦν ἀπηλλαγμένος
ἐκείνων τῶν κενῶν δοξῶν καὶ κεκαθαρμένος χρυσὸν μὲν καὶ ἄργυρον ὥσπερ
τοὺς ἄλλους λίθους περιορῶν ὑπερβαίνω, ταῖς δὲ σαῖς χλανίσι καὶ τάπησιν
οὐδὲν ἂν μὰ Δι᾿ ἥδιον ἢ βαθεῖ καὶ μαλθακῷ πηλῷ μεστὸς ὢν ἐγκατακλιθείην
ἀναπαυόμενος. τὰ δὲ τοιαῦτα τῶν ἐπεισάκτων ἐπιθυμιῶν οὐδεμία ταῖς ἡμετέραις
ἐνοικίζεται ψυχαῖς· ἀλλὰ τὰ μὲν πλεῖστα ταῖς ἀναγκαίαις ὁ βίος ἡμῶν ἐπιθυμίαις καὶ ἡδοναῖς διοικεῖται, ταῖς δ᾿ οὐκ ἀναγκαίαις ἀλλὰ φυσικαῖς μόνον
οὔτ᾿ ἀτάκτως οὔτ᾿ ἀπλήστως ὁμιλοῦμεν.

7. Καὶ ταύτας γε πρῶτον διέλθωμεν. ἡ μὲν οὖν πρὸς τὰ εὐώδη καὶ κινοῦντα
ταῖς ἀποφοραῖς τὴν ὄσφρησιν οἰκείως ἡδονὴ πρὸς τῷ τὸ ὄφελος καὶ προῖκα
καὶ ἁπλοῦν ἔχειν ἅμα χρείαν τινὰ συμβάλλεται τῇ διαγνώσει τῆς τροφῆς.
ἡ μὲν γὰρ γλῶττα τοῦ γλυκέος καὶ δριμέος καὶ αὐστηροῦ γνώμων ἐστί τε
καὶ λέγεται, ὅταν τῷ γευστικῷ προσμιγέντες οἱ χυμοὶ σύγχυσίν τινα λάβωσιν·
ἡ δ' ὄσφρησις ἡμῶν πρὸ τῶν χυμῶν γνώμων οὖσα τῆς δυνάμεως ἑκάστου πολὺ
τῶν βασιλικῶν προγευστῶν σκεπτικώτερον διαισθανομένη, τὸ μὲν οἰκεῖον εἴσω
παρίησι τὸ δ' ἀλλότριον ἀπελαύνει καὶ οὐκ ἐᾷ θιγεῖν οὐδὲ λυπῆσαι τὴν γεῦσιν
ἀλλὰ διαβάλλει καὶ κατηγορεῖ τὴν φαυλότητα πρὶν ἢ βλαβῆναι· τἆλλα δ'
οὐκ ἐνοχλεῖ, καθάπερ ὑμῖν, τὰ θυμιάματα καὶ κινάμωμα καὶ νάρδους καὶ φύλλα
καὶ καλάμους Ἀραβικούς, μετὰ δεινῆς τινος καὶ δευσοποιοῦ φαρμακίδος
τέχνης, ᾗ μυρεψικῆς ὄνομα, συνάγειν εἰς ταὐτὸ καὶ συμφοιτᾶν [40] ἀναγκάζουσα,
χρημάτων πολλῶν ἡδυπάθειαν ἄνανδρον καὶ κορασιώδη καὶ πρὸς οὐδὲν οὐδαμῶς
χρήσιμον ὠνουμένους. ἀλλὰ καίπερ οὖσα τοιαύτη διέφθαρκεν οὐ μόνον πάσας
γυναῖκας ἀλλὰ καὶ τῶν ἀνδρῶν ἤδη τοὺς πλείστους, ὡς μηδὲ ταῖς αὑτῶν ἐθέλειν
συγγίγνεσθαι γυναιξίν, εἰ μὴ μύρων ὑμῖν ὀδωδυῖαι καὶ διαπασμάτων εἰς ταὐτὸ
φοιτῶεν. ἀλλὰ κάπρους τε σύες καὶ τράγους αἶγες καὶ τἆλλα θήλεα τοὺς
συννόμους αὑτῶν ταῖς ἰδίαις ὀσμαῖς ἐπάγεται, δρόσου τε καθαρᾶς καὶ λειμώνων
ὀδωδότα καὶ χλόης συμφέρεται πρὸς τοὺς γάμους ὑπὸ κοινῆς φιλοφροσύνης,
οὐχὶ θρυπτόμεναι μὲν αἱ θήλειαι καὶ προϊσχόμεναι τῆς ἐπιθυμίας ἀπάτας καὶ
γοητείας καὶ ἀρνήσεις, οἱ δ' ἄρρενες ὑπ' οἴστρου καὶ μαργότητος ὠνούμενοι
μισθῶν καὶ πόνου καὶ λατρείας τὸ τῆς γενέσεως ἔργον, ἄδολον δὲ σὺν καιρῷ
καὶ ἄμισθον Ἀφροδίτην μετιόντες, ἢ καθ' ὥραν ἔτους ὥσπερ φυτῶν βλάστην
ἐγείρουσα τῶν ζῴων τὴν ἐπιθυμίαν εὐθὺς ἔσβεσεν, οὔτε τοῦ θήλεος προσιεμένου
μετὰ τὴν κύησιν οὔτε πειρῶντος ἔτι τοῦ ἄρρενος. οὕτω μικρὰν ἔχει καὶ ἀσθενῆ
τιμὴν ἢ ἡδονὴ παρ' ἡμῖν τὸ δ' ὅλον ἡ φύσις. ὅθεν οὔτ' ἄρρενος πρὸς ἄρρεν
οὔτε θήλεος πρὸς θῆλυ μῖξιν αἱ τῶν θηρίων ἐπιθυμίαι μέχρι γε νῦν ἐννόηκασιν.
ὑμῶν δὲ πολλὰ τοιαῦτα τῶν σεμνῶν καὶ ἀγαθῶν· ἐῶ γὰρ τοὺς οὐδενὸς
ἀξίους . . .

8. Οὕτω δὲ φαῦλοι καὶ ἀκρατεῖς περὶ τὰς εἰρημένας ἐπιθυμίας ὄντες ἔτι
μᾶλλον ἐν ταῖς ἀναγκαίαις ἐλέγχονται πολὺ τῷ σωφρονεῖν ἀπολειπόμενοι τῶν
θηρίων. αὗται δ' εἰσὶν αἱ περὶ βρῶσιν καὶ πόσιν· ὧν ἡμεῖς μὲν τὸ ἡδὺ μετὰ
χρείας τινὸς ἀεὶ λαμβάνομεν· ὑμεῖς δὲ τὴν ἡδονὴν μᾶλλον ἢ τὸ κατὰ φύσιν
τῆς τροφῆς διώκοντες ὑπὸ πολλῶν καὶ μακρῶν κολάζεσθε νοσημάτων, ἅπερ
ἐκ μιᾶς πηγῆς ἐπαντλούμενα τῆς πλησμονῆς τοῖς σώμασι παντοδαπῶν πνευ-
μάτων καὶ δυσκαθάρτων ὑμᾶς ἐμπίμπλησι. πρῶτον μὲν γὰρ ἑκάστῳ γένει ζῴου
μία τροφὴ σύμφυλός ἐστι, τοῖς μὲν πόα τοῖς δὲ ῥίζα τις ἢ καρπός· ὅσα δὲ
σαρκοφαγεῖ, πρὸς οὐδὲν ἄλλο τρέπεται βορᾶς εἶδος οὐδ' ἀφαιρεῖται τῶν
ἀσθενεστέρων τὴν τροφήν· ἀλλ' ἐᾷ νέμεσθαι καὶ λέων ἔλαφον καὶ λύκος
πρόβατον ᾗ πέφυκεν. ὁ δ' ἄνθρωπος ἐπὶ πάντα ταῖς ἡδοναῖς ὑπὸ λαιμαργίας
ἐξαγόμενος καὶ πειρώμενος πάντων καὶ ἀπογευόμενος, ὡς οὐδέπω τὸ πρόσφορον
καὶ οἰκεῖον ἐγνωκώς, μόνος γέγονε τῶν ὄντων παμφάγος. . . .

9. ἀλλ' ἡ τῶν θηρίων φρόνησις τῶν μὲν ἀχρήστων καὶ ματαίων τεχνῶν
οὐδεμιᾷ χώραν δίδωσι· τὰς δ' ἀναγκαίας οὐκ ἐπεισάκτους παρ' ἑτέρων οὐδὲ
μισθοῦ διδακτὰς οὐδὲ κολλῶσα μελέτῃ καὶ συμπηγνύουσα γλίσχρως τῶν
θεωρημάτων ἕκαστον πρὸς ἕκαστον ἀλλ' αὐτόθεν ἐξ αὑτῆς οἷον ἰθαγενεῖς καὶ
συμφύτους ἀναδίδωσι. τοὺς μὲν γὰρ Αἰγυπτίους πάντας ἰατροὺς ἀκούομεν
εἶναι, τῶν δὲ ζῴων ἕκαστον οὐ μόνον πρὸς ἴασιν αὐτότεχνόν ἐστιν ἀλλὰ καὶ
πρὸς διατροφὴν καὶ πρὸς ἀλκὴν θήραν τε καὶ φυλακὴν καὶ μουσικῆς ὅσον
ἑκάστῳ προσήκει κατὰ φύσιν. παρὰ τίνος γὰρ ἡμεῖς ἐμάθομεν νοσοῦντες ἐπὶ
τοὺς ποταμοὺς χάριν τῶν καρκίνων βαδίζειν; τίς δὲ τὰς χελώνας ἐδίδαξε τῆς

---

[40] Adopting Wyttenbach's reading in place of συμφαγεῖν.

ἔχεως φαγούσας τὴν ὀρίγανον ἐπεσθίειν· τὰς δὲ Κρητικὰς αἶγας, ὅταν περι-
πέσωσι τοῖς τοξεύμασι, τὸ δίκταμνον διώκειν, οὗ βρωθέντος ἐκβάλλουσι τὰς
ἀκίδας; ἂν γὰρ εἴπῃς, ὅπερ ἀληθές ἐστι, τούτων διδάσκαλον εἶναι τὴν φύσιν,
εἰς τὴν κυριωτάτην καὶ σοφωτάτην ἀρχὴν ἀναφέρεις τὴν τῶν θηρίων φρόνησιν·
ἣν εἰ μὴ λόγον οἴεσθε δεῖν μηδὲ φρόνησιν καλεῖν, ὥρα σκοπεῖν ὄνομα κάλλιον
αὐτῇ καὶ τιμιώτερον, ὥσπερ ἀμέλει καὶ δι' ἔργων ἀμείνονα καὶ θαυμασιωτέραν
παρέχεται τὴν δύναμιν· οὐκ ἀμαθὴς οὐδ' ἀπαίδευτος, αὐτομαθὴς δέ τις μᾶλλον
οὖσα καὶ ἀπροσδεής, οὐ δι' ἀσθένειαν ἀλλὰ ῥώμῃ καὶ τελειότητι τῆς κατὰ
φύσιν ἀρετῆς, χαίρειν ἐῶσα τὸν παρ' ἑτέρων διὰ μαθήσεως τοῦ φρονεῖν
συνερανισμόν. ὅσα γοῦν ἄνθρωποι τρυφῶντες ἢ παίζοντες εἰς τὸ μανθάνειν
καὶ μελετᾶν ἄγουσι, τούτων ἡ διάνοια καὶ παρὰ φύσιν τοῦ σώματος καὶ
περιουσίᾳ συνέσεως ἀναλαμβάνει τὰς μαθήσεις. ἐῶ γὰρ ἰχνεύειν σκύλακας
καὶ βαδίζειν ἐν ῥυθμῷ πώλους μελετῶντας, ἀλλὰ κόρακας διαλέγεσθαι καὶ
κύνας ἄλλεσθαι διὰ τροχῶν περιφερομένων. ἵπποι δὲ καὶ βόες ἐν θεάτροις
κατακλίσεις καὶ χορείας καὶ στάσεις παραβόλους καὶ κινήσεις οὐδ' ἀνθρώποις
πάνυ ῥᾳδίας ἀκριβοῦσιν ἐκδιδασκόμενοι καὶ μνημονεύοντες εὐμαθείας ἐπίδειξιν
εἰς ἄλλο οὐδὲν οὐδαμῶς χρήσιμον ἔχουσιν. εἰ δ' ἀπιστεῖς ὅτι τέχνας μανθάνομεν,
ἄκουσον ὅτι καὶ διδάσκομεν. αἵ τε γὰρ πέρδικες ἐν τῷ προφεύγειν τοὺς
νεοττοὺς ἐθίζουσιν ἀποκρύπτεσθαι καὶ προΐσχεσθαι βῶλον ἀνθ' ἑαυτῶν τοῖς
ποσὶν ὑπτίους ἀναπεσόντας· καὶ τοῖς πελαργιδεῦσιν ὁρᾷς ἐπὶ τῶν τεγῶν ὡς
οἱ τέλειοι παρόντες ἀναπειρωμένοις ὑφηγοῦνται τὴν πτῆσιν. αἱ δ' ἀηδόνες
τοὺς νεοσσοὺς προδιδάσκουσιν ᾄδειν· οἱ δὲ ληφθέντες ἔτι νήπιοι καὶ τραφέντες
ἐν χερσὶν ἀνθρώπων χεῖρον ᾄδουσιν, ὥσπερ πρὸ ὥρας ἀπὸ διδασκάλου γεγονότες.
καταδὺς δ' εἰς τουτὶ τὸ σῶμα θαυμάζω τοὺς λόγους ἐκείνους, οἷς ἀνεπειθόμην
ὑπὸ τῶν σοφιστῶν ἄλογα καὶ ἀνόητα πάντα πλὴν ἀνθρώπου νομίζειν.

10. ΟΔ. Νῦν μὲν οὖν, ὦ Γρύλλε, μεταβέβλησαι σύ, καὶ τὸ πρόβατον
λογικὸν ἀποφαίνεις καὶ τὸν ὄνον;

ΓΡ. Αὐτοῖς μὲν οὖν τούτοις, ὦ βέλτιστε Ὀδυσσεῦ, μάλιστα δεῖ τεκ-
μαίρεσθαι τὴν τῶν θηρίων φύσιν, ὡς λόγου καὶ συνέσεως οὐκ ἔστιν ἄμοιρος.
ὡς γὰρ οὐκ ἔστι δένδρον ἕτερον ἑτέρου μᾶλλον οὐδ' ἧττον ἄψυχον, ἀλλ' ὁμοίως
ἔχει πάντα πρὸς ἀναισθησίαν· οὐδενὶ γὰρ αὐτῶν ψυχῆς μέτεστιν· οὕτως οὐκ
ἂν ἐδόκει ζῷον ἕτερον ἑτέρου τῷ φρονεῖν ἀργότερον εἶναι καὶ δυσμαθέστερον,
εἰ μὴ πάντα λόγου καὶ συνέσεως, ἄλλα δὲ μᾶλλον καὶ ἧττον ἄλλων πως
μετεῖχεν. ἐννόησον δ' ὅτι τὰς ἐνίων ἀβελτερίας καὶ βλακείας ἐλέγχουσιν
ἑτέρων πανουργίαι καὶ δριμύτητες, ὅταν ἀλώπεκι καὶ λύκῳ καὶ μελίττῃ παρα-
βάλῃς ὄνον καὶ πρόβατον· ὥσπερ εἰ σαυτῷ τὸν Πολύφημον ἢ τῷ πάππῳ σου
τῷ Αὐτολύκῳ τὸν Κορίνθιον ἐκεῖνον Ὅμηρον. οὐ γὰρ οἶμαι θηρίου πρὸς
θηρίον ἀπόστασιν εἶναι τοσαύτην, ὅσον ἄνθρωπος ἀνθρώπου τῷ φρονεῖν καὶ
λογίζεσθαι καὶ μνημονεύειν ἀφέστηκεν.[41]

3. *Gryllus.* Let us then speak. But we must begin first with the
virtues upon which you rate yourselves so highly, saying that you
differ greatly from the beasts in justice, prudence, fortitude, and
others. Now answer me, wisest of mortals; I have heard you telling
a story to Circe of the land of the Cyclôpes, which, though neither
ploughed nor planted by any one, is so good and fertile that it bears
all sorts of fruits and herbs spontaneously. Do you prefer this
country or your own goat-feeding and stony Ithaca, which, being
cultivated with great labor and hardship, yet returns to the husbandmen only a small and scanty crop? Do not be angry and answer contrary to the evidence from love of your country.

[41] Ed. Bernardakis, Leipzig, 1895, VI.

Ulysses. But there is no need to lie. I love and honor my own fatherland and country more; but I praise and admire theirs.

Gryllus. Hence we must conclude that things are as the wisest of men has said: that there are some things to be praised and approved, others to be preferred by choice and affection. And I suppose you to believe the same concerning the soul. For the same is true in regard to the soul as the country; that the best produces virtue like spontaneous fruit, without labor and toil.

Ulysses. Let it be as you have said.

Gryllus. Then you confess that the souls of beasts are the more perfect and more fertile in the production of virtue; for without any command or instruction — as if unsown and unploughed — they produce and increase according to nature that virtue which is fitting for each.

Ulysses. And in what kind of virtue, Gryllus, do the beasts share?

4. *Gryllus.* Rather ask in what virtues they do not share in a higher degree than the wisest of men? Look, if you please, upon fortitude in the first place, of which you boast so much, nor do you hide your head when called " the bold " and the " city-stormer," when indeed, knave that you are, by tricks and artifices you deceive men who understand only the simple and noble way of making war, ignorant altogether of fraud and falsehood, and by giving to your knavery the name of virtue, which never admits knavery. But you should observe the combats of beasts, both one against another as well as against yourselves, how straightforward and artless they are, and how with an open and naked courage they defend themselves with genuine strength. And afraid neither of the law that conscripts them nor that against deserters, but fleeing battle at the dictates of nature alone, they hold out to the last and protect the unconquered. For they are not conquered when their bodies are worsted, nor do they give in to their feelings, but they die in battle. And though many are dying, their strength withdraws into the spirited part somewhere and, collecting itself in some organ of the body, takes its stand against the victor, and pants and fumes until at length it fails like a fire that goes out. But there is no crying for quarter, no begging of mercy, no acknowledgement of being beaten; nor will the lion be a slave to another lion, nor the horse to a horse, from cowardice, as one man is a slave to another. . . .

Whence it is apparent that the beasts are naturally inclined to be courageous. But that the daring of men is contrary to nature, most noble Ulysses, you may especially learn from this. In beasts nature keeps an equal balance of strength and the female is in no way inferior to the male, but undergoes all necessary toils and fights in defence of her young. . . . [He gives examples.] From this it is apparent that women do not by nature share fortitude with men, for if they did, there would be equal strength in both. So that you exercise a fortitude necessitated by law, not free and voluntary, but subservient to customs and censure, made up of words and adventitious opinion. And yet you undergo labor and dangers, not out of real valor, but because you are more afraid of other things. Therefore, as among your companions he that first makes haste to snatch up the light oar does it not because he despises it, but because he is afraid of and shuns the heavier, so he that endures a blow to avoid a wound and defends himself against an enemy to preserve himself from wounds and death, does it not out of courage against the latter but out of fear of the former. Thus your fortitude appears to be prudent fear; and your courage a knowing timidity, which understands how to do one thing in order to avoid another.

In short, if you believe yourselves superior to the beasts in fortitude, why do your poets call those who fight most valiantly against their enemies, "wolf-breasted," "lion-hearted," and compare them to wild boars; but never call lions "man-hearted," or compare the strength of the wild boar to that of a man? But as they call the swift "wind-footed" and the beautiful "godlike," hyperbolizing in their similes, so they make their comparisons of the fearful in battle with their superiors. The reason is because the coloring and testing of fortitude is courage. The beasts make use of this unmixed in their combats, but in you, being mixed with reason, like wine diluted with water, it gives way before danger and loses its opportunity. And some of you deny that courage is generally needed in battle, and therefore, laying it aside, make use of reason, speaking well insofar as defensive security is concerned but shamefully in regard to strength and vengeance. Is it not, therefore, beside the point for you to complain of Nature, because she did not furnish your bodies with goads and teeth and crooked claws to defend yourselves, when at the same time you would deprive the soul of her natural weapons and curtail them?

5. *Ulysses.* Ah me, Gryllus, you seem to me to have become a fearful sophist, grunting from your hog's snout and yet arguing so vigorously to your point. But why have you not all this while discoursed on temperance?

Gryllus. Because I thought you would first contradict what I have already said. But you are in haste to hear what I have to say concerning temperance, both because you are the husband of a very chaste wife and you believe yourself to have set us an example of temperance by despising the charms of Circe. And yet in this you differ in no wise from the beasts in self-control, for neither do they desire to have intercourse with their betters, but they find their pleasures and loves among those of their own species. It is no wonder then, if — like the Mendesian goat in Egypt, which, it is said, when shut up with several beautiful women, was never stirred to copulate with them, but was passionately excited by she-goats — you, though greatly given to erotic pleasures, since you are a man do not wish to lie with a goddess. And thousands of crows, cawing about the fame of Penelope's chastity, make it laughable and expose it to contempt, for each of them, if the male dies, remains a widow, not for a short period, but for nine generations of men; so that any one of those crows surpasses in chastity your fair Penelope nine times over.

6. But since you believe me to a sophist, I shall follow a certain order in my speech, defining temperance, and then dividing desire according to its several kinds. Temperance, then, is the limitation and

ordering of our desires, abolishing the superfluous and extravagant and ruling those that are necessary by a sense of fitness and moderation. In desires you may observe a thousand variations.[42] The desire for meat and drink is both natural and necessary, but erotic desires which have their source in nature may be restrained without any inconvenience. These are therefore called natural but not necessary. Those, however, which are neither natural nor necessary, but instilled from without by vain opinion, through want of a sense of decency, come very close to concealing all your natural desires with their number, like a foreign horde pouring into a country and swamping the native citizens. But the beasts, having souls unsullied and unmixed with adventitious passions, and living lives as distant from vain opinion as from the sea, are inferior to you in the elegance and luxury of their living, but their temperance and their control of their desires require no protection against many internal and external longings. Formerly gold struck me myself no less than it now strikes you as a possession comparable to no other, and silver and ivory had me in their power. . . . But now, altogether freed and purged of those vain opinions, I tread gold and silver under my feet as I do other minerals; nor did I ever sleep more sweetly in your blankets and rugs than I now do, by Zeus, covered over in deep soft mud. None of those adventitious desires resides in our souls, but for the most part our life is accustomed to necessary desires and pleasures; and as for those pleasures which are not necessary but only natural, we enjoy them only with order and moderation.

7. Let us then consider these. The pleasure peculiarly affecting the sense of smell with sweet odors and effluvia, besides having an inherent value which is simple and freely given, also is serviceable for distinguishing foods. For the tongue is said to be the judge of sweet, sour, and tart, only when the juices are mingled with the faculty of taste and have become fused with it. But our smell, before the taste, being the judge of the power of each thing, distinguishes more accurately than the royal tasters, and on the one hand admits what is proper and on the other rejects whatever is unsuitable. Neither does it permit it to touch or molest the taste, but accuses and declares its harmfulness before it does any injury. Yet it does not trouble us with other things, as it does you, with incense, cinnamon, nard, malobathrum, and Arabian reed, forced to unite and interpenetrate with a kind of fearful and deep-dyed apothecary's art, called "unguent-boiling," and at great expense to furnish unmanly and girlish delight, profitable or useful for nothing whatsoever. But being such, it has not only corrupted all women but most men, so that they are unwilling to unite with their own wives, unless they embrace all perfumed with ointments and powders. But sows, she-goats, and other females attract the boars, he-goats, and the males of their species by their own proper scents, and smelling of the pure dew, the meadows, and the fresh grass, they are stimulated to copulation by common affection. The females without coquetry or the practice of tricks and charms and false refusals excite desire and the males, stimulated with rage and frenzy, do not purchase the act of generation with wages and labor and servi-

---

[42] For the division of desires which follows, cf. IV, 26, p. 153, above.

tude, but seek a guileless and unpaid Aphrodite at the proper season, a goddess who in the spring, as she puts forth the buds of plants, likewise awakens the desires of animals, but immediately quenches them again, so that neither the female admits the male after conception nor the male attempts to mount the female. And thus pleasure has but small and weak honor among us, but Nature is everything. So that even to this very day the desires of the beasts never stimulate the coupling of male with male and female with female. But many examples of such things are found among your honored and good, for I pass by those not worthy of remembrance. . . . [He gives examples.]

8. Since men are so wicked and persistent in the desires we have been speaking of, they are proved to be more intemperate than the beasts, even in those things which are necessary, that is, in eating and drinking. The pleasure of these things we always enjoy with reference to utility. But you, pursuing the pleasure rather than the natural end of eating, are punished with many great diseases, which, arising from the single fountain of superfluity, fill your bodies with all sorts of spirits difficult to expel. Now for each species of beast exists one sort of food, which is in conformity to its nature; for some there is grass, for some roots, and for others fruits. Those which are carnivorous never feed on any food other than meat, nor do they rob the weaker of their nourishment. But the lion permits the deer, and the wolf the sheep, to feed upon their natural diet. Man, however, driven by his gluttony, eats everything for his pleasures' sake. He tries all things, tastes all things; and, as if he did not know what was his proper and characteristic food, alone of all creatures is omnivorous. . . .

9. The prudence of the beasts has no place for useless and vain arts. And the necessary are not given them by others nor taught for pay, neither by study do they build up and glue their theorems clammily together, one upon the other, but each learns from himself alone whatever is of his own nature and innate. Now we hear that the Egyptians are all physicians, but each of the beasts is not only innately endowed with the art of healing but also with that of procuring its food and building up its strength, and of self-defence, and of music, too, so far as is proper for them according to their nature. For from whom did we hogs learn to run to the rivers, when we are sick, to look for crabs? Who taught the tortoises, when they have eaten vipers, to take origanum? Who taught the Cretan goats, when shot with arrows that stick in their bodies, to take dittany, which when eaten expels the darts? If you should say — what is true — that Nature is the teacher of these things, you acknowledge the prudence of the beasts to have the most authoritative and wisest source. If you think one ought not to call this reason and prudence, it is time for you to find out a finer and more honorable name for it, as, it cannot be denied, it exhibits a power greater in its effects and more wonderful than either — not untaught nor without education, but self-taught rather and complete; not weak, but because of the vigor and perfection of its natural virtue caring nothing for the gathering in of prudence which others attain by instruction. Whatever, moreover, men in their luxury and sport do through learning and study, our understanding acquires even when it is contrary to

the nature of our bodies, because of our excellent powers of comprehension. For think of puppies that learn to track the quarry and colts that learn to dance in rhythm; of crows that speak and dogs that leap through whirling hoops. Horses also and bulls in the theatre have been taught to lie down, to dance, to assume perilous postures and movements very difficult even for men, and, since they remember them, they prove that they can learn even things which are useless to them. If you doubt that we learn arts, know that we teach them too. For partridges teach their young to escape the hunter by concealment, lying upon their backs with a clump of earth in their claws. And you may observe the old storks upon the house tops guiding their young when they first try out their wings. Nightingales teach their young to sing, and those which have been caught when young and bred by hand sing worse, as if they had been taken away from their teachers before the proper time. So that since I have been put in this body, I wonder at those arguments by which I was persuaded by the sophists to believe that all creatures except men were devoid of reason and mind.

10. *Ulysses.* Now then, Gryllus, that you are changed, do sheep and asses also appear rational to you?

Gryllus. From these very creatures, best of men, Ulysses, the nature of the beasts is especially to be observed as it is, neither devoid of reason nor understanding. For as one tree is neither more nor less than another without a soul, but all are alike in their insensibility — for none of them is endowed with soul — so it would seem that no animal would be slower than another in understanding nor more unteachable than another, if all did not partake of reason and understanding, though some in a less, some in a greater degree. But you must consider that the stupidity and laziness of some is proof of the cleverness and subtlety of others, when you compare a fox, a wolf, or a bee with a sheep or ass. The same would appear if you should compare yourself to Polyphemus, or your grandfather, Autolycus, with Homer's Corinthian. For I do not believe there is such difference between beast and beast in reason and understanding and memory, as between man and man.[43]

---

[43] Translation based on that of Sir A. J., which first appeared in the late seventeenth century and was reprinted in Boston in 1871.

The concluding sentence in our quotation was reproduced by Montaigne in his *Apology for Raymond Sebond*, causing a veritable scandal in the seventeenth century, See *Essais*, ed. Villey, Paris, 1922, II, 183. Many of the themes illustrated in the above passages appear again, as a part of the argument for Scepticism, in Sextus Empiricus, *Hyp.* I, 60-78; see R. G. Bury's ed., *Loeb Class. Lib.*, 36 ff.

I. PRIMITIVISM IN ANCIENT WESTERN ASIA (MESOPOTAMIA AND ISRAEL)

BY

W. F. ALBRIGHT

In pre-Hellenic Western Asia there existed, properly speaking, only one great culture, that of the Tigris-Euphrates Valley, with its three main geographical divisions, Babylonia, Assyria, and Northwestern Mesopotamia. For practical purposes most recent writers include all three under the term " Mesopotamia," following good classical precedent. All surrounding cultures of that age, including the Elamite, the Mitannian, the Hittite, the Phoenician, the Israelite, and other less commonly known ones, are, strictly speaking, branches of it, though the degree of dependence varied greatly, and influences radiating from Egypt and the Aegean were by no means negligible, especially in Palestine and Syria. Nor should we underestimate the significance of local features of relatively autonomous origin. Only the Mesopotamian cuneiform literature and the partly contemporary literature of Israel provide us with enough material to study the spread of ideas coming under the general designation of " primitivism."

PRIMITIVISM IN MESOPOTAMIA

Thanks to the vast and constantly increasing mass of published cuneiform literature, covering three millennia, according to the lowest chronological estimate, we are extremely well informed today with regard to Babylonian thought. During the eighty years that have elapsed since this literature became first accessible, as a result of the brilliant combinations of the first decipherers (1845-1855),[1] there has been steady progress in its interpretation, through the use of the rigidly scientific method introduced by Friedrich Delitzsch, the founder of the Assyriological school which prevails today.[2] Systematic analysis of Babylonian thought has in general kept pace with the interpretation of the texts, though premature attempts to reduce it to a rigid system by Lenormant,[3] and later by Hugo Winckler,[4]

---

[1] The best account of the decipherment of cuneiform is still that of Rogers, *History of Babylonia and Assyria*, Vol. I, chapters I-VII.

[2] Delitzsch and Haupt were the founders of the modern school of cuneiform grammar and lexicography; cf. the writer's remarks, *Beiträge zur Assyriologie*, Vol. X, 2, p. xiii ff.; *Oriental Studies Dedicated to Paul Haupt* (Leipzig, 1926), p. xxi ff.

[3] See especially *La magie chez les Chaldéens* (Paris, 1874) and the German and English editions of this work.

[4] His views are scattered through the volumes of his *Altorientalische Forschungen*, as well as through numerous brochures. The most convenient sketch of them will

Alfred Jeremias,[5] and Hermann Schneider,[6] have done nearly as much harm as good.

Owing to the complexity and difficulty of the cuneiform script, as well as to other causes, the literature and learning of Mesopotamia were almost exclusively in the hands of priestly guilds, which formed narrow circles of specialists, jealous of their prestige and power. Thus there was a guild of *bārū,* who devoted themselves exclusively to divination, a guild of *kalū,* or temple musicians, etc., etc.[7] The scribes (*ṭupsharru*) were much given, especially in certain periods, to deliberate mystification, by which they made it more difficult for outsiders to penetrate into the arcana. At the same time, their love of systematization and habit of cataloguing everything in sight make it possible for the modern scholar to do what the layman could not have done then without insuperable difficulties. The frequent injunction in the colophons of late copies of mythological and magical texts, " let the adept (literally, ' knower ') instruct the adept " (*mūdū mūdā likallim*), is very characteristic of the priestly attitude toward their knowledge.[8]

The inevitable result of guarding inherited wisdom, especially in a society where intellectual progress was as slow as it was during most periods of Mesopotamian history, was to over-emphasize the antiquity of this wisdom. Hence the Babylonians traced it back to the antediluvian age, to the time of the kings who were before the Flood (*sharrāni sha lam abūbi*).[9] These kings, whose number varies from eight to ten in different recensions of the cuneiform royal lists, reigned from 10,800 to 72,000 years each, the numbers varying in the three known recensions.[10] The kings of the earlier postdiluvian dynasties only receive up to 1200 years each in the four available recensions of the royal lists,[11] a reduction showing that the

be found in his *Himmels- und Weltenbild der Babylonier,* Leipzig, 1901. Winckler founded the so-called pan-Babylonian school, whose only living representative is Alfred Jeremias; cf. *Jour. Am. Or. Soc.* Vol. LIV, pp. 124-6.

[5] See especially his work, *Handbuch der altorientalischen Geisteskultur,* 2nd ed. Berlin, 1929. In a later brochure, *Der Kosmos von Sumer* (Leipzig, 1932), the same author indulges in even wilder speculations, verging dangerously close to theosophy. Students who are not Assyriologists cannot be warned too strongly against the views of Jeremias.

[6] *Kultur und Denken der Babylonier und Juden,* Leipzig, 1910.

[7] The best general account of the priestly classes or guilds is given by Meissner, *Babylonien und Assyrien,* Vol. II (Heidelberg, 1925), p. 61 ff.

[8] Cf. Jeremias, *Handbuch der altorientalischen Geisteskultur,* Leipzig, 1913, p. 13, but care must be taken not to follow him in his extreme deductions with regard to the existence of a " Geheimlehre."

[9] Cf. Zimmern in Schrader's *Keilinschriften und das Alte Testament,* 3rd ed. p. 537.

[10] See Langdon, *Oxford Editions of Cuneiform Texts,* Vol. II (London, 1923), p. 1 ff.

[11] Published by Poebel, *Historical Texts,* Philadelphia, 1914 (see especially Ungnad, *Zeitschrift für Assyriologie,* Vol. XXXIV, p. 1 ff.); Langdon, *op. cit.;* Scheil, *Revue d'Assyriologie,* Vol. XXXI (1934), p. 149 ff.

Babylonians regarded the age of man as becoming progressively less. While there are gaps and uncertainties in detail, the two main recensions assigned a duration of 432,000 or 456,000 years, respectively, to the antediluvian age. The principal recensions agree on placing the Deluge at a date which would correspond to between 34,000 and 35,000 B. C.

According to Babylonian mythological tradition, all wisdom was taught men by seven beings known as the "ancient *apkallē* who were before the Flood (*sha lam abūbi*)." [12] To judge from the explanations given in the cuneiform vocabularies, the term *apkallu* meant "master of a craft, branch of learning; wise man *par excellence.*" Two different forms of the myth of the seven prediluvian master wise men are known to us. According to one of them, found in several texts, the seven came from seven early Babylonian cities, and are represented as monsters (*ūmu*) with bird-faces or with fish-bodies. [13] According to the other, the seven arose from the sea in the reigns of different antediluvian kings. [14] These monsters, the first of whom was the famous Oannes (Bab. *uwwānu,* "master craftsman"), were also provided with fish-bodies. There can be no doubt that the fish-bodies mean that the monsters in question were regarded, at least at one stage of the growth of this myth, as the offspring of Ea, god of wisdom, normally represented as having the body of a fish and the upper part of a wild goat. Since Ea was the god of the sea, the origin of the secondary form of the myth, deriving the monsters from the sea, is clear. In no case can the Oannes myth be utilized for any conclusions with reference to supposed southern origin of the Sumerian civilization.

The natural corollary to this conception of the primeval origin of wisdom was that there was no wisdom at the very beginning of man's existence; man lived a life like that of the animals, free both from the benefits and from the pains of organized sedentary society. It is clear from several passages in cuneiform literature that the Babylonians were keenly aware of the differences between themselves and the nomads, and between themselves and the animals. As a rule, the nomads are spoken of with contempt, and the inferiority of animals is stressed, but a striking exception is found in the Gilgamesh Epic, especially in its Old Babylonian recension (dating from about the twentieth century B. C. in its present form). [15]

In the Gilgamesh Epic we are told that the goddess Aruru (otherwise

---

[12] See Zimmern, *loc. cit.*

[13] Zimmern, *Zeitschrift für Assyriologie,* Vol. XXXV, pp. 151-4.

[14] See Zimmern, *Die Keilinschriften und das Alte Testament,* 3rd ed. p. 535 ff.; Langdon, *op. cit.* p. 4.

[15] The best edition of the cuneiform text of the Gilgamesh Epic is now that of Thompson, *The Epic of Gilgamesh,* Oxford, 1930, and the best translation is that of Schott, *Das Gilgamesh-Epos,* Leipzig (Reclam), 1934. Cf. also Thompson, *The Epic of Gilgamish,* London, 1928, and Ebeling in Gressmann's *Altorientalische Texte zum Alten Testament,* 2nd ed. pp. 150-198.

known as the creatress of mankind) moulded and gave life to an anthropoid being of heroic form, called Engidu. The latter wandered over the plain with the gazelles, hairy and naked, eating grass and drinking water with the beasts. When the hunter tried to attack the animals as they came to the watering place, Engidu opposed him, and forced him to give up the hunt. Finally the hunter appealed to Gilgamesh, king of Erech, who sent a sacred courtesan to seduce the wild man. The latter went to Engidu's haunts, disrobed herself before him, and he had intercourse with her for seven days and nights. Weary of the liaison, Engidu tried to return to his gazelles, but they fled before him; "the beasts of the field fled from his body"—which had been corrupted by its contact with civilization. Then the erstwhile wild man gave way to despair, until the woman persuaded him to follow her to Erech. She divided her clothing with him, took him to a camp of shepherds, where she fed him milk and bread, followed by seven great measures of beer. Thereafter he washed his body, anointed his skin, put on men's clothing, and turned his newly found weapons against the beasts, protecting the shepherds. There can be no doubt that this story has important points of contact with the biblical story of the Fall of Man.[16]

The story of Engidu reflects the condition of the first men, which is described in the so-called Uttu poem, written down in Sumerian before the end of the third millennium B. C.[17] Enki (Ea), god of the sea, and his consort Ninsikilla were assigned a place by the gods in the island of Tilmun (modern Baḥrein in the Persian Gulf). Before Enki's first intercourse with his consort the condition of mankind is described with the following words:

> " In Tilmun the raven did not cry,
> The *dar* (bird) did not utter the *dar's* cry,
> The lion did not slay,
> The wolf did not carry off the lambs,
> The dog did not (attack) the resting kids,
>
> The doves did not lay (eggs),
> A sick eye did not say, 'I am a sick eye,'
> A sick head did not say, 'I am a sick head,'
> An old man did not say, 'An old man am I.'
> An old woman did not say, 'An old woman am I,'
>
> 'A man has dug a canal,' one did not say,
> An overseer did not go around in his arrogance (?),
> 'A liar has lied (?),' one did not say."

[16] For the interpretation of this episode see Jastrow, *Am. Jour. Sem. Lang.* Vol. XV, p. 200 ff. (antiquated, but still suggestive); Gressmann, *Das Gilgamesch-Epos* (Göttingen, 1911), pp. 92-101; Albright, *Jour. Am. Or. Soc.* Vol. XL, 319 ff. 327 ff.

[17] See Langdon, *Sumerian Epic of Paradise, the Flood, and the Fall of Man*, Philadelphia, 1915; Albright, *Jour. Am. Or. Soc.* Vol. XXXIX, 65 ff. (with the literature there cited); Witzel, *Keilinschriftliche Studien*, part 1 (1918), p. 51 ff.; Langdon, *Le poème sumérien du paradis*, Paris, 1919; Albright, *Jour. Am. Or. Soc.* Vol. XLII, p. 197 ff.

Several obscure lines are omitted from this rendering. The picture illustrated by the above lines is that of a state of life where wild beasts were peaceful and did not prey on one another, where there was no disease or old age, where there was no sexual intercourse and no offspring (stated more explicitly, it would seem, by some of the untranslated lines), where there was no agriculture (no irrigation), and no organized society — in other words, a primeval paradise. The rest of the poem, so far as preserved, is mainly devoted to a description of the *hieros gamos* of Enki and his consort, which brought fertility into existence, with the creation of plants and gods particularly stressed. Since its interpretation is beset with difficulties, owing mainly to the elliptic style, we need not discuss the rest.

Another Sumerian poem from the same period, and from the same Uttu cycle, also describes the condition at the beginning, when mankind had been created, but had not learned the art of living.[18] Men did not know how to make bread or beer, or clothing of woven stuff, but lived in the reed-thicket. Then they were taught how to plant grain, to raise domestic animals, and to build houses of brick, etc.

The existence of different accounts of man's beginnings, and of different, often mutually exclusive, cosmogonies, almost inevitably led to the development of a theory of successive world-ages. When equally sacred myths and narratives were handed down to a scribal school, a very common way of harmonizing them was to keep everything, either by incorporating all variants into a composite production, or by simple addition. In this way, heterogeneous myths of cosmogony or cosmology were adopted, the result being a more complex myth or group of myths. An excellent illustration is provided by the Epic of Creation (*enūma elish*), where several cosmogonies are combined into a complex genealogical system.[19] Again, in the Uttu myth cited above we have the motive of the first *hieros gamos* repeated several times, with striking variations, not the least of which is that the goddess appears each time with a different name, derived from the cult of the mother-goddess in a different city.

The clearest account of a succession of creations and destructions is found in the Atrakhasīs Epic, numerous longer and shorter portions of which have survived from different periods.[20] Like most of the cuneiform " epics " of mythological type, the later forms go back to an Old Baby-

---

[18] See Witzel, *Keilinschriftliche Studien*, Part 5 (1925), p. 106 ff.

[19] For analyses of the Creation Epic on the basis of the latest material for its text see Langdon, *The Epic of Creation*, Oxford, 1923, and Furlani, *La religione babilonese-assira*, Vol. II (Bologna, 1929), p. 2 ff.

[20] For recent treatments see Clay, *A Hebrew Deluge Story in Cuneiform*, New Haven, 1922 (the translation is corrected by Luckenbill, *Am. Jour. Sem. Lang.* Vol. XXXIX, p. 153 ff. and Albright, *Am. Jour. Sem. Lang.* Vol. XL, p. 134 f.) ; Ebeling in Gressmann's *Altorientalische Texte*, 2nd ed. pp. 201-6. For new material since these treatments see Boissier, *Revue d'Assyriologie*, 1931, p. 91 ff. and Ebeling, *Tod und Leben nach den Vorstellungen der Babylonier* (Berlin, 1931), pp. 172-7.

lonian recension, put into writing before the nineteenth century B. C. In this text we learn that mankind repeatedly aroused the wrath of the gods, who determined to put an end to the race, once by drought and famine, another time by pestilence, again by a great deluge. Each time man is saved by the intervention of a being named *Atrakhasīs* (lit. " the very wise one "). How many of these partial destructions of the human race were included in the three tablets of the epic we do not know. It would appear, however, that drought was employed twice as a means of extermination, though the fragmentary nature of our document makes it possible that the same episode is recapitulated in different connections. Since at least three separate destructions, perhaps four, are mentioned in the extant portions of the text, and since the number seven plays an important rôle in it, occurring at least three times, it may well be that there were seven partial destructions of mankind. The seven interventions of Atrakhasīs would then correspond to the seven appearances of the master wise men before the Flood. It is interesting to note that the master wise man (*apkallu*) Adapa [21] is also called *Atrakhasīs*.[22] This would indicate a certain relation between the two mythic cycles or conceptions in question. It should be added that the hero of the Flood narrative in the Gilgamesh Epic, Utnapishtim, is also called by the name *Atrakhasīs* in the latter epic,[23] so there can be no doubt that the Flood of the Atrakhasīs Epic is the same as that of the Gilgamesh Epic. In an unpublished paper the writer has called attention to the dependence of the Israelite and especially of the later Jewish Elijah cycle on the Babylonian conception of Atrakhasīs.[24] This idea continues in modified form in the Moslem beliefs about el-Khidhr. The Gnostic conception of the reincarnation of certain ancient worthies in later personages is also characterized by the succession of seven,

---

[21] The demigod Adapa is also called *ummān Adapa* in the so-called " Persian Verse Account of Cyrus," published by Sidney Smith; see the latest treatment by Landsberger and Bauer, *Zeitschrift für Assyriologie*, Vol. XXXVII, p. 90, n. 3, and the previous discussion by Smith and Albright referred to there. Both by the appellations *apkallu* and *ummānu*, and by the fact that he is called " offspring of Eridu " (*mār Eridu*), he is identified with the antediluvian wise men mentioned above, so that Landsberger's suggestion that the curious writing of *ummān* in this passage is connected with the use of the term *ūmu*, " monster," for the seven *apkallē* is confirmed. If we try to identify him with one of the names preserved in Greek transcription by Abydenus and Apollodorus, after Berossus, the best chance is offered by the Ανωδαφος of Abydenus, which may be a corruption of *Ωαναδαφος, a perfect transcription of *Ummān Adapa* (pronounced *Owwanadap* in Neobabylonian); for the latter see especially Zimmern, *Die Keilinschriften und das Alte Testament*, 3rd ed. p. 536.

[22] See Jensen, *Assyrisch-babylonische Mythen und Epen* (Berlin, 1900), p. 92, line 8.

[23] Gilgamesh Epic, XI: 196.

[24] Cf. the abstract printed in the *Johns Hopkins University Circulars, New Series,* 1919, No. 6, p. 22.

and probably depends in part upon the same conceptions, since several of the personages are intimately connected with the Babylonian Flood-hero.[25]

Numerous attempts have been made to connect the cuneiform totals for the duration of the antediluvian period, or of the reigns of individual kings, with Indic mythological speculation. That there is a connection can hardly be doubted, since the *kaliyuga* and the antediluvian age of Berossus both last 432,000 years, a number which can hardly have arisen independently in Babylonia and India. However, nothing like a cycle of world-years has yet been discovered in Mesopotamia. It is highly probable that a " world-year " of 36,000 common years formed by days of a century each was known, for the following reasons. Sargon II of Assyria says in two passages in his inscriptions that an " age of the moon-god " (*adū Nanna*) had elapsed since the last previous conquest of Melukhkha and Cyprus, i. e., since the time of Sargon I of Accad.[26] Now Nabonidus of Babylonia, who lived nearly two hundred years later, fixes that time at 3200 years earlier, evidently following well-established scribal theory. The " age of the moon-god " would thus be 3000 years, or thirty days of a century each.[27] In a recently published text Shamshī-Adad I of Assyria places the end of the Dynasty of Accad seven *dāru* before him, i. e., about seven centuries, according to our best-attested chronological data; the *dāru* (= Arab. *dahr,* " century ") would represent the unit of this system of computation.[28] Again, the Ḥarrānian system reckoned the world-year as 36,525 Julian years, i. e., as a Julian world-year composed of days of a century each.[29] This unit presumably replaced a similar one of 36,000 years, i. e., a luni-solar world-year, such as was employed in ordinary business and astrological computations.

Since the number 36,000 and its multiple, 72,000, occur so frequently in all three recensions of the Babylonian list of antediluvian kings, it seems clear that a conception like that sketched in the preceding paragraph was known to the Babylonians before the end of the third millennium. In the Greek period it is probable that the Mesopotamians launched out into very far-reaching cosmological and astrological speculations, partly based on the discovery of the precession of the equinoxes during the Persian period.[30] There can be little doubt that there is some connection between late Babylonian speculation and the elaborate cosmogonic and cosmological theories

[25] Cf. provisionally Albright, *Am. Jour. Sem. Lang.* Vol. XXXVI, p. 287 ff.

[26] Cf. Jeremias, *Handbuch der altorientalischen Geisteskultur* (Leipzig, 1913), p. 198.

[27] Cf. Albright, *Jour. Am. Or. Soc.* Vol. XLIII, p. 328; *Revue d'Assyriologie,* Vol. XVIII, p. 94, n. 2. Contrast Jeremias, *op. cit.* p. 193 ff.

[28] Cf. Albright, review of Woolley's *Ur Excavations,* Vol. II, in the *American Journal of Archaeology,* 1935.

[29] Chwolsohn, *Die Ssabier und der Ssabismus,* Vol. II, p. 443.

[30] See Schnabel, *Zeitschrift für Assyriologie,* Vol. XXXVII, 1 ff. Schnabel's conclusions have been accepted by virtually all competent historians of astronomy.

of the Hindus, as described by Dumont in the present volume. In the same way, the Indic conception of the seven *dvipas* must be connected in some way with the corresponding Babylonian idea of the seven *nagē* (" districts, islands "), beyond the encircling ocean, and also occupied by strange beings.[31]

PRIMITIVISM IN ISRAEL

Since Palestine lay in the extreme southwestern corner of the basin of Mesopotamian cultural influence, we need not be surprised to find less direct influence from this direction than from the neighboring land of Egypt. This situation is reflected in the literature of Israel, where Egyptian influence is strong, in spite of the numerous ties binding Israel to Mesopotamia. When we survey the principal streams of Mesopotamian influence, we find clear-cut Mesopotamian sources for the stories of the Flood, the antediluvian patriarchs, and the dispersion of mankind, as well as a persistent tradition of the Mesopotamian origin of the Hebrew people. It may be added that the tendency now is to accept the fundamental historicity of this last tradition.[32] We also find strong Canaanite influence on Hebrew literature and Hebrew conceptions, though it is not yet possible to evaluate it. The discovery of part of the long-lost Canaanite mythological literature at Ugarit (Rās esh-Shamrah) since 1930 gives us material for the ultimate solution of this hitherto elusive problem.[33] Canaanite culture, though independent in its later development, was unquestionably influenced considerably by the higher Mesopotamian civilization, and many elements belonging to the latter were transmitted to Israel through the former.

The writer believes that nearly all the stories in the first chapters of Genesis are of North-Mesopotamian origin, and would thus go farther than is warranted by the direct comparison of Hebrew and cuneiform literature. In favor of this view are numerous facts and considerations.[34] Very important negative support may now be derived from the total absence of any reference to these stories in the Canaanite mythology as described by Philo of Byblus and as now found in original texts at Ugarit. We are, therefore, not justified at all in regarding the Hebrew cosmogony as reflecting Canaanite myths.

[31] Cf. Weidner, *Boghazköi-Studien*, Part 6, 1922, p. 85 ff.

[32] Cf. provisionally Böhl, *Das Zeitalter Abrahams*, Leipzig, 1930; Albright, *The Archaeology of Palestine and the Bible* (New York, 1932), pp. 139 f. 209 f. 237; Lewy, " Les textes paléo-assyriens et l'Ancien Testament " (*Revue de l'Histoire des Religions*, Vol. CX, 1934, pp. 29-65), *passim*.

[33] Cf. especially Virolleaud's numerous papers in *Syria* since 1930 and the discussion and bibliography given by Friedrich, *Ras Schamra* (Leipzig, 1933), and Albright, *Journal of the Palestine Oriental Society*, Vols. XII, p. 185 ff. XIV, p. 101 ff.

[34] Since the writer expects to discuss this subject at length in the near future, and there is no space for a lengthy discussion, he refers to his forthcoming treatment elsewhere.

The Israelites shared with the Babylonians the belief in the ten ante-diluvian heroes who lived much longer than more recent men. With them they also shared the belief in a great Flood, marking the end of an era of human activity, as well as the conception of a line of heroes after the Flood, with ages decreasing more or less uniformly until historic times were reached. The Hebrews drew a logical conclusion from this tendency to shorter and shorter lives, that there was a time at the beginning when man was healthier and happier than he ever was in later ages. Consequently, the first man was placed in a primeval paradise, localized in the land of Eden, in the region from which the two Mesopotamian rivers, the Tigris and Euphrates, sprang.[35] That Eden was also the name of a district in northwestern Mesopotamia is probably not accidental.

It is not our purpose to make a literary or documentary analysis of the story of Paradise and the Fall of Man.[36] We note that man lived in a well-irrigated terrestrial paradise, that he was naked, without any arts or crafts, and that he consorted with the animals. Whether man was then immortal does not appear; from the present narrative (Gen. 2: 9, 17) it would seem that he was, but v. 22 suggests the contrary. In any case he was still ignorant of moral distinctions, not having eaten from the forbidden tree " of the knowledge of good and evil." After the Fall this was all changed, just as in the Babylonian story of Engidu, cited above.

There is some reason to believe that the conception of world-ages was not unknown to the Israelites, the first age being brought to a close by the Flood, and the second one by a cataclysm which was to destroy all mankind but a righteous remnant.[37] The increasing wickedness of man after the initial creation, as well as after the Flood, is stressed.

So far the conceptions which we have sketched are not appreciably different from similar ones known from cuneiform literature. Among the Israelites, however, there was a form of cultural primitivism which has not yet been found among the Mesopotamians. This is the nomadic ideal of the prophetic age, to which attention was first called by Budde in 1895.[38]

---

[35] See the discussion and literature cited in the writer's paper, " The Location of the Garden of Eden " (Am. Jour. Sem. Lang. Vol. XXXIX, p. 15 ff.)

[36] For the latest critical literary treatment, with references to the available literature, see Begrich, Zeitschrift für die Alttestamentliche Wissenschaft, Vol. L (1932), p. 93 ff.; for additional material on the mythological and iconographic motives in these stories cf. Albright, Am. Jour. Sem. Lang. Vol. XXXVI, p. 280 ff.

[37] Cf. especially Gunkel, Schöpfung und Chaos in Urzeit und Endzeit (Göttingen, 1895), passim; Jeremias, Das Alte Testament im Lichte des alten Orients, 3rd ed. (Leipzig, 1916), p. 111 ff. Jeremias' theories are in part too strongly influenced by his pan-Babylonian bias to be taken seriously. Attempts to determine the world-age conceptions underlying the numerical system of the P document and later systems (traceable in the Samaritan and Greek recensions of the Pentateuch, as well as in the Book of Jubilees) have recently been made by Bork and Jepsen (Zeitschrift für die Alttestamentliche Wissenschaft, Vol. XLVII (1929), pp. 206 ff. 251 ff.).

[38] Budde's first paper on this subject appeared in The New World, Vol. IV (1895),

According to the Hebrew traditions regarding the Patriarchal Age, the ancestors of Israel were semi-nomads, living partly as shepherds and partly as peasants, but without fixed abode, as a rule.[39] According to these traditions, they were forced to wander in the desert for nearly forty years, between the Exodus and the Conquest of Canaan. Hence the later Israelites had their attention constantly called to the fact that their forefathers did not live as they did, and that increasing luxury and debauchery, as well as loss of property and of personal freedom on the part of the debtor class, could be explained as the result of agricultural life. This explanation was rendered even more plausible by the fact that the disabilities of civilization were not found among the nomads who wandered in the deserts to the east and south of Israel.

It can hardly be accidental that the first recorded instance of this reaction toward the nomadic state of society dates from the middle of the ninth century B. C., when some five generations of organized civic and commercial life from the accession of Solomon to the death of Ahab, had developed the tendency to concentrate wealth and to live luxuriously to a point where both the oppressed classes and the prophetic reformers of the Elijah school became bitter in their opposition. A zealous Yahwist named Jonadab, son of Rechab, probably an adherent of Elijah and Elisha, then commanded his followers, who became known as Rechabites: " You shall drink no wine, neither you nor your sons forever; and you shall build no house, nor sow seed, nor plant, nor own a vineyard; but you shall live in tents all your lives, so that you may live long in the land where you sojourn " (Jer. 35: 6-7). It is true that the testimony comes from a period more than two centuries and a half after the first appearance of Jonadab (II Kings 10: 15-6), but there is no valid reason to doubt the attribution of these prohibitions to him.[40]

In the collections attributed to the prophets Amos, Hosea, Isaiah, Jeremiah, and their contemporaries, from the middle of the eighth century on, there are numerous references to the nomadic ideal. The prophets often refer to the time when Israel was in its infancy and wandered in the desert. They oppose the Yahwistic cult itself, in so far as it was bound up with agricultural ritual of pagan origin. What is even more interesting, they picture the restoration of a pious remnant after the great cataclysm

---

pp. 726-45. For the fullest discussion, with additional references to the literature, see Flight, " The Nomadic Idea and Ideal " (*Jour. Bib. Lit.* Vol. XLII, pp. 158-226), especially p. 209 ff. Like many scholars with a thesis to prove, however, Flight has included passages where the exegesis he offers is not supported by the context. In numerous recent publications of Sellin, especially on the Book of Hosea, the latter has employed this principle with more or less success.

[39] Cf. Albright, *The Archaeology of Palestine and the Bible*, p. 130 ff. with the references there given to the literature on this subject.

[40] Cf. Eduard Meyer, *Die Israeliten und ihre Nachbarstämme* (Halle, 1906), pp. 84 ff. 132 f.

which closes their age, in terms of nomadic life. Thus Hosea says: "And Ephraim said, 'Truly I am rich; I have found myself wealth '— but all his toil will not suffice for the guilt which he has incurred. I am Yahweh your God; from the land of Egypt (I will bring you), and again I will make you live in tents, as in the days of old" (Hos. 12: 9-10). The reference to the land of Egypt is rhetorical; Israel will be brought out of its present sinful and wealth-loving state, just as Israel was brought out of Egypt.

TRACES OF PRIMITIVISM IN EGYPT

In Egypt, which attained the highest degree of cultural refinement reached by the ancient Near East, we find surprisingly few indications of ideas belonging in our horizon. The extraordinary independence of Egypt in its cultural evolution appears here again. This negative evidence can hardly be due to the defectiveness of our information, since every new discovery makes it clearer that a large proportion of the Egyptian literary compositions which had been put into writing, has now been recovered by the Egyptologist, at least in fragmentary form. That this is true appears particularly from the fact that most important Egyptian compositions, as well as many unimportant ones, survive in several papyrus and ostracon copies.

The Egyptians, like the Mesopotamians and Hebrews, believed that the earliest dynasties of their legendary history held sway for fabulously long periods. This we know from the fragments of the Turin Papyrus (thirteenth century B. C.), which establish the antiquity of the material preserved in more or less corrupt form by the successors and epitomizers of Manetho, as well as in the Sothis Book and in Diodorus.[41] Thus, e. g., the Turin Papyrus assigns a total of either $23,200 + x$ or $36,620 + x$ years to all the dynasties before Menes, the first historical king of Egypt. Diodorus allows the period of divine rule a total of nearly 18,000 years, while Eusebius seems to give the first two dynasties of gods 13,900 years. But it is to be noted that dynasties of gods, not of men, are referred to. Similarly, Egyptian cosmogony has a great deal to say about the origin and the history of the gods, but singularly little to tell us about human origins. There is no Flood story and no clear reference to primordial wisdom among the Egyptians. The reign of Osiris and the age of the "Servants of Horus" are referred to not infrequently in Egyptian literature, but there is no suggestion that those ages were paradisaical. It is not until Greek times that we find the reign of Osiris on earth pictured as a golden age. To be sure, future discoveries may show that this conception antedates Greek influence.

In Egyptian secular literature the note of pessimism is exceedingly common, and two whole categories of compositions are essentially pessi-

[41] See Eduard Meyer, *Aegyptische Chronologie* (Berlin, 1904), Ch. IV.

mistic, but neither of them suggests an escape through chronological or cultural primitivism. Times are bad, and are growing worse — but they never were really good. There is no future, no divine justice; man's only escape from misery is through hedonism or through suicide. Many texts of the " prophetic " type describe the degeneracy of the present and predict the return of better times under a new king, but none of them points to a golden age in the past. The oscillation between periods of prosperity and decline seems never to have developed into a theory of world-ages, as among the Mesopotamians.

Lovejoy has well suggested that the remarkably exaggerated interest of the Egyptians in life beyond the tomb reduced their incentive to seek for an emotional escape from present ills in some form of primitivism. Belief in the complex vicissitudes and the rich after-life of the soul in the other world thus took the place of exoticism and cultural primitivism in more sophisticated cultures.

II. PRIMITIVISM IN INDIAN LITERATURE

BY

P.-E. Dumont

The most conspicuous manifestation of primitivism in the Indian literature is the doctrine of the *Yugas*. The orthodox Hindus recognize four
Yugas or ages of the world. They are called *Kṛta, Tretā, Dvāpara* and
Kali after the four sides of the Indian die; *Kṛta,* the lucky one, being the
side marked with four dots, *Tretā* that with three; *Dvāpara* that with two;
Kali, the losing one, that with one dot. These names are very old; they
already occur in the Vedic literature, that is, in texts which are not later
than the ninth century B. C. Still, as in Vedic times the gamblers did not
play with dice marked with dots, but with the nuts of the Vibhīdaka-tree,
the names *Kṛta, Tretā, Dvāpara* and *Kali,* in the Vedic texts, are not the
names of the four sides of the die, but the names of the four throws of
dice in the old game. In one verse of the *Aitareya Brāhmaṇa* the names
Kṛta, Tretā, Dvāpara and *Kali* are already referred, by the commentator,
to the Yugas, but I think that the commentator is wrong.

In the epics and the Purāṇas the belief with regard to the four Yugas
has become a fully established doctrine. The general idea is that the proportion of virtue and the length of each Yuga conform to the number of
dots marked on that side of the die after which it is named. In the *Kṛta
Yuga,* virtue (*dharma*) was perfect and fully present in men, but it diminished by one quarter in every succeeding age till in the *Kali Yuga* only one
quarter of *dharma* remains. The same proportion holds good with regard
to the duration of the several ages. Each of these ages is preceded by a
period called dawn and is followed by another period of equal length called
twilight, each being equal to one-tenth of the Yuga. The duration of the
Yuga is computed by divine years consisting each of 360 human years.
Thus the *Kṛta Yuga* lasts $4000 + 400 + 400 = 4,800$ divine years; the
Tretā Yuga $3000 + 300 + 300 = 3,600$ divine years; the *Dvāpara Yuga*
2400 divine years; the *Kali Yuga* 1200 divine years; and the period of the
four Yugas together, technically called a *Mahāyuga,* 12000 divine years, that
is 4,320,000 human years.[1]

Possessed of the desire to express mythically the infinity of time, the
Hindus have combined the doctrine of the Yugas with the doctrine of the
Kalpas into a fanciful system of universal chronology. According to that
system, one Mahāyuga is followed by another, one thousand of them form
a Kalpa; the Kalpa is the length of time from a creation to a destruction

---

[1] Cf. H. Jacobi's article in Hasting's *Encyclopaedia of Religion and Ethics,* I,
p. 200 ff.

of the world; and there are periodical creations and destructions of the world again and again. Such is the general common doctrine. But we have good reasons to presume that originally the Mahāyuga comprised the whole existence of the world.

From our point of view the interesting fact is that the history of mankind, in the course of that long period which comprises the four Yugas — Kṛta Yuga, Tretā Yuga, Dvāpara Yuga and Kali Yuga — analogous to the four ages of man — childhood, youth, adult life and old age — is conceived as a long degeneration.

This fact clearly appears in the descriptions of the Yugas. There are in the epics and in the Purāṇas many passages which describe either the four Yugas or one of the Yugas. In spite of the prolixity of the style and the useless repetitions usual in the epics, some of these passages are really interesting. The following descriptions I have collected in the Mahābhārata, the Vāyu Purāṇa and the Mārkaṇḍeya Purāṇa will show better than any comment, how primitivism is represented in the Indian doctrine of the four ages of the world.[2]

The Four Ages and Chronological Primitivism

S. E. II, 1.   *Mahābhārata,* Vanaparvan, 149, 11 ff.:

> The Kṛta age is that age in which righteousness is constant. In that age everything had been done (kṛta), and nothing remained to be done. Duties did not then languish; nor did the people decline. In that age there were neither Gods, Dānavas, Gandharvas, Yakṣas, Rākṣasas, nor Pannagas; no buying or selling went on; the Vedas were not classed as Sāman, Ṛg and Yajus; man's life was effortless (there was no manual labor); the fruit of the earth was obtained by mere wish; no disease or decline of the organs of sense arose through the influence of age; there was no malice, weeping, pride or enmity; no contention, no lassitude, no hatred, cruelty, fear, affliction, jealousy, or envy. In that age Nārāyaṇa (Viṣṇu), the soul of all beings, was white. In that age the creatures were devoted to their duties. They were alike in the object of their trust, in their behavior and in their knowledge. In that age, the classes, alike in their functions, fulfilled their duties, were unceasingly devoted to one deity, and used one formula, one rule, one rite. Though they had separate duties they had but one Veda, and practised one duty. By works connected with the four successive orders of life, and dependent on conjunctures of time, but unaffected by desire or hope of reward, they attained the supreme felicity.

S. E. II, 2.   *Mahābhārata,* Vanaparvan, 149, 23 ff.:

> In the Tretā age, sacrifice commenced, righteousness decreased by a fourth, Viṣṇu became red.

---

[2] In the translations of the Mahābhārata I follow J. Muir (*Original Sanskrit Texts*) and Pratāpa Chandra Rāy (*The Mahābhārata*) with some corrections. The translations of the Vāyu Purāṇa are revised from J. Muir's *Original Sanskrit Texts.*

In that age the men were devoted to truth and to righteousness dependent on ceremonies. The sacrifices appeared and various holy rites and ceremonies.

In the Tretā age men acted with an object in view, seeking after reward for their rites and their gifts; and no longer disposed to austerities and to liberality from a simple feeling of duty.

In that age they were devoted to their own various duties and to religious ceremonies.

S. E. II, 3. *Mahābhārata,* Vanaparvan, 149, 27 ff.:

In the Dvāpara age righteousness was diminished by two quarters; Viṣṇu (the supreme Being) became yellow and the Veda fourfold. Some studied four Vedas, others three, others two, others one, and some none at all. The scriptures being thus divided, ceremonies were celebrated in a great variety of ways; and the people, although being occupied with austerities and the bestowal of gifts, became full of passion. Owing to ignorance of the one Veda, Vedas were multiplied. And now from the decline of the quality of goodness few only adhered to truth. When men had fallen away from goodness, many diseases, desires and calamities, caused by destiny, assailed them, by which they were severely afflicted, and driven to practice austerities. Others desiring enjoyments and heavenly bliss, offered sacrifices. Thus, when the men had reached the Dvāpara age, they declined through unrighteousness.

S. E. II, 4. *Mahābhārata,* Vanaparvan, 149, 33 ff.:

In the Kali age righteousness remained to the extent of onefourth only. In that age of darkness Viṣṇu (the supreme Being) became black. Practices enjoined by the Vedas, works of righteousness and rites of sacrifice ceased. Calamities, diseases, fatigue, anger and other faults, distresses, anxiety, hunger, fear prevailed.

Thus, as the ages revolve, righteousness declines, and when righteousness declines, the people also decline.

S. E. II, 5. *Mahābhārata,* Śāntiparvan, Mokṣadharma, 231 (B. 232), 23 ff.:

In the Kṛta age righteousness exists in its entirety along with Truth. No knowledge or object came to man of that age through unrighteous or forbidden means. In the other ages, duty, ordained in the Vedas, is seen to gradually decline by a quarter in each. Sinfulness grows in consequence of theft, untruth, and deception. In the Kṛta age, all persons are free from disease and crowned with success in respect of all their objects, and all live for four hundred years. In the Tretā age the duration of life decreases by a quarter. It has also been heard by us that, in the succeeding ages, the words of the Vedas, the periods of life, the blessings uttered by the Brāhmaṇas and the fruits of Vedic rites, all decrease gradually. The duties set down for the Kṛta age are of one kind; those for the Tretā age are otherwise; those for the Dvāpara age are different; and those for the Kali age are otherwise. This is in accordance with that decline that marks every succeeding age. In the Kṛta, asceticism occupies the foremost place. In the Tretā, knowledge is foremost.

In Dvāpara, sacrifice is said to be the foremost. In the Kali age, only gift is the foremost.

S. E. II, 6. *Mahābhārata,* Śāntiparvan, Mokṣadharma, 268 (B. 267), 18 ff.:

Men of remote and remoter times were capable of being governed with ease. They were very truthful in speech and conduct. They were little disposed to disputes and quarrels. They seldom gave way to wrath, or, if they did, their wrath never became ungovernable. In those days the mere crying of " *fie* " on offenders was sufficient punishment. After this came the punishment represented by harsh speeches or censures. Then followed the punishment of fines and forfeitures. Now, however, the punishment of death has become current. The measure of wickedness has increased to such an extent that even by slaying one, others can not be restrained.

S. E. II, 7. *Mahābhārata,* Śāntiparvan, Mokṣadharma, 268 (B. 267), 32 ff.:

In the Kṛta age, kings should rule their subjects by adopting ways that are entirely harmless. In the Tretā age, kings conduct themselves according to ways that conform with righteousness fallen away by a fourth from its full complement. In the Dvāpara age, they proceed according to ways conforming with righteousness fallen away a half, and in the age that follows, according to ways conforming with righteousness fallen away by three-fourths. When the Kali age sets in, through the wickedness of kings and in consequence of the nature of the epoch itself, fifteen parts of even that fourth portion of righteousness disappear, a sixteenth portion thereof being all that then remains of it. Then, by adopting the first method, that is the practice of harmlessness, anarchy would set in. Therefore, the king should award punishments, considering the period of human life, the strength of human beings, and the nature of the time that has come.

S. E. II, 8. *Mahābhārata,* Śāntiparvan, Mokṣadharma, 207, 37 ff.:

In those times (in the Kṛta age), men lived as long as they chose to live, and were without any fear of Yama (the god of Death). Sexual intercourse was then not necessary for perpetuating the species. In those days offspring were begotten by fiat of the will. In the age that followed, the Tretā age, children were begotten by touch alone. The people of that age even were above the necessity of sexual congress. It was in the next age, in the Dvāpara age, that the practice of sexual intercourse first began to prevail among men. In the Kali age, men have come to marry and live in pairs.

S. E. II, 9. *Mārkaṇḍeya Purāṇa,* 49, 9-11 and 28-29:

At that time, in the Kṛta age, women had no monthly discharge, and they consequently bore no children although sexual intercourse was practised. They brought forth just pairs of children once at the close of life. From that period commenced the birth of twins, and such offspring was once only born to these creatures by a mental effort, in meditation. . . . In the Tretā age, in the course of time, passionate affection sprang up suddenly among human beings. By reason of the occurrence of passionate affection, menstruation occurred month by month, and conception frequently took place.

S. E. II, 10. *Vāyu Purāṇa*, 8, 64-65:

Contemplation is declared to be supreme in the Kṛta age, and knowledge in the Tretā age; sacrifice began in the Dvāpara age; liberality is the highest merit in the Kali age.

The Kṛta age is goodness, the Tretā age is passion, the Dvāpara age is passion and darkness; in the Kali age it is to be understood that darkness prevailed, according to the necessary course of the ages.

S. E. II, 11. *Mahābhārata*, Bhīṣmaparvan; Jambūkhandanirmāna, 10, 5 ff.:

Four thousand years are specified as the duration of life in the Kṛta age, three thousand in the Tretā, and two thousand in the Dvāpara. There is no fixed measure in the Kali age. In the Kali age embryos die in the womb, as well as children after their birth.

In the Kṛta age men of great strength, goodness, wisdom and virtue were born opulent and beautiful, and also munis (ascetics) rich in austere fervour, energetic, mighty, righteous and veracious.

In the Tretā age beautiful, well formed, valorous, bow-carrying, heroic Kṣatriyas, distinguished in battle, were born. In the Tretā age all sovereigns were Kṣatriyas. In the Tretā age heroic Kṣatriyas were born, long-lived, great warriors, excellent archers in the fight, and living subject to authority.

In the Dvāpara age all four classes are produced, energetic, valorous, striving for victory over one another. In the Kali age are born men of little vigour, irascible, covetous and mendacious. During that period envy, pride, anger, delusion, ill-will, desire and cupidity prevail among all beings.

S. E. II, 12. *Mahābhārata,* Vanaparvan, 183, 63 ff.:

The first-born Prajāpati (Lord of the creatures) created the bodies of corporeal creatures pure, spotless, and essentially righteous. The holy men of old, partaking of Brahma's nature, were not frustrated in the results at which they aimed; they were religious and truth-speaking. Being all like gods, they ascended to the sky and returned at will. And they died when they desired, suffered few annoyances, were free from disease, accomplished all their objects, endured no oppression. Self-subdued and free from envy, they beheld the gods and the mighty prophets, and had a clear perception of all duties. They lived for a thousand years and had each a thousand sons.

Then at a later period of time, the inhabitants of the earth became subject to desire and anger and subsisted by deceit and fraud. Governed by cupidity and delusion, devoted to carnal pursuits, the sinful men by their evil deeds walked in crooked paths leading to hell.

S. E. II, 13. *Vāyu Purāṇa,* 8, 47 ff.:

In the Kṛta age the human beings appropriated the food which was produced from the essence of the earth and they acted according to their pleasure, enjoying mental perfection. They were characterized neither by righteousness nor unrighteousness; they were marked by no distinctions. Their age, happiness, and form were alike; they were neither righteous nor unrighteous. They were produced each with authority over himself. . . . They suffered no impediment, no susceptibility to the pairs of opposites (like pleasure and pain, cold and heat), and no fatigue. They frequented mountains and seas, and did not dwell in houses. They never sorrowed, were full of the quality of goodness, and supremely happy; they moved about at will and lived in continual delight. There were at that time no beasts, birds, reptiles, egg-born animals or hellish creatures (for these animals are produced by unrighteousness), no roots, fruits, flowers, productions of the seasons, nor seasons. The time brought with it every object of desire and every enjoyment. There was no excess of heat or cold. Produced from the essence of the earth, the things which those people desired sprang up from the earth everywhere and always, when thought of. That perfection of theirs both produced strength and beauty and annihilated disease. With bodies which needed no decoration, they enjoyed perpetual youth. From their pure will alone twin children were produced. Their birth was the same and their form was the same, and they died together. Then truth, contentment, patience, satisfaction, happiness and self-command prevailed. They were all without distinction in respect of form, term of life, disposition and actions. The means of subsistence were produced spontaneously without forethought on their part. In the Kṛta age they engaged in no works which were either virtuous or sinful. And there were no distinctions of classes or orders, and no mixture of classes. Men acted towards each other without feeling of love or hatred. In the Kṛta age they were all born alike in form and duration of life, without distinction of lower and higher, with abundant happiness, free from grief, with hearts continually exulting, great in dignity and in force. There existed among them no such things as gain or loss, friendship or enmity, liking or dislike. . . . They neither desired anything from one another, nor showed any kindness to each other. . . .

S. E. II, 14. *Vāyu Purāṇa*, 8, 74 ff.:

After the evening of the Kṛta age, the Tretā age succeeded. . . . When the evening of the Kṛta age had died out, perfection disappeared from among the creatures who survived at the commencement of the Tretā age. . . . When that perfection had perished, another perfection arose. The subtle form of water having returned to the sky, rain began to be discharged from the thundering clouds. The earth having once received that rain, trees resembling houses were provided for those creatures. From them all means of enjoyment were produced. Men derived their subsistence from them at the beginning of the Tretā age. Subsequently, after a great length of time, owing to their alteration (degeneration), the passions of desire and covetousness arose in their hearts uncaused. . . . Then owing to their alteration (degeneration) and owing to that fated time, all those house-like trees perished. When these had been destroyed, men, disturbed and agitated, but genuine in their desire, longed after that perfection which they had lost. Then those house-

like trees appeared to them; and among their fruits yielded clothes
and jewels. On these trees too, in every cavity, there was produced
without the aid of bees, honey of great potency, having scent, colour,
and flavour. By this means they subsisted at the beginning of the
Tretā age, delighted with this perfection and free from trouble.
Again, through the lapse of time, becoming greedy, they seized by
force those trees, and that honey produced without bees. And then
owing to that misconduct of theirs, occasioned by cupidity, the Kalpa
trees, together with their honey, were destroyed here and there. As
but little of their perfection remained, owing to the effects of the
period of twilight, the pairs of opposites (as pleasure and pain, cold
and heat) arose in men, and they became greatly distressed by sharp
cold winds, and heats. Being thus afflicted by these opposites, they
adopted means of shelter, and to counteract the opposites they re-
sorted to houses. Formerly they had moved about at their will, and
had not dwelt at all in houses; but subsequently they abode in such
dwellings as they found suitable and pleasant in barren deserts, in
valleys, on mountains, in caves, and they took refuge in fortresses,
in a desert surrounded by perpetual water. As a protection against
cold and heat they began to construct houses on even and uneven
places, according to opportunity and at their pleasure. Then they
measured out towns, cities, villages, and apartments. . . . These
places having been made, they next constructed houses, and as
formerly there were trees formed like houses, so did they now begin
to erect the houses, after repeated consideration. Some boughs are
spread out, others are bent down, others rise upwards, while others
again stretch horizontally. After examining thus by reflection how
the different boughs of trees branch out, they constructed in like
manner the apartments of their houses. . . . Having adopted these
means of defence against the opposites (cold and heat) they devised
methods of subsistence. The Kalpa trees having been destroyed,
along with their honey, these creatures, afflicted with thirst and
hunger, became disquieted by dejection. Then again another perfection arose for them, a perfection which fulfilled the purpose of
subsistence: rain at their pleasure. . . . When the drops of water
first reached the ground, then from the conjunction of the waters
and the earth plants sprang among them, which bore flowers, roots
and fruits. Fourteen kinds of plants, cultivated and wild, were
produced without ploughing or sowing, as well as trees and shrubs
which bore flowers and fruit at the proper season. This was the
first appearance of plants in the Tretā age, and by them men subsisted at that period. Then there again arose among them, universally, desire and cupidity, through a necessary process, and as a
result of the Tretā age. They then appropriated to themselves, by
force and violence, rivers, fields, hills, trees, shrubs, and plants. . . .
When men had thus become opposed to each other, through their
misconduct, while they struggled together, the plants were destroyed,
being seized with their fists like gravel. Then the earth swallowed
up the fourteen kinds of cultivated and wild plants, in consequence
of the influence exerted by that Tretā age: for men had seized again
and again the fruit, together with the flowers and leaves. After
the plants had perished, the famished people, becoming bewildered,
repaired to Svayambhū, the Lord of creatures, seeking the means of

subsistence. Knowing what they desired, and determining by intuition what was proper to be done, the Lord Brahmā Svayambhū, knowing that the plants had been swallowed up by the earth, milked them back. Taking the mount Sumeru as a calf, he milked this earth. When this earth (which is like a cow) was milked by him, roots were produced again in the ground. . . . When these plants, though created, did not afterwards grow, the divine Brahmā Svayambhū devised for the people means of subsistence depending on labour effected by their hands. From that time forward the plants were produced and ripened through cultivation. The means of subsistence having been provided, Svayambhū the Lord established divisions among men according to their tendencies. . . . [There were Brāhmans, Kṣatriyas, Vaiśyas and Śūdras.] But after the system of the four classes had been in all respects established, those men, from infatuation, did not fulfill their several duties. . . . Having become aware of this fact, the Lord Brahmā prescribed force, criminal justice, and war, as the profession of the Kṣatriyas. He then appointed the duty of officiating at sacrifices, the study of the Veda and the receipt of presents to be the functions of the Brahmans. The care of cattle, traffic and agriculture, he alloted as the work of the Vaiśyas; and the practice of mechanical arts and service he assigned as that of the Śūdras.

S. E. II, 15. *Mahābhārata,* Vanaparvan, 190, 9 ff.:

Mārkaṇḍeya said: . . . O bull of the Bharata race, in the Kṛta age everything was free from deceit and guile and avarice and covetousness; and morality, like a bull, was among men, with all the four legs complete. In the Tretā age, sin took away one of these legs, and morality had three legs. In the Dvāpara age, sin and morality are mixed half and half, and accordingly morality is said to have two legs only. In the dark age of Kali, morality, mixed with three parts of sin, lives by the side of men. Accordingly, morality then is said to wait on men, with only a fourth part of itself remaining. Know that the period of life, the energy, the intellect, and the physical strength of men decrease in every Yuga! The Brāhmaṇas and Kṣatriyas and Vaiśyas and Śūdras, in the Kali age, will practise morality and virtue deceitfully, and men in general will deceive their fellows by spreading the net of virtue. And men with false reputation of learning will, by their acts, cause Truth to be contracted and concealed. And in consequence of the loss of truth, the lives of men will become short. And in consequence of the shortness of their lives, they will not be able to acquire much knowledge. And in consequence of the littleness of their knowledge, they will have no wisdom. And for this, covetousness and avarice will overwhelm them all. And wedded to avarice and wrath and ignorance and lust, men will entertain animosities towards one another, desiring to take one another's lives. And Brāhmaṇas and Kṣatriyas and Vaiśyas with their virtues contracted, and divested of asceticism and truth, will all be reduced to an equality with the Śūdras. And the lowest orders of men will rise to the position of intermediate ones, and those in intermediate stations will, without doubt, descend to the level of the lowest ones. Such, o Yudhiṣṭhira, will become the state of the world at the end of the Yuga. Of robes, those will be regarded the best that are made of flax, and of grain, the Koradūṣaka will be regarded the best. At that time men will regard their wives as their only friends. And men will live on fish, and milk goats and sheep, for cows will be extinct. And towards that period, even they that are always observant of vows will become covetous. And opposed to one another, men will, at such a time, seek one another's lives; and divested of prayer, people will become atheists and thieves. And they will dig the banks of streams with their spades and sow grains thereon, and even those places will prove barren for them at such a time. And also men who are devoted to ceremonial rites in honor of the deceased and of the gods, will be avaricious and will also appropriate and enjoy what belongs to others. The father will then enjoy what belongs to the son; and the son what belongs to the father. . . . And the Brāhmaṇas speaking disrespectfully of the Vedas, will not practise vows, and, their understandings clouded by the science of disputation, they will no longer perform sacrifices and oblations. And deceived by the false science of reasons, they will direct their hearts towards everything mean and low. . . . And sons having slain their fathers, and fathers having slain their sons will incur no opprobrium. And they will frequently save themselves from anxiety by such crimes, and even glory in them. And the whole world will be filled with barbarian (mleccha) behaviour and notions, and ceremonies and sacrifices will cease, and joy will be nowhere, and general rejoicings will disappear. And men will rob the possessions of helpless persons, of those that are friendless, and of widows also. And possessed of small energy and strength, without knowledge, and addicted to avarice and folly and sinful practices, men will accept with joy the gifts made by wicked people with words of contempt. And the kings of the earth with hearts wedded to sin, without knowledge, and always boastful of their wisdom, will challenge one another from desire of taking one another's life. And the Kṣatriyas also, at that time, will become the thorns of the earth. And filled.with avarice, and swelling with pride and vanity, and unable and unwilling to protect their subjects, they will take pleasure in inflicting punishments only. And attacking and repeating their attacks upon the good and the honest, and feeling no pity for them even when they will cry in grief, the Kṣatriyas will rob these of their wives and wealth. And no one will ask for a girl for purposes of marriage, and no one will give away a girl for such purposes, but the girls will themselves choose their lords. And the kings of the earth, with souls steeped in ignorance, and discontented with what they have, will rob their subjects by every means in their power. And without doubt the whole world will become barbarian. And the right hand will deceive the left; and the left, the right. And men with false reputation of learning will contract Truth, and the old will betray the senselessness of the young, and the young will betray the dotage of the old. And cowards will have reputation of bravery, and the brave will be cheerless like cowards. And, towards the end of the Yuga, men will cease to trust one another. . . . And sin will increase and prosper, while virtue will fade and cease to flourish. And Brāhmanas and Kṣatriyas and Vaiśyas will disappear, leaving no remnants of their orders. And all men will become members of *one* common order, without distinction of any kind. And sires will not forgive sons and sons will not forgive sires. And wives will not wait upon and serve their husbands. . . . And both men and women will become perfectly free in their behaviour and will not tolerate one another's acts. . . . And no one will listen to the words of others, and no one will be regarded as a preceptor by another. And intellectual darkness will envelope the whole earth, and the life of man will then be measured by sixteen years, on attaining to which age death will ensue. And girls of five years of age will bring forth children, and boys of seven or eight years of age will become fathers. And the wife will never be content with her husband, nor the husband with his wife. And the possessions of men will never be much, and people will falsely bear the marks of religion, and jealousy and malice will fill the world. And no one will be a giver in respect to anyone. And the inhabited regions of the earth will be afflicted with dearth and famine, and the highways will be filled with lustful men and women of evil repute. . . . And all men will adopt the behaviour of the Barbarians, become omnivorous without distinction, and cruel in all their acts. And, urged by avarice, men will, at that time, deceive one another when they sell and purchase. . . . And people will, without compunction, destroy trees and gardens. And men will be filled with anxiety as regards the means of living. And overwhelmed with covetousness, men will kill Brāhmanas and appropriate and enjoy the possessions of their victims. . . . And when men will begin to slay one another, and become wicked and fierce and without any respect for animal life, then will the Yuga come to end. And even the foremost of the best classes, afflicted by robbers, will, like crows, fly in terror and will speed and seek refuge in rivers and mountains and inaccessible regions. And always oppressed by bad rulers with burdens of taxes, the foremost of the best classes will, in those terrible times, take leave of all patience and do improper acts by becoming even the servants of the Śūdras. And Śūdras will expound the scriptures, and Brāhmanas will wait upon and listen to them, and settle their course of duty accepting such interpretations as their guide. And the low will become the high, and the course of things will look contrary. And renouncing the gods, men will worship bones and other relics deposited in walls. . . . These all will take place at the end of the Yuga, and know that these are the signs of the end of the Yuga. And when men become fierce and destitute of virtue and carnivorous and addicted to intoxicating drinks, then does the Yuga come to end. And when flowers will be begot within flowers, and fruits within fruits, then will the Yuga come to end. . . . And the earth will soon be full of Barbarians, and the Brāhmanas will fly in all directions for fear of the burden of taxes. . . . And the course of the winds will be confused and agitated, and innumerable meteors will flash through the sky foreboding evil. And then the Sun will appear with six others of the same kind. And all around there will be din and uproar, and everywhere there will be conflagrations. . . . And fires will blaze up on all sides. And travellers, unable to obtain food and drink and shelter even when they ask for these, will lie down on the wayside, refraining from urging their solicitations. And, when the end of the Yuga comes, crows and snakes and vultures and kites and other animals and birds will utter frightful and dissonant cries. . . . And men abandoning the countries and directions and towns and cities of their occupation, will seek for new ones, one after another. And people will wander over the Earth, uttering, " Oh father! Oh son!" and such other frightful and heart-rending cries.

CULTURAL PRIMITIVISM

As the praise of ancestors and the praise of prehistoric ages are manifestations of primitivism, so the praise of Nature and the praise of a simple life lived in a state of nature, far from the noise and the luxury of the city, may also be considered as an expression of primitivism. The latter mood also is largely represented in the Indian literature.

The hero Rāma has been banished by his father the king Daśaratha. He must renounce the throne, he must abandon all the pleasures he enjoyed in his palace, and he has to live fourteen years in exile, in the forest. But his faithful wife Sītā and his courageous brother Lakṣmaṇa have resolved to accompany him. Clothed only in garments of bark, the banished ones are living a hard and simple life in the Citrakūṭa hills.

One time Rāma, showing to Sītā the surrounding landscape, addressed her with the following quite romantic lines:

S. E. II, 16. Rāmāyaṇa. Book II, Canto 94 (3-7; 10; 14-16; 18-19);
Canto 95 (3; 17-18):

> Neither the loss of my kingdom, O my darling, nor the separation from my friends grieves my heart, when I see this charming mountain. Look, darling, on this mountain full of many different kinds of birds and adorned with heaven reaching peaks which abound in minerals. Abounding in minerals, some parts of that king of mountains have the appearance of silver, some have the appearance of blood, some are of a yellowish-red colour, some shine like diamond, some like the blossoms of the Arka-plants and the Ketala-trees, some like the Jyotīrasa-gems. Full of many birds, full of all sorts of deer, inhabited by harmless tigers, hyenas and bears, that mountain shines. . . . Full of charming shade-trees which are loaded with flowers and fruits, this mountain displays glorious beauty. . . . Who is the man who would not be delighted by the breeze blowing from the caves (of that mountain), laden with the many perfumes of various flowers, a pleasant fragrance? If I spent many autumns here with you, irreproachable spouse, and with Lakṣmaṇa, sorrow would not overcome me, for I am delighted in this charming mountain with its wonderful peaks, in this charming mountain where there are so many flowers and fruits and birds of every kind. . . . O Sītā, do you enjoy with me the charm of that Citrakūṭa-mountain, when you see all these various aspects attuned to body, speech and heart? My fathers, who have passed away, the royal saints, said, O queen, that living in a forest like this is immortality, that it is for eternal bliss after death. . . .
>
> Look at this charming Mandākinī river, adorned with wonderful islets, inhabited by wild geese and cranes, and full of flowers. . . . Here, bathing three times every day, living on honey, roots and fruit, I shall not long for (the great city of) Ayodhyā nor for royal sway,

since I am with you (my darling). For there is no man who, seeing this charming river, and its water troubled by herds of elephants, its banks where elephants, lions and apes come to drink, its beautiful flowers and its blooming trees, would not become happy and free of pain.

The feeling for external nature and the admiration of beautiful scenery have, of course, inspired many poets in many countries; and certainly the glorification of nature in their poems is not necessarily a consequence of primitivistic ideas. But when the poets consider Nature as a consoler and as a refuge, when they long for a simple life in a state of nature, and consider it as the best way to escape the troubles and sorrows of the corrupted social life of their time, this *Naturgefühl* is often connected with primitivistic tendencies. Such a feeling connected with primitivistic tendencies is often expressed in the works of Indian literature: in lyric and dramatic poetry as well as in the religious poems which exalt the simple life of the ascetics in their hermitages.

The Śakuntalā, for instance, the masterpiece of the great poet Kālidāsa, gives us idyllic pictures of the hermitage of Kanva, where the charming girl Śakuntalā and her two friends Priaṃvadā and Anasūyā lead a simple and happy life, under the protection of the ascetics, among the flowers, the trees and the tame antelopes of the gardens. By the spirit which pervades it, this picture, made by a poet who was used to living among the luxuries and the intrigues of the court of some great Indian prince, recalls to mind that taste for pastoral poetry that developed in the 16th, 17th and 18th centuries in the aristocratic society of some European courts.

Here is a characteristic stanza of the first act of the Śakuntalā. Looking at the hermit-girls who are just coming to water the young plants of the hermitage, King Duṣyanta exclaims: " How sweet is the appearance of these girls! If this charming figure, difficult to be found in the inner apartments of palaces, belongs to people living in a hermitage, then indeed the shrubs of the garden are surpassed in excellencies by the shrubs of the forest."

We have seen that soft primitivism is largely represented in Indian literature. It is questionable whether hard primitivism is really well represented there. It is true that there are many texts which praise the anchorite who, clothed only in garments of bark, drinking only the water of the brooks, eating only roots and fruits, is living a simple and hard life in the forest. But, although there may be here an influence of hard primitivism, we must remember that the principal object of the hard life of the ascetic is not health, strength and happiness in this world, but the acquisition of moral merit, bliss in heaven, and final release.

THE NOBLE SAVAGE

The sort of primitivism represented in the classical literature by the legends concerning the Hyperboreans and the Scythians is represented in the Indian literature by the legends concerning the Uttara-Kurus and the inhabitants of Śakadvīpa. In the Aitareya Brāhmaṇa (a Vedic text perhaps of the ninth century B. C.), the Uttara-Kurus are still a historical people, and they are located in the North, beyond the Himālaya. But in the Epic and later literature they have assumed a wholly mythical character.

The following passage of the Mahābhārata will give an idea of the legends concerning the Uttara-Kurus.

S. E. II, 17. *Mahābhārata,* Bhīṣmaparvan, 7, 2 ff.:

> On the Northern side of the Meru mountain are the sacred Northern Kurus. The trees there bear sweet fruits, and are always covered with fruits and flowers. All the flowers there are fragrant, and the fruits of excellent taste. Some of the trees again yield fruits according to the will of the plucker. There are again some other trees that are called milk-yielding. These always yield milk and the six different kinds of food of the taste of amṛta (nectar). Those trees also yield cloths and in their fruits are ornaments. The entire land abounds with golden sands. A portion of the region there, extremely delightful, is possessed of the radiance of the ruby or diamond, of the lapis lazuli or other jewels and gems. All the seasons there are agreeable and nowhere does the land become miry. The tanks are charming, delicious, and full of crystal water. The men born there have dropped from the world of the celestials. All are of pure birth and all are extremely handsome in appearance. There twins (of opposite sexes) are born and the women resemble Apsaras (celestial nymphs) in beauty. They drink the milk, sweet as Amṛta (nectar), of those milk-yielding trees. And the twins grow up equally. Both possessed of equal beauty, both endowed with similar virtues, and both equally dressed, both grow up in love like a couple of Cakravākas. The people of that country are free from illness and are always cheerful. Ten thousand and seven hundred years they live, and never abandon one another. A class of birds called Bhāruṇḍa, furnished with sharp beaks and possessed of great strength, take them up when dead and throw them into mountain caves. . . .

According to other passages of the Mahābhārata, in the country of the Uttara-Kurus women enjoy sexual liberty. They live in perfect freedom, unrestrained by rules of any kind regulating their conduct and motions, and there is no feeling of jealousy among men and women. (Cf. *Mahābhārata,* Anuśāsanaparvan, 102.)

Another mythical country where people are supposed to live in perfect happiness is *Śākadvīpa,* the island of the Śāka trees.

That island is of twice the extent of India. The states there are full of righteousness and the men never die. There is no famine. The people are

full of forbearance and great energy.   There are seven mountains decked
with jewels and many rivers.   Since the hue of those mountains is dark,
the people residing there are dark in complexion.   The people there are
virtuous and all the four orders are devoted to their respective occupations.
There is no instance of theft.   Free from decrepitude and death, and gifted
with long life, the people there grow like rivers during the season of rains.
In these provinces there is no king, no punishment, no person who deserves
to be punished.   Conversant with the dictates of duty, they are engaged in
the practice of their respective duties and protect one another.   (Cf. *Mahābhārata*, Bhīṣmaparvan, 11.)

This survey of primitivism in ancient India is very incomplete, for I
have omitted examining some important parts of the Sanskrit literature,
the whole Buddhistic literature and the whole Jaina literature.   But it may
suffice to show that primitivism is largely represented in India, and that, in
that country where the burden of the old traditions so heavily weighs upon
life, the tendency to imagine that the far remote prehistoric times were the
golden age in which virtue and happiness prevailed, is as strong as in any
other country.

APPENDIX

SOME MEANINGS OF 'NATURE' [1]

Necessarium est ante omnia aequivocationem huius nominis Natura
e medio tollere, et multiplices eius significationes assignare.

J. T. Giliolus, _Disputatio demonstrans_
primum movens immobile . . . non esse
Naturam, 1635.

A. _Senses of_ physis _and ' nature' in literary and philosophical usage from which ethical and other normative uses are derived._

1. Genesis, birth. An infrequent sense of _physis_, though etymologically primary. (Herodotus, VII, 134; Aristotle, _Met._ 1014b 17.)
2. The congenital or inborn qualities, characters or talents of a person, in contrast with the effects of instruction or training: ' nature ' _vs._ ' culture '. (Democritus, _Fragm._ 33 and 183; Plato, _Republic_, 409d, 410b.) Hence _physikos_ and _naturalis_, as applied to human qualities or skills, mean native, not needing to be learned, as opposed to _didaktos_. (Cf. Pindar, _Ol._ IX, 100 ff.; II, 93 ff.; the Hippocratic Essay _On Law_, II.)
3. Any distinguishing characteristic of anyone or anything, especially its sensible appearance. (Homer in _Od._ X, 303, and many later writers.) According to Beardslee, " this is throughout Greek literature the predominant use of the word." (_The Use of_ ΦΥΣΙΣ _in Fifth Century Greek Literature_, 1918, p. 2.)
4. With reference either to the body or mind of the individual: one's disposition, constitution, bent or temperament. (A frequent use in the Hippocratic medical writings; cf. Beardslee, pp. 32-3, 35.)
5. In the _Hippocratica_ frequently: the body. (Cf. Beardslee, p. 35.)
6. Also often in _Hippocratica:_ generic human nature (i. e. the physical nature of man), with express or implied contrast with the specific

---

[1] This list is not intended as a substitute for a dictionary article. The development of meanings of _physis, natura_, and the derivatives of the latter in modern European languages, is treated as a single semasiological process, of which the greater part belongs to the history of the Greek word. A number of minor senses of the terms in question have been omitted. The enumeration is, however, designed to include the more significant normative meanings of the term, to suggest how some of these arose, to indicate the relations of congruity, implication or opposition between various significations, and to contribute in some degree towards the realization of the desideratum expressed in the motto by a seventeenth-century philosopher. Modern senses have been included, but the list is in great part a conspectus of uses of ' nature ' separately dealt with in various parts of this volume.

characters of other animals. (Hippocr. *On Diet*, I, vi, 486, 490; cf. Beardslee, pp. 36, 39, 45.)

7. Also in *Hippocratica:* the normal state or functioning of an organ, in contrast with deranged conditions. (*On Airs, etc.* II, 58; cf. Beardslee, p. 37); similarly, in ordinary use, *para physin* means abnormal.

8. The permanent and fundamental character (of a person), in contrast with transient manifestations or superficial appearances. (Sophocles, *Philoct.* 902, *Ajax,* 472; the orator Antiphon, 2, 2, 1.)

9. In the pre-Socratic physiologers, *physis* generally and primarily means the intrinsic and permanent quality or qualities of (physical) things, 'what things really are.' Probably derived from 2, 3, 8. (Aristotle, *Phys.* 193a 9; cf. Lovejoy, *Philos. Rev.* 1909, p. 369; Beardslee, pp. 11-16, 54-67.)

10. In some of the physiologers (and, according to Burnet, in their prevailing usage): *physis* = the underlying, primary and permanent substance, matter in its fundamental 'nature'; derived from senses 8 and 9. (Burnet, *Early Greek Philosophy,* 2nd ed. pp. 12 ff.; but see Beardslee, pp. 65 f.)

11. By virtue of the distinction (implicit in 9 and 10) between sensible appearances and physical things as they are 'in themselves,' *physei* ('by nature') becomes equivalent to 'objectively' (Theophrastus, *De sensibus*, 63, 70).

12. According to certain interpreters, *physis* in the physiologers means 'becoming,' 'the formation of things,' 'the process of cosmic development,' 'the world story'; (cf. Woodbridge, *Phil. Rev.* 1901, p. 359; Millerd, *On the Interpretation of Empedocles*; Heidel, Περι Φύσεως 1909; but see Beardslee, *op. cit.* pp. 63-65).

13. The cosmic law or the general scheme of things, conceived as the ground of all particular details in that scheme. Cf. Euripides, *Troades*, 886.

14. The physical world as a whole; "the sum of things as constituted by the elements and the cosmic laws and processes." (According to Heidel, *op. cit.* the primary sense of *physis* in the physiologers.) Cf. Euripides, *Fragm. inc.* 910; Philolaus(?) in Diels, *Fragm. der Vorsokratiker,* I, p. 239, *Fragm.* 1; Plato, *Lysis*, 214b. Probably derivative from 9, 10.

15. By a hypostatization—often passing into vague personification—of the idea of causality contained in 13: the general cause of phenomena, the universal originating or moving power. (Cicero, *De re pub.* III, i, 1; *De fin.* V, xiii, 38; *De nat. deor.* I, xx, 53. Cf. *natura naturans* in Neoplatonism and Spinoza, and *natura naturata* in some uses; Philo Jud. *De opificio mundi,* I, 3). As personified, especially 'Mother Nature' (Cicero, *Paradoxa*, 14; Montaigne, *Essais,* I, 30: *notre belle et puissante mère Nature*; cf. 38.) The term in this sense tends to become a substitute for 'God as efficient cause.'

16. The universe in its entirety; 'everything.' (Critias, *Fragm.* 19, Diels; Plato, *Cratyl.* 400a; Aristotle, *Met.* 1074b 3, 1075a 11.)

17. Probably by a fusion of the ideas in 2, 13, 15, arises the general philosophic antithesis of 'nature' and 'culture' or 'art'; here *physis* or nature is a generic or collective name for that which arises without human effort and contrivance, in contrast with that which man produces through his purposive action. (Hippocrates, *On Diet*, I, vi, 486, *On Epidemics*, VI, v, 314; Democritus, *Fragm.* 33; Plato, *Laws*, 888e-890a; Cicero, *De fin.* IV, 16. A favorite antithesis in Aristotle, e. g. *Phys.* 194a 21. Cf. Shakespeare, *Winter's Tale*, IV, Sc. iii, 86-97.)

18. As expressing a kindred distinction *within* animal or human nature, the natural, or that which arises *physei*, is the innate, spontaneous, instinctive, unreflective, in contrast with that which is acquired by experience, individual or social, or depends upon deliberation and reasoning. (Aristophanes, *Clouds*, 1078; Plato, *Republic*, 375e, 530c, *Apol.* 22c; Aristotle, *Politics*, I, 1252a 28; Cicero, *De finibus*, III, v, 17; cf. Rousseau, *Disc. sur. l'inégalité*, Pt. I: '*Tel est le pur mouvement de la nature, antérieur à toute réflexion.*')

19. By a related but slightly different distinction, an individual's nature is that part of his character or tendencies which is 'not in his own power,' which is outside of the sphere of his will and for which he is not responsible. (Ar., *Eth. Nic.* 1179b 23, 1114b.)

20. Akin to both 16 and 17 is an aesthetic sense of *physikos* and *naturalis*: simple, genuine, unaffected, in contrast with *technikos* or *artificiosus*, 'consciously artistic, showing deliberate design'; applied to literary styles (Dionysius Hal. *De Thuc.* 42).

21. As applied to the history of human society, the state of nature is the primeval or archaic stage; related to 2 and 17. (Varro, *De re rust.* II, i, 3, and innumerable later writers.)

22. Without reference to time, the state of nature is that form of human individual or social life in which only the 'natural' (17, 18) attributes and activities of man are found, in which 'art' has not altered or supplanted 'nature.'

23. More specifically, the state of nature is the condition of human life or of human relations antecedent to, or apart from, organized government. Cf. Cicero, *Pro Sestio*, 91-92; so Hobbes, Locke, Pufendorf, and modern juristic writers generally. All independent states, since they have no common sovereign, are in a state of nature *inter se*, in this sense (Hobbes, *Leviathan*, XIII), as are autocratic sovereigns in relation to their subjects (Rousseau, *État de guerre*, par. 6).

24. By easy metonymy from 3, *physis* signifies a kind, sort, species (Plato, *Repub.* 429d).

25. In the philosophy of Plato, *physis* may mean the generic essence of anything, i. e. the intrinsic or essential meaning of a general concept

(based on 3 and 24). *Physis* or 'nature' thus becomes a synonym of the Platonic Idea. (*Phileb.* 64e, 66a; *Cratylus*, 389c; *Repub.* 597b; *Parm.* 132b.)

26. Since, especially in the epistemological rationalism of modern Platonistic schools, certain ideas or logical essences have fixed and necessary relations to one another, that which is 'by nature' or 'according to the natures of things' comes to mean the system of self-evident and necessary truths expressing the eternal and unchangeable properties of, or relations between, Ideas, especially between the fundamental notions or categories of thought. Cf. the epistemology of such modern Platonists as Cudworth (*Et. and Immut. Morality*, I, 2) and Henry More (*Enchir. Eth.* V). Thus "known 'by (or to) nature'" means self-evident, not in need of proof (cf. Hobbes, *Conc. Body*, I, v, 5).

27. In Aristotle, *physis* may mean the raw material out of which anything is made, in contrast with the finished product (*Metaph.* 1014b 26). Akin to sense 10 and antithetic to 29.

28. In Aristotle, the 'nature' (in a sense akin to 25: *physis kata to eidos*) of any individual thing or specific kind of thing is conceived as the immanent cause or self-active principle of its self-realization, i. e. of its spontaneous growth and action, in contrast with those changes which are due to 'art,' or to any causes external to itself; cf. 17 and 18. (*Metaph.* 1014b 18; *Phys.* 192b 8-23, 199a 15 ff.)

29. Also in Aristotle, the 'nature' of a thing is its 'end' or the good towards which it tends, its final cause, that state in which its 'natural' development culminates (*Pol.* 1252b 33, *Phys.* 194a 28). This later becomes one of the senses of the (social) 'state of nature' (e. g. Robinet, *De la nature*, I, 1761, p. 25).

30. Also in Aristotle, since 'nature' as a whole (senses 14, 15) tends towards the good, 'nature' is the unconscious or conscious striving of imperfect things as a whole towards the realization of the good. (*Phys.* 230b 20, 198b 10-199b 34; *De Gen. An.* 731a 24.)

31. In the Stoic pantheism, 'Nature' is equivalent to 'God,' conceived as identical with the material universe (senses 14 and 15) or its constitutive substance, the 'cosmic fire,' but at the same time as purposive, rational and perfect (Stoic optimism). (Diog. Laert. VII, 156; Zeno in Cicero, *De nat. deor.* II, 57-8.) A kindred use is common in subsequent forms of pantheism; cf. Spinoza, *Deus sive Natura*.

32. Probably from 14 and 17, but often with an infusion of senses 15 and 31, arises the modern sense of 'nature' as the out-of-doors, the world of sights and sounds conceived as an object of aesthetic appreciation or a source of religious emotion.

33. Probably in consequence of 7, and of the conception of regularity of operation in nature (in senses 13 and 14), 'natural' in the Hippocratic writings and especially in modern languages, designates any

phenomena or objects which are ordinary and usual, as opposed to the anomalous, the exceptional, or the monstrous.

34. As opposed to the exceptional of a supposed 'higher' origin, i. e. to the supernatural, the 'natural' is that which occurs in accordance with the usual uniformities of 'nature' (sense 13) without intervention of superior powers (Hippocr. *On Airs, etc.* II, 78; a common modern use). Cf. the antithesis in Christian theology of 'nature' and 'grace.'

35. As regular, 'nature' may mean that which happens from intelligible causes or in accordance with uniform law, in contrast with chance. (Democritus, *Fragm.* 176.)

36. In so far as this regularity of operation of 'nature' (in senses 13 and 14) is construed as meaning mechanical causation, 'nature,' especially in some modern uses, comes to mean the world as a mechanical system, and (in particular) 'naturalism' signifies the conception of the world as such a system. The contrast here is with liberty, spontaneity, or final causation. (Cf. Mauthner, *Philos. Wörterb.* s. v. 'Natur.')

37. In the Aristotelian-Ptolemaic cosmography of the Middle Ages, 'nature' may mean the sublunary world, the region of mutability and generation, in contrast with the eternal and immutable heavens. (Cf. references under 38.)

38. Hence personified 'Nature' (cf. 15) often means in medieval allegory the ruler of the sublunary world, *mundanae regionis regina* (Alain de Lille, *De planctu naturae,* Pr. 479a); *Roman de la Rose* (ed. Langlois), 15891-16004: " Nature is under the Mone, Maistresse of every lives kinde " (Gower, *Confessio Amantis,* VIII, 2330); *Interlude of the Four Elements,* 153 ff.

39. In the terms 'light of nature' and 'natural reason' the word is used with special reference to the mode of acquisition of knowledge: the 'light of nature' consists in the ordinary means of acquiring knowledge possessed by every rational being, independently of (a) tradition and instruction (sense 17) and (b) of revelation or supernatural inspiration (sense 34). The terms tend also to carry the connotation of sense 26 (the faculty by which man is acquainted with self-evident and eternal truths).

B. *Normative uses in ethics, politics and religion.*[2]

40. Since, when the general distinction between the subjective and the objectively valid was first applied to ethical judgments and moral codes, *physei* was an already current expression for 'objectively'

---

[2] The uses of the term in the history of aesthetic theories are not here included; an attempt to distinguish them and to indicate their major applications has been made by A. O. Lovejoy, *Mod. Lang. Notes,* XLVII, 1927, pp. 444-450.

(sense 11), that which is objectively valid in the realm of morals came to be identified with that which is good or right by 'nature'; and by a further, primarily verbal, confusion, the latter was construed as equivalent to 'that which is according to nature.' This transition, which was doubtless aided by sense 7, is the critical point in the history of the word.

41. In its ethical application, the notion of the 'objectively' good was, in Greek use, antithetic, not chiefly to individual opinion, but to social custom (*nomos*) or positive law. Hence, that which is 'according to nature' is conceived as opposed to those rules, practices or institutions which are (merely) customary, conventional, traditional. Hence the antithesis of 'nature' and 'custom' in the Greek Sophistic period, sometimes passing into denial of the validity of laws as such; cf. Sophist Antiphon, *Ox. Pap.* XI, 1364; Plato, *Gorgias,* 482e; Euripides, *Bacchae,* 896; Aristotle, *Topica,* 173a 7; and the saying attributed to Democritus: "Injustice is the opposite to nature. For laws are an ill invention, and it befits the wise man not to obey the laws, but to live in freedom." (Diels, *Fragm. der Vorsokr.* II, 54, 2 ff.) A revival of this antithesis of 'nature' and 'custom' was a conspicuous feature of the ethics of the late Renaissance; e. g. Montaigne, Charron.

(The two foregoing senses, however, are purely formal; they designate merely those moral principles, whatever they may be, which *are* objectively valid and are *not* merely arbitrary or conventional. Hence the attempt is made either (a) to derive some concrete practical content for the conception of the objectively, or 'naturally,' right, from one or another of the non-ethical senses, above given (1-39), which had become attached to the word 'nature'; or (b) to establish an association between some such sense and ethical ideas derived from other sources. These processes manifest themselves in the following more definite normative uses of the term):

42. Good 'by nature' are those qualities and modes of action exemplified by physical nature (in sense 14 or 32); these, however, being usually selected or idealized under the influence of traditional moral ideas. Cf. Euripides, *Phoen.* 538-545; Hippocr. *On Diet,* I, vi, 486 ff.; 538-545; Cicero, *De off.* I, xxxiv, 126-7.

43. Good 'by nature' (sense 18) or 'in accordance with the law of nature' is whatever is prompted or required by the instincts common to man and all animals. Cf. Justinian, *Institutes,* I, 2: *jus naturale est quod natura omnia animalia docuit, . . . non humani generis proprium, sed omnium animalium.*

44. Good 'by nature' is any action to which men's impulses or instincts prompt them; ethical naturalism as moral antinomianism (sense 18). (Aristophanes, *Clouds,* 1078; the speech of Callicles in Plato's *Gorgias*; cf. some phases of Montaigne; Diderot in *Supplément au Voyage de Bougainville,* etc.)

45. Good 'by nature' is that social order in which political power coincides with 'natural' power, i. e. in which the stronger rule (Plato, *Gorgias*, 483; *Laws*, 890a).

46. Good 'by nature' is that social order in which those having superior 'natures' rule: ethical naturalism as the principle of aristocracy. (Democritus, *Fragm.* 267, Diels; Plato, *Gorgias*, *loc. cit.*; Aristotle, *Pol.* 1252a 31, 1254a-b.)

47. Good 'by nature' for any individual is the use of any powers which 'nature' (senses 13, 14, 15) gave it—it being assumed that it was 'nature's purpose' that all such powers should be exercised (Aristotle, *Pol.* 1253a 9).

48. Good 'by nature' is that social order wherein each man exercises only the function for which he is 'by nature' adapted and wherein, therefore, those rule who are by nature (i. e. by congenital endowment) best fitted for the specific function of ruling — a modification of 47 involving the further assumptions that (a) 'ruling' is one natural function requiring realization, and that the realization of this conflicts with 44; and (b) that between certain functions and certain capacities an obvious congruity exists, and that — specifically in the case of 'ruling' — the possession of the capacity establishes the right as well as the obligation to exercise the function (Aristotle, *Pol.* 1260a 4-9).

49. Since each species of living being has its distinctive 'nature' (senses 3, 25, 29), and since its good, according to Platonic and Aristotelian teaching, consists in the 'realization' of this nature, that is 'by nature' the good for man which most fully realizes the distinctive attribute of human nature (Cicero, *De fin.* IV, vi, 16, 25; V, 25)— this attribute being diversely defined by Plato, Aristotle, the Stoics, and other ancient and modern writers.

50. In the formula used primarily to express sense 49, *secundum naturam vivere*, that formula, especially in Stoicism, usually also implies harmony with and acquiescence in the general course and purpose of 'Nature' in sense 31. (Cicero, *De Sen.* 5; Marc. Aurel. *Comment.* IV, 23, 48; X, 6): ethical naturalism as cosmical piety, the religion of 'accepting the universe.'

51. Good 'by nature' for the individual is that internal order or organization of the soul in which the part ('reason' or 'conscience') whose nature it is to rule controls the other parts. An ethical doctrine based upon analogy of 48, but with implication also of 29 and 49. ('Justice' in Plato's *Republic*; Aristotle, *Pol.* 1260a 4; J. Butler, *Sermons upon Humane Nature*, II, IV.)

52. Good 'by nature' is that which was, or would be, practised in a 'state of nature' (senses 21, 22): ethical naturalism as cultural primitivism. So probably some Sophists, Cynics, most Stoics, and numerous modern writers of all periods. Associated with the idealization of savages as nearer to 'nature' than civilized man.

53. In modern political theories: 'natural rights' are those which the
individual possesses, or would possess, in a state of nature (senses 23,
52) — i. e. before and independently of the establishment of civil
government. The connotation is colored partly by senses 15, 22, partly
by sense 26; from these largely, the implication of the validity of
'natural' rights is derived. The notion usually presupposes the
consent-theory of government, i. e. the ethical doctrine that no individual can rightfully be coerced by any other individual or group
without his prior consent to be subject to a coercive *régime*, under a
'social contract'; e. g. Hooker, Locke, A. Sidney, Rousseau.

54. (Direct opposite to 52.)   Best 'by nature' for any being is that state
in which its natural development reaches its culminating or final phase
(from sense 29).   A characteristic Aristotelian conception (e. g. *Pol.*
1252b 31), also in various phases of nineteenth-century evolutionistic
ethics and political theory.

55. Obligatory by the 'law of nature' are those actions which conform to
the 'natures of things' (sense 26), i. e. to eternal and self-evident
truths, arising either out of the 'nature of the good' or out of the
'nature of the relations in which moral agents stand to one another':
'nature' as 'right reason' and ethical naturalism as rationalistic
intuitionism in morals: e. g. in the English Platonists of the 17th-
18th centuries; Locke, *Essay*, IV, iii, 18; S. Clarke, *Disc. conc. Nat.
Relig.* 1724, pp. 28 ff.; cf. Stanley, *Hist. of Philos.* 1656, V.   The
actual content of the axiomatic 'law of nature' is diversely given by
different representatives of this way of employing the term.

56. Contrary to 'nature' is any action which may be construed as a way
of asserting or implying that things are what they in fact are not,
i. e. that their 'nature' (senses 3, 25) is not what it is.   (W. Wollaston, *Religion of Nature Delineated*, 1736, Sect. I, iv.)   Passes over
into the following:

57. Contrary to 'nature' is any action which implies that pleasure, by
whomsoever experienced, is not 'by nature' good, or that pain is not
'by nature' evil.   (H. More in *Enchiridion Ethicum*, I, ch. 2 and 6;
Wollaston, *Religion of Nature*, Sect. II, xi, xiv.)   Here universalistic
utilitarianism emerges out of the Platonic conception of conformity
to the 'natures of things' (55).

58. Action in accordance with 'nature' (senses 13, 14) in some empiri-
cistic philosophies is action guided by a due consideration of the
factual 'laws of nature,' with a view to the successful adjustment of
means to an end, the latter being assumed. Cf. some passages in
Cumberland, *De legibus naturae*, e. g. ch. I, ii; d'Holbach, *Système
de la Nature*, Pt. I, ch. 1.

59. Action in accordance with 'nature' is that based upon self-love, as
the spring of action 'natural' to all conscious beings; ethical
naturalism as egoistic hedonism (cf. 18).   (The Sophist Antiphon,

in *Ox. Pap.* 1364; Cicero, *De finibus*, I, 30; Sextus Empir. *Hyp.* III, 194; Pope, *Essay on Man,* Ep. II; Delisle de Sales, *Philosophie de la Nature* (3rd ed. 1777), I, 281-3.)

60. Since the objectively valid is that which is independent of private or local idiosyncrasies (41), and since the 'light of nature' is supposed to be common to all men, 'nature' is the body of truths which are thus universally accessible, and the good or right or valid 'by nature' is identified with that which is actually practised, or at least known and approved, by mankind everywhere, in contrast with merely local or temporary customs; cf. sense 41. (Aristotle, *Nic. Eth.* V, 10; Cicero, *Tusc. disp.* I, 30; *Jus naturale* as equivalent to *jus gentium*, i. e. *quo jure omnes gentes utuntur, Inst. of Justinian*, I, 2 and 11; cf. Hooker, *Eccles. Pol.* I, viii, 9-10.) The principal source of the uniformitarianism or standardizing tendency in 17th-18th century ethics and aesthetics; antithetic to political or moral relativism, and also to the Romantic cultivation of diversity and idiosyncrasy. (Cf. Lovejoy: "The Parallel of Deism and Classicism," *Mod. Philology*, XIX, 281 ff.)

61. When the influence of society upon the individual is conceived as the vehicle of mere conventions (cf. 41) and the source of 'prejudices,' i. e. of beliefs not arising from the pure 'light of nature' (39), not to be found among all peoples uniformly (60), and/or not characteristic of primitive men (52), 'natural' becomes antithetic to 'social' or 'socially generated'; so especially in the pedagogic ideal of keeping the individual apart from society during his formative period. (Cf. Cicero, *Tusc. disp.* II, 2, Beaurieu's *Élève de la Nature*, Rousseau's *Émile*.)

62. When 'nature' (senses 13, 14) is conceived, in accordance with the principle of continuity, as a graded 'Scale of Being,' conformity to nature means the limitation of intellectual ambitions and moral aspirations to those assumed to be appropriate to man's place in the scale: 'not to think or act beyond mankind.' (Cf. Pope, *Essay on Man*, I, 171-192, 241-6.)

63. In ethically dualistic religion, 'natural' has a depreciative sense (perhaps derived from 34 and 44) as antithetic to 'spiritual' or to 'supernatural' or to 'regenerate' or 'twice-born,' and the 'state of nature' is antithetic to the 'state of grace.' For this reason, the dominant tendency of the use of 'nature' as the designation of the moral norm has been adverse to such radical dualism or other-worldliness.

64. In medieval allegory: since Nature (sense 38), as ruler of the sublunary world of generation, has for her especial concern to maintain every species in continuous existence, despite the mortality of individuals, she becomes peculiarly the goddess of procreation and fecundity; hence the prime 'law of Nature' is 'multiply and replen-

ish the earth.' E. g. Alain de Lille in *De planctu naturae, passim*; Jean de Meung in *Roman de la Rose* (ed. Langlois), 16789 ff.; *Interlude of the Four Elements, etc.*

65. In some medieval and Renaissance poety: Since mutability is the characteristic of nature (in sense 37), i. e. of the sublunary world, changelessness is 'against nature.' Hence, with reference to the relations of the sexes, the 'law of nature' is that of free love. Commonly associated with 44 and 52. (Cf. *Roman de la Rose*, ed. Langlois, 13875 ff.; Donne, ' Elegie IV,' ' Confined Love,' ' Progress of the Soul,' I, 191 ff.).

66. As modifying the noun 'religion,' 'natural' or 'of nature' means primarily 'acquired solely by the light of nature' (39) without the supernatural aid of revelation (i. e. deism). But the word in this sense takes on coloring from many other senses, especially from 14, so that the 'religion of nature' tends to mean 'that derived from the study of external nature,' usually with the assumption of the cogency of the argument from the design; or from 26 (a religion whose truths are self-evident and immutable) ; or from 31 (a religion finding its God in 'nature,' i. e. in the universe as a whole) ; or from 60 (that religion which can be held to be actually known *semper, ubique et ab omnibus*) and which therefore (21) existed in the primitive age, is ' as old as the creation.'

INDEX OF CLASSICAL TEXTS

The following index covers Greek and Latin passages cited and translated at length (indicated by prefixed asterisk) and also those summarized or briefly referred to. Page numbers of this volume are in Roman type, those of texts cited in italics.

INDEX OF NAMES AND SUBJECTS

(Numbers in parentheses refer to the English translations of the documents cited. The Supplementary Essays and Appendix are not indexed.)

Abioi, in Aeschylus, 315; in Homer, 288, 315; in Strabo, 290.

Aborigines, of Italy, in Juvenal, 71; in Trogus, 67.

Accius, on identification of Saturnalia and Cronia 56, n. 63.

Achilles, translation of, 291, 292, n. 14.

Achilles Tatius, introduction to Aratus mentioned, 36.

Acorns as man's first food, 70, 71, 95, 370, 371, 373, 380, 382.

Aelian, on Euhemerus, 55; on 'Scythian speech,' 323, n. 65.

Aeschines, on Scythian ancestry of Demosthenes, 324, n. 66.

Aeschylus, on Age of Zeus, 203; anti-primitivism in, 200 (202); on Hyperboreans, 305, n. 33; identifies Hippemolgi and Galactophagi with Scythians, 288; on Palamedes as inventor of number, 202, n. 15; on Scythians, 315, 316.

Aethiopians, as Noble Savages, 348 ff.; in Agatharchides, 349; in Favorinus, 350; in Hanno, 348; in Herodotus, 349; in Homer, 348; in Nicolaus of Damascus, 350; in Pindar, 348; in Scylax, 349.—Their beauty, in Herodotus, 349; in Scylax, 348; no commerce among, 349; follow nature, 349; limitation of desires, ib.; their piety, 350; their simple life, 349.

Aetius, on length of Heraclitean cycle, 80.

Aetna, on Golden Age, 43, n. 40.

Agatharchides, on Aethiopians, 349.

Ages, Legend of, 24 f.; in Aratus, 34; in Babrius, 50; in Firmicus, 75 (76); in Hesiod, 25 (27); in Ovid, 43 (46); in Plato, 156 ff.; in Ps.-Seneca, 50; in Tibullus, 42. See also *Bronze, Golden, Iron, Silver Age.*

Age of Cronus, in Cratinus, 38; in Hesiod, 27; in Plato, 157, 162; survives in Islands of the Blest, 290; and Age of Zeus, Ch. II, B, 53 ff. See also *Age of Saturn.*

Age of Heroes, in Babrius, 50; in Catullus, 24; in Hesiod, 30; in Homer, 23; in Pausanias, 98; in Pindar, 23.

Age of Jupiter, in Firmicus, 75 (76); in Juvenal, 70 (71); in Statius, 68; in Tibullus, 59; in Virgil, 57.

Age of Love, in Empedocles, 32 f., 80.

Age of Saturn, in Firmicus, 75 (76); in Juvenal, 70 (71); in Ovid, 53, 63; in Plutarch, 64; in Silius Italicus, 54; in Tibullus, 59; in Trogus, 67; in Virgil, 57. No agriculture in, 63; no navigation, 61; as post-primitive, 57; and Age of Jupiter, Ch. II, B, 53 ff.

Age of Venus, in Firmicus, 75 (76).

Age of Zeus, in Aeschylus, 203; in Plato, 157.

Agricultural stage, Varro on, 368, 369.

Agriculture, in Golden Age, in Aratus, 34; in Hyginus, 37; in Juvenal, 72; in return of Golden Age, 92; before discovery of iron, 69.—None in Golden Age, in *Aetna*, 43, n. 40; in Fronto, 68; in Lucian, 64; in Ovid, 63; in Oxyrhynchus Papyrus XIV, 58, n. 75; in Ps.-Seneca, 51; in return of Golden Age, Virgil, 87; introduced in Iron Age, Ps.-Seneca, 52.—None in primitive times, Dicaearchus, 94; Diodorus Siculus, 221; Hesiod, 25; Moschion, 216; Ovid, 44; Seneca, 285; Statius, 380; Tibullus, 42; Varro, 368.—None among the Fenni, 361; Germans, 363; Hebrideans, 367; Scythians, 322, 343; avoided by the Scythians, 343.

Alcmaeon, on differentia of man, 389.

Alain de Lille, and Seneca, 281.

Albanians, as Noble Savages, 357 f.

Alcaeus, mentioned Hyperboreans, 304.

Alcibiades, story of his offer of land to Socrates, 124.

Alciphron, on Cronia, 65.

Alcmaeonid, 32.

Alexander the Great, and the Celts, 325; oration of a Scythian chief to, 337.

Anacharsis, Aristotle on, 179, n. 20;

Schol. Aristoph., on Prodicus, 114, n. 24.
Schol. ad Lycophron, 1191 f., on Ophion and Eurynome, 55; *Id. 1232*, on Cronus-Saturn, 56, n. 63.

Schuhl, P.-M., 194, n. 6.

Scylax, on Aethiopians, 349.

Scythians, 215-344; in Aeschylus, 315; Antiphanes, 324; Aristotle, 179, n. 20; Choerilus, 316; Claudian, 343; Clearchus Solensis, 323; Curtius, 337 (338); Dio Chrysostom, 340; Ephorus, 288, 327; Fronto, 339; Herodotus, 306, 322; Hesiod, 327; *Hippocratica*, 316; Homer, 315; Horace, 331; Julian, 339; *Letters of Anacharsis*, 329; Ovid, 333; St. Basil, 342, n. 99; Ps.-Scymnus, 324; in Sophistic oratory, 340; Sophocles, 316; Tertullian, 342; Trogus, 327; Virgil, 331.—Their clothing, 266; their communism, 289; in Horace, 331; in *Letters of Anacharsis*, 330; in Ephorus, 326; in Ps.-Scymnus, 324; in Seneca, 365; in Strabo, 289, 325; in Trogus, 328; their community of wives, in Strabo, 289; degraded by civilization, Strabo, 290 (cf. 340); by wealth, Clearchus, 323; Eichoff on, 287; and Getae, 289; and hard primitivism, 10; in Dio Chrysostom, 340; juristic state of nature, 328; and North American Indians, 289; as noble savages, 315 ff.; their nomadic life, 317; oration of a Scythian chief, 336 f. (338); their physique, *ib.*; sacrifice strangers to Artemis, 73, 339, n. 95; self-sufficiency of, 290; their sterility, 317; technological state of nature, 341.

'Scythian speech,' 323.

'Scythian towel,' 316.

Seasons, differentiation of, after Golden Age, in Ovid, 47.

Self-sufficiency, in Antisthenes, 119; Aristotle, 175; Cynicism, 119 f., 124, 130; Epicurus, 152; Hegesias, 119, n. 9; Plato, 119; Socratic schools, *ib.*; Stoicism, 261; of the Fenni, 361 f.; of the Scythians, 290; and work, in Cynicism, 122. See also *Desires, limitation of.*

'Sell all that thou hast,' in Cynicism, 130.

Seneca, general attitude towards primitivism, 263; on animalitarianism, 400;

anti-primitivism in, 378; cultural primitivism, 265 (269); on Daedalus, *ib.*; on Diogenes, *ib.*; on discovery of the arts, *ib.*; on discoveries of the Wise Man, 267 (272); dispraise of Nordic savage, 365; economic state of nature, 264, 267; effect of theory of cycles on his ethics, 285; on Epicureanism, 267; on ethical state of nature, 264 (268); on fall of man, 267; on Fortunate Isles, 294; on future of science, 378; on the Germans, 364; on liberal studies, 275 (276); on luxury, 266, 285, n. 35; on navigation, 279 (280); on Noble Savage, 266 (271); pacifism in, 267; on physical superiority of animals, 397; on Posidonius's attitude towards riches, 262, n. 17; on his idea of primitive government, 264; on primeval man, 264, 268; on purpose of philosophy, 264; on Scythians, 266; on simple life, 282; on Syrtians, 266; technological primitivism in, 264 (272); virtue an art, 268 (274); on wealth, 285, n. 35.

Seneca Rhetor, and Fortunate Islands, 294.

Senescence, cosmic, in Aulus Gellius, 102; in Dio Chrysostom, 100; in Lucretius, 233, 237 f.; in Seneca, 268 (274), 285 f.; human and cosmic, 98; terrestrial, in Lucretius, 237; in Pliny the Younger, 379. Cf. *Stature, human, decrease in; Nature, denial of her exhaustion.*

Sertorius, and Fortunate Islands, 292, 294.

Servius, on Islands of the Blest, 292; on Saturn, 56.

Seven Sages, visit to Croesus, 398.

Sextus Empiricus, animalitarian themes in scepticism, 420, n. 43; on Critias, 211, n. 29; on Democritus's use of 'nature,' 106, n. 8; on Euhemerus, 56; on human sacrifice to Cronus, 73; on Scythian sacrifices to Artemis, 339, n. 95; on Stoic morals, 260; on Zeno's teachings, 260, n. 4.

Sexual impulse, in Cynic ethics, 121; gratification of, in Antisthenes, 125.

Shakespeare, 'nature' and 'art,' 166, 207.

Shelley, P. B., 92, n. 151.